Employment Rights

Employment Rights

Third Edition

Richard W. Painter and **Keith Puttick**

with Ann Holmes

Pluto Press
LONDON • ANN ARBOR, MI

First published 1993
Second edition published 1998
This edition first published 2004 by Pluto Press
345 Archway Road, London N6 5AA
and 839 Greene Street, Ann Arbor, MI 48106, USA

British Library Cataloguing in Publication Data
A catalogue record for this book is available from the British Library

ISBN 0 7453 2125 9 hardback
ISBN 0 7453 2124 0 paperback

Library of Congress Cataloging in Publication Data applied for

10   9   8   7   6   5   4   3   2   1

Designed and produced for Pluto Press by
Chase Publishing Services, Fortescue, Sidmouth, EX10 9QG, England
Typeset from disk by Stanford DTP Services, Northampton, England
Printed in the European Union by
Antony Rowe Ltd, Chippenham and Eastburne, England

Contents

Authors

The authors of the chapters in this edition are as follows:

Keith Puttick and Richard Painter – Chapter 1
Keith Puttick – Chapters 3–9, 15, 16, 18, 21 and 22
Richard Painter and Ann Holmes – Chapters 10, 11 and 12
Richard Painter – Chapters 2, 13, 14, 17, 19 and 20

Preface

Six years have gone by since the second edition of *Employment Rights*. New Labour has pursued a range of new agendas during that time, the EC Employment and Social Policy programme has been developing apace, and the Human Rights Act 1998 has started to have an impact. A combination of these factors has inevitably produced an expanded coverage of key areas of the subject. Not least of these are pay and work-related benefits (reflecting, no doubt, the high priority given to 'making work pay' schemes like the National Minimum Wage Act 1998 and Tax Credits Act 2002), and holidays and hours (especially after the introduction of the Working Time Regulations 1998); and collective bargaining, with the important, but complex, statutory recognition procedure in the Employment Relations Act 1999 and the changes due to be made by the Employment Relations Act 2004.

When the second edition came out there were plenty of people who doubted the whole idea of 'employment rights'. After a lengthy period of Conservative rule which saw some serious in-roads being made into both individual and collective workplace rights, the first issue was 'do we have any employment rights left?' Second, to what *extent* would New Labour use its sizeable Parliamentary majority to reverse the decline? Would the employment floor of rights – which had all but collapsed by 1997 – be restored, starting with the proposals made in *Fairness at Work* in May 1998? And what *new* rights might we look forward to? In the event the government has pursued a busy programme of law-making, and gone into new and important areas like family-friendly working, reconciling 'work and home', and other initiatives.

The courts have also been as active as ever. Our coverage has been able to include the important trio of House of Lords judgments in *Dunnachie* v. *Kingston-upon-Hull City Council*, *Barber* v. *Somerset County Council* and *Eastwood and Another* v. *Magnox Electric plc*. These highlight the uncertainties still surrounding the subject of remedies. Not surprisingly there have been calls for Parliament to review the position without delay.

We have been joined once again in this edition by our colleague Ann Holmes, who has revised and updated Chapters 10–12.

We would like to say a big thank-you to our families for all their support (and forbearance) while the revisions were being written – and to Pluto Press for all their assistance with this new edition.

Keith Puttick
Richard Painter
Ann Holmes

July 2004

Abbreviations

AC	Appeal Cases
ACAS	Advisory Conciliation and Arbitration Service
All ER	All England Law Reports
BJIR	British Journal of Industrial Relations
CA	Court of Appeal
CAB	Citizens' Advice Bureau
CAC	Central Arbitration Committee
Ch	Law Reports, Chancery Division
CLY	Current Law Yearbook
CPR	Civil Procedure Rules 1998 (SI 1998/3132)
DTI	Department of Trade and Industry
DWP	Department of Work and Pensions
EAT	Employment Appeal Tribunal
EC	European Community
ECHR	European Convention for the Protection of Human Rights and Fundamental Freedoms
ECtHR	European Court of Human Rights
ECJ	European Court of Justice
EOC	Equal Opportunities Commission
Empl. LR	Employment Law Reports
EPA	Employment Protection Act 1975
EPCA	Employment Protection (Consolidation) Act 1978
EqPA	Equal Pay Act 1970
ERA	Employment Rights Act 1996
ET	Employment Tribunal
ETS	Employment Tribunal Service
EWC	European Works Council
HL	House of Lords
HSAWA	Health and Safety at Work Act 1974
HSC	Health and Safety Commission
ICP	Information and Consultation Procedure
ICR	Industrial Cases Reports
ILJ	Industrial Law Journal
ILO	International Labour Organisation
IRLIB	Industrial Relations Legal Information Bulletin
IRLR	Industrial Relations Law Reports
IT	Industrial Tribunal (Employment Tribunal following the change of name in 1998)
KB	Law Reports, King's Bench Division
LRD	Labour Research Department Publications
NIRC	National Industrial Relations Court

NMW	National Minimum Wage
QB	Law Reports, Queen's Bench Division
TULRA	Trade Union and Labour Relations Act 1974
TULR(A)A	Trade Union and Labour Relations (Amendment) Act 1976
TULR(C)A	Trade Union and Labour Relations (Consolidation) Act 1992
TUPE	The Transfer of Undertakings (Protection of Employment) Regulations 1981 (SI 1984/1794)
TURERA	Trade Union Reform and Employment Rights Act 1993
UMA	Union Membership Agreement
WLR	Weekly Law Reports
WTC	Working Tax Credit

Table of Cases

Page numbers where the case is referred to in the text are shown after the dash

Table of EC, ECHR, and International Material

Codes of Practice

Table of Statutory Instruments, Directions, etc.

Table of Statutes

PART ONE

Introduction

Employment Rights: Past, Present and Future

Employment Rights: Introductory Observations

A book about peoples' rights at work needs to offer a perspective on the way the current employment law regime has developed, and is developing. This is important, if only because of the rapidity with which policy becomes legislation, and case law and principles develop. It also needs to address the policy trends, and political and economic ideologies, which play such a decisive part in the shaping of employment laws. A commentary on these is part of any meaningful consideration of the subject. Ideology, in particular, is a powerful catalyst for change in the employment field, as seen with Conservative legislation in the 1980s and 1990s. It is also readily apparent in the continuing influence of Third Way thinking on New Labour employment and social policies. In particular, the Third Way sees a 'middle way' between old-style social democratic values and regulation, and a Conservative, neo-liberal deregulatory agenda.[1]

Attempts are made by employment law commentators, from time to time, to chart what those 'old style' values really were, and the transformation from Old Labour to New Labour. A common theme is that Old Labour focused much of its concern on redistribution, and countering inequalities of income. It was also concerned with empowerment. Among leading labour law gurus like Kahn-Freund an influential (and still valuable) perspective of the employment relationship was that of the employer as a 'bearer of power', and of the isolated worker who was *not* a 'bearer of power'. In its inception Kahn-Freund saw the relationship as 'an act of submission' by the worker. In its operation the relationship generally continued as one of 'subordination' – even if this might be concealed by what he referred to as 'that figment of the legal mind' the contract of employment. On the basis of this analysis, concluded Kahn-Freund, the main mission for labour law is to be a 'countervailing force' to counteract such inequality of bargaining power, which is generally inherent in the relationship.[2] As part of New Labour's ideological transformation it has been argued that such concerns, and preoccupations with redistribution of income and power, have given way to an emphasis on promoting equality of *opportunity* and capabilities: and social rights have become part of a bigger mission, which is to assist workers to participate in the benefits of a stronger labour market, and a more prosperous and competitive economy.[3] It is also the case that a large element in employment law reform since 1997 has been to remove 'barriers to work' and legislate to 'make work pay', as part of the social inclusion agenda.[4] The implementation of that approach began early on with the National Minimum Wage Act 1998, and the Tax Credits Act 1999 (now replaced with the much more comprehensive Tax Credits Act 2002). The 2002 Act undoubtedly provides for such a substantial income transfer from the State to workers that there must be considerable doubt about the adequacy of any analysis that ignores such redistributions. For reasons which are considered in later chapters, including Chapter 22, the increasing levels of financial and other support by the State provide yet another reason why traditional labour law discourses, including those referred to in Hugh Collins' analysis in the 'Productive Disintegration of Labour Law'[5] need to be revised. It is also clear that the bilateral contract-based model, characterised as a predominantly 'private' arrangement between employer and worker needs rapid updating, particularly given the reality that a large section of the labour market now gets a substantial quasi-wage from the State as well as from the employer (in many low-pay cases considerably more than the employer's wage); and that one of the legacies of deregulation of the labour, housing, and other markets, and employers' recognition of the scale of financial support, has been to make such workers heavily reliant on the State. For reasons which are essentially economic, and a mix of competitiveness, macro-economic efficiency, and welfare agendas, the employment relationship has been developing into a tripartite one. In the process, the State has become a significant stakeholder, and there is a growing potential for it to assert its stake when, as it has been doing, it regulates all stages of the employment life-cycle.

A key facet of New Labour thinking in all this has been a pre-occupation with 'personal responsibility', and getting a job to facilitate 'independence'.[6] This focused, initially, on perceptions of individuals' responsibilities to seek employment, and retain it (as part of the government's approach to welfare-to-work, and its New Deal programmes) – but it has progressively extended into other areas of policy and employment. For example, what began as a mild exhortation to employees, and their unions, to help make the 'workplace partnership' ideal work when an early blueprint for reform *Fairness at Work* was published in 1998[7] has since found expression in legal *requirements* to realise this objective – including penalties for not making use of, or following, prescribed dispute procedures before pursuing tribunal litigation options.[8] Another source of employment law that is replete with the language of social partnership, and imbued with its own distinctive set of ideologies about workplace relations, is European Community Law. To the extent that employment law and social policy now takes much of its formal lead from policies of the EC, we need look no further for this than the Treaty Establishing the European Community itself. The original Treaty of Rome was consolidated by the Treaty of Amsterdam and extended by the Treaty of Nice;[9] and it now includes Title VII (arts. 125–130) on Employment. It is supplemented by *Guidelines* drawn up each year by the European Council under art. 128 (2) which Member States are required to take on board in developing and implementing employment policies. Art. 125 sets an important bench-mark for developing new employment regimes, stipulating among other things that Member States and the Community must not only develop a co-ordinated strategy for employment, but one that promotes 'a skilled, trained and adaptable workforce and labour markets responsive to economic change ...' Much of the impetus, and support, for concepts like 'adaptable working' and 'labour market responsiveness' which went into Title VII, and language like the 'dialogue between management and labour', and the 'social partners working together' in Title XI on Social Policy, had their origins in negotiations in the months preceding the signing of the Amsterdam Treaty. The influence of the UK's Prime Minister on the proceedings can also be seen in his address to the EC Council in June 1997 (reported in Hansard, 18 June 1997). Among other things he referred to Europe needing a 'new approach to employment and growth, based on British ideas for competitiveness, introducing more flexible labour markets and employability'. The form of words finally adopted in key parts of the Treaty are also significant in other respects. In art. 127 (2), for example, it asserts that 'The objective of a *high level* of employment shall be *taken into consideration* in the formulation and implementation of Community policies and activities' (emphases added). This, in fact, represented a significant phase in EC employment law history, and in particular a triumph over those Members States' leaders, and countries like Sweden, and the European Trade Union Confederation, who had pressed hard for a wider-ranging mission, and setting an objective of *full* employment. Despite the best efforts of the left and centre-left to do this, and to set some significant new directions for employment and social policy in Europe, including clearer commitments to enshrining 'job security' as part of the formal EC agenda, such opportunities were not taken. The changes eventually agreed have been described as representing little more than a 'weak left turn'.[10]

Nevertheless, a by-product of Amsterdam has been a significantly wider scope for employment legislation in most areas of employment. In developing a Community 'social dimension' there has also been a continuing fusion of employment and other elements of social policy. This can be seen from the lead provisions and 'objectives' in art. 136 of Title XI. This took as its starting point the fundamental social rights of the European Social Charter 1961, and the Community Charter of the Fundamental Social Rights of Workers 1989.[11] But it then identifies, in art. 136 'objectives' such as improving the promotion of employment, improved living and working conditions, 'proper social protection of workers', and the combating of social exclusion. Art. 137 develops the agenda further, enabling the Community to support and complement Member States' activities in areas like improvement of the working environment to improve health and safety, working conditions, social security and social protection, and the protection of workers where their employment contract is terminated. As art. 140 makes clear, in developing the social rights referred to in art. 136 the EC's remit has become one of co-ordinating Member States' action in *all* social policy fields – but particularly those relating to employment, labour law and working conditions, training, social security, prevention of occupational accidents and diseases, and rights of association and collective bargaining.

This has, without doubt, signalled important changes in the UK to the parameters of 'employment rights' as a subject. Whereas the EC and other Member States have, for some time, regarded employment issues as intertwined with social policy in its broader context, UK employment law has had a significantly narrower ambit. Primarily the focus has been, in the UK, on the employment contract, and protective legislation that is superimposed on the contract. For reasons advanced in Chapter 4, the move away from a traditional focus on the contract of employment, and towards an 'employment relationship' has also been accompanied by recognition of other important influences. Not least of these is a discourse that recognises the importance of public law procedures and rights – for example in relation to public sector employment rights.[12] The swathe of anti-union legislation in the 1980s and 1990s, followed by the re-introduction of statutory recognition procedures in the Employment Relations Act 1999, has maintained collective labour relations law as a subject. Wider aspects affecting the employment relationship are no longer segregated off from the subject of 'employment rights'. EC developments, in these respects, have undoubtedly broadened perceptions of the subject in the UK. It is now as much concerned with employment-related issues like welfare-to-work schemes, job creation, reconciling work and family commitments, gender gaps, and States' taxation and benefits systems, as with more traditional areas of employment rights. There is every reason to believe that the UK's action programme will be developed even further to integrate more closely with social policy aspects of employment, for example in legislation to accord greater rights to atypical groups like disabled people, older workers, part-timers, and those on fixed-term contracts. This is particularly seen with the measures to attract and retain such groups in the labour market with tax credits and other incentives.

The point was made in the first edition of this book that underlying the rhetoric and the laws is the reality that economic forces are busily re-shaping the employment landscape and the policy agenda. Falling profitability and demands by employers for more 'competitiveness' were just some of the catalysts for changes in the redundancy laws and collective labour rights, and for dismantling systems for securing rights at work at that time. This was evident when deregulatory agendas, privatisation, and competitive tendering in the public sector quickly led to new employment laws and priorities, and the abandonment of laws that no longer suited employers' requirements. Similarly, the removal of other wage-fixing mechanisms, notably the wages councils (performing an important role in areas of the labour market without developed collective bargaining) suffered the same fate as a direct consequence of such pressures.

The internationalisation of capital and businesses, the transnational nature of production of goods, and the removal of production processes out of so-called 'high-wage' economies into countries with lower labour costs (including Eastern European countries, India and the Far East), raise important issues about the rights of workers in those countries[13] as well as those in employment in the UK and in the rest of the EC labour market. The inability of individual Member States to respond to the scale of the changes brought about by the global movement of capital, and changes in production technology, or to devise employment and welfare programmes which can sustain acceptable levels of employment, has also underlined for EC politicians and planners the necessity for EC-wide programmes. The increasing cost to Member States of income support systems as part of the development of the Social Dimension and in the form of in-work and out-of-work benefits, and employment-related support measures (like tax credits under the Tax Credits Act 2002), has precipitated doubts among some commentators about some of the negative implications of adapting State welfare to reduce employers' labour costs, and making workers increasingly reliant on such income.[14]

The EC's drive towards the creation of the 'flexible labour market', including the promotion of mechanisms to promote 'employability' and 'adaptability' – now imbedded in the Treaty – are the hallmarks of the new thinking. The origins of such ideas, and the impetus for developing them further and in new directions, is now seen as what EC leaders and the EC Commission routinely describe as the 'global challenge'.

Whether the results of these ideas are always likely to be welcomed by European citizens is another matter. Some of the by-products of the flexible labour market, such as 'zero hours' contracts and annualised hours and pay arrangements have been less than welcome: as is the pressure on unions to negotiate new and what can often be less advantageous arrangements in return for 'security of employment' undertakings from employers. These are themes discussed in more detail in later chapters – for example in cases like *Ali* v. *Christian Salvesen* (Chapter 7) which illustrate the pressures unions are increasingly under to trade job security for reductions in pay, hours, and other conditions. A more recent statement of EC and UK policy, in

Full and Fulfilling Employment: Creating the Labour Market of the Future (DTI, 2003), indicates how 'adaptability' expectations on both workers and their employers are being ratcheted up, spelling out that 'A Europe endeavouring to raise its productivity must also concentrate on the flexibility of its labour force. This flexibility encompasses geographical and occupational mobility and skills, as well as the ability of wages and working conditions to adjust to different economic circumstances ...'[15] As one commentator pointed out during earlier phases in these developments, the real thrust of such 'flexibility' is often to shift the risks of business fluctuations from the employer onto the worker.[16]

In the rest of this chapter we chart some of the specific developments and trends that have contributed to the current employment rights regime.

Intervention versus Deregulation: the Origins of the Present System[17]

Despite many centuries of regulatory employment legislation – some of it going back as far as 1349, as discussed in Chapter 7 – or interventions like the Factories Acts dealing with health and safety, and innumerable judicial decisions, observers have looked in vain for what they might recognise as 'labour law' in Britain. Britain has never had a labour law code. So one expert was able to observe in 1959: 'When British industrial relations are compared with those of other democracies they stand out because they are so little regulated by law.'[18] This description of the State's traditional approach to the conduct of British industrial relations, known variously as legal abstentionism, voluntarism or collective laissez-faire, was by the 1970s in need of considerable modification. The droplets of legal intervention discernible in the 1960s assumed torrential proportions during the following decade.

The source of the trend towards regulation can be traced back to a series of Acts which gave employees certain rights which were enforceable in the new industrial tribunals. Namely, the Contracts of Employment Act 1963 (right to minimum period of notice and right to receive in writing major terms and conditions of employment); the Redundancy Payments Act 1965 (employees could claim compensation if their jobs became redundant); the Equal Pay Act 1970 (equal pay for 'like work'); and the unfair dismissal provisions of the Industrial Relations Act 1971.

Indeed, the Act of 1971 was a failed attempt to introduce a comprehensive legal regulation of employment relations in line with the North American model. With its repeal by the Trade Union and Labour Relations Act 1974, we saw a return to the previous policy of legal abstention in relation to collective labour law. A further element in the so-called Social Contract between the labour government and the Trades Union Congress (TUC) was the enactment of legislation such as the Employment Protection Act 1975 (EPA) which created a 'statutory floor' of individual employment rights and gave a degree of legal support for union organisation and collective bargaining. The idea of the 'floor' was to provide legally guaranteed minimum rights which could then be improved upon at the workplace through the encouragement, extension and use of the collective bargaining process.

In radical contrast, the legislation of the 1980s and 1990s, including the five Employment Acts between 1980 and 1990, the Trade Union Act 1984, and the Wages Act 1986, aimed to deregulate so far as employment protection and collective bargaining were concerned. They also imposed major legal restrictions on trade unions and placed major obstacles in the way of the organisation of industrial action.

Strike organisers and trade unions were exposed to court orders and damages by the narrowing of the statutory immunities from judge-made liabilities. In this way, secondary industrial action, solidarity and political strikes, picketing away from the pickets' own workplaces and official action not preceded by ballot were, in effect, made unlawful. Much of that legacy remains in place in the present legal regime.[19] In a way that is unique in UK legal history, unions as private organisations became subject to a pervasive regulatory framework in which their internal rules were overridden, and autonomy removed – usually on the assumption that members needed to be protected against their own organisations. Intervention was also rationalised on the basis of a need to make unions more 'democratic' and to prevent 'abuse of their privileges' – as explained in *Democracy in Trade Unions* (1983, Cm. 8778). In addition, the reduction of strikers' dependants' entitlement to State benefits, and the widening of the employer's freedom to sack strikers without incurring the risk of liability for unfair dismissal, were put in place in order to make individual workers think twice before withdrawing their labour. In some cases legislation rendered industrial action completely unlawful, as the Prison Officers' Association experienced when the Criminal Justice and Public Order Act 1994 was passed.

In addition to the civil law, the Public Order Act 1986 redefined and expanded some of the criminal law offences which were extensively used against pickets in the 1984–85 miners' dispute.

The law and policy relating to collective labour relations are discussed in Part Six below.

Contradictions in Deregulatory Policies?

At first sight there appeared to be a contradiction between the neo-liberal philosophy of the Conservative administration, which essentially believed in keeping the business of the State and the business of government to a minimum, and the highly interventionist policy adopted in relation to trade union reform. There was, in fact, no contradiction. For the free marketeer, the market is the mechanism by which individual wants and desires can be controlled. The only valid function of government is to protect this mechanism from interference. According to this philosophy trade unions maintain a labour monopoly through such practices as the closed shop, and not only distort the market but also infringe the political liberty that the free market offers. The basis of trade union power was seen to be coercion resting on legal privileges which had to be revoked: and it was theorists like Hayek who supplied much of the ideology on which the subsequent assault on unions, was predicated.[20]

While the logic of the 'free market' pointed to the legal restriction of trade unions, it required that most of the burdens of State intervention should be lifted from employers. This became the task of deregulation: to dismantle the legal and bureaucratic controls which, in free market theory, deterred employers, especially small employers, from recruiting labour. Deregulation embraced a wide range of policies, including privatisation, the encouragement of low wages for young workers and – of special concern here – the erosion of legal support for collective bargaining and employment protection. Landmarks in the deregulatory process included:

- The abolition of the procedures under the EPA 1975 and the Fair Wages Resolution (which originated as far back as 1891), designed to establish the 'going-rate' of pay and other conditions in particular industries, and fair wages in companies awarded government contracts.

• The removal of persons under the age of 21 from the protection of the Wages Council system, followed by abolition of the system altogether in 1993.

• The repeal of the Truck Acts 1831–1940, a series of statutes which, albeit in a somewhat complicated, anachronistic and piecemeal manner, offered groups of workers a measure of legal protection against arbitrary deductions from pay and the right to payment in cash.

• The removal of restrictions on working hours and conditions of women. Section 7 of the Sex Discrimination Act 1986 removed all major restrictions on women working shifts (and at night), overtime restrictions, and maximum hours limitations.

• The quadrupling of the qualification period for workers before they could claim unfair dismissal – from 26 weeks in 1979 to two years in 1985.[21]

• A weakening of maternity rights. In particular, firms employing five or fewer employees, were excluded from the provision that employees have a right to return to work after maternity leave.

After the Deregulation and Contracting Out Act 1994 was passed the Act was used, among things, to abolish breaks and the regulation of hours of shopworkers, and to remove certain redundancy procedures that were seen as unduly restrictive on employers' power to determine which staff to retain. In the case of shopworkers the Sunday Trading Act 1994 lifted restrictions on Sunday opening times. This was followed by the Employment Rights Act 1996 which included various opt-out rights for workers in shops and betting shops who did not want to work Sundays. One of the last deregulatory employment measures of the outgoing Conservative government, in the SSP (General) Amendment Regulations 1996, SI 1996/3042, was to allow employers to opt out of the Statutory Sick Pay system, subject to an obligation to pay the equivalent of SSP from the payroll. The purpose was to give employers more control over the terms on which sick pay is paid, as well as to reduce the administrative requirements involved. The removal of State reimbursement of SSP in most cases was, in part, an incentive to employers to introduce stricter systems of control over 'absenteeism'. These changes opened a Pandora's box of non-compliance problems for workers and employers which eventually had to be dealt with by making non-payment of SSP and SMP 'without reasonable excuse' a criminal offence in 2001.

Most of the deregulatory legislation described is still with us, mainly in Acts like the Trade Union and Labour Relations (Consolidation) Act (TULR[C]A) and the Employment Rights Act 1996 (ERA). Similarly, much of the framework regulating unions has remained intact, as pointed out by commentators like Gillian Morris and Timothy Archer.[22] It is also clear that New Labour, like its predecessor, has maintained a mechanism for 'fast-tracking' deregulatory measures. The Regulatory Reform Act 2001 is a potent means of removing unwanted protective legislation.

The Effects of 'Deregulation'

Deregulation, though significant during the Conservatives' period in office, was, in practice, subject to certain constraints or countervailing pressures.

The curtailment of statutory rights at work did not prevent, and may even have encouraged, resort to alternative remedies provided by the common law. For example,

developments saw a greater willingness by the courts to grant injunctions in order
to halt dismissals taking place in breach of a contractually incorporated disciplinary
procedure or to prevent a breach of the employer's other obligations under the
contract (see *Irani* v. *Southampton & SW Hampshire HA* [1985] ICR 590; *Powell* v.
LB Brent [1987] IRLR 466; *Hughes* v. *LB Southwark* [1988] IRLR 55, and the later
cases discussed in Chapters 13, 15 and 18 below). Other cases saw courts upholding
claims for breach of contract against employers based on terms incorporated into the
contract of employment from a collective agreement (see *Rigby* v. *Ferodo Ltd* [1987]
IRLR 516, discussed in Chapter 5).

Furthermore, Conservative governments of the 1980s were forced, mainly on
account of EC requirements, to introduce new measures such as the Transfer of
Undertakings Regulations 1981 SI 1981/1794 ('TUPE'), Equal Pay (Amendment)
Regulations 1983, SI 1983/1794, the Data Protection Act and the Sex Discrimination
Act 1986. EC membership means that UK law is subordinate to the provisions of the
Treaty of Rome, the Single European Act 1986, and the regulations and directives
made under the treaty. For reasons discussed in later chapters, measures like TUPE
have not proved effective, in key respects, in protecting acquired rights affected by
transfers of employers organisations and operations. This prompted changes to the
Acquired Rights Directive 77/187 by the Revised Acquired Rights Directive 98/50.
Nevertheless, the key point was that even at the height of the Conservatives' period
in office the labour market was subject to *some* regulation and legal interventions,
and much of it was EC-driven.

The potency of European regulation was seen with the landmark case of *Barber* v.
Guardian Royal Exchange Assurance Group in 1990 [1990] IRLR 240. In what was – for
UK employers – probably the most important judgment to come from the European
Court of Justice (ECJ) in that period, the court held that occupational pensions payable
under a contracted-out scheme constituted 'pay' under article 119 (now article 141)
of the Treaty of Rome, and so were required to be non-discriminatory in their terms.
This has meant that pensionable ages must be the same for men and women, and
benefits payable must be equal. Where a scheme allows a woman to take a pension
at the age of 60, for example, a man must have the right to insist on the same option,
on the same terms.

As this aspect of EC Law was directly enforceable in the UK, employers had to
act immediately in order to avoid exposure to tribunal claims. UK discrimination
legislation, which allowed discrimination in pension entitlements and benefits, was
largely overridden as a result of the decision in *Barber*: and New Labour inherited a
regime which it was obliged to regulate more closely, which it has been doing through
measures like the Welfare Reform and Pensions Act 1999.

The relationship between UK and EC law, in the context of equal pay, is discussed
in greater detail in Chapter 10 below.

In a number of specific areas the government was on occasion, during this period,
under intense political pressure to legislate to protect workers' rights when, in the
deregulatory environment created, major abuses occurred. In the pensions field, for
example, Robert Maxwell's theft of his employees' pension scheme funds, and the
widespread use by employers of such funds for their own purposes, led to an urgent
consideration of the pensions system by the House of Commons Select Committee
on Social Security and to demands for stricter regulatory legislation.[23]

Maxwell's actions involved, among other things, the uncontrolled use of his
employees' pensions (which in many cases represented a large proportion of their
life savings) as a source of liquidity for his private companies. This served to highlight

a much bigger problem, which was the ability of employers to help themselves to workers' pensions, and use them as a way of financing business operations. In the long run this led to tighter regulation, not just of employers' management of staff pension funds but of the pensions market in general: and giving effect to New Labour's commitment, as part of the *New Welfare Contract*[24] to make pensions and final products more 'secure', Parliament enacted the Financial Services and Markets Act 2000.

If a deregulated labour market produced unforeseen consequences with pensions, then it also produced some curious paradoxes whereby in the enthusiasm to roll back the frontiers of the State the burden could shift from the State to the employer. Two examples of this 'reverse deregulation' was the legislation on Statutory Sick Pay and Statutory Maternity Pay, areas of complex interaction between social security and employment protection. In each case, though, employers are left with significant responsibilities for managing (and in the case of SSP paying for) their workers' in-work 'welfare'.[25]

Deregulation was at its most effective in relation to cutting back State support for collective bargaining. The statutory trade union recognition procedure (ss. 11–16 EPA 1975), the limited right to arbitration where it was claimed that the employer was not observing the 'recognised' terms and conditions for the industry (sched. 11), and the Fair Wages Resolution, all disappeared after 1979; and the Trade Union and Employment Rights Act 1993 saw the removal of the statutory role of ACAS to encourage the development of collective bargaining. New rights for individuals to join the union of their choice, or indeed not to join *any* union if they so wished, further undermined the collective bargaining system, and destabilised voluntary recognition arrangements. Voluntary recognition became the *only* kind of arrangement that was allowed to operate until mandatory statutory procedures were introduced again in 2000 (see Chapter 18).

Despite on-going deregulation, the law continued to have a significant impact in many aspects of employment and labour relations.

The Impact of the Law

The law has always, potentially, been a major tactical weapon in industrial disputes – but no more so than in the 1980s. Employers and, on occasion, disaffected union members, demonstrated a willingness to take or threaten court action. Employers increasingly sought court orders to restrain strikes called without a secret ballot (the most frequent cause of action), but also to prevent secondary action and unlawful picketing. In the face of this legal onslaught, and the removal of their 'blanket immunity' after 1982, unions were forced to centralise authority so as to attempt to avoid liability.[26] The decisive use of legal tactics in disputes which became media *causes célèbres* – the *Stockport Messenger*, Austin Rover, News International, the seafarers' dispute and, above all, the miners' strike – provided the clearest demonstration of the law's potency. In the light of these experiences, and faced with punishing financial consequences and sequestration of assets for non-compliance, unions generally complied with court orders.[27]

The combined effect of the recession of the early 1980s and the legislative assault on trade unions severely weakened organisational strength and militancy. In 1979, 80 per cent of the workforce were covered by collective agreements or by wage councils. By 1996 that figure had fallen to 37 per cent. In 1979 more than 50 per cent of the working population were trade union members. In 1996 trade union membership had fallen to 31 per cent.[28] Throughout the 1960s and 1970s industrial militancy was dubbed the 'British disease' by the media. By 1995, the UK had the fourth lowest strike rate (defined as the number of working days lost due to labour disputes per thousand employees) of the 22 countries in the Organisation for Economic Co-operation and Development (OECD).[29]

While the use of law in industrial disputes was a fairly recent phenomenon, the impact of employment protection law has been felt since the introduction of the right not to be unfairly dismissed in the early 1970s. Unfair dismissal had been the basis for most tribunal applications, and this has undoubtedly encouraged significant changes in industrial relations practices. The evidence of surveys and case studies indicated that the dismissal provisions have generally stimulated the spread and formalisation of grievance and disciplinary procedures, enhanced the role and status of personnel managers and employers' associations and encouraged employers, especially larger ones, in adopting more efficient recruitment and discipline practices. One impact claimed for the legislation has, however, always been rather difficult to substantiate: the negative effect on jobs of the legislation on employment. This view was the impetus for a number of changes which have been wrought to the law since 1979. For example, at different times it has 'neutralised' the burden of proof; introduced the pre-hearing assessment (and, in some cases, the requirement of 'deposits') in an attempt to discourage the continuance of claims which are unlikely to succeed; and increased the qualification period necessary to claim. However, surveys of management attitudes and responses suggest that the legislation only has a minor impact in discouraging recruitment. Apparently, it induces a greater care in selection in order to ensure the right quality of recruits rather than reducing quantity.[30] Research later found that only 8 per cent of firms surveyed expressed reluctance to recruit additional staff on account of the law of unfair dismissal.[31] A further survey did no more than confirm the previous findings.[32]

Other areas of employment law have also had a major impact on both personnel management and collective negotiations practices. The redundancy laws facilitated redundancies by encouraging – in consultation with unions – cash payment for jobs. Union demands have often been confined to the level of payment and a preference for voluntary redundancy. With the advent of the tribunals' jurisdiction to deal with contract-related claims, including those where employers have offered additional payments in return for acceptance of 'voluntary redundancy', the 'cash for jobs' aspect of redundancy laws started to take on a new significance. The gender and race discrimination laws led to the adoption in some workplaces of formal equality policies, though the real impact of the 'equal value regulations' on pay structures remains an open question. As considered in the chapters on discrimination and job loss it has taken three House of Lords' decisions to restore such potency as the regulations had when promulgated.

The law has also played a decisive role in establishing health and safety requirements. For example extending the development of joint safety committees and safety training. Health, safety and the work environment remain a significant area of intervention, and a crucial aspect of workplace rights. In this area, the policy of deregulation clearly failed and, at the instigation of the EC and ECJ judgments, further changes developed, including rights of non-union staff to information, and to be consulted. A central theme has been the general requirement to design work to accommodate the worker's safety and welfare requirements and for work operations to be 'assessed'. This policy was progressively introduced through a series of important measures, assisted by EC Directive 89/391 (the Framework Directive) (see Chaper 16) and now covers many potentially hazardous workplace activities.

The impact of employment laws as they continued to develop during the 1980s and 1990s, notwithstanding a deregulatory environment, and measured purely in terms of their effectiveness in protecting individual claimants, has arguably been relatively minimal. In unfair dismissal, for example, the success rate (around one-third of all cases reaching a tribunal), remained consistently low in the 1990s. Nor was compensation good, with a median award of £2,449 in 1995/96. The tribunals, which are generally supportive of the management prerogative, and managerial perspectives on the 'right to manage', were reluctant to order reinstatement in this period (less than 2 per cent of cases where a remedy was awarded).[33] Similarly, the law has manifestly not eliminated unequal pay or discrimination on grounds of sex or race or union activity, as the Equal Opportunities Commission has repeatedly reported. The effect has been rather on management policies and procedures and collective bargaining.

Overall, as Hepple has observed, there has continued to be an underlying trend towards the 'juridification of industrial disputes ... matters which were once entirely within the sphere of managerial prerogatives or left to collective bargaining, are now directly regulated by positive legal rights and duties.'[34]

Deregulation versus 'Social Europe'

Whereas the UK government continued down the 'deregulation' path well into the 1990s, with measures such as the Employment Act 1989 (giving effect to deregulation measures set out in the 1986 White Paper *Building Business ... not Barriers*) – for example by exempting employers in undertakings with less than 20 employers from specified employment law requirements – the EC in this period set itself an entirely different course, with very different priorities. These included the principles enunciated in the European Commission's *Charter of Fundamental Social Rights*.[35] The Charter represented principles on the future of European workplace policy, and proposed significant social and employment rights for EC citizens. These included, for example, a right to 'fair remuneration' and annual paid leave, and the right to belong to a union. It also provided the basis of calls for minimum rights in relation to holidays and working time – now implemented by the Working Time Directive (EC Dir. 93/104), and in the UK the Working Time Regulations 1998 (see Chapter 8).

Other aspects of the Charter, for example those establishing rights to 'equal treatment', 'participation' in decision-making processes, and in redundancy situations were, of course, anathema to a UK government pursuing a very different ideological agenda. The first batch of draft directives to implement Social Charter principles were adopted by the European Commission in the 1990s. Dealing with working time, pregnant employees (EC Dir. 92/85) and various aspects of part-time and temporary work (EC Dirs. 97/81 and 98/23), the directives have required major amendments to UK law.

The United Kingdom government strongly opposed the Charter, and continued to resist much of the detailed legislation designed to implement it, on the ground that it would lead to excessive regulation and would impede rather than foster the creation of jobs. Indeed, Mrs Thatcher famously described the Charter as 'inspired by the values of Karl Marx and the class struggle'. It was, therefore, unsurprising when at the meeting of the European Council in Strasbourg in December 1989 the UK was the only dissenting voice among the 12 on the question of the Charter's adoption.

At the Maastricht summit in December 1991, the UK continued to strongly resist the expansion of EC legislative activity in the area of social policy. Nevertheless, the Treaty on European Union which resulted from the negotiations was signed by the heads of all 12 Member States at Maastricht on 7 February 1992. The accompanying protocol and agreement, though, which extended the scope of the qualified voting procedure into new areas of social policy covered only 11 states – the UK being in a minority of one. The basis of the protocol was that all Member States apart from the UK 'wish to continue along the path laid down in the 1989 Social Charter'.

The UK's situation was further complicated by the fact that the Commission retained its powers within the framework of the EC of 12 to propose and press for directives in the 'social' field on the basis of the existing EC Treaty.

At Maastricht, the 11 States agreed to use qualified majority voting (as introduced by the Single European Act 1986) in 1997 in several key areas, including:

- improvement of the working environment to protect workers' health and safety;
- working conditions;
- the information and consultation of workers;
- equality between men and women with regard to labour market opportunities and treatment at work;
- the 'integration' of people excluded from the labour market.

This caused immediate problems in relation to measures the EC was keen to enact using those provisions. Not least of these was the directive on working hours and holidays (Dir. 93/104/EC concerning the organisation of working time), which had been adopted by the EC Commission in 1990. This was not unreasonable given the co-relation between excessive hours of work and accidents, and the recognised effects of stress at work. It was not, however, how the UK government saw things, and, in a belated attempt to block progress on the measure, it launched an unsuccessful action in the European Court of Justice against the directive.[36] This was more than just token resistance to an important social policy initiative which, for years, Member States had been developing. It marked, and may still mark for New Labour, and some important sections of government and business, a fundamental difference of attitude towards the need for legislative intervention. The UK labour market was undergoing (and is still undergoing) massive changes. UK policy was (and still is) in favour of allowing 'atypical' forms of employment, and 'flexibility', to develop with a minimum of control, permitting new working arrangements to develop. The removal of statutory obstacles to this process was a key strand in the deregulatory philosophy. Notwithstanding the ECJ's rejection of the UK case against working time regulation, there were still concerns about the manner in which the working time directive operated. This prompted the government's acceptance of a right for employees to 'agree' longer hours than those prescribed – something that has not been changed by New Labour, to date, even though the 'opt-out' has been seen as watering down the directive's fundamental purposes. As part of an EC-initiated review, which may lead to changes by 2005, the TUC concluded that the UK's scheme of implementation, especially the opt-out, is 'seriously flawed' (*Working Time Directive Review 2003: The Use and Abuse of the 'Opt-out' in the UK* [Feb. 2004]). The issue is considered further in Chapter 8.

Current Policies and Future Directions

The continuing influence of Europe on our employment system, and as a major source of new workplace rights, can be seen in a number of key areas. Not least of these is in anti-discrimination legislation. These aspects are developed in later chapters. But among other new legislation has been EC Council Directive 2000/78. This establishes a general framework for equal treatment in employment. Its impact can be seen, most potently, on key areas like disability rights, and in UK implementing legislation (the Disability Discrimination Act 1995 [Amendment] Regulations 2003, SI 2003/1673, from 1 October 2004). Among other things, the regulations restructure the Disability Discrimination Act, Part 2 and introduce new aspects of 'discrimination', including harassment.

In what has been seen as one of the most important employment law reforms of the last decade, Council Directive 2000/78/EC has opened the door to UK legislation against age discrimination, and following consultations on the DTI's proposals in *Equality and Diversity – Age Matters* anti-age discrimination regulations came in to operation from 1 October 1996.

Closely linked to these developments, which are picked up in different contexts in later chapters, the incorporation of the European Convention for the Protection of Human Rights and Fundamental Freedoms (the ECHR), has added to the momentum of European intervention. As in other areas of the legal system, Employment Tribunals and courts dealing with employment matters are not only obliged to take into account Convention rights, they must address specific aspects of such rights in areas like due process, and the right to a fair trial (art. 6); family life and privacy (art. 8); discrimination (art. 14); and the right to 'possessions' (art. 1 of protocol 1) – a process that as John Bowers QC and Jeremy Lewis have described in *Employment Law and Human Rights*[37] is plainly impacting on substantive rights as well as procedural aspects of appeals.

That said, one of the concerns with human rights must be with the discretion which it vests in judges to determine and shape 'rights'. The ECHR's articles are replete with opportunities for restrictions to be introduced on public policy and other grounds, as seen with cases like *X* v. *Y* [2003] IRLR 561. In that case a person who worked with young people, promoting 'personal development' – having been cautioned for an offence involving consensual sex with another man – was dismissed. On appeal his claim that ECHR art. 8 (and a right to privacy) and art. 14 (discrimination) should have been taken into account failed. The EAT concluded that, given the nature of his work, such rights operated more restrictively and in the employer's favour. However, this is a judicial position which could now be wrong in the light of EC legislation, given effect since the case by the Employment Equality (Sexual Orientation) Regulations 2003, SI 2003/1661.

The election of New Labour in May 1997 led to a wide-ranging reappraisal of employment policy, in relation to both individual and collective employment rights. However, as anticipated in the last edition of this work, this did not prompt any rush to radically overhaul Conservative legislation. Whilst the government signalled its willingness to act quickly on selective issues, it adopted a cautious approach to many aspects of Employment Law reform.

On collective issues there were concerns about its slow progress in implementing election promises to introduce statutory union recognition mechanisms. In particular, in what became a litmus test on its willingness to acede to unions' views, it would not be drawn for some while on the important question of whether legislation should require, in a recognition ballot, a majority of employees working for the employer or simply those voting in the ballot, before a recognition obligation could be established. Early experience of such problems, with disputes like Grunwick,[38] when this issue was highly problematical for ACAS, no doubt prompted caution. Its reluctance to reverse the ban on Prison Officers' Association members taking industrial action – a restriction introduced by the Criminal Justice and Public Order Act 1994 – also caused considerable consternation, and led to the POA threatening industrial action over the issue in February 1998.

Apart from the legislative proposals in the White Paper *Fairness at Work* (summarised below), the most significant step taken in the aftermath of the government's victory was the decision to take the UK into the EC's Social Chapter, thus ending the Conservative opt-out and committing the UK to the full range of measures developing in the employment and social policy field. Its commitment to the implementation of the 1998 EC Commission *Guidelines on Member States Employment Policies*, and immediate adoption of the UK's 'Action Plan' in 1998, marked an important step towards full integration of EC policies and laws on employment rights in the UK.

On a different European front, the government's commitment to incorporate the European Convention of Human Rights and Fundamental Freedoms fully into UK law, by enacting the Human Rights Act 1998, has introduced yet a further mechanism by which employment rights are developing further. Among other things it provides opportunities for Convention-related rights (such as the 'right to family life' and the 'right of association') to be raised directly in UK court or tribunal proceedings.

In addition to an early commitment to adopt pro-active labour market policies putting its *Welfare to Work* and *New Deal* programmes into operation,[39] and early legislation like the National Minimum Wage Act 1998, Employment Rights (Dispute Resolution) Act 1998, the Working Time Regulations 1998, SI 1998/1833, and the Tax Credits Act 1999, the centrepiece of Labour's reform proposals was *Fairness at Work*. This was a White Paper which undertook to replace the notion of conflict between employers and employees with the promotion of 'partnership' (taken from the White Paper's Foreword written by the Prime Minister). Proposals, and issues for consultation, fell under three broad headings: New Rights for Individuals; Collective Rights and 'Family-Friendly' Policies.

New Rights for Individuals

The government made proposals in *Fairness at Work* to:

1. reduce the qualifying period for unfair dismissal claims to one year
2. abolish the maximum limit on awards for unfair dismissal
3. introduce legislation to index-link limits on statutory awards and payments 'subject to a maximum rate'.

It also invited views on changes to tribunal remedies, and whether further action should be taken to address the abuse of 'zero hours' contracts but 'without undermining labour market flexibility'.

In the event, there were, indeed, changes: namely to reduce the qualifying period for unfair dismissal to one year, and raise the 'cap' on compensatory awards (but not to remove it altogether) – and otherwise restructure remedies (as discussed in Chapter 14). One of the main weaknesses in the unfair dismissal regime, namely the inability of successful complainants to get an effective order ensuring that they get their job back (or another job), either through reinstatement or re-engagement, did *not* feature in the reforms. Nor has there been any indication since 1998 that New Labour even wants to move in the direction of regulating the labour market in such a way.[40] Proposals to deal with the problem of 'zero hours' contracts were not pursued. Nor has there been much intervention to secure the rights of atypical workers other than in order to comply with EC law. When this has been done, for example by the Part-time Workers (Prevention of Less Favourable Treatment) Regulations 1998, SI 1998/1551 the implementing scheme has generally made it difficult to secure the objectives intended, as illustrated by cases like *Matthews and Others* v. *Kent and Medway Towns Fire Authority* [2003] IRLR 732.

Collective Rights

The government gave clear commitments, among other things, to establish a statutory machinery to enable employees to have a trade union recognised by their employer where the majority of the relevant workforce wanted this; and to regulate both recognition and derecognition. It also undertook to change the law so that, in general, those dismissed for taking part in lawfully organised official action should have the right to complain to a tribunal of unfair dismissal (a right now contained in the Trade Union and Labour Relations [Consolidation] Act 1992 s. 238A). It also undertook to bar out discrimination by omission on grounds of trade union membership, non-membership, or union-related activities. In most respects, the government delivered on these proposals – even if there were concerns that they might have gone further in key respects. In particular, there has been on-going controversy about some aspects of the statutory recognition procedure that is now in TULR(C)A Schedule A1. A detailed consideration of the scheme, and criticisms of it, is provided in Chapter 18. As an overview point, though, a major, principled objection that was made – aired at the time the Employment Relations Act 1999 introduced the legislation – was that the threshold of support among workers which a union would have to demonstrate, i.e. a majority of the workers actually voting, *and* at least 40 per cent of all the workers in the unit, was simply too difficult. For this and other reasons, the leader of the GMB union at the time, John Edmonds, called the scheme a 'flawed jewel'. Another objection has been that even when it has become clear to the Central Arbitration Committee that a majority of employees in the proposed bargaining unit support the union and recognition, a ballot may even at that point be required before recognition can, finally, be ordered. For example the CAC may determine that a ballot would be 'in the interests of good industrial relations'; or if it seems that a 'significant number of union members' do not want the union to conduct collective bargaining on their behalf. Such further hurdles are controversial for a number of reasons, but mainly because they could well provide a hostile (and determined) employer a final late attempt to block recognition. At the very least it is an approach that is often likely to put additional pressure on workers when an employer may well seek to *reduce* the level of initial support for the unit. On the other hand, if a ballot is required, and is then won by the union, it will crystallise the support for new bargaining arrangements. In July 2002 the government announced a review of the operation of the Employment Relations Act 1999, including the recognition scheme. Needless to say, in order to reverse the decline in collective bargaining, and collective rights that resulted from Conservative anti-union legislation, it is important that any refinements made to the scheme get it right. As a result of that review the Employment Relations Act 2004 (as it will be) is due to make important changes designed to improve the recognition system. However, the changes do not address all the concerns identified by the TUC in its representations in *Modern Rights for Modern Workplaces* (2002).

In what remains another key area of concern for unions, the operation of statutory 'immunities', cases like *Willerby Holiday Homes Ltd* v. *UCATT* [2003] EWHC 2608 (where the union was sued successfully for damages for a two-week strike after failures to observe pre-strike balloting and notification procedures) have highlighted the vulnerability of unions in the face of courts' strict adherence to industrial action rules. Despite such cases, the Employment Relations Act 2004 is set to *add* to unions' pre-strike requirements, including rules on notification, and entitlement to take part in ballots.[41]

Other New Labour Changes

The Employment Relations Act 1999 gave effect to most of the other proposals in *Fairness at Work*, referred to above, usually after extensive consultations with employers' organisations and unions. These are considered in the chapters of this book dealing with dismissal and grievance procedures, and unions. Among a number of changes still to be made (from October 2004) are procedures that will provide a new framework for workplace dispute resolution. Details were provided by the government in *Dispute Resolution Regulations: Government Response to Public Consultation* (20 January 2004). Among other things this requires:

- employers to activate a three-stage statutory disciplinary/dismissal procedure before issuing 'warnings' or suspending on full pay;
- a modified two-stage procedure in cases of gross misconduct;
- a statutory grievance procedure route which can apply even if employment has ended;
- extension of time limits for bringing tribunal claims in cases where a grievance procedure would also give rise to such a claim.

The scheme builds on important changes put in place under the Employment Act 2002. These include a new s. 98A (1) in the Employment Rights Act 1996 whereby an employee who is dismissed is to be regarded as unfairly dismissed if (a) one of the procedures in Schedule 2, Part I to the 2002 Act applies, (b) the procedure is not completed, and (c) the failure is wholly or mainly attributable to failure by the employer to comply with the requirements. Dismissal is generally made an easier process for employers in many cases. As long as the minimal procedural 'steps' in the statutory procedures are followed it is difficult for an employer's action to be characterised as unfair. The steps are not particularly demanding, and, subject to the operation of contractral or statutory requirements, consist of little more than providing the employee with a 'statement of grounds' detailing information about the allegation, conduct, etc.; a reasonable opportunity to consider a 'response'; and then a meeting between the employer and employee which can then end in dismissal. The only other core requirement (in cases where the contract or collective procedures do not add to the minimum statutory requirement) is the right to an internal appeal. The process is considered in more depth in Chapter 14, but what also made these changes particularly controversial was the further change, in s. 98A (2), whereby even if there *is* a 'failure' by the employer to follow a procedure, a dismissal does not necessarily thereby become 'unfair'. This is because the failure is not to be regarded for the purpose of s. 98 (4) (a) as 'by itself' making the employer's action unreasonable if the employer, at that point, can show that he would have dismissed *anyway* – even if he had followed the procedure. This approach has the overall effect of reducing the scope for asserting procedural failures as a basis of unfair dismissal, and the impact of *Polkey* 'procedural fairness'.

There are many facets to these important changes, and reasons why they can be criticised. What they were intended to do, plainly, was reduce the number of applications reaching the Employment Tribunals. Indeed the Explanatory Notes to the legislation indicated that the government expected applications to go down by anything between a quarter to a third. The rationale for the changes was not justice. It was, very explicitly, competitiveness – achieved by reducing employers' operating costs (and legal costs in defending cases); and public expenditure savings, mainly in the public funds spent on administering the tribunal system. As Bob Hepple QC and Gillian Morris have contended, the decline in collective procedures may have led to a growth in individual rights: but the government has, unfortunately, chosen to limit them – ostensibly on grounds of costs (something that has also been happening in other European countries like Spain and Italy). The result, they say, is a 'moment of crisis' for employment law in Europe as States try to hold back the 'irreversible demands for enforcement' of such rights. As far as the 2002 Act changes are concerned, they characterise these as privatising enforcement through 'management-controlled procedures' in preference to public tribunals.[42]

Family-Friendly Policies

In this important and developing area of employment rights, the proposals in *Fairness at Work* included a right to maternity leave of 18 weeks extended maternity leave, and parental leave. It was also envisaged that the contract of employment should continue during the whole period of maternity or parental leave (unless expressly terminated by either party, by dismissal, or resignation). There would also be similar rights for employees to return to their jobs after parental leave, as available in relation to maternity-related absences from work.

Parental leave for adoptive parents, and a right to 'reasonable time off' for family emergencies, applicable to all employees regardless of length of service, would be introduced.

As with other areas of reform, family-friendly legislation has proven to be something of a mixed bag. It did not feature at all in the first major employment legislation of the government, the Employment Relations Act 1999. However, when the first tranche of legislation on family-friendly policies did come, with the Maternity Leave and Parental Leave etc. Regulations 1999, SI 1999/3312 (the MPLR), it created two periods of maternity leave along the lines put forward in *Fairness at Work* – i.e. an 'ordinary' period, followed by the option of a further period of 'additional' leave. It also introduced parental leave for a period of up to 13 weeks. The Employment Act 2002, and the Paternity and Adoption Leave Regulations 2002, SI 2002/2788, later proceeded to extended entitlements in this area in a number of important ways, giving effect to EC legislation but on the basis of the specific proposals for implementation set out in *Work and Parents: Competitiveness and Choice – A Framework for Paternity Leave*

(DTI, May 2001). Ss. 1–16 brought in paternity leave and adoption leave, and new State benefits to facilitate take-up of leave.
Specifically:

- two weeks' paternity leave following the birth of a child, or else placement of a child for adoption for up to two weeks, assisted by Statutory Paternity Pay (SPP);
- adoption leave for up to one year to facilitate the adoption of a child, assisted by Statutory Adoption Pay (SAP) for up to 26 weeks.

Whilst the 1999 regulations introduced parental leave, this was not a right to *paid* leave, even if in practice paid paternity leave in some form or other was provided by a minority of employers. In practice the lack of financial support served, demonstrably, to inhibit take-up of the leave right. Another concern was that leave could take a variety of forms, and was not available on an established *general* basis, even for workers within a particular organisation. Accordingly, in 2002 the scheme was developed to provide a universal legal right to two weeks' paid paternity leave – a right which could also be asserted in addition to the right of 13 weeks' parental leave. In the case of a disabled child the leave period rises to 18. SPP and SAP are State-financed, so that employers can recover most of the expenditure they incur, or in some cases all of it, with the Inland Revenue being the lead welfare agency involved in assisting employers to manage payments; Paternity and Adoption Leave Regulations 2002, SI 2002/2788, and the Statutory Paternity and Statutory Adoption Pay (General) Regulations 2002, SI 2002/2822.

Maternity Leave

The government announced in 2001 that ordinary maternity leave would be increased to 26 weeks – followed by 26 weeks *additional* maternity leave, giving a potential total leave period of one year. The changes were implemented by s. 17 of the 2002 Act, the Employment Rights Act 1996, s. 71 (4), and changes to the MPLR, which also deal with rights to return to work. As important to leave rights are the benefits which facilitate take-up. To reflect the extension of the core ordinary period of leave, Statutory Maternity Pay, as managed by the employer (with an adjudication and default role given to the Inland Revenue), and Maternity Allowance, as adjudicated and paid by the Department for Work and Pensions to women who may not be eligible for SMP, were both extended and improved in key respects to coincide with the 2002 Act's changes. Among other things guidance to employers managing SMP is much clearer, and in cases where there are delays in making payments prosecution is one of the possibilities introduced to secure better compliance.[43]

Flexible Working

Of the various changes signalled in *Fairness at Work*, this may prove to be the most problematic. It has also, to some extent, been a disappointment for those expecting more. In *Work and Parents, Competitiveness and Choice* (DTI, 2000), the government developed its proposals for giving workers with the required service qualifications the right (now in the ERA ss. 80F–80I, and the Flexible Working [Eligibility, Complaints and Remedies] Regulations 2002, SI 2002/3236) to *apply* to their employers for a change in their terms and conditions to facilitate 'flexible working'. This falls well short of expectations, and certainly is less than the anticipated right to such an arrangement – even if it was always understood that there are practical difficulties in negotiating such arrangements. Broadly, the purpose of the scheme is to facilitate care for a child, particularly with changes relating to working hours, and times of work. There are a number of concerns with the scheme, including the likely obstacles to a successful application – with wide-ranging potential grounds for refusal by an employer, including the burden of additional costs, inability to reorganise work among existing staff, and detrimental impact on performance. As Naomi Feinstein and Adam Turner have said in a commentary on the scheme *The Right to Work Flexibly – Placebo or Panacea*[44] there was 'a general consensus that this was a pretty toothless law', and 'window dressing'. On the other hand, research has been showing a growing number of applications – and a corresponding level of 'seriousness' on the part of employers in deciding how to respond.[45] As the research seems to indicate, this may be due in part to a concern that refusals may attract potential sex discrimination claims, or other negative repercussions.

The government is committed to reviewing the operation of the scheme in 2006. In *Balancing Work and Family Life: Enhancing Choice and Support for Parents* (DTI, 2003) it has already identified the possible 'next steps' in its family-friendly working strategy, including the targeted use of tax and National Insurance exemptions to provide incentives for employers to support better childcare provision; revising arrangements in the Tax Credits Act 2002 for providing tax credits for the childcare element in Working Tax Credit (see Chapter 22); and generally making improvements to family leave arrangements, and the financial support provided. Research by Claire Callender and Rosalind Edwards, *Caring and Counting: The Impact of Mothers' Employment on Family Relationships*,[46] indicated that current flexible working arrangements, and policies, are likely to be of limited help; and that it will take significant changes on the parts of employers and government to make much impact on the negative effects felt by many parents – especially those with jobs and pre-school children.

The scheme, and its operation and shortcomings, are discussed further in Chapter 8.

PART TWO

Individual Rights

CHAPTER 2

The Gateways to
Employment Rights

Context

The employment protection legislation was drafted principally with full-time, permanent employees – so-called core workers – in mind. The legislation of the mid-1970s which established the 'statutory floor of employment rights' effectively excluded millions of workers from its protections because they were considered to be self-employed, or failed to qualify through lack of continuity of employment. Indeed, it may well be argued that, if the policy behind the legislation was to protect those workers which collective bargaining could not reach, the groups who were excluded – the 'peripheral workers' – were the ones in greatest need of protection.

It is a paradox that at the very moment the contemporary structure of labour law was erected, the labour market started a rapid transformation, both in terms of composition and structure, leaving even more workers engaged, for instance, as part-timers, casuals, homeworkers, or as part of a government training scheme on the margins of employment protection.

Part-time workers constitute the largest group of peripheral workers. Trends in the UK labour market in recent years show a marked increase in part-time work as full-time work has declined. Labour Force surveys show that about 6 million people (25 per cent of all employees) now work less than 30 hours a week, women constituting around 90 per cent of this total and married women accounting for some three-quarters of all part-timers.[1] Most of the growth in the number of part-time jobs and the increase in part-timers as a proportion of the workforce has resulted from changes in the structure of the labour market. Manufacturing, traditionally employing few part-timers, has declined, while the services sector, which has always engaged a relatively large number, has grown.[2]

While the increase in part-time working since the 1960s may be explained by appreciation by employers of the benefits in terms of lower overheads, increased productivity and greater flexibility engendered by the use of part-time labour, there are serious disadvantages from the worker's point of view, not least the low rate of pay relative to full-time employment.[3] A House of Lords committee which examined the problems of part-time workers made this comment on the part-time worker's vulnerability:

Part-time employees, while contributing significantly to the development of the economy and to the flexibility of the productive system, are as a group still behind their full-time colleagues in regard to wage rates, access to training and the promotion and the provision of other benefits. This is both economically self-defeating and socially unacceptable, not least when it reinforces other types of discrimination such as that between male and female employees.[4]

As will be seen, this economic vulnerability is compounded by the status and continuous service requirements of our employment protection law, with the result that a significant number of part-timers have been excluded from rights to redundancy pay, minimum notice periods, statutory guarantee payments, maternity leave, maternity pay or protection against unfair dismissal.[5]

As the use of part-timers increased in the 1980s, this was also paralleled by a marked, though less spectacular, growth in the use of temporary and casual workers. The definitions of a temporary employee covers a number of arrangements: fixed-term contracts; agency temping; casual work; seasonal work. Research by the Institute of Employment Studies[6] suggests that three-quarters of employers in most industrial sectors hire temporary workers. Just over 1 million employees were temporary workers in 1985, compared with over 1.5 million in 1996. Of these, 720,000 worked part-time. Whilst women make up 48 per cent of all employees, 55 per cent of temporary workers are women. It was found that the proportion had grown since 1980 and was on a rising trend. It appears that newer rationales for the engagement of temporary workers (associated with 'flexible manning' policies) are increasingly seen by employers to be important, though traditional rationales (holiday, sickness and absence cover, etc.) still exist.

Interestingly, the growth in temporary work appears to have slowed. According to the Labour Force Survey, the share of employment accounted for by different forms of temporary work (fixed-term contracts, agency workers, casual and seasonal workers) has been falling since 1997, although the overall numbers of temporary workers has increased since 1992 and now stands at over 1.6 million.

According to the Labour Force Survey, the proportion of the workforce in non-permanent employment increased from 5.5 per cent to 6.2 per cent between 1992 and 2001, against the background of a 12 per cent increase in total employment.

However, within the non-permanent employment group, there has been a substantial growth in the number of temporary agency workers – the Labour Force Survey indicates a 253 per cent increase between 1992 and 2001. Growth in agency work across the EU is one factor driving the European Commission's proposal for a directive offering employment protection to agency workers. As will be seen below, the ambiguous employment status of agency workers leaves them legally vulnerable. The proposed Directive on the Working Conditions of Temporary Agency Workers applies an equal treatment principle to agency workers as compared to similar permanent workers in the user company in respect of certain 'essential employment conditions'. On agency workers' rights, see now SI 2003/3319 and Chapter 3.

As with part-time work, the vast majority of 'temps' are women (two-thirds) and are concentrated in personal services, semi- and unskilled manual occupations. However, the survey does suggest that a small but growing proportion of temporary workers is to be found in managerial, technical and professional work.

In legal terms, temporary workers are at least as, and perhaps more, vulnerable than their part-time counterparts. Once again, problems of employment status and continuity present themselves, while those engaged on fixed-term contracts could, until recently, be lawfully be required to sign away redundancy and unfair dismissal rights should the employer not renew the contract.[7]

Employee Status

The number of people who are self-employed increased from almost two million in 1977 to over three million in 1996. The distinction between contracts of employment and self-employment is of fundamental importance, because only 'employees' qualify for employment protection rights such as unfair dismissal, redundancy payments and minimum notice on termination. Wider protection is provided under the Health and Safety at Work Act 1974 and under the discrimination and equal pay legislation which applies to those both under a contract of service and a contract 'personally to execute any work or labour', so including the self-employed. As we shall see below, a recent trend has been to extend the scope of some of the newer employment protection rights to a broader catergory of 'workers'. This definition has been adopted by the Public Interest Disclosure Act 1998, the Working Time Regulations 1998 and the National Minimum Wage Act 1998.

Given the fundamental importance of the distinction, it is unfortunate that the formulation of the test of employee status has come from the courts and tribunals rather than from statute. The only guidance on the question in the legislation is so completely circular as to be absolutely useless.[8]

The case law on this subject is confusing and contradictory. Historically, the leading approach was to apply the test of 'control', that is, could the employer control how, when and where the worker was to work – if so, that worker was an employee. However, as nowadays many employees possess skills not held by their employers, control as the sole determinant of status was rejected. Along the way the test of 'integration' was floated, that is, whether the worker was fully integrated into the employing organisation, but the test was never widely adopted. The modern approach has been to abandon the search for a single test and adopt a multifactorial test, weighing up all the factors for and against the existence of a contract of employment to determine whether the worker was 'in business on his own account'.[9]

Factors which are influential include:

- The method of payment (payment on a commission basis is indicative of self-employment).
- The degree of control exercised over the worker. For example, the worker may be subject to a disciplinary code laid down by the employer.
- If the worker supplies his/her own tools and equipment, this may point to self-employment.
- Can the worker hire his/her own helpers and who bears the risk of loss and chance of profit?
- The payment of sickness and holiday pay indicates the existence of a contract of employment.

Recent case law involving the question of the status of temporary and casual workers has seen an emphasis placed on the concept of mutuality of obligation as a possible factor in the equation. In other words, there must be reciprocal obligations on the employer to provide work for the employee and on the employee to accept that work.

The implications of this test for workers with irregular working patterns are highly disadvantageous – at least if it is applied in a strict sense. The dangers are highlighted in the case of *O'Kelly* v. *Trusthouse Forte plc* [1983] IRLR 369. In this case, the Court of Appeal was not prepared to find that 'regular' casual waiters were employees, even though they had a well-established and regular working relationship with Trusthouse Forte. It was held to be quite 'unreal' to maintain that the long-standing arrangement, which involved a reliance by the employer on its regular casuals, and the regulars receiving priority in the allocation of work, involved the essential 'mutuality of obligation' to classify these casuals as employees. Mutuality was lacking because technically they could refuse work when it was offered, even though in practice they did not do so because refusal would result in removal from the regular casual list.

The sort of narrow reasoning seen in *O'Kelly* is also to be found in the judgment of the EAT in *Wickens* v. *Champion Employment* [1984] ICR 365, where 'temps' engaged by a private employment agency were not accorded employment status because of the lack of binding obligation on the part of the agency to make bookings for work and the absence of any obligation by the worker to accept them. (Cf. *McMeecham* v. *Secretary of State for Employment* [1997] IRLR 353, where the Court of Appeal held that a temporary worker can have the status of employee of an employment agency in respect of each assignment actually worked, notwithstanding that the same worker may not be entitled to employee status under his general terms of engagement.) A return to the *Wickens* approach is again in evidence in *Montgomery* v. *Johnson Underwood Ltd* [2001] IRLR 275, CA. Mrs Montgomery was registered with an agency and was sent to work as a receptionist for the same client company for more than two years. Following her dismissal, she named both the agency and the client as respondents. The employment tribunal and the EAT both held that she was an employee of the agency, but this view was rejected by the Court of Appeal. Buckley J stated that 'mutuality of obligation' and 'control' are the 'irreducible minimum legal requirement for a contract of employment to exist'. According to Buckley J, 'a contractual relationship concerning work to be carried out in which one party has no control over the other could not possibly be called a contract of employment'. In Mrs Montgomery's case, there may have been sufficient mutuality, but a finding of fact that there was no control by the agency was fatal to the argument that she was an employee of the agency. At the same time, there was insufficient mutuality of obligation to find that the hirer was the employer or that any contract at all existed between the agency worker and the hirer.

Yet more confusion relating to the status of agency work was introduced by the decision of the Scottish EAT in *Motorola* v. *Davidson and Melville Craig* [2001] IRLR 4. Davidson worked for Motorola as a mobile telephone repairer. His contract was with Melville Craig, who assigned him to work for Motorola. Motorola paid Melville Craig for his services, and Melville Craig paid Davidson. Davidson was largely subject to Motorola's control. They gave him instructions, provided tools, and he arranged holidays with them. He wore their uniform and badges, and obeyed their rules. If Davidson chose not to work for Motorola, that might have breached his contract with Melville Craig, but not a contract with Motorola. The agreement between Motorola and Melville Craig gave Motorola the right to return Davidson to them if they found him 'unacceptable'. His assignment was terminated by Motorola following a disciplinary hearing held by one of their managers. Mr Davidson claimed unfair dismissal against Motorola who maintained that he was an employee of Melville Craig. However, the employment tribunal concluded that there was sufficient control to make Motorola the employer and the EAT agreed. In the view of the EAT, in determining whether there is a sufficient degree of control to establish a relationship of employer and employee, there is no good reason to ignore practical aspects of control that fall short of legal rights. Nor is it a necessary component of the type of control exercised by an employer over an employee that it should be exercised only directly between them and not by way of a third party acting upon the directions, or at the request of the third party. (Cf. *Hewlett Packard Ltd* v. *O'Murphy* [2002] IRLR 4, EAT and *Dacas* v. *Brook Street Bureau (UK) Ltd* [2004] IRLR 358.)

In the *O'Kelly, Wickens, Montgomery* and *O'Murphy* decisions there is no recognition of the policy considerations of protecting workers from anti-union employers (*O'Kelly*) or providing job protection rights for 'marginal' workers (*Wickens, Montgomery, O'Murphy*).

A more liberal approach is to be found in the majority judgments of the Court of Appeal in *Nethermere (St Neots) Ltd* v. *Gardiner and Taverna* [1984] IRLR 240. Here, homeworkers making clothing on a piecework basis were accorded employee status on the basis that the regular giving and taking of work over a period of time evidenced the necessary mutuality of obligation. This was so even though the workers were under no obligation to undertake a particular quantity of work and in certain weeks did no work at all. As Lord Justice Stephenson put it:

I cannot see why well-founded expectations of continuing homework should not be hardened or refined into enforceable contracts by regular giving and taking of work over periods of a year or more, and why outworkers should not thereby become employees under contracts of service.

A growing subcategory of temporary workers is those on 'zero hours' contracts. The employment status of such workers is cloaked with uncertainty. In their pure form, 'zero hours' contracts require workers to be on call but specify no hours of work and no work is guaranteed. A variant arrangement is the 'min-max' contract where minimum hours are specified. Such arrangements have gained in prevalence in recent years and are most likely to be found in sectors such as retail, banking and the public sector, including health and local authorities. A recent survey of selected organisations found that just over a fifth used 'something which could be described as zero-hours contracts'. Almost all the employers surveyed (80 per cent) said that their zero-hours workers were employees and the authors concluded that this was probably the case given the evidence relating to the employees' limited right to refuse work and the degree of control and integration (Katherine E. Cave, *Zero Hours Contracts: A Report into the Incidence and Implications of Such Contracts*, Huddersfield: University of Huddersfield, 1997). In the light of subsequent developments in the case law, this might be regarded as an overly optimistic conclusion.

In *Carmichael* v. *National Power plc* [1999] IRLR 43, tour guides worked on a 'casual as required' basis. The House of Lords found that the parties' relationship was not intended to subsist during the period when the respondents were not working as guides and that there was no mutuality of obligation such as to give rise to a global contractual relationship of employer and employee existing between the periods of work.

A number of wider implications flow from *Carmichael*. The decision has erected significant obstacles in the way of any attempts to extend employment status to casual workers. Furthermore, it could be used by employers to try to question the employment status of other workers on the margins of employment protection, for example, agency workers and homeworkers. Finally, 'highly evolved' HR practitioners have always faced an uphill struggle in trying to convince line managers that it was not sufficient to label a worker as 'casual' and then assume that they possessed no employment rights. The *Carmichael* decision does not aid the HR manager's cause (see P. Leighton and R.W. Painter, 'Casual Workers: Still Marginal after all these Years?', *Employee Relations*, vol. 23, Nos 1 & 2, 2001, pp. 75–93).

The confusions which abound in this area are multiplied because of the view that the question of employment status is one of mixed fact and law rather than a pure question of law (see *O'Kelly* v. *THF* above). As a result, the powers of the EAT and Court of Appeal to interfere with decisions of industrial tribunals on status are much reduced and the chances of inconsistency thereby heightened. Those who regretted the adoption of this view, welcomed the House of Lords decision in *Davies* v. *Presbyterian Church of Wales* [1986] IRLR 194, where it appeared that Lord Templeman unequivocally held that whether the claimant was an employee was a pure question of law. That case, in which *O'Kelly* was not referred to, turned entirely upon the construction of a document, whereas *O'Kelly* had to be decided partly on the interpretation of various written documents and partly on inferences to be drawn from the parties' conduct. This difference was seized upon by the Court of Appeal in *Hellyer Brothers Ltd* v. *McLeod* [1987] IRLR 232 in order to distinguish *Davies* and to continue to apply the *O'Kelly* approach: viz. an appellate court is entitled to interfere with the decision of a tribunal on whether the applicant was employed under a contract of employment only if the tribunal had misdirected itself in law or its decision was one which no tribunal properly instructed could have reached.

More recently, the Privy Council in *Lee* v. *Chung* [1990] IRLR 236 adopted a similar approach to that taken in *McLeod*, holding that, in the ordinary case, whether or not a person is employed under a contract of employment is not a question of law but a question of fact to be determined by the industrial tribunal. *Davies* v. *Presbyterian Church of Wales* was described as an exceptional case where the relationship was dependent solely on the construction of a written document.

After a period of uncertainty, where it was not clear whether the courts would allow the stated intentions of the parties to determine the matter of status, the courts adopted the view that the subjective intention of the parties will not override what in other respects has the attributes of a contract of employment.

In *Young and Woods Ltd* v. *West* [1980] IRLR 201, West, a sheetworker, requested that he be treated as self-employed. This was accepted by his employer and, although there was no difference between his working conditions and the 'employees' he worked alongside, doing the same job and under the same level of supervision, he was paid gross of tax. When West's job was terminated, he claimed that he was an employee after all and therefore entitled to claim unfair dismissal. The Court of Appeal held that, despite West's arrangement with his employer, he was really an employee and that the tribunal had jurisdiction to hear his complaint. (Cf., however, *Stevedoring and Haulage Services Ltd* v. *Fuller* [2001] IRLR 627.)

The Employment Relations Act 1999, s. 23 gives the Secretary of State power to confer employment rights on non-employees. Unless and until this is done, a typical worker's rights are dependent on the above catalogue of confusing and contradictory case law.

Continuity of Employment

Even for those classified as 'employees', many workers were unable to claim employment protection because they lacked the requisite continuity of employment. Generally, the law required employees to have worked for the employer for at least 16 hours per week for a minimum of two calendar years before they could mount a claim for unfair dismissal or redundancy payments. Those who worked between 8 and 16 hours per week had to accrue five years' service in order to bring a complaint. Only in exceptional cases was no period of qualification required, e.g. dismissals relating to union membership and activities or to non-unionism and sex and race discrimination. Recent EC-inspired case law has brought about a dramatic change to the situation.

First, the House of Lords ruled in *R v. Secretary of State for Employment, ex parte EOC* [1994] IRLR 176 that the hours thresholds for claims of unfair dismissal and redundancy constituted indirect discrimination against women workers contrary to European Law. As a consequence, the government was forced to introduce the Employment Protection (Part-time Employees) Regulations 1995 (SI 1995 No. 31), which came into force on 6 February 1995. The Regulations repeal various provisions of what was sched. 13 of EPCA 1978 so that periods of part-time service will now count in computing the employee's continuous service under the legislation. This ensured that employees working fewer than 16 hours per week had only to complete two years' service with their employer before they qualified for the right to claim unfair dismissal and redundancy pay.

The next development was a challenge to the two-year continuing rule itself in *R v. Secretary of State for Employment, ex parte Seymour-Smith* [1995] IRLR 464. The Court held that in 1991, the two-year qualification period was incompatible with the principle of equal treatment enshrined in Directive 76/207. The Court granted a declaration that the two-year threshold, introduced in 1985, constituted unlawful direct discrimination for which the government could not provide objective justification. The reason for the decision was that statistics for the relevant periods showed that the threshold had a disproportionate effect on women: fewer women could qualify because of their different career paths. As to justification, it was asserted by the government that the law had been changed in order to maximise employment opportunities, but the Court was of the view that there was no evidence that it had succeeded. According to Lord Justice Neill:

On that evidence, the threshold of two years is neither suitable nor requisite for attaining the aim of increased employment. It follows that this discriminatory measure had not been justified.

The Court granted the Employment Secretary the right to appeal to the House of Lords. On appeal, the Lords discharged the declaration on the grounds that it served no useful purpose since it neither enabled the employees to claim unfair dismissal (the Directive not having direct effect against the applicants' private sector employers) nor directed the government that UK legislation had to be amended, since the declaration made was limited to May 1991 (1997 ICR 31). The House of Lords has, however, adjourned consideration of whether the qualifying period, as applied to the applicants, was contrary to European Law until the ECJ has ruled on the following questions:

1. Does an award of compensation for breach of the right not to be unfairly dismissed under national legislation such as the ERA constitute 'pay' within the meaning of article 119 [now 141] of the EC Treaty or that of Directive 76/207 (the equal treatment directive)?
2. If the answer to the question is 'yes', do the conditions for determining whether a worker has a right not to be unfairly dismissed fall within the scope of Article 119 or that of the Equal Treatment Directive?
3. What is the legal test for establishing whether a measure adopted by a Member State has such a degree of disparate effect as between men and women as to amount to indirect discrimination for the purposes of Article 119 [now 141] of

the EC Treaty unless shown to be based upon objectively justified factors other than sex?

4. When must this legal test be applied to a measure adopted by a Member State? In particular at which of the following points in time, or at what other point in time, must it be applied to the measure:

   (a) When the measure is adopted?
   (b) When the measure is brought into force?
   (c) When the employee is dismissed?

5. What are the legal conditions for establishing the objective justification, for the purposes of indirect discrimination under Article 119 [now 141], of a measure adopted by a Member State in pursuance of its social policy? In particular, what material need the Member State adduce in support of its grounds for justification?

The European Court of Justice [1999] IRLR 253 ruled as follows:

1. A judicial award of compensation for breach of the right not to be unfairly dismissed constitutes pay within the meaning of Article 119 [now 141] of the EC Treaty.
2. The conditions determining whether an employee is entitled, where he has been unfairly dismissed, to obtain compensation fall within the scope of Article 119 [now 141] of the Treaty. However, the conditions determining whether an employee is entitled, where he has been unfairly dismissed, to obtain reinstatement or re-engagement fall within the scope of Directive 76/207/EEC of 9 February 1976 on the implementation of the principle of equal treatment for men and women as regards access to employment, vocational training and promotion and working conditions.
3. It is for the national court, taking into account all the material legal and factual circumstances, to determine the point in time at which the legality of a rule to the effect that protection against unfair dismissal applies only to employees who have been continuously employed for a minimum period of two years is to be assessed.
4. In order to establish whether a measure adopted by a Member State has disparate effect as between men and women to such a degree as to amount to indirect discrimination for the purposes of Article 119 [now 141] of the Treaty, the national court must verify whether the statistics available indicate that a considerably smaller percentage of women than men is able to fulfil the requirement imposed by that measure. If that is the case, there is indirect sex discrimination, unless that measure is justified by objective factors unrelated to any discrimination based on sex.
5. If a considerably smaller percentage of women than men is capable of fulfilling the requirement of two years' employment ..., it is for the Member State, as the author of the allegedly discriminatory rule, to show that the said rule reflects a legitimate aim of its social policy, that that aim is unrelated to any discrimination based on sex, and that it could reasonably consider that the means chosen were suitable for attaining that aim.

The case returned to the House of Lords for consideration in the light of the European Court's response to the questions posed. No issues arose on the first two questions, it being accepted that the claim fell within Article 119 [now 141]. The House of Lords allowed the appeal and dismissed the application. In finding the 1985 increase not discriminatory, three Lords (Lords Goff, Jauncey and Nicholls) held that any adverse effect was justified and two (Lords Slynn and Steyn) held that there was no significant adverse effect in the first place.

By the time the above case was decided, the discriminatory effect of the service qualification was reduced with the introduction of the requirement for one year's continuous service for unfair dismissal applicants – though it remains at two years for redundancy payments claims (Unfair Dismissal and Statement for Reasons for Dismissal [Variation of Qualifying Period] Order 1999, SI 1999/1436). The period of continuous employment is relevant not only for determining whether an employee is *qualified* to make claim for unfair dismissal, redundancy payments, etc., but also for calculating the *amount* of compensation. The statutory provisions attempt to ensure that 'continuity' is preserved despite certain changes of employer and certain periods where the employee is away from work.

Continuity: Change of Employer (ERA 1996, s. 218)

Normally only employment with the present employer counts. But there are six circumstances set out in s. 218 in which a change of employer does not break continuity. These include a transfer which occurs on the death of an employer, a change in the constitution of a partnership which acts as an employer and where an Act of Parliament causes one corporate body to replace another as employer. The two most important situations provided are given here.

The first is if a trade, business or undertaking is transferred, the period of employment at the time of transfer counts as a period of employment with the transferee. In other words, the transfer does not break continuity (s. 218 [2]).

In order for this provision to operate, the business must be transferred as a going concern; a mere sale of the physical assets of the business is insufficient. An example of this distinction is provided by *Woodhouse* v. *Peter Brotherhood Ltd* [1972] ICR 186. In this case the nature of the business changed after the transfer from the manufacture of diesel engines to the manufacture of compressors and steam turbines. The Court of Appeal held that in this situation there was only a transfer of physical assets and not a transfer of a business.

In the important case of *Melon* v. *Hector Powe Ltd* [1980] IRLR 477, Lord Frazer thought that essential distinction between the transfer of a business or part of business and the mere sale of assets was 'that in the former case the business is transferred as a going concern so that the business remains the same business in different hands – whereas in the latter case the assets are transferred to the new owner to be used in whatever business he chooses. Individual employees may continue to do the same work in the same environment and they may not appreciate that they are working in a different business, but that may be the true position on consideration of the whole circumstances.'

What counts as the essence of the business? In many cases a decisive factor will be the transfer of the 'goodwill', that is, the acquisition of the right to trade with the transferor's former customers. Machines, and other property, do not possess this essential quality. It is also likely that if the product changes after transfer then the 'business' has not been transferred.

In *Crompton* v. *Truly Fair (International) Ltd* [1975] ICR 359, for example, it was held that there was only a change of ownership of the physical assets where a factory, together with its machinery, was sold and was used for the manufacture of men's trousers, whereas the premises had originally been used for the manufacture of children's clothes.

Until relatively recently, this provision was thought only to preserve continuity where the employee is employed in the business 'at the time of the transfer'. Consequently, a gap between the employee's employment with the transferor and employment with the transferee would break continuity. In *Macer* v. *Abafast* [1990] IRLR 137, the EAT adopted an alternative purposive interpretation of the provision and held that periods of employment accrued with the old employer at the time of the transfer could be added to the period of employment with the new employer and that any gap in employment 'which is related to the machinery of transfer' should not break continuity.

In *Macer*, it was admitted that the new owners had deliberately attempted to break the applicant's continuity by creating a gap of more than one week before the transfer transactions commenced. The EAT decided that continuity was preserved and that he was entitled to maintain his claim for unfair dismissal.

In approaching the construction of the provision, the EAT felt that

> the Court should lean in favour of that interpretation which best gives effect to the preservation of continuity of service and hence to the rights of the employee, and to obviate and discourage a tactical manoeuvre which seeks to avoid the clear intention of Parliament.

(See also *Clark and Tokey Ltd* v. *Oakes* [1997] IRLR 564 EAT.)

The second key circumstance providing continuity of employment is that if the employee is taken into the employment of an 'associated employer', the period of employment with the old employer counts as a period of employment with the 'associated employer' (ERA 1996, s. 128 [6]).

The definition of this concept is to be found in ERA 1996, s. 231, which states that '... any two employers are to be treated as associated if one is a company of which the other (directly or indirectly) has control, or if both are companies of which a third person (directly or indirectly) has control'.

Two major issues arise from this definition. First, 'control' means voting control rather than de facto control. In *Secretary of State for Employment* v. *Newbold* [1981] IRLR 305, Mr Justice Bristow stated: 'In the law affecting companies, control is well recognised to mean control by the majority of votes attaching to the shares exercised in General Meeting. It is not how or by whom the enterprise is actually run.'

Second, the definition has been held to be exhaustive, so that only companies can be associated – local authorities or health authorities fall outside the definition (see *Gardiner* v. *LB Merton* [1980] IRLR 472).

In *Hancill* v. *Marcon Engineering Ltd* [1990] IRLR 51 it was held that the word 'company' can include an overseas company if the overseas company can be likened in its essentials to a company limited under the Companies Act. Thus, Mr Hancill was able to count his period of employment with an American subsidiary in order to meet the qualifying period of service for claiming unfair dismissal.

The Transfer of Undertakings (Protection of Employment) Regulations 1981
These complex regulations overlay additional rules which apply where there
is a change of employer. They provide for the automatic transfer of contracts of
employment, collective agreements and trade union recognition in the case of certain
business transfers, impose a duty on employers to inform and consult recognised trade
unions and hold any dismissal in connection with such transfers automatically unfair
unless it occurs for an 'economic, technical or organisational' reason. This latter
aspect of the regulations will be discussed in greater detail in Chapter 15 below.

None of the provisions of the regulations operates unless there is a 'relevant transfer'
under reg. 3 (1), that is, 'a transfer from one person to another of an undertaking
situated immediately before the transfer in the UK or a part of one so situated'. An
undertaking was defined by reg. 2 (1) to include 'any trade or business but does not
include any undertaking or part of an undertaking which is not in the nature of a
commercial venture'. Under the Trade Union Reform and Employment Rights Act
1993 (TURERA) the definition was extended to cover non-commercial undertakings.
This is designed to bring UK legislation into line with EC law.[10] The implications of
this change for those workers involved in contracting out of services and compulsory
competitive tendering are discussed in Chapter 15 below. It would appear that under
ERA 1996, s. 218 a mere transfer of assets which falls short of a transfer of the
undertaking as a going concern will fall outside the regulations. Subsequently, the
ECJ has enunciated the test as whether a stable economic entity has been transferred.
In *Schmidt* v. *Spar- und Leihkasse der Früheren Ämter Bordersholm, Kiel and Cronshagen*
[1994] IRLR 302, it was held that there could be a transfer of contracted-out cleaning
services, even where the services are performed by a single employee and there is
no transfer of tangible assets. Contrast this approach to the later holding in *Süzen* v.
Zehnacker Gebäudereingung GmbH Krankenhausservice [1997] IRLR 255, ECJ, that an
activity does not, in itself, constitute a stable economic entity. Consequently, the ECJ
stated, the mere fact that a similar activity is carried on before and after a change of
contractors does not mean that there is a transfer of undertaking. In the case of a
labour-intensive undertaking with no significant assets (e.g. contract cleaning), the
Süzen approach will mean that there will generally be no transfer unless the new
contractor takes on the majority of the old contractor's staff. This opens up a huge
gap in the protection offered by the Acquired Rights Directive and TUPE.

The Effect of a Transfer on the Contract of Employment
The important change wrought by the regulations is to override the position at
common law and provide that a transfer does not terminate the contracts of the
employees of the business. Instead, contracts continue with the substitution of the
transferee as employer and the transferee taking all the transferor's 'rights, powers,
duties and liabilities under or in connection with any such contract' – reg. 5 (1)
and (2).

By virtue of reg. 5 (3), however, this transfer of liability will only occur where the
employee was employed in the undertaking 'immediately before the transfer'.

Different divisions of the EAT reached different conclusions on the precise
interpretation of the phrase 'immediately before the transfer'. This conflict of authority
was apparently resolved by the decision of the Court of Appeal in *Secretary of State
for Employment* v. *Spence* [1986] IRLR 248 that only when employees are employed
at the very moment of a business transfer does the purchaser take over the vendor's
liabilities under or in connection with the existing employment contracts. In other

words, a business purchaser could not be made liable for dismissals carried out by the vendor before the transfer.

The scope of this decision is now heavily constrained by the judgment of the House of Lords in *Litster* v. *Forth Dry Dock & Engineering Co Ltd* [1989] IRLR 161. The House of Lords holds that liability for a dismissal by the vendor prior to the transfer passes to the purchaser if the employee has been unfairly dismissed for a reason connected with the transfer.

Although reg. 5 (3) provides that liability is to be transferred only where the employee is 'employed immediately before the transfer', in order for the regulations to give effect to the EC Employee Rights on Transfer of Business Directive 77/187 as interpreted by the ECJ, reg. 5 (3) must be read as if there were inserted the words 'or would have been so employed if he had not been unfairly dismissed in the circumstances described in reg. 8 (1)'.

Without such a purposive interpretation, the regulations would, according to Lord Keith, 'be capable of ready evasion through the transferee arranging with the transferor for the latter to dismiss its employees a short time before the transfer becomes operative', thereby leaving the employees, as in this case, with 'worthless claims for unfair dismissal' against an insolvent vendor (see also *P Bork International A/S* v. *Forgeningen af Arbejdsledere i Danmark* [1989] IRLR 41).

The approach advocated by the House of Lords is in two stages. First, it must be determined whether the dismissal by the vendor was unfair within the meaning of reg. 8. If yes, then unfair dismissal liability under reg. 5 passes to the purchaser, even if the dismissal was not, in temporal terms, immediately before the transfer. Second, it is only where the dismissal does not breach reg. 8 that the construction of 'employed immediately before the transfer' laid down in *Spence* continues to apply. So, if the reason for the dismissal is unconnected with the transfer, liability passes to the transferee only if the employee had not been dismissed before the moment of transfer.

Continuity: Periods away from Work

An employee's service may be continuous in a statutory sense even where the employee has been away from work for certain periods.

First, ERA 1996, s. 212 (1) makes it clear that any week during the whole or part of which an employee's relations are governed by a contract of employment counts in computing the employee's period of employment. This is so whether the employee is actually at work or not. It follows that periods of absence from work by reason of sickness or pregnancy will count as periods of continuous employment without reliance on any other provision so long as the contract of employment has not been terminated.

Second, even where an employee is away from work and no longer has a contract, service may still be deemed to be continuous in certain situations should the employee eventually return to work. These situations are set out in ERA 1996, s. 212 (3):

(i) Absence through sickness or injury, provided the absence does not exceed 26 weeks.

(ii) Up to 26 weeks absence wholly or partly because of pregnancy or confinement (for example, where a woman with less than two years' service with her employer has been dismissed while absent because of pregnancy and is later re-employed by that employer).

(iii) The whole of statutory permitted absence for leave on the grounds of pregnancy or confinement.

(iv) Absence through a 'temporary cessation of work'. This phrase has caused some difficulty; two decisions by the House of Lords and one by the Court of Appeal have provided guidance on its interpretation. The first authority is *Fitzgerald* v. *Hall Russell Ltd* [1970] AC 984, where it was held that the phrase refers to the cessation of the individual employee's work for some reason: there is no need to show that 'at the same time the whole works would close down or a department was closed down or a large number of other employees were laid off at the same time' (Lord Upjohn).

This decision also states that in order to determine whether the absence is temporary it should be viewed in the context of the employment relationship as a whole. With the benefit of hindsight, we should be able to determine whether the absence was of a transient nature.

The second important House of Lords authority is *Ford* v. *Warwickshire County Council* [1983] IRLR 126. The applicant in that case was a teacher who had been employed by the county council under a series of consecutive short-term contracts, each for an academic year, for a total of eight years. There was, therefore, a break between the end of one contract and the beginning of the next. The House of Lords held that what is now ERA 1996, s. 212 (3) (b) could apply in order to preserve the continuity of her employment. In the course of his judgment, Lord Diplock offered the following guidance:

> The continuity of employment for the purpose of the Act is not broken unless and until looking backwards from the date of the expiry of the fixed-term contract on which the employee's claim is based, there is to be found between one fixed-term contract and its immediate predecessor an interval that cannot be characterised as short relative to the combined duration of the two fixed-term contracts.

This approach is undoubtedly of benefit to many workers, such as part-time or temporary teachers, and makes it much more difficult for employers to avoid the employment protection laws by offering a succession of fixed-term contracts. However, it may not be appropriate where patterns of employment are not regular, as they were in Ford's case, but are subject to fluctuation. To look only at a particular period of unemployment and to compare that period with the combination of the periods either side could lead to some unjust results.

This issue arose before the Court of Appeal in *Flack* v. *Kodak Ltd* [1986] IRLR 258. In this case, Mrs Flack had been employed by Kodak in its photo-finishing department over a number of years for periods which fluctuated markedly. Following her final dismissal, she and the other 'seasonal employees' claimed redundancy payments. A tribunal, purporting to follow what Lord Diplock had said in *Ford* with regard to temporary cessation, rejected their claim. In coming to this conclusion, the tribunal confined itself to a purely mathematical comparison of the gap in employment falling within the two years preceding the final dismissal with the period of employment immediately before and after that gap. Both the EAT and Court of Appeal thought that this was the wrong approach in the context of this particular case. They were of the view that the correct approach was to take into account all the relevant circumstances, and in particular to consider the length of the period of employment as a whole. While it was true that the only absences from work on account of temporary cessations of work which were relevant for the purposes of redundancy payments and unfair dismissal claim qualifications were those which occurred during the two years prior to the dismissal, the characterisations of those cessations as temporary may be crucially affected by the whole history of the employment. As Sir John Donaldson put it: 'A long gap in the course of a longer period of work extending over many years might well be considered temporary, whereas if the same gap occurred in the course of a shorter period it would not.'

(v)   Absence from work 'in circumstances such that by arrangement or custom' the employee is regarded as continuing in the employment of the employer for all or any purposes.
       It would appear that in order to fall within this provision, the arrangement or understanding must be established at the time the absence commences (see, for example, *Murphy* v. *A. Birrell & Sons* [1978] IRLR 458). The absences that might be encompassed could be leave of absence arrangements, employees placed upon a 'reserve list' to be called upon as necessary and employees on secondment. A number of commentators argue that the EAT's broad application of the sub-paragraph in *Lloyds Bank Ltd* v. *Secretary of State for Employment* [1979] IRLR 41 is no longer good law following the judgments of the Lords in *Ford*. In the *Lloyds* case, the EAT held that where an employee works on a one-week-on and one-week-off basis, the weeks which she does not work count towards continuity by virtue of what is now ERA 1996, s. 212 (3) (c). This was despite the fact that the side note to the provision reads 'Periods in which there is no contract of employment'. In the Lloyds case a contract did exist throughout the period of employment. In the Ford case, the House of Lords placed considerable emphasis on the requirement that there be no subsisting contract before the provision could operate. On that basis, the authority of the Lloyds case looks decidedly shaky. See also *Curr* v. *Marks & Spencer plc* [2003] IRLR 74, CA.

In *Morris* v. *Walsh Western Ltd* [1997] IRLR 562, the EAT held than an employer's ex post facto agreement to treat the period of an employee's absence from work as a period of unpaid leave was insufficient to preserve his continuity of employment. As a matter of statutory construction, an 'arrangement' whereby an employee is treated as continuing in employment must be in place when the employee is absent from work, not afterwards.

Strikes and Lock-outs
If an employee takes part in a strike or a lock-out, the beginning of the period of employment is treated as postponed by the number of days between the start of the strike or lock-out and the resumption of work (ERA 1996, s. 216). In other words, the period of the industrial dispute does not count towards continuity, but it does not break it.

The Case for Reform[11]

In this chapter we have examined the complexities surrounding the two major gateways to employment protection and the particular problems they pose for those whose work is temporary, part-time or casual.

Commentators such as Hepple[12] and Leighton[13] have long argued for a radical change of approach by our legislators, maintaining that any reform in this area is likely to be frustrated if statutory rights continue to rest on the nebulous concept of the 'contract of service'. Hepple has proposed that the 'contract of service' should be replaced by a broad definition of the 'employment relationship' between the worker and the undertaking by which s/he is employed. The relationship would continue to be based on a voluntary agreement between the worker and the undertaking to work in return for pay, but 'it would be a contract of a new kind, one that encompassed both the intermittent exchange of work for remuneration and the single continuous contract'.

Hepple accepts that this protection should exclude genuinely independent workers, those 'in business on their own account', but argues that there can be no watertight legal definition of who is 'independent'. He proposes a statutory presumption that the worker is covered by the legislation, with the burden of proof on the employer should it be alleged that the worker is independent.

In *Fairness at Work*, Cmnd 3968, May 1998, the government invited views on whether legislation should be introduced to extend the coverage of some or all of existing employment rights by regulation to all those who work for another person, not just those employed under a contract of employment.

Indeed, a number of the new employment protection rights have been extended to the broader category of 'workers'. This definition has been adopted by the Public Interest Disclosure Act 1998, the National Minimum Wage Act 1998 and the Working Time Regulations 1998.

The definition is set out in ERA 1996, s. 230 (3) which states that a 'worker' is an individual who has entered into or works under –

(a) a contract of employment, *or*
(b) *any other contract ... whereby the individual undertakes to do or perform personally any work or services for another party to the contract* whose status is not by virtue of the contract that of a client or customer of any profession or business undertaking carried on by the individual. (original emphasis)

In addition, the Employment Relations Act 1999, s. 23 empowers the Secretary of State to extend employment rights to workers who are not currently covered. In July 2002, the government issued a discussion document as part of a review it was carrying out in relation to statutory employment rights (see *Discussion Document on Employment Status in Relation to Statutory Employment Rights*, DTI, July 2002, URN 02/1058). The government invited views on, *inter alia*, the following:

- What the costs and benefits of extending the scope of some or all employment rights may be for small businesses, other organisations and working people.

The Discussion Document identified the case for and against extending statutory employment rights. The arguments for extending the coverage included:

- There are concerns that some working people are being excluded from employment rights due to technicalities relating to the type of contract or other arrangement they are engaged under. Examples of these might be some agency workers, the clergy or labour-only subcontractors. These working people may, in practice, do the same type of work as employees, may be subject to similar demands in that they may have equally little autonomy over when and how they do their work in practice and may be economically dependent on a single source of work. There may be a fairness case for giving them the same protection as employees.

- Extending employment rights may guarantee protection for more atypical workers and increase working peoples' willingness to take up atypical work, knowing their rights are secured. The numbers of atypical workers in the UK labour market remains surprisingly low and the extension of rights may increase the take-up of atypical work arrangements.
- Extending certain rights could increase clarity in the law. It may remove anomalies in the coverage of some employment and other rights. For example, some non-employee workers may have a right to receive statutory maternity pay (SMP), but would not automatically have a right to take maternity leave or a right not to suffer detriment for reasons of pregnancy. This may be confusing for both employers and workers. Extending rights to all workers may also increase certainty and clarity for working people who are on the employee/ non-employee borderline and their employers if a single definition were used in employment rights legislation, or fewer different definitions were used. This may particularly help small businesses.
- The numbers of working people who would be affected by adopting the definition of 'worker' is likely to be low and the extension could bring significant benefits to the working people concerned and ensure they feel more valued. Work providers may be more willing to integrate more peripheral workers into their permanent workforce through investment in training and this could result in more high performance workplaces.
  ...(N.B. DTI research on employment status estimates that adoption of the definition of 'worker' would be likely to increase the numbers covered by employment rights by 5% (Burchill, B., Deakin, S., Honey, S., The Employment Status of Individuals in Non-Standard Employment, (1999) URN 98/943 no.6, EMAR Employment Relations Research Series, DTI, London))

Arguments against extending protection included the following;

- If non-employees have a broader range of statutory employment rights, employers might increase their demands on them or the degree of commitment they expect of them. This could reduce flexibility for these working people. Some atypical workers may enjoy a higher remuneration package than other workers because they do not have the same employment rights protection. The government would appreciate views on whether an extension of employment rights would fundamentally change the nature of the relationship between certain work providers and working people.
- Extending certain rights may reduce employers' willingness to offer atypical working arrangements. The government is seeking evidence of the effects of extending employment rights on overall employment rates and opportunities for people. Extending some rights, such as maternity rights and the right to unfair dismissal may increase administrative burdens on business. The effect could be significant in certain sectors such in the temporary agency work sector, where there may be a high proportion of non-employee workers. In addition, there may be a risk that extending some rights to certain categories,

such as agency workers, could lead to a reduction in demand for such working people.

• Legislation extending employment rights may be unnecessary to allow some working people to achieve a work-life balance. Some working people with looser employment relationships may in practice be able to exercise the same rights to time off as those on a contract of employment, even in the absence of statutory protection. Non-employees may be able to choose to work around domestic commitments or public duties and could refuse offers of work coinciding with periods where they would want to take maternity and parental leave. Some working people may be given certain benefits, such as parental leave, maternity leave or time off for emergencies, despite the absence of a legal requirement to do so.

• There may be set up costs for business, especially small businesses, in the extension of rights. For instance, some small businesses who rely on non-employee workers would be especially affected by the extension of certain rights which involve putting in place certain procedures, such as the right to a written statement of reasons for dismissal, right to written statement of terms and conditions and the right ot an itemized pay statement.

• Using a 'worker' definition more widely in employment rights legislation would not remove differences between the definitions used in employment rights legislation and for tax purposes. It might not increase the clarity of employment status across different jurisdictions.

• Extending employment rights to all workers may not significantly reduce uncertainties over status, since disputes over status would still ultimately needed to be decided by a tribunal.

The closing date for responses to the Discussion paper was 11 December 2002 but, at the time of writing, no proposals have been forthcoming from the government.

What is surprising is that relatively few individuals will gain access to the full range of employment rights if the 'worker' definition was generally adopted – a further 5 per cent of the workforce according to the DTI research referred to above. Also, as the Discussion Paper implicitly recognises, the adoption of the 'worker' definition will not necessarily enfranchise that many more individuals or remove uncertainties over status if the definition receives a restrictive interpretation by the courts and tribunal. If this occurs we will have replaced the problems surrounding the employee/self-employed divide with a whole new set of problems around the borderline between the worker and the self-employed (e.g. see *Smith* v. *Hewitson and Hewitson t/a Executive Coach Catering Services* EAT/489/01).

What is clear is that as work organisational forms become become more complex through arrangements such as agency working, private finance initiatives, franchising etc., there is an increasing mismatch between the legal construct of an employment relationship involving a single employer and a single employee and the reality for the employee who may be subject to more than one 'employer'. For this reason Earnshaw, Rubery and Cooke have proposed that 'one way forward would be to recognise that for certain purposes more than one entity may be the employer of a single group of employees, so long as this did not lead to buck-passing ... We could indeed envisage the answer to the question "Who is the employer?" should depend on the reason for the question being asked. For instance, if the question arises because an employee has been injured at work, the person who should be deemed to be the employer is the one who has the greater control over the working environment and input into devising the relevant systems of work. If, on the other hand, the employer seeks redress in respect of the loss of his or her job, one should consider not only who has the *right* to discipline, but also who in reality has the greater influence over that person's job tenure.'

Earnshaw et al. also offer an alternative approach which would be simply to extend the scope of certain rights and obligations beyond the immediate employer in ways already adopted by the discrimination legislation. Agency workers are protected against discrimination by the client organisation in which they are placed not because the client is viewed as the 'employer' but because the duty not to discriminate unlawfully is extended to the person to whom the client workers are made available for work (SDA 1975, s. 9, RRA 1976, s. 7) (J. Earnshaw, J. Rubery and F.L. Cooke, *Who is the Employer*, London: Institute of Employment Rights, 2002).

EC Initiatives Relating to Atypical Workers

The Part-time Workers (Prevention of Less Favourable Treatment) Regulations 2000 (SI 2000/1551)

The EC has been concerned for some while to ensure that part-time workers receive no less favourable treatment than full-time workers. There are a number of policy considerations for this, including recent rapid increases in part-time and 'atypical' working within Member States; and the need to promote labour market objectives of 'employability', and conditions generally in which workers are going to remain in employment rather than leave work to take up out-of-work State benefits. The principles of equal treatment in respect of terms and conditions of employment and the application of statutory employment protection is recognised in most other European Member States (see, for example, the French *Code du Travail*, Article L212–4–2). However, the translation of this principle into an EC directive was, for many years, opposed by the UK's Conservative government on the grounds of the negative employment effect it would allegedly create.

The Directive on Part-time Work (EC Directive 97/81) was the result of an earlier Framework Agreement between the 'social partners' (employers, unions and public sector employers). The Directive itself is open to criticism in that it allows governments to exclude casual workers from the definition of part-time worker entirely (clause 2), while the equal treatment of part-time workers is subject to the possible justification of special conditions on objective grounds. The range of objective grounds envisaged include time worked and an earnings qualification. Such qualifications have proved to be an effective means of excluding part-time workers from employment rights. (See J. Rose, 'Marginal Notes? Gender and the Contract of Employment', in A. Morris and T. O'Donnell, (eds), *Feminist Perspectives on Employment Law*, London: Cavendish, 1999; M. Jeffrey, 'Not Really Going to Work? "Atypical Work" and Attempts to Regulate It', *ILJ*, vol. 27 (1998), pp. 193–213.)

On 1 July 2000 the government brought into force the Part-time Workers (Prevention of Less Favourable Treatment) Regulations 2000 (SI 2000/1551) in order to implement the Directive. The Regulations define a full-time worker as a person who is 'paid wholly or in part by reference to the time he works and, having regard to the custom and practice of the employer in relation to workers employed ... under the same type of contract, is identifiable as a full-time worker' (reg. 2 [1]).

A worker is defined as part-time 'if he is paid wholly or in part by reference to the time and, having regard to the custom and practice of the employer in relation to workers employed by the worker's employer under the same type of contract, is not identifiable as a full-time worker' (reg. 2 [2]).

The key equality of treatment principle is set out in reg. 5 which states:

5(1) A part-time worker has the right not to be treated by his employer less favourably than the employer treats a comparable full-time worker –

    (a) as regards the terms of his contract; or

    (b) by being subjected to any other detriment by any act, or deliberate failure to act, of his employer.

(2) The right conferred by paragraph (1) applies only if –

    (a) the treatment is on the ground that the worker is a part-time worker, and

    (b) the treatment is not justified on objective grounds.

(3) In determining whether a part-time worker has been treated less favourably than a comparable full-time worker the pro rata principle shall be applied unless it is inappropriate.

(4) A part-time worker paid at a lower rate for overtime worked by him in a period than a comparable full-time worker is or would be paid for overtime worked for him in the same period shall not, for that reason, be regarded as treated less favourably than the comparable full-time worker where, or to the extent that, the total number of hours worked by the part-time worker in the period, including overtime, does not exceed the number of hours the comparable full-time worker is required to work in the period, disregarding absences from work and overtime.

This means part-timers are entitled to:

(a) the same hourly rate of pay (subject to reg. 5 [4] on overtime);

(b) the same access to company pension schemes;

(c) the same entitlements to annual leave and maternity/parental leave on a pro rata basis;

(d) the same entitlement to contractual sick pay; and

(e) no less favourable treatment in access to training.

In the draft form of the Regulations, the government proposed to confine their coverage to 'employees' not 'workers' (draft reg. 1 [2]). As a consequence, many economically dependent workers – such as Mrs Carmichael – would have been disenfranchised from significant parts of the framework of employment protection. Ultimately, the government responded to the threat of legal action from the TUC and broadened the coverage of the Regulations.

Regulation 2 (4) sets out the requirements for the full comparator:

A full-time worker is a comparable full-time worker in relation to a part-time worker if, at the time when the treatment is alleged to be less favourable to the part-time worker takes place –

(a) both workers are –

    (i) employed by the same employer under the same type of contract, and

      (ii)   engaged in the same or broadly similar work having regard, where relevant, to whether they have a similar level of qualifications, skills and experience; and

  (b) the full-time worker works or is based at the same establishment as the part-time worker or, where there is no full-time worker working or based at that establishment who satisfies the requirements of sub-paragraph (a), works or is based at different establishments and satisfies those requirements.

Despite the broadening of the coverage of the Regulations to 'workers' – as opposed to 'employees' – the Regulations, as originally enacted, retained the potential to disenfranchise many economically dependent workers from the scope of their protection. This was because comparisons under the Regulations could only be employed under the Regulations between an actual comparator (cf. the SDA and RRA) employed under the same contract. Thus, for example, a part-time worker employed on a fixed-term contract could not compare his or her treatment with that of a full-time worker employed on a permanent contract – see reg. 2 (3). It was clear that the Regulations needed to be amended to comply with the Fixed-term Work Directive, 1999/70/EC. Consequently, the reference to a different category of fixed-term contracts was removed by the Amendment Regulations 2002 SI No. 2035 as from 1 October 2002. As a result, fixed-term and permanent workers will be regarded as 'employed under the same contract', although the fact that a worker is on a particular type of contract may be justification for less favourable treatment. The only cases in which a claim may be made without reference to an actual full-time comparator are set out in the Regulations. Broadly, these exceptions cover (a) a full-time worker who becomes part-time (reg. 3) and (b) full-time workers returning to work part-time for the same employer within a period of less than 12 months (reg. 4).

    Matthews v. *Kent & Medway Towns Fire Authority* [2003] IRLR 732. EAT is an illustration of how narrowly the Part-time Workers Regulations were drafted. This was a test case brought by some 12,000 retained firefighters alleging that they had been treated less favourably than full-time firefighters, especially as regards their exclusion from the Firemen's Pension Scheme. The claim fell at the first statutory hurdle. Regulation 2 (4) specifies that a part-time worker can only bring a comparison with a full-time worker if both workers are 'employed by the same employer under the same type of contract'. Regulation 2 (3) sets out what are regarded as different types of contract. These include 'employees employed under a contract that is not a contract of apprenticeship' and a residual category of 'any other description of worker that it is reasonable for the employer to treat differently from other workers on the ground that workers of that description have a different type of contract'. The EAT held that retained fire workers have a 'different type of contract' and that it was reasonable for the employers to treat them differently.

    The thrust of this decison is that employers can continue to single out part-time workers for unfavourable treatment in respect of fringe benefits, for example, so long as no full-time workers are employed on the same type of contracts.

    The impact of the Regulations may not be devastating. Even the DTI's Regulatory Impact Assessment, which accompanied the draft Regulations, evidences their likely limited effect when it states:

> There are approximately 6 million part-time employees in Great Britain – all of whom will benefit from added security. We estimate that 1 million have a comparable full-time employee. Equal treatment could directly benefit 400,000 part-time workers through increases in pay and non-wage benefits.

In other words, less than 17 per cent of all part-time workers work alongside a potential full-time comparator and less than 7 per cent stand directly to benefit through increase in pay and non-wage benefits.

The right of part-timers not to be treated less favourably than a comparable full-timer applies only if the treatment is not justified on objective grounds (see reg. 5 [4], above). The Explanatory Note accompanying the Regulations states that:

Less favourable treatment will only be justified on objective grounds if it can be shown that the less favourable treatment:

(i)   is to achieve a legitimate objective, for example, a genuine business objective;

(ii)   is necessary to achieve that objective; and

(iii) is an appropriate way to achieve the objective.

Unfair Dismissal and the Right not to be Subjected to Detriment
Regulation 7 renders it unlawful to dismiss a worker or subject him or her to any detriment on the grounds that s/he has:

(i)   brought proceedings against the employer under these Regulations;

(ii)   requested from his employer a written statement of reasons under regulation 6;

(iii) given evidence or information in connection with such proceedings brought by any worker;

(iv)   otherwise done anything under these Regulations in relation to the employer or any other person;

(v)   alleged that the employer has infringed these Regulations; or

(vi)   refused (or proposed to refuse) to forgo a right conferred on him by these Regulations, or

that the employer believes or suspects that the worker has done or intends to do any of the things mentioned above.

An unfair dismissal under reg. 7 does not require the qualifying period generally required for unfair dismissal claims.

The rights set out in the Regulations are exercisable by complaint to an employment tribunal. Regulation 6 provides a right for the employee to receive a written statement of reasons for less favourable treatment within 21 days of the request.

Where a tribunal finds that a complaint of less favourable treatment presented to it under the Regulations is well-founded, it may, *inter alia*, order the employer to pay such compensation which is just and equitable in all the circumstances (reg. 8 [7], [9]). The calculation will not include injury to feelings (reg. 8 [11]).

A further amendment to the Regulations came into force on 1 October 2002. It covers access to occupational pension schemes (reg. 8). The amendment removes the limitation on remedies following a complaint relating to access to, or treatment under, an occupational pension scheme. As originally enacted, reg. 8 (8) stated that where an ET has upheld a complaint from a part-timer for equal access to an occupational pension scheme, the remedies which it orders may not go back further than two years. This time limit was originally inserted to ensure consistency with existing equal pay and pensions legislation, which provides that employer contributions to a pension scheme may not be backdated by more than two years. In *Preston* v. *Wolverhampton*

Healthcare Trust [2001] IRLR 237, the House of Lords ruled that the two-year time limit on backdating contravened EC Law and could no longer be maintained. As a consequence, the government propose to amend the Part-time Workers Regulations to remove the two-year limit.

The Fixed-term Employees (Prevention of Less Favourable Treatment) Regulations

Background

In 1999, the European employers' associations and trade unions (the 'Social Partners') negotiated the European Framework Agreement on fixed-term work. The Framework Agreement aims to prevent fixed-term employees from being less favourably treated. It also aims to limit the scope for using a succession of fixed-term contracts to employ the same person and to improve access to training and information on permanent jobs for workers on fixed-term contracts. The European Council agreed to make the Framework Agreement legally binding through the EC Directive 1999/70/EC of 28 June 1999. The Directive was implanted in the UK by the Fixed-term Employees (Prevention of Less Favourable Treatment) Regulations which came into force on 1 October 2002.

Aims of the Regulations

The overall aim of the Regulations is to seek to ensure that fixed-term employees should not be treated less favourably than comparable permanent employees on the grounds they are fixed-term employees, unless this is objectively justified.

Who is Covered?

The Regulations apply to: employees on contracts that last for a specified period of time or will end when a specified task has been completed or a specified event does or does not happen. Examples include employees covering for maternity leave and peaks in demand and employees on task contracts such as setting up a database or running a training course.

The Regulations define 'permanent' employees as those who are not on fixed-term contracts. These employees may more generally be referred to as employees on contracts for an indefinite or indeterminate term.

The Comparator

Fixed-term employees can compare their conditions to: employees who are not on fixed-term contracts and are employed by the same employer to do the same or broadly similar work. Where relevant the comparator should have similar skills and qualifications to the fixed-term employee. If there is no comparator in the establishment, a comparison can be made with a similar permanent employee working for the same employer in a different establishment.

Less Favourable Treatment

Less favourable treatment can occur when a fixed-term employee does not get a benefit, whether it is contractual or not, that a comparable permanent employee gets or is offered. For example, permanent employees could be given free medical insurance which fixed-term employees do not receive. Alternatively, membership to the scheme is open to all provided that they pay a contribution to the annual premium, but permanent employees are allowed to pay on a monthly basis, whereas fixed-term employees have to pay their contribution 'up-front' in one lump sum.

A fixed-term employee could also be less favourably treated than a permanent comparator because, even though their contracts are the same, the permanent employee receives non-contractual benefits which are not given to fixed-term employees e.g. an annual bonus.

By the same token, the fixed-term employee could be subject to a disadvantage not experienced by a permanent employee. For example, where fixed-term employees are selected for redundancy purely because they have fixed-term contracts.

Objective Justification

Employers should ask themselves the question: 'is there a good reason for treating this employee less favourably?' They should give due regard to the needs and rights of individual employees and try to balance those against business objectives.

Less favourable treatment will be justified on objective grounds if it can be shown that the less favourable treatment –

- is to achieve a legitimate objective, for example a genuine business objective;
- is necessary to achieve that objective;
- is an appropriate way to achieve that objective.

Objective justification may be a matter of degree. Employers should therefore consider whether it is possible to offer fixed-term employees certain benefits, such as annual subscriptions, loans, clothing allowances and insurance policies, on a pro rata basis. Sometimes, the cost to the employer of offering a particular benefit to an employee may be disproportionate when compared to the benefit the employee would receive, and this may objectively justify different treatment. An example of this may be where a fixed-term employee is on a contract of three months and a comparator has a company car. The employer may decide not to offer the car if the cost of doing so is high and the need of the business for the employee to travel can be met in some other way.

Employers need to consider whether less favourable treatment is objectively justified on a case-by-case basis.

When applying the equal treatment requirement, employers can objectively justify different terms and conditions for fixed-term employees in two different ways:

(i) By showing that there is an objective justification for not giving the fixed-term employee a particular benefit or for giving him or her the benefit on less good terms. This approach is used in other discrimination law, including sex discrimination and race relations law and the Regulations preventing part-time workers from being treated less favourably than comparable full-time ones.

(ii) By showing that the value of the fixed-term employee's total package of terms and conditions is at least equal to the value of the comparable permanent employee's total package of terms and conditions.

A comparison needs to be made, either on a term-by-term basis or on a package basis.

Comparing Conditions Term by Term

Employers and employees may take what may be called a 'term-by-term' approach to equal treatment. This means that every individual term of a fixed-term employee's employment package should be completely the same, or if appropriate the same on a pro rata basis, as the equivalent term of the comparable permanent employee, unless a difference in the term is objectively justified. For example, if a permanent employee is paid £350 per week, has 25 days annual leave per year and receives an annual clothing allowance of £500, the same conditions should apply to a fixed-term employee (on a pro rata basis if appropriate), unless objectively justified.

The Package Approach

The Regulations provide in particular that less favourable treatment in relation to particular contractual terms is justified where the fixed-term employee's overall package of terms and conditions is no less favourable than the comparable permanent employee's overall package.

Employers will be able to balance a less favourable condition against a more favourable one, provided they ensure a fixed-term employee's overall employment package is not less favourable than that of a comparable permanent employee. Employers will not be prevented from paying higher up-front rewards in return for reduced benefits elsewhere if the overall package is not less favourable. This is what is meant by a 'package approach'.

The value of benefits should be assessed on the basis of their objective monetary worth, rather than the value the employer or employee perceives them to have.

Employers can still objectively justify not giving a particular benefit if they choose to use a package approach. Employers do not have to make up for the value of a missing benefit if they can objectively justify not giving it. If a package approach is used, it will be objectively justified for a fixed-term employee to have a less favourable overall package than a comparable permanent employee, if the difference consists in one or more terms that it is objectively justified not to give the fixed-term employee. Example of using the package approach: A fixed-term employee is paid £20,800 per year (£400 per week) which is the same as a comparable permanent employee but gets three days fewer paid holiday per year than comparable permanent employees. To ensure that the fixed-term employee's overall employment package is not less favourable, their annual salary is increased to £20,970. (£170 is added on, since this is the value of three days' holiday pay. A day's holiday pay is worked out as annual salary divided by 365.)

Seeking Reasons for the Treatment

A fixed-term employee has a right to ask their employer for a written statement setting out the reasons for less favourable treatment if they believe that this may have occurred. The employer must provide this statement within 21 days.

Limiting the Use of Successive Fixed-term Contracts

The use of successive fixed-term contracts will be limited to four years, unless the use of further fixed-term contracts is justified on objective grounds. However, it will be possible for employers and employees to increase or decrease this period or agree a different way to limit the use of successive fixed-term contracts via collective or workforce agreements. For the purposes of this part of the Regulations, service accumulated from 10 July 2002 will count towards the four-year limit. There is no limit on the duration of the first fixed-term contract, although if a contract of four years or more is renewed, it will be treated from then as permanent unless the use of a fixed-term contract is objectively justified.

If a fixed-term contract is renewed after the four-year period, it will be treated as a contract for an indefinite period (unless the use of a fixed-term contract is objectively justified). A fixed-term employee has a right to ask their employer for a written statement confirming that their contract is permanent or setting out objective reasons for the use of a fixed-term contract beyond the four-year period. The employer must provide this statement within 21 days.

The End of the Redundancy Waiver
Any redundancy waiver that is included in a fixed-term contract which is agreed, extended or renewed after 1 October 2002 will be invalid.

Information on Permanent Employment Opportunities
Fixed-term employees should receive information on permanent vacancies in their organisation.

Task and Contingent Contracts
From 1 October 2002, the end of a task contract that expires when a specific task has been completed or a specific event does or does not happen (a 'contingent contract') will be a dismissal in law. The non-renewal of a fixed-term contract concluded for a specified period of time is already a dismissal in law. Employees on these task contracts of one year or more will have a right to a written statement of reasons for this dismissal and the right not to be unfairly dismissed. If the contract lasts two years or more and the contract is not renewed by reason of redundancy, the employee will have a right to a statutory redundancy payment.

Other Employment Rights
From 1 October 2002, employees on fixed-term contracts of three months or less will have a right to statutory sick pay and to payments on medical suspension, guarantee payments and the right to receive and duty to give a week's notice after one month's continuous service. These new notice requirements only apply to a termination of the contract before it is due to expire. This will put these fixed-term employees on the same footing as permanent and fixed-term employees on longer contracts.

Remedies
If fixed-term employees believe they are being less favourably treated than a comparable permanent employee because they are fixed-term or that their employer has infringed their rights under the Regulations, then they may present their case to an employment tribunal.

An Improvement in Protection but ...
The EC Directive 90/70/EC adopted the broader definition of 'worker'. It is arguable that by restricting the scope of the Regulations to 'employees', the government has excluded those individuals, such as casual or freelance workers, who are most likely to suffer detriment in the first place because of their looser working arrangements. Much the same criticism can be levelled at the exclusion of agency workers from

the scope of the Regulations. Agency workers will have to await the outcome of the political wrangling surrounding the proposed directive on temporary work.

European Commission Proposal for a Directive on the Working Conditions of Temporary (Agency) Workers

Following the breakdown of social partner negotiations on a framework agreement on temporary agency work (TAW) in May 2001, the European Commission had been working on a proposal for a directive on TAW. The Commission published its proposal on 20 March 2002. It has the broad aim of improving the quality of TAW by requiring that temporary agency workers be treated no less favourably than comparable permanent workers in the user enterprise to which the temporary worker is assigned. It also aims to establish a European framework for the use of TAW.

The proposal is currently being considered by the Council of Ministers and the European Parliament. The proposal is subject to the co-decision procedure – that is, it must be agreed by the Council of Ministers and the European Parliament if it is to become law. If the proposal is accepted as a directive, then a transposition date will be set which would give Member States, including the UK, a certain period of time (usually at least two years) to pass appropriate legislation. The government issued a consultation paper on the proposal, the consultation period ended on 18 October 2002 (see *Public Consultation on Commission Proposal for a Directive on the Working Conditions of Temporary (Agency) Workers*, DTI, 2002).

The Commission proposal takes a similar approach to existing directives, negotiated by the EU Social Partners, on Part-time Work and Fixed-term Work. The stated aims of the proposal are to improve the quality of temporary agency work by applying an equal treatment principle to temporary agency workers and to establish a suitable framework for the use of temporary agency work in the EU. It applies to workers employed by temporary work agencies and posted to client companies to work under the supervision of those client companies.

The core principle of the proposal is that an agency worker assigned to work under the control of a client company should not be given less favourable basic employment conditions than a similar permanent worker in that client company, unless this is objectively justified.

The basic employment conditions set out in the directive are: the duration of working time, rest periods, night work, paid holidays and public holidays; pay; work done by pregnant women and nursing mothers, children and young people; and action taken to combat discrimination on the grounds of sex, race or ethnic origin, religion or beliefs, disabilities, age or sexual orientation.

Member States can choose not to apply this equal treatment requirement where temporary agency workers are employed on permanent contracts (these would be where temporary agency workers are paid by the agency in between assignments), where temporary agency workers are covered by collective agreements, or where temporary agency workers' assignments can be accomplished in six weeks or less.

Member States should periodically review restrictions on the use of temporary agency workers and take specified measures to make it easier for them to find permanent jobs.

User companies should give agency workers access to 'social services' provided to permanent workers.

Agency workers should be informed of permanent vacancies in the user company. Clauses banning or having the effect of preventing the conclusion of contracts between an agency worker and a user company at the end of the worker's assignment should be null and void.

Companies using agency workers would need to provide information on the use of TAW when providing information on the employment situation in the company to worker information and consultation bodies.

Agency Work in the UK

In the UK there are estimated to be 700,000 agency workers on temporary assignments at any given time, i.e. around 2.8 per cent of the workforce. Agency work has been in existence since the beginning of the last century and is regulated by the Employment Agencies Act 1973 and the Conduct of Employment Agencies and Employment Businesses Regulations 2003, SI 2003/3319. These are enforced by the DTI's Employment Agency Standards Inspectorate. In addition, certain basic employment rights such as the national minimum wage, working time regulations and health and safety legislation have been specifically applied to agency workers and other statutory rights may apply, depending on the nature of the relationship between the agency and the worker.

The Commission proposal would require significant changes to the current UK legislation, principally to incorporate the non-discrimination obligation. At present the pay and conditions of agency workers are set by the agency according to market principles or collective agreements, generally without reference to conditions in the enterprise to which they are temporarily assigned.

The Commission argues that the directive would improve the working conditions of agency workers and therefore increase the supply of agency workers. In its consultation paper, the government expressed a concern that the directive should not cause a decrease in demand for agency workers, with negative consequences both for agency workers and user enterprises in terms of employment opportunities and flexibility in the labour market.

It went on to argue that 'the present UK regulatory framework offers a balance between flexibility and protection for agency workers, which the government would wish to ensure the proposed directive is broadly compatible with'. The uncertain state of the case law concerning the status of agency workers which we have considered earlier in this chapter would tend to contradict this view.

Responses to the consultation paper were predictable and dependent on whether the respondent was a trade union, employer or agency.

Representatives of business said that equal treatment should be balanced with employment protection and flexibility for employers. They argued that the directive in its current form could remove the incentive for companies to use Temporary Agency Workers (TAWs) and therefore remove employment opportunities for agency workers and restrict labour market flexibility. User undertakings argue that the Directive will mean that it will be more difficult to meet surges in demand and there could be a lower take-up of further education, due to the decreased availability of temporary work.

Union responses reject the argument that the directive will lead to fewer jobs and a rise in unemployment, citing as evidence the rise in employment since the introduction of the National Minimum Wage and the Working Time Regulations.

Agencies argue that the directive will mean fewer temporary workers, due to high levels of bureaucracy and increased cost.

Small business representatives are very concerned that the directive will be especially difficult for small businesses – they will recruit fewer temps, but will not be able to fill the gaps with permanent workers. This would mean that jobs will be lost from the labour market. (see *Summary of Responses to the Public Consultation on the Proposed Directive on Temporary (Agency) Work*, DTI, 2003).

CHAPTER 3

Job Applications and Recruitment

Introduction

Job applicants traditionally, had few, if any, rights. That position has changed, and the pre-appointment stages of employment have become an important aspect of employment law. However, job applicants, candidates for interview, and new starters can still be in a weak position. The prevailing philosophy traditionally was that employers should have unrestricted discretion in the recruitment process. The problem is obviously likely to be greater in workplaces where there is no union, or where union organisation, or influence on recruitment practices, pay and employment conditions, is weak.

As far as selection procedures and appointments are concerned there is no legal right to be interviewed; or, if interviewed, to be appointed to a job that has been applied for, even if the applicant is clearly the best candidate in terms of qualifications and experience. At Common Law employers are entitled to refuse to appoint at all, following an advertisement. Having made an appointment they may go on employing their chosen candidate, even where they have based their decision on mistaken information, or act for malicious or improper reasons.[1] This position has only been partially improved by legislation designed to tackle race and sex discrimination, anti-union recruitment practices, and disability. There are also criteria, such as age, used by employers to impose job qualifications which can preclude well-qualified people from employment and promotion opportunities, and which are often patently unfair. In some employment sectors it is not uncommon to be precluded from appointment for being 'over-experienced'. In January 1998 the government announced that it would not be outlawing ageist recruitment practices. Since then EU law has addressed age and other areas of discrimination in recruitment (for example on grounds of sexual orientation, religion and disability). This has been assisted by the addition of new Social Policy provisions by the Treaty of Amsterdam facilitating anti-discrimination legislation as part of a wider employment and social policy programme. Council Directive 2000/78/EC requires Member States to prohibit age discrimination, and in the UK the Department of Trade and Industry paper *Equality and Diversity: Age Matters* (DTI, 2 July 2003) has signalled that regulations will come into operation on 1 October 2006 including a 'general prohibition' of direct and indirect discrimination on grounds of age (but with 'justification' defences).

In one significant area of institutionalised discrimination, wages, the National Minimum Wage Act 1998 and regulations permit lower wages to be paid to younger workers on appointment. It is not expected that the new age discrimination laws will change this.

General

Restrictions on an employer at the recruitment stage, and rights for job applicants and new starters, operate through one or more possible sources, and these are discussed below.

National and Local Collective Agreements

These may be relevant if there are union-agreed minimum pay scales and conditions at the workplace. In particular an agreement may specify the rate of pay and terms on which staff appointed to a particular post, with particular experience and so on, should start. The union will usually want to ensure the agreement is operating correctly because of implications for other staff. If a letter of appointment or other evidence of the conditions of employment provide for the terms of collective agreements to apply to the employment, then a failure to apply those terms could be a breach of contract (see further Chapter 4 below). Enforcing such provisions may, however, be difficult in practice. Following appointment, there may be scope for the appointee to assert rights which she or he may have, to receive pay or conditions applicable under a collective agreement – especially if such collective terms are 'incorporated' into the appointee's individual contract.

Legislation on Recruitment: Sex and Race

Equal pay and discrimination and equal opportunities law (see Chapters 10–12 below) include rules restricting employers' discriminatory practices. Key rights which relate to pre-appointment procedures and recruitment include:

- *Sex Discrimination Act 1975 (SDA)* ss.1 (direct and indirect discrimination against women); 2 (discrimination against men); 2A (gender re-assignment); 3 (discrimination on grounds of marital status); 4 (victimisation); 6 (1) (a) (arrangements made for the purpose of determining who should be offered employment); 6 (1) (b) (terms on which employment is offered) a provision which displaces the Equal Pay Act 1970 s. 1 (1) as it would otherwise apply to the terms on which employment is offered (s. 8); 6 (1) (c) (refusing or deliberately omitting to offer employment); 6 (2) (a) (the way the employer affords access to opportunities for promotion, transfer or training, or to any other benefits, facilities or services [or by refusing/omitting to afford access]); 6 (2) (c) (dismissal, or subjection to 'any other detriment'); s. 38 (advertising).
  Employers are, in general, unable to pursue affirmative or positive action programmes (subject to very limited exceptions) aimed at giving preferential treatment to one gender over the other. These are generally contrary to restrictions on direct discrimination in s. 1 (1) (a) (as with the RRA 1976) and depending on the exact circumstances may also be contrary to the Equal Treatment Directive EC 76/207; *Kalanke v. Freie Hansestadt Bremen* [1995] IRLR 660, ECJ. Under s. 6 (1) (a) an employer may not discriminate in terms of the *arrangements* made for determining who is to be employed. The combined effect of s. 6 (1) (b)–(c), 2 (a), (b) is to prevent discrimination in such post-appointment matters as the terms on which employment offers are made;

refusal, or deliberately omitting to offer, employment on the basis of sex; and access to opportunities for promotion, transfers and training, and benefits, facilities, and services. In some cases the discriminatory act or omission will take the form of dismissal, or in subjecting a person to 'detriments'; sub-ss. (1) (b)–(c), (2) (a), (b). The concept of a 'detriment' is potentially wide-ranging. S. 6 rights must, however, be read in conjunction with exceptions, including 'genuine occupational qualification' that enable acts or omissions that would otherwise be discriminatory (s. 7).

- **Race Relations Act 1976 (RRA)**. Broadly, the rules are similar to the SDA. Discrimination at the appointment and recruitment stages of employment can be *direct* under s. 1 (1) (a). Specifically, a person discriminates against another in any circumstances relevant for the purposes of the Act if, on racial grounds, the employer treats (or would treat, if appointed) a person less favourably than he would treat other persons. Or discrimination can be *indirect* under s. 1 (1) (b). Notably, if the employer applies to the person a requirement or condition which is applied to equally to others not of the same racial group, but (i) which is such that the proportion of persons of the same racial group as that other who can comply with it is considerably smaller than the proportion of persons not of that racial group who can comply with it; and (ii) which he cannot show to be unjustifiable irrespective of the colour, race, nationality or ethnic or national origins of the person to whom it is applied; and which is to the other person's detriment because he cannot comply with it. Case law on occasion has suggested that the 'requirement or condition' generally needs to be of a kind that a job applicant has been *required* to comply; see the Court of Appeal case of *Meer* v. *London Borough of Tower Hamlets* [1988] IRLR 399. Other key RRA provisions include ss. 2 (victimisation); 3 (meaning of 'racial grounds', 'racial groups', etc. – the Act's definition of 'racial grounds' extends to colour, race, nationality or ethnic or national origins); 4 (discrimination in the arrangements made for determining job offers, terms, etc.); 5 (exceptions for 'genuine occupational qualifications'); 10 (extension to partnerships); 11 (trade unions, membership rights, etc.); 14 (employment agencies); and 29 (discrimination in advertising).
- **Employment Equality (Sexual Orientation) Regulations 2003, SI 2003/1661**, in effect since 1 December 2003, and making it unlawful, in employment or vocational training matters, to discriminate on grounds of sexual orientation (meaning sexual orientation towards persons of the same sex, opposite sex, or to both persons of the same and opposite sex). Discrimination can be direct or indirect, and includes victimisation and harassment. Part II relates to recruitment and appointments processes.[2]
- **Employment Equality (Religion or Belief) Regulations 2003, SI 2003/1660**, in effect from 2 December 2003, making it unlawful to discriminate on grounds of religion, religious belief, or similar philosophical belief (extending to discrimination that is direct or indirect, and victimisation and harassment) – and applying to recruitment, appointments, etc.

Codes of Practice

There are Codes of Practice, official guidance, etc., issued by the key bodies dealing with discrimination, and these provide valuable sources of information and guidance.

The Equal Opportunities Commission publish a Code of Practice for the Elimination of Sex and Marriage Discrimination. This contains, among other things, guidance on the steps it is reasonably practicable for employers to take to ensure that their employees do not in the course of their employment act unlawfully contrary to the SDA, and to promote equality of opportunity between men and women, and prohibit discrimination against men. It clarifies the scope of s. 6 in all its key areas, including s. 6 (2) (a) which bars out direct and indirect discrimination on grounds of sex or marriage in the way an employer affords access to promotion, transfers or training – and practical guidance is given on such matters as appraisal systems, promotion and 'career development patterns', policies and practices regarding selection for training, day release, and personal development. Age limits on access to training and promotion should be questioned particularly in the context of the developing legislative framework to counter ageism at work.

The Code of Practice on Race Relations is also directed at providing guidance on policies to eliminate discrimination and enhance equal opportunity. Although not law in itself, if its recommendations are not observed this may result in breaches of the law where the act or omission falls within any of the specific prohibitions in the RRA – and the guidance is linked to the main provisions of the RRA. Key parts of the recommendations apply to recruitment, transfer, training and dismissal. This includes sources of promotion and training (ss. 4, 28); selection criteria and tests which avoid direct and indirect discrimination (ss. 24, 28); the scope of the genuine occupational qualification provisions (s. 5); performance appraisals (s. 4 [2] [b]); advertising practices (ss. 29–31); and the scope of positive action to encourage training for members of particular groups (s. 38).

The Disability Rights Commission also provides important guidance on advertising, recruitment, internal promotions, etc.: in some cases this is backed up by legislation; see the Code of Practice for the 'Elimination of Discrimination in the Field of Employment against Disabled Persons or Persons who have had a Disability' (SI 1996/1396). In some cases key provisions in the DDA directed at disability discrimination on recruitment and appointments is backed up by regulations such as the Disability Discrimination (Employment) Regulations 1996, SI 1996/1456.

ACAS produces guidance on discrimination in the workplace, and this can be accessed on their website.[3]

Employers, particularly in the public sector, frequently state that they are 'equal opportunity employers', and have policies on this – but this does not necessarily increase their legal liabilities. Public authority employers may not, in practice, implement such policies, as shown, for example, by the Crawford Report into discriminatory practices in the London Borough of Hackney.[4]

Wages Regulation; Minimum Wage

Following abolition of Wages Councils by the Trade Union Reform and Employment Rights Act 1993, the UK had no formal system for establishing minimum pay, other than in areas like agricultural wages (through wage-setting by the Agricultural Wages Board). Such a mechanism has been recommended by the International Labour Organisation (ILO) since the 1920s. The National Minimum Wage Act 1998 has, however, created a national minimum wage system ensuring employers pay wages at or above a fixed level, although enforcement is always going to be a problem in the same way it was for earlier systems. The low level at which it is set means many low-paid workers still depend on State benefits and 'tax credits' (see further Chapter 7 [Pay] and Chapter 22 [Employment Benefits]).[5]

Employment Agencies and Business Regulations

If an applicant is going through an employment agency the agency must provide information about the job's pay and conditions, and comply with other standards: for example charging practices, details of employment status that would be involved, and other information about jobs arranged (including health and safety risks). Details are in regulations issued at the end of 2003.[6] Agencies are subject to requirements governing employment practices under some of the legislation referred to below, for example in relation to anti-union practices under the Trade Union and Labour Relations (Consolidation) Act 1992. On the other hand, legislation like the Disability Discrimination Act 1995 does little to assist the position of disabled people seeking work, or getting work, from agencies where the agency provides the work. This is an aspect of the 1995 Act which has been much criticised by disability groups.

Disability Legislation

The inadequacy of the disability legislation, such as it was, to deal with widespread discrimination against disabled people was illustrated by measures like the Disabled Persons (Employment) Act 1944. This was supposed to require every employer with more than 20 staff to employ a quota of registered disabled people (specifically 3 per cent of those on the payroll). In practice, a very small proportion of employers complied. If a disabled person did get a job there were no specific legislative provisions to protect him/her from discrimination on disability grounds whilst in post, so that a dismissal could, for example, be treated as 'fair' on occasions when it might 'disturb' the business.[7]

In 1995 the Disability Discrimination Act (the DDA) was introduced by the Conservative government. Whilst the DDA assists people with a 'disability' within the scope of s. 1 (1), i.e. those with a 'physical or mental impairment which has a substantial and long-term adverse effect on his ability to carry out normal day-to-day activities' (as to which see *Goodwin* v. *Patent Office* [1999] IRLR 4 and *College of Rippon and York St John* v. *Hobbs* [2002] IRLR 185) disabled workers can still experience significant discrimination and insecurity at work. The disabled workforce still earns substantially less than able-bodied workers (a fact officially acknowledged by the social security system by preferential in-work payments through Jobseeker's Allowance and the 'disability element' in Working Tax Credit). This has been just one of many characteristics of disability discrimination in the UK employment scene. The other is the difficulties people with a disability have in even getting an interview for jobs which they could do, as shown by the cases summarised on the Disability Rights Commission website at www.drc.org.uk.[8]

The 1995 Act makes it unlawful to discriminate against a disabled employee by treating him or her less favourably than others for disability-related reasons, and the employer cannot show that this is 'justified', s. 5 (1). A duty is also imposed on employers to make adjustments to premises and work arrangements to assist disabled persons to be accommodated. This applies where the 'arrangements' made by the employer, or physical features of the premises the employer occupies, 'place the disabled person concerned at a substantial disadvantage in comparison with persons who are not disabled'. The duty on the employer is then 'to take such steps as it is reasonable, in all the circumstances of the case, for him to have to take or to prevent the arrangements or feature having that effect': this is the duty to make reasonable adjustments (s. 6 of the Act). The section gives examples of the sort of 'steps' that might be required. These include altering hours, allowing time off, modifying equipment, and providing supervision.

As far as recruitment practices are concerned, s. 4 of the Act renders it unlawful to discriminate, for example, in the arrangements made for determining employment offers (e.g. advertising and interviewing procedures), or in the *terms* of employment afforded. The section also extends to opportunities for promotion, transfer, training, or the receipt of 'any other benefits'. Dismissal, or subjection to 'any other detriment', is also covered.

Criticisms of the Act are wide-ranging, but key problems are with the narrowness of the definition of 'discrimination' in s. 5, and of 'disability' in s. 1. Both these terms, as they are defined, tend to limit the scope of protection available. The reliance on tribunal complaints, unsupported by Legal Services Commission assistance, has put complainants at a disadvantage. However, the Disability Rights Commission (established under the Disability Rights Commission Act 1999) provides advice and other support. If a tribunal finds a complaint well-founded it is required to take such steps as it considers 'just and equitable'. This includes, in accordance with s. 8:

(a) making a 'declaration of rights'
(b) ordering compensation to be paid
(c) recommending that the employer take, within a specified period, action appearing to the tribunal to be reasonable in all the circumstances of the case for the purpose of 'obviating or reducing the adverse effect on the complainant of any matter to which the complaint relates'. Failure to implement such a recommendation can lead to an increased award of compensation, and can include an element for 'injury to feelings'. Complaints must be presented within three months of the act complained of. See further Chapters 14 and 21.

Changes are made to the DDA, SDA, RRA, etc., including discrimination in recruitment and appointments, as a result of EC Directive 2000/78. On disability see the Disability Discrimination Act 1995 (Amendment) Regulations 2003, SI 2003/1673 (from 1 October 2004).

Among other things, the regulations:

• apply the legislation to *most forms of employment*, self-employment, etc. (not just 'employees'), and encompass office-holders, directors, people wanting/ undertaking work experience, and others at present outside the scheme;
• extend coverage in the DDA Part 2 to *access to employment*, work placements, and *agencies* providing access to employment;
• apply the DDA to those who have had disabilities in the past, i.e. 'past disabilities';
• bar out *'justification' of direct discrimination*, and restrict the scope for justifying *indirect* discrimination: resulting in some key modifications and repeals of DDA sections;
• provide new and wider-ranging definitions of *'discrimination'*;

- extend coverage to *discrimination occurring after the employment relationship has ended* ('post-termination' discrimination) – something that is relevant, for example, to references, post-termination benefits, etc.

'Rehabilitation' of Offenders Rules

Under the rules in the Rehabilitation of Offenders Act 1974 previous convictions can become 'spent' after the specified rehabilitation period.[9] For details of the scheme, reference must be made to the Act itself (and in particular s. 5 and Tables A and B), but subject to exclusions (and reductions for those under the age of 18, young offenders, and others, for sentences of up to six months' imprisonment the period is seven years) and for sentences of between six and 30 months it is ten years. Fines are normally subject to a five-year period. Sentences of over 30 months cannot be spent, and certain occupations like nurses and doctors, teachers and social workers are outside the scope of the Act. As long as the post does not come within such an excepted category, a spent conviction need not be declared in job applications and questions on forms enquiring about previous convictions do not have to be answered. Questions about convictions can be answered in the negative. There is no sanction in the Act, though, or specific protection if an employer discriminates against an ex-offender *before* the employment begins. If a tribunal complaint for unfair dismissal is brought after commencement, *and* the applicant is otherwise eligible to claim, it is possible to succeed if all the employer is relying on is a spent conviction.[10] On the unfair dismissal aspects, including qualifying periods, see Chapter 14 below.

Workers from Overseas

EC nationals, and since 1 July 1992 non-EC spouses of EC nationals (in most cases), are not generally subject to work permit requirements or other restrictions on working or setting up a business in the UK. This also applies to citizens of the European Free Trade Association (EFTA) countries. Non-EC nationals are subject to work permit and other requirements, however. For those who need a work permit this must be obtained when applying for a visa or entry clearance: and the permit usually runs for a period starting with the date leave to enter the UK is granted. For those already in the UK an application must be made for a 'letter of permission'. Restrictions may apply under the Immigration Act 1973 and regulations (including 'conditioning' procedures preventing work, claims for State benefits, etc.); and under the Asylum and Immigration Act 1996, s. 8, and Nationality, Immigration and Asylum Act 2002. Guidance can be obtained from the Home Office website at www.HomeOffice.gov.uk in the 'Work Permits' part of the Immigration and Asylum section. Permits are dealt with by Work Permits (UK) on behalf of the Immigration and Asylum Directorate. Department of Work and Pensions and Jobcentre Plus centres also give guidance. The criteria for obtaining a work permit are, primarily, that the applicant has special skills and experience needed for the job, and that a 'resident worker' or someone in the European Economic Area (EEA) is not available to fill the vacancy. There are also relevant categories of employee (such as 'key' worker, employment in the national interest, senior executive). Business people and company representatives may also be permitted entry under the immigration rules. Working without a work permit when one is required is extremely risky. Apart from the action that can be taken by the immigration authorities, the employment contract is potentially 'illegal', which means there may be no employment protection and dismissal may be fair. Conditions can be imposed on work permits, for example with regard to the types of work that may be undertaken, social security claims etc., and a breach of conditions can lead to the permit being revoked.

Workers from outside the UK are entitled to be paid the National Minimum Wage; and have 'working time' rights (see guidance at the website at www.dti.gov.uk). In practice it is difficult for workers working in the informal economy, including asylum-seekers and those 'subject to immigration control', who should not be working (but who in many cases will either have no State welfare support, or minimal support), to enforce employment rights. As a response to the tragic deaths of Chinese workers who drowned in Morecambe Bay while collecting cockles, the government belatedly supported a Private Member's Bill to set up a scheme of licensing and enforcement of 'gangmastering' (involving the recruitment and deployment of workers). The Gangmasters (Licensing) Act 2004 is unlikely to deal with most of the employment and welfare needs of atypical groups of workers like asylum-seekers and others working illegally. In many cases their contracts, being unlawful, are likely to be unenforceable, and the Act only regulates 'licensable conduct'. The Act does not make lawful the employment of workers legally excluded from the labour market.

In-work welfare support is generally not available for those working illegally. For migrants entering the UK from new Eastern European EC countries (from 1 May 2004) who are able to find employment the full range of employment rights, including Working Tax Credit, Child Tax Credit, and Child Benefit are available. However, they will not be able to obtain the full range of welfare support until they have been working legally for a minimum of 12 months without interruption (Chris Pond MP, Parliamentary Under-Secretary of State, Department of Work and Pensions on 27th February 2004, House of Commons Hansard col. 585W; and see SI 2004 Nos. 775 and 1232).

Legislation against Discrimination on Union Grounds

It is unlawful to refuse to employ a person on union membership grounds, or for employment agencies to refuse to provide their services on such grounds. The legislation, the Trade Union and Labour Relations (Consolidation) Act 1992 (TULR[C]A) ss. 137 and 138, was originally based on proposals in a consultative paper 'Removing Barriers to Employment' (1989). A key policy objective was directed against workplace arrangements where new staff are expected either to join a union, or to pay the equivalent of union dues to charity. The scope of the legislation is now wider than that, however, and makes anti-union discrimination unlawful; see, generally, TULR(C)A Part III, but particularly ss. 137–145, and ss. 152, 153. A refusal to employ is unlawful, in particular, if it is because a person:

- is, or is not, a union member;
- does not agree to become, or to cease to be, a union member;
- is unwilling to accept a requirement to make payments, or suffer pay deductions, for not being in a union.

Another part of the legislation (s. 137 [4]) is directed against 'labour supply' arrangements whereby a union supplies workers to employers from among its members. If a non-member applies and is refused a job where this arrangement operates it may be presumed that the refusal was because s/he was not a member.

'Refusal to employ' occurs, or can be presumed to occur, in a variety of situations, such as refusing to entertain or process an application, including union-related conditions in an advertisement, or attaching unreasonable conditions to a job offer.

Tribunal complaints can be made and compensation paid up to the same limits that apply to unfair dismissal compensation. Unions and 'third parties' can be joined as defendants in a tribunal claim.

Case law on the subject, and in particular the 'refusal to employ' right in s. 137, have shown that it can in some cases be difficult to show that discrimination has resulted from union membership, as opposed to 'personal' attributes, or the employer's perceptions of an applicant's 'attitude'. In *Harrison* v. *Kent County Council* [1994] ICR 434, EAT, however, it was held that tribunals could conclude that rejection of an applicant on such grounds *could* be linked to their previous union membership while in a similar job.

Advertisements and Job Offers

Advertisements are subject to standards as to accuracy and content set by advertising standards bodies and the media themselves, as well as the criminal law and anti-discrimination legislation. The contents of an advertisement can also cause an employer problems in other ways. Collective agreements may restrict, or impose conditions on, job advertising – for example, by requiring a job to be advertised or filled *internally*, or requiring it to be advertised on the same terms that existing job-holders are employed. The contents of a job advertisement are not, in contract terms, normally regarded as an 'offer' which can thereupon be formally 'accepted'. The advertisement is usually just the start of a 'negotiating' phase. Advertisements and their contents can be good *evidence* of terms, and could become 'contractual' – that is, any specific details on pay, hours and other conditions could be treated as terms of the contract which the employer can be held to. This could be the case where, for example, there is no subsequent letter of appointment modifying what is promised in the advertisement, or the conditions on which you are employed are unclear after you have started.[11] If no written statement of 'initial particulars' is issued, as is required within two months under the Employment Rights Act 1996, section 1, the contents of the advertisement could be referred to when asking a tribunal to determine what your terms are (see Chapter 4 below).

In legal terms an employment contract is not formed until an offer of terms, which must normally include the main terms dealing with the most important aspects of the job such as pay,[12] has been made and that offer has been accepted. Without those key elements of offer and acceptance there is no contract. It is important to confirm acceptance formally by letter. Although tribunals and courts can infer from the parties' conduct, and where service has been rendered, that a contract of employment has come into being (*Thorn* v. *London Corporation* (1875) LR 10 Exch 112), and will usually accept other evidence, such as appearing for work or starting a job, a letter of acceptance avoids complications.

In practical terms there is usually no problem provided a letter of appointment, or statement of terms, is issued confirming the details of what has been agreed. These should make it clear whether the employment is 'permanent' (that is, it will continue indefinitely, subject to termination by notice or other legal reasons), or whether it is for a 'fixed term'.

Validity of Employment Contracts

Employment contracts, particularly at the stage of their formation, are generally subject to the same rules as other contracts,[13] for example they may be invalidated (or subject to rules governing contractual performance) if misrepresentations are made by one side; or if performance is impossible either because of the fault of a party or because of a factor outside anybody's control. 'Non-performance', or 'breach' as it is better known, is discussed in Chapters 4 and 5. One problem, which is important because of the effect it can have on a worker's employment, is 'illegality'. This is particularly relevant to workers in occupations where the scope for employers to break the law is increased. Employees often bear the consequences of this in employment terms.

Legislation can have the effect of making an employment contract void or unenforceable, for instance if a job requires a licence and one has not been obtained. Work permits have already been referred to, but there are many other examples which could render the contract void. The exact consequences of illegality will depend on the particular legislation, and the circumstances in each case.

If a contract is illegal from the start, as for example where it is agreed that wages will be paid in cash or as 'expenses' to avoid tax, employees will normally not be allowed to rely on the contract. In practical terms this means an employee could not sue to recover any arrears of pay that are due, or enforce other parts of the contract. If an *employer* sets up a pay system which defrauds the Inland Revenue, but without telling the employees concerned, an employee may still be able to rely on the contract, but only while s/he is unaware of what has been going on. This was decided in an unfair dismissal case where the EAT decided the claim could only be maintained if the applicant did not know that the wages system was being run fraudulently.[14] More recent case law has tended to relieve employees of the consequences of illegality – for example in sex discrimination cases where employers have raised the illegality of their own actions (such as withholding tax and NI contributions after promotions) in an attempt to defend discrimination cases.

'Conditional' Job Offers

A job offer can be made conditional. For example, the employer might make it a condition of the employment that the appointee must produce evidence of qualifications before starting. References have also become a normal practice so that it is always wiser to assume that a job offer is going to be subject to the new employer receiving satisfactory references before the employment begins. For this reason it is always advisable not to resign from an existing job until it is clear that this last hurdle has been safely jumped. It is generally for the new employer to decide if a reference is needed and then, when it is received, whether it is satisfactory or not.

Example
Mr Wishart was offered a job as information officer at the National Association of Citizens' Advice Bureaux 'subject to the receipt of satisfactory written references'. The reference referred to his absenteeism record, which included 23 days off in the preceding year. The offer was withdrawn. The court decided the offer was conditional and the employer was entitled to decide the condition had not been satisfied.[15]

Existing or previous employers are not legally obliged to provide a reference. If the employer refuses to provide one then in practice there will be little, if anything, that can be done. It is probably just customary to provide one, rather than a legal obligation. In some employment contracts such a commitment may have been stipulated. They are also sometimes included as part of a termination agreement – something which is more common with senior staff or as part of a termination package. If a reference is given by the employer the reference can contain an assessment of the worker's record and performance, and include views about aptitude and suitability for the job applied for. The employer has a 'qualified privilege' to make negative statements, but this would not extend to views which are malicious and false and which could amount to defamation. In some cases, though, the employer could be sued for damages if it can be shown that there has been a lack of care and inaccuracies in the preparation of a reference. In the leading case on this the judge described the reference as being so bad as amounting to the 'kiss of death' to the applicant's career in insurance. He held that points in the reference suggesting, or implying, that the applicant was dishonest had been negligently included. The House of Lords subsequently explained the legal basis of an employer's duties when preparing references. The duty is essentially contractual, i.e. based on implied obligations in the employment contract. It also derives from a 'duty of care' once the responsibility has been taken on.[16]

As far as the prospective employer's use of references is concerned there is usually no legal remedy available against that employer even if the information relied on is unfair or inaccurate. This also raises the issue of employers' use of organisations which hold 'black-lists' of people on the jobs market. Such use is restricted by TULRA and employment protection provisions in relation to trade unionists. A further problem is the insistence by some new employers on accessing medical records to verify statements in applications about absenteeism and health. It is now possible to get access to doctors' records (Access to Medical Reports Act 1988), and to do so, employers may try to require the applicant or appointee to obtain access to their records and then allow them to read them for vetting purposes. That person has a right to see records, and to query their contents *before* the employer sees them, and could, of course, resist such requests. In the context of the Disability Discrimination Act 1995 such vetting is only subject to limited regulation, and further clarification is expected in a Disability Act 2004. In the meantime, there is a developing case law on DDA rights at the appointments stage, assisted by DRC guidance and the Code of Practice on the *Elimination of Discrimination in the Field of Employment against Disabled Persons or Persons who have had a Disability* (SI 1996/1396); and see the DRC website for cases on recruitment and appointments discrimination.

As well as general legal requirements that apply to the keeping of personnel data that could be used for references and other purposes, for example in the Data Protection Act 1984, employers are also subject to confidentiality restrictions. This means that data provided to an employer, for instance on application forms marked 'confidential', or obtained in other ways during the employment, should *not* be divulged to third parties unless this is authorised by the worker concerned, or by law.[17]

Withdrawal of Job Offers

Normally, as soon as there has been 'acceptance' of an effective 'offer' of employment a contract (and contractual rights and duties) come into operation. If the employer does not allow an appointee to start work there is a breach of contract, and an action for damages is normally possible. In practice it is not necessarily worth an employer's while suing in such cases because the amount of damages that can be recovered is normally limited. This will depend, however, on the scope of the 'loss' – and the position may be different with some types of contracts.

The withdrawal of a job offer can be extremely serious for an employee, especially if she or he has given up another job on the strength of the employer's promise. In such cases the exact amount of damages obtainable, if any (or compensation that can be demanded in settlement of legal proceedings) will depend on the particular circumstances. It may be very limited, and amount to no more than the equivalent pay for the notice period required to terminate the contract. If a specific period of employment was envisaged when the contract was made, it could be the equivalent of what would have been payable under the contract. This is particularly relevant to fixed-term contracts. Similarly, termination before the necessary qualifying service for unfair dismissal (and other ERA and TULR[C]A rights) is obtained is problematic. However, the ET will have jurisdiction to consider claims for loss based on the contract at termination, as in *Durrant* v. *Financial Collection Agency Ltd* (2002) EAT (Appeal No. EAT/1325/00). In that case the appellant was a well-paid IT manager, and he was dismissed after the employer said he had failed to complete a six-month probationary period. The disciplinary procedure provided that if the company was dissatisfied with conduct or performance then he would be advised of this orally – and, where appropriate, a period would be set for the required standard to be achieved. A final warning would then be given if at the end of that period conduct or performance was still 'unsatisfactory'. Failure to attain a satisfactory level of conduct or performance by the end of the second period meant he could have his job terminated. His manager was concerned about the appointee's performance, and this lack of confidence increased after a period of three weeks' absence. He was then dismissed. A complaint was made to the ET, and a claim for compensation lodged: but the tribunal concluded that the manager knew, or must have known, that he had to improve, and that his work was 'crucial to the company'. An appeal succeeded, however. The tribunal did not have regard to the disciplinary procedures governing dismissal, and these formed part of the manager's contract of employment, thereby providing the basis for compensation for breach of contract.

In a leading case a company offered jobs and higher pay to staff working for another company. They were told the jobs would last for six months. After they accepted and left their jobs the offers were withdrawn. It was held that compensation should be awarded and this should be based on the representations made about the promised employment. Compensation was payable based on the likely period of employment, but was reduced to take into account a proportion of pay that would have been paid for the climatic conditions they would have been working in had they actually commenced employment (the new jobs were in the Shetland Islands). The representations had, said the court, amounted to a separate, or 'collateral' contract between the workers and the employer.[18]

Internal Appointments and Promotions

The exact terms on which internal appointments and promotions are made, and the procedures that apply, will usually depend on contract terms and any collective agreements or arrangements that the employer operates. Once interviews have taken place and an appointment has been made employers are not usually entitled to withdraw an offer, and other dissatisfied applicants will find it difficult to challenge the decision.

Example

Mrs Powell worked for Brent Council, and she applied for and got promotion to a post as a principal benefits officer. She was told on the telephone by a senior officer that she had been selected. Meanwhile another candidate started a claim under the grievance procedure in respect of the procedures used for the appointment. The council decided there had been a breach of the 'equal opportunities code of practice'. Mrs Powell was told she would not be appointed, and the job was due to be re-advertised. She successfully claimed that she had been appointed to the post, and obtained a temporary injunction stopping the post being advertised or filled pending a decision whether she had been properly appointed.[19]

CHAPTER 4

The Contract of Employment

Introduction

Employment Law is probably the most heavily regulated area of 'private law' in the UK legal system. Yet State interventions in the employment relationship are not just a recent phenomenon. As early as 1349 the Statute of Labourers (23 Edw. III) bound servants to their masters, irrespective of the terms of any 'contract'. This followed the period of labour shortages after the Black Death. Among other things this statute prevented servants seeking pay rises, compelled them to work at pre-plague pay rates, and made it an offence to leave the employment before the end of their legal term.[1] The Statute of Artificers 1562 (5 Eliz. c. 4) maintained this regulatory tradition, forming part of what has been called the corporative system, with complex controls over prices, wages, and labour mobility.[2] The late Victorian period was also a period in which contracts of employment remained heavily regulated, sometimes rendering them largely ineffectual as a means of providing secure employment terms, or rights. Legislation like the Employers and Workmen Act 1875 among other things enabled a county court wide discretion, in the event of disputes, to completely end or re-write contract terms, and substitute new terms that would operate in accordance with the court's order. This was facilitated in large measure by the fact that most contracts of employment operated 'at will', and with a minimum of express provision or rights for the worker. In the case of *Keates* v. *Lewis Merthyr Consolidated Collieries Ltd* [1911] AC 641 at 642–644, Lord Atkinson observed that the Act had enlarged county court powers

in a most remarkable way. The court may now, under this very section (s. 8), give relief which not only was never claimed by either of the parties litigant, but which is directly in conflict with the relief claimed, and *setting at naught the rights they respectively insist upon*. For instance, if an employer should sue his workman for damages for breach of contract by refusing to do the work he had contracted to do, and the workman insisted that the work he refused to do was not work which under his contract he was bound to do ... the county court judge, in defiance on this insistence [can] *dissolve the contract, apportion the wages earned under it, and award damages, presumably for its breach, or for its termination, as the case may be* to either of the parties litigant. Not one of which things was claimed by any one concerned ... It is obvious that this *quasi-parental jurisdiction* was conferred in the interest of industrial peace, and should not be hampered by rules of pleading ...

In combination with a statutory regime typified by the earlier Master and Servant Act 1867, which superimposed restrictions on both sides of the contract (and which in the case of workers maintained the tradition of reinforcing a coercive Common Law system with criminal sanctions affecting many aspects of contract formation, wage negotiation, and leaving the employment), it is difficult to conclude that contract, as opposed to statutorily regulated status, played a significant role in shaping employment relations until relatively recently.

Yet in the modern context the employment relationship is still, notionally at least, founded on a bilateral, contractual relationship – with much of it focusing on contract terms agreed, and operating, at a private level. This remains so even when it is supplemented by statutory terms – as with the equality term inserted by the Equal Pay Act s. 1, or the statutory implied terms and dispute resolution and dismissal and disciplinary procedures introduced by the Employment Act 2002. In itself this does not say much about the wider role employment contracts play, or their value and interaction with other legal sources that shape employment relations. Despite their continuing importance, employment contracts are not necessarily the *only* repository of employment rights and responsibilities for most workers – especially given the way legislation impacts on (or even completely displaces) core areas of the employment contract, including wages, working time, and the general working environment. It is also clear, at the same time, that contracts have a much wider function in the construction and operation of the employment relationship than simply being a source of terms and conditions, or the final destination of many important collectively agreed elements that contribute to the overall bargain. Apart from providing a gateway to statutory rights – particularly when it assists 'employee' status – contract terms can then have a complex interaction with all the other main sources of employment law. The main one, legislation, has now, itself, been knocked off the top of the hierarchy of sources of employment rights and duties by a higher set of regulatory norms in the form of ECHR Convention rights: a subject operating predominantly in the control of judges, in the UK and the European Court of Human Rights in Strasbourg. As considered later in this chapter, employment law, a subject still in many ways operating predominantly in the private domain and through the medium of the contract, has started to be affected in some significant ways by the ECHR, the Human Rights Act 1998, and judicial perceptions of what 'Convention rights' demand.

In considering employment contracts it may be better to talk of 'employment relationships' – particularly as it provides a more effective focus for all the various facets that now make up the employer–employee (or worker) relations. The chief exponent of this, Bob Hepple, in an influential article 'Restructuring Employment Rights',[3] offered a variety of reasons, a key one being that the legislative floor of rights being developed by Parliament would be jeopardised if it continued to just superimpose on the Common Law contract of service. That has, indeed, proved to be right in many ways. More recently, Mark Freedland in *The Personal Employment Contract*, has suggested that employment law is 'deeply, perhaps even irrevocably, committed to a contractual analysis of the individual employment relationship'.[4] He does, however, broaden the analysis into other areas of contracts for personal work which are wider than the category of contracts of employment, and this corresponds to some extent to Hepple's notion of the 'contractual employment relationship'.

In the modern context, relationships depend on one or more legal sources, and regulatory mechanisms. They include:

- the individual contract of employment;
- collective agreements and procedures, the terms of which may be incorporated into the individual contract (but which often may not, despite their importance or potential impact on the relationship);

- other workplace agreements, procedures, etc., which affect individual workers: examples include 'workforce agreements' used for the purposes of regulating working time;
- legislation (including UK, EC and ECHR laws). Increasingly a source of terms, rights and responsibilities – but also regulation of the relationship: in many cases the interventions are welfare-led, examples being the national minimum wage, working time restrictions, and the equal pay 'equality clause', all of which, in effect, re-write core terms of the contract. In this way contracts become an instrument of distributive (or 'corrective') justice between the parties, as well as pursuing wider welfare agendas;[5]
- custom and practice.

Whilst the vast majority of employment relationships are, indeed, contract-based, some workers hold a position, post, or office, where there is *no* contractual nexus of any kind with an employer. In other cases the employment may be subject to a *mix* of contractual and other relations, i.e. a hybrid. Thus 'office holders', according to the EAT in *Johnson* v. *Ryan* [2000] ICR 236, can be characterised in a number of ways. They can comprise of individuals whose position is determined exclusively in terms of the office they hold, and have no contract; or they are people with office-holder titles or status, but who are, basically, employees working to a contract of service; or they can be people whose position straddles office-holder *and* employee status. The issue is an important one because in some cases, notwithstanding the absence of any written contract terms, a person may display the characteristics of an employee – such as carrying out functions under supervision, or other organisational hierarchy. Building on that, a court or tribunal may then, in effect, *construct* the terms of a contract around that fact, supplying if necessary core terms relating to pay, hours and responsibilities. Directors are just one such group. Typically, having worked for what may be years without a written service agreement (or other formal indication of anything other than holding the office of director under the Companies Act 1985), they seek 'employee' status. Very often this is for the purpose of securing statutory rights (such as the right not to be dismissed in the ERA Part X), but not unusually for the purpose of securing implicit rights under their contract not to be deprived of accrued rights. Employee status is not incompatible with the office and status of company director – especially if the functions undertaken include day-to-day management or other activities for their company.[6] On the other hand some groups are unable, it would seem, to get to do that – and for a variety of reasons.

The absence of any obvious 'employer' as the other party/side to the employment relationship can be problematic for some groups, who are then left in a similar position to those characterised as working to a contract for services, or with self-employed status. This is considered in Chapter 2. One such group that illustrates the point are priests, and the effect is that that cannot be treated as working under a contract of employment: they are no more than an ecclesiastical office-holder.[7] Similarly, and for what are essentially policy reasons, the courts have also been reluctant to treat shareholders with a majority of the issued shares in a company as employed under a contract of employment, with their company being on the other side of the contract.[8] However, as the *Bottrill* case, cited at Note 6 above, and the later case of *Sellars Arenascene Ltd* v. *Connolly* [2001] IRLR 222 suggest, there is no reason *why*, in principle, one status (shareholder, priest, etc.) should not also operate in tandem with an employment relationship founded on a contract of employment. This may be appropriate, and enables the contract on which that status is predicated, however notional, to be a conduit for statutory rights like redundancy, protection from unfair dismissal, etc. Although contracts of employment can be presumed to exist, and be treated as in operation on the back of a working relationship (with or without any formal 'contract' or documentary evidence to sustain it) the absence of at least *some* indication of contractual or quasi-contractual relations or characteristics will generally be problematic, as indicated in *Hewlett Packard Ltd* v. *O'Murphy* [2002] IRLR 4.

For reasons which need to be considered further, the characterisation of employment as a *contractual* relationship has become difficult to sustain. Apart from anything else, with the increasingly important role of *other* stakeholders in the employment relationship, including the State, it has become difficult to see the employment relationship as just a bilateral one between employer and employee.

Consideration is given in this chapter to the way employment contracts are formed, and how they operate.

Before that, however, it is necessary to address further the concept of contractual rights.

Contractual 'Rights'

In the United Kingdom context the contract of employment has traditionally been seen as the cornerstone of the employment law system, dealing with key terms on pay, working hours and holiday entitlements. In many cases this continues to be so, although in reality such core areas of the employment relationship no longer operate *exclusively* in the private domain of the contract, but are regulated by legislation (as later chapters dealing with pay, working time, and annual leave will show). In practical terms the majority of employment disputes are concerned either with what is actually in the contract, that is to say what has been agreed, whether it has been effectively included, and the *scope* of its terms: but also the interaction of the contract and regulatory legislation. It is wrong to assume, however, that the employment relationship is governed *entirely* by the contract terms that exist between the employer and the employee, and legislation. Apart from specific terms which the employer may rely on, including implied terms (see below), an employer may also be able to rely on a general power to do things for the purpose of managing the business. This is a power sometimes referred to as 'management prerogative'. Unless there are clear contractual entitlements which might inhibit or prevent an employer relying on such a general management power, for example if a 'no smoking' policy is introduced,[9] then legal action to prevent such general management powers is difficult.

Disagreements about contract rights and liabilities may be resolved through resort to a grievance or disputes procedure (which may be necessary to avoid a reduced award; see Chapter 14), or using arbitration processes of the kind now in operation since May 2001 under the ACAS Arbitration scheme; see the ACAS Scheme (Great Britain) Order 2004, SI 2004/753 and TULR(C)A, s. 212A. Otherwise disputes are dealt with in the adversarial system of tribunals and courts. In fact most workers do not necessarily make much use of the courts during their employment, largely because of the costs, uncertainties about the likely outcome, and the problems of pursuing disputes with employers while still working for them.

Despite the problems and the other difficulties which stem from the contract system's dependency on legislative and judicial interventions, and on the results of an adversarial system of courts and tribunals, for most people the contract does represent an important safeguard of their employment rights. Similarly, in the collective sphere, collective agreements are an important formal written record and a benchmark by which unions can gauge their success. As well as providing a form of protection of workplace rights they are a spring-board for future negotiations and collective organisation for advancing members' interests. Some trade union commentators have seen the process of negotiation of collective terms and their incorporation into the individual contract of employment as unions' central role.[10]

Contractual Rights in Practice

How significant, though, are contract terms in *reality* as a means of safeguarding employment rights? Although employment case law illustrates how important it is in evidential and formal terms to have a written statement confirming rights, and this assists as the essential legal basis for any 'guarantees' the law may give them, there is a powerful argument that in reality the observance of workplace rights and duties depends much more heavily on non-legal considerations, such as goodwill, economic pressures on the employer's business, the existence and effectiveness of a union organisation (if staff are in a union), and other extra-legal factors. It is also significant that there can be various aspects of a job which are not dealt with by the contract at all, and workplace 'rights' may rely on assumptions and 'understandings' – what may be seen as a kind of mutual self-interest and operational understandings – rather than on any sort of formal definition. Although most employers look to the contract to give them the disciplinary power they need, larger employers will also rely on a much wider range of employment 'human resource management' practices to get workers to do what they want, as an early study showed.[11]

Even where employment terms and procedures are recorded and established in detailed individual contracts and collective agreements, and even when these are reinforced by strong union organisation, this is no guarantee that employment institutions, including court and tribunal processes, can necessarily provide a framework for ensuring they *are* observed and are 'secure'. Nor does it follow that an employer will not try to 'roll back' contractual provisions, and rights which developed during the employment relationship. This is an enduring theme at both the individual and collective levels. There is no such thing as sanctity of contract in Employment Law. The point was clearly shown in May 1991 when, in one well-publicised incident, Rolls Royce unilaterally decided that it would not be paying wage rises, even when these were provided for in contracts and collective agreements. Employees were then sacked and simultaneously offered re-engagement on new terms – which did not include a pay increase! Such a large and well-known employer's readiness and ability to do this, even if there were doubts about whether it had been done correctly in legal terms (see Chapter 13 below on termination), came as a considerable shock to many people at the time. In other landmark cases employers sought to remove displace contract rights *and* union representation when 'personal contracts' were introduced: and less advantageous employment terms and pay rises were offered to those refusing to enter into such individually negotiated personal contracts. The House of Lords refused to protect this entitlement by treating it as 'action short of dismissal' on grounds of union membership; and generally interpreted TULR(C)A (as it was worded at the time) in ways which facilitated such incursions into bargaining procedures and union members' accrued rights.[12] In another well-publicised dispute in 1997 British Airways sought to unilaterally cut back on payments paid to cabin staff. The move led to lengthy industrial action.

Notwithstanding that the contract of employment may contain explicit, as well as implicit, guarantees on such matters as pay rises, promotion, overtime requirements and pay, and so forth, the reality is that because an employer will generally have a stronger hand throughout the duration of the employment relationship such rights can remain highly tenuous. There are a variety of legal and non-legal explanations for this, which are discussed further in later chapters, but it is worth identifying some of the key stages at which a person's employment rights can be vulnerable. In the first year of service an employee runs a gauntlet of possible dismissal because the 'qualifying period' for going to a tribunal will not have been established. The point is underlined by the way the tribunals and courts approach the problem of staff being dismissed before they have served the necessary period of continuous service. Basically, an employee who has been dismissed before that length of service has been completed will not be able to make a tribunal claim for unfair dismissal. This is the position even if proper contractual notice, had it been given, would have given the claimant the required time; *Morran v. Glasgow Council of Tenants' Associations* [1998] IRLR 67. This means that changes in employment conditions during that period could not, for example, be challenged in a constructive dismissal claim (although other court or tribunal action may be possible, including ET complaints about 'unauthorised' deductions (see Chapter 5). Another period during which contractual rights can be extremely vulnerable is during a 'reorganisation' of the employer's business, when significant changes to rights under employment contracts can often be justified in tribunal proceedings (see Chapter 5 below).

The time at which work entitlements are particularly at risk, of course, is when an employer's business is in financial trouble, or caught up in insolvency procedures. At that time the management may well have been displaced, and employment responsibilities may have switched to 'administrators' and others (see Chapter 15). An increasingly important phase for many people and one which can impact severely on a job, is when a new employer takes over. This is often the cue for a new management to introduce changes and reinterpret existing contractual arrangements, working practices and procedures.[13] Such 'transfers' may require the new employer to carry out existing obligations to employees, as discussed in Chapters 14 and 15. Improvements made by the Revised Acquired Rights Directive 98/50/EC, for example for public sector workers when 'outsourcing' occurs have improved the position to some extent.

Underlying everything is the point that for many workers their contract of employment can often contain terms which are highly disadvantageous, even to the point of being outrageously unfair. This can be seen with things like powers to deduct pay for lateness or imposing compulsory overtime, requiring changes of work base at short notice, deduction of pay for 'bad workmanship' and 'under-performance' and so forth. This is not just the result of the contract system itself,[14] but to the imbalance in bargaining power which is usually inherent in the employment relationship. This generally gives an employer a strong hand at the outset in fixing terms and conditions, and subsequently in modifying and applying them. This position was not helped by the 'deregulation' process between 1979 and 1997,[15] and which in many respects continues in response to labour market changes and pressures. Apart from the introduction of a national minimum wage, and working time restrictions, there are few other minimum safeguards built into an employment contract by law (or which the law forces an employer to leave *out*); and there is no pervasive legal test of 'reasonableness' (unlike other areas of contract rights such as consumer transactions)[16] which operates to prevent exploitative employment terms.

It is, no doubt, this aspect of an employer's and employee's 'freedom of contract' which is attractive to most employers and inward investors when they assess the UK employment regime.

The last Conservative government's policy of maintaining 'flexibility' in employment relationships, and resisting legal obligations on employers with regard to key matters such as working hours, job mobility, and working practices, was clearly stated in 1992.[17] This was, in part, an ideological 'response' to EC initiatives on working hours, reconciling work and family commitments, and other developments which it saw as a threat to a flexible labour market.

New Labour has continued that priority, with a wish to avoid excessive regulation of the employment contract and in its continuing commitment to 'the flexible labour market'. Indeed, in June 1997 the Prime Minister referred to Europe needing a 'new approach to employment and growth, based on British ideas for competitiveness, introducing more flexible labour markets and employability'.[18] The EC responded favourably, with the adoption of new employment guidelines focusing on the twin themes of 'employability' and 'adaptability'.[19]

Enforcing Contractual Rights

Assuming an employment contract contains terms which are capable of protection through legal remedies, the difficulties in *enforcing* contractual rights must be borne in mind. There are various reasons for this. Some are to do with the absence of financial assistance and representation for tribunal and court claims. Others include the problems associated with having to sue an employer, and jeopardising the job and the goodwill that may exist. This is a practical consideration affecting both union and non-union workers. It is also a major problem when employers seek to impose changes to employment contracts (as discussed in Chapter 5).

Contract Terms and Conditions

Employment contract details are rarely all contained in a single written document which sets out each side's rights and obligations. Only in a small minority of cases, for example senior managers and certain groups like sales staff who might have a detailed 'service agreement', might this be the position. For the majority of employees this is not the case and a typical contract of employment can derive from a variety of possible sources. These include:

- verbal statements and promises;
- statutory written statements;
- written evidence;
- collective agreements;
- rule books, notices, and the like;
- custom and practice;
- implied terms.

Verbal Statements

A contract of employment can be based entirely on a verbal arrangement and there is generally no requirement that such oral contracts must be evidenced in writing.

This means that an employee would be able to rely on an informally made agreement for most purposes. For example, a person who has undertaken work for someone else with no preceding formalised arrangement could go to a tribunal or county court for an order be paid for any work done.[20] If the evidence supports this, the claim could be dealt with on the basis that a contract of employment (or for services) came into existence when the work started. In some cases it may be possible to claim damages if the job does *not* materialise, particularly if shown specific contractual rights have been infringed.

Constructing the Contract

In practice the employment contracts usually depend on a mixture of verbal and written evidence, and failing that the court or tribunal may be willing to infer agreement on certain points. The courts have, however, laid down stricter limits on how far they will go in helping the parties in this way by maintaining that it is not their job to write or rewrite contract terms.[21] As already observed, employment contracts can be like commercial contracts and be set out in one comprehensive agreement. In most cases, though, they derive from a variety of sources.

The key sources of contract terms are considered in the sections that follow.

Express Terms: Statutory Written Statement

An employee must, within two months of starting work,[22] be given a written 'statement of initial particulars' which contains:

(i)   the names of the employer and the employee;
(ii) the date when the employment began;
(iii) the date on which continuous employment began (taking into account any employment with a previous employer that counts towards that period).

The statement must contain particulars which are accurate as at a specified date which is not more than seven days before the statement (or the 'instalment' of the statement) is issued of the following particulars:

(a) The scale or rate of pay, or the method of calculating pay.
(b) The intervals at which remuneration is paid (for example, weekly or monthly).
(c) Any terms relating to hours of work, including normal working hours.
(d) Any terms relating to holidays, public holidays and holiday pay (including entitlement to accrued holiday on termination of employment precisely calculated); sickness and injury (including any provision made for sick pay); pension and pension schemes.
(e) The length of notice which is required to be given or which should be received to terminate the job.
(f) The title of the job which the employee is employed to do, or a brief description of the work involved.
(g) The period of employment if it is not permanent, or date it ends if it is for a fixed term.

(h)   The place(s) of work (including an indication of where the work is if there is more than one place).
(i)   Any collective agreements which directly affect the terms of the employment.
(j)   Details of any employment for more than one month outside the UK (including duration, remuneration, and benefits or additional remuneration involved).

The Act requires most information to be communicated directly in the statement itself. Reference can be made to the ERA Part I for the exceptions to this. The Employment Act 2002 relaxed the requirements imposed on employers to some extent, for example by enabling particulars to be given in other documents (ERA, s. 7A), or in the form of a contract of employment or letter of engagement before the employment begins (ERA, s. 7B). If there are no particulars to be entered under any of the paragraphs above, that fact must be stated in the statement. Information about incapacity for work due to sickness or injury (including sick pay), pensions, or notice obligations or rights, can be contained in other documents to which employees are referred, as long as they are reasonably accessible to them. The matters dealt with in (i)–(iii), and paragraphs (a)–(c); (d) as it relates to holidays and holiday pay; and (f) and (h) must all be included in one single document.

Status of the Statement

The legal status of the statutory statement provided by an employer is not always clear in any particular case. If a statement is signed by the employee, when it has been provided, not just as a receipt but as if it were a contract in itself, it is possible that a tribunal could treat the document as a 'contract' in the same way as a written contract. Otherwise the statement should only be regarded as *evidence* of what was agreed.[23] In the latter case, the practical significance of this is that if the employee believes the statement is incomplete, or does not agree that the statement accurately records what was actually agreed, or if the position has changed since the employment began, the accuracy of the statement can be contested in a tribunal or in court proceedings.[24] Reference may be made to the ERA ss. 11, 12 for the precise scope of the ET's powers: but when a reference is made to a tribunal (which can be either while the employee is working or after the employment has ended) it can determine what particulars *ought* to have been included or referred to in the statement.

If there is a later change in any terms of the kind referred to the employer must issue a *further* statement, giving particulars of the change, in most cases 'at the earliest opportunity', but in any case not longer than one month after the change (section 4, ERA). This requirement does not, in itself, give an employer the right to make changes which have not been properly agreed. Unfortunately, it is not unusual for employers to see it that way, and to introduce changes by simply issuing such amending statements, and then expecting staff not to object. See further, on such changes and whether they are effective, Chapter 5. However, it is necessary to consider the potential for such statements of changes, after they have been issued, to be the basis for effective variation of contract terms. The ERA s. 4 (1) states: 'If after the material date, there is a change in any of the matters particulars of which are required by sections 1 to 3 to be included or referred to in a statement under section 1, the employer shall give to the employee a written statement containing particulars of the change.' This is underlined by s. 4 (3) which deals with the time by which the statement must be given, i.e. 'at the earliest opportunity, and in any event, not later than (a) one month after the change in question ...'

This begs the question whether there *has* been an effective 'change'. In contract terms some changes which the employer has sought to impose may not, in law, be effective to change the contract of employment. So, as with s. 1 initial statements (which are only *evidence* of how the employer sees the matter: see the observations of Brown-Wilkinson J in the *Daniel* case cited in Note 23 above), an s. 4 statement is only evidence (the employer's evidence) of the status of the change. The problem is that an employee may object to the change, and do nothing about that objection. In this case, in the absence of protest at being asked to work in accordance with the change, is there implied or tacit agreement to accept the change? If it does not have immediate effect, such as an alteration in working hours, or wages, said Brown-Wilkinson J in another leading case *Jones* v. *Associated Tunnelling Co Ltd* [1981] IRLR 477, it may be asking too much for an employee to be 'taken to have assented to the variation'. There is a further dimension to the problem, however. What happens in a case where an employee is asked to agree to new terms and conditions, and a method of indicating agreement to the change is specified but not, in the event, used by the employee? According to *Chitty on Contracts*[25] an offer requiring acceptance to be expressed or communicated in a certain way can generally *only* be accepted in that way. Although acquiescence in the change, or a different mode of acceptance is a possibility, if an offeree does *nothing* in response to an offer (which is a proposed change) in the absence of agreement he or she is *not* bound by its terms. The general rule is that there can be no 'acceptance' by silence, and it is difficult in the case of employment contracts to base it on an employee's subsequent lack of response, conduct or inaction.

In *Aparau* v. *Iceland Frozen Foods plc* [1996] IRLR 119 the EAT (reversed by the CA in 2000, [2002] IRLR 116) adopted the approach in *Jones* when it was said that:

> to imply an agreement to vary or to raise an estoppel against the employee on the grounds that he has not objected to a false record by the employers of the terms actually agreed is a course which *should be adopted with great caution* .... Even if he does read the statement and can understand it, it would be unrealistic of the law to require him to risk a confrontation with his employer on a matter which has no immediate practical impact on the employee. For those reasons, as at present advised, we would not be inclined to imply any assent to a variation from *a mere failure by the employee to object to a unilateral alteration by the employer* of the terms of employment contained in a statutory statement. (emphasis added)

In the context of the process envisaged by the ERA s. 4, it is necessary to differentiate between those situations in which the employer and employee have *already* agreed to changes (for example through the agency of a collective agreement), and situations in which agreement is needed but has not yet been obtained. In the former case the function of an s. 4 statement is merely to record the change *after* it has happened. Changes which are non-contractual, in the sense that they do not formally require agreement of the employee (such as changes in the employer's discretion, or within the scope of management prerogative). The fact that the procedure in the ERA ss. 11, 12 for referring statements to a tribunal extends to s. 4 (1) variations still leave it open, on such a reference, for the tribunal to determine if new contract terms have been agreed. They can decide the particulars which ought to have been included or referred to, or amend or substitute them: and the tribunal appears to have a wide discretion under s. 12 (2) for deciding how to proceed.

Going to a Tribunal

An employee can ask a tribunal to decide[26] what particulars ought to be included in a statement if one has not been issued: or it does not comply with what is required.

Disagreements over the terms which ought to have been included in a statement can arise at any time: but often arise when the job is ending, or has already ended. In this case it is important to note that applications must normally be brought within three months of termination of the employment ceasing; see the ERA, s. 1 (4).

Other Consequences

As a further consequence of failures to comply with the ERA s. 1, the Employment Act 2002 s. 38 enables tribunals to make awards for non-compliance under jurisdictions listed in Schedule 5 to the 2002 Act (including key ones like equality clauses, discrimination, unauthorised deductions, unfair dismissal, and redundancy).

Written and Other Evidence

If no statutory statement has been issued, or if it is inaccurate, other written evidence of what has been agreed may be available and can be relied on as evidence in proceedings under ERA ss. 11, 12 to show what *should* have gone into the statement. Examples include letters of appointment, internal memos and job advertisements.

Advertisements can be particularly important if they offer entitlements which, for one reason or another, are not repeated in the formal offer or statement of terms. For example, an advertisement which offers participation in a profit-sharing scheme as part of the remuneration package may well be creating a contractual right – even if the point is not repeated in later documentation.

A tribunal can, of course, hear evidence of what was said in the periods before and after appointment. This is necessary before a tribunal can determine whether a person has 'employee' status or not, and whether he or she therefore *has* a right to a s. 1 statement. The leading case on this, in the House of Lords, is *Carmichael and Leese v. National Power plc* [1999] IRLR 43 and important guidance about the tribunal's note in proceedings was given by Lord Hoffman.

Collective Agreements

Incorporating Terms by 'Reference'

The contents of documents like collective agreements are often expressly 'incorporated' into the contract. Typically, a written statement or letter of appointment will state that the employee will be working in accordance with the employer's published conditions of service, and that those conditions may be subject to change from time to time in accordance with any new collective agreement made. If it does say that, or a similar form of words is used, any changes in such conditions will usually mean that employees are subject to that process. They can also apply to staff who are not necessarily members of the union making the bargain as long as the terms of its 'recognition', and bargaining practices, extend to bargaining for them. In this case the employees' terms and conditions are automatically amended in line with the terms of any new collective agreements.

This process of amending and updating workers' terms and conditions is a distinctive feature of UK Employment Law and collective labour relations, and is facilitated by the collective labour relations processes operating throughout many areas of industry. The process by which changes can take effect using this system, even when individuals may object to the effects of such changes, has been illustrated by cases like *Burke* v. *Royal Liverpool University Hospital NHS Trust* and *Ali* v. *Christian Salvesen Food Services Ltd*, discussed in Chapters 7 and 18. It is also facilitated by the collective bargaining procedures underpinned by law, and inserted into TULR(C)A Schedule A1 by the Employment Relations Act 1999 Schedule 1. These assist recognition of trades unions by employers for bargaining purposes, and are considered further in Chapter 18. It is important to note, though, that the precise manner in which bargaining takes place, agreements are made, and then periodically varied, depend on the scope of arrangements in operation in any case, and whether these have been made voluntarily or 'declared' by the CAC. The bargaining process itself, including arrangements made for revising agreements, may take the form of a legally enforceable contract, subject to specific performance: and will have other legal attributes, as provided by Schedule A1.

When collective agreements result in changes to existing terms and conditions they will, as a general rule, be incorporated in to individual employees' terms, and if this is appropriate (given what they do, their aptness for incorporation, etc.) they have legal effect. Accordingly, subject to exceptions in Part I of the ERA, individuals are entitled to be advised in writing of changes affecting them 'at the earliest opportunity' and in any case not later than one month after the change in question; s. 4 (3). The ERA s. 6 requires collective agreements and other documents affecting staff, and to which employees may be referred for the purposes of complying with Part I, to be 'reasonably accessible'.

Legal Effects of Collective Bargaining

Before a collective agreement is changed agreement will usually have been reached beforehand between the union and employer (or employer's organisation). But prior agreement is not always essential *before* changes are legally effective. In particular it may not be required if the particular service condition has not become part of a worker's contract of employment and there are no other legal constraints on the employer withdrawing or altering a benefit.

Example
Employees of a local authority were employed according to the authority's published terms of service. But in this particular case the changes did *not* require prior agreement with the union representing the authority's staff before they could be made. It was held that the council could unilaterally withdraw a non-contributory life assurance scheme. The case appears to have been decided on the basis that the employer, under the scheme, had the ability to modify the scheme periodically. The form of words used in the employee's letter of engagement was a standard one, namely that the post was subject to the conditions of service laid down by a national joint council and as supplemented by the Authorities' Rules, and 'as amended from time to time'. However, the decision is inconsistent with other precedents, and has been criticised.[27]

Crossing the 'Bridge'
The process by which terms of documents are incorporated in this way is sometimes described as a 'bridge' between the individual worker's contract and the document

in question. Unfortunately in some cases this system clearly operates to the worker's disadvantage, as in the last example. It is also the case that collective bargaining can produce an 'escalator' effect – with the escalator going down as well as up, and facilitating agreements that produce worse working conditions (as in the *Burke* case). It is important to note, though, that rights which have become part of the individual contract of employment (particularly if they are concerned with pay and other rights which the courts are more inclined to protect) may well be protected from change unless the individual's consent is given, or his/her union agrees the change. Those rights may have 'crossed the bridge' from another document, or may have been part of the contract since the employment began.

Example

Mr Robertson's appointment letter said that incentive bonus scheme conditions would apply to workers in his type of employment. A collective agreement dealt with the actual calculation of bonus payments. Later he received a statutory statement which said that any bonus which may become due would be calculated by reference to the rules of the scheme in force 'at the time'. The part of the collective agreement containing the scheme was later terminated (which the employer could do by simply giving notice to the union of its termination). The corporation thereupon stopped paying bonuses, and Mr Robertson and his colleagues suffered a significant pay cut as a result.

He successfully sued in the county court. On appeal the employer argued that his right to bonus ended when the collective agreement was terminated. This argument was rejected. The appointment letter had created a contractual right, and even if the employer could terminate the *collective* agreement Mr Robertson's right to bonus, which was in his own contract, went on. The employer could not, therefore, simply stop paying.[28]

Although this case was an example of how employment rights which are (or have become) part of the individual's contract may survive such actions of an employer, a problem remains, and it is one which has important implications for many workers whose employment rights are contained in collective agreements. Not all incorporation case law produces the favourable result (from the employees' standpoint) achieved in *Robertson*. Such rights will always be vulnerable so long as collective arrangements and procedures remain legally unenforceable.[29] The reason why collective arrangements are likely to remain unenforceable are complex. From an employer's perspective the system preserves flexibility, and enables concessions made in previous bargaining rounds to be re-negotiated or bought out. From a union perspective unenforceability at the collective level does not necessarily prevent enforceability at the individual member's level (on the *Robertson* principle): and it generally suits workers and their unions to maintain a situation in which employers are unable, legally, to enforce many of their rights under a collective agreement. The system can clearly operate as a double-edged sword for both sides.

For further discussion of the incorporation of collective agreements into the individual worker's employment contract, see Chapter 18.

Other Methods of Incorporation

If there is no express provision made in the individual contract of employment which specifically incorporates a collective agreement or other document, can incorporation be achieved by *other* means?

In an attempt to rationalise, at least in legal terms, the industrial relations practice whereby work arrangements are collectively made and then automatically applied to individual workers, a number of approaches have been put forward. No one approach is entirely satisfactory and often in cases where courts or tribunals have seemingly accepted incorporation as a matter of course the basis on which they have done so is far from clear. As Lawton LJ observed in the *Marley* case (Note 27 above), there has been a 'long judicial history to the problem of incorporation'.

Incorporation by Implication

In some cases collectively agreed work arrangements are applied to individuals on the basis that this can be *implied*. This is obviously easier in situations where the tradition, in a workplace, of making and applying collective arrangements in this way is well established. This is based on the assumption (although the point is not always clear) that an implied term can be found in the individual contract that the particular collective term or arrangement can apply. However, the courts go further and require that the collective term, or procedure, must also be appropriate for incorporation.

Although there can be significant problems involved in the practical application of this process, and in particular there does not seem to be a clear rationale for why some collective terms are capable of incorporation while others are not, the practice has been established for some while.[30]

The leading case of *Alexander* (Note 28 above) illustrates some of the difficulties that can occur.

Example

Workers at Standard Telephones and Cables plc (STC) were made redundant and argued that this was in breach of contract as the company had failed to select staff on the basis of LIFO (last in first out) as provided for by a collective agreement. This procedure was, they said, incorporated into their individual contracts and the failure to follow it entitled them to claim damages. The judge decided that the statutory statements did not provide a basis for expressly incorporating the provisions of the agreements which established length of service as the criterion for selection. He accepted that incorporation could be implied, but this required evidence that this was *intended* by the parties to the contract. He did not consider such an intention could be inferred from the evidence, including the agreements and other documentation: nor did he believe the redundancy provisions were 'apt' for incorporation. Nor did he like the idea that an agreement which was not enforceable at the collective level could be relied on, as a contract term, by individuals. As observed in the earlier case of *National Coal Board v. National Union of Mineworkers* [1986] IRLR 439, collective agreements may be important to individual workers, but it did not follow that they were intended to be legally enforceable at the suit of an individual worker.

A very different approach was taken in the Scottish case of *Anderson v. Pringle of Scotland Ltd* [1998] IRLR 64 (Court of Session) – assisted, though, by findings that trust and confidence remained between the employer and employee. This enabled the court to make an order restraining dismissals in breach of collectively agreed redundancy procedures. The case is authority for the proposition that in appropriate cases collective arrangements and procedures *can* create legal rights as between individuals and the company. In *Alexander* the judge, in contrast to *Anderson*, appeared to regard it as axiomatic that an employer that dismisses some staff for redundancy (while retaining others) has less trust and confidence in the staff *not* retained. The notable point is the disparity in approaches taken to incorporation North and South of the border.

Now that the Employment Rights Act 1996 ss. 1–3 have reduced the opportunities for incorporation by reference (by requiring most terms to be expressly set out in the individual employee's statement) it may, perhaps, in practice be harder (particularly for employers) to try to rely on incorporation by implication.

Collective Agreements as 'Custom'

One authoritative labour lawyer, partly in an attempt to advance the case for more extensive incorporation of collectively agreed procedures and rights, suggested that collective agreements operate, in relation to the individual contract, as a form of 'crystallised custom'.[31] Put simply, this approach proceeds on the basis that individual contracts can include terms and conditions which are normally followed as workplace custom and practice.

It is difficult to see, though, how most modern collective arrangements operate in the same way as customarily established terms (see the section on custom and practice below); and, despite its attractions, the concept has not become established in practice as a means of demonstrating incorporation.

Agency

Another possible way in which incorporation is sometimes explained is on the basis of 'principal' and 'agent'. So long as the employee (the principal) gives the union (the agent) power to negotiate and make contractual terms, it might be said that the union has power to make and change its members' conditions, and this may make an express clause or other mechanism unnecessary.

Although this relationship does help to rationalise many of the problems in this area, and may be relied on in appropriate cases, it cannot be adopted as a *general* basis for incorporating collective terms whenever there is no express incorporation clause. For one thing, a union may not necessarily enjoy agency rights for all the workers it 'represents'. This is illustrated, for example, by the fact that in many workplaces the union may well 'negotiate' for non-union staff and members of other unions as well as its own members. But it generally does so not as an agent but because the individual contracts of those non-union and other staff state that their terms will be in accordance with the collectively agreed arrangements that the union negotiates. Alternatively, it is generally understood that the employer simply applies those arrangements in practice to such staff once they have been agreed.

There is another practical problem in relying on agency as a medium of incorporation. This is the possibility that members may well want to withdraw their authority from the union. In this case the result may be that any collective agreements that are made will not apply to that member as they have not been incorporated effectively into his/her contract.[32] To address the potential implications for collective bargaining processes in other cases employers now tend to ensure that, on apointment, it is made clear that collective terms apply to all staff eligible to join the union in question (or, simply, 'all staff' in the areas they wish the arrangements to cover).

Rule Books, Notices and the Like

Workplace rules and notices are ways in which the employer can exercise managerial power, but they do not necessarily amount to terms of a contract in themselves. They are used in different ways and for a variety of purposes at most workplaces, and their status will depend on a number of factors.

Their contents might already have been agreed, for example as a collective issue. In this case they could, in appropriate cases, be treated as if they had been incorporated into individuals' contracts and thereby acquire contractual force. To satisfy the requirements of the Employment Rights Act 1996, ss. 1–3, they may also need to be specified in the individual employee's statement of particulars.

Even without such a specific reference in the contract, some workplace conditions might have become so well known that they acquire contractual force. An example of this was a case where sick-pay arrangements were posted on a works noticeboard.[33] Sick pay, like incapacity arrangements and pension provision, is now a matter which could be specifically dealt with in a document like a rule book which is reasonably accessible to the employee (ERA, ss. 1 [4] [d] [ii], [iii], and 2).

Apart from these possibilities, notices, circulars and rules can (depending on the particular circumstances) be regarded as no more than 'information' or, at best, management instructions. In the latter case these can nevertheless be important, as in some circumstances ignoring them might well amount to a breach of the contractual obligation to carry out employers' orders.

Custom and Practice

Terms can be incorporated into a contract on the basis of custom and practice, either in the particular industry or in the workplace itself. With workers increasingly getting written statements of terms which cover most of their workplace rights and duties this mode of incorporation is becoming less important. There have, though, been examples of employers seeking to rely on what they have claimed to be established practice, usually to justify action like pay deductions or downgradings. In one important 2003 case,[34] for example, the EAT rejected the employer's argument that because short-time working (and reduced pay) had been introduced before (even though there was no express term permitting this) such a power operated by 'custom and practice'.

In order to succeed it must be shown that the practice is well established and generally accepted, although it is an arguable point whether the worker concerned must necessarily be aware of the practice on commencing work.[35] In the modern employment context the argument that an employer has not applied the alleged practice consistently, or on the basis that it is an established managerial right, may be significant. In one case[36] a 'chargeman' was demoted and had his pay cut. The employer tried to justify this by pointing out that this had been done before with the agreement of the individuals concerned. It was held that this did not entitle the employer to take such action. The previous occasions did not, in themselves, establish a managerial *right* in such cases.

Implied Terms

An important kind of contractual term is one which can be *implied*. Although most workers' terms will be dealt with in one written form or another there may well be aspects of the employment relationship which have not been specifically dealt with, or which are not dealt with in any of the ways already mentioned. In this case a court or tribunal may fill the gap or omission by deciding what the contract *ought* to say in order to make it workable or meaningful. In *Scally and Others* v. *Southern Health and Social Services Board* [1992] IRLR 523, for instance, the House of Lords ruled that there should be an implied term requiring the employer to inform workers of any rights they have under collective agreements or arrangements, or other conditions which could give rise to personal benefits and of which they might otherwise not be aware (such as options under employees' pensions schemes). What has come to be called the 'Scally implied duty', is generally satisfied if employers use reasonable means to communicate important information (like options for dealing with accrued benefits). A 2003 case, has held that this could, for example, be done by attaching proposed changes and alternatives to pay slips.[37]

Broadly speaking, implied terms come within one of two possible categories. The first comprises terms which are implied in the particular employment relationship: so-called 'factual' implied terms.

'Factual' Implied Terms

These include terms which are 'necessary' and which the parties might be assumed to have agreed on had the point been considered. For example, it has been held that an implied right to sick pay may be introduced into the contract. The leading case on this form of implication is *Mears* v. *Safecar Security Ltd*, discussed in Chapter 8. The case is particularly relevant in providing guidance on the way tribunals should proceed for the purposes of dealing with 'references' under the ERA ss. 11, 12. The essential question, and 'starting point', said the Court of Appeal, is to determine if a term has been agreed expressly 'by word of mouth or by necessary implication'. If not, it has to find a suitable implied term based on 'all the facts and circumstances', including the subsequent actions of the employer and employee, conduct of the parties, etc. Later clarification of the process indicates that if the evidence does *not* point to an 'agreement' between the parties, or it is not clear what they *would* have agreed, tribunals should not then proceed to 'invent' implied terms; *Eagland* v. *British Telecommunications plc* [1992] IRLR 323, CA. Perhaps as important, though, was the guidance given in *Howman & Son* v. *Blyth* [1983] ICR 417, whereby tribunals should then go on to consider *how* the implied terms should operate in any case. For example, when inserting an implied duty to pay wages or sick pay during periods of absence from the workplace, in deciding the amount required, and the duration of payment, reference can be made to evidence of what is the 'common position', and practice, elsewhere in industry. This suggests, to some extent, a fusion between constructing terms based on implied intent, assumptions, and wider custom and practice.

In practice, courts and tribunals bring to bear a wide range of policy considerations in deciding such points, including their own view of the particular case and what they perceive to be generally desirable. In one case, for example, it was held that an implied right to an annual salary rise was not 'reasonable' and had not been established on the particular facts. But this finding was reinforced by the view than an implied right to annual pay rises 'ought not' to be regarded as established in industry.[38]

'Law' Implied Terms

A second way of implying terms derives from implications which can be made in general about what is appropriate in the employment relationship. On this basis a number of important terms may be held to exist by operation of law in every contract unless they are ousted or modified by expressly agreed arrangements. Employers' duties under this head include the obligation to pay wages and to take reasonable care of employees' safety. The implied duty to pay wages, for example where an employee works additional hours, *may* enable the court or tribunal to determine the appropriate pay due. In certain cases there may be an implied duty to provide some types of staff with work, for example people who need to maintain their work skills or business connections. Such duties may, however, be modified or even completely removed by express clauses. For instance, an employer may include in the contract a term permitting suspensions without pay, or short-time working without pay. This would modify the normal implied duty to go on paying wages irrespective of work-flow problems. Or, as is increasingly common with performance-related pay systems, contracts may specifically exclude implied pay rights. It is now quite normal for more senior staff to be subject to so-called 'garden leave' clauses. These override implied rights and may, if valid, entitle their employer to send them home without work until their employment comes to an end.

Apart from the likelihood that employers will have substantially modified the position by express clauses, there may well be judicial interventions which override any rights which a worker might otherwise have. For example, what had hitherto been assumed to be a well-established right to continue to be paid wages without interruption until the contract is terminated, has been modified and held to be subject to the principle of 'no work, no wages'. Essentially this meant, in the case in question,[39] that as the worker concerned was not working 'normally' (due to industrial action), the normal obligation to pay wages would be suspended.

The reluctance of the courts to infer implied rights in collective agreements, particularly where these have been reached as a compromise between the objectives of the union and the employer is illustrated by the 1997 case of *Ali* v. *Christian Salvesen Food Services Ltd*, discussed in Chapter 7.

The importance of implied terms becomes particularly clear in the context of the statutory right not to be unfairly dismissed and constructive dismissal. In both cases it may be necessary to rely on breaches by the employer of implied terms, for example to maintain the elements of 'mutual trust and confidence' essential in working relationships.

Employees' duties include the following:

- to obey orders (see Chapters 13 and 14 below for examples);
- to show 'fidelity' (a term which may be broken in a wide variety of ways; see Chapter 9 for examples);
- to maintain mutual trust and confidence;
- to exercise reasonable care in carrying out duties during the employment;
- to co-operate.

The importance of these duties in the context of day-to-day working arrangements is obvious, and is illustrated throughout the chapters that follow. In the collective sphere, they can be useful to employers faced with action in the form of a withdrawal of 'goodwill'. This may, depending on the form it takes, be treated as a breach of contract (allowing the employer to take sanctions), as seen from judicial observations in *Ticehurst and Thompson* v. *British Telecommunications* [1992] IRLR 219, CA.

'Implication', Rights and Employment Obligations

From its inception, the employment contract requires the employer and employee to perform the contract in accordance with its terms, and with 'good faith'.

This is usually taken to mean doing things in a way that the parties themselves would have expected when the employment terms were agreed, but also (rather more uncertainly) in accordance with what implied requirements dictate. The point is illustrated, for example, by cases where the courts have taken action against workers 'working to contract' or 'to rule',[40] or where the courts have ruled that an employer had abused a power to require overtime working by habitually demanding that staff work unacceptably long hours, as in the junior hospital doctor's case.[41] Other areas of implied terms have been progressively developing and these too, have tended to highlight the same uncertainty. On what basis can, and should, the courts introduce implicit requirements – in many cases in pursuit of judicial agendas that are far from transparent.

A difficult issue in employment law, that has not been satisfactorily resolved, is the extent to which an employer *is* required to exercise rights and powers under the contract 'reasonably'. That was certainly one way of interpreting the result in the junior hospital doctor's case. A better way, perhaps, was to conclude that reliance on powers to work lengthy or 'unsocial' hours may, in strict contract terms be permitted. But that this could, in some circumstances, then be prevented by the court if to do so would mean the employer then falls foul of other implied terms, for example to take reasonable care of employees' health and welfare; or to maintain the trust, mutual respect and 'mutual confidence'. An interesting discussion of cases, and new directions, in relation to the obligation of mutual trust and confidence is provided in an article 'Beyond Exchange: The New Contract of Employment'.[42] Among other things, it argues that attempts to contract out of responsibilities implied on the basis of this principle should be barred out on public policy grounds.

A similar approach to constraining an employer's reliance on express terms, and exercising powers to dismiss (as shaped by legislation on unfair dismissal, and statutory redundancy regime), can be seen in action when it is deployed as a means of blocking dismissals when an employee's accrued rights are jeopardised. A valuable case study to illustrate this can be seen in *Jenvey* v. *Australian Broadcasting Corporation* [2002] IRLR 520 (High Court).

In that case Mr Jenvey was employed under a series of fixed-term contracts. His employer wanted to vary his contract and employ him part-time, with a reduction in pay and benefits. He refused to accept the change and asserted his right to continue in his post unchanged, and without being subject to variations. A year later he went to the tribunal, as the matter was still unresolved, and sought a 'written statement of initial particulars' under the ERA s. 1. The matter was then settled, however, and for the time being at least he continued as a full-time worker.

A month later he was told his fixed-term contract would not be renewed. He thereupon began unfair dismissal proceedings. The tribunal found that the principal reason for his dismissal was that he had commenced proceedings asserting his right to a s. 1 statement. On this basis, and assisted by the ERA s. 104 (which renders dismissals for asserting a statutory right 'unfair') the dismissal was automatically 'unfair'. The tribunal also found a redundancy situation, and that he would have been entitled to redundancy compensation of up to £58,000. As the upper limit (at the time of the case) was £12,000 he commenced proceedings in the High Court, having reserved that right. He claimed that the employer was in breach of contract under the contractual scheme. He sought from the High Court, successfully, an implied term that in the event of a redundancy situation arising the employer would not use its powers under the contract in a way that would remove his entitlement to contractual benefits (including pay, accrued benefits, etc.) other than for 'good cause'.

The argument, which the High Court accepted, was similar to the approach used in long-term sickness cases such as *Aspden* v. *Webbs Poultry & Meat Group (Holdings) Ltd* [1996] IRLR 521 (another busy area in which implied terms now operate). I.e. there should be an implied term either preventing, or at least limiting, the right to dismiss. Specifically, dismissal should not be an option available to the employer if the result would be to deprive employees of accrued sick pay and other sickness/disability rights – or rights which the employee was still in the *course* of accruing. In the case itself, held the court, the contract was not lawfully terminated simply by giving notice. Damages were to be assessed on the basis of what the claimant would have been entitled to redundancy, and to take into account other benefits had his employment continued and he had been dismissed for redundancy.

The *Aspden* case highlights the potential that implied terms have to inhibit the exercise by an employer of their powers. In that case Mr Aspden had been employed as a company manager since 1978. He had sick leave following a heart attack in 1983. Following a management buy-out, a permanent health insurance scheme for staff was established. A key term was that employees would get amounts equivalent to three-quarters of their last salary while they were wholly incapacitated from work. Payments would commence 26 weeks after incapacity, and *continue* until death, retirement, or the date on which he or she ceased to be an eligible employee. Unusually, there was no contract term or other 'long stop' procedure limiting this. In 1986 he entered into a written contract, based on a format adopted before the new PHI scheme was introduced, and this contained a general power of the company to terminate the contract, and a power to terminate it in the event of prolonged illness. It provided for full salary in the first three months of absence (less National Insurance benefits received) – then half salary for the next three months. In the event of a further period of absence, or if he should be unable to work/discharge his duties for a total of 183 days (whether he was working or not) in any 12 consecutive calendar months, the company could terminate the contract by notice. Otherwise the contract only catered for termination without notice for gross misconduct – or by either party giving three months' notice for any reason. The company was not doing well, and Mr Aspden had been demoted. He was also told he would not get a pay increase (despite provision for this in his contract). After a further dispute with the company he had further heart problems, and was off on sickness leave for seven weeks. After a return to work he was then off work again. Despite GP sickness certification, the Managing Director told him he thought he was 'malingering'. While he was still off work sick he was dismissed. He claimed damages for wrongful dismissal, contending that there was an implied term that, except for summary dismissal, the company would *not* terminate his contract – at least while he was 'incapacitated'. Without such an interpretation, he said, his rights under the PHI scheme could be frustrated, very easily, by an arbitrary dismissal. A separate claim for unfair dismissal was settled after ACAS's intervention (with a £7,500 settlement). The High Court upheld his claim, and agreed that there *should* be an implied term restricting the company's ability to dismiss (except on 'summary' grounds). Accordingly, on the basis of that term the company was in breach of contract by dismissing him: he collected damages for wrongful dismissal (with an off-set for his unfair dismissal award).

In a similar case, *Villela* v. *MFI Furniture Centres Ltd* [1999] IRLR 468, again in the High Court, a fork lift truck driver had a continuing entitlement to receive PHI scheme benefits. The effect of this, held the court, was that he should have the benefit of an implied term that he would *not* be dismissed – something that was necessary to give 'efficacy' to the arrangements that had been made when the scheme was introduced. This result was assisted by the employer's failure to bring changes that would have altered his rights to his attention. Had the changes been agreed, or been effective, his contract would have provided for scheme benefits to end at the point he left his employment (and this would not have precluded termination by dismissal as a means of bringing contract entitlements to an end).

In cases like *Aspden* and *Villela* the courts have demonstrated how, in appropriate case, implied terms can be used to restrict dismissal, or make employers pay significant amounts as the price of breaching such terms.

There are, however, *other* important aspects to the way implied terms are developing, and being used. For example, a breach, or threatened breach, of a term characterised as 'fundamental' is the basis for a constructive dismissal claim – an option explored further in Chapter 14. But the thrust of this is that if an employer *is* guilty of conduct which is a significant breach 'going to the root of the contract of employment, or which shows that the employer no longer intends to be bound by one or more 'essential terms', then building on Common Law approaches to repudiation an employee who has been adversely affected by the employer's action can either elect to affirm the contract (and continue working), or accept the breach has brought the contract to an end (and leave the employment). This is now given statutory form by the ERA s. 95 (1) (c) – a system which has also been extended, adapted, and used, in discrimination legislation – for example in the Sex Discrimination Act 1975 s. 6, and the Disability Discrimination Act (DDA) s. 4. In *Commissioner of Police of the Metropolis* v. *Harley* [2001] IRLR 263 the EAT concluded that the phrase 'by dismissing him' in the DDA s. 4 (2) (d) does *not* include constructive dismissal. More recently, though, it has been held that it *does* (for the purposes of asserting important disability rights, and securing a 'purposive interpretation'): see, for example *Catherall* v. *Michelin Tyres plc* [2003] IRLR 61 and *Meikle* v. *Nottinghamshire County Council* EAT 26 Sept. 2003.

The fact that the courts have opted to go down the road of requiring a *contract* test (rejecting early attempts to develop a more generalised 'unreasonableness' approach, and building on early statements of principle such as in *Western Excavating (ECC) Ltd* v. *Sharp* [1978] QB 761, CA) begs the question to what extent breaches of *implied* terms can be utilised by tribunal litigants. The answer is clear enough. As long as the implied term is an important one, and the breach (and the circumstances of it) is sufficiently serious in its impact on the relationship, it can be used. The implications of this are wide-ranging, as seen by cases like *Malik* v. *Bank of Credit and Commerce International (in Liquidation)* [1997] IRLR 462, HL. That case, and others since then, confirm that a breach by the employer of the implied duty to maintain trust and confidence comes within this category, 'since it necessarily goes to the root of the contract'; *Woods* v. *W.M. Car Services (Peterborough) Ltd* [1981] ICR 666 at 672.

Trust and Confidence

The 'trust and confidence' route to asserting and maintaining employment rights, and cases like *Woods* and *Malik*, are discussed in a valuable analysis by Mr Justice Lindsay, President of the Employment Appeal Tribunal, in 'The Implied Term of Trust and Confidence'.[43] As he notes in that article, as more cases relating to this important implied term are heard fresh questions will arise for answer. For example, can the term be expressly excluded, and, if it is, could the Unfair Contract Terms Act come into play? Can the term apply to the self-employed – a significant question given, as he says, that 'the growth in this form of employment has been remarkable'.

And can the term be amended or its operation confined? Perhaps one of the most difficult questions facing employment contract-based rights at present is what are the limits on remedies, and the type of damage, for which compensation can be paid after a breach of the implied term? An important constraint was re-affirmed by the House of Lords in the leading case of *Johnson* v. *Unisys Ltd* [1999] ICR 809; [2001] UKHL, p. 13; [2001] IRLR 279, HL. This appeared to confirm the principle laid down in *Addis* v. *Gramophone Co Ltd* [1909] AC 488 whereby damages cannot be recovered for the manner of a wrongful dismissal, injured feelings, and the consequential difficulties of getting new employment. Yet, as Mr Justice Lindsay has pointed out, *Addis* and *Johnson* together 'lead to distinctions which have very little appeal to common sense'. The difficulties presented by *Johnson* v. *Unisys*, including the restrictions on pursuing contract-based remedies in the courts, having failed to get a meaningful level of compensation from the tribunal system, are considered in Chapter 14. It would appear that breaches of the implied trust and confidence term which result in dismissal cannot give rise to damages awards for any period after the contract has ended – whereas injuries and loss arising from situations where the contract subsists, such as the costs and on-costs of a wrongful suspension from employment, *can* be compensated! This distinction was translated into a successful claim and award in the case of *Gogay* v. *Hertfordshire County Council* [2000] IRLR 703, CA – a case of psychiatric injury resulting from an unjustifiable *suspension* of a care worker in a children's home. In that case Lady Justice Hale commented on the 'strange result' whereby the local authority was liable for damages for wrongly suspending the care worker while investigating possible abuse of a child. She noted that the employer 'would have done better had they dismissed rather than suspended her'.

Guidance from the House of Lords in *Dunnachie* v. *Kingston-upon-Hull City Council* [2004] UKHL 36 now confirms that compensation for dismissal can *not* include 'non-economic loss'. However, damages for psychiatric injury caused prior to dismissal are possible; *Eastwood and Another* v. *Magnox Electric plc*; *McVabe* v. *Cornwall CC* [2004] UKHL 35.

Cases like Transco plc (formerly *BG plc*) v. *O'Brien* [2002] IRLR 444, CA illustrate the wide range of more mainstream employment situations in which the implied 'trust and confidence' term may be relied on. In that case the employer mistakenly assumed that Mr O'Brien was not an employee with 'permanent' status, and did not offer him a revised contract of employment (with enhanced redundancy terms). Despite an apparent lack of malevolent intent this was treated by the ET, and on appeal, as breach of the implied term of trust and confidence.

Trust and confidence, as a requirement, manifests itself in many ways. A key one, however, gives employees protection against personal abuse in the form of dictatorial behaviour, violent outbursts, and bad language directed by a manager at a subordinate. In the leading case of *Horkulak* v. *Cantor Fitzgerald International* [2003] IRLR 756 (High Court), this facet of the term was said to derive from the general duty of co-operation between the parties to an employment contract, and this means the personal aspects of the relationship need to be maintained. Even if a job is subject to high standards of performance, those legitimate demands of the employer must be balanced by a fair system of enforcement, and the level of rebuke must be proportionate to the alleged failing. Use of foul language and abuse undermines self-esteem and dignity, as the facts of the case revealed; and on that basis the employee was entitled to resign and sue the employer for damages for wrongful dismissal.

Duty of Care: Bullying and Harassment

Trust and confidence is not the *only* implied term which assists the constructive dismissal or wrongful dismissal routes. There are others which underpin the employment relationship, and in some cases they straddle the contractual and tort-based liabilities of an employer. An increasingly important term, but also a problematic one in practice, is the 'duty of care'. Again, like trust and confidence, which Lord Steyn in the *Malik* case described as a 'standardised term implied by law', operating like 'default rules', the duty of care has long been a basis for requiring employers to implement Common Law duties to employees. It is also an important basis for obtaining compensation if people are injured at work. Yet the difficulties associated with bringing actions based on the implied duty of care are now well understood. They came to a head in what are now the leading cases on stress and psychiatric injury *Hatton* v. *Sutherland* [2002] ICR 613; [2002] EWCA Civ. 76 and *Barber* v. *Somerset County Council* [2004] UKHL 13.[44] These highlight what can, in many cases, prove to be three insurmountable hurdles which have to be jumped. First, demonstrating that the employer even owed a *duty of care*, based on sufficient knowledge and awareness of the problems facing an employee before the duty can even arise; second, showing that there has been a *breach*; and then showing *injury caused by the breach* i.e. that the injury, illness, etc., complained of was, on the evidence, clearly attributable to that breach.

In some cases the allegation of a breach of duty of care is assisted where the evidence also points to harassment or bullying. In one of the four appeals considered in *Hatton* v. *Sutherland* (that of Mrs Jones) – the only employer's appeal not to succeed – the case was clearly assisted by the aggravated behaviour of the claimant's line manager. This has highlighted the growing scope for claims in cases where there has been bullying and harassment – not only by employers and their managers, but by co-workers. In *Waters* v. *Commissioner of Police of the Metropolis* [2000] 4 All ER 934, the appellant was a police officer who had complained to her reporting sergeant and other officers that she had been raped by a fellow officer while they were both off duty. She sued the Commissioner of Police as her employer, contending that in breach of contract and of statutory duties to her, and negligently, he had failed to deal properly with her complaints. Among other things he had permitted officers to harass and victimise her. Implicit in this was that he was vicariously liable for the acts of officers under his command who had harassed after her complaint about the other officer she alleged had assaulted her. The case undoubtedly took the implied terms in a contract, and potential breach of duty of care, into new territory. The claim was struck out, and appeals against to the High Court and Court of Appeal both failed. By the time the case got to the House of Lords it focused on whether there was the scope for a cause of action in negligence, or other tort committed by the Commissioner. In particular, could he be held vicariously liable under the Police Act 1964, s. 48, or indeed for *any* other act or omission?

Among the acts she complained of before the Lords was ostracism by fellow officers, including refusal to support her while she was on duty; harassment; and victimisation. She attributed most of these incidents to her belief that other officers reviled her because she had broken the police force's 'team rules' by complaining of sexual acts by a fellow officer. A claim before a tribunal, alleging breaches of the Sex Discrimination Act 1975 had also, by then failed before the tribunal, the EAT and the Court of Appeal. So things were not, at that point, looking good for her.

The House of Lords allowed her appeal in a landmark ruling. Among other things it held that there was 'an arguable case' on these facts. Nor did it matter that people working for organisations like the police were able to use separate statutory routes for complaint such as the grievance procedure in the Police (Discipline) Regulations 1985. This did not preclude either a negligence or contract-based claim. The bar on suing the police in negligence for the manner in which they investigate crimes, or deal with allegations, did not restrict the claimant bringing an action – particularly given that her claim related to wider employment issues.

In the course of his speech, Lord Slynn in the House of Lords observed that:

> If an employer *knows* that acts being done by employees during their employment may cause physical or mental harm to a particular fellow employee and *he does nothing to supervise or prevent such acts, when it is in his power to do so*, it is clearly arguable that he may be in breach of his duty to that employee. It seems to me that he may also be in breach of that duty if he can foresee that such acts may happen and if they do, that physical or mental harm may be caused to an individual. (emphasis added)

Implied Terms and Constructive Dismissal

As will be considered further in Chapter 14, implied terms may, in some cases, be the basis for claiming unfair dismissal in appropriate cases. However, the difficulties in sustaining breach of duty cases (as seen in *Hatton* and *Waters*) have now been transposed into the 2003 case-law on constructive dismissal – as shown by leading cases like *Marshall Specialist Vehicles Ltd* v. *Osborne* [2003] IRLR 672. In that case a finance director suffering the effects of overwork had a meeting with the managing director to discuss ways of reducing her workload, and getting assistance from the company. Nothing transpired at that meeting, and believing that she could get no assistance, she resigned – and then claimed constructive dismissal. The claim failed. Whilst the duty of care, as an implied contract term *could* be used as a basis for claiming unfair dismissal (as it could for other contract-based, as well as tortious, remedies) the claimant never got past 'stage 1' of any unfair dismissal claim. I.e. she failed to even demonstrate a dismissal. In particular, said the EAT, the company's 'inaction' could not amount to a fundamental breach entitling her to resign and say she had been 'dismissed'.

Human Rights and Contractual Terms

The Human Rights Act 1998 (HRA), which came into operation in October 2000, provides the means by which ECHR Convention rights can be relied on in UK law, courts and tribunals. ECHR articles like the right not to be subject to inhuman or degrading treatment (art. 3), to respect for private and family life (art. 8), freedom of expression (art. 10), freedom of association and assembly and association (art. 11), the prohibition on discrimination (art. 14), and the protection of property and possessions (art. 1 of the First Protocol), can in some cases be relevant to the employment relationship, even though it is primarily a private relation. Among other things the employment relationship operates within a larger relationship between the State and citizens which is subject to ECHR requirements and standards. The ECHR, and the way the HRA implements it, requires courts and tribunals as public authorities to act lawfully for the purposes of the Convention (HRA s. 6), and 'so far as it is possible to do so', to read and give effect to legislation in a way which is compatible with Convention rights (HRA s. 3). This means, as Sir Gavin Lightman and John Bowers QC have said, that some provisions are *particularly* relevant to UK employment law.[45]

To appreciate the ECHR's potential impact on UK employment rights it is necessary to appreciate that the scheme contains express exceptions to the rights it confers, as can be seen in arts. 8–11. There are also *implicit* exceptions where there is 'objective and reasonable justification', as with art. 14 and discrimination. In some cases, notably art. 3, there are no exceptions, express or implied.

Cases being brought in employment tribunals are, increasingly, being influenced by employees' Convention rights. This is also apparent in the process of determining the scope of exceptions – including those impacting on the public interest. Employers and the public, too, have rights. In the important case of *X* v. *Y* [2003] IRLR 561, an employee working for a charity and with young offenders was cautioned for an offence with another male person in a public toilet. He did not tell his employer about the incident. When the employer learned about the incident, six months later, it dismissed him for gross misconduct. The ET dismissed his case, and with it the argument that the employer's action breached art. 8 and 14 rights. The EAT rejected his appeal, and held that transitory sexual encounters in public lavatories did not come within the scope of protection given by art. 8 (1) to 'private life' – and this, in turn, meant that art. 14 rights in relation to discrimination were not engaged. The earlier case of *ADT* v. *UK* (2000) 9 BHRC 112 was distinguished. Despite the result in *X* v. *Y*, the implicit rights under the contract of employment, as well as specific Convention rights in areas like sexuality and dignity, are well-established in ECHR jurisprudence, as confirmed in ECtHR cases like *Lustig-Praen and Beckett* v. *United Kingdom* (1999) 29 EHRR 548, ECtHR – a case in which the dignity and Convention rights of gay servicemen and -women were asserted and upheld. The Strasbourg court rejected the defence raised by the government that restrictions on gay servicemen and servicewomen were necessary or justified; and it confirmed that the government's actions against gay service personnel in their employment terms (and in administrative action against them, and the UK legislation that sustained it) were contraventions of the Convention.

Whilst decisions like *X* v. *Y* are controversial and highlight how employment rights are still dependent on judicial perceptions about the impact of a person's sexuality on their work – an issue that will almost certainly have to be revisited in future cases coming before the tribunals given the impact of legislative rights in the Employment Equality (Sexual Orientation) Regulations 2003 (SI 2003/1661)[46] – they do represent a step forward when the position is compared with the pre-ECHR/October 2000 position and court decisions. In deciding the case, the EAT doubted, for example, whether an earlier case on gay rights at work of *Saunders* v. *Scottish National Camps Association* [1980] IRLR 174 could now be good law. In that case it was held that a worker in a youth campsite could be fairly dismissed for no better reason than he was gay, assisted no doubt by perceptions at that time of how the trust and confidence requirement should work.

Regulatory Bodies and the Employment Relationship

The operation of art. 8 and other relevant ECHR articles, such as art. 1 of Protocol 1, has also been subjected to public interest factors in cases where regulatory bodies seek to impose conditions on professionals and on the way working conditions under a professional contract is allowed to operate. In *Whitefield* v. *General Medical Council* [2003] IRLR 39 (Privy Council) a doctor was convicted of conspiracy to defraud the NHS, and after his release from prison the General Medical Council's professional conduct committee judged that his fitness to practise was impaired by severe depressive illness. Conditions were therefore imposed on his registration, directed at monitoring his alcohol consumption, taking blood and urine samples, attending Alcoholics Anonymous, and limiting his working hours. He complained that the conditions were unreasonable and oppressive. His case did not succeed, though. The Privy Council did not accept there was an infringement of art. 8 (1); even if there was, it was permitted by art. 8 (2), as the conditions were made in pursuit of a legitimate aim (the protection of health and the rights and freedoms of others, including patients). Nor, held the Privy Council, was there any infringement of his rights to practise, and impact on 'possessions' (such as his job) in terms of any employment rights he may have under art. 1 of Protocol 1 of the Convention. Although the court did not need to go further with its judgment, and consider whether the doctor had an 'economic interest' to protect, it was satisfied that the conditions imposed were not sufficient to deprive him of any 'property' he might have.

The effect of the judgment would appear to be that whilst a job, and the right to work and practise a profession (and enjoy it and the rewards from it), is potentially a form of 'possession' – a point that did not need to be decided in the specific case – regulatory bodies like the General Medical Council are generally able to 'control' professions and employment using reasonable conditions if this is needed in the public interest.

CHAPTER 5

Workplace Change

Introduction

Workplace change is one of the major issues in modern employment law. In some cases the change process is regarded by the law as exclusively within the employers' control, and therefore usually outside the scope of legal regulation. Examples of this include management decisions to alter the physical working environment, moving staff around the particular location (subject to contractual terms on 'mobility'), and general day-to-day management matters. Staff changes like promotions are likewise normally a matter for management – although in this case the process may be subject to requirements considered in the last chapter, and the operation of collective procedures and customary arrangements. Staffing matters may also be subject to the operation of implied terms like 'trust and confidence'. For many workers, particularly if they are not in a union, there may be minimal rights to participate in workplace decision-making, however much the decisions and resulting changes impact on their working lives.[1] The procedural requirements associated with changes linked to reorganisation and redundancies may well dictate requirements for an employer to consult with staff affected, and union or employer representatives. This is considered in the later chapters on termination of employment, unfair dismissal, redundancy, and collective bargaining. Although EC legislation and policy has increasingly been directed at improving rights to consultation and 'participation',[2] for example on the establishment of works councils and the provision of information about the employer's business, the UK has often been slow to implement such rights.

An illustration of the difficulties there have been in securing effective participatory rights can be seen in relation to consultation about redundancies. This is one of the most difficult aspects of workplace change and reorganisation, and it is inextricably linked to wider issues of workplace changes, and the principles and requirements governing the way they should be managed. Originally, measures like the EC Redundancy Consultation Directive 1975/129 (as later modified, for example by EC Directive 1992/56) were implemented in the UK in ways which simply required employers to consult, but with minimal responsibilities beyond giving notice of intended dismissals and 'listening' to unions' responses: and without necessarily any commitment *beyond* that. Management prerogatives in relation to the change process have, in practice, not been accompanied by much more than lip service to the idea of workforce involvement. Collective agreements have always been able to supplement such bare legal requirements: but these in most cases are limited to superimposing procedural steps on a system in which substantive power remains with the employer. On occasions attempts have been made to utilise the law by seeking court orders to slow down or restrain reorganisations entailing job losses – but with mixed success, as the case law on redundancies, considered in Chapter 15, shows. It is also fair to say that court processes and legal remedies are not well developed. Even when a strong case appears to have been made out that employers should be required to abide by agreed procedures (and there is scope for treating collective procedures as incorporated into individuals' contracts) the courts have been reluctant to interfere in employers' management of the change process. This is a significant deficit in UK employment rights, and it is typified by cases like *Alexander and Others* v. *Standard Telephones and Cables Ltd* (discussed in Chapter 15). The best that can be said is that legislation – primarily EC-driven – has started to move away from a non-negotiable decision-making culture, and more in the direction of more meaningful rights to information and discussion.

Significant problems began early in the history of the collective redundancies system, and were characterised by a reluctance by UK employers and governments to fully implement EC requirements the way they should be. In the aftermath of the ECJ's decision in *Commission of the EC* v. *United Kingdom* EC Case C-382/92 [1994] IRLR 392, that EC rules on consultation procedures were not being properly given effect, amendments were made to TULR(C)A s. 188.[3] Nevertheless, the resulting position still had controversial aspects to it. Among other things the changes made in 1995 to s. 188 enabled employers to consult with non-union staff representatives, even where there might be a union that was recognised by the employer for such purposes. A further round of legislation in 1999 (discussed in Chapter 15) produced the present regime. Yet the current ss. 188, 188A remain problematic in many ways – and even after planned changes to consultation rights in 2004 have sought to address the on-going concerns. The bottom line is that ultimate control over most aspects of the redundancy process – including decisions to initiate changes and reorganisations, and to dismiss, redeploy, retain staff and otherwise alter existing working conditions – remain with the employer. In many ways the change process continues to be largely non-negotiable. The employer retains considerable discretion over whether to proceed with planned reorganisations and job reductions; over the timing of announcements and 'plans' (and thus the timetable); and, ultimately, whether to respond to alternatives and counter-proposals. The consultation regime leaves the employer with considerable control on the question of who to talk with, particularly in non-union workplaces. In this case a decision may be made by an employer who does not like what is being said to opt to consult with new employee representatives rather than existing ones (a course of action which may trigger an election for new arrangements under s. 188A). Sanctions for non-compliance by an employer with consultation, information and other requirements are also, arguably, inadequate as a means of securing consultation requirements. It is also the case that the lay union and employee representatives on whom consultation arrangements depend remain vulnerable to victimisation during and after disputes, and when there are reorganisations and opportunities for staff cuts, as the case law on TULR(C)A ss. 146, 152, 153, and 189 continues to show.[4]

TUPE and Organisational Changes

Similar considerations have affected the development of the 'transfers' system under the Transfer of Undertakings (Protection of Employment Act) 1981 (TUPE) (SI 1981/1794), and in the operation of the consultation regime in regs. 10–11A. But the shortcomings in the TUPE regime, particularly in the context of the bigger issue of workplace changes in general, run deeper than just a deficit in the information and consultation part of the regime.

With something as significant as a transfer of ownership, and given the interests and concerns employees are bound to have when faced with such a transition, it might be assumed that, at the very least, staff should have the basic right to know the identity of their new organisation early on in the process. This is not, however, a feature of the system, as demonstrated in *Secretary of State for Trade and Industry* v. *Cook* [1997] IRLR 150. Employees affected by transfers also experience many other difficulties, either in the pre-transfer stages or post-transfer when attempts are made to assert acquired rights against new owners. In particular, and perhaps in ways that should have been anticipated earlier in the life of the history of the Acquired Rights Directive 77/187 and TUPE, the 'economic, technical and organisational' (ETO) defence (in reg. 8) has been demonstrating its capacity to defeat even the most basic objectives of preserving employees' acquired rights at times of change. In particular, the principal objective of enabling employees' acquired rights to cross the transfer bridge between the existing employer and the transferee employer – and then form part of the transferee employer's obligations – appears to be increasingly at risk in a number of key aspects. Apart from the initial difficulty workers and their organisations can face in demonstrating that TUPE even applies, and that the employer's transaction is within the scope of TUPE as a 'relevant transfer', the regulations are often ineffectual in preventing certain kinds of pre-transfer dismissal, and variations in even the most basic, core terms and conditions of the employees transferring.

The Wilson Case

An example has been provided by *Wilson and others* v. *St Helens Borough Council; British Fuels Ltd* v. *Meade and Baxendale* [1998] IRLR 706, HL. In the first of the two appeals (held together) a county council, Lancashire, had financial problems in its management of a managed school. It therefore gave notice to the trustees that it would cease to be a managed school from the end of September 1992. St Helens, a borough council, then agreed to take it over from the start of October that year, but subject to conditions, including that it would not involve charges on its resources. There was an agreement with the union that staff cuts would be implemented; that the staffing complement would go down from 162 to 72; and that staff transferred to St Helens would be appointed to new posts. Lancashire agreed to redeploy those not transferring. With a day to go before the transfer the staff were dismissed for redundancy. The Borough Council had negotiated new terms and conditions for the staff: but these involved worse conditions. A number of the staff claimed that the changes entailed unlawful deductions in wages by St Helens, and that their wages (as paid by Lancashire) should not change. The tribunal found that TUPE applied, i.e. that it was a 'relevant transfer', but that their dismissal was for an ETO reason – and that the changes to their working conditions had already been agreed, making the variation legally effective. The EAT, on appeal, allowed an appeal – primarily because the changes were clearly part of the bigger scheme under which St Helens agreed to the transfer. As they were transfer-related they were ineffective: so the original terms on which they were working continued, in law, to be effective. Its decision, on the face of it, appeared correct – especially as ECJ case-law makes it clear that employees cannot waive rights given by Dir. 77/187, even when the overall position is beneficial, or the changes do not make the employment position of the affected staff any worse.[5]

In further appeals, though, the Court of Appeal reversed the EAT, and this was upheld by the House of Lords. Lord Slynn observed that 'the overriding emphasis in the European Court's judgments is that the existing rights of employees are to be safeguarded if there is a transfer'. But then he added that the exact scope of what this *means* is left to *national* law. In particular it is national law, i.e. the UK employment regime, which decides what to do if there is a dismissal, and the extent of any other related employment rights from that point. Nor is there any general Community right, it would seem, for an employee to continue in employment if such a right does not already exist in national law. Plainly this is not an aspect of acquired rights which is safeguarded in the UK. Normally the terms of the contract go with the transferred employee on a transfer. But where the transferee does *not* take on the employees who have been dismissed the dismissals are not, under UK law, rendered a nullity. If employees are dismissed, and then resume work (but on new terms after the transfer), the question arises whether there has been a valid 'variation' of their contractual and acquired rights (including statutory rights) 'by conduct'. In a key passage Lord Slynn did not accept that a variation can only be invalid for TUPE purposes if it is agreed on, or as part of, a transfer itself. In some cases it could, he pointed out, be due to the transfer (and for no other reason) – even if it came later in time. In what is, perhaps, one of the more contentious parts of the judgment, he went on to say that there had to come a time when the link with the transfer is 'broken', or is 'no longer effective'. On the facts of the case the dismissal process *was* 'effective'. The home, he said, could not have continued without 'radical organisational changes' which would reduce its running costs. Accordingly, the changes were for an ETO reason, as the tribunal had found.

The case is clearly an important one, and provides insights into some important limitations of TUPE in protecting acquired rights. It also highlights, at the same time, some of the practical realities facing the interest groups involved in such cases, particularly when financial problems dictate a need to take actions which TUPE does not address other than through a less than clear set of ETO principles. Basically, the case emphasised how TUPE is simply *not* an effective way of protecting the interests of employees who have been dismissed prior to a transfer, and as part of a wider reorganisation scheme. In particular, it does not have the ability to allow employees and unions, as of right, to preserve acquired rights in the form of pre-dismissal working conditions against the transferor employer. This has been seen with the case of *Celtec Ltd* v. *Astley and others*[6] when the Lords referred a series of questions to the ECJ, one of which arose from the words in reg. 3 (1) of the TUPE Regulations concerning the transferor's rights and obligations under the contract of employment. Specifically, it queried whether there is a particular point in time at which a transfer is completed: and if so how can that particular point in time be identified?

Clearly this is just one facet of unfinished business since *Wilson* which requires elucidation. But in many ways much of the confidence in TUPE as a means of assisting employees to preserve accrued rights at times of changes in ownership, and reorganisational changes generally, has gone. As one commentator, Mark Freedland, has said of the *Wilson* case 'this evolution of a notion of sub-contractual sub-transfer does less than justice to the notion of transfer of contractual rights and obligations which is embodied in the Acquired Rights Directive and implemented by the TUPE Regulations'.[7]

What is also becoming clear, since *Wilson*, is that employers faced with financial problems, or who simply want to change staff working conditions to reduce labour costs, are increasingly using the 'share transfer' route to avoiding the impact of TUPE. In *Brookes* v. *Borough Care Services* [1998] IRLR 636, for example, a local authority established a company to manage care homes for the elderly in its area. The care homes and staff were thereupon transferred to the company BCS. Another organisation,

CLS, then made a bid to take BCS over, which was accepted by the authority. At that point the EAT had given its judgment in *Wilson*, and this led the parties to believe they could not negotiate changes to staff terms and conditions that would require the transferee to maintain the changes. Accordingly they opted to circumvent TUPE by transferring the operation by the 'share' ownership route – i.e. whereby the transferor becomes the holder of at least the majority of the issue shares in a business (if not all the shares). In this case CLS became the sole shareholder of BCS, with CLS members becoming directors of BCS. The employees continued to be employed by BCS. Not unreasonably Brookes and other employees went to a tribunal arguing that in reality there *had* been a transfer, and that adopting a purposive construction to TUPE and what it is meant to do by way of protecting their acquired rights the tribunal should pierce 'the corporate veil'. The case was rejected, partly on the basis that there were genuine 'operational reasons' for CLS not taking on the management of the homes. Brookes' arguments on appeal that the transaction was plainly engineered, and was for the clear purpose of avoiding the TUPE Regulations, were rejected.

'Misinformation' and Transfers

In the course of organisational changes, and the consultation processes that accompany workplace change, it has become clear that employers do owe duties to employees not to give wrong information. There may also be some significant contract-based rights, including a duty of care owed to staff by a new transferor employer. In the case of the employer with whom staff are working (and who are being advised to agree to changes and transfer of their employment) the duty is generally formulated as an implied term of the contract to take reasonable care in making statements as to the likely impact of the changes on their interests. The transferor, as the prospective employer, may also be liable, but in tort, based on negligent misstatement (for example if misrepresentations are made about future employment benefits, pension rights, etc.). The key principles were explained in the leading case of *Hagen* v. *ICI Chemicals and Polymers and others* [2002] IRLR 31, High Court.

Cases like *Wilson*, *Brookes* and *Hagen* raise doubts about the ability of statutory interventions like TUPE to provide an effective system that secures acquired rights in the process of reorganisations and business transfers. Despite changes made to implement the Revised Acquired Rights Directive 98/50/EC which serve to improve TUPE – for example to preserve occupational pension and severance rights of public sector workers when there is 'outsourcing' – the scheme is still ineffectual in many respects. This has also, to some extent, been mirrored by other recent problem areas where statutory rights should be protecting employees during the process of workplace change. A key one is the Working Time Regulations scheme which operates as a bar to the imposition of increases in hours and the removal of break periods. In practice, though, such protection can be evaded by the use of 'opt-outs' and the expectation by employers that staff will agree to them.

Before that, though, it is worth considering the impact of corporate law systems on employment rights.

Corporate Law and Business Changes

Entrenched attitudes towards the employer's 'right to manage' are sometimes shared by union traditions that support such a demarcation between the management and union functions. The management 'prerogative to manage', including the power to initiate changes, is, in any case, strongly underpinned by the law. A particularly pervasive factor derives from the Company Law position on management power. Essentially, it is a company's board of directors that is charged with the legal power to make day-to-day management decisions – a power that cannot even be shared with shareholders, let alone other stakeholders like employees. Company Law regards directorial power as absolute, and indeed it is the source, in law, from which subordinate managers below the board derive and exercise day-to-day powers. As Table A of the model regulations provide, 'Subject to the provisions of this Act, the memorandum and the articles and to any directions given by special resolution, the business of the company shall be managed by the directors who may exercise all the powers of the company.'[8]

The management system of a company then hinges on the arrangements made for delegation of management authority from the board. But it is clear from the case law that the UK corporate system is antithetical to any notions of power-sharing, least of all with employees. As discussed in Chapter 15, directors and managers are only subject to minimal obligations to take into account the interests of employees as a group during corporate restructurings, and in deciding on closures of operations and resulting job losses. Thus s. 309 of the Companies Act 1985 merely enables directors to *have regard* to the interests of employees, for example at times of reorganisations and insolvencies.[9] The section is designed, primarily, to give legal authority to company directors to make management decisions that might otherwise be unlawful. It also legitimises expenditure on redundancies and severance payments, and decisions to keep company operations working or to shut them down; see cases like *Re Saul D. Harrison & Sons plc* [1995] BCLC 14.

Just as the courts in the Company Law regime are usually reluctant to intervene in arguments about the merits of the management of companies, for example during business transfers or reorganisations, employment tribunals and courts are, similarly, abstentionists when it comes to disputes about the merits (or otherwise) of corporate workplace changes. This is evident from leading cases like *Moon v. Homeworthy Furniture (Northern) Ltd* [1976] IRLR 298 in which employees' arguments that a factory closure after industrial action was unnecessary (and could not be justified) would not be considered. There are, however, aspects of protective legislation in which judicial processes do at least entail review of management decision-making.

The Relevance of the Contract

In the last chapter consideration was given to how workplace rights and obligations can become 'contractual', and how this is the basis on which rights and obligations can become legally enforceable. That said, one of the realities of workplace changes and reorganisations is how employment contracts can often prove to be ineffectual as a means of protecting rights, and blocking change.

In practice, in the UK context, there are many 'rights' which workers could quite reasonably claim are, or by practice have become, established 'entitlements'. Unfortunately, in legal proceedings many of these may prove to be or are treated by the courts and tribunals, as 'non-contractual' – and therefore largely susceptible to change without prior agreement. Given the inherent imbalance in bargaining power between employers and workers, it is unlikely that many of the areas in which 'management discretion' operates could ever be properly protected through the medium of the contract of employment alone. As Wedderburn has observed in *The Worker and the Law*, 'The contract of employment exhibits an individualism which necessarily ignores the economic reality behind the bargain. The parties are not equal, even in their ability to go to law'.

It is therefore as important now as it ever was to look to *other* ways, including union organisation at the workplace, collective agreements and legislation to provide such protection. It is also necessary to consider the development of more recent consultative systems like works councils as a means of mitigating the imbalance of workplace power.

Trade unions, through the collective bargaining system and participation, have traditionally had a key role in both fighting and facilitating the process of change. But there is no general recognition in the UK, either by the government or employers, that employees (or their unions) *should* have a right of co-determination in relation to key issues affecting the business and the people working for it. There is often a reluctance among some UK trade unions to depart from traditional approaches to dealing with the process of workplace change, and to adopt new consultative procedures like works councils. There are differences about how such systems could assist in the UK context, and these are often a regular feature of debates within the trade union movement – particularly as the very concept of a works council plainly cuts across more traditional forms of representation, and is contentious for that reason alone.[10] Given the way the EC's works council and consultation/participation legislation is formulated, however, it is becoming clear that these organisations do offer at least a modest potential to be important forums in which workers can have a voice in day-to-day workplace management issues. In response to criticisms that they are essentially talking shops, with little teeth (and in many cases largely controlled by employers) the counter-argument has been that they can, on occasion, assert workers' rights strongly. For example Jessica Learmond and Jeffrey Roberts have highlighted works councils role (including initiating court action) in fighting Renault's programme of plant closures.[11] It is also apparent that the legislators have targeted workplace reorganisation, and the change process, as an important part of the remit of works councils. Primarily for such reasons, one leading European employment law academic, Prof. Roger Blanpain, has described the European Works Councils Directive – affecting the largest companies in Europe, with more than 1,000 employees, and operating across more than two EC Member States – as the 'kiss of life'.

A different kind of forum, the national works council (NWC) is in the process of being set up in the UK and other EC countries in accordance with another EC Regulation 2002/14. For present purposes an important feature of the system is that there are some significant rights to access key information and consultation rights. These are under provisions which extend to 'anticipatory measures'. I.e. situations in which reorganisations pose a threat to employment; and when decisions about to be made by employers are likely to lead to substantial changes in work organisation or changes in contractual relations – including collective redundancies and business transfers.[12] As with recognition agreements, which can be required of the employer (as discussed in Chapter 18), NWCs can be imposed on an employer by *default* if conditions are met. There are, however, some important 'let-outs' – particularly in relation to confidential information – enabling listed companies regulated by stock markets to withhold information in certain circumstances (including at times when negotiations are in progress for sales and acquisitions, transfers, etc.).

The importance of such EC initiatives in the context of workplace change can also be seen with a number of other directives. These not only provide important minimum safeguards; but also operate as a 'block' on changes to core working conditions which, for many workers in the UK would never otherwise have been possible. These include the Council Directive on working time,[13] with its minimum rest periods, paid holidays, and maximum hours for weekend and night work. They have also produced minimum rights concerning work part-timers and those working to fixed-term contracts and other 'atypical' workers which have also served as a restraint on changes which would otherwise impact negatively on such groups. In the context of the flexible labour market, and rapidly changing patterns of working, it is becoming difficult to describe some kinds of employment as 'atypical', any more: but the prevalence of such forms of working has also dictated a need for some significant legislative interventions to restrict employers imposing unacceptable working conditions on such groups.[14]

The Courts' Approach to Workplace Changes

Before discussing the legal issues in detail, it is worth making several general points about the current legal approach to workplace change. In particular, it is immediately apparent that the law places more emphasis on *some* aspects of the employment relationship than on others. Protection (or financial compensation) is more likely for changes to 'core' areas of the employment relationship like pay or other monetary entitlements than for changes to the way in which a job is organised or performed. To some extent this just reflects the low priority which the law has given employees' rights as stakeholders in the organisations in which they work (compared with more immediate concerns such as the prompt payment of wages), and compared with the emphasis it has given to the needs and priorities of the owners of enterprises. It is this issue, which UK company law has never addressed, that lies behind EC policies to develop worker involvement in boards and management structures – and which is the impetus behind other initiatives for developing EC employment and social policy, and the 'social dimension'.[15]

Despite what sometimes seems to be the illogicality of differentiating between different types of change (and affording different levels of protection) the courts have attempted to rationalise their approach in several ways. First and foremost, decisions to impose change, and the choice of *means* for implementing them, are generally treated as part-and-parcel of management's 'prerogative to manage'. Rather like the royal prerogative, though, management prerogative is one of those curious features of the UK workplace scene which nobody really understands, but, with the assistance of the courts, has nevertheless acquired an almost mystical quality. It means that management has significant discretion to make decisions on most matters affecting the conduct of the enterprise. Even if other parties' views might be heard, at the end of the day these are entirely within management's exclusive control. Second, an employer's need for 'flexibility', particularly in relation to business reorganisations, is considered to be of paramount importance, even if it means that contractual rights may suffer. As can be seen from the 'business reorganisation' cases, this approach has meant that tribunals can, and do, routinely place a higher priority on an employer's business needs than on the rights of the employees affected.

The principal exception to his approach relates to changes which impact on remuneration. Even in that area of employment rights, however, the courts have been slow to interfere in changes which serve the perceived higher purpose of organisational change. They also, on occasion, facilitate inroads into *statutory* rights. This is evident from the way in which EAT decisions in 2003 resulted in employers being given a green light to 'roll up' holiday pay required by the Working Time Regulations (WTR) with ordinary wages, as long as this is in line with guidance on *how* this can be done. Specifically, as *Marshalls Clay Products Ltd* v. *Caulfield* [2003] IRLR 552, EAT has confirmed – and this is in line with earlier Court of Appeal guidance in *Gridquest* v. *Blackburn* [2002] IRLR 604 – using a contractual term for rolled-up pay introduced by employers which identifies an express amount or percentage as an *addition* to basic pay is not unlawful under the WTR reg. 16 (1).

These features look set to go on being important for the foreseeable future. From the courts' point of view the right of management to introduce change is facilitated by a corresponding duty on employees to *accept* change, and help to make it work.[16] This position is underpinned by the pervasive view that employment contracts are substantially different in nature from other kinds of contracts. For example, it is said that, unlike other kinds of contract, they cannot remain 'static' and the parties must therefore accept the need for flexibility in their interpretation. The practical consequence of this, as we shall see, is that it is often employees who are called upon to shoulder the negative consequences of their employers' changing business needs. Such a requirement to accept changes imposed unilaterally by one contracting party on another would, of course, be completely unacceptable in commercial or other contract situations.

Changing Working Conditions

Non-contractual Conditions

Changes can be made to non-contractual conditions without prior agreement, and in most cases without giving rise to any legal redress. The withdrawal of a purely discretionary bonus, for example, would not involve the infringement of any legal rights.[17] In another case, *Wandsworth LBC* v. *D'Silva* [1998] IRLR 193 the Court of Appeal held that a 'Code of Practice' on sick leave, which detailed arrangements on taking leave, was not contractual. The employer could therefore unilaterally change it. Except in exceptional circumstances where the employer's conduct (and the *way* in which changes have been carried out) could be said to amount to a breach of the trust and confidence term, or constructive dismissal,[18] there is little that can be done in such situations.

The concept of a discretionary or non-contractual scheme must be contrasted, however, with schemes which are part of the individual contract, and are 'contractual' but which then enable the employer to *vary* their terms without prior consent. This can be the case even where the scheme incorporates rights like incentives payments into the individual contract with the power to make changes. This can be the case even when *other* aspects of the scheme, including wages and general working conditions can only be varied by *agreement*. It is also significant in such cases that the power to make unilateral changes may be implied into the contract, as explained in *Airlie* v. *City of Edinburgh District Council* [1996] IRLR 516, Scottish EAT.

'Contractual' Conditions and Statutory Rights

If the entitlement or condition *is* contractual, or if the change involves statutory rights (or action taken against the employee for trying to assert them) there are a number of possibilities. Specifically, there are four matters to be considered:

- *permitted* changes;
- changes by *agreement*;
- terminating *and replacing* the contract and substituting new working conditions;
- breach of contract: this requires consideration of possible responses by the worker.

Permitted Changes

The employer may well be allowed under the contract to make the changes in question. It is obviously to an employer's advantage to make sure that contracts and job descriptions are worded in such a way that they enjoy maximum flexibility in the sort of work that can be required, and how it is to be done. If there is any doubt about this the courts will look at what the employer could ask the person to do under the contract, as well as at what he or she may have actually been doing since starting.[19]

In the leading case on the introduction of new technology the starting approach was to examine carefully the way existing jobs were done, and to compare this with the way the jobs would be done following the planned changes.

Example
Clerical and tax officers at the Inland Revenue worked on the administration of the PAYE system. When the system was computerised the Inland Revenue Staff Association initially wanted to co-operate. Its attitude changed when no guarantees were given that there would not be redundancies. The staff thought that the Inland Revenue was not entitled to require them to work with the new computerised system. They tried to get a High Court order to confirm that, and to ensure that they would continue to be paid while not using the new system. It was held that, although the job content of some jobs would be changed by the new requirements, and methods of working would undoubtedly change, the tasks to be performed were still in most cases within the terms of the original job descriptions. Although the jobs would be done in a different *way*, they were still the same jobs. The judge then proceeded to hold that those staff were subject to the implicit obligation to co-operate with the employer in making reasonable changes. Until they were prepared to adapt to the new requirements the Inland Revenue was held to be entitled to stop paying them.[20]

Implementing Permitted Changes
Even if the contract *does* allow an employer to make changes in working conditions, those changes should be implemented in a reasonable way which makes it possible to carry them out. If the employers do not do this their conduct can amount to a breach of the implied contractual duty of confidence and trust that is in every employment contract.[21]

Although this is an important principle which offers some protection against the worst effects of one-sided contracts or reasonable changes (as considered by Douglas Brodie in the article referred to in Chapter 4), its scope in any particular case may be uncertain.

Example

Mr White worked in the rubber mixing department of a factory. He asked to be moved to lighter work but this was refused. His attendance record deteriorated and, after a warning, he was later moved to another department where he had to accept a significant drop in pay. His contract had a 'job flexibility' clause which read: 'The Company reserves the right, when determined by requirements of operational efficiency, to transfer employees to alternative work and it is a condition of employment that they are willing to do so when requested.' The tribunal decided that this power was subject to two implied conditions, namely that the transfer should be exercised in a reasonable way and that there should be no pay cut without prior agreement. As the company had broken those terms Mr White had been constructively dismissed. The EAT reversed this decision. If there is an express power to transfer it is wrong to make that power subject to a 'reasonableness' requirement. The employer would only be acting wrongly if, for example, there were insufficient grounds to justify the move or the decision was 'capricious'. On the pay point they ruled that as long as employers act within their contractual rights, and their management power to move workers to other departments, any loss of income involved as part of such a change would not involve a breach of contract.[22]

Changes by Agreement

If the entitlement or condition in question is 'protected' as it cannot be readily changed by the employer under the contract (and it is not possible for the employer to make changes), it will be necessary to vary that contract. In line with ordinary contract principles, such variation can only be achieved by agreement, either with the individual concerned or through the collective bargaining process. For example, the change could be formally agreed either on a one-to-one basis or as part of a wider consultation and agreement affecting other workers (see Chapter 18 below, on collective agreements).

In practice changes are often agreed as part of a package of new arrangements. In order to make the variation legally effective something will usually have to be offered in return by the employer. In contract terms 'consideration' is important, and without it the change could be legally ineffective. For example, if you verbally agree to come in to work earlier than usual without extra pay, time off in lieu, or some similar arrangement, the employer would find it difficult to claim that such an agreement amounted to a formal change in your conditions. It is for this reason that employers usually include a pay rise, or other tangible benefit, as part of any package involving changes – for instance where they are seeking individuals' agreement to new contracts.

In some circumstances the law *presumes* that there has been agreement. This might occur where you have not objected to a change, or your agreement could be inferred from your conduct: a possibility identified by Lord Slynn in the case of *Wilson and others v. St Helens Borough Council* in the context of business transfers and reductions in pay and conditions (discussed above). It is therefore essential that employees do not give the appearance of accepting changes they do not want to agree to. As long as they make clear their objections to a proposed or imposed change it will be possible to avoid this risk (see the section on terminating and replacing the contract below). In another case it was held by a tribunal that agreeing to be laid off on a previous occasion did not prevent the worker concerned from arguing that the employer was not legally entitled to lay staff off on a later occasion.[23]

Past practice in the particular workplace has, on occasion, been seen as the basis for inferring or implying terms – and giving powers to employers to make changes which appear to be incompatible with established contractual rights. This is, perhaps, one of the aspects of the *Wilson* case which has caused a lot of concern. As already indicated, though, there remains a tendency for the courts and tribunals to try to avoid inferring agreement on the basis of past understandings or practices – particularly in the area of core terms like working hours and wages. This can be seen in cases like *International Packaging Corporation (UK) Ltd* v. *Balfour* and others, discussed in the next chapter, in which employers sought to impose reductions in hours, pay and conditions unilaterally.

Formal Notification of Changes

Employers are required to notify employees affected by changes by updating their written statement of particulars. This is done by issuing a written statement to them giving the new 'particulars' 'at the earliest opportunity' and, in any event, not later than one month after the changes in question.[24]

Terminating and Replacing the Contract

One option open to an employer who wants to make changes is to terminate the existing contract by formally giving the required notice, and then offering new terms and conditions under a new contract. An example of an employer attempting this, but withdrawing from it under pressure, was Rolls Royce in 1991. It was also threatened by British Airways during the 1997 dispute referred to in Chapter 4. There are, however, very few publicised examples of how employers have done this successfully.

For such action to be legally effective, though, the employer must make it clear that the contract *is* being terminated. It is not enough to simply notify employees of change.

Example
Six school canteen workers employed by Hertfordshire County Council received letters giving them notice that their contracts would be changed with effect from a given date. The changes included a reduction in pay. The letters, from the county education officer, went on to say: 'I hope you will continue in the meals service.' The staff carried on working but made it clear, through their union, that they did not accept the changes. It was held that the employer's action did *not* have the effect of terminating their employment. It merely confirmed the employer's intention to break the contract. By carrying on work, it could not be implied that the women concerned had accepted a new contract. They were therefore entitled to be paid their arrears of wages due under their contract.[25]

Breach of Contract: Responses

If an employer is in breach of contract, particularly in relation to important terms like wages, the employee may have an election as to how to respond. As considered in Chapter 14 a constructive dismissal claim is a possible option. Specifically, under the ERA s. 95 (1) (c) the employee could resign (with or without notice), and if this *is* subsequently accepted by the tribunal as a situation that merited such a response, this will be a 'dismissal' in law, paving the way for an unfair dismissal claim under the ERA Part X. There are many uncertainties associated with this option, including the possibility that the ET will *not* treat the employee as 'dismissed'. A leading case on the test to be adopted in constructive dismissal cases where the employee seeks to rely on breach of the employer's implied duty to maintain trust and confidence (where action was taken publicly against a manager in front of subordinates) was *Morrow* v. *Safeway Stores plc* [2002] IRLR 9. The difficulties, however, are also shown in cases where breach of the employer's 'duty of care' is alleged – as in cases of overwork and work-related stress (see Chapter 16).

In the leading case the House of Lords confirmed that workers faced with repudiatory action, such as a unilaterally imposed change in wages, can elect whether to accept the change or reject it.

Example

Workers at Ferodo Ltd, including Mr Rigby, were told that their wages were to be cut as a result of the company's financial problems, and following the company's failure to agree pay reductions and other changes with their union. He carried on working under protest. It was held that his contract terms, including rate of pay, had not changed given that neither he nor his union had agreed to a change. The fact that he had continued working over a period (of several years), during which he was paid less wages, and in accordance with the changes, did not mean the changes could take effect and had become legally effective. He had continued to object to the changes in terms while 'affirming' his intention to remain in his job. Nor did his job end when the new terms were imposed. As he had not agreed to the changes, and had continued to protest about them, he was entitled to pursue a claim for breach of contract, and be paid arrears of wages.[26]

A reduction in pay without agreement can sometimes be treated as a breach of contract on the more general ground that it undermines the implied term of trust and confidence.[27]

Unauthorised Deductions

An alternative response to non-payment of wages or other amounts due, which can be made while remaining in post, is to make a complaint to an Employment Tribunal of an unauthorised wage deduction. Under the Employment Rights Act 1996 s. 13 (3) where the total amount of wages paid on any occasion is 'less than the total amount of the wages properly payable' the deficiency is normally treated as deduction. S. 27 of the Act gives 'wages' a wide definition, and it includes fees, bonuses, commission, holiday pay, or 'other emolument referable to his employment, whether payable under his contract or otherwise' Statutory Sick Pay, and Statutory Maternity Pay. Typically, a deduction can occur when sick pay is improperly withheld, as illustrated by leading cases on this considered in Chapter 7.[28] In some cases, however, where the dispute focuses on the way pay is calculated under the contract, the tribunal may not have jurisdiction under Part II of the 1996 Act.[29]

Responding to Imposed Changes

The position described in the last section, and the case examples referred to, look easy. They suggest that all that employees objecting to changes need to do is refuse to accept any proposed changes and sit tight on the basis that the law will protect the employee's interests. The reality is that workers can be put under great pressure; and a refusal to accept changes may result either in threats of dismissal, or in being forced to resign.

Although the exact rights a person has will depend on the circumstances of the particular case, there are several possibilities for responding to an employer's action in trying to impose new working conditions. If the contract was only terminable on notice, and the job has ended, and wages have not been paid for the notice period, it will normally be possible to seek damages (or compensation) for that loss. In Chapter 14 unfair dismissal claims, including constructive dismissal, are discussed in further detail. There may also be scope for a redundancy payment if the change imposed has meant that the job being done has come to an end – or it has changed so significantly that it is not the same job anymore. Compensation may in such cases be enhanced by an unfair dismissal element (see Chapter 15).

Claiming Unfair Dismissal

Unfair dismissal claims are difficult, and their outcome is uncertain. Employers can often successfully defend claims on the basis that they have acted reasonably in proposing new terms, and dismissal has been necessary in order to make necessary changes. Tribunals can, and do, often decide that a dismissal linked to such reorganisational changes is 'fair'.

Example
Mr Harper was employed by Chubb Fire Security Ltd as a sales representative. Sales declined and he was offered new contract terms which involved a pay cut, and which required him to cover a different area. He was sacked after refusing the new terms. The tribunal held the dismissal to be unfair. The employers won an appeal. The EAT said that what mattered was the reasonableness of the employer in dismissing Mr Harper. Specifically, they formulated the question as follows: 'Was Chubb acting reasonably in dismissing Mr Harper for his refusal to enter into the new contract? In answering that question the tribunal should have considered whether Chubb was acting reasonably in deciding that the advantages to them of implementing the proposed reorganisation outweighed any disadvantage which they should have contemplated Mr Harper might suffer.' The case was therefore returned to the tribunal for reconsideration.[30]

Claims for unfair dismissal, including cases where employers have forced changes on staff as part of reorganisations, company restructuring exercises, and other forms of workplace change, are discussed further in Chapters 13 and 14. It may be seen from such cases, however, including an important 1997 case on unfair dismissal and redundancy,[31] that employers may be able to rely on the statutory defence of 'some other substantial reason' (known better by its abbreviated name SOSR) to justify workplace changes. Such imposed changes might otherwise constitute an infringement of employees' rights. The availability of the SOSR reason to employers dismissing staff as part of a reorganisation was confirmed by a 1997 Court of Appeal decision in *Parkinson* v. *March Consulting Ltd* [1997] IRLR 308, CA.

Unlawful Action: Threats of Dismissal

In order to obtain an employee's agreement to changed working conditions, for example new hours or pay arrangements, an employer may threaten disciplinary action or even dismissal. If the employer's action involves changes or actions which are unlawful the employee may be put in a difficult situation. An example of this might be where the employer could be subject to criminal law sanctions if tax or National Insurance fraud is involved; or health and safety actions proposed are illegal. Cases being brought which have utilised the Public Interest Disclosure Act 1998 (discussed in Chapter 9) have shown how many instances of criminal activities are being undertaken – and in sectors as diverse as financial services, community care provision, and road haulage. In doing this employers often seem to expect staff to go along with and collude in unlawful activities. The 1998 Act itself specifically singles out employers' criminal acts as within the scope of the scheme: and the main purpose of this part of the scheme is to provide people with a measure of protection if it becomes necessary to disclose such illegal behaviour (in the ERA s. 43B [1]). To appreciate the way the scheme works, and the rights of employees to 'disclose' employers' actions, it is necessary to be aware that an employer is *not* entitled to require an employee to commit an illegal act. This was confirmed in *Morrish* v. *Henlys (Folkestone) Ltd* [1973] ICR 482.

If action taken or threatened by an employer relates to an employment right in the ERA or other employment legislation, which the employee is asserting, such as the right not to have wage deductions made, working time or NMW entitlements, the right to seek flexible working arrangements, tax credits, or all the other employment rights in the ERA Part X ss. 99–107, the threat, or action, will generally give rise to an unfair dismissal claim. This is shown by two important 1996 and 2002 cases on 'assertion of a statutory right' as the basis for a claim.[32]

CHAPTER 6

Reductions in Work

Lay-off and Suspension

Employers hit by a downturn in business will want to reduce their operating costs as quickly as possible. To do this they will be looking to cut their labour costs and on-costs, including wages bills. In some industries and areas of work this is habitually done through redundancy – that is, by dismissals which may be justified in legal terms by a reduction in the employer's labour requirements (see Chapter 15 below). In other situations, though, employers will opt for more temporary measures; in particular, lay-off or suspension. This has the advantage, if the employer *is* legally able to do it, of keeping the workforce together while at the same time paying reduced wages or no wages at all. Needless to say this is not necessarily what employees want – especially given the uncertainty such action produces, and problems that may be experienced in accessing replacement income from State benefits.

An employer is not entitled to lay staff off work, reduce pay, or otherwise substantially change working conditions, unless there is an express or implied power to do so in the contract, or in a collective agreement, or, exceptionally, under customary procedures. The principle that an employer's contractual obligations must continue to be met despite difficulties in performing those obligations, will normally mean that wages should continue to be paid – unless the contract or collective agreement provides otherwise. As the *Rigby* v. *Ferodo Ltd* case discussed in the last chapter illustrates (and the company initially tried), ageement to vary or suspend the contract will have to be negotiated if the employer does not have the authority to unilaterally introduce changes in pay and conditions.

In practice, though, employers increasingly try to ensure that contracts and collective agreements *do* give them the right to employ staff 'flexibly', lay them off, introduce short-time working, or take other temporary measures. Arrangements will usually be in force to reduce pay, by restricting it either to the level of the minimum statutory 'guarantee payments' that must normally be paid by law (see below), or to levels which are *better* than the statutory requirements. Even if an agreement *appears* to give the employer powers to lay off or reduce earnings there may be scope to challenge whether those powers can be used in the particular circumstances.

Example
Workers were laid off and their normal wages withheld. This was done, despite normal work being available, because of an industrial dispute. The employer decided the situation was covered by lay-off powers in the national agreement. The agreement provided for guaranteed employment and pay, but it also said that the guarantee could be suspended if there was a dispute. The workers claimed that there could be no suspension under the provision while there was work available which they could do. The claim succeeded. The agreement did not give employers

a general right to suspend and there was no customary right in the industry giving them such a power. It was held that normal wages should have continued without interruption.[1]

Transfers and Other Changes

Employers may be able to introduce changes in working conditions on a temporary basis, for example by requiring staff to transfer to other work. Such temporary changes, or reorganisations, are different from the kind of permanent changes considered in the last chapter, i.e. redundancies, transfers to other organisations and variations in pay and conditions (as in the *Wilson* case). Depending on what the contract or collective procedure says, the transfer to other work may or may not involve a change in wages or other working conditions.[2]

Responding to Unauthorised Changes

If an employer tries to lay a worker off, or introduce short-time working or similar, when there is no power to do so one 'response' may be resignation followed by a claim for constructive dismissal.[3] Rather than opting to leave and claiming unfair dismissal (or possibly redundancy: see Chapter 15 below), with results that are unpredictable, it may in some circumstances be better to continue in the job, but insist on being paid. If an employer does not respond to requests to comply with the contract terms it is generally advisable to utilise internal grievance or 'dispute' opportunities *before* pursuing legal options like complaints to a tribunal, or bringing a claim based on breach of contract while remaining in post. The claim should obviously cover any arrears of wages due. But it might also include compensation under other heads, such as lost opportunities to earn commission or overtime. There may also be express or implied obligations of other kinds which could have been affected – for example, the opportunity to practise or develop skills in the person's particular profession or field.

Alternatives to breach of contract claims when short-time working and pay reductions are made without authority may be available, and for various reasons these may be a better option to pursue. One is a complaint that the reduction is an unauthorised deduction in wages under the ERA s. 13. The following 2003 case illustrates its use.

Example
Mr Balfour and his colleagues normally worked a basic 39-hour week. Falling orders led the company to unilaterally introduce short-time working, and this meant reductions in wages. The ET found that there was no express term authorising this, but then said such authority could be implied on the basis of custom and practice. However, the changes were held to be 'unauthorised deductions' as they had not been authorised in the workers' contracts, contrary to the ERA s. 13 (1) (a); and there had been no notification in writing of the existence and effects of powers to reduce wages, as needed by ERA s. 13 (1) (b). The EAT overturned this. They held that the reductions were indeed 'unauthorised deductions'. But they went on to confirm that there was no basis for a power to impose changes, and the evidence did not support a power to impose short-time working. The fact that the

employers had made reductions in the past, even if this was done on the basis of agreement at the time of such reductions, was not, the EAT held, the basis for finding a more open-ended, general agreement to reduce hours and pay every time the employer wanted to introduce short-time working.[4]

Even if an employer is entitled to lay off or keep staff on short-time working, there may be scope for bringing a redundancy claim if this is protracted, and the necessary conditions are satisfied (ERA 1996, ss. 147–154; and see Chapter 15 in this book on redundancy).

Statutory Guarantee Payments

Payments under the statutory scheme[5] can be claimed from the employer if:

- the employee has been continuously employed for not less than a month ending with the day for which payment is being claimed (or he or she has been continuously employed for *three* months if employed on a fixed-term contract of three months or less or a job is being done which is not expected to go on for more than three months); and
- there is a diminution in the requirements of the business for the work he or she is employed to do; or
- there is any other 'occurrence' affecting the employer's business relating to the work done.

'Occurrences' for this purpose include problems like power failures and interruptions in the supply of raw materials and parts; but the legislation specifically disqualifies anyone who is not working because of

- strikes, lock-outs and other industrial action involving other staff, or employees of an associated employer; or
- a refusal to accept suitable alternative work, or to carry out reasonable requirements for ensuring their services are available.

The entitlement is normally calculated (in accordance with the ERA s. 30) by multiplying the guaranteed hourly rate – a week's pay divided by the hours normally worked – by the number of hours of the workless day. There is, in any case, a maximum level of entitlement for each workless day. This can be paid for a maximum of only five days in any three-month period. Any contractual pay paid on a workless day reduces the employer's obligation to make guarantee payments. Other sources of income (for example, private insurance scheme payments) do not affect the statutory entitlement. On the position where the employer's contract has been varied (or a new contract is entered into) in connection with short-time working s. 30 (5) may be considered. Specifically, the computation provisions in s. 30 (2), (3) operate as if for references to the day in respect of which the guarantee payment is payable there are substituted references to the last day on which the *original* contract was in force. This is designed, in part, to prevent variations removing eligibility for continuing income.

There may also be scope for claiming State benefits in some circumstances during periods of reduced working – for example when reduced wages enable recipients of Working Tax Credit to require the Inland Revenue to increase their awards.[6]

Court Action and Tribunal Complaints

If wages or other entitlements are due, but have not been paid, a claim in the tribunal or county court will usually be appropriate. If guarantee payments are due and have not been properly paid a claim should be made to the tribunal within three months of the workless day (ERA 1996, s. 34 [2]).

CHAPTER 7

Pay

Wages Rights and the Law

For most workers wages, and the various elements that go to make them up, are probably the most important part of their job.[1] At the heart of the employment relationship lies the wage–work bargain.[2] This is a concept which, notionally at least, operates on the back of a two-way, bilateral contract agreed at the outset by the employer and worker. It is based on the idea that, having agreed the contract's terms, including wages aspects, the consideration for work undertaken for an employer is wages, and the consideration for wages and other remuneration and benefits is work. The wage–work model still produces potent effects. This was seen in the way the House of Lords in 1987 used it to construct a principle that if a worker is *not* working normally, and is delivering *less* than the agreed level of performance, the employer may withhold wages.[3] However, while the traditional bilateral contract model may be an accurate description of the way the wages element of the employment relationship works for many workers it is not the *full* story.

In an area of the law which, traditionally, has been one of the most heavily regulated in the legal system, it is the wages part of it that has been, and still is, probably where much of the State's legislation operates. Historically, the law has often closely regulated most facets of wages, including the level at which they may be fixed, the rights and duties of the parties on matters like deductions, and, of course, the processes by which wage rates can be increased. This includes the way collective bargaining processes can operate to provide the means of negotiating wage rates for incorporation into the individual contract (see Chapters 4 and 19); and State control over the ability of unions to take effective action to put pressure on employers to bargain meaningfully (see Chapter 5, and later chapters on unions and bargaining).

In terms of the *level* at which pay should be set, illustrations of legislative interventions to regulate wages go back a long way, as seen with the Statute of Labourers 1349. Among other things this bound workers to their masters during the period of labour shortages caused during the plague periods known as the Black Death. The Act compelled them to work at the lower, pre-plague wage rates.[4] Later legislation like the Statute of Artificers 1562, and Employers and Workmen Act 1875, and other measures discussed in Chapter 4 continued that tradition of State restrictions on pay.

Precedents for the idea that the State and its institutions should go further than just intervening in the employment relationship, and actually take responsibility for relieving the *effects* of low pay and in-work poverty, had been set by the Poor Laws as early as 1388.[5] The system was called 'outdoor relief'. Later, there were parts of the UK where legal intervention was essential to *maintain* wage levels at times of crisis: an example being the Speenhamland system in the 1790s at the time of the Napoleonic Wars, when magistrates fixed the minimum wages of labourers.[6] In Scotland, the poverty caused by the Highland clearances prompted a need for Destitution Boards to be set up to relieve in-work poverty, and thereby maintain a live population (and workforce).[7] The eighteenth century also produced the idea that the tax system could be used for intervening to raise wages and household income. The pioneer of the modern tax credit, Thomas Paine – when writing his classic *The Rights of Man* and pamphlets on the subject – was able to draw on plenty of precedents for wage regulation (as well as a fairer tax system to reduce the indignities of 'the working poor'); and in many ways such ideas form the basis of the modern tax credits scheme.

As considered in Chapter 1, interventions in later periods, including wartime, post-Second World War periods of 'pay restraint', and the operation of wages councils, all highlight the point that wages are a major focal point for State regulation in different ways. In the modern context, the introduction of the national minimum wage, considered in more depth later in this chapter, marked a key stage in the process. However, the important role of tax credits is also significant. For a large section of the UK's labour force, though, notably those assisted by tax credits, the concept of 'wages' has undergone a massive transformation. Tax credits represent part of a complex trilateral pay arrangement which completely transforms the model of a bilateral private bargain between the employer and worker. Essentially, tax credits provided for under the Tax Credits Act 2002 now provide the means by which the worker (and indirectly his or her family) receive, through the payroll, a substantial part of their income from a third party, the State (see Chapter 22). Intentionally, the way this important part of the pay package is delivered through the payroll, and alongside occupational wages, was intended to remove the stigma of it being seen as a State welfare benefit. In effect, after 1999 it created a secondary 'wage'.[8] The system now provides such a wage, and other support, for nearly 6 million families in the UK;[9] and is being extended under the 2002 Act to workers aged over 25, who do not have children, but who work more than the prescribed weekly hours (see Chapter 22).

Arguably, the role now played by the tax credits system, in providing considerable support for wages, and supplementing them by what might be termed a quasi-wage, means traditional perceptions of the wage work–work bargain should be revisited, and perhaps termed the wage–work–welfare bargain.

As seen in the 'Rona and Children' example in Chapter 22, workers in less well-paid employment can receive considerably more income from the State and the tax credits system each week than from their occupational wage. In Rona's case her annual wages from her employer are £6,500; her 'quasi-wages' are over £11,000. Equally significant, though, is that if at any time during the year of the award earnings go down – for example if overtime hours reduce, or a person is demoted – the State's wage in the form of the Working Tax Credit goes *up*.

The problems which can occur in relation to wages will be considered in relation to each key stage of a job, that is:

- at recruitment;
- during the employment;
- on termination.

Before doing this, it is necessary to refer to the relevance of employment status to the most common types of pay systems which are in operation.

Employment Status and Wages

The key feature of most contracts of employment is that in return for the performance of service wages will be paid, usually at agreed weekly, monthly or other intervals. In practice this system applies to most employees – and it also extends to many workers with contractor, or self-employed status. If there are differences, then they are likely to be, first, that the pay intervals may not be so regular. In fact in a contractor's employment, or so-called 'task contract', there may just be a one-off payment. Second, contractors will in most cases be paid without deduction of tax, National Insurance, or other deductions and are usually required to be responsible for their own tax and National Insurance.

Apart from these differences the legal ground rules on pay are generally the same whatever a worker's status. Those rules will depend, first and foremost, on what is provided for in the contract.

As far as legislation on pay is concerned, a worker's rights will – as with other rights – depend on whether the employment status involved brings him or her within the particular statutory protection in question. This would mean, for example, that a person who is not an 'employee' would be excluded from the chance to bring an unfair dismissal complaint if the wages were unilaterally reduced. This is because an unfair dismissal complaint in which constructive dismissal is alleged would require the complainant to have 'employee' status (see Chapter 14 on unfair dismissal). This can pose considerable difficulties for groups like agency workers who are provided to employers who may be responsible for most day-to-day aspects of the job. In some cases, though, the agency may be responsible for pay and, possibly 'discipline'. Is such a worker an 'employee'? If so, is the agency or the secondary employer the 'employer'? Guidance in the leading case of *Brook Street Bureau (UK) Ltd* v. *Dacas* [2004] EWCA Civ. 217 is that just because an agency pays the worker does not, in itself, make her the employee of the agency. If control is exercised by the secondary employer then it may be appropriate for the tribunal to conclude that the worker is an employee of that employer if there is sufficient mutuality and reciprocity (on the principle explained in Chapter 2). In the case itself the Court of Appeal directed that tribunals must in all such cases consider if an implied contract of employment had come into operation between the worker and the 'end-user', i.e. the client employer of the agency. The case highlights significant problems given that large numbers of local authority staff are employed in this way through agencies who are responsible for their pay. In the case itself a cleaner was provided to Wandsworth Council over a period of four years and had been trying, unsuccessfully, to show that she was the agency's employee. The ET's decision that she was neither the employee of the Council nor of the agency was overturned, and the majority concluded that 'all the pointers' were to her being the Council's employee.

In the case of pay it is worth noting that the scope of the Employment Rights Act 1996 provisions dealing with wages deductions is wider than most other employment rights, for example the right not to be unfairly dismissed. By s. 230 (3) of that Act it applies to 'workers', i.e. those working under a contract of service (employees), *or* under 'any other contract' whereby somebody undertakes to do or perform personally any work or services.

In some workplaces an important part of the wages package, namely the sickness and disability benefits provided when a worker is off sick or has an accident, is underwritten by permanent health schemes made by the employer with insurers. If the insurers do not accept a claim the payments may not be payable. In this case it will be difficult for the worker to get payment unless it can be shown that there was a right to the payments under the contract of employment; *Briscoe* v. *Lubrizol Ltd* [2000] ICR 694. If, on the other hand, there is a duty to pay sick pay, even after insurers have stopped reimbursing the employer, then the employer can be the subject of an 'unauthorised deduction' claim under the ERA s. 13; *Jowitt* v. *Pioneer Technology (UK) Ltd* [2002] IRLR 790. On sickness absence, and sick pay rights while away from work, see Chapter 8.

Pay Systems

There are a number of pay systems in operation and each system has its own characteristics. These have an important bearing on pay rights and obligations, and on how the courts and tribunals deal with them.[10] The two most important and commonly used systems are time rates and payment by results. As will be seen later in this chapter in the discussion of the National Minimum Wage scheme there are variants of these two main systems including 'time work', 'salaried hours work', 'output work', and 'unmeasured work'.

Time-rated Pay

The main feature of this system is that the workers are paid at the agreed rate provided for in the contract. Subject to anything in the contract, that rate must continue to be paid *without variation* and irrespective of the quality of work performance, and generally without reference to productivity, output, and so on. Most people's pay comes within this category, although it is increasingly common for pay to have a mix of time-related pay and other elements, such as discretionary bonuses or performance-related pay.

Payment by Results (PBR)

In this case earnings *will* vary over a given period, and PBR systems will link the level of earnings to whatever performance criteria are in the contract. PBR systems all require some form of 'performance' and, of course, some form of assessment. That system may operate by using objectively ascertainable criteria (such as the number of 'pieces' produced per hour in the case of piecework). Otherwise it may lay down criteria which give management much wider discretion in ascertaining whether performance targets have been met (for example, where performance bonuses are payable to groups of employees following an assessment of their contribution to company profits). Even if bonuses, supplements, etc, are 'discretionary' the employer may be in breach of contract by refusing to pay them, or pay them at a fair level, if no reasonable employer would have exercised the discretion that way; *Clark* v. *Nomura International plc* [2000] IRLR 766, High Court; and *Mallone* v. *BPB Industries Ltd* [2002] ICR 1045.[11]

In most cases PBR systems are used to supplement wages. This is a feature of most commission systems, although for groups of workers like sales staff who are employed on commission the guaranteed pay salary element is usually only a small part of their total earnings. Most employers operating PBR systems will try to build into those systems as much flexibility as possible to give themselves the freedom to introduce changes to their schemes, for example by altering conditions of eligibility, the methods of calculation, targets to be reached and so on. Such flexibility is not uncommon in the pay of white-collar staff in some Japanese and European companies, and employers may seek to introduce such systems in order to regulate performance more closely.[12]

If the earnings include a PBR element there are a number of problems that can arise. These include a lack of opportunity to meet performance targets (or otherwise satisfy the criteria for entitlement), underpayment, and unilateral alterations in the computation methods which the employer uses. In quite a few cases the staff involved complain that they have never really been clear what the performance standards of the job are, or have been since the job began! Another difficulty is that other key elements of the renumeration package, such as holiday pay, may be linked to, or calculated by reference to commission systems which are complex. In any case they may not produce a fair outcome for the worker concerned. Thus in the 2003 case of *Evans* v. *The Malley Organisation Ltd* [2002] EWCA Civ. 1834 [2003]; ICR 432 a sales representative was paid a basic wage, and commission only became payable once a client had paid at least a quarter of the fees due to the employer. This was usually not until nine months later! His holiday pay was, in turn, assessed on the basis of his normal basic rate. After he resigned the employer assessed the holiday pay he was due by reference to just his basic wage, disregarding any commission. The tribunal rejected his claim to include the commission element, invoking the Employment Rights Act 1996 s. 221 (2). Although the EAT allowed his appeal, the Court of Appeal reinstated the tribunal's approach. It concluded that in such PBR cases where the worker has 'normal working hours', and the renumeration does not vary with the amount of work done in the period, it was right to use just that basic amount as his week's pay when calculating holiday pay.

It is necessary to look now at the basic wages law principles that apply to most jobs.

'Flexible' Contracts and Variable Pay

Flexible working arrangements have become increasingly common. These may, for example, provide for variable hours each week, or indeed *no* guaranteed hours. Indeed, the employer may just require the employee to be 'on-call' or 'on standby', or otherwise work in ways which are more responsive to the employer's changing needs. This may be useful to the employer and in some cases may have been agreed with the employee, for example after a formal request for flexible working under the Employment Rights Act 1996, s. 80F has been agreed. This may not always prove to be such an advantageous system for staff, however: e.g. because of the uncertainty about earnings and other unwelcome consequences, such as being prevented while on standby from undertaking *other* work. If the worker gains too much control over the arrangement, for example by having the ability to refuse the offer of work when it comes, this may deprive the relationship of the necessary reciprocity needed for 'employee' status; see the *Brook Street Bureau (UK) Ltd* v. *Dacas* case discussed above. It may also make in-work social security benefit and tax credits claims very difficult, particularly if the person is not continuously employed, or if hours of work vary greatly (see Chapter 22).

Wages at the Recruitment Stage

The wages for a job are often decided upon by the employer before the appointment is made. For this reason it is not usually realistic, in most people's cases, to talk about wages terms being 'negotiated'. Nevertheless, any promises or statements made, whether at the interview or before, and whether in writing or just verbally, may be important, as they could be enforceable if there is sufficient evidence to rely on later. So the advertisement for the job could be decisive, for example, if there are arguments later.[13] If your letter of appointment states that you will receive a particular benefit that is likely to be treated as giving you a contractual right to that benefit: and that entitlement will continue unless it is effectively changed or ended.[14]

In the absence of specific agreement the law may imply a duty to pay expenses, or cover any costs[15] involved in carrying out a job. This cannot be relied upon with any certainty, and it is safer to clarify the position at the outset. The right to be paid any costs or expenses incurred is limited to what is reasonable.

Even if wages have not been agreed, as long as it is implicit that wages will be paid the *court* is able to decide what is a reasonable wage.[16] What the law cannot do, though, is decide whether the wages which have been agreed are adequate,[17] even if they are obviously unfair. Low pay can be supplemented by State in-work benefits and tax credits, and Housing Benefit and Council Tax Benefit. Under the National Minimum Wage Act 1998 a national minimum wage, supported by 'tax credits' (see Chapter 22), now operates (see below). The ineffectiveness of such in-work benefits for some workers in atypical forms of employment has been highlighted by commentators including one of the authors.[18]

Once an offer has been made and accepted, and the job has begun, the employer's wages obligations will begin. If, following acceptance of a job offer, the employer tries to withdraw the offer, there may be scope for legal action to obtain compensation. There is the danger, of course, that having resigned from an existing job on the strength of an offer of a new job, the latter new job may never materialise! The leading case on this,[19] and the scope for compensation based on compensation and loss of opportunity to make wages (and based on a 'collateral contract'), is discussed in Chapter 3 above.

Wages Problems during the Employment

The Obligation to Pay Wages

Once the job has started the employer is obliged to pay the agreed wages, at the correct rate, at the correct time, and as otherwise provided for in the contract. That obligation will normally continue until the contract ends. The main exceptions to this are where wages conditions are varied (see Chapter 5), or if workers are laid off or suspended without pay (see Chapter 6). Otherwise a departure from what has been agreed will usually amount to a breach of contract. Unilateral changes to wages, especially reductions which have not been agreed, are generally seen as 'repudiatory' action entitling the employee to elect to either continue in employment (and sue for breaches, arrears of unpaid wages, etc as in *Rigby* v. *Ferodo Ltd*, discussed in Chapter 5); pursue an 'unauthorised deduction' claim under the ERA Part II; or accept the breach has ended the contract and leave to pursue other remedies.

An alternative response to an unauthorised reduction, or to a change in the way wages are calculated, is to resign and pursue an unfair dismissal claim in the tribunal.

Example
Mr Mooney's contract as a salesperson entitled him to a salary plus 1 per cent commission on sales. The company decided to change this to a commission paid on sales over a specified target figure. This was held to be a breach of contract entitling him to claim for constructive dismissal, particularly as it was unclear at the time of the change what the effects would be on Mr Mooney's earnings.[20]

As well as not reducing pay, or changing the basis on which pay can be earned, an employer should not make it impossible or difficult for the agreed level of earnings to be achieved. If it has been agreed, or it was understood when the job began, that a particular level of earnings could be earned, then this is what must be paid. If there is a dispute over non-payment, compensation for any lost earnings will normally be based on this principle.

Example
A photo-journalist was employed by *Picture Post* on a retainer of £10 per week, and on the basis that he would be paid for the photographs and other work accepted for publication. It was held that he should have been given six months' notice, instead of the two weeks he actually received. In assessing his compensation for wrongful dismissal the court took into account what the parties envisaged he would have been able to earn in that six-month period.[21]

National Minimum Wage

In addition to observing any express or implied contractual obligations affecting the level at which wages are paid, an employer must comply with statutory regulation. For a lot of workers in the UK the two main Acts dealing with this are: the Tax Credits Act 2002, which among other things requires the employer to comply with 'start notices' and other Inland Revenue directions, and pay any amounts of Working Tax Credit due, and to show the amounts paid on the itemised pay statement required by the ERA s. 8 (see, further, Chapter 22); and the National Minimum Wage Act 1998.

The National Minimum Wage (NMW), provided as part of the scheme in the 1998 Act, and the Minimum Wage Regulations 1999, SI 1999 No. 584 (as they are amended from time to time), is the product of proposals in New Labour's White Paper *Fairness at Work* (Cm 5968, May 1998). The idea of minimum wage setting is not a new one in the UK, however. The most important precedents are the Fair Wages Resolutions 1891–1983. Minimum wages in particular industrial sectors of the labour market, especially where union organisation was poor, and collective bargaining was weak (or non-existent), were fixed by Trade Boards or Wages Councils[22] in the period from 1909. These were probably less to do with philanthropy, and the promotion of the welfare of workers and their families, than a perceived need among some industrialists to restrict what they saw as uncompetitive practices, including low wages paid by other manufacturers operating 'sweated trades'. This was certainly one of the priorities expressed by Winston Churchill when he was President of the Board of Trade. Regulation of wages was undertaken by the Trade Boards, and later by Wages Councils, as they operated under the Wages Act 1986.[23] The latter were finally abolished by the Thatcher government in the Trade Union Reform and Employment Rights Act 1993.

As Bob Simpson has observed in a comprehensive analysis of the background to the NMW, the history of British labour relations since the advent of the modern industrialised market economy has been dominated by pay issues.[24] Much of the debate over the desirability of a minimum wage focused (and still focuses) on the *level* at which it is set and on issues of social and economic policy. As Simpson also notes, there have also been a number of important strands to the NMW's 'social' element, including the fulfilment of ideas about a 'family wage', the unacceptability of rates of pay which leave workers in poverty, and concerns about whether the use of social security should or should not be used as a form of State subsidy towards employers' labour costs.[25] On the latter point, however, the enactment of the Tax Credits Acts 1999 and 2002 has, in fact, *continued* the process of what are essentially State top-ups for low wages, using the social security and tax systems for re-distributing income out of tax revenues. This has been part of the active labour market policies, and 'making work pay';[26] and can be linked, too, to objectives of maintaining competitiveness by transferring some of the burden of maintaining 'competitiveness' away from employers and to the State and the taxpayer.[27] On the 'economic' side of the argument, the issues about the NMW are even more contentious, with forceful arguments being advanced for and against it given its effects on employment and the competitive position of employers in international markets.[28]

There are a number of concerns about the NMW, including the likelihood that a large number of people are working outside the scope of its protection – either because of exemptions or because of ineffective enforcement. This was an issue which came to the fore in February 2004 after the deaths in Morecambe Bay while harvesting cockles for gangmasters for £5 a day. There is also on-going concern about the low level at which it is fixed – an aspect of the system which the UK's NMW shares with other systems in Europe and America. As Sachdev and Wilkinson comment in *Low Pay, the Working of the Labour Market and the Role of the Minimum Wage* (1998, Institute of Employment Rights), the NMW, to be credible, has to be sufficiently high to guarantee a living wage for a reasonable number of hours worked, with as few exceptions as possible. Exemptions allowing workers to be employed at below the minimum wage risks undermining the NMW's integrity by providing opportunities for substituting cheaper labour. The counter-argument, of course, is that if the NMW is fixed *too* high the risk of economic dismissals is increased; and employers, inevitably, will re-locate jobs to countries where wages, and other labour costs and on-costs, are lower.

NMW Scheme

The National Minimum Wage Act 1998, as supplemented by the National Minimum Wage Regulations 1999, SI 1999 No. 584, which are amended from time to time, provides that a person who qualifies for the NMW *must* be remunerated by his or her employer for work done in any 'pay reference period' at a rate which is not less than the national minimum wage; s. 1. To qualify, an individual must be a 'worker', who is working (or ordinarily works) in the UK under his contract, and who has ceased to be of compulsory school age. The Secretary of State prescribes the NMW in the form of a single hourly rate of remuneration, having regard to recommendations made by the Low Pay Commission. The NMW operates in accordance with a system of determining the hourly rate which is in s. 2 and the 1999 regulations.

S. 54 defines 'worker', 'employee', 'employment', and other key terms. Among other things, a contract of employment means a contract of service or apprenticeship, whether express or implied, and (if it is express) whether oral or in writing. The definition of a 'worker' in s. 54 (3) is the same as that used for the Working Time Regulations 1998, SI 1998 No. 1833, and so extends to most workers other than the self-employed. Specifically, it means an individual who has entered into or works under (or, if the employment has ceased, worked under)

(a)   a contract of employment; or
(b)   any other contract, whether express or implied and (if it is express) whether oral or in writing, whereby the individual undertakes to do or perform personally any work or services for another party to the contract whose status is not by virtue of the contract that of a client or customer of any profession or business undertaking carried on by that individual.

Unlike other employment rights which require a period of qualifying service, the right to be paid the NMW operates immediately for most workers, subject to exceptions. The scheme covers most agency staff and home workers.

However, it was held in *Wolstenholme* v. *Post Office* [2003] ICR 546 that the NMW, as well as other rights given to 'employees' in relation to unfair dismissal, and 'workers' in relation to unauthorised deductions from wages, does not to extend to groups like sub-postmasters. The absence of personal service, and the fact that they provide their own premises and equipment, and run what are, basically, businesses, takes them outside the scope of s. 54 (3).

Exclusions from the NMW
Reference must be made to the NMW regulations for the details, but some workers do *not* qualify for the NMW, including those listed in Part II. Among those excluded by reg. 12 are:

- workers under the age of 18;
- workers who have not attained the age of 26, and who are working under a contract of apprenticeship within the scope of reg. 12 (3) (or treated as such), and who are within the first 12 months of that apprenticeship or have not attained the age of 19;
- certain prescribed training, work, and education schemes in reg. 12;
- workers attending a higher education course which includes work experience for up to a year; and
- those being provided with shelter and other benefits (including money benefits) in return for performing work.

Workers undertaking the kinds of 'work' defined in reg. 2 (2) while residing in the family home of the employer and who satisfy other conditions, such as au pairs and family members participating in the running of a family business, are also outside the scope of the NMW's protection; reg. 2 (2).

Reduced Rate of NMW
Other groups, including those dealt with by reg. 13, qualify for the NMW: but they only do so at a reduced rate. These include workers:

- aged over 18 but who are under 22; or
- aged 22, and who are within the first six months after the commencement of their employment (and who have not previously been employed either by that employer or by an associated employer); and who have agreed to take part in 'accredited training'. This is defined in reg. 13 (3), but includes preparation for a vocational qualification approved under the Further and Higher Education Act 1992, or training which leads to an external qualification (approved under the Learning and Skills Act 2000 for the purposes of s. 97 of that Act) on at least 26 days between the commencement of their employment or, if later, the day on which they entered into the agreement and the end of the six-month period.

Calculating the NMW

The NMW Regulations lay down the method for ascertaining whether the NMW has been paid or not: and thus whether the employer has complied with the law.

It is always necessary to consider the detailed legislation, and how it applies in any particular case: but an outline of how the scheme works can be provided. The starting-off point is to identify the worker's 'pay reference period'. This is either a month or, if wages are paid by reference to a shorter period, that period; reg. 10. It is then necessary to calculate the number of hours worked, and the method used depends on whether the work system used is time work (regs. 3, 15), salaried hours work (regs. 4, 16), output work (regs. 5, 17) or unmeasured work (regs. 6, 18). Time spent on training at a place other than the normal place of work is treated as time work; reg. 19. Time work includes any time spent while being available at or near a place of work for the purpose of doing time work and is required to be available for such work. There are exceptions to this however: notably when the worker's home is at or near the place of work, and the time is time that can be spent at home; or when suitable facilities for sleeping are provided at or near the place of work and the period in question is used for sleeping; s. 15 (1), (1A). Even if workers may only be actively engaged while they are actually undertaking a particular form of work, such as answering the telephone, for the purposes of the NMW scheme they are nevertheless to be treated as working, and therefore entitled to be paid at the NMW rate. This was established in a Court of Appeal case on nurses being on 'standby' for an emergency service.[29]

Most forms of money payments paid during the pay reference period, or else in the following period in respect of that pay reference period, or later in certain cases – for example if they are made in respect of work done in that period, and satisfy conditions laid down in reg. 30 – count towards 'the total of remuneration' to be taken into account; reg. 30. Reg. 31, as supplemented by regs. 32–37, clarifies the way any reductions from such payments are to be taken into account, including costs of providing living accommodation.

To determine whether the NMW has been paid or not, reference must be made to reg. 14, 14A, and related provisions. Basically, the hourly rate paid to a worker is identified by dividing the total amount of remuneration assessed in the pay reference period, using the formula in reg. 14 (2), by the number of hours completed, as calculated under reg. 14 (3). The hourly rate at which the worker is entitled to be remunerated in respect of his or her work in any pay reference period is the rate, prescribed under the regulations, in force on the first day of that period.

The result of that calculation can then be compared with the prescribed NMW rate for that worker.

In some cases this can be far from straightforward. For example, in the case of 'unmeasured work' the worker would normally include all the hours of work spent in carrying out contractual duties; reg. 27. However, this is displaced where there is a 'daily average' agreement under reg. 28. This can make a significant difference to a worker's NMW, as shown by *Walton* v. *Independent Living Organisation Ltd* [2003] IRLR 469. Julie Walton worked as a carer looking after older and disabled people in their homes, sometimes spending long periods on site, and being required to remain on the premises for 24 hours a day. Within that period, though, 6 hours and 50 minutes was recorded as being the actual time needed, on average, to complete 'tasks'. She was paid £31.40 per day. She argued, unsuccessfully, that her hours were 24, not 6 hours and 50 minutes. The Court of Appeal concluded that she was not working 'time work' within reg. 3, but 'unmeasured work' to which regs. 27, 28 applied. Accordingly, the NMW rate was reached by dividing £31.40 by 6 hours 50 minutes, producing £4.60 – and this complied with the (then) NMW of £3.60 an hour.

Records

An employer is obliged to maintain records in respect of a worker who qualifies for the NMW 'sufficient to establish that he is remunerating that worker at a rate at least equal to the NMW', and 'in a form which enables the information kept in respect of a pay reference period to be produced in a single document'; s. 9 of the NMW Act and reg. 38 of the regulations. A worker may require his employer to produce any relevant records, and, accompanied by any other person he thinks fit, inspect and examine them (and copy them) if he believes on reasonable grounds that he is or has been paid in any pay reference period less than the NMW. The procedures to be followed are set out in ss. 10, 11 of the Act, and include providing the employer with a 'production notice'. The employer must give the worker reasonable notice of the place and time the records will be produced; s. 10 (7).

Workers who are 'employees' will generally be given the information they need about their pay as a result of the Employment Rights Act 1996 s. 8 requirement to provide an itemised pay statement. However, s. 12 of the NMW Act 1998 enables regulations to be made about NMW written statements in other cases.

Enforcement

There are several systems of monitoring compliance, and of enforcement.

Inland Revenue enforcement officers can require records to be produced, and can require 'explanations' of the records or additional information; and can enter premises at reasonable times to exercise their powers; s. 14. The Act also contains other enforcement powers, and these include the ability to serve enforcement notices on the employer requiring remuneration to be paid in accordance with the notice; s. 19. As a result of the National Minimum Wage (Enforcement Notices) Act 2003 officers can now issue enforcement notices which relate to one or more past pay reference periods, and this can be done in cases where the worker is no longer employed by the employer who has failed to pay the NMW; s. 19 (2A), (2B). This has reversed the EAT's decision in *Inland Revenue Commissioners* v. *Bebb Travel plc* [2003] ICR 201, EAT; [2002] IRLR 783. If there is non-compliance with an enforcement notice an officer can sue on behalf of the worker (on the basis of unauthorised deductions contrary to s. 13 of the Employment Rights Act 1996); or in other kinds of civil proceedings that might be available to the worker for recovery; s. 20. Workers are assisted by reversal of the normal burden of proof in civil proceedings, so that a presumption operates that she or he qualifies for the NMW unless the contrary is established; s. 28. A financial penalty procedure for non-compliance is in s. 21. It is, in any case, a criminal offence to refuse or wilfully neglect to remunerate a worker for any pay reference period at a rate below the NMW: and there are also offences relating to failures to keep proper records, making false entries, obstructing inspectors, etc.; ss. 31–33.

Dismissal in NMW Cases

A worker is also to be taken as entitled under his or her *contract* to be remunerated in respect of any difference in remuneration received and the rate that should have been received under the legislation; s. 17. The significance in practical terms of this is workers may also start proceedings in an Employment Tribunal, or, if necessary, in the county court. There is protection against unfair dismissal or other 'detriment'; ss. 18–26. Under the Employment Rights Act 1996 s. 104A an employee who is dismissed is to be regarded as unfairly dismissed if the reason (or if, more than one, the principal reason) is connected with action taken to secure the NMW, prosecution of the employer, or where the employee qualifies or might qualify for the NMW.

Non-payment of Wages; Delays in Payment

Non-payment of wages may occur for a number of reasons. If it is due to unacceptable delay, or repeated delays, which are more than just an inadvertent error in the payment system, this may entitle the worker to immediately leave and claim unfair dismissal. This was the case, for example, where a barmaid's weekly wages for the week ending 28 June were not received until 5 July (and those due for 12 July did not get paid until 7 August).[30] On the other hand a delay might not be sufficiently serious to enable a claim to succeed. An example would be where the causes are outside the employer's control, or are not tantamount to treating the employment as at an end.[31]

The most practical step to take, in most cases, if confronted with non-payment or a delayed payment is to formally require the employer, in writing, to make payment. If this does not produce results, it may then be necessary to consider options, including the use of an internal grievance procedure (to give the employer an opportunity to make good the missed payment). A failure to pay wages may in appropriate cases amount to an unauthorised 'deduction' and entitle the employee to recover unpaid amounts (see below).

Non-payment might be deliberate, for example, where the employer says staff are not working 'normally'. Although the principle 'No work: no pay' may be relied upon by employers in appropriate situations (see Chapter 19), it will *not* be relevant where action like a work-in or work to contract does not involve a breach of contract or 'industrial action'. An example of this is where an employer who is experiencing falling orders or financial problems unilaterally imposes short-time working, and cuts staff wages. Unless this is permitted by the contract, expressly or impliedly, or it has been formally agreed, the change will be an 'unauthorised deduction', as held in *International Packaging Corporation (UK) Ltd* v. *Balfour and Others* [2003] IRLR 11, EAT (see below). Nor will the principle necessarily apply where the employer *allows* somebody to carry on working in their normal way but then refuses to pay. In a leading case, which has already been referred to in the context of lay-offs, the worker concerned was able to take advantage of this principle. In such cases the duty to pay wages may remain unaffected.

Example
Mr Bond was a maintenance setter in an engineering factory. Following a dispute over bonus pay arrangements the setters, including Mr Bond, refused to work on certain machines but otherwise worked normally. Although they had 'withdrawn their co-operation' the employer allowed them to carry on working. Later the company informed them not to come in to work unless they were going to work normally. The dispute was later settled but the employer refused to pay Mr Bond for five days he continued to work, and for two other days when the company's action prevented him working. It was held that under his contract, and the relevant collective agreements, he should have been paid for four of the days he had been allowed to work and for two days when he was ready and willing to work but the only thing preventing him working was the company's action.[32]

Pay during Industrial Action

As industrial action generally involves a breach of contract by the worker, the employer is usually entitled to withhold wages. So even if the employer has not dismissed the worker – either because of statutory protection from dismissal (for example during a period of 'protected action' under TULR[C]A 1992 s. 238A), or elects not to dismiss during a period when dismissal *was* an option – wages can be withheld where it is clear that workers were deliberately refusing to perform contractual duties. The position may be less clear, however, in cases where employees are working within the terms of their contracts: or where the employer has either accepted *partial* performance of the required duties, or waived defective performance. The scope for this was shown in the *Bond* case, above. See, further, Chapter 19.

Pay Increases

Whether a worker has a right to an increase or not will depend on what the contract says, or on what has been agreed when or since the job began. Employers are sometimes not averse to forgetting about promised pay rises, and digging their heels in when it comes to upgrading and other forms of increases. In all cases, though, the question depends on the precise wording of the terms of employment, or on the effects of any relevant collective agreement which deals with pay upgradings and pay scales. It may also depend on what happens in practice in the particular organisation, especially with other workers.

The courts, for their part, have sometimes tended to interpret contracts, and apply collective agreement provisions on pay enhancements, in a restrictive way. In one leading case, for example, a lecturer paid on the Burnham national agreement saw her workload expanding rapidly, and assumed that she was entitled as of right to a regrading and pay increase. The court, however, took a totally different view. Even if the prescribed workload for a higher grade had been passed there was not, it said, an *automatic* right to be regraded.[33] On the other hand it might be argued, in appropriate cases, that a refusal to at least consider regrading after an application for one, where there was a reasonable expectation that it should be considered, would undermine 'trust and confidence'.

Annual Pay Rises

Employers' organisations in Britain are generally opposed to any general entitlement to annual pay rises.[34] The courts, in turn, have also pronounced that there is no general legal right to such a rise.[35] Despite this limitation, there may well be scope for insisting on a pay rise if, for example, *other* comparable staff have received one, or it would be reasonable to infer a right to one in the particular circumstances – for instance after taking on a greater workload or responsibilities. Unfortunately the courts and tribunals have only gone so far as saying that an employer should not act unfairly in refusing a pay rise, or should not act arbitrarily or capriciously so as to break the implied duty of mutual trust and confidence.[36] In another case a *Daily Mail* journalist challenged his employer's refusal to pay him an increase (which had been paid to other staff), because he had refused to accept a new personalised contract and, in effect, wanted him come out of collective bargaining arrangements with his union. His challenge was on the basis that he was being penalised for his trade union membership and activities, and participation in collective procedures – and the case, eventually, went all the way to the European Court of Human Rights before he won.[37]

Other Rises, Bonuses, Additional Payments

Unless the contract, or a collective agreement, gives a clear contractual right to this type of payment it can be difficult, in practice, to force the employer to make it. The problem is usually two-fold. First, is there a right to receive a payment? Second, assuming there is such a right is it possible to identify the *amount* involved; and does that depend on a procedure or process that can be the subject of a tribunal or court order? As already noted above in the discussion of discretionary pay systems and *Clark* v. *Nomura International plc*, even if payments depend on employers' discretion, the employer should act reasonably in the way they operate the system. Many arrangements are, in fact, non-contractual and therefore it is difficult to demonstrate a right to even be *considered* for a rise for that reason. This was the position in a leading case where the promise was to pay salary plus such bonus, if any, as the directors would 'from time to time determine'.[38] Another case illustrates the problem of *maintaining* the value of any payments that have been made:

Example
A headteacher's extra duties and responsibilities were rewarded by additional pay. That payment was fixed at 62 per cent of the payments made to assistant teachers. Later the level of the assistant teachers' payments were increased, but the authority refused to award a proportionate rise. The court held that, as the

payment was only 'discretionary' (and had not become a contractual entitlement, for example by being regularly paid) the head was unable to insist as a legal right on its value being maintained.[39]

Correct Payment – Itemised Statements

As a way of trying to ensure that workers can check they have been paid correctly, the ERA[40] requires an employer to provide a written statement that itemises the pay which is due, either before or at the time of payment. The statement must show, specifically:

- the gross amount;
- the amounts of any variable or fixed deductions from the gross amount;
- the net amount of wages or salary payable; and where different parts of the net amount are paid in different *ways*, the amount and method of payment for each part-payment.

In the case of fixed deductions the employer is entitled (under ERA s. 9), instead of detailing the deductions separately on each occasion, to give an aggregate amount if a 'standing statement' of the various deductions has been provided. Such statements must be updated if necessary and reissued every 12 months. Deductions must, in any event, be authorised (either by law or by the contract), and this is discussed further in the next section.

If a proper itemised statement has not been given, or a question arises as to the particulars which should have been included (or referred to), a complaint can be made to an employment tribunal under the ERA ss. 11 and 12. The tribunal can decide what particulars should have been included.

Deductions

ERA Restrictions

The ERA[41] prohibits an employer from making a deduction from the wages of a worker or from receiving a payment from him or her, unless:

- the deduction, or payment, has statutory authority (tax and National Insurance would come into this category), or is authorised by the worker's contract; or
- the worker has previously signified in writing his/her agreement or consent to the making of the deduction.

Wages for this purpose are any sums payable to a worker in connection with his/her employment, including bonuses, commission, holiday pay and other 'emoluments' referable to the employment. It also includes guarantee payments, and other entitlements like statutory sick pay and statutory maternity pay.[42] Payments in the nature of a non-contractual bonus are specifically treated as wages (and are to be treated as payable on the day payment is made); s. 27 (3). Certain payments are not, however, subject to the rules on deductions. Details are in s. 27 (2), but they include payment by way of an advance under a loan arrangement, or advance of wages, expenses, pensions, redundancy or other payments related to retirement, and other payment to the worker other than in his/her capacity as a 'worker'.

To deal with situations where it is not clear why there has been a shortfall in pay (for example, where an itemised statement has not been provided) the Act treats any situation in which the total amount paid is less than the total amount payable as a deduction. There is an exception to this if the deficiency is due to an error made in working out the gross wages.[43]

Disputes over Entitlement

Non-payment of wages may, however, be due to an employer maintaining there is no contractual entitlement to the amount claimed. The employer may also assert a right to be able to withhold payments. For example there may be a power to withhold sick pay if illness was brought on by the employee's 'misconduct' as in *Manchester City Council* v. *Thurston* [2002] IRLR 319. In that case, though, the council was still held to have made an 'unauthorised deduction' as the employee's illness pre-dated the alleged misconduct; and in any case they should have exercised discretion to pay him.

If the tribunal lacks jurisdiction to treat the matter as an 'unauthorised deduction' under Part II of the ERA, it may be necessary to make a claim for damages or other sum in the courts, or under the ET's powers in the Employment Tribunals Extension of Jurisdiction (England and Wales) Order 1994 (SI 1994, No. 1623).[44] The problems of asserting a legal right to be paid wages (or that there has been an 'unauthorised deduction' for the purposes of the ERA s. 13) in a flexible labour market where employers are operating what may be complex pay systems, is illustrated in the important Court of Appeal case of *Ali* v. *Christian Salvesen Food Services Ltd* [1997] IRLR 17. In that case, workers' overtime pay was paid in accordance with a system in their collective agreement. It required them to have worked for at least 1,824 hours each year. As they had been made redundant before they were even able to reach that figure (but had worked more than their basic 40 hours each week), the question was whether the employer's refusal to pay them for their overtime worked constituted an unauthorised deduction. The EAT held that it did. This was on the basis that an implied right to payment for hours worked over and above the basic 40 hours should be *inferred*. The Court of Appeal overturned that decision. The collective agreement, said the court, needed to be concise and clear, and was a compromise between the desire of the union to have an assured weekly wage, and the wish of the employer to avoid expensive overtime costs. There was no enforceable 'right' to pay from that point, and therefore there had been no 'deduction'.

For an 'unauthorised deduction' to have taken place it is necessary to have wages (or other amount) 'properly payable' under the contract – and in some cases it may not be possible for the worker to show this. Leading cases on this include *New Century Cleaning Co. Ltd* v. *Church* [2000] IRLR 27 (in which a majority of the Court of Appeal held that window cleaners paid under a team piecework system could not show that a 10 per cent cut in their earnings amounted to a deduction from wages to which they had a legal entitlement). Similarly, in *Hussman Manufacturing Ltd* v. *Weir* [1998] IRLR 288, EAT, when an employer introduced a three-shift system, and moved a worker to another shift (where workers were paid less) – something they were entitled to do without his agreement – this did not result in an 'unauthorised deduction'.

Other Remedies

An unlawful deduction or non-payment can, of course, have other legal consequences. As well as being the basis of a possible claim for constructive dismissal it may in some cases, in ways that are particularly helpful for higher-paid employees, be the basis for starting a wrongful dismissal action (see Chapters 13 and 14 below).

Exceptions

There are a number of important exceptions to the rules prohibiting deductions and payments.[45] The practical effect of these is that disputes over the sums in question (which may be due to alleged 'overpayment' for example) may have to be dealt with as a dispute over the contract and the parties' rights (in the courts) under it, rather than under the procedure in the ERA Part II.

Details are in the legislation, and need to be consulted: but in summary the exceptions, as provided for in the ERA 1996, s. 14, are:

- deductions made, or payments received, in relation to overpayment of wages or expenses;
- deductions, or payments, as a result of statutory disciplinary proceedings (something that can be particularly relevant to certain public sector workers, for example in the emergency services);
- deductions required under statutory procedures, like attachment of earnings orders;
- payments to third parties authorised by a worker (in a signed and dated document) to be made on his/her behalf;
- deductions, and payments to the employer, resulting from industrial action (for example, where the employer wants to recoup wages paid during a dispute);
- deductions made with prior written agreement for the purposes of satisfying court or tribunal orders.

Where pay deductions are the result of an agreed collective agreement, the terms of which are incorporated into individual workers' contracts, they cannot be challenged as an 'unauthorised deduction' by employees affected by the cut; *Burke v. Royal Liverpool University Hospital NHS Trust* [1997] ICR 730.

Strike or Other Industrial Action

An employer is entitled to withhold wages during periods of strikes or other kinds of industrial action, at least to the extent that the worker *is* taking industrial action, for example by being in breach of the implied duty of 'fidelity'; *Ticehurst and Thompson v. British Telecommunications* (discussed in Chapter 4). In such cases the ERA s. 14 (5) prevents an employee claiming an 'unauthorised deduction'; and the employer's action would have to be disputed in the courts rather than under the ERA Part II procedure; *Sunderland Polytechnic v. Evans* [1993] IRLR 196.

Retail Workers' Protection

The 1986 Wages Act (the ERA's predecessor) was designed to give workers in retail employment extra protection, particularly as employers in the retail sector have long been accustomed to recouping losses for stock shortages by imposing penalties on their workers. This generally takes the form of deductions from wages or demands for payments.

Although the current provisions are a long way short of what is needed, and at the end of the day still allow employers considerable powers, the additional protection it provides does assist, either by:

- limiting the *amounts* of wages that can legally be deducted (or which can be the subject of payments to the employer); or
- staggering the *times* when deductions and payments to employers are possible.

The starting point is that, as with other workers, any deduction (or payment received) must be authorised by law or by the contract. The ERA ss. 17–22 then deals specifically with retail employment.

Deductions for cash shortages or stock deficiencies can be made on a pay day, but the deduction (or payment required) must not exceed one-tenth of the gross amount payable on that day.[46] Any balance that is still owed must be carried forward to subsequent pay days, and the 10 per cent limit will apply on each of those successive days. There is no restriction applicable to a retail worker's 'final instalment' of wages, and a worker could in this case be subject to substantial deductions and demands for payment. The obvious point here is that the legislation in effect, gives the green light to employers to sack workers and avoid these limitations.[47]

Time Limits and Other Requirements

Among other things, the ERA provisions (mainly ss. 20 and 21) require that deductions or demands must be made within 12 months of the cash shortage or stock deficiency being established by the employer. If a series of deductions is being made in relation to a cash shortage or stock deficiency, the employer need only make the first deduction within the 12-month period. If the shortage or deficiency was not reasonably 'discoverable' the period will only start to run from when it *was* reasonably discoverable.

As far as payments are concerned, any payment is unlawful unless:[48]

(i) there has been previous written notice of the total amount claimed by the employer; and
(ii) the following main requirements have been met, namely that the demand for payment is:

- in writing on a pay day;
- not made earlier than the next pay day after the day the worker is notified of the full amount due;
- not made outside the 12-month period after the shortage or deficiency was discovered (or should reasonably have been discovered);
- not in excess of 10 per cent of gross wages on the particular pay day.

On the last point, it is possible that the employer might try to make a combination of deductions and demands for payments on a particular pay day. In this event the 10 per cent limit applies to the total value of such deductions and demands.

Tribunal Complaints: ERA 1996, ss. 23–27

Complaints of infringements of the ERA's provisions are regulated by complaints and enforcement procedures in ss. 23–27. Basically, a complaint should be made to the employment tribunal within three months of the deduction being made, or the payment being received. The tribunal can order the employer to pay back any money due.[49] In an important 1997 case it was confirmed that underpayment of wages in the form of non-payment of 'commission' can be dealt with by a tribunal for the purpose of the time limit. Time starts to run from the contractual time when payment is due in such cases.[50] Otherwise time starts to run for the purpose of the time limit from the date of the payment from which a deduction is made; or, in the case of a payment, when the payment is received by the employer; s. 23 (3).

The tribunal does not normally have jurisdiction unless there has been a 'deduction', or non-payment of contractual wages or payments on termination. Employees have a right not to be dismissed for asserting their rights.[51]

Overpayments

As noted above, 'overpayments' of wages or expenses are not subject to the usual restrictions in the ERA on deductions. If a worker is mistakenly overpaid, the employer's ability to recover it depends, among other things, on a distinction which the law makes between overpayments resulting from 'factual' errors – for example, miscalculations, wrong information – and errors of law, or which have been made because the law has been misunderstood.

Factual errors will normally mean the overpayment can be recovered. Legal errors will make the issue more difficult. In some circumstances, namely where employees have been led to believe they are entitled to the money and have acted on the misunderstanding to their detriment (by spending it, or taking on debts expecting to use it, for instance), the employer may be prevented from recouping the payment. In the leading case *Avon CC* v. *Howlett* [1983] 1 All ER 1073 a teacher was regularly overpaid whilst on sick leave. Although this was caused by mistake of fact the employer could not recover the amounts as he had been led to believe the money was his own, and as a result his financial position had changed and affected (for example through loss of State benefits). Accordingly the employer was stopped from recouping any part of the overpayments.

If wages are paid in advance and the employer tries to recover them, its success will depend on what the contract provides. In many cases, though, this will be down to whether or not an obligation to repay can be inferred from the circumstances in question. It is not uncommon, for example, for sales staff to be overpaid commission – sometimes called 'advance commission'[52] – or expenses which have not been earned by the time they leave or are sacked. Although the position depends on the circumstances and contract provisions in each case, in one important case it has been held that there is no implied obligation to repay.[53]

CHAPTER 8

Holidays, Working Hours and Absence from Work

Holidays

Until the government implemented the EC's Working Time Directive in 1998[1], there was no general obligation in UK law to give workers holiday leave. Nor, unless this was provided for in the contract, collective agreement, custom and practice, or wages council order, was there a duty to pay holiday pay or wages during leave periods. While bank holidays and recognised public holidays are customarily accepted by most employers as holiday days, this has not been obligatory and employers have not had to pay their staff for them.

The EC has long had a clear position on workers' need for, and rights to, holiday. This has taken the form of a non-binding Recommendation on minimum holiday entitlements for workers.[2] The EC's Working Time Directive (Dir. 93/104/EC) now provides, among other things, for paid annual leave, rest breaks, and maximum weekly working hours. Member States were supposed to have implemented its provisions, primarily through legislation, by November 1996. In the event, UK workers did not benefit from changes in UK law until 1 October 1998. Following the White Paper *Fairness at Work*, para. 3.18 it was estimated that over 2.6 million full- and part-time workers – many in industries like catering, retail and hotel work – received three weeks' holiday a year (rising to four weeks in 1999).

In practice many employers accept the importance of paid annual holiday leave, and individual contracts and collective agreements have traditionally contained detailed provisions and given employers control over *when* leave is taken, and making payments conditional on compliance with conditions.[3]

Until the Working Time Regulations 1998 established a general minimum statutory entitlement to paid annual leave for UK workers disputes focused mainly on the operation of contractual leave arrangements, and payment problems (note, for example, the case example in the last chapter on the withholding of holiday pay on termination). This point is also illustrated by a county court case:

Example
Mr Tucker and other members of the TGWU at a car plant were opposed to seeing changes made to their existing holiday arrangements. In particular they objected to losing two recognised holiday days, the August bank holiday and New Year's holiday, in order to get a week off after Christmas from 27 December to 31 December. The company assured them in writing that statutory holidays would not be transferred except by mutual agreement between management and all the unions represented at the plant. The works committee, on behalf of the management and some of the workforce's unions, later agreed the proposed new

arrangements, but Mr Tucker and his colleagues still objected. They confirmed that they intended to take holidays on the August bank holiday and the New Year holiday. In a county court action to claim unpaid holiday pay it was held that they were not obliged to accept changes to their holiday arrangements. Management had neither an express nor any implied right to change holiday terms without their consent. Although a collective agreement enabled staff to be required to take public holidays on dates agreed between the company and the unions, the undertaking given by the company required any changes made to be approved by all the unions at the plant, and this had not happened.[4]

Working Time Regulations 1998: Introductory Points

Minimum annual leave and working time rights are now provided in a regulatory regime in the Working Time Regulations 1998, SI 1998 No. 1833 (the 'WTR'), as amended. These implement EC legislation, including Dir. 93/104/EC on working time and the Young Workers Directive (Dir. 94/33/EC), in the UK from 1 October 1998.

They deal with four main aspects of working time:

- annual leave
- maximum weekly working time
- minimum periods of daily and weekly rest breaks
- regulation of night work, shift work, and work patterns.

They extend rights to 'workers', defined in the same terms as for the National Minimum Wage (see the section 'NMW Scheme' in Chapter 7), and apply to individuals who undertake 'to do or perform personally any work or services for another party to the contract ...' In *Byrne Brothers (Formwork) Ltd* v. *Baird* [2002] IRLR 96 this was held to extend annual leave rights to building workers even though they had signed a standard 'subcontractor's agreement' form which purported to exclude holiday pay, sick pay, or pension rights. They qualified for rights under the scheme as they undertook work 'personally', and did not do so, for example, as a separate business undertaking.

The Working Time Directive has not had a happy history in the UK. This is not, perhaps, surprising. As Nick Adnett has pointed out in *European Labour Markets*,[5] the UK (unlike other European countries) has no tradition of regulating working hours and an estimated 16 per cent of employees normally work over 48 hours a week compared with an EU average of less than 7 per cent. The UK also has, he says, the EU's highest proportion of workers subject to night and Saturday working. This, he argues, helps to explain the government's resistance to the Directive. The Conservative government unsuccessfully contested it, and in particular the validity of its adoption as a health and safety measure using the qualified voting procedure that applied to art. 118a of the Rome Treaty (now art. 138); *United Kingdom* v. *Council of the European Union* [1997] IRLR 30, European Court of Justice.[6] Having lost that case, though, the UK then delayed implementing the measure until 1 October 1998. It should have been in operation by 23 November 1996; art. 18 (1). Although it has been held in the UK courts that the Directive does not have 'direct effect' so as to confer leave rights, and rights to compensation, in respect of periods prior to implementation, when workers may have lost out as a result of the delay,[7] failures to implement properly have continued to cause difficulties, for example in relation to 'night worker' status.[8] In one important respect, the UK's imposition of a 'qualifying service' requirement, a challenge was mounted by the union BECTU. In *R v. Secretary of State for Trade and Industry, ex parte Broadcasting, Entertainment, Cinematographic and Theatre Union* [2001] IRLR 559 (European Court of Justice) the union argued, successfully, that a requirement in reg. 13 (7) (now revoked) had unlawfully tried to make the four weeks' annual leave entitlement dependent on the worker having 13 weeks' service. In concluding that such a requirement is not permitted, the European Court of Justice held that a worker's right to annual leave 'must be regarded as a particularly important principle of Community social law from which there can be no derogations'.

Although a worker's contract of employment (whether through collective arrangements or otherwise) can provide for *better* working time arrangements, the WTR are important in establishing minimum rights of general application across most employment sectors in the UK. Exceptions are in Part III (regs. 18–27A), and among those excluded are workers in the air, rail, road, sea, sea fishing sectors, doctors in training: and those where 'characteristics peculiar to certain specified services' such as the armed forces, police, and some civil protections services 'inevitably conflict' with the WTR provisions; reg. 18. Also excluded from WTR rights to maximum weekly hours, night working restrictions, daily rest, weekly rest periods, and rest breaks are workers engaged in unmeasured working time (reg. 20) and prescribed 'special cases' (reg. 21). There are also some exceptions in relation to aspects of the daily rest and weekly rest period provisions for shift workers in some cases (reg. 22).

Collective agreements and workforce agreements may modify or exclude the application of night work, daily rest, weekly rest provisions. For 'objective or technical reasons', or 'reasons concerning the organisation of work', they can modify the application of the normal 17-week reference periods by the substitution of a different period not exceeding 52 weeks in relation to particular workers or groups of workers; reg. 23. If WTR rights are excluded by regs. 21 or 22, or are modified under reg. 23, then the employer must wherever possible permit *equivalent* periods of compensatory rest or afford appropriate protection to safeguard the worker's health and safety; reg. 24.

The rest of the WTR scheme deals with enforcement, remedies, opt-outs, and the use of workforce agreements.

A more detailed analysis of the UK working time regime, including annual leave rights and their operation, is provided below.

Absence from Work: Sickness

If workers are unable to attend work as a result of sickness or injury their rights to time off and pay will usually be dealt with in their contracts. Although most workers are now covered by contractual sickness and injury arrangements, assisted by the Statutory Sick Pay scheme (see below), there can be problems if no express arrangements have been made, or if leave schemes are unclear.

As a general principle unavoidable absence due to sickness and temporary incapacity from work does not bring an employment contract to an end. Historically, as long as the worker was ready and willing to work, but was temporarily incapacitated, the contract continued unless and until it came to an end, or was brought to an end by the parties. This is still, broadly, the position. However, an employer may wish to dismiss a worker who is (or has been) on sick leave; and will generally do so under one or more of the potentially fair heads in the unfair dismissal provisions in the ERA s. 98 (1), (2) – and particularly 'conduct' (for example for excessive absence, or abuse of the sick leave and pay scheme), or 'capability' (for example in long-term sickness situations).[9] However, in appropriate cases, particularly if there is a lengthy, on-going absence from the workplace, and there is no reasonable prospect of a return to work, the contract may be 'frustrated': in which case there is no 'dismissal', and therefore no right to bring an unfair dismissal claim.[10] Similarly, there is no 'dismissal' if there has been a genuine and effective agreement to terminate the contract. These and other aspects of sickness-related termination and dismissal are considered in more depth in Chapters 13–15.

To the question of whether a worker should be paid, either wages or sick pay, during periods of incapacity from work, generally depends on the contract and its exact terms. The ERA s. 1 (4) (d) (ii) requires any terms and conditions relating to incapacity for work due to sickness or injury, 'including any provision for sick pay', to be included in the statement of initial particulars given to an employee. In the absence of such express provision the position will depend on other factors, including the practices in the particular workplace when staff are away from work. As the case-law shows, though, it may be difficult to demonstrate that other workers in a comparable position *are* routinely paid sick pay.[11] Historically, the 'duty to pay wages' has generally been regarded as continuing – at least while the contract subsisted. But this has always been subject to any terms of the contract provided that wages would *not* be paid, or would be paid at a reduced rate. Inroads into this position started to be made from the 1940s onwards by cases like *Petrie* v. *Macfisheries Ltd* [1940] 1 KB 265[12] and *Orman* v. *Saville Sportswear Ltd* [1960] 3 All ER 105. In the absence of express provision, and custom and practice as a basis for importing sick leave and pay rights into a person's contract, the position will depend on whether a right may be implied. In *Mears* v. *Safecar Security Ltd* [1982] IRLR 183, CA, the leading case on the subject, the judge at first instance, Mr Justice Slynn in the EAT relied on *O'Grady* v. *M. Saper Ltd* [1940] 2 KB 469 where it was said:

> Was it agreed that the man should be paid when he was ready and willing to work, or that he should be paid only when he was actually working? ... In this case ... there was abundant evidence that the terms, not express but no doubt implied ... were that he should not be paid wages whilst he was sick. Conclusive evidence of that is furnished by the fact that on at least three occasions during the time he had been employed he was not paid wages when he was away sick, and he acquiesced in that position.

In *Mears* itself the employer had failed to include the required 'particulars' on sick pay in the statement given to a security guard. A reference was made to a tribunal requesting that a duty to pay sick pay should be included in what is now the ERA s. 1 particulars, on the basis that it should be implied. The tribunal declined to do so, saying the evidence did not support this. The Court of Appeal upheld them, but also provided guidance on how, in the absence of compliance by an employer with the ERA s. 1, a tribunal should determine a reference to it under the ERA s. 11 (1) requiring it to determine sick pay 'particulars'. The starting point is to determine if a term has been agreed expressly 'by word of mouth or by necessary implication'. If not, it has to find a suitable implied term based on 'all the facts and circumstances, including the subsequent actions of the employer and employee, conduct of the parties, etc.

Later clarification of the judgment, and of the process of identifying 'particulars' on a reference to a tribunal under the ERA ss. 11, 12, indicates that if the evidence does not point to an 'agreement' between the parties, or it is not clear what they *would* have agreed, a tribunal should not 'invent' a term.[13] This may be right in principle, but it does not address the problem of what the position should be when there is a lack of evidence or documentary material to go on. Should it, for example, be resolved in favour of the employee, resorting to a presumption that wages should be paid? A further problem for a tribunal, on an s. 11 reference deciding whether to imply a term – assuming the evidence indicates an implied term to pay sick pay or wages is called for – is how *much* to pay (and over what *period*). This may require consideration of what the general practice is in the industry, or nationally.[14]

Although SSP assists employees who are away sick, there will be many cases where *Mears*, implied terms, and custom and practice becomes relevant – for example if SSP is not payable (or has ceased to be payable); or where staff are ineligible for SSP for other reasons, including status and low earnings. It is not unusual for employees' statements of initial particulars to make no provision about sick pay, or earnings during absences from work – or to include particulars which are inaccurate, and which need a tribunal to hear evidence about what they should provide. If no particulars on sick pay are provided the statement should make it clear that there is *no* provision: otherwise a reference to a tribunal may be appropriate.

Sick Pay and Absences in Notice Periods

In the ERA, Part IX ss. 87–91 helps to ensure that an employee who has been given notice of termination (or has given it), and is 'ready and willing to work' but is incapable of work because of sickness and injury (or is absent for other reasons like maternity leave, holidays, etc.), retains rights to be paid. Payments of sick pay, SSP, SMP, etc., go towards meeting the employer's wages liability. In the case of an employee 'without normal working hours' the employer's liability is conditional on the employee being 'ready and willing to do work of a reasonable nature and amount to earn a week's pay'; s. 89 (2).

Sickness, Incapacity and Disability: State Support

If an employer does *not* pay wages during sickness, or the contract only provides for *reduced* wages (or limited amounts of sick pay), State benefits become particularly important – either as replacement earnings or as an income/wages top-up.[15] In the context of workers who have had an injury or on-going incapacity, the Tax Credits Act 2002 provides for important earnings supplements. For example, in the case of a claimant who has had an injury or illness, and whose hours have reduced as a result, as long as they are more than 16 hours a week Working Tax Credit is payable (with contractual sick pay, SSP, Incapacity Benefit etc., being gateways to eligibility). In many cases WTC pays more money than a worker gets from occupational wages, especially if she or he is earning low wages near to the NMW. It can also assist those on maternity leave, including periods of maternity-related illness or incapacity.

For a person who has a 'disability' within the meaning of the Disability Discrimination Act 1995 an employer has a duty, among other things, to consider making 'reasonable adjustments', including perhaps a change in hours, place of work, periods away from work for medical reasons, job requirements to be undertaken, etc.; s. 6. WTC clearly facilitates such changes, given that one of the factors to be considered under s. 6 (4) is the 'financial and other costs' that would be incurred, and 'the extent of the employer's financial and other resources'. Accordingly, WTC and State support (including support from schemes like Access to Work, and in some cases the Community Care system), ought to be considered as part of the process of asking an employer to assist in making changes that could facilitate retention in employment.

Sickness Absences and Statutory Sick Pay

Statutory Sick Pay (SSP) provides important earnings replacement income for eligible employees for a period, or periods, of up to a total of 28 weeks. The key provisions are in the Social Security Contributions and Benefits Act 1992 (the SSCBA) ss. 151–163, and the SSP (General) Regulations 1982, SI 1982/894. As explained in the government's proposals in *Income During Initial Sickness* (1980, Cmnd 7864), the purpose of the SSP scheme is to provide a minimum 'floor' of income after an initial three-day 'waiting period'. Although it is still, notionally, a State benefit the removal of State support for employers (through National Insurance offsetting) by the Statutory Sick Pay Act 1994 has meant it is probably better described as a State-regulated occupational benefit. The State subsidy has been restricted since 1994. Although an entitlement to SSP, once established, does not affect the employee's right to receive any additional *contractual* sick pay, the payment of such employer's contractual payments discharge the liability to pay SSP. In practice, many employers do not pay any more than SSP, or the equivalent, although they may also 'top up' SSP with contractual sickness benefits, in some cases over a longer period than 28 weeks – partly as a means of managing sickness absence.

The fact that SSP is still treated as a State benefit, rather than a source of occupational income, has been underlined in the EAT case of *Taylor Gordon & Co Ltd v. Stuart Timmons*.[16] This is a case in 2003 which confirms that although non-payment of SSP is within the scope of the ERA Part II restrictions on 'unauthorised deductions' (as SSP is within the definition of 'wages' in s. 27 [1] [b]) when employers do not pay it (or pay less than they should) disputes should proceed through the Inland Revenue and Tax Commissioners 'route'. Among other things the EAT noted how the Inland Revenue has the power, or liability, to pay SSP when employers do not. For the details, see the SSP (General) Regulations reg. 9A and Inland Revenue guidance.

Although the employer administers and pays SSP, if an 'issue' arises about payments, including eligibility, the point can be referred for decision to the Inland Revenue; Social Security Contributions (Transfer of Functions, etc.) Act 1999, s. 8 (1) (f), (g). Decisions of the Inland Revenue can then be contested, usually within a time limit of a month.[17]

SSP is only payable:

- to 'employees'[18]
- in respect of qualifying days of absence due to incapacity for work. Specifically, if the conditions in the Act are satisfied the employer is liable to make a Statutory Sick Pay payment in respect of a 'day of incapacity'.[19]

If the claimant is not eligible for SSP, s/he may, instead, be eligible for short-term Incapacity Benefit (normally paid from the first day of sickness), but normally subject to the claimant's National Insurance contributions record (see the Incapacity Benefit section below). In practice, this may be difficult for employees without at least a year's continuous service in the three years preceding the year of claim, paying enough NI contributions in that time. Otherwise, Income Support may be claimed by an incapacitated worker if he or she is eligible. SSP entitlement cannot be excluded by the employee's contract of employment, and agreements which purport to exclude, limit or modify the SSP provisions, or require an employee to contribute to the employer's SSP costs, are void.[20]

Certain types of employees are not eligible, including those whose average total pay before deductions in the eight weeks before incapacity was less than the amount on which NI contributions are payable (the Lower Earnings Limit for NI contributions).

The legislation contains the detail, but the main exclusions from entitlement are people who are:

(i)   Over pensionable age.
(ii) Working under a contract for less than three months. A worker who has been employed for at least three months, even if this is on a series of 'one day' contracts, may qualify.[21]
(iii) Sick when they are due to start a new job.
(iv) Pregnant and within their statutory maternity pay or maternity allowance period.
(v)   Not at work due to a trade dispute where they work, except where they do not participate or have a direct interest in the dispute.

SSP is not payable for the first three qualifying days in any period of entitlement or, against any one employer, to an aggregate amount above his or her 'maximum entitlement'. Nor is it payable beyond the entitlement limit of 28 times the weekly SSP rate.[22] However, social security benefits like Income Support may be available in this case and where the person is excluded from SSP or Incapacity Benefit.

Details of entitlements and eligibility criteria is in guidance leaflets available from the Inland Revenue (for SSP) and the Department of Work and Pensions (for Incapacity Benefit and other benefits) and these should be referred to. Key points[23] are that:

- The employee must be incapable as a result of disease, or bodily or mental disablement, from undertaking the work expected under his or her contract.
- The day of incapacity claimed for must be within a 'period of incapacity' of four or more consecutive days. Periods of incapacity can be treated as continuous if they are within a fortnight of each other.
- Part-timers are eligible subject to satisfying SSP conditions.
- If period of SSP entitlement for the year has not ended. SSP is paid for up to 28 weeks in any period, or in any year (after that claim State sickness benefits).
- SSP does not have to be paid if necessary and reasonable certification procedures, including completion of a sickness claim form or continuing sickness form, have been followed.[24]
- Although employers can require notification of absence due to sickness, there are restrictions on what can be required – for example, medical evidence does

not have to be given at the same time as notification, and notification cannot be required, if the employee is away for more than a week, at more than weekly intervals.[25]

• The Inland Revenue can determine eligibility points, and otherwise assist if SSP has not been properly paid.[26]

Working Hours

Introduction

UK law has traditionally left working hours to be dealt with by the contract of employment and through the collective bargaining process – i.e. at a private law level between the employer and worker.

The main exception to this has been the statutory regulation of the working hours of women, young persons, and children, some of which goes back to restrictions in the Factory Acts 1844 and 1847. Most restrictions on children and young persons have been repealed by the Employment Act 1989. Health and safety-related restrictions, other than those in the WTR, are generally now catered for in regulations made under the Health and Safety at Work etc. Act 1974, and the Management of Health and Safety at Work Regulations 1999, SI 1999/3242. Many of the restrictions on women's hours of work have been progressively removed, mainly by anti-sex discrimination legislation – particularly as a result of the EC Directive 76/207 on equal treatment, including the Sex Discrimination Act 1986 (which lifted limits on overtime and night work). The Employment Act 1989, especially s. 1, enables pre-1975 and other restrictions that discriminate to be overridden. Plainly, protective legislation has played a significant role in maintaining stereotypes of women, and generally inhibiting equal opportunities (as noted by a report by the Equal Opportunities Commission, *Health and Safety Legislation – Should We Distinguish between Men and Women* in 1979). However, protective legislation continues in a variety of forms, including legislation like EC Directive 92/85 on pregnant workers, and in the Employment Rights Act 1996. For workers in general there are also restrictions on working hours in legislation like the Transport Act 1968 (for drivers), Mines and Quarries Act 1954 (on mining restrictions), and Shops (Early Closing Days) Act 1965 (for retail workers).

There are also health and safety regulations (including those made under the Health and Safety at Work etc. Act 1974, s. 15) that entail restrictions on working hours, or require rest periods and breaks,[27] in relation to specific vocations or work activities, as with the Health and Safety (Display Screen Equipment) Regulations 1992, SI 1992/2792. Risk assessments carried out under health and safety legislation, including the Management of Health and Safety at Work Regulations 1999, SI 1999/3242, may also result in restrictions or limits on the amount of time a particular worker is employed on particular tasks or activities. In some cases the regulation of hours is the product of a *mix* of WTR restrictions, collective arrangements, and health and safety regulations. Thus WTR reg. 6 (7) requires an employer to ensure that no night worker whose work involves 'special hazards' or 'heavy physical or mental strain' (as identified in a collective agreement, workforce agreement, or risk assessment under the Management of Health and Safety at Work Regulations 1999) works for more than eight hours in any 24-hour period of night work.

Excessive Hours/Overwork: Civil Liability

Whilst most restrictions are now contained in the WTR, or specific regulations, a further factor acting as a form of control on working hours is civil liability. At Common Law an employer owes a duty of care to workers, requiring among other things a 'safe system of work', and safe working. The scope for civil claims for damages is well-established, and based on principles in leading cases like *Wilsons and Clyde Coal Co. Ltd* v. *English* (discussed, together with the other cases below in this section, in Chapter 16). Employers are liable, potentially, for physical injuries; but also if they know, or should have realised, that overwork and stress in any particular case can produce psychological harm and psychiatric injury. As considered in Chapter 16, legal liability can be based on tort grounds, including breach of the duty of care if a duty of care (based on the employer's knowledge) is demonstrated. However, there must also be a breach; and the injury must demonstrably have resulted from that breach. These requirements may, in practice, be difficult to maintain, as shown by the leading cases of *Hatton* v. *Sutherland* and *Barber* v. *Somerset County Council* discussed in Chapter 16. As a general principle employers are also responsible for ensuring that demanding contract terms on hours are operated reasonably, particularly if they are likely to result in injury to health, stress, etc. This was illustrated by the junior hospital doctors' case *Johnstone* v. *Bloomsbury Health Authority* [1992] QB 333. That duty is probably now assisted by the explicit statutory formulation in the WTR regs. 4 (2), 5A(4) and 6 (2). Other contract-based remedies in cases where a worker has been required to undertake excessive hours (for example, when this has forced them to resign) include, potentially, compensation following a 'constructive dismissal'. Again, the difficulties of bringing such cases, which require clear evidence of breach of a fundamental term (even though this can include a breach of the implied duty of care for the worker's health), have been shown by cases like *Marshall Specialist Vehicles Ltd* v. *Osborne*. This case is also considered in Chapter 16.

Working Time Restrictions

The EC Working Time Directive requires that 'working hours' should normally be organised in a way that ensures that there is

- work of no more than an average of 48 hours each week (including overtime);
- a minimum daily rest period of 11 consecutive hours in any 24-hour period;
- a minimum uninterrupted break of at least 24 hours each week (generally including Sundays);
- a limitation on night work: normally no more than an average of 8 hours in 24-hour work periods);
- 20-minute breaks in shifts or periods of more than 6 hours.

Workers in some industries are be subject to exceptions on maximum hours, breaks, etc; for example some transport workers, fishermen, doctors and those in some emergency services.

The Limit on Weekly Hours

The WTR reg. 4 (1) provides that a worker's working time, including overtime, in any 'reference period' which applies must not exceed an average of 48 hours for each seven days. However, a worker can make an agreement with the employer (which can either be for a specified or indefinite period) – in an agreement in writing that complies with requirements in reg. 5 – to work *above* the limit; reg. s. 4 (1), 5. Subject to an agreement for a different period of notice (which can be up to three months), the agreement can be ended by the worker. He or she must give not less than seven days' notice in writing to the employer. It is the employer's duty to 'take all reasonable steps, in keeping with the need to protect the health and safety of workers', to ensure compliance with the limit; reg. 4 (2).

The Reference Period

Subject to reg. 4 (4), (5) and any agreement under reg. 23 (b), the reference period is as follows:

(a) where an agreement provides for the regulation to apply in relation to successive periods of 17 weeks, then it is each such period
(b) in any other case *any* period of 17 weeks in the course of his employment; reg. 4 (3).

If a worker has worked for his employer for *less* than 17 weeks, the reference period is the period that has elapsed since he started work; reg. 4 (4).

To identify the worker's average working time over seven days during a reference period the following formula, as provided for in reg. 4 (6), is used:

$$\frac{A + B}{C}$$

Where: **A** is the aggregate number of hours worked during the reference period; **B** is the aggregate number of hours working time in the period beginning immediately after the end of the reference period and ending when the number of days in that subsequent period equals the number of 'excluded days' during the reference period; and **C** is the number of weeks in the reference period.

B is a necessary element in the formula because in any given 'reference period' there may well be days when the worker is *not*, in fact, working (e.g. because of a holiday). Accordingly, such 'excluded days', as they are called, must be replaced using days in the next period that follows. 'Excluded days' include days of annual leave, sick leave and maternity leave; reg. 4 (7).

Limits on Working
In a leading High Court case on the operation of the scheme *Barber* v. *RJB Mining (UK) Ltd* [1999] IRLR 308[28] confirmed that on the facts of that case the employees were entitled not to work in periods which would take them over the statutory limit (see, further, below on enforcement of the WTR scheme).

Night Work

Night working is also regulated. Under the WTR reg. 6 a night worker's normal hours of work in his or her reference period must not exceed an average of eight hours for each 24-hour period; and it is the employer's duty to take 'all reasonable steps' to ensure this is complied with by all night workers.

The reference periods used are laid down by reg. 6 (3) as:

(a) where a relevant agreement provides for reg. 6 to apply in relation to successive periods of 17 weeks, then it is each such period, or
(b) in any other case, any period of 17 weeks in the course of his employment.

If a worker has worked for *less* than 17 weeks for the employer, the reference period is the period that has elapsed since starting work.

A night worker's average normal hours of work for each 24 hours during a reference period is identified using the formula

$$\frac{A}{B-C}$$

where **A** is the number of hours in the reference period which are normal working hours for that worker; **B** is the number of days during the reference period; and **C** is the total number of hours in the reference period comprised in rest periods spent by the worker in pursuance of his entitlement under reg. 11 (the weekly rest period), divided by 24.

'Night worker' is defined in reg. 2 (1) as a worker

(a) who, as a normal course, works at least three hours of his daily working time during night time, or
(b) who is likely, during night time, to work at least such proportion of his annual working time as specified for the WTR in a collective or workforce agreement.

In the case of *R v. Attorney-General for Northern Ireland ex parte Burns* [1999] IRLR 315 (Northern Ireland Court of Appeal), 'normal course' was held to mean someone for whom night working is a regular feature of his or her employment.

As already noted above, reg. 6 (7) restricts to a maximum of eight hours in any 24-hour period working that involves 'special hazards' or 'heavy physical or mental strain'.

Health Checks

Another important feature of the scheme is that night workers are entitled to be given a free health assessment before taking night work, and that follow-up assessments are undertaken at 'regular intervals'; reg. 7.

If a medical practitioner has advised the employer that a worker is suffering from health problems connected to the worker's night work, and it is possible for the employer to transfer the worker to work to which the worker is suited, and which means he or she will not be night working, the employer *must* transfer the worker; reg. 7 (6).

Young Workers

Regs. 5A, 6A, as added to the scheme in 2002,[29] and 7, impose restrictions on the working time of a young worker (defined in reg. 2, but broadly someone aged

15–17). The key points are that his or her working time must not exceed (a) eight hours a day, or (b) 40 hours a week.[30] If on any day, or during any week, there is more than one employer the working hours are aggregated for the purpose of the limit. A 'week' starts at midnight between Sunday and Monday. There is then a bar on working in the 'restricted period',[31] which is the period between 10 p.m. and 6 a.m. or, where the contract provides for working after 10 p.m., the period between 11 p.m. and 7 a.m. Subject to work of an 'exceptional nature' an employer must not assign a young worker to work during the restricted period unless there has been the opportunity of a free assessment of his/her 'health and capacities' before taking up the assignment (unless there has already been an assessment on an earlier, and the employer has no reason to believe that that assessment is no longer valid). There must then be assessments 'at regular intervals'.[32] Young workers must also be provided with daily and weekly rests periods, and daily rest breaks.[33]

Other Key Requirements

Patterns of Work
As considered below, although the WTR scheme includes minimum rest periods, if the employer's 'pattern of work' puts the health and safety of a worker at risk, in particular because the work is 'monotonous or the work-rate is predetermined', the legislation requires that the worker must be given 'adequate rest breaks'.[34] This is the subject of official guidance, but at the very least it requires work practices to be reviewed regularly to address the likely risks that such work may create, and then implementation by the employer of the results of the review.

Records
Employers must keep adequate records showing compliance with WTR limits in regs. 4–7, and retain them for two years from when they were made.[35]

Daily Rest
Workers are entitled to a rest period of not less than 11 consecutive hours in each 24-hour period of working. For a young worker, he or she is entitled to a rest period of not less than 12 consecutive hours in each 24-hour period, except that this minimum rest period may be interrupted in the case of 'activities involving periods of work that are split up over the day or of short duration'.[36]

Weekly Rest Period
Workers are entitled under reg. 11 to an 'uninterrupted rest period' of not less than 24 hours in each seven-day period. The employer can determine, as alternatives, either (a) two uninterrupted periods of not less than 24 hours in each 14-day period, or (b) one uninterrupted period of not less than 48 hours in each 14-day period.[37] A young worker is entitled to a rest period of not less than 48 hours in each seven-day period in which he works for his employer, subject to interruptions in the case of activities involving periods that are split up over the day, or of short duration – and in some cases where this is justified by technical or organisational reasons. But the reduction must not be to less than 36 consecutive hours.[38] The regulation contains provisions for determining when periods begin, and are to be taken. They also make it clear when periods do or do not include, or affect, rest breaks.[39]

Rest Breaks

If an adult worker's daily working time lasts more than six hours she or he is entitled to a rest break; reg. 12 (1). Subject to any applicable collective agreement or workforce agreement this is an uninterrupted period of at least 20 minutes 'which shall be consecutive if possible'; and the worker is entitled to spend it away from the worker's workstation if there is one. For a young worker a 30-minute break period is required after four and a half hours' working time: if there is more than one employer this is determined by aggregating the numbers of hours worked for each one.[40]

Exceptions to WTR rights are in Part III (regs. 18–27A) of the regulations, and include excluded sectors; unmeasured working time; special cases and shift work; collective and workforce agreements; 'compensatory rest'; and certain 'young workers' exceptions, and have in some cases already been referred to. Reference should be made to Part III itself for the detailed provisions.

Annual Leave: The WTR Scheme

Although a worker's contract of employment can provide for better annual leave time, and arrangements for taking it, a statutory scheme of minimum leave in each leave year is prescribed in the WTR regs. 13–17. Exceptions are in Part III and, in effect, remove the annual leave (and pay) right from some groups; reg. 18.

Subject to the position where workers start their job after the leave year has begun, and so only get a proportion of their entitlement (see below), a worker is entitled to four weeks' annual leave. Holiday pay is normally paid on the basis of the worker's 'week's pay', and the ERA ss. 221–224 apply when determining the amount. As held in *Bamsey and Others* v. *Albon Engineering Ltd* [2003] ICR 1224, EAT, when working out what a 'week's pay' is reference can also be made to the ERA s. 234 to see what the worker's 'normal working hours' are.[41] The leave year, for this purpose, begins in accordance with reg. 13 (3):

(a) on the date during the calendar year provided in a 'relevant agreement' (which means a workforce, collective or other agreement in writing which is legally enforceable as between the worker and employer); or

(b) if there are no relevant agreement provisions which apply:

   (i) if the worker's employment began on or before 1 October 1998, on that date and on each subsequent anniversary of that date; or

   (ii) if it begins *after* 1 October 1998, then it starts on the date on which that employment begins and each subsequent anniversary of that date.

Special arrangements apply to agricultural workers.[42]

If the date on which the worker's employment begins comes later than the date on which (under a relevant agreement) the first leave year begins, the leave entitlement in that leave year is a *proportion* of the leave period. This is equal to the proportion of that leave year remaining on the date on which the employment begins.[43] If, as a result of this rule, the period of leave entitlement is (or includes) a proportion of a week, that proportion is determined in days. Any fraction of a day is then to be treated as a *whole* day.[44]

Leave 'Instalments'

Leave under reg. 13 can be taken in instalments, but it may only be taken in the leave year in respect of which it is due.[45] Nor can it be replaced by a payment in lieu except if employment is terminated; reg. 13 (9) (b).

If a worker's employment ends during the leave year, and on the date termination takes effect ('termination date') the proportion he has taken of leave to which he is entitled in the leave year under reg. 13 (1) differs from the proportion of the leave year which has expired, reg. 14 (1) applies. If the proportion of leave taken is less than the proportion of the leave year which has expired, the employer must make a compensatory payment in lieu of leave.[46] If there is a 'relevant agreement' covering the point it will be the sum provided for in it. Otherwise, if there is no such agreement, it will be a sum equal to the amount of holiday pay due[47] calculated using the formula

$$(A \times B) - C$$

where A is the period of leave entitlement under reg. 13 (1); B is the proportion of the worker's leave year that expired before the termination date; C is the period of leave taken by the worker between the start of the leave year and the termination date.

A relevant agreement can, and usually does, require workers to compensate their employers – either by making a payment, undertaking additional work, or otherwise – if the proportion of leave already taken exceeds the proportion of the leave year which has expired. If there is no such agreement, or it does not deal with the point, an employer may not make deductions from wages when the job ends. Nor can the worker be treated as receiving an 'overpayment of wages' for the purposes of the ERA s. 14 provisions on unauthorised deductions, as held by the case *Hill* v. *Chapell* [2003] IRLR 19, EAT.[48]

Leave Dates

A worker can take leave on days that have been elected by giving the employer notice in accordance with the scheme's requirements: and the right to be paid for annual leave, if asserted, arises even while the worker is away from the workplace on sick leave, as confirmed in *Kigass Aero Components Ltd* v. *Brown* [2002] IRLR 312, EAT.[49] The worker's choice of days can be restricted, however, in line with the employer's requirements as to days when leave should be taken (or not taken) if notice of this has been given by the employer.[50] Rights or obligations under the provision regulating leave taking can be varied or excluded by a relevant agreement.[51] Special rules apply to a worker taking leave in the first year of employment: broadly, only leave which is deemed to have accrued to that point, as modified in accordance with any 'relevant agreement' (less any days already taken), can be taken.[52]

Payment of Holiday Pay; Contract/WTR 'Overlaps'

As already noted, payment for annual leave under the WTR is based on 'a week's pay' for each week of leave, and the ERA ss. 221–224 is applied, with modifications, for this purpose; reg. 16. Such payments should not affect any other rights of a worker to remuneration under his contract (so-called 'contractual remuneration'). Any contractual remuneration paid to a worker for a leave period will go towards discharging any liability of the employer; and, conversely, any payment of remuneration under the WTR will go towards discharging an employer's liability for contractual remuneration in respect of the same period. This part of the scheme has produced some significant problems, particularly when it is claimed by the employer that holiday pay is incorporated into (or 'rolled up' with) other remuneration. In principle the practice seems wrong, and inconsistent with Working Time Directive objectives; and it might be expected that the inclusion of holiday pay in a rolled-up rate should be treated as void given the bar on 'contracting out' in WTR reg. 35 – a position adopted by the EAT in 2003 in Scotland in *MPB Structures Ltd* v. *Munro* [2003] IRLR 350 CS; [2002] IRLR 601. However, in *Marshalls Clay Products* v. *Caulfield* [2003] IRLR 552 a different approach has been taken, and guidance has been provided indicating that in some cases such arrangements are *not* necessarily unlawful.[53] In particular, in its decision the EAT confirmed that a contractual term for rolled-up pay, which identifies an express amount or percentage as an addition to basic pay is not unlawful under the WTR reg. 16 (1). Reference must be made to the judgment for the more detailed guidance it gives, but among other things the EAT's guidance makes clear that certain kinds of 'rolled-up' provision will be unlawful, notably:

- if the contract is silent on holiday pay;
- the contract excludes liability for/entitlement to holiday pay;
- contracts which purport to include holiday pay, but without specifying an amount.

In *Robinson-Steele* v. *R.D. Services Ltd* (2004, ET Case 1800174/04) an ET referred to the ECJ the question of whether allowing pay for annual leave to be included in a worker's hourly remuneration and paid as part of working time (but not as part of a period of leave actually taken) is consistent with EC Dir. 93/104, art. 7; and does art. 7 (2) preclude ETs giving employers 'credit' for such payments when giving applicants remedies?

It is possible that a worker may have an entitlement to a rest period, rest break or annual leave both under the WTR and a contract provision. If so, he or she may not exercise the two rights separately, but can take advantage of whichever right, in any particular respect, is the more favourable.[54]

WTR Rights: Enforcement

Detailed provisions on enforcement are in the WTR Part IV.[55] In summary, though, there are several forms of liability, and ways of securing WTR rights.

An employer who fails to comply with 'relevant requirements'[56] including duties relating to reasonable steps to ensure compliance with weekly working hours limits, limits on night work, patterns of work, records and compensatory rest periods commits a criminal offence.[57] Inspectors of the Health and Safety Executive, or in some cases a local authority (under the Health and Safety [Enforcing Authority] Regulations 1998, SI 1998/494) are responsible for a range of provisions. These include:

- compliance with the 48-hour limit;
- night-working restrictions, health assessments, and assessments of young workers;

- arrangements for transfers to day working;
- rest breaks;
- maintaining records;
- compensatory rest periods/health and safety protection arrangements if limits are modified by collective or workforce agreements.

Employment Tribunal Complaints

Workers may also present complaints to an Employment Tribunal that the employer has refused to permit them to exercise working time and leave rights;[58] or has failed to pay amounts of leave pay, or pay for leave that is outstanding at termination of employment. Details of time limits are in reg. 30, but in summary in most cases a complaint must be brought within three months of the date on which it is alleged the right should have been permitted; or, in the case of payments of holiday pay, from the date the payment should have been made. The tribunal has limited powers to extend the period within which a complaint should have been made if it is satisfied that it was not reasonably practicable for the complaint to have been brought within the time limit.[59]

Non-Payment of Holiday Pay: 'Deduction'

A failure to pay holiday pay that is payable under the WTR is also a 'deduction' for the purposes of the ERA Part II, assisted by the inclusion in the definition of 'wages' in the ERA s. 27 (1) (a) of 'holiday pay'. Tribunal powers in relation to unauthorised deductions, including those made from a final instalment of wages (ERA s. 22), apply to contractual holiday pay and payments due under the WTR, as confirmed in cases like *List Design Group Ltd* v. *Douglas* [2003] IRLR 14, EAT; and *Hill* v. *Chapel* [2003] IRLR 19, EAT (and see the cases cited at Note 49 above). Exceptionally, as in the case of *Barber* v. *RJB Mining (UK) Ltd* [1999] IRLR 308 (High Court)[60] it may be necessary to seek a court order declaring the rights and obligations of the parties under a contract or collective agreement. In that case a declaration was granted that the workers concerned were not obliged to undertake further working until their average hours reduced to below their maximum weekly limit. The case also, in effect, makes it clear that WTR weekly limits on hours take effect as contract-based restrictions.

Employment Protection

The ERA[61] contains important protective legislation directed at workers who have been subjected to a 'detriment' by their employers for refusing to comply with WTR limits, or refusing to forgo WTR rights, signing workforce agreements or opt-outs, taking proceedings against the employer, etc. The unfair dismissal system in the ERA Part X has also been modified to extend rights not to be unfairly dismissed, or selected for redundancy, after refusing (or proposing to refuse) to comply with requirements in contravention of WTR restrictions; or for asserting rights, failing to sign workforce agreements, failing to enter into, vary, or extend other agreements with the employer, etc.[62]

Taking Time Off

The starting point for considering time off is that it is implicit in the nature of the employer–employee relationship that employees are normally required to be ready and available for work at all times during their agreed working hours. If the job itself requires any time away from the workplace, then a right of absence for that purpose might be implied, or operate on the basis of custom and practice. However, the basis on which such 'time away' operates requires agreed procedures to be followed properly. Otherwise specific permission to be away generally needs to be obtained for what would otherwise be treated as an unauthorised absence. Attendance at work during the hours prescribed by the contract may, perhaps, be seen as an essential element in the mutuality of obligation, and reciprocity, traditionally demanded of employees in the employment relationship. In 1845, in *Turner* v. *Mason* (1845) 14 M & W 112, a court held that whilst it might have been 'unkind and uncharitable' to prevent a domestic servant having time off to visit her seriously sick mother, being away from her duties without permission on just one occasion was sufficient to make her dismissal lawful. That decision may be compared with the case of *Stanley Cole (Wainfleet) Ltd* v. *Sheridan* [2003] ICR 297, EAT which reached a very different conclusion. Namely, that giving an employee a final written warning for leaving her workplace for an hour without permission was not only 'disproportionate' – it amounted, in the circumstances, to a fundamental breach of contract by the employer entitling her to resign and go on to win an unfair dismissal claim.[63] With some jobs, where the worker has a degree of control over their working time, including working hours while working at home, the fact that they can take time off when they wish to do so does not necessarily deprive them of 'employee' status.[64] To some extent the precise scope of attendance requirements, and the potential for any flexibility in their operation, will depend on the type of work being undertaken, as well as the understandings and expectations the employer and employee have developed as the relationship has developed.

Family-Friendly Leave Rights

Although statutory rights to time off have been superimposed on this contractual position, those rights were generally limited until the late 1990s to work-related activities like trade union functions and health and safety committee work. Outside commitments, with the exception of 'public duties' and jury service, never figured very highly until EC social legislation became concerned with reconciling work obligations with family and domestic commitments. This was one of the reasons why the Conservative government opted out of the Social Chapter of the Maastricht Treaty in December 1991.[65] However, the UK government has been committed (since May 1998) to developing 'family-friendly' policies, including longer maternity leave and better State benefits to facilitate it; parental leave; and leave for 'family emergencies', and related rights.[66]

The courts' and tribunals' approach to time off for non-work-related reasons has not, traditionally, been very favourably disposed to workers' needs. They have been reluctant to place even domestic emergencies ahead of what they see as an employer's workplace priorities.

Example
Mrs Warner worked as a shop assistant in Stourport. Her son had been taken ill, suddenly, with diabetes and when he was allowed out of hospital, on a Saturday, she expected to be able to be with him on his arrival home to supervise his insulin injections and meals. She tried unsuccessfully to get the day, or even just the morning, off. She left work and later tried to get some compensation for unfair dismissal. Her claim was rejected. There was no entitlement to time off, even in an emergency, that could be implied into all employment contracts. Mrs Warner's lawyer tried to argue that in this day and age an employer should sometimes have to cope with the effects of an employee's domestic emergency.[67]

It was suggested by the EAT in the case that a right to time off could be more readily implied in the case of larger organisations where the effects of a person's temporary absence may not be so significant as with a small employer. That was as good as it got until Parliament intervened in 1999 with a right to reasonable time off to assist dependants.

What follows is a summary of key statutory rights to time off, including entitlements in the ERA Part I (ss. 50–63C), starting with that important right.

Time off for Dependants

In order to give effect to EC Directive 96/34/EC on the framework agreement on parental leave,[68] Parliament, in the Employment Relations Act 1999, introduced a right to unpaid 'dependants' leave'. Details are in the legislation,[69] but, basically, an employee is entitled to be permitted by the employer to take 'a reasonable amount of time off during working hours' to take action which is necessary to provide assistance for a dependant. This means a spouse, child, parent, or person who lives in the same household as the employee, otherwise than as an employee, tenant, lodger or boarder (and certain others who reasonably rely on the employee for assistance, arrangements, etc.). The right arises if that person falls ill, gives birth or is injured or assaulted, or if it becomes necessary to make care arrangements, or in consequence of a death of a dependant. It also assists if there is an unexpected disruption or termination of care arrangements. Reversing *Warner*, it also extends to dealing with an incident which involves a child of the employee which 'occurs unexpectedly in a period during which an educational establishment which the child attends is responsible for him'.

The right depends on (a) telling the employer the reason for the absence as soon as reasonably practicable, and (b) except where (a) cannot be complied with until after the employee has returned to work, telling the employer for how long the absence is expected.[70] An employee can make a complaint to an Employment Tribunal that leave has been unreasonably refused.[71] If an employee is dismissed for excessive absenteeism, the tribunal must if necessary first consider to what extent any leave *is* permitted by the 'time off for dependants' provisions. This should take into account, among other things, that leave is only available if it is reasonable and necessary. Other factors may also be relevant, such as the closeness of the relationship between the employee and dependant. The EAT has made it clear, though, that an employee is not entitled to unlimited amounts of time off – especially if, after initial periods away, the need to have leave may no longer be 'unforeseen'; *Qua* v. *John Ford Morrison* [2003] ICR 482, EAT.

'Protected Workers': Sunday Working

The ERA contains measures designed to enable workers to be away from work on Sundays. They are mainly directed at shop workers and betting workers, and enable them to opt out of such working. They provide for requirements to be 'unenforceable' unless the worker has completed an 'opting-in' notice, or has expressly agreed to undertake Sunday work.[72]

Dismissal of a 'protected worker' is unfair if the reason (or principal reason) is that s/he refused to undertake Sunday work (ERA 1996, s. 101).

Union Officials

Officials of a trade union, if the union is recognised by their employer (see Chapter 18 below on recognition), are entitled to reasonable time off during working hours to carry out their duties.[73] The exact amount of time is whatever is 'reasonable in all the circumstances' having regard to the ACAS guidance in a Code of Practice on *Time Off for Trade Union Duties and Activities* (Code of Practice). The Employment Act 1989 limited the scope for time off under this head, largely because the government thought the existing provisions were being applied too generously.

Time off is now restricted to the time which an employee, who is an official, needs for duties prescribed in the TULR(C)A s. 168. These include duties which, as such an official, are related to or connected with collective bargaining, and which are listed in s. 178 (2) of the Trade Union and Labour Relations (Consolidation) Act 1992: and in relation to which the union is recognised by the employer. It also extends, for example, to consultation on redundancies and undertaking industrial relations training which is relevant to carrying out union duties.

Such officials must be paid for time off as an official on the basis of what would have been their normal pay on the day in question. If their pay varies with the amount of work they do then it is calculated by reference to average hourly earnings.[74]

If time off is refused, or is not paid for, a complaint can be taken to a tribunal (ss. 168 [4], 172).

Union Activities

Union members are entitled to a reasonable amount of unpaid time off for union activities. So, too, are union representatives, if the union is recognised by the employer.[75] The activities which this important right covers are organisational activities. As ACAS Code of Practice No. 3 states: 'To operate effectively and democratically, trade unions need the active participation of members.' It goes on to refer to things like attending workplace meetings to discuss and vote on the outcome of negotiations with the employer voting in union elections, and meetings with full-time officials to discuss issues 'relevant to the workplace'.

In practice many employers are prepared to agree detailed arrangements on time off under this head (and in relation to union officials) which can take into account local circumstances. This is recognised in the Code, and is obviously advantageous from the union's point of view.

Tribunal complaints can also be brought for refusals under this head.

Employee Representatives

Employees who are representatives of an independent trade union, or an elected employee representative, or candidate to be elected, is entitled to reasonable, paid time off, e.g. to consult on issues like a transfer of the undertaking or proposed redundancies (ERA ss. 61–63; and on protection from a 'detriment' or dismissal see the ERA ss. 47, 103).

Safety Representatives and Committees

Safety representatives, including those appointed by the union under the Health and Safety at Work Act 1974 (see Chapter 16 below), must be given paid time off to carry out their functions under the Act. I.e., functions like consultation with the employer, monitoring hazards and compliance with safety arrangements, investigating dangerous occurences and complaints by employees, and making representations to the employer, for instance. This is laid down by the Safety Representatives and Safety Committees Regulations 1977 SI 1977/500, but important guidance is also given in the HSC Codes of Practice on *Safety Representatives and Safety Committees* (1978) and *Time Off for the Training of Safety Representatives* (1978). Time off also extends to attendance at safety committee meetings, which operate in accordance with s. 2 (7) of the 1974 Act and regulations like the Health and Safety (Consultation with Employees) Regulations 1996.[76]

Safety representatives must also be given paid time off to attend safety courses. Basic training, as soon as possible following appointment, should be provided (para. 3); and further training will depend on whether or not it is reasonable for particular representatives to attend given their responsibilities.[77]

The ERA s. 44 provides protection to representatives against victimisation in respect of their work. For further details of health and safety representatives' rights in the 1974 Act, see s. 2 (7), the Employment Rights Act 1996, ss. 100, 105 (3) and Chapter 16.

Public Duties

There are a number of public duties for which an employer must give unpaid leave. The time off must be 'reasonable in all the circumstances', having regard to how much time is required in question, the time off already taken, the circumstances of the employer's business, and the effect of the absence on its running.[78] The duties include: Justice of the Peace, local authority membership, statutory tribunals, National Health Service trusts and health authorities, school managing or governing bodies, and prison and other penal institutions' boards of visitors. Complaint to a tribunal of failure to permit time off may be made within three months of the failure (ERA, s. 51 [1], [2]).

Redundancy and Job-hunting

Employees with two years' continuous service who have been made redundant are entitled during the period before notice runs out to reasonable time off during working hours to look for work and to arrange training to help future employment prospects.[79]

Jury Service; and Armed Forces Reservists

Employees summoned for jury service must be given leave to attend by their employers unless they have been excused service (Juries Act 1974). Travelling, subsistence allowances and payments for lost earnings are paid in accordance with fixed rates. Reservists called up for service have employment rights, including rights to retention, reinstatement, etc., after their service (with preservation of continuity of service). Details, including requirements as to notification to employers about returning to work, reinstatement, etc., are in the Reserve Forces (Safeguard of Employment) Act 1985. See also the Reserve Forces Act 1996 on reservists' absences, employer registrations, etc.

Pension Schemes: Employee Trustees

The employer in relation to an occupational pension scheme is required to give any employee who is a trustee of that scheme paid time off during working hours for the purpose of performing trustee duties or undergoing training relevant to those duties; ERA ss. 58–60.

Young Persons' Study or Training

An employee who is aged 16 or 17, and who is not receiving full-time secondary or further education, and who has not attained a prescribed 'standard of achievement', is entitled to reasonable amounts of time off during working hours. This is to undertake study or training leading to a qualification that would lead to attainment of the standard, and which would be likely to enhance his or her employment prospects with the employer 'or otherwise'; ERA ss. 63A–63C.

Pregnancy, Parental Leave, and Proposed Changes

Introductory Points

Maternity leave arrangements are a key factor in ensuring that women get equal opportunities with men at work and in the jobs market. It is also the right of women, and men sharing responsibilities in relation to childcare, to be able to reconcile work and home commitments fairly. This is implicit in the equal treatment clause (Clause 16) of the EC's Community Charter of the Fundamental Social Rights of Workers 1989. Specific family rights now derive from EC legislation like EC Directive 92/85 on pregnant workers and workers who have recently given birth or are breastfeeding. This was implemented by the Employment Relations Act 1999, ERA ss. 71–75, the Management of Health and Safety at Work Regulations 1999, SI 1999/3242, and changes to the social security legislation, including SMP and Maternity Allowance rights in the Social Security Contributions and Benefits Act 1992. The legislation now extends to encompass wider family-related leave entitlements including paternity leave, and leave from work for the purposes of facilitating adoption. Key measures include the EC Directive 97/75 on parental leave (as implemented by the UK's Maternity and Parental Leave, etc. Regulations

1999, SI 1999/3312, the Paternity and Adoption Leave Regulations 2002, SI 2002/2788, and UK legislation like the Employment Act 2002 introducing enhanced leave maternity pay rights, and new benefits such as Statutory Paternity Pay, Statutory Adoption Pay. There is, now, easier and improved access to Maternity Allowance for women who are not 'employees', or who have low earnings that exclude them from Statutory Maternity Pay.

UK maternity leave legislation providing a general right to maternity leave, and affording leave entitlements (supported by financial support through the Statutory Maternity Pay [SMP] system) – and coupled with protection against unfair dismissal – only came in to UK law in 1975. The Employment Protection Act 1975 had its roots in Europe and art. 118A of the EC's Rome Treaty (now art. 137). However, the scheme contained qualifying service conditions and other significant limitations on the exercise of leave rights, and made no provision for parental leave until 1999. In practice take-up is still inhibited by financial disincentives, including the restriction of paid paternity leave to two weeks on top of the unpaid 13 weeks parental leave available since 1999. As with SMP and Statutory Sick Pay, some employers clearly resent what they see as the administrative burden of paying Statutory Paternity Pay. EC Directive 92/85 has led to significant improvements in UK legislation, notably by removing service requirements as a precondition for leave and by providing for contractual entitlements to continue during the leave period. A big exception to this is pay. Although there is no reason why arrangements should not be made with an employer for normal pay to continue during the leave, EC and UK rules only provide for minimum maternity pay entitlements. The legislation sets standards which can be improved on in collective agreements and individual arrangements. Indeed, the official expectation since the reforms, put forward by the government in *Work and Parents: Competitiveness and Choice* (December 2000) is that family-friendly policies, and arrangements aimed at improving workers' 'work–life' balance, *should* be developed further at the workplace level. To that end the Maternity and Parental Leave etc. Regulations 1999, reg. 21 (considered in more detail below) facilitate take-up of any 'more favourable' rights which arise under contractual and collective arrangements.

Maternity, Paternity and Parental Leave

Family-related leave, and leave-related pay and benefits, rights now operate at a number of points in a parent and family's life. A key one, though, is when an employee is pregnant and she needs time away from work, before and after the pregnancy. Similarly, a partner may need leave, particularly in the period after childbirth. In many cases employers may already have in place supportive and 'family-friendly' arrangements to facilitate staff to take leave, for example for the purposes of ante-natal classes or attendances at clinics in the lead-up to childbirth. Others will not, indeed may be hostile, and actively discriminate against staff – especially when leave and pay rights are requested and asserted. Indeed, as the case-law unfortunately shows, detrimental and discriminatory action may begin soon after a woman informs her employer of her pregnancy, or intended leave. Partners of women may also experience negative treatment from their employer when asking for time off, for example when 'time off for dependants' rights, parental leave, or paternity leave (see below) are sought. For that reason the ERA and regulations provide rights for employees not to be subjected to a 'detriment', or any 'deliberate failure to act', in relation to leave taken for family and domestic reasons (s. 47C), or asserting rights to flexible working, for example after childbirth or other family changes (s. 47E). If she or he is dismissed for such 'family reasons' the dismissal will be regarded as unfair (s. 99). As is sometimes the case, if an employee is dismissed for asserting her or his 'working time' rights (including the rights not to work above the weekly limit, to take rest breaks, annual leave, etc.) the ERA makes such a dismissal 'unfair' (s. 101A).

Ante-natal Care

A pregnant employee, who on the advice of a registered medical practitioner midwife or health visitor or has made an appointment to attend ante-natal care sessions, is entitled to paid leave for such care.[80] This right is not dependent on previous service. It is, however, necessary to be employed under a contract of employment: so some workers who may not have 'employee' status can sometimes experience difficulties from this point. It is also necessary to be able to show the employer proof of an appointment. Generally an employer cannot insist on appointments being at out-of-work hours, and should not be able to impede take-up of this important leave right.

Changes in Hours/Work Arrangements

An employer is under a duty to undertake a 'suitable and sufficient' assessment of the risks to a woman who is an employee if her work could pose a risk to her, or to her baby, in accordance with the Management of Health and Safety at Work Regulations 1999, SI 1999/3242. A 'self-employed' worker is responsible under the regulations for arranging their own assessment. Health and safety arrangements for preventative and protective measures must then be taken (reg. 5). Regs. 16–18 extend procedures to new or expectant mothers, and these can include, in appropriate cases, alterations to her working conditions and hours of work; reg. 16 (2). If this is not reasonable, or would not avoid the risk, suspension from work is required; reg. 16 (3). Failing to carry out a risk assessment, and implementing its results, could in some circumstances be sex discrimination, as indicated in an important EAT case.[81]

Suspension on Medical and Maternity Grounds

The ERA 1996, Part VII (ss. 64–70) contains rights for employees who are suspended on medical grounds as a result of legislation and health and safety regulations, including the right to be paid while still being employed or not undertaking alternative work. Employment may contravene statutory restrictions on working in some types of employment, and this may be apparent if the employer has carried out a 'risk assessment' as required by health and safety legislation (primarily the Management of Health and Safety at Work Regulations 1999, SI 1999/3242). Part of that scheme includes important rights for women suspended from work after requirements, or recommendations in a Code of Practice under the Health and Safety at Work Act 1974, s. 16 in the case of a woman who is pregnant, has recently given birth, or is breastfeeding a child. Key parts of the legislation include a right to be offered suitable alternative work that is available *before* being suspended. Suspended employees are entitled to normal pay unless suitable alternative work has been offered and unreasonably refused (s.68). A complaint of non-payment may be made to a tribunal (s. 70).

Maternity Leave Period

All women who have 'employee' status are entitled to be absent from work during an ordinary maternity leave period, and this right is available as soon as the employment has begun; ERA s. 71. An 'ordinary leave period' is calculated in accordance with the Maternity and Parental Leave etc. Regulations 1999, SI 1999/3312, as amended ('the MPLR') (ERA s. 71). By s. 71 (4) and the MPLR reg. 9 she is generally entitled to the benefit of terms and conditions (other than pay) which she would have but for her absence, and to return from leave to a job in line with the regulations.

Ordinary Leave Period

The right to ordinary leave under s. 71 is available provided the conditions in MPLR reg. 4 are satisfied. Reference should be made to the details of reg. 4 (and see ACAS guidance),[82] but in summary the main requirements to be satisfied are that:

- no later than the 15th week before her expected week of childbirth, or, if that is not reasonably practicable, as soon as is reasonably practicable, the employee must notify her employer of:

  (i)   her pregnancy
  (ii) the expected week of childbirth
  (iii) the date on which she intends her ordinary maternity leave period to start (in writing if the employer requests this): this date may not be earlier than the beginning of the 11th week before the expected week of childbirth. The date she gives may later be varied provided she notifies the employer of the change at least 28 days before the date varied, or 28 days before the new date, whichever is earlier. If that is not reasonably practicable then notification should be as soon as is reasonably practicable.

- if requested to do so by the employer, she must produce for inspection a certificate from:

  (i)   a registered medical practitioner
  (ii) a registered midwife
  (iii) stating the expected week of childbirth.

'Early' Returns

If an employee who has started a period of maternity leave wishes to return to work earlier than the end of her ordinary leave period or additional leave period (see below), she must give her employer not less than 28 days' notice of the date on which she intends to return; MPLR reg. 11.

Duration of Leave

The ordinary maternity leave period operates in accordance with the MPLR regs. 4–7. It usually continues for 26 weeks from its commencement – or until the end of a two-week 'compulsory maternity leave' period prescribed by s. 72 (and the MPLR reg. 8): or later if the employee is subject to other restrictions; reg. 7 (1)–(3). Its commencement is determined by reg. 6. Normally, though, this means the earlier of either (a) the date the employee notified the employer of her intention to start leave, or (b) the day which follows the first day after the beginning of the fourth week before the expected week of childbirth on which she is absent from work wholly or partly because of pregnancy.

Additional Maternity Leave

If the leave-taker is eligible for ordinary maternity leave, i.e. she has fulfilled the prescribed conditions (including notifications), and at the beginning of the 14th week before the expected week of childbirth, has been continuously employed for not less than 26 weeks, she is entitled to an 'additional maternity leave' period; s. 73 and MPLR reg. 5.

The additional leave period commences on the day after the last day of her ordinary maternity leave period; MPLR reg. 6 (3). It normally continues until the end of a period of 26 weeks or, if she is dismissed before then, at the time of the dismissal; MPLR reg. 7 (5).

Employer's Notifications
An employer who has been notified of the date on which an employee's ordinary maternity leave period will commence (or has commenced) is required to notify the employee of the date on which maternity leave (whether ordinary, additional, or both) will end. Details of the dates by which the employer must do this are in reg. 7 (7).

Return to Work: Job and Conditions

A woman who has been on ordinary maternity leave – or a period of parental leave of four weeks or less which is within the scope of the MPLR reg. 18 (1) – is entitled to return to the job in which she was employed before her absence; ERA s. 71 (4) and MPLR reg. 18 (1).

If she takes additional maternity leave, or the other forms of leave referred to in reg. 18 (2), she is entitled to return to the job she was in before her absence unless that is not reasonably practicable for the employer to permit this: in which case, the right is to return to 'another job which is both suitable for her and appropriate for her to do in the circumstances'; reg. 18 (2).

More specific details of what the right to return means are set out in reg. 18A. In summary, the 'right of return' after maternity or parental leave means the right to return –

(a)   with her seniority, pension rights and similar rights –
     (i)   in a case where she is returning from additional leave, or consecutive periods of statutory leave, which included a period of additional maternity or additional adoption leave, as they would have been if the period or periods prior to that leave were continuous with the period following it;

(ii) in any other case, as they would have been if she had not been absent, and

(b) on terms and conditions not less favourable than those which would have applied if she had not been absent.

In the case of the additional maternity leave and additional adoption leave provisions, the periods of leave are subject to the rights to equal treatment, including rights under pension schemes in the Social Security Act 1989.

Redundancy

The right of return in reg. 18 does not apply if it is not practicable by reason of redundancy for a leave-taker's employer to continue employing her under her existing contract. If this is the case, though, the ERA s. 74 and reg. 10 provides a number of important rights, particularly in relation to suitable alternative employment (and non-compliance by the employer with regulations, including dismissals which are treated as unfair under the ERA Part X). If there is a suitable available vacancy, for example, she is entitled, before the end of her employment under her existing contract, to be offered alternative employment with the employer (or any successor, or associated employer) under a new contract which complies with the 'suitability' requirements in MPLR reg. 10 (3) in terms of the kind of work involved, place of work, etc. In some cases an employer may be reluctant to appoint a leave-taker to a job that is available, or could be made available – particularly, as the case-law sometimes shows, if there are doubts about the leave-taker's return to work. If a post can be filled, and it is 'suitable', then it *should* be treated as available to that employee; *Community Task Force* v. *Rimmer* [1986] IRLR 203.

Protection from 'Detriment'; Unfair Dismissal

An employee is entitled under the ERA s. 47C and the MPLR reg. 19 not to be subjected to any detriment by an employer (by any act, or deliberate failure to act) which relates to a range of family and domestic reasons – including pregnancy, childbirth or maternity; ordinary, compulsory or additional maternity leave; or parental leave, paternity leave, or taking time off for dependants. The ERA s. 99, in conjunction with the MPLR reg. 20, also makes dismissals (including selection for redundancy) relating to leave for such family reasons unfair.

A significant feature of the obligations of the employer during the additional maternity or parental leave period is that 'trust and confidence', and other prescribed duties, must be maintained. Reciprocally, the leave-taker's implied obligation of 'good faith' is specifically maintained; reg. 17.

On discrimination aspects of leave-taking, see Chapter 11; and on unfair dismissal, see Chapter 14.

Parental Leave

In the Employment Relations Act 1999 Parliament introduced a right to parental leave. This takes effect in the ERA ss. 76–80, and the MPLR Part III (ss. 13–21) and related provisions. Basically, an employee with one year's continuous service and who has, or expects to have, responsibility for a child, is entitled to be absent from work on parental leave for 13 weeks (18 weeks if the child is entitled to Disability Living Allowance); MPLR regs. 13, 14. Reg. 15 provides details of when the leave may be taken, but in summary, and subject to exceptions, an employee cannot exercise the leave right after the child's fifth birthday – or, if the child is adopted, on or after (a) the fifth anniversary of the date the placement began, or (b) the child's 18th birthday, whichever is the earlier. Parental leave can be taken by women as part of a maternity leave arrangement, notably as an extension to it. It is also possible to agree other necessary arrangements for take-up, including weekly periods – either through individual arrangements, collective agreement, or workforce agreement (as provided for in Schedule 1 to the MPLR). Failing that, default procedures in Schedule 2 operate, including requirements as to notices to the employer, postponement of leave by the employer, maximum periods during a year, etc.; reg. 16.

An employer must maintain obligations and terms and conditions under the employee's contract as if he or she had not been absent (s. 77). In the case of periods of leave of four weeks or less, which was an isolated period of leave, or the last of two or more consecutive periods of statutory leave which did not include any period of additional maternity leave (or additional adoption leave, or a period of more than four weeks), employees are entitled to return to the job in which they were employed before their absence. Otherwise, for the longer periods detailed in reg. 18 (2) the 'right of return', if it is not reasonably practicable for the employer to permit a return to the same job, the right is a right to return to another job which is both suitable and appropriate in the circumstances. Reg. 18A details the other 'incidents' that should accompany the right of return. As with additional maternity leave, the implied obligations of trust and confidence, and terms and conditions relating to notice of termination, compensation in the event of redundancy, and disciplinary and grievance procedures, must be maintained. Conversely, employees continue to be bound by the obligation of 'good faith', and other requirements, while they are away; reg. 17.

Employees do not have to be paid during parental leave, although there is nothing to prevent contractual arrangements being made which *do* provide for wages or other payments and benefits.

Tax Credits and Benefits in Leave Periods

Take-up of leave rights is facilitated by the availability of tax credits and State benefits: and an important feature of the Working Tax Credit system is that claimants are treated as continuously employed during periods of maternity and parental leave if conditions are met. In periods when earnings go down State support will go up.[83]

Employment Act 2002: Parental and Adoption Leave

The 2002 Act, ss. 1–16, extended leave rights in connection with paternity and adoption. As already noted, it improved the length of the maternity leave period, so that a woman is entitled to a 26-week ordinary maternity leave period and a two-week additional maternity leave period – assisted by Statutory Maternity Pay (or Maternity Allowance) for 26 weeks (payable for the first six weeks at a level of 90 per cent of her average weekly earnings). Details of entitlements, claims procedures, etc., are in the Paternity and Adoption Leave Regulations 2002, SI 2002/2788 ('the PALR') and other regulations; and in ACAS guidance.

It also introduced Statutory Paternity Pay and Statutory Adoption Pay. In summary, the Employment Act 2002 introduced:

Two weeks' paid paternity leave. This enables the father of a child to take leave (for up to two weeks) for care purposes. This is where he

(a) has been continuously employed for a period of not less than 26 weeks ending with the week immediately preceding the 14th week before the expected week of the child's birth;
(b) is either (i) the father of the child or (ii) married to (or is the partner of) the child's mother, but not the child's father, and
(c) has, or expects to have (i) if he is the child's father, responsibility for the upbringing of the child or (ii) if he is the mother's husband or partner but not the child's father, the main responsibility (apart from any responsibility of the mother) for the upbringing of the child; PALR reg. 4 (1), (2).

An applicant for paternity leave may be eligible sooner than the 26-week service period, or otherwise under other 'responsibility' criteria in some circumstances; PALR reg. 4 (3)–(5). Leave can be taken in one week periods or in two consecutive weeks, and must be taken within 56 days of the date of the child's birth, or placement for adoption; ERA ss. 80A–80E and PALR regs. 5–14 (with protective legislation relating to 'detriments' and unfair dismissal in regs. 28, 29).

Adoption leave consisting of 'ordinary adoption leave' of 26 weeks (subject to special provisions relating to disrupted adoption placements, redundancy and dismissal during the leave period, and 'early' returns from leave), and additional leave of up to 26 weeks; ERA ss. 75A–75D and PALR regs. 15–27 (with protective legislation relating to 'detriments' and unfair dismissal in regs. 28, 29).

In conjunction with such leave-taking, benefits (managed by the employer, as with SMP and SSP, and also under the supervision of the Inland Revenue) are now payable, namely:

- Up to two weeks' Statutory Paternity Pay (SPP)
- Up to 26 weeks' Statutory Adoption Pay (SAP)

Detailed provisions on take-up and leave rights are in the MPLR and Statutory Paternity and Statutory Adoption Pay (General) Regulations 2002, SI 2002/2822. See also Chapter 22.

Flexible Working

Employees who meet the qualifying conditions have a right under the ERA ss. 80F–80I, and the Flexible Working (Eligibility, Complaints and Remedies) Regulations 2002, SI 2002/3236 (the 'FWR') to formally apply to their employers for a change in their terms and conditions to facilitate 'flexible working'. Applications may be made using the ACAS Flexible Working Application Form.[84] An employee must have been continuously employed by the employer for not less than 26 weeks, and be the mother, father, adopter, guardian or foster parent of the child – or be married to, or be the partner of, the child's mother, father, adopter, guardian or foster parent. She or he must have, or expect to have, responsibility for upbringing the child; FWR reg. 3. The application must comply with the requirements in s. 80F, and in particular must be made before the 14th day before the day on which the child concerned reaches the age of six or, if disabled, 18.

The purpose of applying for the change is to facilitate care for a child, if qualifying conditions in the 2002 regulations are met. The changes relate to:

- working hours;
- times of work;
- where, as between home and a place of business of the employer, work is required; or
- other aspects of employment specified in the regulations.

Refusals of Requests

The employer must deal with applications in accordance with the regulations, and the Flexible Working (Procedural Requirements) Regulations 2002, SI 2002/3207 ('FW[PR]'); and can only refuse them in one or more of nine specified cases (in s. 80G). Permitted grounds of refusal include the burden of additional costs, inability to reorganise work among existing staff, detrimental impact on performance, and detrimental impact on quality. Following receipt of an application for a contract variation the employer must hold a meeting with the applicant within 28 days; and then give a notice of the decision within 14 days. Decisions are subject to appeal within the organisation and ET complaints; FW (PR) regs. 3–15.

A tribunal may order a reconsideration of an application, and order compensation; ss. 80H, 80I. Breaches of procedure regulations entitle an employee to make a complaint to a tribunal (under s. 80H), when an application has not been disposed of by agreement (or withdrawn). Complaints may also be made for failures to hold meetings with the employee, or to notify a decision (FWR reg. 6); and if an employer does not permit the applicant to be accompanied by a 'companion' at meetings; FW (PR) regs. 14, 15. Protection against detriment and dismissal in connection with the flexible working rights is given by the regulations, and by the ERA s. 104C.

As Naomi Feinstein and Adam Turner have said in a commentary, *The Right to Work Flexibly – Placebo or Panacea*,[85] when this new right was introduced there was 'a general consensus that this was a pretty toothless law', and 'window dressing'. More recent appraisals have suggested the scheme opens up important rights; and avenues for bringing sex discrimination claims, especially given the underlying sex discrimination that may be associated with refusals. Indeed it may be that this is a factor explaining why, according to a survey cited by Feinstein and Turner,[86] employers are responding to claims 'seriously'. However, as these commentators point out, the tests for an employer's valid refusal under the scheme, and under sex discrimination law, are different. The flexible working legislation, they say, allows the employer to give a

subjective explanation provided they cite one of the specified grounds whereas sex discrimination law requires the tribunal to strike an objective balance between the discriminatory effect of the refusal and the needs of the business when deciding whether an employer's refusal is justified.

CHAPTER 9

Conflicts of Interest, Competition and Confidentiality

Introduction

Staff are subject to a raft of implied duties to their employer. As well as dealing with issues like attendance at work, obedience to lawful orders, and the other mainstream employment requirements discussed in earlier chapters, they can *also* extend to such matters as care of the employer's property, confidentiality, the disclosure of 'know-how', enticing staff away to work for a new business, and bars on working for other organisations and competitors.

Aside from implicit obligations and restrictions there is nothing to stop an employer including *express* contractual terms to reinforce, clarify or add to these – tailored to meet the specific needs of the organisation. It is not uncommon for an employer, when a perceived threat is looming, to require staff to enter into new, more restrictive arrangements. In *Euro Brokers* v. *Rabey* [1995] IRLR 206, for example, as soon as the employer became aware that a competitor was recruiting staff, it entered into new, more restrictive contracts requiring longer periods of notice. In the event of an employee wanting to leave, but giving inadequate notice of termination (or no notice), the contract provided that the employer could thereupon elect to waive the breach and hold the person to the terms of the agreement for up to six months. In the particular circumstances, and given that the court accepted that such a period of 'garden leave' was necessary to protect the firm's 'customer connections', and to recruit new traders, an injunction to enforce the new terms against the employee was issued.

However, even without such express limitations implied terms can be very potent. Requirements and restrictions are, for the most part, extensions of the general, implicit duties requiring 'faithful service', 'reasonable skill and care', and the preservation of confidentiality and trade secrets. In general, and in rather more pervasive terms, the ingredient that binds together the rest of the mix is that a worker should not engage in activities that are damaging to the employer's interests. Nor should they undermine trust and confidence. That principle is easily stated. But as in the other areas in which it operates, such as constructive dismissal, the precise parameters are hard to define. This is, in part, due to the fact that trust and confidence is still a developing concept, as suggested by a judge writing on the subject.[1]

There are a number of public interest and other factors which alleviate the effects of restrictions, and which dictate that workers also have rights. For example, in the absence of an express restraint, and where there are no obvious justifications (such as protection of commercial secrets, or adverse impact on the worker's performance caused by excessive working), an employer should not seek to restrict employees unduly from working in their own time. In the case of ex-employees, restrictions by a former employer may well be unenforceable – particularly if they go beyond what the law permits as reasonable or necessary to protect legitimate interests or secrets post-termination. A mix of Common Law and statutory rights protect staff (and the public interest) from unreasonable and unjustifiable restraints, particularly if their effect is to stifle competition or prevent a person exercising knowledge, experience and skills in new employment.

Restrictions on disclosure of employers' 'secrets' have also, to some extent, been eased by other statutory interventions, for example the Public Interest Disclosure Act 1998, which in some situations can protect 'whistleblowers' who reveal information about their employers' misdeeds. Cases which define what is, or is not, 'confidential information', including *Attorney General* v. *Guardian Newspapers Ltd and Others* (No. 2) [1988] 3 All ER 545, HL (which marked the end of the *Spycatcher* saga) have also, to some extent, liberalised what is still a highly restrictive regime preventing information reaching the public domain from ex-civil servants.

In the rest of this chapter legal obligations and restrictions are considered as follows:

(1) Responsibility for Property and Money
(2) Working for Other Employers
     –   In-Service Restrictions
     –   Restrictions on Ex-Employees
(3) Information and Know-how
(4) Employees' Defences to Alleged Breaches of Confidentiality
(5) 'Whistleblowing': Public Interest Disclosure Act 1998
(6) Intellectual Property: Patents and Copyright

(1) Responsibility for Property and Money

Employees are subject to the operation of the ordinary criminal law. Among other things this means potential liability for dishonestly appropriating an employer's property, putting in dishonest expenses claims, and other activities which could be interpreted as theft, or obtaining property, or pecuniary advantage, by deception.[2] The duty of fidelity, which is implied into all employment relationships for this purpose, will also make employees liable to reimburse an employer for losses. Secret profits gained as a result of the employee's position, and which should be disclosed to the employer, may in some circumstances have to be paid over to the employer.[3] If the worker does not take sufficient care of property, for example if negligent when looking after it and this results in it being stolen, damages may be recovered to compensate for the loss. Reasonable skill and care must also be exercised by staff. In the leading case a bank manager was held to be personally responsible for not using sufficient care and skill in giving customers credit facilities without checking their creditworthiness.[4]

Property or money to which an employer is entitled must be accounted for. This would include money or funds in any other form which should be coming into the employer's business. This point is illustrated in the case of receipts from shop sales. Shopworkers are required to account for these immediately and can have pay deducted to make up for any stock shortages and till deficiencies for which they are responsible (see Chapter 7 on restrictions on employers' rights to deduct and demand payments). As well as accounting to the employer, there is also the risk of dismissal or disciplinary action, as in the case of a shopworker borrowing money from the till without authority.[5] More recent case law like *Neary* v. *Dean of Westminster* [1999] IRLR 288 shows a failure to disclose 'profits' – in that case from an organist's recording and other activities – may undermine trust and confidence. It is not, however, every case in which an employee has 'fiduciary' status, and thus becomes liable to account for profits and property (or to make restitution); *Nottingham University* v. *Fishel* [2000] IRLR 471.[6] In that case, whilst it was clear that the defendant, a researcher, was making money from his 'outside work', in order to require him to account to the employer for this evidence of his fiduciary relationship had to be shown.

(2) Working for Other Employers

Some employers try to impose tough restrictions on working for other employers, and might even try to bar it altogether. Others may not object, particularly if 'moonlighting' or other part-time work supplements the low wages they pay. Not surprisingly, though, employers with trade secrets, customer lists or other information or special interests to protect will be much more likely to try to restrict their staff working for competitors or having outside interests.

In-service Restrictions

Employees are normally free to do what they want in their spare time, that is, outside their normal working hours. During their working hours they are not entitled to undertake other work without the employer's permission; *Wessex Dairies* v. *Smith*.[7] In the case itself a milkman was also in breach of his duty of fidelity by canvassing customers ahead of his departure from the job, when he was due to set up in business on his own account. There are also examples of employers successfully preventing staff working in their spare time where the work is done for a competitor and there is scope for that work resulting in damage to the employer's business in some way, such as revealing to competitors information about secret manufacturing processes. In appropriate cases a company that is employing the staff of a competitor may be restrained from doing so by an injunction.[8] If there is no risk of this kind then an employer is not generally entitled to restrict such part-time work without an express restraint clause.

Example
Mr Froggatt was sacked from being an 'odd-job man' (as his job was described in the tribunal), after being employed for nearly five years. The employer found out that other workers had been working for a rival upholstery company; and because Mr Froggatt had also been going to the other company's premises assumed he had also been working there. The dismissal was held to be unfair. The fact that the other company was in competition with the employer did not, in itself, mean the employees could be stopped from spare-time working, or that they could be dismissed for doing so. It had to be shown that such work actually damaged the employer, and the nature of Mr Froggatt's work for the rival company did not contribute very seriously to the competition between the companies. Nor did it interfere with any of the work for the employer, such as overtime obligations.[9]

If the person is subject to an express term restricting part-time work this may be effective in preventing such work. The term's 'enforceability' will be assured if the work also happens to be for a competitor. In the case example above, the result might have been different if the employee was subject to an express clause, for example making overtime compulsory, as there would then have been a conflict between the employer's requirements and the part-time work. Express restrictions are more commonly used to limit the activities of more senior staff.

Restrictions on Ex-employees

Employers are much more restricted in their ability to prevent ex-employees working. In fact the position changes as soon as notice to leave is given, or if the employee simply leaves a job to work elsewhere. First, subject to any valid and enforceable express restraints that are capable of restricting the employee during the notice period (or which carries over into the period after the effective date of termination) the employee is entitled to make use of skills, knowledge, connections etc.[10] Second, the employer can not simply prevent the departing employee starting up a new business, or working for a competitor, just because it *is* 'competition'.[11] There are, however, cases where defendants have been stopped by a court order from working for a rival organisation before the required notice has expired, and where there is an express bar on working for competitors. The courts will not usually make such orders unless significant harm would be caused to the former employer's business resulting from misuse of confidential information.[12] There are cases where an employee's access to trade secrets, details of manufacturing processes, and confidential information during his employment provide a clear basis for *continuing* restrictions after the relationship has ended. In *Lancashire Fires Ltd* v. *SA Lyons & Co Ltd* [1997] IRLR 113, CA, a manager with unrestricted access to a company's manufacturing processes left to set up his own business using technology developed by the owner of the business (his older brother). He was assisted by another employee, who also had access to such information. The Court of Appeal concluded that the information should be classified as a 'trade secret' in accordance with principles laid down in the leading case on the subject.[13] Based on breach of confidence, and the implied duty of fidelity (given that the 'first steps' taken in setting up the new business were taken whilst still employed), injunctions were issued to restrain the new company's activities. This was not just a case of an ex-employee setting up a new business. The activities went beyond mere 'competition'.

It is increasingly common for employers to put 'garden leave' clauses in contracts, particularly for more senior staff or people in jobs where they have access to confidential data or know-how. Such clauses may prescribe long notice periods, and by requiring notice to be worked out (even when the employee might not be required to do anything) all the in-service restrictions – express and implied (including restrictions based on fidelity, secrecy, etc.) – will generally continue to operate. A court may well refuse to enforce this kind of clause, particularly once it is clear the employment relationship is at an end.

The scope of the restriction may be unreasonably wide, or its duration may be excessive. As considered in the *Euro Brokers* case (see above) a court will look to ensure that the restriction is reasonable, and necessary to protect any genuine interest of the employer's that requires protection. If an employer tries to enforce a clause that is unreasonable, for example in barring out *all* employment, the court can modify its scope. One way of doing is by identifying a specific competitor.[14] It could also reduce the *period* in which the garden leave clause can operate; *GFI Group Inc* v. *Eaglestone* [1994] IRLR 119.

Restraint Clauses

If an employer wants to restrict a person working for other organisations after his or her job has finished, there will have to be a valid 'restraint' clause in the contract. The general rule is that employees are free to work anywhere they want after finishing; and the fact that they might work for a competitor, or even set up a business competing with the ex-employer, is irrelevant. The only basis on which the law permits restraint clauses in some cases is where they are clearly necessary to prevent *unfair* competition, particularly if there has previously been access to confidential data, customer lists, personal contacts with clients, and so on, that could be unfairly exploited. In practical terms it is the ex-employer's job to try to enforce a restraint, such as by trying to obtain an injunction or damages; and the court will expect the employer to demonstrate *why* the clause is necessary.[15]

To be valid and enforceable a clause must be reasonable in terms of:

- duration;
- what it restricts;
- geographical scope;
- 'public interest' requirements;
- maintaining free competition, and people's right to use their work skills.

On this basis, a restraint that tries to bar activities that could not cause any damage to the ex-employer, or which covers geographical areas where the ex-employer clearly does not operate, is likely to be invalid. The general principle, laid down in *Herbert Morris Ltd* v. *Saxelby* [1916] 1 AC 688, is that the restriction will not be enforced if it is unreasonable in terms of duration, and is just preventing competition. There is no 'going rate' by which it is possible to say the time specified in a clause is too long; but clauses stipulating restraint for over 12 months may well be treated as excessive or unnecessary without clear justification.

(3) Information and Know-how

There may be express restrictions on an employee using information required during a job, or these may operate as a result of the implied duty of fidelity. The reasons for this are not always clear but they include a number of factors. First, there is the general principle that people should not collect, disclose or use employer's information, if the objective or result is to harm their employer's interests. Providing information about the organisation to unauthorised recipients is generally a breach of contract, making the person liable to dismissal or other action. For an outsider to induce an employee to break his contract by giving out unauthorised information is also actionable.[16] Second, the law gives certain types of 'sensitive' information special protection. Although employers do not necessarily have any formal proprietorial right over such information (such as the rights that copyright or a patent right would give them), the protection can still be very extensive. The obligation not to disclose confidential information, for example accounts highlighting directors' allegedly 'large payouts', can also mean the *recipients* of such information could be subject to court orders restricting disclosure and requiring the information to be returned. This point was established in a Court of Appeal decision *Camelot Group plc v. Centaur Communications Ltd* [1998] IRLR 80.

While employers can have trade secrets and operational data which it is not unreasonable for them to want to protect, employees also have important rights, in particular the right to make use of, and develop, the knowledge, experience and skills which have been gained in their jobs. Unfortunately, the problem of reconciling these conflicting demands has not been resolved very well. What is more, the courts are still a long way off providing a meaningful definition of what is 'confidential information'. That said, there are a number of leading cases on the subject.

Confidential Information

The key principles have been identified in *Faccenda*, a key Court of Appeal case.[17] In this case, the company employed a sales manager to assist its operations, which included breeding, slaughtering and selling poultry. The manager gained useful sales and other information which he then used when he went into business on his own account, selling chickens from refrigerated vans. There was no express term limiting what he could do *after* he left. The company claimed he had broken an implied duty of confidentiality, specifically by making use of details about customers and their requirements, the best routes to their locations, and the prices the company charged.

After considering the exact scope of the rules about competition with employers and ex-employers, and the type of information involved, the court rejected the employer's claim. The information was not so confidential that it could be covered by an implied prohibition on its use. In particular, the information concerned could not be classed as a 'trade secret'. A number of important points were made which would be relevant in other situations.

In the first place there will obviously be situations in which the information is simply not important enough to be classed as confidential. It is possible, though, for employers to make it clear, either in an express clause or through some other means, that specific types of information *are* to be treated as confidential. Misusing such information *while the job continues* is likely to amount to a breach of contract. Employers may also try to extend restrictions by including restraint clauses in the contract. However, in practice such clauses are much more difficult to justify and enforce.

The court referred to other factors which may assist in deciding whether a confidentiality requirement will operate, including:

- the kind of employment the employee is in – some jobs obviously involve the use of data which can clearly be highly confidential;
- whether the information itself could be of a kind which is a trade secret or requires the same kind of protection;
- whether the information in question can be separated from other information freely available for an employee to use.

Ex-Civil Servants

The principles governing the employment of public sector workers are no different from others. But in practice there may be additional considerations that come into play

– for example when the government seeks to stifle the public's access to information about the workings of government departments or the security services. After a lengthy period following publication of the memoirs of a security services agent, Peter Wright, and protracted restrictions and court orders banning their publication, the House of Lords eventually lifted the bans imposed during the Spycatcher case. In the judgment it gave guidance[18] on the meaning of confidentiality. In particular, it made it clear that it was for the State, as the employer in Peter Wright's case to explain *why* information in any particular case should have the characteristic of confidentiality – and to explain *why* it should not be disclosed. Implicit in this was the need to demonstrate how and why disclosure would be detrimental.

(4) Employees' Defences to Alleged Breaches of Confidentiality

A Common Law defence to disclosure by an employee of confidential information, rooted in the idea that there could on occasions be a higher 'public interest' in permitting information to be given out (particularly to the State and its agencies), is illustrated by early cases like *Weld-Blundell v. Stephens* [1920] AC 956, HL. Although later cases widened this, and encompassed criminal acts and iniquities of the employer brought to the authorities' attention, the Common Law has never developed to the point that it can be said there is a clear, general right of disclosure. Indeed, as has been noted by David Lewis in *Whistleblowing at Work: On What Principles Should Legislation be Based?*,[19] whilst cases like *Initial Services v. Putterill* [1968] 1 QB 396, CA; [1967] 3 All ER 145 confirmed the availability of a defence where the confidential information related to 'any misconduct of such a nature that it ought to be disclosed to others', apart from situations where an employee reports a breach of a statutory duty to a regulatory body they have not provided reliable guidelines about what can be disclosed and to whom. Nevertheless, when faced with a court order to restrain disclosures the defence has offered some scope, albeit limited, for not preventing disclosures to agencies like the Inland Revenue, or regulatory authorities, whilst preserving protection for other information deemed capable of protection by the employer.[20]

(5) 'Whistleblowing': Public Interest Disclosure Act 1998

Employees who reasonably believe there is information which ought to be disclosed are given a measure of protection against dismissal and detrimental action by their employer. This is the result of protective legislation put into the Employment Rights Act 1996, Part IVA, by the Public Interest Disclosure Act 1998. This followed growing unease about the scale of governmental secrecy in Britain, the extensive use of gagging clauses in public sector workers' contracts (the NHS being a good example), and in privatised industries subject to minimal supervision by regulatory bodies.

The scheme is a difficult and convoluted one, but in summary it enables a worker to disclose information to an employer, or other prescribed person. If it is done in accordance with the procedures in the Act he or she will be given the assistance of protective measures. This includes the right not to be dismissed, selected for redundancy, or subjected to a 'detriment' because of the disclosure. A dismissal in the circumstances laid down in the scheme would, indeed, be automatically 'unfair'; ERA ss. 47B, 103A. The normal one-year qualifying service requirement for bringing unfair dismissal claims does not apply, and there is no limit on the size of the compensatory award; ERA s. 124 (1A). Employees utilising the scheme may also apply for interim relief pending the complaint reaching a tribunal for determination; ERA ss. 128–132. The scheme applies to a 'worker', as defined in s. 43K: and this is wider-ranging than the definition in the ERA s. 230 (3).

Disclosures that qualify for protection under s. 43B (1) are that:

(a) a criminal offence has been committed, is being committed or is likely to be committed;
(b) a person has failed, is failing, or likely to fail, to comply with a legal obligation;
(c) a miscarriage of justice has occurred, is occurring, or is likely to occur;
(d) the health or safety of someone has been, is being, or is likely to be endangered;
(e) the environment has been, is being, or is likely to be damaged; or
(f) information tending to show any matter within the above categories has been, is being, or is likely to be deliberately concealed.

It does not matter that the 'failure' is outside the UK, or whether the applicable law is that of another country; s. 43B (2). The disclosure is not protected, though, if the person making it is committing an offence in doing this. So the government thereby preserves one of its main objectives, which is to restrict breaches of national security, infringements of official secrets, etc. S. 43B (4) also stipulates that a disclosure of information in respect of which a claim to legal professional privilege (or the Scottish equivalent) could be maintained in legal proceedings is *not* a qualifying disclosure if it is made by a person to whom the information has been disclosed in the course of obtaining legal advice.

Category (b) above has been the subject of litigation, and guidance. Among other things this has confirmed, in a case where an employee had raised a health and safety issue about inadequate on-site supervision (for which he was then summarily dismissed), that a breach of an employment contract is potentially a 'failure to comply with a legal obligation' within the scheme. On that basis the case was remitted back to a tribunal for re-determination by another tribunal. The pre-conditions, though, in line with the scheme, are that the employee must reasonably believe a breach of contract has happened (or is happening, or is likely to happen): and there must be a 'disclosure' of this; *Parkins* v. *Sodexho Ltd* [2002] IRLR 109, EAT.

A qualifying disclosure is made under s. 43C if the worker does it in good faith –

(a) to his or her employer, or
(b) where the worker reasonably believes that the relevant failure relates solely or mainly to –

   (i) the conduct of a person other than his employer, or
   (ii) any other matter for which a person other than his employer has legal responsibility,

   to that other person.

If a worker makes a qualifying disclosure to a person other than his employer, under a procedure authorised by the employer, then it is treated by the scheme as made to the employer; s. 43C (2).

Disclosures may also be made, and be 'qualifying disclosures' under the scheme, if they are made to certain *other* designated people, namely:

- Legal advisers (s. 43D)
- Ministers of the Crown, members of the Scottish Executive, etc., if this done in good faith by individuals appointed under legislation by such Ministers (s. 43E)
- Other 'prescribed persons' in any order made by the Secretary of State: in this case the disclosure must be made in good faith, and relate to a failure within the description of matters for which that person is described; and the allegation must be 'substantially true'; s. 43F and the Public Interest Disclosure (Prescribed Persons) Order 1999, SI 1999/1549. The order lists specific authorities, regulatory agencies, for designated purposes.

Disclosure in certain 'other cases' (s. 43G), and where the matter comes within an 'exceptionally serious failure' category (s. 43H), are also given 'qualifying disclosure' status. Reference must be made to the details in these provisions. Among other things the disclosure must be made in good faith, not be for the purposes of 'personal gain', and, somewhat vaguely, when 'in all the circumstances of the case' it is 'reasonable' to make the disclosure. In deciding this, regard is to be had, in particular, to factors listed in s. 43G (3). These include the identity of the person to whom disclosure is made; and the seriousness of the relevant failure. A further consideration is whether the failure is continuing or likely to recur; and whether in making the disclosure to an employer the worker complied with procedures authorised by the employer. This has been a controversial part of the scheme, particularly as it tends to give employers in the public sector the opportunity to limit publicity and minimise damaging revelations. In terms of employment rights, though, it makes it harder to gauge at what point the worker *is* actually entitled to go to a third party such as a newspaper to reveal concerns they have.

The 'other cases' head is notable in that a worker may disclose information to someone *other* than the employer or a 'prescribed person' under the s. 43F procedure. In order to do so, though, and to be accorded protection, one of the three conditions in s. 43G (2) must be met. I.e. the worker must either reasonably believe that she would be subject to detriment if she (or he) made the disclosure to the employer or a prescribed person; *or*, where there is no 'prescribed person' to whom disclosures may be made under s. 43F, she must reasonably believe that evidence relating to the failure will be concealed or destroyed if a disclosure is made to the employer; *or* there must have been a previous disclosure to the employer or a prescribed person of substantially the same information.

Contract 'Bars' on Disclosure

A contract of employment, or other agreement, which purports to preclude a worker from making a protected disclosure is void; s. 43J.

(6) Intellectual Property: Patents and Copyright

Employees' rights to exploit and otherwise benefit from their inventions and designs remain very limited although legislation has improved the position. The usual presumption has been that anything done in the employer's time belonged to the employer. Specifically, an implied term generally treated the employee as a trustee of the invention, holding it for the benefit of the employer (coupled as a general rule with a duty to disclose it to the employer). The position was particularly advantageous to an employer if it could be said the design work was done in the employer's time, or was made possible by equipment available from the employer.[21] In some cases before 1977 employers could, and often did, lay claim to the work done in employees' own time – especially where it could be argued that the tasks employees were required to do for the employer, or use of the employer's resources, facilitated that work.

The Patents Act 1977, s. 39, now makes it clear that an invention made by an employee, as between him and his employer, is *only* to be taken to belong to the employer for the purposes of the Act (but also for all other purposes) in either of these two cases:

(a)   it was made in the course of the normal duties of the employee or in the course of duties falling outside his normal duties, but specifically assigned to him, and the circumstances were such that an invention 'might reasonably be expected to result from the carrying out his duties'; or

(b)   the invention was made in the course of the duties of the employee and, at the time of making the invention, because of the nature of his duties and 'the particular responsibilities arising from the nature of his duties he had a special obligation to further the interests of the employer's undertaking'.

Any other inventions made by the employee are treated, as between him and the employer, as belonging to the employee; s. 39 (2).

That position has been largely maintained, without change, since 1977 apart from a new s. 39 (3) added by the Copyright, Designs and Patents Act 1988, which clarifies that the employee's rights, under the section, to an invention does not necessarily infringe any copyright or design right to which an employer may be entitled in any document or model relating to the invention. Case law has reinforced the legal rights of an employee under the section: and in particular the legislation has been applied in a way that overrides any clauses in the contract of employment that might detract from them. So, unless the employee is *employed* to invent or design things and actually do such work, or there are some other 'special obligations' under the contract, for example because of the seniority of the job, the invention is generally going to be found to be the employee's property. This was illustrated by the leading case of *Reiss Engineering Co. Ltd* v. *Harris* where a manager's invention was treated as his own property. He was not employed as an inventor or a designer; and he had no 'particular responsibilities', or 'special obligations' to his employer within the meaning of s. 39 (1) (b).[22] Where the employer successfully patents an invention the Act provides for compensation if it is of 'outstanding benefit to the employer' and it is 'just' that compensation should be paid. It may also be payable if any benefits received are inadequate, although the scope for obtaining compensation under the Act is excluded if compensation is payable under a relevant collective agreement (s. 40). Compensation principles and amounts are dealt with under ss. 40, 41. It may be necessary for an application to be made to the Patents Court or Comptroller-General of Patents within prescribed time limits, and in accordance with the Patent Rules 1995, SI 1995, SI 1995/2093. Generally, compensation is based on a 'fair share' of the benefits from the invention taking into account factors listed in s. 41 (4) such as the nature of employee's duties, effort and skill used, and the employer's contribution.

'Authorship' rights in an employee's work will usually depend on who owns the copyright in the work in question. This is relevant to written material, designs and software programs, among other things. In this case anything produced in the course of the employment will normally belong to the employer under the Copyright, Designs and Patents Act 1988.[23] The position depends on the particular contract of employment, and what it provides – and this may modify or dispace the employer's rights.

The 1988 Act has regulated employee rights in many other aspects of the employment relationship – but in general have not provided much more by way of additional entitlements for staff. An example is the creation of IT systems like databases. In this case, unless contractual agreements provide to the contrary a database produced in the course of an employee's employment will generally belong to her employer.

Discrimination

Equal Pay

Background

A victim of sex discrimination may have possible legal remedies under:

- European Community law
- The Equal Pay Act 1970
- The Sex Discrimination Act 1975.

In recent years the impact of Community law has substantially increased as a result of radical decisions of the European Court of Justice in such cases as *Barber* v. *Guardian Royal Exchange Assurance Group* [1990] IRLR 240 and *Foster* v. *British Gas plc* [1990] IRLR 353. As we shall see, Community law will override domestic law in the event of a conflict. Indeed on two occasions the UK government has been hauled before the European Court by the European Commission because it failed to comply with its obligations under the Treaty of Rome.

In *EC Commission* v. *United Kingdom of Great Britain and Northern Ireland* [1982] IRLR 333, the UK was held to have failed fully to implement Council Directive 75/117/EEC on equal pay. The government was forced to amend the UK's legislation on equal pay in order to comply with the ruling, and to allow equal value claims in addition to claims based on 'like work'. In *EC Commission* v. *United Kingdom* [1984] IRLR 29 the ECJ ruled that British law on sex discrimination did not comply with EC standards because among other things it did not apply non-legally binding collective agreements and that its exemptions regarding small firms and private households were too wide. Once again the government had to introduce legislation, the Sex Discrimination Act 1986, in order to accommodate both that ruling and the ECJ's decision in *Marshall* v. *Southampton and South West Hampshire Area Health Authority (Teaching)* [1986] IRLR 140, where it was held that the imposition of discriminatory retirement ages for men and women offended the Equal Treatment Directive (76/207).

The issue of qualifying periods denying part-time employees access to employment rights and therefore discriminating against females was considered in *R* v. *Secretary of State for Employment, ex parte EOC* [1994] 2 WLR 409 and *R* v. *Secretary of State for Employment, ex parte Seymour-Smith & Perez (No. 2)* [2000] IRLR 263. Whilst it was held that a two-year qualifying period for unfair dismissal complaints had a disparately adverse impact on women so as to amount to indirect discrimination contrary to Article 141, the House of Lords concluded that the Secretary of State had objectively justified the requirement by providing evidence that to reduce the requirement might inhibit the recruitment of part-time employees and had shown that it was unrelated to any discrimination based on sex.

If the complaint centres on unequal terms and conditions of employment (whether about pay or not) then there may be a remedy under the Equal Pay Act

(EqPA). However, the complainant must be able to point to a person of the opposite gender who is treated more favourably – there is no such thing as the hypothetical man or woman under this legislation.

If there is no remedy under the EqPA, then a possible claim under the Sex Discrimination Act (SDA) should be investigated. This Act covers a wide range of discriminatory practices as well discrimination in employment. Within the employment field, it covers not only those in employment but also applicants for jobs. It also makes unlawful discrimination on grounds of marital status within employment. The law relating to discrimination is discussed in the next chapter.

European Community Law

The Treaty of Rome

The general rule is that the articles of the treaty cannot be enforced directly by the individual citizen against a Member State. The citizen must wait for the government to legislate and transform its international treaty obligation into domestic law. There are, however, some exceptions to this rule and the European Court of Justice has held that article 141 of the treaty (dealing with equal pay) creates a directly enforceable right for the individual (see *Kowalska* v. *Freie und Hansestadt Hamburg* [1990] IRLR 447).

Article 141 states:

> Each Member State shall ... maintain the application of the principle that men and women should receive equal pay for equal work.
>> For the purpose of this Article, pay means the ordinary basic or minimum wage or salary and any other consideration, whether in cash or in kind, which the worker receives, directly or indirectly, in respect of his employment from his employer.
>
> Equal pay without discrimination based on sex means:
>
>> (a) that pay for the same work at piece rates shall be calculated on the basis of the same unit of measurement;
>> (b) that pay for work at time rates shall be the same for the same job.

Even though two groups of staff, one predominantly male and the other predominantly female, perform almost identical tasks, they may not be employed on the 'same work' within Article 141 where they have different qualifications which bring different skills to the job - so held the ECJ in *Angestelltenbetriebstrat der Wiener Gebietskrankenkasse* v. *Wiener Gebietskrankenkasse* [1999] IRLR 804.

The categories of 'pay' as interpreted by the courts continue to grow. In *Lewen* v. *Denda* [2000] IRLR 67, the ECJ held that a Christmas bonus constituted 'pay' as it was a benefit granted in connection with employment.

The Directives

The treaty is supplemented by directives made by the Council of Ministers. Under art. 249 of the treaty, a directive is 'binding as to the result to be achieved' but the form and method of achieving the result is left to the individual Member State.

In certain circumstances, however, a directive may be held to be directly enforceable. In *Van Duyn* v. *Home Office* [1975] 3 All ER 190, it was held that a directive could be enforceable by an individual and that this depended on whether the directive was 'clear, precise, admitted of no exceptions, and therefore of its nature needed no intervention by the national authorities'.

A good example of a directive found to have a direct effect is to be found in *Marshall* v. *Southampton and South West Hampshire Area Health Authority (Teaching)* [1986] IRLR 140. Miss Marshall had been employed by the Health Authority for 13 years before being dismissed shortly after she reached the age of 62, despite the fact that she had expressed a willingness to continue her employment as a senior dietician until she reached the age of 65. The sole reason for her dismissal was that, as a woman, she had passed 'the normal retirement age' applied by her employers to female employees. The ECJ held that the dismissal of a woman solely because she had reached the qualifying age for state pension where that age is different for men, constituted discrimination on grounds of sex contrary to the Equal Treatment Directive (76/207). The directive was held to be directly enforceable by the individual against the Member State, who in this case was also the applicant's employer (a 'vertical' direct effect). However, a directive could not have been relied on had the employer been in the private sector. This is because directives are enforceable only against the state and its organs; they have no 'horizontal' direct effect against private individuals or organisations.

While it is clear that directives can only be enforced against bodies which are 'organs or emanations of the State', there was, until recently, some doubt as to the scope of this phrase. In *Foster* v. *British Gas* [1990] IRLR 353, the House of Lords referred the matter to the European Court for a ruling. The ECJ was prepared to give a wide definition of these terms. It held that a directive that has direct effect may be relied upon in a claim against a body, whatever its legal form, which has been made responsible for providing a public service under the control of the state and has for that purpose special powers beyond those which result from the normal rules applicable in relations between private individuals. This broad approach means that local government, universities and colleges and nationalised industries all clearly now fall within the potential scope of direct effect.[1]

A change of government has seen a more pro-European Union approach resulting in Britain agreeing to a new Social Chapter arising from the Amsterdam Treaty. The treaty re-emphasises the commitment to achieve equality between men and women. Art. 141 is amended to incorporate specific reference to work of equal value.

Equal Pay: Background

When the UK joined the EEC in 1972, the Equal Pay Act 1970 was already on the statute book, although it did not come into force until 29 December 1975. The five-year delay was to give employers time voluntarily to review and alter their pay structures. The Act enabled workers to claim equal pay with a colleague of the opposite gender if their work was the same or broadly similar. However, it gave no remedy if the work was of equal value, unless the jobs had been rated as equivalent under a job evaluation scheme. In *Commission of the European Communities* v. *United Kingdom of Great Britain and Northern Ireland* [1982] IRLR 333, the Commission alleged that the UK equal pay legislation did not comply with the 'Equal Pay' Directive (75/117). The ECJ held that the UK had not adopted 'the necessary measures' and there was 'at present no means whereby a worker who considers that his post is of equal value to another may pursue his claims if the employer refuses to introduce a job classification system'. As a result of this decision the government was forced to introduce the Equal Pay (Amendment) Regulations 1983 (SI 1983 No. 1794) in order to allow equal value claims to be brought. These regulations were accompanied by new and complex procedural rules designed to govern equal value claims before an industrial tribunal.

This complexity, together with the width of the employer's defence (discussed below), raises serious doubts as to whether the government's response adequately implements the 'Equal Pay' Directive and the ECJ's decision. Indeed, the Equal Opportunities Commission has described the current equal pay laws as 'a paradise for lawyers, a hell for women' (see *Equal Pay for Men and Women – Strengthening the Acts*, 1990).

To encourage a more proactive approach by employers with respect to pay inequality, a Code of Practice on Equal Pay was drafted. The Code of Practice came into operation in March 1997. It recommended that all employees adopt an equal pay policy, carry out a pay review and take action to deal with pay inequality. There is some guidance on the stages to be followed in carrying out a review of the pay system. However, as with all codes there is no statutory obligation to adopt the code, although it will be admissible in tribunal proceedings. A Code of Practice was introduced in 2003 which includes guidance on bringing equal pay claims.

The Meaning of Pay

Under the Equal Pay Act, claims are not purely restricted to those concerned with unequal wages or salaries; a claim may be brought in respect of any term in a woman's contract of employment which is less favourable than that of her male comparator. On the other hand, under Community law, the right only applies to pay or remuneration:[2] but is not restricted to contractual entitlements and 'comprises any other consideration, whether in cash or in kind, whether immediate or future, provided that the worker receives it, albeit indirectly, in respect of his employment from his employer' (*Garland* v. *British Rail Engineering Ltd* [1982] IRLR 111 p. 115, per the ECJ).

The European Court has adopted a wide interpretation of 'pay'. In *Garland*, the ECJ took the view that concessionary travel facilities constituted 'pay' and that 'pay' included indirect benefits of this nature which continued to be provided after retirement. In *Worringham and Humphreys* v. *Lloyds Bank Ltd* [1979] IRLR 440, it was held that contributions to a pension scheme paid by the employer in the employee's name were part of the employee's 'pay' for the purposes of the treaty. In *Kowalska* v. *Freie und Hansestadt Hamburg* [1990] IRLR 447, the ECJ held that severance payments made to workers fell within the meaning of 'pay' under art. 119 (now art. 141). such payments being viewed by the court as 'a form of deferred remuneration to which the worker is entitled by virtue of his employment, but which is paid to him at the time of the termination of the relationship'. Thus when a collective agreement provided that severance payments were paid to full-time employees but not to part-timers, the applicant was able to present statistical evidence to show the provision indirectly discriminated against women and was contrary to art. 119 (now art. 141).

Discrimination in the provision of payments made by employers required by certain legislative provisions may also be caught by art. 141, as illustrated by the German case of *Rinner-Kuhn* v. *FWW Spezial-Gebaudereinigung* [1989] IRLR 493. Under German national law, whether a sick employee should continue to be paid was subject to a minimum working hours requirement. In reality fewer women would therefore avail themselves of the provision. The ECJ concluded that art. 119 (now art. 141) applies to national legislation unless the Member State can show that the legislation is justified by objective factors unrelated to any discrimination on grounds of sex.

It is therefore clear from this decision that art. 141 can be relied upon to challenge pay-related national legislation which may have the effect of excluding women from employment protection rights.

'Pay' has been found to include piece work schemes. As a result the pay of two groups of workers, one consisting predominantly of men and the other predominantly of women, is to be calculated on the basis of the same unit of measurement – *Specialarbejderforbendet i Danmark* v. *Dansk Industrie, acting for Royal Copenhagen A/S* [1995] IRLR 648. However, article 141 does not always provide such a positive result. In *Stadt Lengerich* v. *Angelica Helming* [1995] IRLR 216 it was held that payment of overtime rates only where normal working hours for full-time workers were exceeded, did not discriminate against part-time female employees as, in effect, full-time and part-time employees were being treated equally. Notwithstanding, it could be argued that this ignores the fact that part-time employees are predominantly female and, as a result, subject to indirect discrimination as the rule clearly disadvantaged them, since part-time employees would, in this case, have had to work 38 hours per week to obtain overtime pay.

The cases of *Kowalska* and *Rinner-Kuhn*, together with a third (*Bilka-Kaufhaus GmbH* v. *Weber von Hartz* [1986] IRLR 317), clearly establish that indirect discrimination in pay is unlawful. Indirect discrimination occurs when an ostensibly gender-neutral condition or requirement prejudices a substantial proportion of women compared to men. In *Bilka-Kaufhaus*, for example, the exclusion of part-time workers from an occupational pension scheme was held to fall within the ambit of art. 119 (now art. 141) and the benefits provided under such a scheme were 'pay' for the purposes of the article. If the employer seeks to justify a pay practice which in fact discriminates against women workers, the employer must 'put forward objective economic grounds relating to the management of the undertaking. It is also necessary to ascertain whether the pay practice in question is necessary and in proportion to the objectives pursued by the employer.'

The decision in *Enderby* v. *Frenchay Area Health Authority* [1993] IRLR 591 distinguishes between establishing indirect discrimination in pay cases from sex discrimination cases. A speech therapist claimed equal pay based on equal value with male principal grade pharmacists and clinical psychologists employed in the National Health Service; there being £2,500 approximate difference in pay. The ECJ held that there was a prima facie case of discrimination and that the applicant need not identify a requirement or condition or show gender disparate impact in alleging indirect discrimination. Once a prima facie case is established, the onus then moves to the employer to show that the difference in pay is objectively justified. Whilst this has been upheld by the House of Lords in *Ratcliffe* v. *North Yorkshire County Council* [1995] IRLR 439, the EAT in *Staffordshire County Council* v. *Black* [1995] IRLR 234 upheld the criteria used in the Sex Discrimination Act 1975 for establishing indirect discrimination under art. 141.

The decision in *Barber* v. *Guardian Royal Exchange Assurance Group* [1990] IRLR 240 is – for UK employers – probably one of the most important judgments ever to come from the ECJ. The court held that occupational pensions payable under a contracted-out scheme constitute 'pay' under art. 119 (now art. 141) of the Treaty of Rome, and so must be non-discriminatory in their terms. This means that pensionable ages must be the same for men and women, and benefits payable must be equal. Where a scheme allows a woman to take a pension at the age of 60, a man will have the right to insist on the same option, on the same terms.

As art. 141 is directly enforceable in the UK, employers had to respond immediately in order to avoid exposure to employment tribunal claims. The court sought to limit the impact of its decision by ruling that it did not have retrospective effect. This means that any existing employee is entitled to insist on a non-discriminatory pension age, and anyone who has already instituted a discrimination or equal pay complaint will be entitled to have it determined on the basis of *Barber*. UK discrimination legislation, which allowed discrimination in pension entitlements and benefits, is overridden as a result of the decision in *Barber*.

The court also held that redundancy benefits, whether contractual, statutory or voluntary in nature, also constitute 'pay' – so that these must also be offered to women and men on entirely equal terms.

The *Barber* decision also adopts the approach already taken by the House of Lords in *Hayward* v. *Cammell Laird Shipbuilders Ltd* [1988] IRLR 257 that where there is found to be unequal contractual terms, the employer cannot argue that regard should be had to the whole of the remuneration package in assessing whether there is unequal pay. Each of the terms of the contract should be considered separately and individually.

The Part-time Workers (Prevention of Less Favourable Treatment) Regulations 2000 (SI 2000/1551) addresses the issue of indirect discrimination in pay and conditions between full-time and part-time employees.

Who Can Claim Equal Pay?

- The Act applies not only to 'employees' but also to anyone who is employed under 'a contract *personally* to execute any work or labour' (s. 1 [6]). Therefore, unlike the rights to claim unfair dismissal, redundancy payments and the like, self-employed workers are given protection provided 'the sole or dominant purpose of the contract is the execution of work or labour by the contracting party'.[3]
- Again in contrast to many of the other employment rights, there is no qualifying period or minimum period of hours although claims must be brought within six months of leaving employment.
- Employees are generally excluded if they are not in employment at an establishment within Great Britain.
- The right to serve an equal pay questionnaire on the employer has recently been introduced (s. 7B EPA 1970). This is intended to provide an employee with information, which will enable them to decide whether to proceed with an equal pay claim. However, the completion of the questionnaire by the employer is not compulsory and employers have a defence of 'confidentiality'. Although a failure to comply allows an ET to draw an inference which it believes to be 'just and equitable'.

Exclusions

There are three contractual terms which remain unaffected by the 'equality clause':

(a) Terms affected by compliance with the law relating to women's employment. The importance of this exception has been much diminished by the removal by the SDA 1986 of those parts of the Factories Act 1961 which regulated the hours of work of women. This process of deregulation was taken further by the Employment Act 1989 which removed a whole range of restrictions on the types of job which a woman could do. Indeed, the same statute lays down the general principle that any legislation passed prior to SDA 1975 shall be of no effect in so far as it imposes a requirement to do an act which would amount to direct or indirect sex discrimination.

(b) Terms giving special treatment to women in connection with pregnancy or childbirth. This allows employers to provide maternity leave without risking an equal treatment challenge from their male workforce.

(c) Terms related to death or retirement, or to any provision in connection with death or retirement. The significance of this exception has been much reduced as a result of the influence of EC law. First, the SDA 1986 now makes it unlawful to provide for differential retirement ages as opposed to pension ages. Second, the decision in *Barber* renders unlawful any differential treatment paid under an occupational pension scheme. Finally, under the Social Security Pensions Act 1975 it is unlawful to deny either gender equal access to an occupational benefits scheme.

The Right to Equal Pay

The Comparator

The legislation protects men and women equally. However, it is essential for the applicant to have a comparator of the opposite sex. Before embarking on an equal pay claim, it is crucial that the female applicant can identify a man with whom to compare herself. If there is no man whose contract can be compared to that of the woman, then she will have no chance in her equal pay claim. This is because, in contrast to a claim under the Sex Discrimination Act, the applicant is not allowed to compare herself with a hypothetical male.[4]

The woman may select the comparator of her choice; it is not the job of the employment tribunal to reject her choice and select a comparator who appears to the tribunal to be more appropriate.[5] Where an applicant cannot name her comparators, she is not barred from bringing a claim as long as she can show a prima facie case. The employment tribunal can order discovery of the relevant names.

Under the Equal Pay Act, it was necessary to show that there was a time when her comparator and she were employed contemporaneously on like work, work rated as equivalent or work of equal value. Once again our domestic law has proved to be narrower in scope than Community law. As a result, even if a woman cannot show that her comparator was in contemporaneous employment, she may bring a claim under art. 141 as opposed to the Equal Pay Act. This was established in the important case of *Macarthys Ltd* v. *Smith* [1980] IRLR 210.

Mrs Smith became trainee manageress of the stockroom on 21 January 1986, and manageress on 1 March. She claimed equal pay with her predecessor as stockroom manager, a Mr McCullough, who had left on 20 October 1975. The majority of the Court of Appeal held that she could not succeed in her claim under the Equal Pay Act because its wording clearly required contemporaneous employment. However, the court was less certain as to whether she could bring her claim using art. 119 (now art. 141) and they referred that issue to the ECJ. The ECJ held that under the Treaty of Rome Mrs Smith could compare herself with a predecessor. The decision in *Diocese of Hallam Trustee* v. *Connaughton* [1996] IRLR 505 now permits comparison with a successor.

Section 1 (6) EPA 1970 requires the applicant to show that s/he is either employed by the same employer as the comparator or an associated employer at the same establishment or at an establishment where common terms and conditions are being observed. Generally, this will not be problematic if the applicant is employed at the same establishment as the comparator. However, if she is employed by the same or an associated employer but at a different establishment, then she has no claim unless common terms and conditions of employment are observed at both establishments either generally or for the relevant class of employee.

In *Leverton* v. *Clwyd County Council* [1989] IRLR 28, the phrase 'same employment' was given an expansive definition by the House of Lords, offering to applicants the prospect of an enlarged pool from which to choose comparators. In this case the applicant and her comparators were employed under the same collective agreement at different establishments – she being a nursery nurse and they being clerical staff. Although there was a difference in the hours worked and the holidays received, the House of Lords concluded that the correct construction of s. 1 (6) called for a comparison between the terms and conditions of employment observed at the establishment at which the woman was employed and the establishment at which the men were employed, and applicable either generally, as in this case, or to a particular class or classes of employees to which both the woman and men belonged; she was therefore in the 'same employment' for the purpose of s. 1 (6). In effect the issue is whether the applicant would have been employed under the same contract had she been doing the same job at her comparator's establishment.

However, the court of session upheld the decision of the ET in *South Ayrshire Council* v. *Milligan* [2003] IRLR 153 in deciding that a male primary school teacher could claim equal pay with male secondary school head teachers by naming as comparator a female colleague on the same or less pay than himself, who, in her own equal pay claim had cited as comparator the male secondary head teacher. This recognises that such contingency claims are valid and will be allowed to proceed.

The decision in *British Coal Corporation* v. *Smith* [1996] IRLR 404 has introduced a degree of flexibility by holding that common terms are 'substantially comparable on a broad basis rather than being the same'. This test would be satisfied therefore if the comparator were to be employed on similar terms and conditions if his post were at the same establishment as the applicant.

In *South Ayrshire Council* v. *Morton* [2002] IRLR 257 the Court of Session held that a teacher employed by a local education authority in Scotland was entitled to bring an equal pay claim comparing herself with a teacher employed by a different education authority in Scotland within article 141. However, the decision of the ECJ in *Lawrence* v. *Regent Office Care Ltd* [2002] IRLR 822, whilst not precluding such comparisons limits them to situations where the differences identified can be attributed to a single source for which there is an identifiable body/person responsible.

The issue of broadening the scope of the comparator continues to engage the Tribunals. The CA in *Allonby* v. *Accrington & Rossendale College* [2001] IRLR 364 referred the issue of whether a person employed by an agency could compare themselves with an employee of the opposite sex at an establishment in which they were placed by the agency to the ECJ. The Advocate General's opinion has now been received and the ECJ has been asked to rule on whether art. 141 can be relied on where the pay differences cannot be attributed to a single source as no entity can be held responsible for the difference or its elimination (2-4-03 case 256/01). For the ECJ's response, see [2004] IRLR 224.

An even more flexible approach has been suggested by the EAT in *Scullard* v. *Knowles* [1996] IRLR 344. This case suggests that s. 1 (6) can be displaced by art. 119 (now art 141) and therefore extends the range of employment to the same 'establishment or service', thereby increasing the scope for public sector employees to make equal pay claims.

Grounds on Which Equality can be Claimed

There are three different types of comparator on which to base the claim:

(a)   the man employed on like work with the applicant;
(b)   the man employed on work rated equivalent to that of the applicant; and
(c)   the man employed on work which is of equal value to that of the applicant.

Like Work

This is defined as work which is the same or of a broadly similar nature where the differences (if any) between the applicant does and what her comparator does are not of practical importance in relation to terms and conditions of employment (s. 1 [4]).

In *Capper Pass Ltd* v. *Lawton* [1977] ICR 83, the EAT stated that a two-stage inquiry should be adopted in determining whether people were engaged in like work. First, is the work the same, or, if not, is it of a broadly similar nature? To this latter question a broad approach should be adopted, without a minute examination of the differences between the jobs. Second, if the work is broadly similar, are the differences of practical importance?

Mrs Lawton was a cook providing lunches for up to 20 directors in a company director's dining room. She was held to be entitled to pay equal to that earned by two male assistant chefs who provided 350 meals per day in the company canteen.

In *Electrolux Ltd* v. *Hutchinson* [1986] IRLR 410, the EAT stated that in order to amount to a difference of practical importance it must be shown that, as well as being contractually obliged to undertake the additional different duties, the duties are actually performed to a significant extent.

In this case, men and women worked on the same track in the manufacture of refrigerators and freezers, but while all the men were paid on Grade 10, 599 out of the 600 women received rather lower wages on Grade 01. The company argued that the men had additional contractual obligations: they had to transfer to totally different tasks on demand and work overtime as and when required. The EAT focused on how frequently the men did the work; how often they were required to work on a Sunday; and what kind of work they did in those unsocial hours. The EAT came to the conclusion that in reality the work was like work.

The Time the Work is Done

The orthodox view is that tribunals should ignore the time when the work is done in comparing the two jobs. In *Dugdale* v. *Kraft Foods Ltd* [1977] ICR 48, the applicant sought equality with a male night-shift worker and it was held that they were employed on like work. The EAT held that 'in the context of the Equal Pay Act ... the mere time at which the work is performed should be disregarded when considering the differences between the things which the woman does and the things which the man does' (Judge Phillips, p. 53). It is the nature of the work which must be considered. The tribunal went on to say that it remains permissible to pay an unsocial hours bonus or night-shift premium to the men as long as the basic pay remains the same. This was confirmed in *Calder & Cizakowsky* v. *Rowntree Mackintosh Confectionery Ltd* [1993] IRLR 212.

The *Dugdale* decision was distinguished in *Thomas* v. *NCB* [1987] ICR 757, where the EAT held that female canteen assistants employed during the day were not engaged in like work with a male employed alone and at night. The effect of this decision is to make the time when the work is done relevant to the consideration of like work if it results in additional responsibility; for example, as in this case, working alone.

Additional Responsibility

A factor such as responsibility may be decisive where it can be seen to put one employee into a different grade from another with whom comparisons are being made. In *Eaton Ltd* v. *Nuttall* [1977] IRLR 71, a male production scheduler handling 1,200 items worth between £5 and £1,000 in cash and a woman scheduler handling 2,400 items worth below £2.50 each were held not to be engaged on broadly similar work – an error on the part of the man would be of much greater consequence.

Conversely (or perhaps perversely), it has been indicated that if a woman's work is more onerous or responsible than a man's, she may not be considered to be engaged in like work, even if she is less well paid (see *Waddington* v. *Leicester Council for Voluntary Services* [1977] ICR 266). An applicant in this situation is now able to bring an equal value claim since the decision of the ECJ in *Murphy* v. *Bord Telecom Eireann* [1988] IRLR 267.

Work Rated as Equivalent

A woman may claim equal pay with a man even though she is not doing like work, if her job has been 'rated as equivalent' to that of the man. The work will be rated as equivalent if the jobs of the comparator and applicant

> have been given an equal value, in terms of the demand made on the worker under various headings (for instance, effort, skill and decision) on a study undertaken with a view to evaluating in those terms the jobs to be done by all or any of the employees in an undertaking or group of undertakings, or would have been given an equal value but for the evaluation being made on a system

of setting different values for men and women on the same demand under any heading (s. 1 [5]).

In *Bromley* v. *H & J Quick Ltd* [1988] IRLR 249, the Court of Appeal held that in order to fall within s. 1 (5), a job evaluation study must be 'analytical' in the sense that it must analyse the jobs covered by it in terms of the demands made on the worker under various headings (such as points assessment or factor comparison). Therefore, job evaluation studies based on 'felt fair' comparisons of 'whole jobs' (such as job ranking, paired comparisons or job classification) will not suffice and will not prevent the applicant bringing an 'equal value' claim under s. 1 (2) (c).

If no job evaluation has been carried out, under this part of the Act, there is no legal requirement for the employer to conduct one. It was, of course, this flaw in the legislation which lead to the introduction of the Equal Pay (Amendment) Regulations 1983. They purport to implement the Equal Pay Directive 75/117 by enabling an employee to insist that a job evaluation study should be carried out.

Work of Equal Value

An equal value claim is allowed if the applicant is engaged in work which, not being work in relation to which the provisions on like work or work rated as equivalent apply, 'is, in terms of the demands made on her (for instance under such headings as effort, skill and decision), of equal value to that of' her comparator – s. 1 (2) (c).

In *Pickstone* v. *Freemans plc* [1988] IRLR 357, the House of Lords refused to accept that the presence of a man doing like work to Mrs Pickstone prevented her from making a claim for equal pay for work of equal value using another man as a comparator. Lord Keith considered that to accept this construction of s. 1 (2) (c):

would leave a gap in the equal work provision, enabling an employer to evade it by employing one token man on the same work as a group of potential women claimants who were deliberately paid less than a group of men employed on work of equal value with that of the women. This would mean that the UK had failed yet again to fully implement its obligations under art 119 of the Treaty and the Equal Pay Directive and had not given full effect to the decision of the European court in *Commission of the European Communities* v. *UK*. It is plain that Parliament cannot possibly have intended such a failure.

The Procedure in Equal Value Claims

The complex procedural rules governing equal value claims were contained in the Industrial Tribunals (Constitution and Rules of Procedure Regulations 1993 (SI 1993/2687) Schedule 2; the Sex Discrimination and Equal Pay (Miscellaneous Amendments) Regulations 1996 (SI 1996 No. 438) and SI 1996, No. 1757). They are now in the Employment Tribunals (Constitution and Rules of Procedure) Regulations 2001, SI 2001/1171.

The procedure for lodging a complaint with the employment tribunal under the equal value provisions is largely the same as for other proceedings, but with modifications, reg. 11 (3), Sched. 3; that is, proceedings may be instituted by the applicant while she is still employed by the respondent employer or within six months of the termination of her employment (s. 2 [4]). A copy of the originating application is sent to ACAS, which may endeavour to promote a settlement.

Furthermore, the employment tribunal may hold a pre-hearing review and, if the contentions of one of the parties appears to have no reasonable prospect of success, it may give a warning as to costs if the case is taken further (rule 7). Modified rr. 4–23 apply.

At the full hearing, the tribunal may invite the parties to apply for an adjournment for the purpose of seeking a settlement. Assuming that no settlement has been reached and before proceeding further, the tribunal must consider whether it is satisfied that there are no reasonable grounds for determining that the work is of equal value – s. 2A (1) (a) (b). The idea behind this provision is that only hopeless cases would be weeded out and that if there is an arguable case of any kind, the claim should proceed with any doubt resolved in favour of the applicant.

The Equal Pay (Amendment) Regulations 2003, SI 2003/1656 amended s. 2A (1) by removing the 'no reasonable grounds' proviso which will allow all applicants in equal value cases to put evidence before the ET re a prima facie case. Where there has been a job evaluation, the ET can allow a case to proceed if it believes the job evaluation is tainted by discrimination. The ET may request an independent expert to prepare evidence on whether a job evaluation scheme is based on a discriminatory system; SI 2001/1171, Sched. 1, reg. 10A (1).

Where the two jobs have already been evaluated under a job evaluation scheme as unequal, the tribunal must dismiss the application if 'there are no reasonable grounds for determining that the evaluation contained in the study was made on a system which discriminates on grounds of sex' (s. 2A [2]), that is, whether 'a difference or coincidence between values set by that system on different demands under the same heading or different headings is not justifiable irrespective of the sex of the person on whom those demands are made' (s. 2A [3]).

Where the applicant has overcome the obstacles presented by the filtering process described above, the employer may ask the tribunal to consider the defence that the difference in pay is genuinely due to a material factor which is not a difference in gender.

If the 'genuine material factor' defence is raised by the employer at this stage and rejected, it may not be raised again after an independent expert's report has been received on the equal value claim. This follows the decision of the employment tribunal in *Hayward* v. *Cammell Laird Shipbuilders Ltd* [1984] IRLR 463, which determined that employers who wish to put forward the genuine material factor defence should raise it at this preliminary stage. The employers in that case did not pursue the defence at the initial hearing and, as a result, were unable to raise it at the hearing following reception of the independent expert's report. We give a detailed examination of the material factor defence below.

With the exception of the cases where the tribunal decides that the claim is hopeless or that the genuine material factor defence is established, under the procedure the tribunal may require an expert is drawn from a panel nominated by ACAS, to prepare a report. The 'expert's report' procedure is regulated by r. 10A. The expert, if appointed, is obliged to take into account all information supplied to him/her and sends to the parties a written summary of the information and representations. In addition, the expert is under a duty to take no account of the difference of sex and at all times to act fairly.

Failure to comply with any of these requirements may lead to a tribunal finding that the expert's report is inadmissible. In addition, the report may not be admitted if the conclusion contained in the report is one which, taking due account of the information supplied and representations made to the expert, could not reasonably have been reached; or if for some other material reason (other than disagreement with the conclusion that the applicant's work is not of equal value or with the reasoning leading to that conclusion) the report is unsatisfactory.

The employment tribunal sets a date by which the independent expert must send his/her report to the tribunal. The independent expert should also provide progress reports. This is to overcome some of the criticism directed at the length of equal value proceedings. The independent expert must give notice in writing to the employment tribunal if s/he is likely to fail to meet the designated date.

The procedure provides a number of avenues for the obtaining of information which may lead a tribunal to decide not to admit a report. The tribunal itself may, at any time after it has received the report, require the expert to explain in a reasoned written reply any matter contained in his/her report or to give further consideration to the question. A copy of the expert's reply must be sent to each of the parties and they must be allowed to make representations.

In addition, each party, having been sent a copy of the expert's report, may make representations and call witnesses on the question of admissibility. The expert is compellable as a witness and may be subject to cross-examination. Furthermore, any party, after giving reasonable notice to the tribunal and any other party, may call one expert witness who may also be cross-examined.

If the report is admitted, it is ultimately for the tribunal to decide whether or not the jobs are of equal value. At this stage, the tribunal may still hear evidence from experts or other witnesses, but the rules introduce an important limitation. No party may give evidence or question any witness on any matter of fact on which a conclusion in the expert's report is based. The only exceptions to these restrictions are where the matter of fact is relevant to, and raised in connection with, a genuine material factor defence; or where a party's refusal to comply with a tribunal order for information or documents has prevented the expert from reaching a conclusion on the equal value issue.

Even where the conclusion of the expert is not shown to be unreasonable and is admitted into evidence, this does not mean that the employment tribunal is obliged to accept its conclusions.

In *Tennents Textile Colours Ltd* v. *Todd* [1989] IRLR 3, the following guidance was provided by the Northern Ireland Court of Appeal:

- The burden of proof remains at all times with the applicant, and is not transferred even if the expert's report favours the applicant. (This can pose a major difficulty for the applicant if the tribunal cannot decide whether to follow the independent expert's report or that produced by the employer's expert. An applicant may be forced to commission her own expert report with all the attendant cost and complexity.)
- Conversely, the applicant is under no greater burden of proof if the report of the independent expert is not favourable to her case.
- The tribunal may reach a conclusion opposed to that of the independent expert without concluding that the report is obviously wrong; the normal burden of proof on the balance of probabilities is applicable.
- The findings of fact made by the expert are not binding. It can be argued that they are wrong, unreliable or that some are more important than others. The power of challenge exists despite the limited grounds for challenging the report before it has been admitted into evidence.

How Equal is Equal Value?
There are conflicting views on this question. In *Wells* v. *F. Smales & Son (Fish merchants)* (IT unreported; see 2 EOR 24 [1985]), the expert's report had concluded that 9 out of 14 claimant fish packers were engaged in equal or higher value work than a male labourer. The remaining 5 claimants' jobs had received scores ranging from 79 per cent to 95 per cent of the score accorded the job of the comparator. While accepting all the expert's findings of fact, the employment tribunal adopted a broad-brush approach and concluded that all of the claimants were engaged in work of equal value in that 'the differences between them and the comparator are not relevant nor make real material differences'.

This approach should be contrasted with the much narrower view adopted by the employment tribunal in *Brown* v. *Cearns & Brown Ltd* [1985] IRLIB 304, where the expert's report concluded that the applicant's work was worth 95 per cent of her comparator's. The ET declined to hold that the work was of equal value as 'it was not of precisely equal value'.

Currently the broad-brush approach is the acceptable approach for determining equal value. It was upheld by the ET in *Pickstone* v. *Freemans plc* (1993) 28811/84 following reference from the House of Lords that the female warehouse operatives were employed on work of equal value with male checker warehouse operatives, even though the women only scored 19 on the evaluation compared to the male comparitor score of 22. The ET recognised that it was difficult for a system of evaluation to attain 100 per cent precision. Interestingly, the ET chose to disagree with the independent expert's report which found against the women.

As we have seen, it is now clear that 'equal' includes 'higher'. Therefore, a woman employed on work of higher value than her male comparator may make an equal value claim (*Murphy* v. *Bord Telecom Eireann* [1988] IRLR 267).

The Genuine Material Factor Defence

It is a defence in equal pay cases if the employer can show that the variation between the woman's contract and the man's contract is genuinely due to a material factor which is not a difference in gender (s. 1 [3]). In the case of like work or work rated as equivalent claims, that factor must be 'a material difference between the woman's case and the man's', whereas in the case of equal value claims the factor 'may be such a difference'.

Following the decision of the House of Lords in *Rainey* v. *Greater Glasgow Health Board* [1987] IRLR 26, it would now appear that, despite this difference in wording, the ambit of the defence is probably the same in all three types of equal pay claims. In this case the major issue relating to the scope of the defence was whether the material factor justifying the difference in pay could encompass 'market forces': 'Given that men have traditionally been able to demand higher rewards in the labour market, the acceptance of market force arguments has serious implications for the degree of protection offered by the equal pay legislation.'[6]

In *Clay Cross (Quarry Services) Ltd* v. *Fletcher* [1979] ICR 1, the Court of Appeal held that the phrase 'difference between the woman's case and the man's' meant that only factors relating to the 'personal equation' of the employees could constitute a defence to a like work claim. As a result, it was not acceptable to defend a variation in pay on the grounds that the male clerk had been the only suitable candidate for the job and could only be persuaded to take it with the offer of more money than that paid to the existing female clerk. As Lord Denning put it: 'If any such excuse were permitted, the Act would become a dead letter. Those are the very reasons why there was unequal pay before the statute. They are the very circumstances in which the statute was intended to operate' (at p. 4).

Subsequently, as we have seen, pressure from the EC forced the government to introduce the equal value claim. Given its free market philosophy, the government was concerned that the *Fletcher* approach would prevent employers paying the market rate for labour. Therefore, in reluctantly introducing the equal value claim, it took the opportunity to change the wording of the material factor defence. The substitution of 'must' by 'may' was designed to allow the 'market forces' argument as a defence in equal value claims.

The government need not have worried because in *Rainey* v. *Greater Glasgow Health Board*, the court took the *Fletcher* interpretation of the scope of the defence in like work and work rated equivalent claims was unduly restrictive.

Mrs Rainey, a prosthetist employed by the NHS in Scotland, claimed equal pay with a male prosthetist, Mr Crumlin, who earned over £2,000 a year more. Mrs Rainey and Mr Crumlin had broadly the same qualifications and experience, but Mr Crumlin had been recruited from private practice, where salaries were much higher, in order to establish a prosthetic service within the NHS. Mrs Rainey, who had been recruited directly from the NHS, had her salary determined according to the appropriate Whitley Council scale; Mr Crumlin's salary was based upon agreements between his union and private contractors. All those paid at the higher rate were men and, with one exception, all those on the lower rate were women. It was conceded that they were engaged on 'like work' within s. 1 (4) of EqPA.

The Employment tribunal found that there was a genuine material difference other than gender within s. 1 (3), because each was paid according to a different pay scale because of their different mode of entry into the NHS. Mrs Rainey's appeals to the EAT and Court of Session, Inner House, were dismissed. Mrs Rainey also unsuccessfully appealed to the House of Lords. The House of Lords held that a genuine material difference should not be limited purely to personal factors between the man and the woman, but could include extrinsic ones such as economic factors, provided that they could be justified on objective grounds. In Mrs Rainey's case it had been shown that it was essential to pay a higher salary to prosthetists recruited from private practice in order to obtain the personnel necessary to establish the new prosthetic service in the NHS and this constituted a genuine material difference other than a difference of gender.

The decision of the House of Lords in *Strathclyde Regional Council and Others* v. *Wallace* [1998] IRLR 110 upholds the principle that where a difference in pay is explained by genuine factors not tainted by discrimination, this is sufficient to raise a valid defence and there is no further burden on the employer to justify anything under s. 1 (3); see *Parliamentary Commissioner for Administration* v. *Fernandez* [2004] IRLR 22.

In *Glasgow City Council* v. *Marshall* [2000] IRLR 272 the HL decided that where an employer has established an absence of sex discrimination, he is under no obligation to objectively justify the disparity in pay. Although in the case of *Brunhoffer* v. *Bank der Osterreichischen Postsparkasse* [2001] IRLR 571 the ECJ suggested that employers were required to objectively justify such factors even though there was no sex discrimination.

The case of *Brunhoffer* (above) in pre-empting the Burden of Proof Directive (Dir 97/80) places the onus on the applicant to establish a *prima facie* case and then shifts the burden of proof to the employer to show that the difference in pay is objectively justified and not tainted by discrimination.

Some Examples of Genuine Material Factors

Location

Employees who work in London may be paid more in order to compensate them for the higher cost of living in the capital or may be expected to work fewer hours.

In *Navy, Army and Air Force Institutes* v. *Varley* [1976] IRLR 408, Mrs Varley, a female clerk employed in Nottingham, claimed to be entitled to the same shorter working hours as male clerks employed in London. Both male and female clerks in Nottingham worked for the same number of hours (37). NAAFI workers in London (of either gender) worked a 36-hour week. It was held that the different places of employment constituted a material difference.

'Red-circling'

In cases of reorganisation or regrading employers will often transfer workers from a higher-grade job to one of lower status but preserve their wages at the previous higher rate. This is known as 'red-circling', and as a result workers will often find themselves in the same grade and doing the same job alongside workers who are paid more. Depending on the circumstances, red-circling may amount to a material difference between the cases of particular men and women.

In *Snoxell* v. *Vauxhall Motors Ltd* [1977] IRLR 123 EAT, Mrs Davies and Miss Snoxell were quality inspectors at Vauxhalls. Though doing the same work as men, they were on a lower grade and paid less. In 1970 the job of quality inspector was downgraded. All the existing female quality inspectors and all new entrants to the job were put into the lower grade. But the men who had been on the higher grade were red-circled and retained their higher wages. In 1976 the women claimed parity. The EAT held that the employers could not shelter behind the red-circle defence. It could not be a genuine material difference if it owed its existence to past sex discrimination – which was the situation in this case.

Where employers seek to establish the red-circle defence, they must do so with respect to every employee who, it is claimed, is within the circle. If an employer subsequently lets an outsider into the red circle, the defence will probably fail because the woman will find it easier to demonstrate that the original reason for the red circle is not the real reason why she is being treated less favourably (*United Biscuits* v. *Young* [1978] IRLR 15 EAT).

In assessing the validity of the defence, it is relevant for an employment tribunal to take into account the length of time which has elapsed since the red circle was introduced, and whether the employer has acted in accordance with good industrial relations practice in the continuation of the practice (*Outlook Supplies Ltd* v. *Parry* [1978] IRLR 12 EAT).

Part-time Work

A crucial issue in the equality debate has been whether it is legitimate to discriminate against part-time workers in terms of pay and conditions. This is a key issue because over 90 per cent of all part-time workers are women, so differential treatment of part-time workers is indirect discrimination against women. Can part-time work constitute a genuine material difference?

In *Handley* v. *H Mono Ltd* [1979] ICR 147, a female machinist, working a basic 26-hour week at £1.61 per hour, claimed an equal hourly rate to a man employed on like work who worked a 40-hour week at £1.67 per hour. It was held that there was a material difference between her case and his because part-time workers contributed less to productivity. His machine was fully utilised for 40 hours per week, whereas hers was used for 26 hours only and remained idle when she was not at work.

This decision can be read as accepting the difference in part-time and full-time work as itself legitimating unequal treatment. However, in *Jenkins* v. *Kingsgate (Clothing Productions) Ltd No. 2* [1981] IRLR 388 EAT, it was held that it was not sufficient for the purposes of s. 1 (3) for the employer to show that he had no intention of discriminating on grounds of sex or that he intended to achieve a legitimate objective. Section 1 (3) should be understood as imposing on the employer the burden of proving that a variation in pay between a man and a woman employed on equal work is objectively reasonably necessary in order to achieve some objective other than an objective related to the gender of the worker.

This view has now been sustained by the decision of the ECJ in *Bilka-Kaufhaus GmbH* v. *Weber von Hartz: 170/84* [1986] IRLR 317. In this case it was held that, under art. 119 (now art. 141), a policy which has the effect of creating a pay differential between men and women undertaking like work – in this case, giving occupational pension rights to full-time workers only – may only be justified if 'the means chosen for achieving that objective correspond to a real need on the part of the undertaking, are appropriate with a view to achieving the objective in question and are necessary to that end'.

Differential Grades

It would appear that a pay difference resulting from a different grade or pay scale will be justified provided that the payment schemes do not discriminate on grounds of gender.

The early case law suggested that a pay difference resulting from a different grade or pay scale would be justified provided that the payment scheme did not discriminate on grounds of gender. However, this ignored the concept of indirect discrimination in relation to pay where jobs predominantly carried out by females were paid less than jobs predominantly carried out by men, yet could be determined as being of equal value. Fortunately, as we shall see, there have now been inroads into the use of differential grades as a means of avoiding equality in pay. First, we shall consider the early case law.

In *Waddington* v. *Leicester Council for Voluntary Services* [1977] IRLR 32, Mrs Waddington was recruited as a community worker and paid under the national scale for social workers. She was put in charge of an adventure playground project and a playleader, a man, was appointed to assist her. His salary was paid according to the scale for youth leaders and community centre wardens. Both salary scales were nationally negotiated. The male playleader, despite being responsible to Mrs Waddington, received a higher salary. The EAT sent the case back to the employment tribunal in order reconsider whether they were employed on like work (see above). However, they also commented they had first thought that, in any event, Mrs

Waddington's claim must fail under s. 1 (3) because of the operation of nationally negotiated pay scales, but again they left this for the employment tribunal to decide on the ground that evidence might be forthcoming which showed an element of discrimination in the practical operation and application of the scale.

In *Reed Packaging Ltd v. Boozer* [1988] IRLR 333, the complainants were employed as dispatch clerks and paid in accordance with the staff pay structure negotiated with ACTSS. They brought a claim comparing their work with that of a male dispatch clerk paid £17 a week more on the basis of a pay structure for hourly paid workers negotiated with GMBATU. The EAT held that the employers had made out a defence under s. 1 (3). There had been no suggestion that either of the two pay structures was sexually discriminatory and there was no reason why the fact of separate pay structures could constitute a material factor defence. As a result, pay as determined in accordance with separate pay structures was 'an objectively justified administrative reason' for the unequal pay.

This has been the subject of the following powerful criticisms:

> Such an approach is plainly superficial: the fact that each pay structure operates internally without bias does not explain why there were two pay scales nor why she was on one and he on another.

> If, as is common, the manual workers are mainly men and the staff workers are mainly women, the fact that the manual workers are paid more for the same work would seem to be a classic illustration of indirectly discriminatory pay since in order to receive higher pay for work of equal value you must be covered by the manual worker agreement, a requirement which has a disproportionately adverse impact on women. On this reasoning, to hold that the mere existence of the two schemes is itself an 'objectively justified administrative reason' for the inequality is a distortion of the concept. There is no 'objective justification' rather it is precisely the kind of administrative convenience that, in accordance with the *Bilka-Kaufhaus* test should no longer suffice as a defence.[7]

One of the most significant decisions to date which has reduced the negative impact of the earlier case law is that of the ECJ in *Enderby v. Frenchay Health Authority and the Secretary of State for Health* [1993] IRLR 591. This was a test case concerning equal value claims by speech therapists. The applicants claimed that they were employed on work of equal value with male principal grade pharmacists and clinical psychologists employed in the National Health Service whose salary exceeded theirs by about 60 per cent.

At the employment tribunal, the employers denied that the work was of equal value, but argued, in any event, that the variation in pay was genuinely due to a material factor: the separate negotiating structures by which the pay for the relevant professions was determined. The employers argued that there was no sex discrimination within the professions or in the negotiations. They pointed to the fact that speech therapists had been considered in the past to be a profession auxiliary to medicine and had been treated as such in the national negotiations, whereas clinical psychologists had been treated as comparable to scientists such as physicists and biologists.

The applicants pointed out that the speech therapists, as well as the other professions which had been treated as auxiliary to medicine, were overwhelmingly composed of women. There was a far greater proportion of men in the higher grades in the comparator professions. It was accepted that the negotiations had not been conducted with the deliberate intention of treating women less favourably, but it was argued that the salaries of speech therapists were artificially depressed because of the profession's predominantly female composition. It was argued that the employer's pay policy indirectly discriminated against women in that the outcome of negotiations had an adverse effect upon women and was not justifiable.

The employment tribunal dismissed the complaints and the EAT dismissed the complainant's appeal. The EAT upheld the employment tribunal's view that the employers had established a material factor defence by showing that the variation in pay 'arose because of the bargaining structure and its history which was not discriminatory, and from the structures within their own professions which were also non-discriminatory'. Collective agreements were to be properly considered under the headings of genuine material factors or justification under EC law. The EAT could not accept the appellant's submission that a collective agreement can never justify the difference in pay even if it is untainted by gender.

The case proceeded on appeal to the Court of Appeal which requested a ruling from the ECJ – it is this ruling which is of such importance. Firstly, as we have seen, where an applicant is claiming indirect discrimination in relation to pay, they need not identify a requirement or condition or show gender-based disparate impact in alleging indirect discrimination. Indirect discrimination will be presumed whenever there is significant statistical evidence to show that a predominantly female group of workers is doing work of equal value but is being paid less than a male group of workers. The onus then moves to the employer to show that the difference is objectively justified.

Secondly, it makes inroads into the market forces defence. This is no longer a blanket defence to a claim of indirect discrimination. The ECJ felt that, where market forces is pleaded, the tribunals must assess what proportion of the pay differential can be attributed to market forces as objectively justified by the employer. This may result in applicants being awarded proportional equal pay rather than nothing where the market forces defence is successful.

Following the decision in *Jamstalldhetsombudsmannen* v. *Orebro Lans Landsting* [2000] IRLR 421, if the applicant shows that the employer's pay policies have an adverse impact on considerably more women than men, the employer will have to objectively justify these policies. Again this is in line with the Burden of Proof directive which has been implemented in the UK by the Sex Discrimination (Indirect Discrimination and Burden of Proof) Regulations 2001, SI 2001/2660.

Finally, the fact that the respective rates of pay of two jobs of equal value were arrived at by collective bargaining processes which, although carried out by the same parties, were distinct and conducted separately and without any discriminatory effect within each group is not sufficient justification for the difference in pay between these two jobs. Following *Enderby* the House of Lords in *Ratcliffe* v. *North Yorkshire County Council* [1995] IRLR 439 had to consider what needed to be established to prove indirect discrimination in pay and whether competitive tendering could be used as a genuine material factor defence under s. 1 (3). The facts of *Ratcliffe* are as follows. Following a job evaluation scheme the jobs of catering assistants were rated as being of equal value to those of refuse collectors and leisure attendants employed by the council. The same rate of pay was duly awarded. However, the school meal service was put out to competitive tendering and as a result it was decided that the catering staff could no longer be paid on the basis of local government terms and conditions. The catering staff were duly dismissed and re-employed at lower hourly rates. It was held that (per Lord Slynn) in applying the EPA 1970 there was no need to introduce a distinction between direct discrimination and indirect discrimination in pay. The issue was whether equal treatment had been accorded for men and women employed on like work or work rated equivalent. In this case it had not. The next stage was to decide whether the s. 1 (3) defence was satisfied. The House of Lords upheld the ET finding that there was a genuine material factor which explained the difference in terms, namely the need to keep women's wages competitive with the commercial catering organisations. Those organisations employed almost exclusively female workforces which were prepared to work for low rates of pay because it was the only type of work that they could fit around their childcare responsibilities. However, that material factor was due to the difference of sex, since it arose 'out of the general perception in the United Kingdom and certainly North Yorkshire that a woman should stay at home to look after the children and if she wants to work, it must fit in with that domestic duty'.

It is clear that if cases continue to follow the *Enderby* decision, the effectiveness and acceptability of s. 1 (3) defences where tainted by sex will gradually be limited and will require far greater evidence from the employer wishing to defeat equal pay claims.

The ECJ has in the past taken a more purposive approach when considering pay structures which appear on the surface to be gender neutral. Indeed, the ECJ has shown itself prepared to look behind superficially gender-neutral pay structures. In *Handels-OG Kontorfunktionaernes Forbund i Danmark* v. *Dansk Arbejdsgiverforening (acting for Danfloss)* [1989] IRLR 532, a Danish trade union claimed that the pay practices of Danfloss were in breach of the Equal Pay Directive. In accordance with a national collective agreement, the employer used a job classification system to establish basic pay for each grade. Within the grade, however, the collective agreement allowed the employer to give increments on the basis of the employee's flexibility – defined as including capacity, quality of work, autonomy and responsibilities – and on the basis of training and seniority.

The union demonstrated that within a pay grade the average pay of men was 6.85 per cent higher than that of women and said that therefore the system was discriminatory, contrary to EC law.

The court held that in respect of 'flexibility', it was acceptable for an employer to reward the 'quality of work' done by an employee, because this was totally neutral from the point of view of gender. If the application of such a criterion did result in systematic unfairness to female workers, that could only be because the employer applied it in an 'abusive manner', it being 'inconceivable that the work carried out by female workers would generally be of a lower quality'. Therefore, the employer may not justify 'quality of work' as a basis for additional increments where it systematically works to the disadvantage of women.

Where flexibility refers to the adaptability of the worker to variable work schedules and places of work, this criterion may also operate to the disadvantage of female workers who, as a result of 'household and female duties', may have greater difficulty in organising their time flexibly. In such a situation the employer must show that adaptability is important to the specific duties of the particular worker and objectively justifiable. Similar considerations were held to apply in relation to additional pay for vocational training.

The court took a different approach in relation to seniority. In its view, even though the criterion of seniority, like that of vocational training, may result in less favourable treatment of female workers, seniority goes hand in hand with experience which generally places workers in a better position to perform their duties. Therefore, it is permissible for the employer to reward it without the need to establish the importance which it takes on for the performance of the specific duties of the particular workers.

The effect of this important decision is that merit pay systems which in practice work to the disadvantage of women can be attacked as unlawful. The ECJ also held that the burden of proof rests on employers to show that their pay practices are not discriminatory and are justifiable.

The decision in *Enderby* is starting to have an impact. In *British Road Services* v. *Loughrin* [1997] IRLR 92, it was confirmed following *Enderby* that the mere existence of separate pay structures based on different collective agreements did not amount to objective justification sufficient for the purposes of a s. 1 (3) defence. Nor was it necessary for the group claiming equal pay to be 'almost exclusively' women, a 'significant number' would suffice for the employer to have to establish the defence.

Different qualifications and professional training which bring different skills to the same job may justify a difference in pay, so held the ECJ in *Angestelltenbetriebstrat der Wiener Gebietskrankenkasse* v. *Wiener Gebietskrankenkasse* [1999] IRLR 804.

Longer service or seniority may no longer justify a difference in pay as it may have an adverse impact on women. *Crossley* v. *ACAS* (1999) 620 IRLB 12; *Cadman* v. *HSE* [2004] IRLR 29.

Remedies

In order to make an equal pay challenge the worker must apply to an employment tribunal. The Equal Pay (Amendment) Regulations 2003 maintain the time limit for bringing equal pay claims at six months from the end of the employment. Although to provide some flexibility the time limit will run from six months from the date on which the 'stable employment relationship' ends. This allows employees on non-standard contracts, for example, term time contracts for teachers, to have rights within the EPA 1970. In any event the time limit will not commence in cases where the employer deliberately concealed relevant facts, until the employee knew of those facts. The six-year limitation has been challenged successfully in *Kells* v. *Pilkington plc* [2002] IRLR 693 in which the EAT held that there is no rule of law restricting the period of events in respect of which an equal pay comparison can be made to six years before the date of the application. S. 2 (5) is concerned with the period of compensation, not the period during which comparison is acceptable. If the claim is successful the applicant may recover arrears of pay for a period of up to two years prior to the date on which proceedings were started. An order for the payment of damages rather than back-pay will be made where the employer has broken a term of the contract not directly related to pay, such as a term relating to holiday entitlement. The limit on compensation of up to two years' back-pay was successfully challenged as being in breach of EC law in *Levez* v. *TH Jennings (Harlow Pools) Limited* (No. 2) [1999] IRLR 764.

An employer may apply to an employment tribunal for a declaration of the rights of the employer and employee where there is a dispute about the effect of an equality clause (s. 2 [1A]). The Secretary of State has the power to bring proceedings on behalf of the employee where it is not reasonable to expect her to bring the proceedings herself (s. 2 [2]). To the best of our knowledge, this power has never been exercised.

EqPA s. 2 (4) does provide that no claim may be brought before a tribunal unless the applicant has been employed by the employer in the six months preceding the date of the application to the tribunal. The Equal Pay Act (Amendment) Regulations 2003, SI 2003/1656 amend the period in respect of which back-pay is awarded. This is in line with the decision of the ECJ in *Levez* v. *TH Jennings (Harlow Pools) Ltd (No. 2)*.

Collective Enforcement

Prior to the coming into force of the SDA 1986 a collective agreement containing differential provisions for men and women could by EqPA s. 3 be referred to the Central Arbitration Committee at the request of any party to the agreement or the Secretary of State. EqPA s. 3 has now been repealed by the SDA 1986 which provides that collective agreements (whether legally enforceable or not) are deemed automatically unenforceable and void in so far as they provide for the inclusion in a contract of employment of a provision which contravenes EqPA s. 1. But this provision does not provide individuals, such as prospective employees, with a remedy (SDA 1975, s. 77; SDA 1986, s. 6).

Again, European law offers a more effective approach. In *Kowalska* v. *Freie und Hansestadt Hamburg* [1990] IRLR 447, the ECJ held that terms in a collective agreement which indirectly discriminate against women – for example, by favouring full-timers over part-timers – can be challenged directly under art. 141. The court also rejected the employers' argument that the correct approach is to declare the term void and leave it to the parties to find a solution – the remedy adopted by UK law. Instead, the court took the view that workers should be treated equally proportionate to their hours of work. So in this case part-time workers were entitled to the severance payments available to the full-time workers on a proportionate basis.

The SDA 1986 s. 6 (4A) seeks to remedy the defect in UK law by allowing individuals to challenge in an employment tribunal the validity of terms of a collective agreement which may be applied to them where the terms may contravene the principle of equal treatment.

The Effectiveness of the Legislation

After the EPA came into force in 1970, it did appear to have some initial effect in reducing the gap between male and female pay. Women's earnings as a proportion of men's rose from 63.1 per cent in 1970 to a peak of 75.7 per cent in 1977. But little inroad has been made since then and, despite the legislation, women's average hourly earnings have remained stubbornly at around 81 per cent of men's for the last decade. The 2000 New Earnings Survey shows that the pay gap between men and women has not changed significantly and indeed the 2002 survey shows a slight increase in the gap. However, in real terms the gap is still significant with men earning on average 18 per cent more than women (2003 New Earnings Survey).

The ineffectiveness of the legislation in mirrored in the number of claims made each year. Claims under the Act declined rapidly to reach an all-time low of 35 in 1983. The introduction of the new equal value claim in 1984 increased claim activity but the success rate has remained low.

Table 10.1: Equal Pay Applications Registered by Employment Tribunals

1998–99	1999–00	2000–01	2001–02
7,222	4,712	7,153	5,314

The number of equal pay claims registered with ETs in 2002–03 fell by 42 per cent to 3,077 – less than half the number of applications made in 2000–01.

Defects in the Legislation

Procedural Complexity and Delay

As has been noted earlier, the equal value regulations are massively complex. During the House of Lords debate on them Lord Denning described them as 'beyond compare – no ordinary lawyer would be able to understand them – the industrial tribunal would have the greatest difficulty and the Court of Appeal would probably be divided in opinion'. This prediction has proved accurate, with the lack of clarity in the regulations causing delay in processing complaints. Indeed the president of EAT felt moved to observe that the delays are 'scandalous and amount to a denial of justice to women seeking a remedy through the judicial process'(see *Aldridge* v. *British Telecommunications plc* [1990] IRLR 10). EOC monitoring of the legislation has shown that on average less than 20 claims have been decided each year in the period 1984–89. This and the average length of time of 17 months for a claim to go through the full procedure show the problems created by the legal maze.

In their report 'Equal Pay For Men and Women: Strengthening the Acts' (1990), the EOC put forward a series of proposals aimed at simplifying and speeding up the procedure and increasing access to justice. These include:

- Requiring members of tribunals to have specialised training in the identification of gender bias in pay structures and collective agreements.
- Cases involving important questions of fact or law to be transferred straight to the EAT for initial hearing upon the application of both parties or on the initiative of the tribunal, and with the consent of the EAT.
- The requirement for a tribunal to determine that there are no reasonable grounds for the equal value should be abolished, as it operates as an 'unjustified fetter on individuals seeking access to the legal process'. Tribunals already have sufficient powers to 'weed out' hopeless claims – such as striking out a claim because it is 'frivolous or vexatious', or through the pre-hearing assessment review/assessment procedure.
- An employer's job evaluation study should no longer operate as a bar to an equal value claim.

At present an existing job evaluation scheme such as is described in s. 1 (5) of the Equal Pay Act, namely a study which is analytical and covering the jobs in question, acts as a bar to a claim if there are no reasonable grounds for determining that it is based on a sex discriminatory system. This provision covers a study which may have been in existence for several years and which is unlikely to have been introduced for the purpose of eliminating sex discrimination from the pay structure. It is more likely to reflect traditional expectations of employees and employers with a tendency to undervalue women's work, and as a result may well contain hidden and unintentional sex discrimination which is very difficult to identify without the most searching enquiry.[8]

- Some independent experts should be appointed on a full-time basis and there should be a chief independent expert charged with the responsibility of setting standards, providing initial and continuing training, publishing guidelines on job evaluation, reviewing the equal value procedures, ensuring that the investigations are completed within the agreed timescales.
- Independent experts, within 14 days of receiving an equal value question from the tribunal, should provide written notification of the estimated time for completion of their report.
- Parties should be required to respond to an independent expert's invitation to supply information or to make comments or representations within a period laid down by statute.
- Independent experts should be granted access to employers' premises within 14 days of making the request and tribunals should have the power to make an order for access.

As we have seen the Equal Pay Act (Amendment) Regulations 2003 attempt to facilitate the process for the applicant.[9]

The Equal Pay Task Force has called for mandatory equal pay reviews to be carried out by employers. It also believes that the procedure in equal pay cases needs to be streamlined and that the absence of a comparator should not be a bar to an equal pay claim. A study by the Equal Pay Task Force looks at the consequences of the gender pay gap and wants the gap reduced by 50 per cent within the next five years and eliminated within eight years (Just Pay – Report of the Equal Pay Task Force (2001) EOC). The EOC in its annual report 1999–2000 has also pressed for reforms to the current legislation. It wants a simpler and quicker procedure for equal pay claims as well as a duty imposed on employers in cases where there has been a successful claim to produce an action plan to remove inequities in its pay systems.

The EOC's report *Equality in the 21st Century: A New Approach* (1998) makes a number of recommendations which propose amendments to the current equal pay provisions; some are highlighted as follows:

Employers should be placed under a statutory duty to review their pay systems and pay structures, in line with the EOC Code of Practice and should identify areas of potential and actual pay inequality between men and women which cannot be objectively justified.

- Employers should be required to publish the results of their reviews to their employees.
- In the absence of a review or if such a review appears inadequate or unfair, the EOC should be empowered to intervene and set objectives and programmes for employers by means of directions.
- The EOC should be empowered to bring proceedings against an employer for non-compliance.

The Material Factor Defence

As stated earlier, the decision of House of Lords in *Rainey* permits the market forces argument to be used by an employer in all equal pay claims (that is, in like work cases as well as in equal value cases). If this concept is applied in a largely unrestricted manner, it undermines the equal pay legislation. After all, the very *raison d'être* of the equal pay legislation is that men are more powerful actors in the labour market than women. While the EOC does not propose the removal of the market forces defence, probably on the grounds that it is too well embedded in both UK and EC law for it to be removed, the Commission does argue for certain restrictions on the scope of the material factor defence. First, the employer should be under a statutory obligation to justify a differential pay practice by showing that it corresponds to a real need on the employer's part, is appropriate with a view to achieving the objectives pursued, and is necessary to that end (the *Bilka* test). Second, the employer should be obliged to show that the whole of the pay inequality has been caused by the material factor or factors relied on. This was not the approach favoured in *Enderby* v. *Frenchay Health Authority and Secretary of State for Health* [1993] IRLR 591, although proportionality was. Finally in this context, the EOC proposes that the use of the material factor defence should only be permitted on one occasion and then only after there has been a finding of equal value.

The Lack of Collective Enforcement Mechanisms

The Act does not provide for an application to be made by a representative or a class or group of employees; it only provides a remedy for the individual employee. Similarly, although trade unions may lend their support to individual equal pay claims as a way of pressurising employers to revise discriminatory pay structures, employers are under no legal obligation to do so; they may prefer to meet the cost of each individual equal pay claim as it arises. The current situation places the employment tribunals under quite unnecessary administrative strains in dealing with multiple applications from individual members of the same bargaining group (for example, the application by Enderby was one of 1,395 equal value applications from speech therapists). It also acts unfairly against other employees engaged in the same or broadly similar work, because they will be forced to institute equal pay claims unless the employer is prepared to extend the tribunal's decision to them.

In order to remedy this state of affairs, the EOC proposes:

- There should be a statutory requirement that all employees in the same employment as a successful applicant who do the same or broadly similar work should be entitled to the same award including back-pay.
- Where the source of the pay discrimination is a term or provision in a pay structure or collective agreement the respondent employer should notify the employment tribunal within a specified period that the term or provision has been modified or removed.
- Employment tribunals or a similarly constituted body should be given jurisdiction to determine allegations of discrimination in the terms of collective agreements and pay structures on the application of any interested party including the EOC.

- Such a body should be empowered to make orders for the modification or removal of sex discriminatory terms in collective agreements and pay structures.[10]

The 'Hypothetical Male'

A major flaw in the Act is the fact that it provides no remedy for the woman whose work is undervalued but who has no male colleague who is in the same employment and engaged on like work, work rated as equivalent or work of equal value to her own. She cannot compare her situation with that of the 'hypothetical man' and what he would have been paid to do the work. As a result the Act does not begin to tackle the root of the problem. Women's employment is largely segregated and certain jobs are seen as 'women's work'. These jobs tend to be low paid and badly unionised and lack male comparators.

The EOC advocates the replacement of the Equal Pay Act and Sex Discrimination Act with a unified Equal Treatment Act. One benefit of the merger would be a legislative code which would be less complex and more accessible. But another advantage would be the importation of the 'hypothetical male' comparator – allowed in sex discrimination cases – to equal pay claims. The statutory comparisons – like work, work rated as equivalent and equal value – would remain the normal concepts under which the vast majority of equal pay cases would be decided.

Nevertheless, the adoption of the test of discrimination from the Sex Discrimination Act under which the criteria may not only be that employers treat the underpaid woman less favourably than they actually treat a man but also that they treat her less favourably than they *would* treat a man, would permit a wider range of comparisons to be made. This alternative to the three statutory comparisons would be invoked only as a last resort in exceptional circumstances.

Initiatives to Promote Equality in Pay

In January 1998 the EOC provided written evidence in support of a national minimum wage to the Low Pay Commission. Their evidence supported the statistic that there are 4 million women in Britain in low paid jobs.[11] The EOC stated that 'women are particularly vulnerable to low pay and will benefit disproportionately from the introduction of a national minimum wage'. It is also believed that the national minimum wage will go some way to tackling the low pay of part-time employees; eight out of ten of which are female.

The National Minimum Wage Act 1998 provides that all workers over compulsory school age have the right to be paid the national minimum wage and this right will be extended to agency and home-workers. The national minimum wage is set at a single hourly rate by the Secretary of State.

Where a worker discovers that s/he is not being paid the national minimum wage, s/he will have the right to recover the difference in pay from the employment tribunal or a civil court. The onus will be on the employer to prove that the worker does not qualify for the national minimum wage. Employers may be subject to criminal sanctions for failing to pay the wage or keep records or falsify records.

The national minimum wage is subject to revision from time to time, but is set (as at 2003) at £4.40 for adults (Oct 2003) rising to £4.85 (Oct 2004). For 18–21 year olds, it is £3.80 (Oct 2003) rising to £4.10 in October 2004. The possibility of introducing a national minimum wage for 16–17 year olds is being considered. The Low Pay Commission monitors the rate. The Inland Revenue acts as the enforcement agency, requiring employers to keep adequate records for scrutiny on request. Inland Revenue officers may issue enforcement notices which require the employer to pay workers any arrears of pay.

The Equal Pay Task Force has called for mandatory equal pay reviews to be carried out by employers. It also looks at the consequences of the gender pay gap; Just Pay – Report of the Equal Pay Task Force (2001) EOC 13.[12]

CHAPTER 11

Race and Sex Discrimination

Discrimination has been long established in employment and yet legislation seeking to outlaw it has been introduced relatively recently.

Racial discrimination in employment was brought within the scope of the law for the first time by the Race Relations Act 1968. Under the Act, the Race Relations Board was given the power to investigate complaints of discrimination in employment and, if conciliation failed, to initiate civil proceedings. The Race Relations Act 1976 provided the victim of racial discrimination with direct access to the ordinary courts and tribunals without the necessity of seeking the approval of a government-appointed agency. Moreover, the Act encompassed not only direct discrimination but the more subtle forms of indirect discrimination.

It might be expected that the passage of the wider-ranging 1976 Act would make discrimination much less common. In fact, many studies of recruitment and of the position of black workers during the 1970s and 1980s have demonstrated continuing discrimination in employment. For example a survey conducted over 1984/85 found that one-third of employers directly discriminated against black and Asian applicants.[1]

Similarly, in relation to sex discrimination, despite the legislation and at least some attitudinal change, the idea that there is 'women's work' and 'women's wages' remains firmly rooted in our society. As we saw in the previous chapter, the Equal Pay Act has only managed to close marginally the earnings gap between men and women and women's work continues to be concentrated in traditionally low-paid and low-grade occupations.[2]

Of course, it would be naive in the extreme to expect that legislation by itself can eradicate discrimination. Nevertheless, as Steve Anderman has argued:

it is possible for legislators to take a more or less robust view of the use of legislation to produce social change ... [I]n shaping the content of the legislation the concern of legislators is not to remove discrimination at all costs. There is in their minds a trade-off between the desirability of helping women to achieve greater equality of treatment and opportunity and the effect of social regulation on industry.[3]

In this chapter, we argue that the content of the legislation and the way the judges have interpreted it evidence a marked reluctance to intervene in management decision-making in the interests of helping to bring about social change.

Where to Find the Law

The law relating to discrimination is to be found in two principal statutes, the Sex Discrimination Act 1975 (SDA) and the Race Relations Act 1976 (RRA). As was seen in the previous chapter, sex discrimination in pay and other contractual terms is dealt with separately under the Equal Pay Act 1970 (EqPA 1970), as amended by the Equal Pay (Amendment) Regulations 1983. Both the SDA and RRA encompass discrimination in employment, education and in the provision of goods and facilities, services and housing – though this chapter will focus on the employment field.

There are Codes of Practice for the elimination of racial discrimination as well as codes relating to age discrimination and disability. The Codes of Practice lay down guidelines for good employment practice, but they are not legally actionable themselves. However, the Codes are admissible in evidence at a hearing and an employment tribunal can 'take into account' any relevant provision in reaching its decision. In addition there is a separate Code of Practice on measures to combat sexual harrassment.[4]

As stated in the previous chapter, the UK's law on sex discrimination has been much affected by the influence of the standards laid down by the European Community. Like the EqPA, the SDA was the subject of a successful complaint by the Commission to the ECJ that the UK had fallen short of the standards required by the Equal Treatment Directive (76/207) (*EC Commission* v. *United Kingdom of Great Britain and Northern Ireland* [1984] IRLR 29). As a result of both this case and the subsequent decision of the ECJ in *Marshall* v. *Southampton and South West Hampshire Area Health Authority (Teaching)* [1986] IRLR 140, the SDA 1986 was passed in an attempt to bring the UK law in line with EC standards. Further movement towards compliance is evident in certain of the provisions of the Employment Act 1989, and the Employment Rights Act 1996.

There are considerable changes to the domestic discrimination provisions as a result of the Race Discrimination Directive (Dir. 2000/43); the Equal Treatment Directive (Dir. 2002/73) and the EU Framework Directive (2000/78). The Race Directive is the first EU Directive to prohibit race discrimination. It is being implemented through the Race Relations Act 1976 (Amendment) Regulations 2003, SI 2003/1626. It introduces a new definition of indirect discrimination, and racial harassment; changes the burden of proof and introduces a new genuine occupational qualification dependent on a particular race or ethnic or national origin. It should be noted that colour and nationality are not covered by the Directive but are within the RRA.

The revised Equal Treatment Directive does not have to be implemented until 2005 but will result in changes to the definition of sexual harassment; a new definition of direct discrimination and indirect discrimination, revised genuine occupational qualifications, explicit rights re pregnancy, promotion of equal treatment, and extension of current legislation to pay discrimination.

The Framework Directive prohibits discrimination on grounds of sexual orientation, religion, disability and age and will be phased in.

Sex and race discrimination have received a specific focus in the legislation, but, of course, there other reasons why people are victimised. In the following chapter we will examine employers' duties to people with disabilities, and discrimination against gay men, lesbians and those workers with AIDS or who are HIV positive. Discrimination against workers because of membership/non-membership or participation in the activities of a trade union is covered by ERA 1996 and is discussed in our chapters on unfair dismissal and collective bargaining.

Sex and Race Discrimination:
Who is Covered by the Legislation?

The rules relating to discrimination in employment cover not only those who work or seek to work under a contract of employment but also those under contract personally to execute any work or labour (self-employed workers).

Individuals engaged in government training schemes have been held not to fall within this definition (see *Daley* v. *Allied Suppliers* [1973] IRLR 14) but, as a result of revisions to both discrimination statutes, any person providing or making arrangements for the provision of training facilities is now covered (RRA 1976 s. 13 as amended; SDA 1975 s. 14 as amended).

Contract workers supplied by an agency – for example, office temps and certain construction workers – are within the scope of the legislation (SDA s. 9; RRA s. 7). The law makes express provision for such workers because it will usually be the client for whom the temp works – as opposed to the agency with whom the temp is 'in employment' – who will have most control over working conditions. In *Harrods Limited* v. *Ms Remmick* [1997] IRLR 9 the EAT confirmed that Section 7 RRA 1976 applied to the staff of concessionaires, who were then entitled to protection from discrimination under the legislation. For Section 7 to apply there must be a contract of employment between the individual contract workers and their employer; and a contract made between the employer of the workers and the principal under which the employer is under an obligation to supply workers. In this particular case there was such a contract between the workers and the person who supplied them to the principal.

EC law has generally utilised the term 'worker' rather than employee. Workers include not only employees, but also independent contractors who personally undertake work. The term worker is used in the National Minimum Wage Act 1998 (see *Edmunds* v. *Lawson* [2000] IRLR 391) and the Part-Time Workers (Less Favourable Treatment) Regulations 2000, SI 2000/1551. The Secretary of State for Employment has the power to extend existing statutory rights to workers by virtue of s. 23 Employment Relations Act 1999.

The Acts extend the umbrella of protection beyond those bodies with which the worker is 'in employment' to include:

- Trade unions and employers' associations (RRA s. 11; SDA s. 12) – it is unlawful to discriminate in the terms on which membership is offered, refused or varied, in the way in which access is provided to benefits, facilities and services or in subjecting them to any detriment.
- Qualifying bodies (RRA s. 12; SDA s. 13) – it is unlawful for a body which can confer an authorisation or qualification which is needed for, or facilitates, engagement in a particular profession or trade to discriminate against a person by refusing or deliberately omitting to grant an application, or by withdrawing or varying the terms upon which the authorisation or qualification is awarded. Examples of such bodies might be the Law Society, British Medical Association and even the British Judo Association when exercising its discretion to grant a referee's licence (*British Judo Association* v. *Petty* [1981] IRLR 484).
- Employment agencies (SDA s. 15; RRA s. 14) – it is unlawful to discriminate by deliberately denying an employment agency's services, or in the terms

upon which it offers its services, or in the way in which it provides its services. The definition of employment agency in the legislation is wide enough to encompass a university careers office and state employment services, in addition to private profit-making concerns.

- Partnerships (RRA s. 10; SDA s. 11) – partners must not discriminate against a woman partner nor against a woman seeking a partnership. This provision used to apply only to partnerships of six or more but this was removed by the SDA 1986. The six or more rule continues to apply in the context of race discrimination.

The Race Relations (Amendment) Act 2000 makes indirect discrimination by public authorities unlawful in respect of the way in which they carry out their functions. It also imposes a duty on public authorities to eliminate unlawful racial discrimination and provide equality of opportunity. A similar amendment has been introduced by the Sex Discrimination Act 1975 (Amendment) Regulations 2003, SI 2003/1657.

Geographical Limitations

In order to qualify to bring a case, the complainant must be employed at an establishment in Great Britain, so a worker who works wholly or mainly outside Great Britain cannot claim (SDA s. 10; RRA s. 8). The exclusion does not apply to employment on board a ship registered in Great Britain, or to employment on an aircraft or hovercraft registered in Britain and operated by a person who has his/her principal place of business, or is ordinarily resident, in Britain, unless the work is done *wholly* outside Great Britain.

In *Haughton v. Olau Line (UK) Ltd* [1986] IRLR 465 CA, the employers were based at Sheerness and the worker spent the majority of working hours on a ship outside UK territorial waters. She was held to be outside the coverage of the Sex Discrimination Act because the ship on which she worked was German-registered.

In *Deria v. The General Council of British Shipping* [1986] IRLR 108 CA, Somali seamen were refused employment on a British ship requisitioned for service during the Falklands War. The vessel unexpectedly completed its voyage in Southampton rather than Gibraltar, as originally planned. The Court of Appeal construed the section as meaning that 'employment is to be regarded as being at an establishment in Great Britain unless the employee does or is *to do* his work wholly outside Great Britain'. The seamen's claim was excluded, notwithstanding that the ship actually sailed in British waters, since it was not contemplated that those who were employed would work within territorial waters when the applicants were refused employment. However, the decision in *Bossa v. Nordskess Ltd and another* [1998] (2/3/98) makes it clear that art. 48, which enshrines the right to work anywhere in the EC, may override the exclusion.

Discrimination and Third Parties

Liability for unlawful discrimination is not confined to the discriminator him/herself.

Vicarious Liability

Principals are liable for the acts of their agents carried out within the scope of their authority and employers are liable for unlawful acts of discrimination by employees committed in the course of their employment (SDA s. 41; RRA s. 32). For example, if you claim that the personnel officer of Capital plc discriminated against you in a job interview, you can sue both the officer and the company. An employer will not be liable for acts which are clearly outside the employee's course of employment. It was thought that, in order to decide if this applied, the courts had to determine whether an act was merely an unauthorised or prohibited mode of carrying out an authorised act (if so, the employer is liable) as distinct from an act which is outside the sphere of employment (no vicarious liability). So, for example, in *Irving* v. *Post Office* [1987] IRLR 289 CA, the Post Office was not vicariously responsible under the Race Relations Act for racially abusive words written on an envelope by a postman, since the postman was not acting in the course of employment. The act of writing on the envelope did not become part of the manner in which the postman performed his duties merely because he did it while on duty. His employment provided the opportunity for his misconduct, but the misconduct formed no part of the performance of his duties, was in no way directed towards the performance of those duties, and was not done for the benefit of his employer. However, this created a loophole through which employers could avoid liability as illustrated in *Irving* v. *Post Office (Supra)*. The common law test was applied initially in *Jones* v. *Tower Boot Co Ltd* [1995] IRLR 529. The EAT found that colleagues who subjected their workmate to racial harassment by deliberately branding him with a hot screwdriver and whipping him were not acting within the course of employment. On appeal the Court of Appeal [1997] IRLR 168 reversed this decision by ruling that 'the RRA 1976 has to be interpreted in line with its legislative purpose which is as much to eliminate the occasions for discrimination as it is to compensate its victims or punish its perpetrators. The purposive approach requires the phrase "in the course of employment" to be given a broad interpretation according with its normal meaning and not limited to the principles of vicarious liability that apply under the common law principles of tort.'

The importance of this decision cannot be underestimated as prior to this the employer was permitted to escape liability for serious acts of discrimination due to the restrictive interpretation of the words 'course of employment'. The anomaly created was that the more serious the act of discrimination, the less likely would be the liability of the employer. In those circumstances it was questionable how sexual and racial harassment in particular, would ever be eliminated.

However, if the act of discrimination is not within the course of employment, the fact that it is racially or sexually motivated will not sustain a claim of vicarious liability. In *Sidhu* v. *Aerospace Composite Technology Ltd* [2000] IRLR 602, a family day out was organised by the employer. A racial assault took place, which was found by the CA not to be in the course of employment. It should also be noted that where the employer is found not to be vicariously liable, the Tribunals may find the employee personally liable – *Yeboah* v. *Crofton* [2002] IRLR 634.

In addition, employers have a statutory defence if they can show that they took such steps as were reasonably practicable to prevent the commission of an act (SDA s. 41 [3]; RRA s. 32 [3]). Certain commentators and, indeed, the Commission for Racial Equality have questioned why employers need this additional protection, seeing it as open invitation to dismiss claims on the basis of very limited preventative action on the part of the employer. A prime example of this tendency is the decision in *Balgobin v. London Borough of Tower Hamlets* [1987] IRLR 401 EAT, discussed below in the section on sexual harassment.

Aiding and Abetting

A person who aids another to commit an unlawful act of discrimination is treated as having committed an unlawful act of 'the like description'. Employees or agents who cause their employer or principal to be vicariously liable are treated as if they aided their employer's or principal's unlawful act. For example, if you are the victim of sexual harassment you can sue both the harasser and your employer.

A person has a defence to aiding if it can be shown that s/he acted in reliance on a statement by the discriminator that the act which was aided was not unlawful and that it was reasonable to rely on that statement.

Other Unlawful Acts

False or Misleading Statements

A person who knowingly or recklessly makes a statement to another that a particular act would not be unlawful, is guilty of a criminal offence and is liable on conviction in a magistrates' court to a fine not exceeding level 5 on the standard scale (RRA s. 33 [4]; SDA s. 42 [4]).

Pressure to Discriminate

Direct or indirect pressure to induce or attempt to induce a person to discriminate is unlawful (RRA s. 31 [1], SDA s. 40). The inducement can take the form of either a threat or a promise. An attempted inducement is not prevented from being unlawful because it is not made directly to the person in question, provided that it is made in such a way that the other is likely to hear it. So if A, the works manager, tells B, an employee, that another employee, C, will be sacked unless B discriminates against D, an Asian, in selecting candidates for a job, A is guilty of an unlawful act. Enforcement of this provision is vested in the EOC and CRE.

Instructions to Discriminate

It is unlawful for one person who has authority over another, or in accordance with whose wishes that other person is accustomed to act, to instruct him/her to perform a racially or sexually discriminatory act or to procure or attempt to procure the doing of such an act (RRA s. 30; SDA s. 39). Once again, enforcement of these provisions is the sole responsibility of the EOC and CRE.

Advertisements

An employer must not cause to be published an advertisement which indicates, or might reasonably be understood to indicate, an intention to discriminate (SDA s. 38 [1]; RRA s. 29).

In relation to sex discrimination it is provided that the use of a job description with a sexual connotation (such as 'waiter', 'salesgirl', 'postman', or 'stewardess') shall be taken to indicate an intention to discriminate, unless the advertisement indicates an intention to the contrary.

Only the EOC or CRE can bring proceedings in respect of discriminatory advertisements.

There are two exceptions to the rules against discriminatory advertising:

(i) where it is an advertisement for employment outside Great Britain which discriminates other than by reference to colour, ethnic or national origins (RRA s. 29 [3]);

(ii) where the advertisement is for a job in which there are genuine occupational qualifications for employing a person of a particular race, colour, ethnic or national origin or sex.

Discrimination is Unlawful if Based Upon:

(a) Racial grounds (RRA ss. 1, 3)
(b) Gender (SDA ss. 1, 2)
(c) Marital status (SDA s. 3)

Racial Grounds

'Racial grounds' are defined as any of the following grounds: colour, race, nationality or ethnic or national origins.

Case law suggests that 'ethnic origins' is a wider concept than 'racial origins' and brings groups within the scope of the Act who would otherwise be unprotected. So in *Mandla (Sewa Singh) v. Dowell Lee* [1983] AC 548, the House of Lords finally decided that Sikhs constituted a distinct ethnic group. The word 'ethnic' did not require the group to be distinguished by some inherited racial characteristic.

Lord Fraser provided the following guidance:

For a group to constitute an ethnic group in the sense of the 1976 Act, it must, in my opinion, regard itself, and be regarded by others as a distinct community by virtue of certain characteristics. Some of these characteristics are essential; others are not essential but one or more of them will commonly be found and will help to distinguish the group from the surrounding community. The conditions which appear to me to be essential are these: (1) a long shared history, of which the group is conscious as distinguishing it from other groups, and the memory of which it keeps alive; (2) a cultural tradition of its own, including family and social customs and manners, often but not necessarily associated with religious observance. In addition to these essential characteristics the following characteristics are in my opinion relevant; (3) either a common geographical origin, or descent from a number of common ancestors; (4) a common language, not necessarily peculiar to the group; (5) a common literature peculiar to the group; (6) a common religion different from that of neighbouring groups or from the general community surrounding it; (7) being a minority or being an oppressed or dominant group within a larger community, for example a conquered people (say, the inhabitants of England shortly after the Norman Conquest) and their conquerors might both be ethnic groups – A group defined by reference to enough of these characteristics would be capable of including converts, for example people who marry into the group, and of excluding apostates. Provided a person who joins the group feels himself or herself to be a member of it, and is accepted by other members, then he is, for the purposes of the Act, a member.

This test was applied in *CRE* v. *Dutton* [1989] IRLR 8, where the Court of Appeal had to determine whether gipsies were a racial group. It concluded that using the narrower meaning of the word 'gipsies' as a 'wandering race of Hindu origin' rather than the larger, amorphous group of 'travellers' or 'nomads', the evidence was sufficient to establish that gipsies are an identifiable group defined by reference to ethnic origins. The evidence was that gipsies are a minority with a long-shared history and a common geographical origin. They have certain customs of their own. They have a language or dialect which consists of up to one-fifth of Romany words in place of English words. They have a repertoire of folk tales and music passed from one generation to the next.

Discrimination on grounds of national origin is discrimination on racial grounds within the meaning of s. 3 (1) RRA 1976 as confirmed by the EAT in *Northern Joint Police Board* v. *Power* [1997] IRLR 610. In this particular case, an Englishman claimed that he had not been shortlisted for the post of Chief Constable of the Northern Constabulary because he was English rather than Scots. 'National origins are ascertained as identifiable elements both historically and geographically which at least at some point in time reveal the existence of a nation.' On that basis, so the EAT held, there was no doubt that both England and Scotland were once separate nations. The EAT, however, confirmed that the applicant could not bring his claim on the basis that he had been discriminated against on grounds of his 'ethnic origin', as the Scots, the English and the Welsh did not fall within the definition of racial group in s. 3 on the basis of having different 'ethnic origins'. 'Ethnic origins' had to have a racial flavour to it.

However, there are still problems faced by those whose status may fall between race and religion such as Muslims and Jews. It is clear in these cases that if the reason for the discrimination is based solely on religious grounds, then no breach of the RRA has occurred.

Discrimination on the grounds of religion is not expressly covered by the Act[5] but a number of religious groups may fall within the definition of an ethnic group following the approach adopted in *Mandla*.

In *Seide* v. *Gillette Industries Ltd* [1980] IRLR 427 EAT, it was held that 'Jewish' could mean a member of a race or a particular ethnic origin as well as a member of a particular religious faith, and can therefore fall within the scope of the Act.

More recently, however, in *Dawkins* v. *Department of the Environment* [1993] IRLR 284, the CA was not prepared to accept that a refusal to offer a job to a Rastafarian because he would not cut his hair was discrimination against an ethnic group. In the CA's view, Rastafarians were no more than a religious sect and as such were not sufficiently distinct from the rest of the Afro-Caribbean community. Moreover, they had not established a separate identity by reference to their ethnic origin.

However, it should be noted that the EU Employment Framework Directive (Directive 2000/78) prohibits discrimination on the grounds of religion, amongst other things. The Directive has to be implemented by December 2003. This has resulted in the Employment Equality (Religion or Belief) Regulations 2003, SI 2003/1660.

Sex

As with the Equal Pay Act, the SDA applies equally to discrimination against men and women (SDA s. 2 [1]).

Marital Status

SDA s. 3 makes it unlawful to discriminate against a married person in the field of employment. It remains lawful, however, to discriminate against a person because s/he is single.

Types of Discrimination

The main heads of claim for the complainant under the RRA and SDA are either direct discrimination, indirect discrimination or victimisation.

Direct Discrimination

This occurs when one person treats another less favourably, on the grounds of gender, marital status or race, than s/he treats or would treat a person of another gender, marital status or race.

However, you should note the slightly different wording between the RRA and the SDA. Under the RRA discrimination is based on 'racial grounds' whereas under the SDA, discrimination against a woman has to be 'on the grounds of her sex'. The wider phrase under the RRA brings transferred discrimination within its remit. This means that discrimination may take place where a person is treated less favourably because of another person's race. For example, in *Showboat Entertainment Centre Ltd v. Owens* [1984] ICR 65, Owens, who was white, was dismissed from his job as a manager of an amusement centre for failure to obey an order to exclude black people. Unlawful discrimination was held to have taken place. The concept of transferred discrimination has, on the whole, been underutilised. However, the case of *Weatherfield Ltd t/a Van and Truck Rentals v. Sargent* [1998] IRLR 14 provides a good example of its usage. In this case Mrs Sargent, a white European, was instructed to inform 'coloureds and Asians' that no vehicles were available. She felt she had been put in an intolerable position and consequently resigned. The EAT held that there had been a breach of s. 1 (1) (a) RRA.

Unlike the EqPA which requires an actual comparator, the SDA and RRA allow comparison to be made with how a hypothetical person would have been treated.

Where there is no actual comparator, the onus is on the ET to construct a hypothetical one, so held the CA in *Balamoody v. United Kingdom Central Council for Nursing, Midwifery and Health Visiting* [2002] IRLR 288. Failure to do so is an error in law. In *Shamoon v. Chief Constable of the Royal Ulster Constabulary* [2003] IRLR 285, the HL emphasised that where there is no actual comparator whose circumstances are the same, the statutory comparison should be how a hypothetical comparator in those same circumstances would be treated.

As Anne Morris and Susan Nott observe:

To allow motive to justify directly discriminatory behaviour detracts from any attempt to achieve equality of opportunity since it legitimises and perpetuates gender-based prejudice. If direct discrimination were acceptable on the basis that, for example, an employer genuinely believed that one woman working in an all-male workshop would find life very difficult, this would frustrate attempts to eliminate discrimination. Indeed, the deep-rooted assumptions that can lead to a woman receiving less favourable treatment may not be regarded by the person who holds them as discriminatory, and, arguably, the practical effect of allowing a consideration of motive would be to reduce dramatically the number of instances of direct discrimination.[6]

In *R* v. *Birmingham CC ex parte EOC* [1989] IRLR 173, the House of Lords formulated a simple test for establishing direct discrimination as follows:

(i) Was there an act of discrimination? If the answer is in the affirmative:
(ii) But for the complainant's gender (or race), would s/he have been treated differently, i.e. less favourably?

In *James* v. *Eastleigh BC* [1989] IRLR 318, the Court of Appeal failed to apply the test expounded in the Birmingham County Council case and it required another trip to the House of Lords to clarify matters.

Eastleigh Council allowed free swimming for children under the age of three and for persons who had reached the state retirement age. Mr and Mrs James were both aged 61 and both were retired. When they went swimming Mr James had to pay whereas Mrs James had free admission. Mr James alleged this was a breach of s. 29 (1) (b) of the SDA (discrimination in the provision of a service). The Court of Appeal held that there was no act of direct discrimination within s. 1 (1) (a). In order to establish direct discrimination 'one must look at the reason why the defendant treated the plaintiff less favourably, not to the causative link between the defendant's behaviour and the detriment to the plaintiff'. In this particular case it was accepted by the court that the reason for adopting the policy was 'to aid the needy' and was therefore not on the grounds of gender.

Mr James' appeal to the House of Lords was upheld (see [1990] IRLR 289). The majority of the House of Lords laid down a 'but for' causative test for determining whether there had been direct discrimination – that is, 'would the complainant have received the same treatment from the defendant but for his or her sex'. The determinative question is whether gender is the ground for the alleged decision; why the employer discriminated is irrelevant. An employer acting with the best motive may still fall foul of the legislation – *Grieg* v. *Community Industry* [1996] ICR 356.

Direct discrimination may be inferred from the facts. This was recognised both in *Noone* v. *North West Thames Regional Health Authority* [1988] IRLR 195 and *King* v. *The Great Britain China Centre* [1991] IRLR 513. The decision in *King* lays down the test for inferring discrimination and recognises the difficulties in providing conclusive evidence in many cases that discrimination has taken place. The CA stated 'though there will be some cases where, for example, the non selection of the applicant for a post or for a promotion is clearly not on racial grounds, a finding of discrimination and a finding of a difference in race will often point to the possibility of racial discrimination. In such circumstances, the tribunal will look to the employer for an explanation. If no explanation is then put forward, or if the tribunal considers the explanation to be inadequate or unsatisfactory, it will be legitimate for the tribunal to infer that the discrimination was on racial grounds.'

A further aid in establishing discrimination can be found in the case of *Zafar* v. *Glasgow City Council* [1998] IRLR 36 in which the HL ruled that the test for establishing discrimination is not based on consideration of the conduct of the hypothetical reasonable employer. Whether an employer has acted reasonably or not is irrelevant in establishing whether there has been less favourable treatment.

In *Shamoon* (above) the HL also offered revised guidance on establishing direct discrimination. It was suggested that the first question should be why was the complainant treated less favourably? This would allow the ET to infer discrimination at this stage or to conclude that it was not on grounds of sex or race. This approach in effect reverses the approach laid down in *Zafar*. However, it is unclear whether this revised approach is applicable in all cases.

Finally the Race Relations Act 1976 (Amendment) Regulations 2003, SI 2003/1626 and the Equal Treatment Amendment Directive Dir. 2002/73 introduce a new definition of direct discrimination. For race it is as follows: 'A person (A) discriminates against another if – (a) on grounds of religion or belief, race, A treats B less favourably than he treats or would treat other persons'; and for sex discrimination: direct discrimination occurs 'where one person is treated less favourably on grounds of sex than another is, has been or would be treated in a comparable situation'. It is hoped that when the Directive is implemented the revised definition will be the same in the main statutes. The revised race definition does not permit any justification for the act of discrimination.

The Race Relations Act 1976 (Amendment) Regulations 2003 and the Equal Treatment Amendment Directive also introduce explicit provisions making racial and sexual harassment unlawful. Both are based on 'unwanted' conduct on the part of the recipient and cover not only the 'violation of the recipient's dignity' but also 'the creation of an intimidating, hostile, degrading, humiliating or offensive environment for the recipient'.

The Equal Treatment directive extends sexual harassment to sex-related and sexual harassment and includes verbal, and non-verbal acts such as displaying pornographic images or sexually explicit emails. Both definitions are in line with the EC Code of Practice on sexual harassment at work.

Sexual Harassment

Successive surveys of women's experience have shown that sexual harassment in the workplace is widespread. Commenting on the empirical data documenting the incidence of sexual harassment at work in the EC Member States, Michael Rubenstein concludes that:

> sexual harassment is not an isolated phenomenon perpetrated by the odd socially deviant man. On the contrary it is clear that for millions of women in the EEC today, sexual harassment is an unpleasant and unavoidable part of their working lives.[7]

Despite the significance of this problem, there was no specific reference to 'sexual harassment' in the legislation. Indeed, it was not until the mid-1980s that it was firmly established that sexual harassment constituted direct discrimination under the SDA. This recognition came in *Strathclyde Regional District Council* v. *Porcelli* [1986] IRLR 134, the first case on sexual harassment to reach the appellate courts. The complainant, Mrs Porcelli, was a laboratory technician employed by the regional council in one of its schools. She claimed she had been unlawfully discriminated against when she had been compelled to seek a transfer to another school because of a deliberate campaign of vindictiveness against her by two male colleagues, some of it of a sexual nature. She claimed that the regional council was vicariously responsible for the behaviour of the two men.

The employment tribunal, while accepting that the men's behaviour had been extremely unpleasant, rejected her application. The tribunal was of the view that a man who had been disliked would have been treated equally badly, although the tribunal agreed that the unpleasantness would have been of a different nature.

The EAT rejected this argument and allowed Mrs Porcelli's appeal. The council's appeal to the Scottish Court of Session was dismissed. According to the court, even if only some of the treatment complained of was sexually oriented, there was less favourable treatment on grounds of sex. What mattered was the treatment, not the motive for it, and therefore if any material part of the treatment included elements of a sexual nature to which the woman was vulnerable, but a man would not be, then she had been treated less favourably on grounds of her sex. It was also held that conduct falling short of physical contact could still constitute sexual harassment.

Mrs Porcelli was eventually awarded £3,000 damages for the injury to feelings and stress which she had experienced.

In *Bracebridge Engineering* v. *Darby* [1990] IRLR 3, it was concluded that a single act of a 'serious' nature will support a claim of sexual harassment. Employees committing such acts may well be acting 'within the course of their employment', which in turn makes their employer responsible. In addition any failure to act on the part of the employer, such as a failure to carry out a serious investigation of the complaint, may allow the complainant to treat herself as constructively dismissed.

In many cases, the victim of sexual harassment will be victimised if she has rejected sexual advances. She may be passed over for promotion or dismissed. In other cases, she will find the situation intolerable and seek a transfer, as in *Porcelli*, or resign, as in *Darby*. But what is the position if she stays at work and makes a complaint to a tribunal? As we shall see, SDA s. 6 requires a victim of sex discrimination to suffer a 'detriment'. If there is no retaliation against her or she fails to resign, does she suffer a detriment within the meaning of the Act? In *De Souza* v. *Automobile Association* [1986] IRLR 103 – a racial harassment case discussed below – the Court of Appeal took the view that harassment will be unlawful if the reasonable employee could justifiably complain about her working conditions or environment. It is not necessary that the result of the discrimination was either a dismissal or some action by the employee such as leaving employment or seeking a transfer.

So far so good, but there are other decisions by the courts and tribunals which are far less supportive to victims of sexual or racial harassment.

In *Snowball* v. *Gardner Merchant Ltd* [1987] IRLR 397, a female catering manager alleged that she had been sexually assaulted by her male district manager. During her cross-examination, she denied that she had talked freely to her fellow employees about her attitude to sexual matters – it was alleged that she had described her bed as a 'play-pen' and mentioned her black satin sheets in conversation with colleagues. It was held by the EAT that the respondent employer could call witnesses in support of the allegation. The view was taken that the evidence was relevant not only to Ms Snowball's credibility but also for the purpose of deciding whether she had, in fact, suffered any detriment or injury to feelings.

This decision has attracted a welter of criticism on the grounds that it has opened the door to the kind of evidence about a woman's moral character and sexual attitudes which has caused so much resentment in rape cases. It is hard to see why a woman's consensual sexual behaviour should be relevant to assessing the degree of hurt she suffers from uninvited and unwanted sexual advances from her boss or a fellow employee. Faced with the prospect of being cross-examined about her sex life, many women will be deterred from making a complaint of sexual harassment.

A similarly offensive attitude to women is to be found in *Wileman* v. *Minilec Engineering Ltd* [1988] IRLR 144, where a victim of harassment was awarded the derogatory sum of £50 based on the fact that the tribunal was allowed to take into account the fact that, on occasions, the applicant wore what were described as scanty and provocative clothes to work. Mr Justice Popplewell stated:

> if a girl on the shop floor goes around wearing provocative clothes and flaunting herself, it is not unlikely that other work people – particularly the men – will make remarks about it; it is an inevitable part of working life on the shop floor. If she then claims that she suffered a detriment, the Tribunal is entitled to look at the circumstances in which the remarks are made which are said to constitute that detriment.

In other words if you wear 'provocative' clothes at work you are 'asking for it'. Yet the way a woman dresses should surely be irrelevant where she has made it clear that the conduct complained of is unwelcome.

We have seen earlier in the chapter that an employer can avoid liability for an act of discrimination committed by an employee in the course of his/her employment by establishing that all such steps as are reasonably practicable have been taken to prevent the conduct in question. The decision of the EAT in *Balgobin and Francis* v. *London Borough of Tower Hamlets* [1987] IRLR 401 suggests that the standard expected of an employer in order to successfully raise the defence is not particularly onerous.

In this case, Mrs Balgobin and Mrs Francis were employed as cleaners in the canteen area of a hostel run by Tower Hamlets. The women complained that between June and October 1985 they had been subjected to sexual harassment by a male cook. Until they complained, management was unaware of the harassment. An inquiry was held in October 1985 into the complaint, but the management was unable to determine the truth of the matter. Thereafter, the two women and the cook continued to work together.

While accepting that sexual harassment had occurred, the majority of the EAT rejected the women's arguments that the employer had produced no evidence that it had taken such steps as were reasonably practicable to prevent the male cook's behaviour. Management did not know what was going on; was running the hostel with proper and adequate supervision of staff; had made known its policy of equal opportunities and, in the majority's view, it was 'very difficult to see what steps in practical terms the employers could reasonably have taken to prevent that which occurred from occurring'. This rather complacent view was reached even though there had been no evidence that the employees had received any training or guidance in the operation of the equal opportunity policy or informed that sexual harassment was unlawful.

Furthermore, the EAT rejected the women's second argument that the employers had discriminated against them by requiring them to continue working with the male cook after the inquiry had been held. The women had not been treated less favourably, for example, than a male to whom homosexual advances had been made.

The EC Council of Labour and Social Ministers adopted a resolution relating to sexual harassment at work (Resolution No. 6015/90). In November 1991, as part of its third action programme on equal opportunities, the European Commission adopted a Recommendation and Code of Practice on the protection of the dignity of women and men at work. The Recommendation asks Member States to

take action to promote awareness that conduct of a sexual nature, or other conduct based on sex affecting the dignity of women and men at work, including conduct of superiors and colleagues, is unacceptable if:

(a) such conduct is unwanted unreasonable and offensive to the recipient;
(b) a person's rejection of, or submission to, such conduct on the part of employer or workers (including superiors or colleagues) is used explicitly or implicitly as a basis for a decision which affects that person's access to vocational training, access to employment, continued employment, promotion, salary or any other employment decisions;
and/or
(c) such conduct creates an intimidating, hostile or humiliating work environment for the recipient.

and that such conduct may, in certain circumstances, be contrary to the principle of equal treatment within the meaning of [the Equal Treatment] Directive 76/207/EEC.

A Commission Recommendation cannot of itself give rise to legal right or liabilities. However, in *Grimaldi v. Fonds des Maladies Professionelles* [1990] IRLR 400, the ECJ ruled that national courts must take such non-binding measures into account, in particular to clarify the interpretation of other provisions of national and Community law. Consequently, an employee who brings a claim of sex discrimination as a result of being the victim of sexual harassment will be able to refer to the Recommendation and Code of Practice in support of her case.

The Code recommends that senior management should develop and communicate a policy statement which should:

- expressly state that sexual harassment will not be permitted or condoned;
- set out a positive duty on managers and supervisors to implement the policy and to take corrective action to ensure compliance with it;
- explain the procedure which should be followed by employees subjected to sexual harassment at work in order to obtain assistance;
- contain an undertaking that the allegation will be dealt with seriously, expeditiously and confidentially, and that complainants will be protected against victimisation;
- specify that disciplinary measures will be taken against employees guilty of sexual harassment.[8]

It is clear from the decision in *Wadman v. Carpenter Farrer Partnership* [1993] IRLR 374 that employment tribunals will expect to see evidence of implementation of the

Code of Practice on sexual harassment. Any oversight on the part of the employer will not be considered favourably.

The ET will also use the Code of Practice as an aid to establishing whether the conduct to which the complainant was subjected, amounted to sexual harassment. For example, in *Insitu Cleaning Co. Ltd* v. *Heads* [1995] IRLR 4 the applicant complained about her manager greeting her with the remark 'Hiya big tits'. The EAT held that the remark was of a sexual nature and that the term 'unwanted conduct' in the Code of Practice referred as much to a single act. As a result an applicant did not have to wait until they were subjected to a second or third remark before bringing a complaint.

Racial Harassment

This can take the form of violence or ostracism and will amount to direct discrimination. Racial insults will also generally amount to racial harassment. However, the complainant may experience greater difficulty in establishing a claim if the insulting remarks are not addressed directly to him/her but are overheard. This is illustrated by the decision in *De Souza* v. *Automobile Association* [1986] IRLR 103, where the Court of Appeal took the view that merely overhearing a racial insult would not amount to less favourable treatment unless the person making the statement 'intended the complainant to either hear what he said or knew or ought reasonably to have anticipated that the person he was talking to would pass the insult on or that employee would become aware of it in some way'.

The case of *Burton* v. *De Vere Hotels* [1996] IRLR 596 raised the important issue of whether an employer can be held liable for the harassment of its employees by third parties who are not in its employment. Miss Burton and Miss Rhule, who were of Afro-Caribbean origin, were employed by De Vere Hotels as casual waitresses. On the night in question they were waiting on 400 guests, all men, and the guest speaker was Bernard Manning. While clearing the tables the women heard Mr Manning make sexually explicit and racially abusive jokes and comments, some aimed directly at them. After Mr Manning's act was over, the guests started to make sexually and racially offensive remarks to both women. The next day the hotel manager apologised to the women for what had happened. The women alleged that their employer had discriminated against them on racial grounds by subjecting them to the detriment of racial abuse and harassment contrary to the Race Relations Act 1976. Initially the ET found that there was racial harassment but that it was Mr Manning and the guests, not the employer who had subjected the women to this and therefore their claims were dismissed. However, the EAT considered that an employer can be viewed as subjecting an employee to harassment if s/he causes or permits the harassment to occur in circumstances in which s/he can control whether it happens or not. The key question was whether the event was something which was sufficiently under the control of the employer that s/he could, by the application of good employment practice, have prevented the harassment or reduced the extent of it. If s/he could, then the employer had subjected the employee to harassment. Applying this to Miss Burton's case, it was held that the employer could have prevented or reduced the extent of the harassment but had failed to do so.

The decision in *Burton* v. *De Vere Hotels* has now been overruled by *MacDonald* v. *Advocate-General for Scotland*; *Pearce* v. *Governing Body of Mayfield Secondary School* [2003] IRLR 512 in which the HL held that the failure to protect employees from sexual or racial abuse by third parties was not discrimination as it was not related to the sex or race of the employees.

One major problem in establishing harassment was the fact that it had to fall within the direct discrimination provisions which were not designed to cover acts of harassment. However, as a result of the Equal Treatment Amendment Directive (Dir. 2002/73) and the Race Discrimination Directive (Dir. 2003/43), new regulations will introduce explicit provisions to cover sexual and racial harassment.

Other statutes afford some protection from harassment, both in the workplace and in public. Section 4A of the Public Order Act 1986 provides for the offence of intentional harassment involving the use of threatening, abusive or insulting words or behaviour or disorderly behaviour or displaying any writing, sign or other visible representation which is threatening, abusive or insulting, thereby causing another person harassment, alarm or distress. This offence may be committed in a public or private place except a dwelling.

The Protection from Harassment Act 1997 creates both a criminal offence and a statutory tort for acts of harassment. Harassment is prohibited if it is a course of conduct which the perpetrator knows, or ought to know, amounts to harassment of another. A breach of the criminal provision may lead to a fine or imprisonment. However, a civil remedy of an injunction and damages is also available.

Finally, the Crime and Disorder Act 1997 creates an offence of racially aggravated assault as well as restrict anti-social behaviour which causes harassment and distress to two or more persons who are not of the same household. Application will be restricted to public places.

Pregnancy-related Dismissals

A dismissal on the grounds of pregnancy or a connected reason is automatically unfair and the question of how the employer would have treated anyone else is irrelevant (ERA 1996, and see Chapter 14). A woman can still challenge a pregnancy dismissal by way of the sex discrimination legislation. An initial difficulty here is the fact that SDA s. 5 (3) requires that when comparing how a man would have been treated the comparison must be such that 'the relevant circumstances in the one case are the same or not materially different'. This provision persuaded the majority of the EAT in *Turley* v. *Allders Department Stores Ltd* [1980] IRLR 4 to hold that a pregnancy-related dismissal was not unlawful discrimination because there is no masculine counterpart to pregnancy. More recently, this approach has been rejected and a woman could succeed if she could show that a man in comparable circumstances (such as one who was going to be absent on grounds of sickness) would have been treated better than she was (*Hayes* v. *Malleable Working Men's Club* [1985] IRLR 367).

While the recognition of pregnancy-related dismissals as direct discrimination is to be welcomed, the reasoning used to gain that protection – comparing the treatment of a healthy pregnant woman with a sick man – is unfortunate to say the least.

This issue resurfaced in *Webb* v. *EMO Air Cargo Ltd* [1991] IRLR 124. Ms Webb was employed to replace another employee, Ms Stewart, during the latter's pregnancy. She was informed of this at interview. Two weeks after starting work, Ms Webb discovered that she too was pregnant. She informed the company and was dismissed. Her complaint of sex discrimination was rejected by both the ET and EAT. Applying the test in *Hayes*, it was held that the company had not treated Ms Webb less favourably than it would have treated a man who had been recruited for the same purpose, but who had then informed the company that he would need a comparable period of leave.

A better approach to the problem was adopted by the ECJ in *Dekker* v. *Stichting Vormingscentrum voor Jong Volvassen (VJW-Centrum) Plus* [1991] IRLR 27, where the court held that unfavourable treatment on grounds of pregnancy is direct discrimination on grounds of gender. The court reasoned that pregnancy is a condition unique to women, so that where it can be shown that unfavourable treatment is on the grounds of pregnancy, that treatment is, by definition, on grounds of gender. A reason which applies 'exclusively to one sex' is in effect inherently discriminatory. Since discrimination on grounds of pregnancy is discrimination on grounds of gender per se, there is no need to compare the treatment of a pregnant woman with that of a hypothetical man.

The import of this decision would appear to be as follows. An employer who refuses to hire (or promote) a woman who is otherwise suitable because she is pregnant or for a reason based on her pregnancy is directly discriminating. Because the discrimination is directly on grounds of gender, it is not capable of being justified. In the court's view, a decision not to hire a pregnant woman because of the financial consequences of her maternity absence should be regarded as being made principally for the reason that the woman is pregnant. That is a reason which can apply to only one gender. Such an act of discrimination cannot be justified on the grounds of the financial consequences for the employer of the woman taking maternity leave. (Since Mrs Dekker was already pregnant when she applied for the job, VJV believed that its insurers would not reimburse the payments that it would have to make to her when she was on maternity leave. If this were the case, VJV would not have been able to afford to employ anybody to provide maternity cover and would be understaffed as a result.)

The court also held that the absence of male candidates for the job was immaterial. According to the ECJ, if the reason for the employer's decision 'resides in the fact that the person concerned is pregnant, the decision is directly related to the applicant's sex. Viewed in this way it is of no importance ... that there were no male applicants.'

It should follow that, to the extent that supremacy must be accorded to the European Court's decision, the comparative approach to pregnancy discrimination that like must be compared with like, followed by the EAT in *Webb*, is no longer good law and should not be followed by the ETs. This is because it is a fundamental principle of EU law that national courts are bound to interpret national law in the light of the aim of an EU Directive as interpreted by the ECJ.[9]

Amazingly, this was not the approach taken when the *Webb* case reached the Court of Appeal [1992] IRLR 116. The court held that dismissal of a pregnant woman for a reason arising out of, or related to, her pregnancy can in law be, but is not necessarily, direct discrimination. Direct discrimination would only occur if the ET were satisfied that a man with a comparable condition would not have been treated in the same way. Dekker's case was distinguished on the facts, an unconvincing attempt being made to limit the effects of *Dekker* to a failure to offer a job to someone who was the best applicant and most able to do the job.

The Court of Appeal instead relied on the decision of the ECJ in another case – *Handels-og Kontorfunktionaerernes Forbund i Danmark (acting for Hertz)* v. *Dansk Arbejdsgiverforening* [1991] IRLR 31 – in which the ECJ held that the dismissal of a woman on grounds of absence due to an illness which arose from pregnancy was not necessarily discrimination on grounds of gender.

After the expiry of her statutory entitlement of 24 weeks' maternity leave from the date of birth, Mrs Hertz was off work for 100 days within a year due to illness arising out of her pregnancy and confinement. This resulted in her dismissal on the grounds of her absence. It was claimed that this offended the equal treatment principle. The ECJ was of the view that, while it was up to Member States to provide a period of maternity leave which allowed women workers to recover from the normal after-effects of pregnancy and childbirth, in regard to an illness occurring after the end of maternity leave there was no reason to distinguish an illness caused by pregnancy or childbirth from any other illness, since though certain illnesses only affect one gender, men and women are equally affected by illness overall. If a woman worker is dismissed because of a pregnancy-related illness but a sick man would have been treated in the same way, there is no breach of the principle of equal treatment.

But *Hertz* was an unusual case with facts which bear little resemblance to *Webb*. Moreover, as in the *Dekker* case, the ECJ held that a woman is protected by the principle of equal treatment from dismissal because of her absence during pregnancy and any maternity leave to which she has a right under national law.

Ms Webb pursued an appeal to the House of Lords, where it was decided that the SDA 1975 does not, on the face of it, make it unlawful for an employer to dismiss a woman because she is pregnant and needs time off work, if a male employee who needed time off work would also be dismissed. The Lords accepted, however, that the EU Equal Treatment Directive may deem such a dismissal to be viewed as direct discrimination, and has requested the ECJ for a ruling on the question.

The definitive decision was finally reached in *Webb* v. *EMO Air Cargo Limited* (No. 2) HL [1995] IRLR 645; the decision of the ECJ being referred back to the House of Lords. The ECJ declared that not only was it contrary to Directive 76/207 to dismiss a woman on grounds of pregnancy, but also that there was no question of comparing the situation of a woman who found herself incapable, by reason of pregnancy, of performing the task for which she was recruited with that of a man similarly incapable for medical or other reasons. However, the ECJ distinguished between pregnant women employed for an indefinite period, who were afforded protection and those on limited-term contracts. The House of Lords confirmed that dismissing the employee in this case because she was pregnant amounted to discrimination, but distinguished the indefinite term from employment for a fixed period. It found that dismissal in the latter circumstances would not be discriminatory, as it would be likely to be perceived as unfair to employers and as tending to bring the law on sex discrimination into disrepute. However, the case of *Caruana* v. *Manchester Airport plc* [1996] IRLR 378 suggests that the principle applies equally to fixed-term contracts.

The ECJ has confirmed that protection of the pregnant woman under article 5 of the Equal Treatment Directive and article 10 of the Pregnant Workers Directive is not restricted to those employed for an indefinite period, but extends to those employed for a fixed term, even though because of her pregnancy, she may be unable to work for a substantial part of the term of her contract – *Tele Danmark A/S* v. *Handels-Og Kontorfunkiunaerernes Forbund; Danmark acting on behalf of Brandt-Nielsen* [2002] IRLR 853. Failure to renew a fixed-term contract on grounds related to pregnancy, constitutes direct discrimination contrary to arts. 2 (3) and 3 (1) of Directive 76/207 – *Jimenez Melgar* v. *Ayuntamiento de los Barrios* [2001] IRLR 848.[10]

Any attempt to avoid the Webb principle by arguing that dismissal is for some reason other than pregnancy will be closely scrutinised. For example, in *O'Neill* v. *Governors of St Thomas Moore RCVA Upper School and Bedfordshire County Council* [1996] IRLR 372 an unmarried teacher became pregnant by a Roman Catholic priest. She was dismissed according to her employer, on grounds of the moral and social implications of her pregnancy. The EAT concluded that the only question was whether the pregnancy was the grounds for the dismissal. If the answer was in the affirmative, discrimination was proven. It did not have to be the sole reason.

Further confirmation that protection for the pregnant woman ceases at the end of the maternity leave period can be found in the case of *British Telecommunications plc v. Roberts and Longstaffe* [1996] IRLR 601 in which the EAT held that once a woman returns to work after maternity leave, the special protection afforded finishes and her treatment is to be assessed by a comparison in which the way a man would have been treated in the same circumstances. However, whilst a woman is pregnant, comparison with a man is inappropriate – see *Iske* v. *P&O European Ferries (Dover) Ltd* [1997] IRLR 401.

The decision in *Caledonia Bureau Investment and Property* v. *Caffrey* [1998] IRLR 110 highlights a potential anomaly between the unfair dismissal and the sex discrimination provisions. In *Caffrey* the EAT held that it was automatically unfair to dismiss a woman for a reason connected with with her pregnancy, even though the maternity leave period had expired. Whilst the EAT also held that it could also amount to sex discrimination as long as any pregnancy-related illness had arisen during the maternity leave period.

However, this ruling ignores the ECJ ruling in *Handels-og Kontorfunktionaernes Forbund: Denmark (acting on behalf of Larson)* v. *Danish Handel and Service (acting on behalf of Fotex Supermarket A/S)* [1997] IRLR 643 which confirmed that it is not automatically sex discrimination to dismiss a woman after her maternity leave has ended because of absence due to pregnancy-related illness, even where the illness first occurred during the pregnancy.

These issues have less significance as a result of the implementation of the Pregnant Workers Directive in the Employment Rights Act 1996, which gives all employees, irrespective of their length of service, a right not to be dismissed on the grounds of pregnancy or childbirth.

Stereotyping[11]
Those who discriminate frequently act on the basis of racial or gender stereotypes. Where the decision is based on such generalised assumptions it may be attacked as unlawful discrimination. For example:

- a refusal to employ women with children because they make unreliable employees (*Hurley* v. *Mustoe* [1981] IRLR 208);
- the dismissal of a woman based on the assumption that husbands are breadwinners (*Coleman* v. *Skyrail Oceanic Ltd* [1981] IRLR 398);
- refusal to second a woman on a training course in the London area, where her husband was employed, because it was assumed that she would remain in London when her course finished and not return to her work in Wales (*Horsey* v. *Dyfed CC* [1982] IRLR 395),
- a refusal to deploy a West Indian prisoner on kitchen work because he showed 'the anti-authoritarian arrogance that seems to be common in most coloured inmates' (*Alexander* v. *Home Office* [1988] IRLR 190).

Rules on Dress
The courts and tribunals allow employers a wide measure of discretion in controlling the image of their establishments, including the appearance of their staff, especially

when those staff come into contact with the public. For example, in *Schmidt* v. *Austicks Bookshops Ltd* [1977] IRLR 360, a rule prohibiting women from wearing trousers at work was not discriminatory where the employers treated both male and female staff equally, with rules governing the appearance of both genders.

This approach was confirmed in *Burrett* v. *West Birmingham Health Authority* [1994] IRLR 7 in which a female nurse, who objected to wearing a cap, was held not to have been treated less favourably on grounds of sex than male nurses who were not required to wear a cap. The requirements to wear a uniform applied equally to male and female nurses. There was therefore no discrimination even though the form of uniform differed for men and women.

Some inroads were made into the decision in *Schmidt* in *McConomy* v. *Croft Inns Limited* [1992] IRLR 562 in which it was held that a public house had unlawfully discriminated on grounds of sex when the publican adopted an admissions policy which prohibited men wearing earrings from entering whilst there was no objection to women. Whilst it was recognised that the ordinary rules of decency accepted in the community might permit or require different dress regulations between men and women, this could not be extended to the wearing of personal jewellery or other items of personal adornment.

The courts had the opportunity but failed to take the initiative in the employment field in *Smith* v. *Safeway plc* [1996] IRLR 456. In this case, Safeway dismissed a male employee because of the length of his hair, which was unconventionally long. However, a female employee with long hair could continue in employment in a similar post. The Court of Appeal ruled that different dress codes for men and women are to be judged on what is 'conventional'. As long as the employer is even handed, then such a policy is not discriminatory, even if its content is different for men and women. It could, of course, be argued that in this day and age, long hair on the part of a man should not be regarded as unconventional. Furthermore, this approach continues to be contrary to the equal treatment directive which upholds the principle that there should be no discrimination whatsoever on grounds of sex.

The Employment Act 1989 provides a limited and specific exception in relation to Sikhs and the wearing of turbans. Section 12 provides that a Sikh working on a building site is exempt from the normal statutory requirement to wear a safety helmet. Employers in the construction industry, therefore, will commit an act of discrimination if they impose such a condition or requirement on Sikhs. Only Sikhs are given this exemption.

Indirect Discrimination

Direct discrimination is aimed at overt and intentional acts of prejudice. However, many forms of discrimination operate in a more subtle and indirect manner. An employer may formulate rules or requirement which, although applying to both genders and all racial groups, actually operate to the disadvantage of one gender or one group. In other words, indirect discrimination consists of acts or practices which are fair in form but unequal in impact: institutional racism or sexism.

Whether unlawful indirect discrimination has taken place depends on the answers to the following four questions:

(i) Has a requirement or condition been applied equally to both genders, marrieds and unmarrieds, or all racial groups? If yes ...

(ii) Is the requirement or condition one with which a considerably smaller number of women (or men), marrieds or persons of a particular racial group can comply compared to those of the opposite gender, unmarrieds or persons not of that racial group? If yes ...

(iii) Has the requirement or condition operated to the detriment of the complainant because s/he could not comply with it? If yes ...

(iv) Can the employer show the requirement or condition to be justifiable irrespective of the gender, marital status or race of the person in question?

However, the Sex Discrimination (Indirect Discrimination and Burden of Proof) Regulations 2001, SI 2001/2660 have introduced a new definition of indirect discrimination into the SDA 1975. The Race Relations Act 1976 (Amendment) Regulations 2003 also amend the indirect discrimination provisions of RRA 1976. The new provisions are as follows:

1. Has a provision, criterion or practice being applied equally regardless of sex, race, religion, belief or sexual orientation?
2. Would it be to the detriment of a considerably larger proportion of women, race, etc?
3. Is the employer able to justify it irrespective of sex, race etc?
4. Is it to the detriment of the complainant?

Point 1 provides greater flexibility and reflects the direction in which the ETs were proceeding in such cases as *Falkirk Council v. Whyte* [1997] IRLR 560. At least until there is case law to clarify the position, it is expected that the other provisions will be applied in a similar way to the existing provisions, as there is considerable overlap; although there may be less dependence on statistical evidence. A further amendment will be made to the provisions on the implementation of the Equal Treatment Amendment Directive (Dir. 2002/73). In considering a possible act of indirect discrimination, the ET should focus on the discriminatory effect of the particular condition and determine whether the employer has objectively justified it – *Sibley v. The Girls' Public Day School Trust & Norwich High School for Girls* (2003) (IRLB 720 p. 7). It is not for the Tribunal to consider wider policies by which that condition may be informed – *Whiffen v. Milham Ford Girls' School* [2001] IRLR 468.

Once a prima facie case has been made out by the complainant the burden of proof shifts to the employer to show that requirement or condition was justifiable irrespective of the gender, marital status or race of the person to whom it applies. The *intention* of the employer is irrelevant in establishing liability, though no compensation will be payable if the industrial tribunal is satisfied that the employer did not intend to discriminate.

Under the Sex Discrimination (Indirect Discrimination and Burden of Proof) Regulations 2001, the complainant need only establish facts from which the Tribunal can conclude that the respondent has committed an act of discrimination. The burden of proof then moves to the respondent to show that he did not commit such an act. In *Barton v. Investec Henderson Crosthwaite Securities Ltd* [2003] IRLR 332 the EAT concluded that the respondent must show that sex, race etc. did not form part of any of the reasons for the discriminatory treatment. If the respondent does not discharge the burden of proof, the ET must find that there has been unlawful discrimination. This goes further than the decision in *King*, which gave the Tribunal some flexibility before inferring that discrimination had taken place.

An interesting application of the concept of indirect discrimination can be seen in *Greater Manchester Police Authority* v. *Lea* [1990] IRLR 372. In this case, the EAT confirmed an ET ruling that, by operating a recruitment policy which generally excluded those in receipt of an occupational pension, the police authority was guilty of indirect discrimination against a male applicant. The EAT was of the view that the scheme was indirectly discriminatory on grounds of sex since, looking at the 'appropriate pool for comparison' (the economically active population of Great Britain), more men (4.7 per cent) than women (0.6 per cent) were in receipt of such a pension, and the policy was not objectively justifiable.

Requirement or Condition

Although some of the case law on the meaning of these words suggests a liberal interpretation, other decisions are highly restrictive.

Some examples of requirement or condition:

- a redundancy procedure with the trade union which provided for part-time workers to be dismissed first, before applying a 'last in, first out' criteria to full-timers (*Clarke* v. *Eley (IMI) Kynoch Ltd* [1982] IRLR 482 – indirect sex discrimination);
- an age bar operated by the civil service which limited candidates for the post of executive officer to those in the 17½ to 28 age range (*Price* v. *Civil Service Commission* [1977] IRLR 291 – indirect sex discrimination);
- a policy that candidates for a job should not have young or dependent children (*Hurley* v. *Mustoe* [1981] IRLR 208 – indirect marital discrimination);
- a refusal to hire persons living in Liverpool 8 where 50 per cent of the population were black (*Hussein* v. *Saints Complete House Furnishers Ltd* [1979] IRLR 337 – indirect racial discrimination);
- to require a person to work full-time – *Briggs* v. *North Eastern Educational and Library Board* [1990] IRLR 181.

This list of examples provides some guidance as to the range of practices which have been held to establish a prima facie indirect discrimination. But, on occasions, the employer may express a 'preference' which may or may not amount to an outright requirement and, in *Perera* v. *Civil Service Commission* [1983] IRLR 166, the Court of Appeal held that this could not amount to indirect discrimination.

In this case, a barrister from Sri Lanka was rejected for a legal post in the civil service. The selection committee assessed all applicants according to a number of criteria: age, practical experience in England, ability to communicate in English and so on. Perera argued that these were 'requirements or conditions', but the court did not agree. None of them were absolute 'musts', without which an applicant could not succeed. The court reasoned that, for example, a applicant whose ability to communicate in English was poor might nevertheless be successful if s/he scored highly on the other factors. The only relevant condition was that the applicant was a barrister or solicitor and this Perera fulfilled.

Perera was applied in *Meer* v. *London Borough of Tower Hamlets* [1988] 399. Mr Meer, who is of Indian origin and a solicitor with local government experience, applied for the job of head of the legal department with Tower Hamlets. Of 23 applicants, 12 were selected for 'long-listing', Mr Meer not being one of them.

The criteria for long-listing was: age, date of admission as a solicitor, present post, current salary, local government experience, London government experience, Inner London government experience, senior management experience, length in present post, and Tower Hamlets' experience. All four of the applicants who had Tower Hamlets' experience were placed on the long-list. Mr Meer contended that this was a requirement or condition which indirectly discriminated against those of Indian origin contrary to s. 1 (1) (b) and s. 4 (1) (a) of the RRA. The CA held that the lower courts were correct in concluding that the criterion relating to Tower Hamlets' experience was not a 'must' and was not therefore a 'requirement or condition' within the meaning of s. 1 (1) (b).

Some doubt has been cast over the approach taken in *Perera* and *Meer* by the decision in *Falkirk Council* v. *Whyte* [1997] IRLR 560. In this case, a selection criterion of managerial training and supervisory experience, which was stated as being a 'desirable' qualification rather than an absolute bar to obtaining the post, was held to be a requirement or condition as it was clear that the qualification operated as the decisive factor in the selection process. Lord Johnstone suggested that it was open to the ET to give a liberal interpretation to what the Sex Discrimination Act means by 'requirement or condition'. If it is shown that qualifying for a particular factor is more difficult for women than men in the workplace, this can be regarded as a requirement or condition in terms of the legislation in relation to applications for a post, particularly when the relevant factor turns out to be decisive.

The uncertainties surrounding the phrase 'requirement or condition' are vividly highlighted by comparing the conflicting approaches adopted in the next three cases.

In *Home Office* v. *Holmes* [1984] IRLR 299, a civil servant who asked to return to work on a part-time basis following the birth of her second child was told that there were no part-time posts available. The EAT held that the obligation to work full-time was a 'requirement' within the meaning of s. 1 (1) (b) of the SDA and indirectly discriminated against women. The EAT also expressed the view that words like 'requirement' and 'condition' are plain, clear words of wide import and there was no basis for giving the words a restrictive interpretation in the light of public policy.

This broad-brush approach, however, was not adopted by the EAT in *Clymo* v. *Wandsworth London Borough Council* [1989] IRLR 241. After having a baby, Ms Clymo, a branch librarian, wanted to job-share with her husband, a senior assistant librarian. Both were employed by Wandsworth but at different libraries. The council had a policy of allowing job-sharing in the library service for lower-level jobs. Wandsworth refused to allow Ms Clymo to job-share with her husband.

The EAT, upholding the decision of the IT, concluded that the employer had not applied a requirement or condition of full-time working; to work 'full-time' was the nature of the job. The EAT also expressed the view that it was not for the tribunal to decide whether a particular job was one which by its nature required full-time work. The decision was one for 'an employer, acting reasonably, to decide – a managerial decision – what is required for the purposes of running his business or his establishment'.

Fortunately, the *Clymo* reasoning was not followed by the Northern Ireland Court of Appeal in *Briggs* v. *North Eastern Education and Library Board* [1990] IRLR 181. Mrs Briggs, a schoolteacher, was required to undertake extra-curricular teaching duties as part of her contract in a promoted post. Following the adoption of a baby daughter, she requested that she be relieved of her after-school obligations. Her request was granted but only on the basis that she would take a demotion.

Mrs Briggs alleged indirect sex and/or marital discrimination on the basis that the requirement of after-school attendance had a significant adverse impact on women and married people. It was held that the after-school attendance stipulation was a 'requirement' or 'condition'.

Preferring the approach adopted in *Holmes* to that in *Clymo*, the court was of the view that the fact that the nature of the job requires full-time attendance does not prevent there being a 'requirement'. (Having managed to overcome this hurdle, Mrs Briggs lost her case on the basis that the after-hours requirement was justified.)

Can a Considerably Smaller Proportion of the Protected Group Comply with the Requirement or Condition?
The courts and tribunals have offered no clear guidance on what proportion constitutes 'considerably smaller'. In the United States many courts have adopted the 'four-fifths rule' – that is, adverse impact is established if there is a 20 per cent difference between the groups under comparison. Indeed, the Commission for Racial Equality has proposed that the UK should adopt the four-fifths rule.

It would appear that the phrase 'considerably smaller proportion' covers the situation where no members of a particular group can comply with the condition or requirement (*Greencroft Social Club and Institute v. Mullen* [1985] ICR 796).

Potential indirect discrimination also falls within s. 1 (1) (b). In *Meade-Hill and NUCPS v. British Council* [1995] IRLR 478 a woman challenged a mobility clause in her contract. The Court of Appeal held that as a greater proportion of women than men were secondary earners, and therefore less able to move, the clause amounted to indirect discrimination, even though it had yet to be enforced.

The complainant must produce evidence – usually in statistical form – to support adverse impact. On the other hand, the EAT has suggested that it is not good policy to require elaborate statistical evidence to be produced.[12]

A recurring problem in establishing indirect discrimination lies in respect of the selection of the pool for comparison. In *Pearse v. City of Bradford Metropolitan Council* [1988] IRLR 379, Ms Pearse, a part-time lecturer, was unable to apply for a full-time post at Ilkley College, where she worked, because the only persons eligible to apply were full-time employees of the local authority. She submitted statistics showing that only 21.8 per cent of the female academic staff employed in the college were employed full-time compared with 46.7 per cent of male academic staff who could comply with the full-time working requirement. The EAT concluded that Ms Pearse had not selected the correct group for comparison. The correct pool for comparison would have been those with the appropriate qualifications for the post, rather than those eligible. Ms Pearse's statistics related to the latter and therefore she failed in her claim.

In *University of Manchester v. Jones* [1993] ICR 474 the Court of Appeal held that the appropriate pool for comparison is all those with the required qualifications for the post, not including the requirement complained of. It further held that the pool cannot be manipulated to fit the applicant's own situation. In this particular case, therefore, the pool could not be restricted to mature graduates, of which the applicant was one, but should include all graduates, since the potential job applicants were all graduates.

Consistency of approach in relation to appropriate pools of comparison is hindered by the fact that in *Kidd v. DRG (UK) Ltd* [1985] IRLR 190 it was held that the choice of pool was an issue of fact within the discretion of the tribunal, which would not normally be open to challenge by appeal unless it was a perverse choice.

A more enlightened approach to the consideration of pools for comparison and statistical evidence can be seen in the decision of the EAT in *London Underground Limited* v. *Edwards (No. 2)* [1997] IRLR 157. Mrs Edwards was a single parent with a young child. She was employed as a train operator. Her rostering arrangements fitted in with her childcare arrangements. However, London Underground announced a new flexible shift system, which would have meant Mrs Edwards having to work either early or late shifts. If she wished to change shifts, she would have had to work a longer shift for the same money. Mrs Edwards was not prepared to work the new system and when negotiations broke down, she resigned and claimed unlawful sex discrimination. The original appeal to the EAT [1995] IRLR 355 allowed the appeal by the employer on the grounds that a pool which consisted of only those train operators who were single parents, was the wrong pool for comparison. The correct pool was that of all train operators to whom the new rostering arrangements applied. The case was referred back to an employment tribunal, who found that 100 per cent of the 2,023 male train operators could comply with the new rostering conditions, whereas 20 of the 21 female train operators could comply, Mrs Edwards being the sole female train operator who could not comply. The ET concluded that the proportion of female train operators who could comply with the new rostering arrangements was considerably smaller than the proportion of male train operators, having regard to the numbers of men relevant to the numbers of women carrying out the job and to its common knowledge about the proportionately large number of women than men in employment with primary childcare responsibilities. The decision of the ET was confirmed by the EAT who held that the tribunal is entitled to consider whether the number of women is so small as to be statistically unreliable and to have regard to the possibility that where there is a very small percentage of women as against the number of men, some kind of generalised assumption may exist that the particular type of work concerned is 'men's' and not 'women's work'.

It is significant that the EAT chose not to adopt a conventional approach in this case by holding that a disproportionate impact had not been shown. Instead, in selecting the purposive approach they were able to recommend adoption of a wider perspective in assessing the disproportionate impact of the condition by looking at the picture as it was at the date of the complaint and as it might be had the small pool of women been larger and statistically significant.

On appeal [1998] IRLR 364, the CA held that, whilst 95 per cent of female train operators compared to 100 per cent of male train operators could comply with the requirement to work early or late shifts, it was still found to have a disproportionate effect on women as when the actual numbers were considered no men were affected.

Moreover, the phrase 'can comply' has been given a generally wide interpretation. In *Mandla* v. *Lee* [1983] IRLR 209, it was stated that it should be read as reading 'can in practice' or 'can consistently with the customs and cultural conditions of the racial group' rather than meaning 'can physically' so as to indicate a theoretical possibility. Similarly, in *Price* v. *The Civil Service Commission* [1977] IRLR 291, the EAT stated: 'It should not be said that a person "can" do something merely because it is theoretically possible for him to do so; it is necessary to see whether he can do so in practice.'

So, in the *Mandla* case it would have been theoretically possible for a Sikh to remove his turban in order meet the school's uniform requirements and, in the *Price* case it was theoretically possible for a woman not to have children in her 20s in order to be able to comply with a civil service entry age maximum of 28 years. But in neither case was it a practical possibility.

Has the Condition or Requirement Operated to the Detriment of the Complainant?

It is insufficient to show that a condition or requirement is indirectly discriminatory; the complainant has to also show that s/he has been disadvantaged by it. The main purpose of this particular hurdle is to prevent hypothetical test cases from swamping the tribunals.

The time to determine whether the complainant has suffered a detriment is the time when the complainant has to comply with the requirement or condition. As we saw earlier, in *Clarke* v. *Eley (IMI) Kynoch Ltd* [1972] IRLR 482 a 'part-timers first' redundancy selection procedure was held to be indirectly sex discriminatory. The employers unsuccessfully tried to argue that the women could have avoided the detriment by becoming full-time workers at some point in the past. This was held to be irrelevant; the women suffered detriment because at the time redundancy selection rule was applied they could not undertake full-time work.

Can the Employer Justify the Condition or Requirement?

The onus of proof is on the employer to show that the requirement or condition which has been applied is justifiable irrespective of the gender, race or marital status of the person to whom it is applied.

In the early days of the legislation, the courts and tribunals adopted a narrow approach to the scope of this defence. In *Steel* v. *Post Office* [1977] IRLR 288, the EAT stated: 'it cannot be justifiable unless its discriminatory effect is justified by the need, not the convenience, of the business or enterprise'.

But the justification test was subsequently weakened and became more generous to the employer. In *Ojutiku and Oburoni* v. *Manpower Services Commission* [1982] IRLR 418, two of the judges in the Court of Appeal took the view that it was not essential for an employer to prove that a requirement was necessary and 'If a person produces reasons for doing something which would be acceptable to right-thinking people as sound and tolerable reasons for so doing, then he has justified his conduct' (Lord Eveleigh). This diluted test was subsequently taken to be the correct one by industrial tribunals.

The third judge in *Ojutiku*, Lord Justice Stephenson, articulated a test based on the approach adopted in *Steel*:

> The party applying the discriminatory condition must prove it to be justifiable in all the circumstances on balancing the discriminatory effect against the discriminator's need for it. But that need is what is reasonably needed by the party who applies the condition.

After a period of uncertainty, the Court of Appeal in *Hampson* v. *Department of Science* [1989] IRLR 69 has now made it clear that it is the test set out by Lord Justice Stephenson which should be adopted in future. As a result, the test for justified indirect discrimination resembles that applied to determine whether unequal pay is justified under EqPA s. 1 (3).

It will be seen that the test for justification requires a balance to be struck between the discriminatory effect of the condition and requirement and the needs of the employer. Therefore, the greater the discriminatory effect, the more compelling the business need must be in order to come within the defence. It also follows there the requirement or condition will not be justifiable if there is a less discriminatory alternative for the employer to achieve the aim.

While the return to the narrower test for justification is to be welcomed,[13] there is still much scope for judicial discretion. As Anne Morris and Susan Nott observe: 'The difficulty is that in balancing the employer's needs against those of a woman who has suffered discriminatory treatment, corporate needs may automatically assume greater weight.'[14]

Victimisation

A separate form of discrimination identified by RRA s. 2 and SDA s. 4 is that of victimisation.

The legislation makes it unlawful to treat anyone less favourably than another by reason that s/he has:

(a) brought proceedings against the discriminator or against any other person under the RRA, SDA or EqPA;
(b) given evidence or information in connection with proceedings brought by any person against the discriminator or any other person under the RRA, SDA or EqPA;
(c) otherwise done anything under or by reference to the RRA, SDA or EqPA in relation to the discriminator or any other person;
(d) alleged that the discriminator or any other person has committed an act which (whether or not the allegation so states) would amount to a contravention of the RRA, SDA or EqPA.

The provisions also cover the situation where the 'discriminator knows the person victimised intends to do any of those things, or suspects the person victimised has done, or intends to do, any of them'.

There is no protection where an allegation which leads to adverse treatment is both false and not made in good faith.

These provisions were enacted in order to protect those employees who took action under the legislation, or who intended to do so, from a hostile response from their employer – a not infrequent reaction. Alice Leonard's survey of successful sex discrimination and equal pay complainants found that:

> Many applicants reported that workplace relationships deteriorated as soon as they filed their case, particularly with employers and managers. Some even reported ill-feeling with fellow workers, and a few were subsequently avoided or insulted in public. For several the situation became untenable: they left their jobs, some before the hearing, and some afterwards. Even worse, a number of applicants actually stated they were dismissed or made redundant because they had brought a case.[15]

Jeanne Gregory's later survey of women who were unsuccessful in their claim paints a similarly depressing picture, with 60 per cent of respondents reporting a deterioration in relations both inside and outside work.[16]

Early developments in the case law cast serious doubts on the effectiveness of the provisions on victimisation. It would appear that it is not sufficient for complainants to show that they were victimised because they brought proceedings against their employers under the discrimination legislation: they have to go further and show that they would not have been victimised for bringing proceedings under a different statute.

In *Cornelius* v. *University College of Swansea* [1987] IRLR 141, the Court of Appeal held that the alleged act of victimisation must relate to the fact the complainant had lodged a complaint under the discrimination legislation. This approach was confirmed in *Aziz* v. *Trinity Street Taxis Ltd* [1988] IRLR 204. In this case a taxi driver was expelled from a co-operative because he was taping conversations to acquire evidence of racial discrimination. This was held by the CA not to amount to victimisation as members of the co-operative would have voted to expel any member who made secret recordings, whatever their purpose, as it amounted to a gross breach of trust.

However, a more enlightened approach which overturns the decision in *Aziz* can be seen in *Nagarajan* v. *London Regional Transport* [1999] IRLR 572. The HL held that the complainant did not have to demonstrate that the respondent had an explicit motive consciously connected to the discrimination legislation. It was sufficient that the respondent's act was 'consciously or subconsciously' influenced by the fact that the complainant had brought proceedings against the employer. The withholding of a reference may amount to victimisation if it is linked to a protected act – see *Chief Constable of West Yorkshire Police* v. *Khan* [2001] IRLR 830.

Finally the EU directives will extend the current legislation to cover post-employment victimisation which was an issue in *Coote* v. *Granada Hospitality Ltd* [1999] IRLR 452 and in this case was found to be outside the Act.

The Scope of Protection against Discrimination

The discrimination legislation makes it unlawful to discriminate at every stage of the employment relationship: advertising vacancies (discussed above), hiring workers, offering promotion, training or fringe benefits, dismissing workers or 'any other detriment'. In order for there to be a detriment, a reasonable worker must take the view that by reason of the acts complained of s/he was disadvantaged in the way s/he would have to work (*De Souza* v. *Automobile Association* [1986] IRLR 103). Some acts are regarded as too insignificant to constitute a 'detriment'. For example, in *Peake* v. *Automotive Products Ltd* [1977] ICR 968, the Court of Appeal took the view that a rule allowing women to leave five minutes early was not a detriment.

Where Gender or Race is a Genuine Occupational Qualification (GOQ)

An employer is permitted to discriminate on grounds of gender in any of the following circumstances (SDA s. 7):

- The essential nature of the job calls for a man on grounds of his physiology; for example, to work as a model. But greater strength and stamina alone are insufficient as qualifications.

- A man is required for authenticity in entertainment. So a film director is not required to interview actresses for the male lead in his film.
- Decency or privacy requires the job to be by a man either because there are men 'in a state of undress at the workplace' (for example, the job of lavatory attendant) or because the job involves physical contact and customers or employees might reasonably object to such contact from a member of the opposite sex. But note that the employer cannot use this exception if there are enough other employees of the appropriate gender to carry out these 'intimate' duties. So in *Etam plc* v. *Rowan* [1989] IRLR 150, a man claimed that he was discriminated against when he was refused employment as a sales assistant in a woman's dress shop. The employer's argument that the job fell within the decency and privacy exception was rejected. The EAT found that, while a sales assistant may be required to work in fitting rooms and to measure women who are uncertain of their size, it would have been possible to ensure that those aspects of the job could have been done by one of the 16 existing female employees without undue inconvenience.[17]
- The job requires workers to live in, there are no separate sleeping and sanitary facilities and it is unreasonable to expect the employer to provide them.
- The job involves working or living in the private home and needs to be held by a man because objection might reasonably be taken to allowing a woman either the degree of personal or physical contact with a person living in the home or the knowledge of the intimate details of such a person's life.[18]
- The job is at a single-sex establishment where persons require supervision or special care and it is reasonable to reserve the job for a person of the same gender – for example, a prison officer.
- The job-holder provides individuals with 'personal services' promoting their welfare, education or similar needs, and those services can 'most effectively' be provided by a man – for instance, a social worker or probation officer.
- The job needs to be held by a man because it is likely to involve work abroad in a country whose laws and customs are such that the job can only be done by a man – for example, work in the Middle East.
- The job is one of two which are held by a married couple – such as a public house manager.

Whether a genuine occupational qualification is a legitimate defence is to be judged at a time when the employer already has female employees. In *Lasertop Limited* v. *Webster* [1997] IRLR 498, Mr Webster replied to a newspaper advertisement for a sales/trainee manager post in a women-only health club. He was told over the telephone that the jobs were for women only. Whether the genuine occupational qualification could be upheld as a defence can only be judged at the time when the alleged act of discrimination took place. In these circumstances, the employer must have already had sufficient female employees at that time who were capable of carrying out the prohibited duties and whom it would be reasonable to employ on those duties without undue inconvenience. At the time Mr Webster was interviewed there were no employees therefore the genuine occupational qualification could operate. The appropriate time for applying a genuine occupational qualification will also be applicable in race discrimination cases.

An employer is allowed to discriminate on the grounds of race in the following circumstances (RRA s. 5):

(i) For reasons of authenticity:

- in entertainment – for example, an actor.
- in art or photography – for example, a model.
- in a bar or restaurant with a particular setting – for example, a waiter or waitress in an Indian restaurant.

(ii) The holder of the job provides persons of that racial group with personal services promoting their welfare, and those services can most effectively be provided by a person of that particular racial group.

In *Lambeth LBC v. CRE* [1990] IRLR 231, the Court of Appeal confirmed that the use of the word 'personal' in the GOQ exception appears to require direct contact between the provider of that service and the client. Therefore, the words are not apt to cover managerial or supervisory posts where there is no face-to-face contact. Consequently, the council's advertisement restricting two managerial posts in its Housing Benefit Department to those of Afro-Caribbean or Asian origin was unlawful.

It is clear that even if only some of the duties of the job fall within the GOQ provisions, it will still be lawful to discriminate in filling the post (RRA s. 5 [3]; SDA s. 7 [3]). In *Tottenham Green Under-fives' Centre v. Marshall (No. 2)* [1991] IRLR 162 EAT, it was held that being of Afro-Caribbean origin was a GOQ for a post as nursery worker because an ability to read and talk in dialect was a 'personal service' even though it was not the most important attribute of the post-holder. As long as the tribunal is satisfied that the duty is not a sham or so trivial it should be disregarded, it is not for the tribunal to evaluate the importance of the duty.

As with the gender GOQs, the above exceptions do not apply if the employer already has employees of that racial group who are capable of being deployed on such duties and it is reasonable to expect such deployment without undue inconvenience.

The Equal Treatment Amendment Directive replaces art. 2 (2) with art. 2 (5) which explicitly preserves the right to have 'genuine occupational qualifications' as long as, where the difference in treatment is based on a characteristic related to sex, such a characteristic constitutes a 'genuine requirement, provided that the objective is legitimate and the requirement proportionate'. This reflects the decision of the ECJ in *Johnston v. The Chief Constable of the Royal Ulster Constabulary* [1986] IRLR 263 and *Sirdar v. The Army Board & Secretary of State for Defence* [2000] IRLR 47. In the former case, sex was held to be a legitimate factor for posts such as prison warders or for policing activities in areas of conflict and in the latter it was a genuine occupational qualification to exclude women from special combat units in the Royal Marines.

Positive Action

As we have seen above, both discrimination statutes impose strict restrictions on the occasions when gender or race is perceived to be a legitimate criterion for appointing somebody to a job. In general terms, positive or reverse discrimination is unlawful in Britain. The limited exceptions to this position do not relate to selection for a post but are restricted to the following:

(a) training boards, employers and trade unions may discriminate in training afforded to members of one gender if during the preceding 12 months there were, in respect of the particular job for which training is being given:

   (i)   no persons of the favoured gender/race doing the job; or
   (ii) the number was comparatively small (SDA ss. 47, 48; RRA ss. 35, 37, 38);

(b) training bodies may favour persons who appear to be in special need of training because of periods for which domestic or family responsibilities have excluded them from regular full-time employment (SDA s. 47 [3]);
(c) trade unions and other similar bodies may reserve seats on elected bodies to members of one gender (SDA s. 49), and organise a discriminatory recruitment campaign, if, during the preceding 12 months, the organisation has no women members or comparatively few (SDA s. 48 [3]).

The ECJ has expressed some doubt about the legitimacy of positive discrimination. In *Kalanke* v. *Freie Hansestadt Bremen* [1995] IRLR 660 it held that a German law which gave equally qualified women preference as against men in selection for public sector jobs in which women were under-represented, were not permissible under the directive since it discriminated against men. The ECJ concluded that national rules which guarantee women 'absolute and unconditional priority' for appointment or promotion go beyond promoting equal opportunities and overstep the limits of the exception to the principle of equal treatment in art. 2 (4) which permits 'positive discrimination' employment measures where women are under-represented in a particular job or grade. However, the decision in *Marschall* v. *Land Nordrhein-Westfallen* [1998] IRLR 39 distinguishes the *Kalanke* decision in holding that national laws giving equally qualified women priority over men for promotion in sectors where they are under-represented may be permissible where there is a 'saving clause' to the effect that women are not to be given priority if reasons specific to the male candidate tilt the balance in his favour. The ECJ felt the mere fact that a male and female candidate were equally qualified did not mean that they have the same chances and therefore preferential treatments 'may counteract the prejudicial effects on female candidates of the attitudes and behaviour found in the recruitment process'. This would not be contrary to art. 2 (1) (4) subject to there being a savings clause, as in this case. The savings clause guarantees the candidates will be subject to an objective assessment which will take account of all criteria specific to the individual candidate and will override the priority accorded to female candidates where one or more of these criteria tilts the balance in favour of the male candidate.

   However the Equal Treatment Directive, the Framework Directive and the Race Directive recognise the legitimacy of positive action in certain circumstances. Member States may therefore adopt measures 'which provide specific advantages in order to make it easier for those under-represented to pursue a vocational activity or to prevent or compensate for disadvantages in professional careers' – art. 141 (4). For example in *Lommers* v. *Minister van Landbouw, Natuurbeheer en Visseij* [2002] IRLR 430, it was used successfully to provide female employees only with access to nursery places for their children while at work. However ring-fencing posts for an under-represented gender, which gives unconditional priority to female candidates will contravene EC law – *EFTA Surveillance Authority* v. *Kingdom of Norway* [2003] IRLR 318; *Abrahamsson* v. *Fogelquist* [2003] IRLR 738.

Changes have already taken place in the UK to allow political parties to select candidates from women-only shortlists – Sex Discrimination (Election Candidates) Act 2002.

Enforcing your Rights

Claim in Time

A complaint must be presented to an ET before the end of the period of three months beginning when the act complained of was committed. The ET has a discretion to hear a complaint which is presented out of time if, 'in all the circumstances of the case, it considers it just and equitable to do so' (SDA s. 76 [5]; RRA s. 68 [5]).

If the act of discrimination continues over a period, the time limit runs from the end of that period (SDA s. 76; RRA s. 68 [7]). For example, in *Calder v. James Finlay Corporation Ltd* [1989] IRLR 55, EAT, a woman was refused a subsidised mortgage on the ground that the benefit was only available to male employees. She left employment eight months after the refusal of the mortgage but lodged her discrimination complaint within three months of the termination of her job. The EAT held that her claim was not out of time. The failure to allow her access to the subsidised scheme was a continuing act of discrimination which lasted up to the day she ended her employment.

Proving Discrimination

Questions of proof are crucial to the outcome of many claims under the legislation. However, the position has been facilitated by the introduction of the Sex Discrimination (Indirect Discrimination and Burden of Proof) Regulations 2001. As a result, once the complainant has established a prima facie case from which the Tribunal can conclude that an act of discrimination has been committed, the Tribunal may uphold the complaint unless the respondent is able to prove that he did not commit the act or it was not tainted by discrimination. (See *Barton v. Investec Henderson Crosthwaite Securities Ltd* [2003] IRLR 332.) However, the decision of the CA in *Nelson v. Carillion Services Ltd* [2003] IRLR 428 suggests that the regulations merely codify the law and therefore the burden of proof in indirect discrimination cases has not changed and remains on the complainant.

The Questionnaire Procedure

The difficulties of proving a discrimination complaint are given some limited recognition by the legislation. Individuals who consider that they may have been the victim of discrimination can issue a questionnaire to the proposed respondent to help them decide whether to bring a claim and, if so, to present their case in the most effective way. The respondent is not compelled to reply to the questions, but if the respondent deliberately and without reasonable excuse does not reply within a reasonable period, or replies evasively, then an ET can draw any reasonable inference from that fact (SDA s. 74; Sex Discrimination (Questions and Replies) Order 1975

(SI 1975 no. 2048); RRA s. 65; Race Relations (Questions and Replies) Order 1977 (SI 1977 no. 842)).

Useful questions might relate to:

- the number of men and women in particular posts and in the workforce as a whole;
- in the case of a failure to recruit or select for promotion, the breakdown by gender of the applicants at the various stages of the appointment process.

Discovery

An ET may, on the application of either side to the proceedings, order disclosure of a document which is relevant to those proceedings. As with the questionnaire procedure, this is a valuable means by which the complainant can develop his/her case.

The House of Lords has set out the following guidance to ETs on how to exercise their powers to order discovery:

- the information necessary to prove discrimination cases is normally in the possession of the respondents, so making discovery essential if the case is to be fairly decided;
- confidentiality of the material is not, of itself, a reason for refusing discovery, but is a factor to be considered. In the case of confidential documents the court or tribunal should examine them to see whether disclosure really is necessary, and if so to consider whether it is possible fairly to preserve confidentiality by covering up the irrelevant parts;
- the test in both the courts and the tribunals is whether discovery is necessary for fairly disposing of the proceedings or for saving costs. (*Science Research Council v. Nasse.*)

Besides grounds of confidentiality, the employer may attempt to resist a request for discovery on the grounds that it is oppressive. For example, it may require the provision of material which can only be made available with difficulty and at great expense; or the effect of the discovery would be to add unreasonably to the length and cost of the hearing.

The value of discovery to the complainant's case can be seen in *West Midlands Passenger Transport Executive v. Singh* [1988] IRLR 186, where the Court of Appeal held that, in attempting to establish direct discrimination, the complainant was entitled to the discovery of statistical evidence which was relevant to his claim. In this particular case, the evidence was a schedule showing the number of white and non-white persons who applied for posts of traffic supervisor with the employers, categorised as to whether or not they had been appointed, covering the two-year period prior to his own unsuccessful application for promotion.

Remedies

On an individual complaint to an ET the following remedies are available if the tribunal considers them 'just and equitable' (RRA s. 56; SDA s. 65).

- declaration
- compensation
- recommendation of action to be taken.

Declaration

This is an 'an order declaring the rights of the complainant and the respondent in relation to the act which the complaint relates' (RRA s. 51 [1] [a]; SDA s. 65 [1] [a]). This order is not enforceable but may have a persuasive influence on the employer.

Compensation

Compensation may be awarded for:

- actual losses, such as expenses and wages
- future losses of wages and benefits
- injury to feelings.

In addition, in cases where the employer has acted maliciously, insultingly or oppressively, the plaintiff can ask for aggravated damages.[19]

Compensation can now be awarded for unintentional, indirect discrimination. There is no longer a statutory maximum compensation limit.[20]

In *Zaiwalla & Co. v. Walia* [2002] IRLR 697 aggravated damages were awarded to reflect the fact that the employer had conducted its defence in a manner deliberately designed to be intimidatory and threatening and to cause maximum distress to the employee. The EAT however felt this was an exceptional case.

Since the removal of the upper compensation limit, awards for injury to feelings have started to increase. In *Chief Constable of West Yorkshire Police v. Vento* [2003] IRLR 102, the CA set out guidelines for ETs in awarding compensation for injury to feelings in discrimination cases; the maximum amount being between £15,000 and £25,000 for serious cases and the lowest award being between £500 and £5,000 – usually where the act is isolated or one-off; and see *Laing v. Essa Ltd* [2004] IRLR 313.

The Law Commission has recommended that exemplary or punitive damages should be available to victims of unlawful discrimination and that employers who are found to be vicariously liable may also be held to be liable to pay punitive damages.[21]

Recommendation

An ET may make a recommendation for specific action, but the scope of the tribunal's action is limited. In particular, there is no general power to order an employer to discontinue a discriminatory practice, other than in relation to the individual complainant.

If the respondent fails to comply with the recommendation, the ET can increase any compensation previously awarded, or, if previously the ET did not award compensation, then it may do so (SDA s. 65 [3] [a]; RRA s. 56 [4]).

The strength of the recommendation as a restraint on an employer's behaviour has been diluted by restrictive interpretations of the scope of the remedy by the judges. In *Noone v. North West Thames Regional Health Authority (No. 2)* [1988] IRLR 530, the Court of Appeal held that an ET had exceeded its powers in recommending that an applicant who had been the victim of a discriminatory selection procedure should be appointed to the next suitable post which became available. It was felt that such positive discrimination would be unfair to other applicants for that post and such action could of itself amount to direct discrimination.[22]

In addition, in *Irvine* v. *Prestcold Ltd* [1981] IRLR 281, the Court of Appeal held that an ET's power to make recommendations for the taking of action does not include the power to make a recommendation that the employer increase the complainant's wages. Money issues were best addressed when the ET decided whether to exercise it power to award compensation.

The Commissions and their Role in Enforcement[23]

The Equal Opportunities Commission (EOC) and the Commission for Racial Equality (CRE) have the following, broadly similar, duties in their respective spheres of operation:

- to work towards the elimination of discrimination;
- to promote equality of opportunity between men and women and racial groups, and to promote good race relations;
- to keep under review the working of the equal opportunities legislation and, as and when necessary, to propose amendments.

Members of the commissions are appointed by the Home Secretary. The commissions are financed from public funds but operate independently of the Crown. Both commissions must publish annual reports.

In order to carry out their duties, the commissions have the power to act in various ways:

- They may assist applicants in the bringing of complaints of discrimination if the case raises a question of principle or it is unreasonable to expect the complainant to deal with the case unaided.
- They may undertake or assist research and education activities and may also issue codes of practice.
- They may conduct formal investigations for any purpose connected with the carrying out of their duties, and this may lead to the issue of a non-discrimination notice to call a halt to particular discriminatory practice. This aspect of their work is worthy of closer attention.

Formal Investigations

The commissions may conduct a general investigation or an investigation into the activities of a particular person or body. They must conduct an investigation if so required by the Secretary of State. There are very detailed procedural rules regulating the steps to be followed in conducting a formal investigation. These requirements have been made more stringent as a result of judicial interpretations, the cumulative effect of which unnecessarily restrict the commissions' role.

A formal investigation cannot take place until terms of reference have been drawn up and notice has been given of the investigation. In the case of a 'general' formal investigation general notice is sufficient, but where the investigation relates to named person the commissions must notify those named. In addition, in a named person investigation, where the commission believes that unlawful discrimination is present, the named person has the right to make oral or written representations and be supported by legal representation.

Since the judgment of the House of Lords in *R v. CRE ex parte Prestige Group plc* [1984] IRLR 355, the power of the EOC and CRE to carry out formal investigations has been considerably narrowed. The Lords held that the CRE could not investigate a named person or organisation unless it believed that such a person or organisation might be acting in breach of the law. The effect of the *Prestige* judgment is to require the Commission to have sufficient evidence to found a belief before it can commence a named person investigation. The limiting effects of this requirement have been described by the EOC as follows:

> There are many situations which give rise to concern that equality of opportunity is being denied, for example where a high degree of job segregation between men and women occurs, but where, in advance of an investigation, there is no evidence as to the reasons why this has come about on which a belief relating to unlawful acts could be based. This is particularly likely to be the case where indirect discrimination is occurring as a result of certain practices and procedures. It is also important to note that, where a particular institution has a monopoly or near monopoly position, the Commission could not conduct a general investigation and is thus precluded from investigating its activities at all unless it can form a belief that unlawful acts may have occurred.[24]

In the circumstances, therefore, it is hardly surprising that both the EOC and CRE have argued for a legislative amendment so as to overturn the *Prestige* decision.

Once the formal investigation is underway, whether or not the Commission has any power to compel the attendance of witnesses and the production of evidence depends on whether it is a general or named person investigation. In the former case, the Commission only has the power to serve notice requiring information where it is authorised by the Secretary of State. In a named person investigation each commission has the power to require information and evidence and this can be enforced by court order.

On completion of investigation, the commissions are required to prepare a report of their findings which must be published or made available for inspection. They are also obliged to make recommendations which appear necessary in the light of their findings. These recommendations may be directed at any person with a view to promoting equality of opportunity; or at the Secretary of State relating to changes in the law.

Non-discrimination Notices

If, in the course of a formal investigation, the Commission is satisfied that a person is committing an unlawful discriminatory act, the Commission must issue a non-discrimination notice (RRA s. 58; SDA s. 67). A notice lasts for five years. The Commission can stop further ('persistent') discrimination within these five years by obtaining an injunction (see below).

A notice can be issued if someone has:

- committed an act of direct or indirect discrimination;
- applied an actual or potential discriminatory practice;

- published an unlawful advertisement;
- issued instructions to discriminate;
- put pressure on an employer to discriminate.

A non-discrimination notice requires the recipient

- not to commit any discriminatory acts;
- to change his/her practices in order to comply with the point above;
- to inform the Commission that s/he has made the changes and what they consist of;
- to take reasonable steps, as specified in the notice, to tell people concerned about the changes;
- to provide information so that the Commission can verify that the notice has been complied with; and
- to give information in a specified form and by a certain date.

Before it issues a non-discrimination notice, the Commission must tell the proposed recipient of its intention, give its reasons, give him/her at least 28 days to make written and/or oral representations, and take these into account.

After a non-discrimination notice has been served on him/her, the recipient has six weeks to appeal to an employment tribunal. It was originally assumed that the appeal was an appeal against the specific requirements of the notice, rather than an opportunity to reopen the case. However, in *CRE* v. *Amari Plastics Ltd* [1986] IRLR 252, the Court of Appeal took the view that the recipient is entitled to contest not only the Commission's requirements as set out in the notice, but also any of the facts relied upon by the Commission. This rerun of the case merely adds to an already unduly cumbersome and lengthy procedure. Lord Denning was moved to remark that the legislative provisions were 'a spider's web spun by Parliament, from which there is little hope of escaping'.

Persistent Discrimination

If, within five years of a non-discrimination notice becoming final, it appears to the Commission that unless restrained the person concerned is likely to commit more unlawful acts of discrimination, it may apply to a county court for an injunction restraining that person from doing so. However, if the employer has not appealed against the non-discrimination notice, the employer must first test the legality of the notice before an employment tribunal. This is a final tortuous twist in a massively cumbersome procedure. The complexities surrounding the formal investigation process go some way to explaining why the commissions have made relatively limited use of their powers.

Future Initiatives to Promote Equality

The EOC published a White Paper entitled *Equality in the 21st Century: A New Approach* (2003), which is a consultative document on proposed legislative amendments to the Sex Discrimination and Equal Pay Acts. The main proposal from the White Paper is the single statute to incorporate both UK and EC law enshrining the principle of a fundamental right to equal treatment between men and women. It is proposed that the statute extends to gender reassignment and sexual orientation. It is further proposed that there should be a shift in the burden of proof once the complainant has established less favourable treatment; that the terms 'direct' and 'indirect' discrimination should be defined; that the provisions on victimisation should be strengthened and that there should be an express prohibition on sexual harassment. The EOC also recommended the introduction of statutory monitoring which would place the employers under a statutory duty to monitor their workforce as well as implement the Code of Practice.

Bob Hepple *et al.*, in *Improving Equality Law: The Options*[25] also make a number of proposals for reform, including a single Act on sex, race and equality law and an Equality Commissioner to enforce all equality legislation. Their proposal extends the scope of the legislation into areas not presently covered, such as religion, politics and sexual orientation, as well as attempting to make the legislation more proactive by requiring employers to monitor the composition of their workforce. Such recommendations are not only timely but should be welcomed as the existing legislative provision is in desperate need of a complete overhaul.

Statutory Developments

Flexible Working
The Flexible Working (Eligibility, Complaints and Remedies) Regulations 2002 and the Flexible Working (Procedural Requirements) Regulations 2002 (SI 2002/3207) supplement the right not to be discriminated under the SDA 1975 by providing a statutory right for parents of young or disabled children to request a 'contractual variation' in respect of working hours, working time or working from home. Any refusal must fall within specified business grounds if it is deemed to be reasonable. An unreasonable refusal will be subject to a maximum of eight weeks' pay in compensation. The right is restricted to employees and does not extend to workers. See, further Chapter 8.

Religion or Belief
The Employment Equality (Religion or Belief) Regulations 2003 (SI 2003/1660) extend the discrimination legislation to make unlawful discrimination on grounds of religion or belief. The Regulations mirror the SDA 1975 and the RRA 1976 in prohibiting direct and indirect discrimination as well as victimisation and harassment. There is no detailed definition of religion or belief and it appears to cover any religion, including minority sects. Belief includes philosophical belief but does not extend to political opinion. No justification of acts of direct discrimination is permitted. There are specified genuine occupational requirements. On recruitment aspects, see Chapter 3.

Part-time Workers
The Part-time Workers (Prevention of Less Favourable Treatment) Regulations 2000 (SI 2000/1551) implement the EC Part-time Workers Directive (Dir. No. 97/81). The Regulations provide specific rights for part-time workers not to be treated less favourably in respect of terms of their contract or by being subjected to a detriment by the employer, in comparison with a full-time worker. It covers

acts of victimisation, but is subject to the defence of objective justification. It also covers full-time workers returning to part-time work or becoming part-time. In *Matthews and Others* v. *Kent & Medway Towns Fire Authority; Royal Berkshire Fire & Rescue Service; Secretary of State for the Home Dept.* [2003] IRLR 732 retained firefighters claimed that they were treated less favourably in being denied access to the pension scheme, sick pay and pay for additional responsibilities compared to full-time firefighters. The EAT held that the retained and full-time firefighters were employed under different types of contract within the meaning of reg. 2 (3) of the Part-time Workers (Prevention of Less Favourable Treatment) Regulations 2000. Neither were they engaged in 'broadly similar' work.

Workers are entitled to request in writing a written statement from the employer giving particulars of the reasons for his treatment. The employer has 21 days in which to reply. This statement may be used as evidence in any legal proceedings.

Any legal action must be commenced within three months of the date of the alleged treatment or if it is a continuing act, the date of the last act. Remedies include a declaration of rights; compensation; a recommendation that the employer takes action for the purpose of obviating or reducing the adverse effect on the complainant. Failure to comply without reasonable justification may result in an increased amount of compensation being paid to the complainant.

EU law continues to champion the cause for part-time employees. In *Steinicke* v. *Bundesanstalt fur Arbeit* [2003] IRLR 892 the ECJ held that a scheme of part-time working for older public sector employees, open only to those who had previously worked full-time, constituted indirect discrimination sex discrimination against an existing part-time worker and was not objectively justified by budgetary or other considerations that encouraged retirement. However there are times where a more pragmatic approach has to be taken as in *Rinke* v. *Arzetammer Hamburg* (Case 25/02 09.09.03) in which the ECJ found that a requirement in a European Directive that training as a general medical practitioner should be full-time was indirectly sex discriminatory, but could be objectively justified on a number of grounds including that it was necessary to adequately prepare practitioners for general practice.

CHAPTER 12

Other Forms of Discrimination

Discrimination against Homosexuals and Transsexuals

After a hesitant start when initially it was determined that there was no protection under the SDA 1975 for discrimination on grounds of sexual orientation (*R v. Ministry of Defence, ex parte Smith* [1996] IRLR 100), limited protection was in theory provided following the decision in *Smith* v. *Gardener Merchant Ltd* [1998] IRLR 510, where the CA, while supporting the decision in *R v. Ministry of Defence*, went on to state that homophobic abuse may be unlawful within the SDA as long as the complainant compares themselves with a homosexual of the opposite sex. However, the need for a 'like with like' comparison continues to impede the progress of the law relating to the discrimination against homosexuals. In *Pearce v. Governing Body of Mayfield Secondary School* [2001] IRLR 669 the applicant was forced to resign from her post as a teacher due to a campaign of homophobic abuse by her students. The CA concluded that the comparator would have to be a male homosexual who would have been treated to the same sort of sexual harassment. Hale LJ concluded that acts of homophobic abuse were capable of contravening art. 8 ECHR when read with the prohibition of discrimination under art. 14. However this decision has now been overruled by the HL [2003] IRLR 512, which concluded that 'gender' does not include sexual orientation; that a comparator is always needed in cases of sexual harassment and in this case the comparator was a homosexual person of the opposite sex.

Following the case of *Smith & Grady* v. *UK* [1999] IRLR 73 in which the European Convention on Human Rights was used successfully to challenge discrimination against homosexuals in the armed forces, it was hoped that the Human Rights Act 1998 would enable the SDA 1975 to be used to protect homosexuals from discrimination. However, doubt has been cast on the applicability of art. 14 ECHR in encompassing sexual orientation – *Secretary of State for Defence* v. *MacDonald* [2001] IRLR 43 and *Salgueiro da Silva Mouta* v. *Portugal* [2001] Fam LR 2, ECtHR.

For a critique of the decision in *MacDonald* – see H.S. Hanne, 'Sexual Orientation and the Sex Discrimination Act 1975', *ILJ*, vol. 30 (2001), p. 324.

However, in implementing the EU Framework Directive (Dir. 2000/78), the Employment Equality (Sexual Orientation) Regulations 2003 (SI 2003/1661) prohibit direct and indirect discrimination in employment on grounds of sexual orientation. Harassment and victimisation are also covered by the Regulations. The Regulations define sexual orientation as:

orientation towards:
a) persons of the same sex;
b) persons of the opposite sex; or
c) persons of the same sex and of the opposite sex.

The definition does not extend to sexual practices and preferences. A wide definition of direct discrimination is incorporated into the Regulations in line with the Directive. As a result, discrimination on the grounds of perceived sexual orientation is covered. There are exceptions within the Regulations, including benefits dependent on marital status. There is still some doubt whether the Regulations therefore comply fully with the Directive. The Regulations encompass unfair dismissal as a potential act of direct discrimination.

Protection from discrimination for transsexuals was provided in *P* v. *S & Cornwall County Council* [1996] IRLR 34 and *Chessington World of Adventure Ltd* v. *Reed* [1997] IRLR 556. These cases led to the Sex Discrimination (Gender Reassignment) Regulations 1991 (SI 1999/1102). However, in *Croft* v. *Royal Mail Group plc* [2003] IRLR 592, the CA held that protection from discrimination depended on the stage reached in the treatment. Until the gender reassignment was complete the correct comparator were employees who were not transsexuals.[1]

Unfair Dismissal

There are relatively few reported cases concerning unfair dismissal on the grounds of homosexuality. The decisions which have been reported display a lack of understanding and, on occasion, hostility towards gay men and lesbians.

The decision in *Saunders* v. *Scottish National Camps Ltd* [1980] IRLR 174 is a prime example. The employee was a maintenance worker at a children's camp. He was dismissed when his employers discovered his homosexuality. He contended that he was able to keep his private life entirely separate from his job and a psychiatrist gave evidence to the IT that his sexual orientation did not create a danger to the children. The dismissal was held to be fair on the basis that a considerable proportion of employers would take the view that the employment of a homosexual should be restricted, particularly when an employee is required to work in proximity to and contact with children. This decision, formed in the face of expert evidence, merely serves to reinforce stereotypical assumptions about gay men. We have seen that operating on the basis of racial and gender stereotyping will amount to unlawful discrimination but apparently the law of unfair dismissal offers little protection against blind prejudice.

A particular difficulty is that it will often be relatively easy for employers to argue that there was some additional factor, over and above mere homosexuality, which prompted them to dismiss. For example, in *Boychuk* v. *H. J. Symons Holding Ltd* [1977] IRLR 395, the EAT upheld an ET's decision that it was fair to dismiss a woman for insisting on wearing a 'Lesbian's Ignite' badge at work. The rationalisation was that a reasonable employer 'on mature reflection' could reasonably have decided that the badge would be offensive to customers and fellow workers. It was not necessary for the employer to wait until business was disrupted or damaged before taking action. As we have seen, employers are given a wide prerogative in terms of dress requirements they can impose on their employees.

The majority of the case law relates to the dismissal of gay men who have been convicted of sexual offences. In *Nottinghamshire County Council* v. *Bowly* [1978] IRLR 252, a schoolteacher with almost 30 years' service was convicted of an offence of gross indecency with a man in a public place and was dismissed from his post. The IT found that the dismissal was unfair because 'there was no satisfactory evidence of any incident suggesting a risk to pupils'. The EAT allowed the employer's appeal, emphasising that the role of the tribunal is not to decide what it would have done in such circumstances, but to decide whether the employers had behaved reasonably in dismissing Mr Bowly. According to the EAT, 'provided they approach the matter fairly and properly and direct themselves correctly, the disciplinary Sub-Committee cannot be faulted in doing what in *their judgment* – is the just and proper thing to do' (our emphasis).

Workers with HIV or AIDS[2]

As with gay men and lesbians, there is no specific legislation offering employment protection to those workers who have contracted AIDS or who are HIV positive. In the US, a number of states have introduced specific legislation to prevent AIDS/HIV sufferers from being discriminated against and from being required to undergo AIDS screening tests.[3] During the passage of the Employment Act 1990 through the House of Lords, the government resisted an attempt to introduce a clause which would have made it unlawful to discriminate against AIDS/HIV sufferers in this country. The government's preferred approach is to encourage employers voluntarily to adopt policies towards AIDS and to educate their workforces as to the non-existent risk of infection in the vast majority of work situations.[4] In the absence of specific legal protection, AIDS/HIV sufferers are forced to rely on general employment law provisions. It has been advocated that HIV/AIDS should also fall within the Disability Discrimination Act 1995, as proposed in the Disability Discrimination Bill 2004.

Discrimination at the Point of Recruitment

With the exception of the law forbidding trade union, gender and race discrimination, employers have a wide prerogative in terms of deciding which workers they employ. As a result, AIDS/HIV sufferers generally have no remedy when they experience recruitment embargoes.

Refusal to employ a candidate for reasons related to AIDS may amount to indirect gender or race discrimination in certain cases. For example, a refusal to employ anybody from a country where the disease was rife would amount to unlawful indirect race discrimination in the absence of justification.

It has also been suggested that a recruitment ban on AIDS/HIV sufferers amounts to indirect discrimination against men, given that the statistical evidence to date shows that AIDS disproportionately affects men. Even if this argument is correct, the employer can still utilise the defence of justification and much will depend on the nature of the occupation. Stronger cases of justification can be made out if the employment is in the medical and emergency services or if the work is to be carried out in a country which requires workers to pass an AIDS test.

Questions at Interview and HIV Screening Tests

It is also lawful to ask job candidates questions about their health records and ask them to undergo medical examinations and have blood tests. Where the job applicant lies about his/her medical condition and is subsequently employed, the employer may well be justified in dismissing the employee when the misrepresentation is subsequently discovered.

Employers can write into the employment contract the power to require an employee to submit to periodic medical checks. However, unless the employer has included such a clause, the worker can legitimately refuse to undergo the test. Even if the employer has the power under the contract to require general medical tests, an attempt to introduce an HIV test as part of the general medical check-up may be seen in most cases as a unilateral extension of the contract and unlawful. An exception would be certain 'high-risk' jobs involving the provision of health services where there is a recognised risk (albeit small) that the virus may be communicated other than by sexual contact. In such occupations, the courts might infer a term in the contract of employment that the employee must undergo an HIV test.

Working Conditions and Dismissal

The government guidance pamphlet 'Aids and the Workplace' emphasises that HIV infection is not of itself sufficient to justify dismissal. Employees with AIDS-related illnesses should be subject to the same procedures and treated no differently than a worker with any other form of illness (see chapter below on unfair dismissal).

In the relatively few occupations where a worker with AIDS/HIV is seen to constitute a health risk to others, dismissal may be justified under 'some other substantial reason', although an employer should first consider deploying the worker in alternative work before terminating the contract.

In other situations, the employer may try to justify the dismissal on the grounds that other workers refused to work alongside the employee. In *Buck* v. *The Letchworth Palace Ltd* (1987)(IT 36488/88, 3.4.87), the dismissal of a cinema projectionist was upheld as fair because, following a conviction for gross indecency, other projectionists refused to work with him. The other projectionists 'viewed his behaviour with disgust', and also feared that their shared toilet facilities might become contaminated with the AIDS virus. Despite the fact that there was no evidence that the employee had actually contracted AIDS, the ET stated that this was not 'a case where the employers took notice of unreasonable prejudices on the part of their employees'. While acknowledging that the fellow workers may have overreacted, the ET held that the employers had acted reasonably in responding to the fears of Buck's fellow workers.

Brian Napier has argued that as a matter of public policy the law should not countenance the approach adopted in *Buck*:

> In the United States, for example, it has been established as a general rule that co-worker or customer preference is not a sufficient defence for an employer who commits a discriminatory act against his employee. But there is no such equivalent legislation in Britain, and there is no real support for this point of view in the cases dealing with unfair dismissal.[5]

Disability Discrimination

We now have the Disability Discrimination Act 1995 and the Disability Discrimination (Employment) Regulations 1996 (SI 1996 No. 1456), which make some attempt to redress some of the inequities that disabled persons meet in the employment field. Whilst the Disability Discrimination Act is based to some extent on the SDA and RRA, it is rather restricted in its application and therefore there must be questions raised about its effectiveness.[6] The Act does not apply to employers with fewer than 15 employees (s. 7). From 1 October 2004 this exclusion will be abolished; and other changes are made by the Disability Discrimination Act 1995 (Amendment) Regulations 2003, SI 2003/1673 from that date. The Act does not apply to the police, armed forces, fire brigade, etc.

The EU Framework Directive also encompasses discrimination on grounds of disability, which will lead to changes to the DDA 1995 by virtue of the Disability Discrimination Act 1995 (Amendment) Regulations 2003. The Directive introduces a specific duty 'to make reasonable accommodations' which is likely to equate to the current requirement regarding 'reasonable adjustments'. New indirect discrimination provisions which are lacking from the existing legislation will be introduced, although there will be a justification defence. Discrimination in respect of pay and related benefits will fall within the indirect discrimination provisions. There will be specific provisions relating to harassment. Some of the occupational exemptions will be removed e.g. police, fire services and the requirement re public authorities and race will extend to disability.[7]

There is also a statutory Code of Practice on 'The Elimination of Discrimination in the Field of Employment' which may be used in evidence before the Tribunal.

Definition of Disability

The duty under the DDA is owed to a disabled person, or a person who has a disability. The Disability Discrimination (Meaning of Disability) Regulations 1996 (SI 1996, No. 1455) attempts to provide a definition. Additional guidance has been produced in 'Guidance on matters to be taken into account in determining questions relating to the definition of disability'. This guidance must be taken into account by an ET in determining whether a person has a right to bring a complaint under s. 3 DDA 1995.

The Act defines 'disabled person' as a person with 'a physical or mental impairment which has a substantial and long-term adverse effect on his abilities to carry out normal day to day activities' (s. 1). Certain conditions are specifically excluded, such as addiction to alcohol or drugs; hay-fever; tendency to set fires; tendency to steal; tendency to physical or sexual abuse of other persons; exhibitionism; and voyeurism; as are disfigurements such as tattoos or body piercing. Persons who are registered disabled at the end of 1996 are to be treated as having a disability for the purpose of the DDA. It appears that the key issue will be not so much whether a person has an impairment, but whether it has a long-term adverse effect on normal day-to-day activities. Mental impairment must, however, be a clinically well-recognised illness. A 'substantial effect' is one which is defined as being more than minor or trivial. Regard must be had for progressive conditions such as cancer, multiple sclerosis and HIV infections. As a general rule, where a person has a progressive condition, s/he will be treated as having an impairment which has a substantial adverse effect from the moment any impairment resulting from that condition first has some effect on ability to carry out normal day-to-day activities. Where the person is undergoing treatment, then the success of the treatment is to be disregarded for these purposes.

There continue to be issues regarding the meaning of 'disability'. The EAT has encouraged employment tribunals to adopt a purposive approach to the construction of the DDA 1995 with explicit reference being made to guidance issued by the Secretary of State and the Codes of Practice (see *Goodwin* v. *The Patent Office* [1999] IRLR 4).

Long-term Effects

These must last at least 12 months or be likely to last from the time of the first onset for at least 12 months, or be likely to last for the rest of the life of the person. Sporadic conditions, such as epilepsy, can still qualify within the meaning of long term, as the likelihood of recurrence should be considered. However, the effects of treatment can be taken into account when considering the likelihood of recurrence of the effects.

One issue centres on the interpretation of 'substantial and long-term effect on his ability to carry out normal day-to-day activities'. In assessing whether a person's ability to carry out such activities is affected, the ET may consider evidence relating to the performance of their duties at work, where those duties include 'normal day-to-day activities' e.g. nursing – *Law Hospital NHS Trust* v. *Rush* [2001] IRLR 611.

The focus for the ET should be on what the applicant cannot do, or can only do with difficulty, not what he can do – *Leonard* v. *Southern Derbyshire Chamber of Commerce* [2001] IRLR 19. Also the impairment and its effect should be considered holistically e.g. an impairment to the hand should be considered in the light of an adverse effect on manual dexterity, ability to lift and carry everyday objects, instead of focusing on particular tasks or issues. Nor should tasks which are gender-specific, e.g. applying make-up, be discounted as not being a normal day-to-day activity solely because it is carried out by women – see *Ekpe* v. *Commissioner of Police of the Metropolis* [2001] IRLR 605.

The onus is on the ET to make its own assessment from the evidence before it, and avoid being overinfluenced by medical opinion rather than fact. Also, where the applicant is receiving medical treatment for the condition, so that the final outcome cannot be determined or the removal of the treatment would result in a relapse, the medical treatment must be disregarded in determining whether there is a substantial adverse effect – *Abadeh* v. *British Telecommunications plc* [2001] IRLR 23. Where expert medical evidence demonstrates that the applicant has a disability which is controlled by medication, it still falls within the definition of disability – *Kapadia* v. *London Borough of Lambeth* [2000] IRLR 699. In *Woodrup* v. *London Borough of Southwark* [2003] IRLR 111 the CA concluded that the onus is on the claimant to prove, using medical evidence, that if the treatment or medication ceased her condition would deteriorate.

Mental impairment has proved a difficult area for the Tribunals. However, the decision in *Morgan* v. *Staffordshire University* [2002] IRLR 190 provides guidance for establishing whether there is evidence of mental impairment in a particular case. The test is quite rigorous. There must be proof of:

- mental illness specifically mentioned in the WHO classification of diseases;
- mental illness specifically mentioned in a publication that has wide professional acceptance;
- medical illness recognised by a respected body of medical opinion;

- a substantial and specific body of medical evidence of mental impairment which neither results from nor consists of a mental illness.

It should be noted that 'anxiety, stress and depression' might not amount in themselves to a mental impairment unless the evidence clearly identifies a clinically well-recognised illness.

In *Power* v. *Panasonic UK Ltd* [2003] IRLR 151 an employee was depressed and was drinking heavily. Addiction to alcohol is outside the scope of the DDA 1995. However, the ET rather than determining whether her depression caused her to be disabled within the meaning of the Act, concluded that her alcoholism caused her depression and therefore that she was not disabled. The EAT concluded that it was not necessary to consider how the impairment was caused. This affirmed the decision in *College of Ripon & York St John* v. *Hobbs* [2002] IRLR 185. Where the alleged disability is actually due to a functional or psychological 'overlay' i.e. where a person claims to be suffering from a physical injury, which the doctor states is due to the individual's psychological state and is not related to any physical pathology, also causes problems for the ET. The applicant is in effect claiming a physical impairment which does not exist whilst the ET must assess whether the mental impairment falls within the DDA 1995 – *Rugamer* v. *Sony Music Entertainment Ltd* [2001] IRLR 644 and *McNicol* v. *Balfour Beatty Rail Maintenance Ltd* [2001] IRLR 644; [2002] IRLR 711, CA.

Progressive conditions, such as cancer and MS, may also pose a problem for the Tribunal in determining whether the claimant has a disability. In *Kirton* v. *Tetrosyl Ltd* [2003] IRLR 353, Mr Kirton underwent surgery for cancer, which left him with a minor incontinence problem. The ET concluded that this did not have 'a substantial long-term adverse effect' on his ability to carry out normal day-to-day activities; nor did they feel that he had a progressive condition within para. 8 sch. 1. On appeal the EAT concluded that the alleged 'progressive condition' was as a result of the surgery, not the cancer. However, the CA held that there was a progressive condition as the medical evidence showed that there was a real possibility of incontinence when this form of surgery was undertaken and therefore the CA was prepared to regard the incontinence as resulting from the cancer. See also *Mowatt-Browne* v. *University of Surrey* [2002] IRLR 235.

Direct Discrimination

Section 4 makes it unlawful for an employer to discriminate against a disabled person and this extends to the same aspects of employment as can be found in the SDA 1975 and the RRA 1976, i.e. recruitment, promotion, dismissal etc. This is currently restricted to direct discrimination (s. 5) and victimisation (s. 55), but will be extended to cover specifically indirect discrimination and harassment by the implementation of the EU Framework Directive in the Disability Discrimination Act 1995 (Amendment) Regulations 2003.

Constructive dismissal also falls within s. 4 DDA 1995 – *Catherall* v. *Michelin Tyres plc* [2003] IRLR 61.

It is therefore unlawful for an employer to discriminate unjustifiably against any person who is currently disabled or has been disabled. Discrimination is further defined in s. 5. An employer discriminates against a disabled person if:

- for a reason which relates to the disabled person's disability;

- he treats him less favourably than he treats, or would treat others to whom that reason does not, or would not apply; and
- he cannot show that the treatment in question is justified.

Under s. 5 (1) (b) the employer is permitted to justify the act of direct discrimination. In order to establish justification under s. 5 (1) (a) and s. 5 (3) the employer must show that 'the reason for the act of discrimination was material to the circumstances of the case and substantial and that he has not, without justification, failed to comply with any duty under s. 6' – *Baynton* v. *Sauras General Engineering Ltd* [1999] IRLR 604.

The key case is *Jones* v. *Post Office* [2001] IRLR 384. The onus is on the ET to judge the employer's decision on the basis of the information available to the employer at that time. It should then consider whether the response by the employer was within the band of reasonable responses.

Lack of knowledge of the disability does not discharge the onus in establishing the justification defence – *Quinn* v. *Schwarzkopf Ltd* [2001] IRLR 67 and *Callagan* v. *Glasgow City Council* [2001] IRLR 724.

The burden of proof is currently on the applicant to establish that they have been treated less favourably because of their disability. The onus then moves to the employer to justify his actions by providing a satisfactory explanation for the applicant's treatment. This will however change when the Disability Discrimination Act 1995 (Amendment) Regulations 2003 come into force.

If the reason for the justification is material to the circumstances of the case, and is a substantial reason, then it is likely to be upheld. An example of its application provided in the Code of Practice for the elimination of discrimination in the field of employment against disabled persons or persons who have had a disability states 'Someone who is blind is not short listed for a job involving computers, because the employer thinks blind people cannot use them. The employer makes no effort to look at the individual's circumstances. A general assumption that blind people cannot use computers would not in itself be a material reason – it is not related to the particular circumstances.'

There is no need for a disabled person to be able to name other people who are actually treated more favourably. As with the SDA and RRA a hypothetical comparison will suffice. The DDA goes on to state that less favourable treatment cannot be justified where the employer is under a duty to make a reasonable adjustment, but fails to do so unless the treatment would have been justified even after the adjustment. Once again examples are provided in the Code of Practice. For example, an applicant for a typing job is not the best person on the face of it, but only because her typing speed is too slow due to arthritis in her hands. If a reasonable adjustment – perhaps an adapted keyboard – would overcome this, her typing speed would not in itself be a substantial reason for not employing her. Therefore the employer would be unlawfully discriminating if, on account of her typing speed he did not employ her and provide the adjustment.

In establishing direct discrimination within the DDA 1995 (s. 5) it is now clear that a 'like with like' comparison is not required. Indeed there is no reference to such a comparison within the DDA 1995. The simple test is 'But for his disability would he have been treated more favourably?' – *British Sugar Ltd* v. *Kirker* [1998] IRLR 624. Following the decision in *Clark* v. *TDG Ltd t/a Novacold* [1999] IRLR 318 in assessing whether an act of discrimination has taken place, the question to be asked is, 'would the employer have dismissed some other person to whom the material reason would not apply?' *Clark* is also an important case for upholding the view that knowledge of the disability on the part of the employer is irrelevant in assessing less-favourable treatment within s. 5.

Less favourable treatment is therefore justified if the disabled person cannot do the job concerned and no adjustments, which would enable the person to do the job, are practicable.

The test for establishing direct discrimination is the same as the SDA and RRA. In *Holmes* v. *Whittingham and Porter* (1997) (Case No. 1802799/97) an epileptic who had one seizure at work was suspended and after a medical investigation was dismissed on the basis that he should not be allowed to work in a forge even though he had been employed there for 30 years. The ET found that he had been unlawfully discriminated against as had he not been an epileptic, he would not have been dismissed, nor would he have been suspended and sent for a medical examination. The issue of justification was not raised.

In determining whether the act of discrimination is justified, 'important health and safety reasons' may be regarded as material and substantial, so held the ET in *Smith* v. *Carpets International UK plc* (1997) (Case No. 1800507/97).The EAT in *Morse* v. *Wiltshire County Council* (1/5/98) 1279/97 has held that the DDA requires ETs to undertake a number of sequential steps when dealing with s. 5 (2). Firstly it must be decided whether a duty is imposed under s. 6 (1). If it is, it must then be decided whether the employer has taken such steps as is reasonable in order to comply with its duty. If it has not, the tribunal must then decide whether the employer has shown that its failure to comply with its duty is justified.

Duty to Make Adjustments

Section 6 DDA 1995 imposes an obligation on employers to make adjustments to their premises or the way in which they operate to prevent disadvantaging disabled persons. Such adjustments are restricted to what is reasonable and the obligation does not come into effect until the employer takes on a disabled person, or a disabled person actually applies or considers applying for the job.

The employer is under a duty to make reasonable adjustments (s. 6). This extends not only to the physical features of the premises, but also to the working arrangements including hours of work, duties etc. An employer is duty bound to consider the adjustments proposed by an employee or applicant, whether they are reasonable and whether their implementation would have avoided the discriminatory act – *Fu* v. *London Borough of Camden* [2001] IRLR 186. However, the onus is not on the employee to suggest adjustments, but on the employer to assess the employee's needs. Although, interestingly, case law in this area suggests that the duty does not apply if the employer was unaware of the disability or could not have reasonably been expected to know that the person had a disability and was likely to be placed at substantial disadvantage in comparison with persons who were not disabled – *Rideout* v. *TC Group* [1998] IRLR 628. In *Mid-Staffordshire General Hospitals NHS Trust* v. *Cambridge* [2003] IRLR 566, the EAT held that it is part of the duty under (1) DDA 1995 to undertake a proper assessment of what is required to eliminate a disabled person's disadvantage. Failure to carry out this assessment amounted to a failure to make 'reasonable adjustments'.

The duty to make reasonable adjustments must be implemented even where the employee is facing disciplinary proceedings which may lead to their dismissal – *Beart* v. *HM Prison Service* [2003] IRLR 238.

If the employer does not know that the person is disabled, or could not reasonably be expected to know, then he will not be liable under this section. For example, in *O'Neill* v. *Symm & Co Ltd* [1998] IRLR 233 the applicant was diagnosed as having ME. A month following this diagnosis she was dismissed, although she had only taken 15½ days sick leave since the beginning of her employment. ME is classified as a separate and recognisable disease of the central nervous system by the World Health Authority – it is therefore a disability. However, her dismissal was deemed not to be unlawful as the employer did not know she had ME, therefore the reason for the dismissal was not disability. The employer could not reasonably have been expected to know she had a disability. Furthermore, the duty only arises where there is a substantial disadvantage. However, where a disabled person is employed or actually applies for a job, then the employer must look at the physical features of the premises, such as access and egress, fixtures and fittings as well as the arrangements for using the premises and the terms on which employment is offered. The Code suggests a variety of steps which the employer may have to take, for example, making adjustments to premises; allocating some of the disabled person's duties to another person; transferring the person to fill an existing vacancy; altering the person's working hours; assigning the person to a different place of work; acquiring or modifying equipment; providing supervision; providing a reader or interpreter; modifying instructions or reference manuals; allowing the person to be absent during working hours for rehabilitation, assessment or treatment and giving the person, or arranging for him to be given training.

Whether it is reasonable for an employer to make adjustments will depend upon a cost–benefit analysis. Clearly the effectiveness and practicability of making an adjustment should be considered, and this will be balanced against the financial aspects; and see *Archibald* v. *Fife Council* [2004] IRLR 197.

Finally, as with all discrimination claims there is a duty to mitigate one's loss. Failure to do so, for example unreasonably refusing an offer of re-employment, will result in a reduction in damages – *Wilding* v. *British Telecommunications plc* [2002] IRLR 524.

Enforcement

A person may make a complaint[8] to an ET on grounds of discrimination or failure to make a reasonable adjustment. The time limit for initiating a complaint is three months from the date of the discriminatory act.

The ET on finding the complaint proven, may make a declaration as to the complainant's rights: make an order for compensation or recommend that the employer takes action which the ET deems to be reasonable in order to obviate or reduce the adverse effect.

The Disability Rights Commission reviews and monitors the legislation. Its functions not only mirror the EOC and CRE in terms of the elimination of discrimination and the promotion of equal opportunities, but it is empowered to assist individuals to enforce their rights and bring representative actions.

There has been a major review of the disability legislation by the Disability Rights Commission – *Disability Equality – Making It Happen.*[9] The review calls for an extension to the DDA 1995 to cover people with HIV and to apply to the Armed Forces; ETs being given the power to issue orders for reinstatement, re-engagement and recommendations to employers to change their practices. It also proposes that progressive conditions be covered from the point of diagnosis, not from when they have an effect on day-to-day activities. It also calls for removal on the restrictions in respect of mental impairment and wants restrictions placed on the use of the justification defence. Finally the review proposes that transferred discrimination should also be unlawful which would then protect carers from discrimination.

Age Discrimination

Whilst age discrimination is outside the remit of the existing legislation, it has at last been put on the agenda by the current Labour government, who stated in their manifesto that they would make age discrimination illegal.[10] It could be argued that there was limited protection for women from indirect discrimination where age ranges were applied to jobs – see *Price* v. *Civil Service Commission* [1977] IRLR 291. However, as we have seen, indirect discrimination is very difficult to establish and recourse to this action could hardly be considered as a proactive response to the problem.

Some of our EC partners have already recognised the need to retain experienced highly trained personnel within the workforce, although such measures are normally dependent upon a strong economy as they are based on incentives to employers to retain or redeploy older employees – see 'Employment Policies and Practices Towards Older Workers: France, Germany, Spain and Sweden'.[11]

The government has published a consultation paper on its proposals for age discrimination legislation.[12] The proposals, if they become law, will make direct and indirect discrimination on grounds of age unlawful, subject to limited justifications. The prohibition will extend to recruitment, selection and promotion as well as terms and conditions.

In addition, workers who wish to do so may have the right to work until aged 70 and will have the right to bring a claim for unfair dismissal if dismissed before then. In *Secretary of State for Trade Industry* v. *Rutherford and others* (2003) EAT 1029/02, the EAT held that unfair dismissal upper age limits do not indirectly discriminate against men. The pool for comparison is the entire workforce. However, the EAT felt that the issue is one of age discrimination and is covered within the consultation paper on age.

PART FOUR

Job Loss

CHAPTER 13

Terminating the Contract

Termination Involving Dismissal at Common Law

- dismissal by notice
- dismissal for fundamental breach
- wrongful dismissal

Termination Not Involving Dismissal

- death or dissolution of the employer
- frustration
- expiry of fixed-term contracts
- mutual agreement

Terminations Deemed to be Dismissals by ERA

- an act of the employer or an event affecting the employer (including death, dissolution of a partnership, or winding up of a company) which has the effect of terminating the contract automatically at common law will be deemed to be a dismissal for the purposes of redundancy but not for an unfair dismissal claim (ERA 1996, s. 136 [5])
- termination of the contract by the employer with or without notice (ERA 1996, ss. 95 [1] [a] and 136 [1] [a])
- the failure to renew a limited-term contract (ERA 1996, ss. 95 [1] [b] and 136 [1] [b])
- where the employee terminates the contract, with or without notice, in circumstances such that s/he is entitled to terminate it without notice by reason of the employer's conduct: 'constructive dismissal' (ERA 1996, ss. 95 [1] [c] and 136 [1] [c])

Terminations Involving a Dismissal at Common Law

Dismissal with Notice

The general principle is that either party to the contract of employment can bring it to an end by giving notice to the other. Once notice is given, it cannot be withdrawn unilaterally.

If the contract is for a fixed period, then the employment cannot be lawfully terminated before the end of that period unless, of course, the employee is in breach of contract or unless the contract provides for prior termination, e.g. by notice.

The length of notice required to bring a contract to an end should be expressly agreed by the parties. If no notice is expressly agreed then the law requires that 'reasonable notice' should be given with the length depending on such factors as the seniority and status of the employee.

Statutory Minimum Periods of Notice

Apart from any contractual provision for notice, an employee is entitled to a statutory minimum period of notice. The employer must give one week's notice to an employee who has between one month and two years' service and then not less than one week's notice for each year of continuous service up to a maximum of 12 weeks for 12 years. In return, the employee must give at least one week's notice of resignation once employed for more than a month (ERA s. 86).

The minimum notice provision does not:

- prevent either party from waiving the right to notice;
- affect the right of either party to terminate the contract without notice in response to a serious breach of contract by the other (see below); or
- prevent the employee accepting a payment in lieu of notice.

Dismissal with Pay in Lieu of Notice

Employers will often decide that it is in their interests not to require dismissed employees to work out their notice. At best such workers will lack motivation and at worst they may try to find a way of getting their own back! When such workers are given pay in lieu of notice, the law regards this as the payment of damages for wrongful dismissal.

Summary Dismissal for Fundamental Breach

The conduct of the employee may be viewed as sufficiently serious to justify immediate termination of employment without notice. In this event, the employee will lose entitlement to both contractual or statutory minimum notice.

Theft of or wilful damage to the employer's property, violence at work, dishonesty and other criminal offences will normally justify instant dismissal. Disobedience to lawful and reasonable orders may justify instant dismissal but not in every case – all the circumstances must be considered. The same applies to the use of obscene language, as can be seen from the rather colourful case of *Wilson v. Racher* [1974] IRLR 114 CA.

Philip Wilson was the head gardener on Mr Racher's estate. He was dismissed following an incident in which Racher accused Wilson of shirking his work and in the course of the ensuing argument Wilson used obscene language. The court found that he had been wrongfully dismissed because his outburst had been provoked by an unfair accusation by this employer.

Terminations which May Not Amount to Dismissal

Frustration

'Frustration' is a legal concept which, if it applies, brings the employment contract automatically to an end. As a result, the employer does not have to go on paying you wages, or to pay you compensation for unfair dismissal, redundancy, or the like.

In order for frustration to apply, there are two essential factors which must be present:

(i) There must be some event, not foreseen or provided for by the parties to the contract, which either makes it impossible for the contract to be performed at all, or at least renders its performance something radically different from what the parties envisaged when they made the contract; and

(ii) the event must have occurred without the fault of either contracting party. Frustration will not operate if it was 'self-induced' or caused by the fault of a party.

Events which have been held to frustrate the contract include the following:

- the conscription of the employee to National Service
- internment as an enemy alien during wartime.

However, frustration arguments have been most frequently employed in the cases of long-term absence through sickness or through imprisonment.

Sickness

In relation to sickness absence, a number of principles will be relevant in deciding whether a contract is frustrated. In *Williams v. Watson's Luxury Coaches* [1990] IRLR 164 the EAT usefully summarised the relevant principles in deciding whether a contract is frustrated through sickness as follows:

- the court must guard against too easy an application of the doctrine, more especially when redundancy occurs and also when the true situation may be dismissal by redundancy;
- although it is not necessary to decide that frustration occurred on a particular date, nevertheless an attempt to decide the relevant date is a far from useless exercise as it may help to determine in the mind of the court whether it is a true frustration situation;
- there are a number of factors which may help decide the issue, including the length of the previous employment; how long it had been expected the employment would continue; the nature of the job; the nature, length and effect of the illness or disabling event; the need of the employer for the work to be done, and the need for a replacement to do it; the risk of the employer acquiring obligations in respect of redundancy payments to the worker who has replaced the absent employee; whether wages have continued to be paid; the actions and statements of the employer, particularly whether the employer has sought to dismiss the sick employee and whether it is reasonable, in all the circumstances, to expect the employer to keep the job open any longer;

- the party alleging the frustration should not be allowed to rely on the frustrating event if that event was caused by the fault of that party.

The case of *Notcutt* v. *Universal Equipment Co Ltd* [1986] IRLR 218 provides a good illustration of the operation of the frustration doctrine. Mr Notcutt had been employed by the same relatively small company as a skilled worker for some 27 years. In October 1983, when two years from retirement age, he suffered a coronary and was thereafter off work. His employer for a time sub-contracted his work on a temporary basis, but this was not wholly satisfactory and, by July 1984, decided to take on someone else if Mr Notcutt was not going to return to work. With Mr Notcutt's permission, the employer sought a medical report from his GP. In that report, the doctor said that he doubted whether Mr Notcutt would ever work again. As a result Mr Notcutt was given 12 weeks' notice of dismissal.

Mr Notcutt took legal advice and was informed correctly that under EPCA (now ERA) he was entitled to sick pay during the notice period, notwithstanding that ordinarily under his contract he was not paid when off sick. He lodged a claim to that effect in the county court. Ultimately, the Court of Appeal decided that the county court judge was correct in finding that Mr Notcutt's contract of employment had been frustrated by an illness which would have probably prevented him from working again. The contract, therefore, was not terminated by the employers and Mr Notcutt was not entitled to sick pay during the notice period.

Imprisonment

In the past imprisonment was thought to be 'self-induced' frustration. More recently, however, the Court of Appeal has ruled that a custodial sentence of six months did have the effect of frustrating a four-year apprenticeship contract which still had 24 months to run. It was felt that it was the sentence passed by the trial judge – as opposed to the employee's criminal conduct – which was the frustrating event. Consequently this was not a case of self-induced frustration (*F.C. Shepherd & Co Ltd* v. *Jerrom* [1986] IRLR 358).

The courts have provided very little guidance as to how long a sentence of imprisonment has to be in order to frustrate the contract. In *Harrington* v. *Kent County Council* [1980] IRLR 353, a sentence of 12 months' imprisonment was found to have frustrated the contract, even though the sentence was later quashed on appeal.

In *Chakki* v. *United East Co Ltd* [1982] ICR 140, the EAT was of the view that in imprisonment cases, whether frustration had occurred could be determined by answering the following questions:

(1) Looking at the matter from a practical commercial point of view, when was it necessary for the employers to decide as to the employee's future and as to whether a replacement ... would have to be engaged?
(2) At the time when the decision had to be taken, what would a reasonable employer have considered to be the likely length of the employee's absence over the next few months?
(3) If in the light of his likely absence it appeared necessary to engage a replacement, was it reasonable to engage a permanent replacement rather than a temporary one?

While frustration arguments may well succeed in exceptional cases, the courts are generally reluctant to apply the doctrine. In *Williams* v. *Watson's Luxury Coaches* (above), the EAT attributed this judicial caution to the view that the doctrine can do harm to good industrial relations, as it provides an easy escape from the obligations of investigation which should be carried out by a reasonable employer. It is therefore better for the employer to take dismissal action.

Fixed-term, 'Task' and Contingent Contracts

Since its introduction, the statutory framework of unfair dismissal has regarded the expiry of a fixed-term contract as a dismissal. The protection offered to those on fixed-term contracts represented a limited recognition on the part of those who drafted the legislation that any other approach would invite employees to employ large sections of their workforce under such arrangements and so avoid liability for unfair dismissal and redundancy payments.

However, this protection was limited for three reasons. First, a dismissal of an employee who comes to an end of a 'temporary' contract may, in the circumstances be held to be fair as 'some other substantial reason'. Second, what was s. 197 of ERA 1996 stated that where an employee was employed on a fixed-term of a year or more s/he could agree in writing to exclude any right to claim unfair dismissal and, if employed for two years, any right to redundancy payments also, should the contract not be renewed at completion of its term. Finally, the Courts drew a distinction between a fixed-term contract, deemed to be a dismissal under the legislation, and a contract for the completion of a particular task at the end of which there is no dismissal. A 'task' contract is discharged by performance of the particular task and cannot give rise to a dismissal – for example, a seafarer engaged for a particular voyage or a worker hired to paint a house (the leading cases on the definition of a fixed-term contract are: *BBC v. Dixon* [1977] IRLR 337, CA; *Wiltshire County Council v. NATFHE and Guy* [1980] IRLR 198, CA). In *Brown v. Knowsley Borough Council* [1986] IRLR 102, EAT the distinction between a fixed-term contract and a contract to perform a particular task was extended to cover contracts terminable on the happening or non-happening of a future event. In that case, a further-education college lecturer, having been previously employed under a number of fixed-term contracts, was then employed under a one-year temporary contract from 1 September 1983 which was expressed to last for only so long as sufficient funds were provided by the Manpower Services Commission (MSC) to support the course which she taught. On 3 August 1984, she was given written notice that, as MSC funds had ceased to be available, her employment would terminate on 31 August 1984. The applicant's claim for a redundancy payment was rejected by the ET and the EAT on the basis that there had been no dismissal and that her contract was terminable on the happening or non-happening of a future event – the withdrawal of MSC sponsorship.

In *Fairness at Work*, Cmnd. 3968, May 1998, para. 3.13, the government undertook to consider possible options for changing the law allowing employees with fixed-term contracts to waive their right to claim unfair dismissal, and to receive statutory redundancy payments. Subsequently, s. 18 (1) of the Employment Relations Act 1999 repealed parts of ERA 1996, s. 197 which permitted agreements to exclude unfair dismissal claims in fixed-term contracts, and so such agreements are void. Finally, the possibility of agreeing a waiver of redundancy payments claims was closed down by the Fixed-term Employees (Prevention of Less Favourable Treatment) Regulations 2002. Any redundancy waiver that is included in a fixed-term contract which is agreed, extended or renewed after 1 October 2002 will be invalid.

The Regulations also amended ERA 1996, s. 95 so as to create a broader protection than that previously offered to those employees on fixed-term contracts in relation to unfair dismissal and redundancy. The definition of the new concept of a 'limited-term' contract in ERA 1996, s. 235, as amended, employees engaged on fixed-term, task and contingent contracts are now covered.

Termination by Mutual Agreement

As with other contracts, a contract of employment may be terminated by the mutual consent of the parties. If the courts were to accept too readily that the contractual relationship had ended in this way then access to employment protection would be severely threatened. As a result statute has intervened by providing that where an employee under notice gives the employer notice that s/he wishes to leave before the expiry of the employers's notice, the employee is deemed still to have been dismissed for unfair dismissal and redundancy purposes and not party to a early termination by mutual consent.

In general, the courts and tribunals have been reluctant to accept the argument that an employee has in reality agreed to give up his/her job and forgo the possibility of an unfair dismissal or redundancy claim.

In *Igbo* v. *Johnson Matthey Chemicals Ltd* [1986] IRLR 215 the Court of Appeal had to consider the effect of an agreement by which an employee agrees that if the employee does not return to work from a period of extended leave by a specified time then the contract of employment will come to an end. In overruling the earlier decision in *British Leyland UK Ltd* v. *Ashraf* [1978] IRLR 330, the Court of Appeal held that these 'automatic termination' agreements were void under what is now ERA 1996, s. 203. This section makes void any provision in an agreement which purports to 'exclude or limit' any provision of ERA 1996. By limiting Ms Igbo's right to claim unfair dismissal, the agreement offended s. 203 (1). Dismissals for overstaying leave, therefore, must be subject to the test of reasonableness and the ACAS advisory handbook, *Discipline at Work*, provides guidance on how such matters should be handled (see p. 42 of the handbook).

A factor which weighed heavily with the Court of Appeal in *Igbo* was that, if such 'automatic termination' were allowed, then there would be nothing to prevent an employer including a term in the contract that if the employee was more than five minutes late for work on any day, for whatever reason, the contract would automatically come to an end. In this way, the protections offered by the unfair dismissal legislation would be non-existent.

For similar policy reasons to those described above the courts have held that a resignation under threat of dismissal may constitute a dismissal (see *Sheffield* v. *Oxford Controls Ltd* [1979] IRLR 133). Whether a contract of employment is terminated by one party alone, or by mutual consent, is a question of fact for the employment tribunal. In *Hellyer Bros Ltd* v. *Atkinson & Dickinson* [1992] IRLR 540, the EAT upheld a tribunal's decision that two trawlermen were dismissed even though the act which brought their contracts to an end was their own act of signing off the crew agreement. Since the company was decommissioning its fleet, the company's request to sign off amounted to a request for the crew's confirmation of an accomplished fact. This was the case even though the employer had not used threats or coercion to force the crew to sign off.

The distinction between a mutual termination on acceptable terms and a forced resignation was crucial to the EAT's decision in *Logan Salton* v. *Durham County Council* [1989] IRLR 99. Mr Logan Salton was employed by the local authority as a social worker. The local authority commenced disciplinary proceedings against him, based on a report from the director of social services which recommended that he should be summarily dismissed. With the assistance of NALGO he negotiated a severance payment which repaid an outstanding council car loan of £2,750 and he signed a written agreement with the local authority that his contract of employment would terminate by 'mutual agreement'. Mr Logan Salton then claimed that he had been unfairly dismissed and that the mutual agreement to terminate was either void as an agreement entered into under duress, or void because it contravened s. 203.

The EAT upheld the tribunal's decision that there had been no dismissal in law. The present case was distinguishable on its facts from that of *Igbo* v. *Johnson Matthey Chemicals Ltd*, relied upon by the appellant. The agreement between the appellants and the respondents was not a contract of employment or a variation of an existing contract. It was a separate contract which was entered into willingly, without duress and after proper advice and for a financial inducement. Therefore the agreement was not caught by s. 203.

So it is not the case that an argument based upon termination by mutual consent can never succeed; for example, where a termination is willingly agreed to by the employee in return for financial compensation, as in *Salton* itself, or under an early retirement scheme, as in *University of Liverpool* v. *Humber* [1985] IRLR 165.

'Constructive Resignation'?

In a number of cases in the 1970s, the EAT was prepared to accept that certain acts of gross misconduct by an employee automatically terminated the contract without the need for the employer to dismiss. A good example of what was known as 'self-dismissal' or 'constructive resignation' is *Gannon* v. *J.C. Firth Ltd* [1976] IRLR 415 where employees 'downed tools' and walked out of the factory, leaving machinery in a dangerous state, and were held to have dismissed themselves by their actions.

Following the Court of Appeal's judgment in *London Transport Executive* v. *Clarke* [1981] IRLR 166 it is clear that self-dismissal arguments will no longer be successful. In this case, the majority of the Court of Appeal held that a contract of employment could not be 'automatically' terminated by a serious breach of contract on the part of the employee: the terminating event was the dismissal by the employer in response to that serious breach.

Wrongful Dismissal

At common law a contract of employment could be terminated by the giving of notice of a length which has been expressly agreed. In the absence of an expressed notice period, the law will imply a period of 'reasonable notice' whose length will depend on the circumstances of the employment. Moreover, the common law allowed an employer to dismiss an employee with no notice at all if the latter's conduct amounted to a repudiation of the contract of employment.

Until the introduction of the statutory right to claim unfair dismissal in 1971, the employer was left with an extremely wide managerial prerogative in the area of discipline given the largely obsolete and unjust legal principles which made up the action of wrongful dismissal. The major weaknesses in the action for wrongful dismissal may be summarised as follows:

- The low level of damages awarded to successful litigants, generally only compensating for the appropriate notice period (see *Addis* v. *Gramophone Co Ltd* [1909] AC 488 and *Bliss* v. *SE Thames RHA* [1985] IRLR 308).
- The inability of dismissed employees to regain their jobs because of the general rule against ordering specific performance of contracts of employment.
- The archaic nature of some of the principles of summary dismissal, reflecting 'almost an attitude of Tsar–serf' (Lord Justice Edmund Davies in *Wilson* v. *Racher* [1974] IRLR 114 CA).
- The lack of procedural protections for most employees, with only so-called office-holders entitled to natural justice and the remedies of public law (see *Ridge* v. *Baldwin* [1964] AC 40).

As stated above, the action for wrongful dismissal was perceived as largely irrelevant in practical terms. However, a number of recent developments have caused us to reassess the position and it may well be that wrongful dismissal cannot be consigned to employment law's lumber room.

As a result of these flaws in the framework of statutory protection, there has been a renewed interest in common law and public law remedies by employees seeking to prevent a dismissal taking place in breach of natural justice or because the power of dismissal has been exceeded.

This is a complex area which is still very much in a state of flux and it is important that you have a clear structure in mind for the presentation of the developments. The discussion of the area can be divided between (a) the public law remedies of judicial review; and (b) the private law remedies of injunctions and declarations.

Public Law Remedies

The holder of a public office has always received special protection over and above that of an employee so that the officer has the right to the protection of natural justice before dismissal. A good example of this position comes from *Ridge* v. *Baldwin* [1964] AC 40, where a chief constable who was dismissed without a proper opportunity to be heard in his own defence was granted a declaration that the decision to dismiss him was a nullity as it was in breach of natural justice.

However, there is immense difficulty in distinguishing a 'protected office' from 'mere employment'. In *Malloch* v. *Aberdeen Corporation* [1971] 2 All ER 1278, Lord Wilberforce was moved to comment that: 'A comparative list in which persons have been entitled to a hearing, or to observation of rules of natural justice looks illogical and even bizarre.'

In Malloch, a Scottish teacher whose employment was regulated by statute was held to be an office-holder and thereby entitled to a hearing. Lord Wilberforce offered a wide definition of the concept and stated that natural justice would only be excluded in those 'pure master and servant cases' where there was 'no element of public employment or service, no support by statute, nothing in the nature of an office or status which is capable of protection'. This statement opened up the possibility that many public sector workers possessed the status of office-holder and could challenge their employers' disciplinary actions by way of application for judicial review under Order 53 of the RSC (now the CPR Part 54).

This potential alternative to unfair dismissal for large numbers of workers was severely restricted by the Court of Appeal in *R* v. *E Berkshire HA ex parte Walsh* [1984] IRLR 278. In this case the judge at first instance accepted the proposition that the employee, a hospital senior nursing officer, was entitled to judicial review of the health authority's decision to dismiss him on the grounds that it was ultra vires and in breach of natural justice. This view was firmly rejected by the Court of Appeal, holding that the relationship between the parties was one of pure master and servant and therefore a matter of private and not public law. According to Master of the Rolls Sir John Donaldson, the remedies of public law were only available to those individuals who were employed by a public authority under terms which were 'underpinned' by statute in one of two ways:

- by statute placing restrictions upon the authority's power to dismiss, or
- by statute requiring the authority to contract with employees on specified terms.

It was not enough, as Mr Justice Hodgson had held at first instance, for the employee to show that he was employed in a senior position by a public authority for public purposes, and that the public had an interest in seeing that public servants were treated lawfully and fairly (see also *R* v. *Derbyshire County Council ex parte Noble* [1990] IRLR 332; *McLaren* v. *Home Office* [1990] IRLR 338; *R* v. *Lord Chancellor's Department ex parte Nangle* [1991] IRLR 343).

Thus our survey of developments in the public law field offer little in the way of alternative or additional protection to the vast majority of employees. Indeed it is the very existence of the right to claim unfair dismissal which is one of the reasons why the courts have taken the view that most workers do not require the additional protection of public law. What of the recent developments in the private law sphere?

Private Law Remedies

We have seen that the courts were traditionally reluctant to force an employer to take an employee back. As regards employees this rule is now enshrined in TULR(C)A 1992, s. 207, which provides that 'no court shall issue an order compelling any employee to do any work or attend any place of work'.

Recent developments in the common law have opened up the possibility of alternative (and perhaps more potent) remedies than those provided by the statutory regime of unfair dismissal.

The decision in *Irani* v. *South West Hampshire Health Authority* [1985] ICR 590 is a good example of this development. The plaintiff was an ophthalmologist who was employed part-time in an out-patient eye clinic. He was dismissed with six weeks' notice because of irreconcilable differences with the consultant in charge of the clinic. No criticism at all was made of his competence or conduct. In dismissing him the employers were in breach of the disciplinary procedure established by the Whitley Council and incorporated into his contract of employment. He sought an injunction to prevent the employers from dismissing him without first following the appropriate disciplinary procedure. The employers argued that this would be contrary to the general rule that injunctions cannot be issued to keep a contract of employment alive. The plaintiff obtained his injunction.

The judge ruled that the case fell within the exception to the general rule for the following reasons. First, trust and confidence remained between employer and employee. The health authority retained complete faith in the honesty, integrity and loyalty of Mr Irani: any breakdown in confidence was between the consultant and Mr Irani, not Mr Irani and the authority. Second, damages would not be an adequate remedy since Mr Irani would become virtually unemployable throughout the National Health Service and would lose the right to use NHS facilities to treat his private patients.

A major landmark is provided by the Court of Appeal's decision in *Powell v. LB Brent* [1987] IRLR 466, in which an interlocutory injunction for specific performance was obtained. Part of the rationale for the general rule that there cannot be specific performance of a contract of employment is that mutual confidence is necessary for the satisfactory working and that this has often been destroyed.

The *Powell* case, in which the plaintiff claimed that she had been given promotion which the council subsequently purported to rescind, is authority for the proposition that the courts will consider granting an injunction to require an employer to let an employee continue in employment if, on the evidence, the employer still retains sufficient confidence in the employee's ability and other necessary attributes for it to be reasonable to make an order. *Powell* was an exceptional case in that dismissal was not an issue and the employee had been working in the new job for some time when the application was heard. As it was not disputed that the plaintiff had done the job satisfactorily and without complaint for over four months, there was no rational ground for the employers to lack confidence in her competence to do the job. Nor was there any basis for supposing that there was any defect in the relationship between her and any other person with whom she worked or with whom she might be expected to have worked.

This decision was applied in the subsequent case of *Hughes v. LB Southwark* [1988] IRLR 55. In this case, the plaintiff social workers successfully obtained an order restraining the council from enforcing an instruction, allegedly in breach of contract, which required them to cease their normal work during part of the week and carry out other work on those days. The mere fact that there was a dispute did not indicate an absence of mutual trust and confidence and there was no question of the employers not having confidence in the employees. On that basis, the judge went on to adopt the approach set out in the *American Cyanamid* case (see p. 458 below) and held that there was a serious issue to be tried as to the allegation of breach of contract since the instruction was 'arguably unreasonable'; that the plaintiffs, unlike the employers, could not be adequately compensated by damages since they would suffer loss of job satisfaction; and that the balance of convenience was in favour of granting the injunction.

Most recently, in *Anderson v. Pringle of Scotland Ltd* [1998] IRLR 64, the Scottish Court of Session granted an issue to restrain an employer from dismissing an employee in breach of the terms of a redundancy selection procedure. The important issue in the case was whether the trust and confidence requirement applied to redundancy selection. In the earlier case of *Alexander v. Standard Telephones and Cables* [1990] ICR 291, the view was taken that it was axiomatic that an employer had less confidence in the employees it proposed to make redundant than in those it proposed to retain. In Anderson, Lord Prosser took a different approach and stated:

If there were any question of mistrust, the position would no doubt be very different; but at least on the material before me, I am not persuaded that there is a true analogy between the respondents' preference for other employees and the need for confidence which is inherent in the employer/employee relationship.

This must surely be correct. Trust and confidence in an employee is not destroyed purely because on an economic downturn. The question for the court is whether the necessary trust and confidence to continue the employment relationship exists, so as to grant the injunction, not whether the employer has even more confidence in the workers it has not selected for redundancy.

These cases suggest a more liberal approach to the granting of orders to restrain breaches of contract, especially concerning the question of continuing trust and confidence. That is not to say that such applications will always succeed. In *Ali* v. *LB Southwark* [1988] IRLR 100, a care assistant was subjected to disciplinary charges following an independent inquiry on grounds of alleged ill-treatment of patients in an old persons' home. An injunction was refused despite claims that the contractual disciplinary procedure was not being adhered to. The employers had lost confidence in the ability of the employee to carry out the job and, pending the findings of the disciplinary hearing, they had lost confidence on reasonable grounds.

It should also be stressed that injunctive relief will be refused if there is evidence that the employee has accepted the employer's breach as terminating the contract. This acceptance might be implied in the electing to claim damages for wrongful dismissal, or in the making of an application for unfair dismissal. In *Dietman* v. *LB Brent* [1987] IRLR 299, the Court of Appeal held that the council was not entitled to dismiss the plaintiff social worker summarily without first affording her a hearing under the contractual disciplinary procedure and that, in any event, on a proper construction of her contract, 'gross negligence' did not constitute 'gross misconduct' as defined by the contract which would justify summary dismissal. The decision emphasises the importance of carefully drafted disciplinary procedures (as well as the importance of following such disciplinary procedures as have been drafted). The contract defined 'gross misconduct' as 'misconduct of such a nature that the authority is justified in no longer tolerating the continued presence at the place of work of the employee who commits' the offence. Examples were then listed, all of which involved an element of intention on the part of the guilty employee and involved conduct which was either dishonest or disruptive. The message here is that if employers wish to have the contractual right to be able to dismiss summarily for 'gross negligence', this should be explicitly set out in the disciplinary rules.

Mrs Dietman was accordingly awarded damages compensating her for the loss of pay she would have received had the proper disciplinary procedure been followed and had she been given proper notice. Her claim for an injunction, however, failed, because by that stage she had by then 'accepted' her employer's repudiation of the contract – she had accepted employment with another authority – with the result that her employment had already come to an end.

In *Wishart* v. *National Association of Citizen's Advice Bureaux* [1990] IRLR 393, the Court of Appeal refused to extend the principle applied in *Powell* v. *LB Brent* to require an employer, by injunction, to take a person into its employment and to keep him in that employment until full trial, when the employer clearly lacked confidence in the prospective employee in the light of unfavourable references.

Mr Wishart had been employed in the CAB since 1986, when he applied for the position of information officer. He was offered the post, and this offer was confirmed in writing 'subject to receipt of satisfactory written references'. The employer received a reference which, although favourable in other respects, mentioned that the employee had taken 23 days sick leave in the previous year. Worried about this level of absences, the employer sought and obtained a detailed breakdown of absences for the previous three years, commenced discussion with Mr Wishart about the nature of the problem, sought advice from the Occupational Health Service, and finally decided that the level of past absenteeism was unacceptable and that the job offer should be withdrawn.

Mr Wishart sought an interlocutory injunction restraining the CAB from readvertising the post. He also sought an order requiring the National Association of Citizens' Advice Bureaux (NACAB) to provide him with employment in his capacity of information officer until trial. Injunctions were granted by the High Court but the employer appealed.

Allowing the appeal, the court felt that the judge was wrong in treating the case as substantially similar to *Powell* and therefore not within the general rule against specific performance of contracts of service. There was no evidence in the present case that the defendants had or had not expressed confidence in the plaintiff. Unlike *Powell*, there was no established employment relationship. The plaintiff had never worked for the defendants and they did not wish to employ him.[1]

A significant development in the area of employee injunctions is seen in *Robb* v. *LB Hammersmith & Fulham* [1991] IRLR 72. Mr Robb was the borough's director of finance. In May 1990, when capital market transactions and interest rate swaps carried out when he was financial controller were declared unlawful, the council invoked the disciplinary procedure relating to capability set out in para. 41 of the Conditions of Service for Chief Officers of Local Authorities. This provides in the first instance for a preliminary investigation to determine whether there is an issue of substance. While this investigation was being conducted, the chief executive instructed Mr Robb to take special leave with pay. Meanwhile there were negotiations as to the possible terms of the termination of the contract. On 5 July, the chief executive wrote to Mr Robb stating that 'in view of your impending termination of service', there was no useful purpose in carrying on with the preliminary investigation and the disciplinary procedure would not be continued.

The negotiations were not successful and on 26 July Mr Robb was summarily dismissed for lack of capability. Mr Robb sought an injunction restraining the employers from giving effect to the purported dismissal until the contractual procedures had been complied with.

The High Court granted an injunction, notwithstanding that the employers had lost trust and confidence in Mr Robb's capacity to do the job. If an injunction is sought to reinstate employees dismissed in breach of contract, so that on reinstatement they can actually carry out the jobs for which they are employed, trust and confidence are highly relevant since, without the employer's trust and confidence the employees' position would be unworkable. In the present case, however, the plaintiff did not seek reinstatement so that he could actually perform his duties and responsibilities. He sought an Order to restore the position as it was before the defendant unilaterally aborted the disciplinary procedure and unlawfully terminated his contract. In such circumstances, the defendant's lack of trust and confidence in the plaintiff's ability to do his job had no relevance to the workability of the disciplinary procedure if ordered by the court. Without the injunction, Mr Robb would lose the opportunity of ventilating his case and justifying himself at the hearings under the procedure. In this sense, damages would not be an adequate remedy.[2]

Damages

Until recently, industrial tribunals had no jurisdiction over breach of contract claims. However, the ministerial power, now contained in the ETA 1996, s. 3, to transfer jurisdiction in order to give employment tribunals the right to determine contract claims was eventually exercised in 1994 (see the Employment Tribunals Extension of Jurisdiction (England and Wales) Order 1994 (SI 1994 No. 1623)). The Order provides that an employee may bring a claim before an industrial tribunal for breach of his/her contract of employment, or for a sum due under the contract, if the claim arises or is outstanding on the termination of the employment. The employer is also able to make such a claim against an employee, but only where the employee has already claimed under the Order. The maximum award that a tribunal can make in respect of a contract claim, or a number of claims relating to the same contract, is £25,000. Certain types of claim are excluded from the tribunal's jurisdiction. Broadly, these relate to claims about the provision of living accommodation, intellectual property (for example, copyright), obligations of confidence on the employee and covenants in restraint of trade.

Calculation
The High Court and county court will normally award damages based on the employee's loss up to the time at which s/he might have been lawfully dismissed with notice under the contract of employment. Net wages for the period in question will form the basis of the calculation, to which will be added commission, bonus and the value of such benefits as company car, pensions, health insurance schemes, meals allowances, holiday pay and profit-sharing schemes. Damages will reflect the net sum the employee would have received after deductions for tax and National Insurance.

Damages for distress or humiliation, however, were not thought to be available (see *Bliss* v. *SE Thames Regional Health Authority* [1985] IRLR 308).

> If there be a dismissal without notice, the employee must pay an indemnity; but that indemnity cannot include compensation either for the injured feelings of the servant, or for the loss he may sustain from the fact that his having been dismissed of itself makes it more difficult for him to obtain fresh employment. (Lord Loreburn in *Addis* v. *Gramophone Co Ltd* [1909] AC 488 HL)

In *Addis*, an employee who was paid at a fixed salary plus commission was wrongfully dismissed and claimed damages under the following heads:

(i)   salary for the six-month notice period;
(ii) reasonable commission for a six-month period;
(iii) damages for the humiliating manner of his dismissal;
(iv) damages for loss of reputation leading to future difficulty in obtaining employment.

The House of Lords held by a majority that only heads (i) and (ii) were recoverable.
However, the long-established approach in *Addis* has now been side-stepped/ overruled by the House of Lords in *Malik* v. *BCCI SA (in liq)* [1997] 3 ALL ER 1 HL. In this case, the House of Lords allowed damages to be recovered by ex-employees

of BCCI Ltd in respect of injury to their reputation allegedly caused by the bank conducting a dishonest or corrupt business. According to Lord Nicholls:

> Employers must take care not to damage their employees' future employment prospects, by harsh or oppressive behaviour or by any other form on conduct which is unacceptable today as falling below the standards set by the implied trust and confidence term.

Their Lordships further held that the implied term may be broken by generally intolerable conduct not aimed at the employee personally. Finally, the reference to 'harsh and oppressive behaviour' in Lord Nicholls' opinion might offer an avenue by which to seek common law redress against bullying and harassment at work. *Malik* involved a claim for breach of contract rather than a dismissal and this distinction was seized upon by the House of Lords in *Johnson* v. *Unisys Ltd* [2001] IRLR 279. In this case, the Lords made it clear that an employee is not entitled to a common law contractual remedy for the *manner* of dismissal. It was held, inter alia, that the contractual duty of trust and confidence does not apply to dismissal or the way in which employment is terminated, so that the employee could not rely on the fact that he was dismissed without a fair hearing to establish a breach on contract. This is because an implied term cannot contradict an express term giving a right to dismiss and because the trust and confidence term is concerned with preserving the continuing relationship, and is inappropriate for use in connection with *the way* the relationship is terminated. However, it has been held that the *Addis* exclusion of damages for injured feelings and mental distress does not cover psychiatric illness, damages for which are recoverable (*Gogay* v. *Hertfordshire County Council* [2000] IRLR 703, Court of Appeal). According to the Court of Appeal in *McCabe* v. *Cornwall County Council* [2003] IRLR 87, *Johnson* did not necessarily exclude a claim for damages for psychiatric injury arising for the alleged breach of the trust and confidence term whenever a dismissal eventuates. Instead, the test adopted by the Court of Appeal in *McCabe* is a factual one of whether the wrongful conduct of the employer formed part of the process of dismissal. If it did, the employee's remedy is confined to unfair dismissal compensation with its statutory maximum. If it did not, damages at common law may be available (see *Eastwood* v. *Magnox Electric plc* [2002] IRLR 447 CA). Guidance by the Lords on appeal ([2004] UKHL 35) now confirms that damages in Common Law actions which accrue before a dismissal *are* available in appropritae cases.

It has been suggested that where the employer breaks the contract of employment by dismissing the employee with no or short notice, thereby depriving him/her of the right to claim unfair dismissal, the employee may be able to claim extra damages representing loss of statutory rights: *Stapp* v. *Shaftesbury Society* [1982] IRLR 326, CA. However, cf. *Harper* v. *Virgin Net Ltd* [2004] IRLR 390.

Reduction of Damages

Any award will be reduced by payment already made by the employer, such as payment in lieu of notice or ex-gratia payments, but will not normally be affected by redundancy payments. Credit will also be given for early payment. This is because damages are supposed to reflect what would have been paid under a contract which may still have some years to run. If receipt of those wages is accelerated – via the payment of damages – then this should be reflected in the final award.

In *Hopkins* v. *Norcross plc* [1992] IRLR 304 QBD, the High Court decided that money received under occupational pension schemes as a result of the termination of employment should not be deducted from damages for wrongful dismissal, unless the pension scheme or the contract specifically said so. The court ruled that a retirement pension is analogous to insurance and is a form of deferred pay to which the employee is entitled in any event.

Compensation for unfair dismissal representing the notice period will be set off against any damages for wrongful dismissal. For an interesting exception to this general rule, see *O'Laoire* v. *Jackel International Ltd* [1991] IRLR 170. This case does not establish as a general rule that unfair dismissal compensation should not be set-off against wrongful dismissal damages, but it does suggest that such a set-off may be impracticable where the employee's loss is in excess of the statutory limit on unfair dismissal awards. An IT hearing of O'Laoire's unfair dismissal complaint assessed his actual loss arising out of his dismissal as £100,700. After the employers failed to comply with an order for reinstatement, O'Laoire received the then maximum compensation award of £8,000. The issue which arose in connection with O'Laoire's claim for damages for wrongful dismissal was whether, in assessing loss of earnings in respect of the contractual notice period, the High Court had correctly held that the unfair dismissal award of £8,000 fell to be deducted in accordance with the rule against double recovery. The Court of Appeal pointed out that it was for the defendant to prove a double recovery for the same loss in order to provide a basis for a set-off. On the facts, that could not be shown since it was impossible to allocate the £8,000 to any one of the particular elements which together made up a loss of over £100,000 – only part of which related to loss recoverable for wrongful dismissal. Thus the defendants could not prove that the £8,000 was attributable to loss of earnings during the notice period (as opposed to some other loss) and the Court of Appeal thought it both unjust and impracticable to make an apportionment. This problem will only arise in cases where the loss exceeds the statutory maximum, so that compensation must be scaled down. In the usual case of loss within the overall limit, the different heads of loss will be expressly allocated by the IT and the rule against double recovery will bar common law damages for loss of earnings during the notice period.

The employee is under a duty to mitigate loss. S/he must make efforts to find alternative employment. This will be particularly relevant in the case of a fixed-term contract with some years to run, but is generally applicable to all dismissals. Any moneys received, or moneys which might have been received had the employee tried to get a job, will be taken into account, as will statutory benefits received. While the employee is under a duty to act reasonably, this does not impose a requirement to accept work at a much reduced status or lower pay.

The Relationship between Wrongful Dismissal and Unfair Dismissal

These are quite distinct remedies. This is not always appreciated by the layperson and you often hear people using the terms interchangeably. They are quite different legal concepts, although it is quite possible for the same conduct by the employer to result in claims under both headings; for example dismissal may have taken place without notice, and therefore be in breach of contract while at the same time being unfair under the ERA. Which action to choose will vary according to individual circumstances. The wrongful dismissal claim is worth considering where:

- the employee is a high earner whose losses in terms of salary and fringe benefits far exceed the relatively low maximum compensation limits set for unfair dismissal (though the increase in the maximum compensation award for unfair dismissal in recent years has made the comparison between the two remedies less stark);

- the employee is prevented from claiming unfair dismissal because s/he lacks sufficient continuity of service, is over retirement age or has failed to lodge a complaint within three months;
- the dismissal is in breach of contract and the employee wishes to keep the contract alive.

Note also that a contract may be terminated lawfully in that proper notice has been given, but unfairly in that there was no fair reason for the dismissal. In such cases, the only action will be unfair dismissal.

Unfair Dismissal	*Wrongful Dismissal*
Time limit in which to lodge complaint is usually three months	Statute of Limitation – six years
Remedies – compensation, reinstatement or re-engagement	Damages are the main remedy
Limit on compensation	No limit on compensation
Forum – employment tribunal (EAT on appeal)	Forum – county court or High Court (appeal to Court of Appeal or, in Scotland, to the Court of Session). But ETs, by virtue of the Employment Tribunals Extension of Jurisdiction Orders 1994 (SI 1994 No. 1623), now have the power to hear claims for breach of contract on termination of employment (up to a maximum of £25,000)
Proceedings relatively informal	Usual court rules and accompanying formality apply
Employee must have been employed for a qualifying period – currently one year – for the majority of dismissals	No qualification period
Employee must not have reached normal retiring age	No age limit
Compensation can be reduced by up to 100 per cent for contributory fault	No account is taken of employee's action in contributing to dismissal
Acts or omissions discovered after dismissal are not relevant to the fairness issue (though they could reduce compensation)	Acts or omissions discovered after the dismissal will be taken into account

Conversely, a dismissal may be held to be fair, but wrongful because the appropriate contractual notice was not provided. In *Treganowan* v. *Robert Knee & Co Ltd* [1975] IRLR 247, an employee was dismissed without notice because of a personality clash between her and her colleagues – she had openly described her sexual exploits and then boasted of a relationship with a young man half her age, and this had created a tense atmosphere in the office which was affecting business. This was held to be a fair dismissal justified under 'some other substantial reason'. However, the tribunal decided that she should not have been dismissed summarily, but should instead have received six weeks' pay in lieu of notice, though it did not have jurisdiction to award this sum. The employee appealed, claiming that the tribunal did have jurisdiction since the lack of notice was capable of making the dismissal unfair. The EAT rejected this argument, holding that, while lack of notice could possibly be of evidential value in deciding some of the points necessary for an unfair dismissal action, it could not per se make a dismissal unfair that was otherwise fair. Now that the Order has been brought into force – allowing claims arising out of breaches of contracts of employment (including actions for personal injury) to be brought before a tribunal – then it will be possible for the tribunal to make the award which was desired in the *Treganowan* case.

With wrongful dismissal, the fairness of the dismissal is irrelevant – the court's concern is only whether the contract has been broken.

Settlement of Claims

The parties to the contract can agree that the employee will not bring or pursue any claim for wrongful dismissal provided that this agreement is supported by 'valuable consideration' – some material benefit to the employee. Employees will usually be asked to sign a receipt which states that they accept the payment in settlement of all claims arising out of or in any way connected with the termination of their employment. Unless this declaration has been signed under duress, it will prevent the employee pursuing a claim for wrongful dismissal any further. However, until recently such a signed declaration would not prevent the employee from going on to make a complaint of unfair dismissal. This could only be prevented if a special form (COT3) was signed in the presence of an ACAS conciliation officer. TURERA amended the relevant provisions to allow the parties to reach a 'compromise agreement' without ACAS involvement. The agreement will have to be in writing and the employee will have had to have received 'independent legal advice from a qualified lawyer as to the term and effect of the proposed agreement' (see now ERA 1996, s. 203 [3]). Following the Employment Rights (Dispute Resolution) Act 1998, the categories of individuals who can give advice on compromise agreements has been extended beyond qualified lawyers. 'A relevant independent adviser' now can be a trade union official or an advice centre worker.

The Act also makes provision for a voluntary arbitration scheme to be drawn up by ACAS which will apply, initially at least, only to unfair dismissal disputes. The scheme came into force in England and Wales from 21 May 2001 – and came into effect in Scotland later that year. Copies of the scheme are available from the DTI website (www.dti.gov.uk).

Terminations Deemed to be 'Dismissals' for the Purposes of Unfair Dismissal and Redundancy Payments

We have seen that statute has extended the concept of dismissal beyond termination by the employer with or without notice to cover the non-renewal of a limited-term contract and cases of 'constructive dismissal'. We have already examined what constitutes a fixed-term contract and below we discuss some of the issues which have arisen in reaction to the two other forms of dismissal: direct and constructive dismissal.

Direct Dismissal (ERA 1996, s. 95 [1] [a])

This is the clearest and most obvious form of dismissal and consequently the concept has not generated the same amount of case law as the other two statutory forms of dismissal. Nevertheless, the following issues have arisen:

'Resign or Be Sacked'
A resignation under threat of dismissal may constitute a dismissal (see *E Sussex CC* v. *Walker* (1972) 7 ITR 280 and *Sheffield* v. *Oxford Controls* [1979] IRLR 133). However, in order to succeed in this argument the employee must establish a certain and immediate threat (*Martin* v. *Glynwed Distribution Ltd* [1983] IRLR 198).

Ambiguous/Unambiguous Words of Dismissal/Resignation
One problem which occasionally arises is whether the words used by the employer amount to a dismissal or not – for instance, they may have been merely intended as a rebuke or uttered in the heat of the moment. The problem can also arise in the reverse, where you the employee use words which the employer chooses to interpret as a resignation.

The legal principles in this area may be summarised as follows:

(a) If, taking into account the context in which they were uttered, the words unambiguously amount to a dismissal (or resignation) then this should be the finding of the tribunal. So where Mrs Southern, an office manager in a firm of solicitors, announced to the partners at the end of a partners' meeting, 'I am resigning', the Court of Appeal held her to her unambiguous statement (*Southern* v. *Franks Charlesly & Co* [1981] IRLR 278).

In *Kwik-Fit* v. *Lineham* [1992] IRLR 156 EAT, the employee, a depot manager, was given a written warning for a relatively minor offence in a public and humiliating way. He threw his keys down on the counter and left. On his claim for unfair dismissal, the issue arose as to whether he had been dismissed or had resigned. Both the tribunal and EAT found that there was a dismissal and that it was unfair.

Mr Justice Wood stated:

If words of resignation are unambiguous then prima facie an employer is entitled to treat them as such, but in the field of employment, personalities constitute an important consideration. Words may be spoken or actions expressed in temper or in the heat of the moment or under extreme pressure ('being jostled into a decision') and indeed the intellectual make-up of an employee may be relevant – These we refer to as 'special circumstances'. Where 'special circumstances' arise it may be unreasonable for an employer to assume a resignation and accept it forthwith. A reasonable period of time should be allowed to lapse and if circumstances arise during that period which put the employer on notice that further enquiry is desirable to see whether the resignation was really intended and can properly be assumed then such enquiry is ignored at the employer's risk.

(b) Where, however, the words employed are ambiguous, perhaps because they were uttered in the heat of the moment, the effect of the statement is determined by an objective test, that is, whether any 'reasonable' employer or employee might have understood the words to be tantamount to a dismissal or resignation.

A rather colourful example is provided by *Futty* v. *D and D Brekkes* Ltd [1974] IRLR 130. Futty was a fish filleter on Hull dock. During an altercation with his foreman, Futty was told, 'If you do not like the job, fuck off.' Futty stated that he interpreted the foreman's words as words of dismissal; the company denied dismissing him. The tribunal heard evidence from other fish filleters as to the meaning they would give to the words used because it was important to interpret the words 'not in isolation – but against the background of the fishdock'. The fish filleters, who had witnessed the incident, did not consider that Futty had been dismissed, and the IT agreed, stating that 'once the question of dismissal becomes imminent bad language tends to disappear and an unexpected formality seems to descend on the parties'. Futty was held to have terminated his own employment.

(c) A dismissal or resignation given in the heat of the moment may be withdrawn. However, it is probable that retraction must follow almost immediately. Once notice of resignation or dismissal is given, it cannot be retracted without the consent of the other party to the contract. It may be that one exception to this general rule is where the words of dismissal or resignation uttered in the heat of the moment can be withdrawn provided the retraction follows almost immediately: see *Martin* v. *Yeomen Aggregates Ltd* [1983] IRLR 49.

Constructive Dismissal (ERA 1996, s. 95 [1] [c])

The problems surrounding this form of dismissal have generated a mass of case law over the years. By virtue of the concept of constructive dismissal, the law treats some resignations as dismissals and therefore extends statutory dismissal rights to those employees who are forced to resign because of their employer's conduct. This form of dismissal may be extremely important in the context of reorganisations where employers may be seeking to introduce changes in terms and conditions of employment.

Under the current definition, which applies to both unfair and redundancy dismissals, it does not matter whether the employee left with or without notice provided s/he was entitled to leave by reason of the employer's conduct.

In the mid-1970s there was a difference of opinion among the judiciary as to the criteria which should be used in order to determine whether a constructive dismissal had taken place. Specifically, a number of decisions suggested that constructive dismissal was not confined, as had been previously assumed, to fundamental breaches of contract, but applied to any case where the employer's behaviour was held to be unreasonable.

Following a period of confusion, the Court of Appeal in *Western Excavating (ECC) Ltd* v. *Sharp* [1978] IRLR 127 clarified matters, rejecting the reasonableness test and holding that a contractual approach was the right one.

The key elements of the concept are as follows:

- Has the employer broken a term of the contract or made it clear that he or she does not intend to be bound by the contract?
- If yes, is the term which has or will be broken an essential or fundamental term of the contract?
- If yes, has the employee resigned with or without notice in response to the breach within a reasonable time?

What constitutes a breach of a fundamental term and how long is a reasonable time? The difficulty in knowing where the employer or employee stand on these and other issues has been compounded by a development which has been referred to earlier in this chapter. This is the recent tendency of the Court of Appeal to hold that many of the issues in unfair dismissal, most notably for the purposes of this discussion the question as to whether there has been a serious breach of contract, are issues of fact alone or mixed fact and law and therefore the findings of employment tribunals are only reviewable following perverse decisions (*Pedersen* v. *Camden London Borough Council* [1981] ICR 74 and *Woods* v. *WM Car Services (Peterborough)* [1982] ICR 693).

In the midst of this uncertainty, however, it is possible to produce a two-part categorisation of acts or omissions which have been held to repudiate the contract by the courts and tribunals:

- First, an employer may break a positive contractual obligation to the employee, for example withdrawal of free transport, or fail to pay wages.
- Second, the employer may insist that the employee agree to a change in existing working arrangements or terms and conditions of employment, for instance a change of shift, or insist that the employee perform duties which s/he is not obliged under the contract to carry out.

Following the adoption of the contractual test by the Court of Appeal in *Western*, a number of commentators argued that it would impose a great restriction on the scope of constructive dismissal claims relative to the more generous reasonableness test. This has not occurred because the EAT has been prepared to hold that contracts of employment generally are subject to an implied term that the employer must not destroy or seriously damage the relationship of trust and confidence between employer and employee. As a result the difference between the *Western* approach and the discredited 'reasonableness' test looks rather slight, as is illustrated by looking at just some of the situations where the implied obligation has been held to be broken:

- Failing to respond to an employee's complaints about the lack of adequate safety equipment (*British Aircraft Corporation* v. *Austin* [1978] IRLR 332).
- Undermining the authority of senior staff over subordinates (*Courtaulds Northern Textiles Ltd* v. *Andrew* [1979] IRLR 84).

- Failure to provide an employee with reasonable support to enable him to carry out his job without disruption and harassment from fellow employees (*Wigan Borough Council* v. *Davies* [1979] IRLR 127).
- A failure properly to investigate allegations of sexual harassment or to treat the complaint with sufficient seriousness (*Bracebridge Engineering Ltd* v. *Darby* [1990] IRLR 3); *Horkulak* v. *Cantor Fitzgerald International* [2003] IRLR 756, QBD; *Stanley Cole (Wainfleet) Ltd* v. *Sheridan* [2003] IRLR 52 EAT.
- Foul language by employer (*Palmanor Ltd* v. *Cedron* [1978] IRLR 303; *Horkulak* v. *Cantor Fitzgerald International* [2003] IRLR 756, QBD).
- Imposing a disciplinary penalty grossly out of proportion to the offence (*BBC* v. *Beckett* [1983] IRLR 43; *Stanley Cole (Wainfleet) Ltd* v. *Sheridan* [2003] IRLR 52 EAT).
- A series of minor incidents of harassment over a period of time which cumulatively amount to repudiation: the so-called last straw doctrine (*Woods* v. *WM Car Services (Peterborough)* [see above]).

The potency of the implied obligation of trust and confidence can be seen in the case of *United Bank Ltd* v. *Akhtar* [1989] IRLR 507, which suggests that even where the contract contains a wide mobility clause employers must still operate the clause in a reasonable manner. Should they fail to do so, it may constitute a breach of contract and entitle the employee to claim constructive dismissal.

Mr Akhtar was a junior ranking and low-paid worker who had been employed by the bank since 1978 in Leeds. A clause in his contract provided:

> The Bank may from time to time require an employee to be transferred temporarily or permanently to any place of business which the Bank may have in the UK for which a location or other allowance may be payable at the discretion of the Bank.

The EAT held that the employee was entitled to treat himself as constructively dismissed by reason of the employer's conduct in requiring him to transfer his place of employment from Leeds to Birmingham at short notice (six days) and with no financial assistance, even if it could be held within the terms of the express mobility clause in the employee's contract of employment. This is because the general implied contractual duty set out in *Woods* v. *WM Car Services (Peterborough)* that employers will not, without reasonable and proper cause, conduct themselves in a manner calculated or likely to destroy the relationship of trust and confidence between employer and employee is an overriding obligation independent of and in addition to the literal terms of the contract.

While the EAT in *White* v. *Reflecting Roadstuds Ltd* [1991] IRLR 331 vigorously insisted that there is no general implied term that the employer must act reasonably, in practice the existence of the implied obligation to maintain trust and confidence will allow industrial tribunals to intervene in an appropriate fashion to override the unreasonable exercise of an express contractual power.

Fairness and Constructive Dismissal

A constructive dismissal is not necessarily an unfair dismissal. Tribunals having first determined whether the elements of constructive dismissal are present will then go on to consider the fairness question under ERA 1996, s. 98 (4). In many cases this will not alter their conclusion, but there may be cases, such as those concerned with business reorganisations, where, although the employee was entitled to resign, the employer's action which prompted the resignation is held to be fair and reasonable in the circumstances.

In *Savoia v. Chiltern Herb Farms Ltd* [1982] IRLR 166, the employers embarked on a reorganisation of duties after the death of one of their foremen. They decided to move Mr Savoia from his role as supervisor in the packing department, following complaints about his performance, and to offer him the dead man's former position: that of foreman in charge of the production department.

Despite the offer of a higher salary, Mr Savoia refused to move to the new post because he was concerned that he would be exposed to conjunctivitis as a result of the heat and smoke in the production department. He refused the employers' offer of a medical examination so that they could judge whether his concerns were well founded.

Both the tribunal and EAT found that he had been constructively dismissed, but that the dismissal was for 'some other substantial reason' and fair. The Court of Appeal upheld the decision on the basis that 'the reorganisation of the business was imperative', and Mr Savoia's 'refusal to be medically examined when he protested that production work was unsuitable for him created a situation which was a substantial reason' for the dismissal and fair.

CHAPTER 14

Unfair Dismissal

The right to claim unfair dismissal has been part of the framework of labour law since February 1972, when it was introduced as part of the now repealed Industrial Relations Act 1971. It was put on the statute book because the common law did not provide adequate protection against arbitrary terminations of employment and also in an attempt to reduce the number of strikes over dismissals.

The Weakness of Protection against Dismissal under Common Law

Under the common law, a contract of employment can be lawfully terminated simply by giving notice of a length which has been expressly agreed. In the absence of an expressed notice period, the common law merely implies a period of 'reasonable notice' whose length will depend on the status of the employee. Moreover, the common law allows an employer to dismiss an employee with no notice at all if the latter's conduct amounted to a serious breach of the contract.

Until the introduction of the statutory right to claim unfair dismissal, the employer wielded immense power in the area of discipline given the largely obsolete and unjust legal principles which constituted the action of wrongful dismissal. The major weaknesses, from the employee's point of view, in the action for wrongful dismissal can be summarised as follows:

- The general failure of the common law action to question the fairness of the employer's decision to terminate the contract: allowing an employer to dismiss for any reason – however arbitrary – provided the correct period of notice was given.
- The low level of damages awarded to successful litigants, generally only compensating for the appropriate notice period which should have been given.[1]
- The inability of the dismissed employee to regain his/her job because of the traditional reluctance of the courts to order reinstatement of the employee.
- The outdated nature of some of the principles of summary dismissal reflecting 'almost an attitude of Tsar–serf', as Lord Justice Edmund Davies observed in *Wilson* v. *M. Racher* [1974] IRLR 114 CA.
- The lack of procedural protections for most employees, with only an ill-defined group of so-called office-holders being entitled to natural justice, including the right to state their case before dismissal.[2]

When 'unfair dismissal' was introduced, the common law action was perceived as largely irrelevant in practical terms. After all, the statutory remedy was concerned with the overall merits of the employer's decision to dismiss and the determination of the fairness of the dismissal also involved a review of the procedure adopted by the employer in taking disciplinary action. Moreover, it did provide for reinstatement or re-engagement as remedies. Wrongful dismissal was seen only to retain a relevance for high-salary earners, particularly if they were employed on fixed-term contracts or had long notice periods.

The Impact of the Right to Claim Unfair Dismissal

The right to claim unfair dismissal is undoubtedly the most significant of the employment rights which were introduced during the 1970s. In quantitative terms, unfair dismissal claims dominate the work of employment tribunals, accounting for the majority of their workload.[3] In addition, the introduction of the claim produced significant changes in employment relations practices during the 1970s, encouraging the reform or formalisation of procedures adopted by employers in taking disciplinary action.

The significance of this particular employment right is further enhanced because it is popularly presented as a powerful, perhaps too powerful, constraint on managerial prerogative. Indeed, there is a potent mythology among sections of British managers that holds that the law relating to unfair dismissal makes it almost impossible to dismiss even the most deserving case. This view persists in the face of judicial decisions, research and statistics which raise serious questions concerning the extent to which the legislative code on unfair dismissal does effectively control management's power of discipline.[4]

By the 1980s commentators had identified the following shortcomings in the action for unfair dismissal:[5]

(a) The generally low success rate of complainants. In 2002/03, 38,612 cases were disposed of (this figure represents a steady decline in unfair dismissal applications in recent years). Of these, about two-thirds did not reach a hearing because they were resolved either through ACAS conciliation or withdrawn, for example, as a result of a private settlement. Of the 9,456 cases proceeding to a hearing, 5,298 were dismissed and 4,158 were upheld, a success rate for employee complainants of 44 per cent. (In 1981 this had reached a low of 23 per cent.)

(b) The few cases in which the reinstatement remedy is awarded. In 2002/03, of the cases upheld, only 16 ended in an order for reinstatement or re-engagement (0.2 per cent of all cases heard).

(c) The low level of compensation. In 2002/03, of the cases upheld by tribunals which resulted in compensation, the median award was £3,225.

(d) The devaluation between 1979 and 1987 of the importance of adhering to fair procedures in unfair dismissal as a result of the application of the test laid down in *British Labour Pump Co Ltd* v. *Byrne* [1979] IRLR 94 (now no longer good law as a result of the Law Lords' decision in *Polkey* v. *AE Dayton Services Ltd* [1987] IRLR 503).

The Resurrection of the Common Law Remedies

Given these flaws in the framework of statutory protection, recently there has been a renewed interest in common law remedies by employees who are seeking to prevent a dismissal from taking place in breach of a contractually binding disciplinary procedure or to restrain some other breach of contract by the employer. The courts have responded by showing a greater willingness to grant court orders to prevent such breaches taking place.[6] Fortunately, the House of Lords reassertion of the importance of procedural fairness in *Polkey* has now restored a degree of potency to unfair dismissal action which had been sadly lacking for some time.

Creeping Legalism

In the decade or so since the introduction of the right to claim unfair dismissal, the amount of case law has multiplied and so has its complexity. As early as 1975 the first president of the EAT, Mr Justice Phillips, was moved to remark: 'The expression unfair dismissal is in no sense a common sense expression capable of being understood by the man in the street' (*Devis* v. *Atkins* [1976] IRLR 16).

The tribunals and the procedure under which they operate were designed to provide a speedy, cheap and informal mechanism for the resolution of disputes over dismissal but the law they have to apply is often of great complexity. It is therefore not surprising that just over one-third of applicants and more than half of respondent employers are legally represented at tribunal hearings.[7] The obvious imbalance in representation between employers and employees which these statistics show underlines the urgent need for the state Legal Aid system to be extended to cover legal representation for workers at such hearings. However, in 1996 the government decided against such an extension (see 'Striking the Balance: The Future of Legal Aid in England and Wales', Cm 3305).

This tendency towards excessive legalism has been recognised by the Court of Appeal and it has attempted to reduce the number of cases coming through on appeal from industrial tribunals to the Employment Appeal Tribunal. First, it has ruled that many issues in employment law are ultimately questions of fact and not questions of law. Given that appeal to the Employment Appeal Tribunal (EAT) is generally restricted to claims that the tribunal has got the law wrong, this is clearly an attempt to return decision-making to the tribunals.[8]

Second, the Court of Appeal has rejected the EAT's practice of laying down guidelines for tribunals to follow when confronted with major problem areas of unfair dismissal law; for example, redundancy procedure, suspected dishonesty, long-term sickness absence. The court felt that too many cases were being appealed on the basis that the tribunal had not followed this guidance and the EAT was being asked to intervene and overturn a tribunal's conclusions on the facts of the case.[9]

There is no doubt that the law of unfair dismissal has become excessively technical, but it may be that the result of the Court of Appeal's attacks on legalism and the proliferation of appeals may be uncertainty and inconsistency. In the absence of established guidelines and precedent, it becomes extremely difficult for lawyers or trade union officials to offer advice to workers on the likely outcome of any particular case and there is every prospect that employment tribunals in different parts of the country can come to diametrically opposed conclusions in cases involving identical facts and with little or no prospect of the EAT resolving the matter on appeal.

Where to Find the Law Relating to Unfair Dismissal

Until relatively recently, the legislation governing unfair dismissal remained largely unaltered, the major amendments being concerned with the introduction of protection for those employees dismissed for non-union membership. The other significant change concerned the qualification period necessary to claim, which was raised from 26 weeks in 1979 to two years in 1985. Following the proposal contained in the government's *Fairness at Work* White Paper (Cm. 3968, May 1998), the qualifying period was reduced to one year with effect from 1 June 1999 (Unfair Dismissal and Statement of Reasons for Dismissal (Variation of Qualifying Period) Order 1999) (SI 1999/1436).

In 1978, an attempt was made to consolidate the legislation in the Employment Protection (Consolidation) Act. After 1978, a number of amendments were made via a succession of Employment Acts, the Sex Discrimination Act 1986, the Trade Union Reform and Employment Rights Act 1993 and a number of pieces of subordinate legislation. As a result, a further consolidation statute was necessary in the form of the Employment Rights Act 1996.

With the election of the Labour government in 1997, further and more far-reaching changes to the unfair dismissal regime have been introduced. The Employment Rights (Dispute Resolution) Act 1998 contains provisions to implement those aspects of the Green Paper, *Resolving Employment Rights Disputes: Options for Reform* (Cm. 2707, 1994), which attracted wide support and required primary legislation. The most significant change under the Act is to grant ACAS powers to fund and provide an arbitration scheme for unfair dismissal claims. This is available as an alternative to an employment tribunal hearing and is voluntary on both sides. After some delay, the ACAS Arbitration Scheme came into force in England and Wales on 21 May 2001 (ACAS hope to offer the Scheme in Scotland by the end of 2001). The Scheme got off to a sluggish start with only one case heard in the first six months of the Scheme's operation (see 'Anyone for Arbitration?', *Employers' Law*, November 2001, pp. 22–3).

In *Fairness at Work*, the government put forward a number of proposals aimed at strengthening the unfair dismissal remedy. These included:

(a)   abolishing the maximum limit on the compensatory award;
(b)   index-linking limits on the basic award, subject to a maximum rate;
(c)   prohibiting the use of waivers for unfair dismissal claims but continuing to allow them for redundancy payments;
(d)   creating a legal right for individuals to be accompanied by a fellow employee or trade union representative of their choice during grievance and disciplinary hearings; and
(e)   reducing the qualifying period for claimants to one year.

The Employment Relations Act 1999 and a ministerial order have implemented these proposals with one exception. The ceiling on the compensation award has not been completely removed but the maximum limit was raised from £12,000 to £50,000. This maximum is automatically indexed to retail prices and with effect from 1 February 2003, is £53,500.

Finally, the Employment Act 2002 contains provisions which will impact on the statutory unfair dismissal regime. New statutory dispute resolution procedures will be set out in detail in regulations and will come into force in October 2004. The statutory procedures introduced by the Act require every employer to implement minimum procedures to deal with disciplinary and dismissal issues, and employee grievances.

We can analyse the law of unfair dismissal in four stages (see Figure 14.1):

- Stage one: has a dismissal taken place?
- Stage two: is the applicant qualified to make a claim?
- Stage three: is the dismissal fair or unfair?
- Stage four: what remedies are available?

Stage One: Has a Dismissal Taken Place?

This was discussed in the previous chapter.

Stage Two: Is the Applicant Qualified to Make a Claim?

The applicant must satisfy the employment tribunal on the following three broad issues:

(1) That the applicant is an 'employee' (the vagaries surrounding the definition of employment status were discussed in Chapter 2 above).
(2) That applicant's employment does not fall within an excluded category and has the requisite continuity of service (see p. 281 and Chapter 2).
(3) That the applicant has presented the claim in time.

Claim in Time

In common with the enforcement of other employment protection rights, an applicant must present a claim (using an IT1 form) to the Regional Office of Employment Tribunals within three months of the effective date of termination (see Chapter 21 below). This time limit is fairly rigorously applied, although tribunals have the discretion to allow a claim to be presented within a reasonable time outside the three-month period where it considers that it was not reasonably practicable for the complaint to be presented in time. The leading cases in this area establish the following:

- The test to be applied in determining whether a late claim should be considered is not confined to whether the applicant knew of the right to claim but extends to a consideration as to whether s/he should have known.[10] In other words, ignorance of rights is not an excuse, unless it appears that the applicant could not reasonably be expected to be aware of them.
- A late claim will not be accepted even though the worker's failure to claim in time was due to a mistake of a 'skilled adviser' such as a lawyer, trade union official or CAB worker.[11]
- It will probably not be regarded as reasonable for the applicant to delay making a claim until the outcome of an internal appeal is known. The balance of authority would now suggest that this would not be a reason for admitting a late claim.[12]

Figure 14.1: Workers Who are Entitled to Bring a Claim for Unfair Dismissal and/or Redundancy Payments

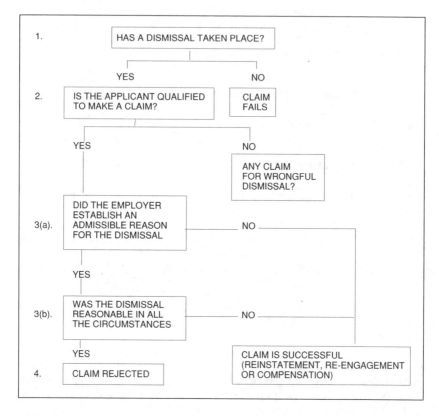

So what excuses are the tribunals to accept as valid reasons for delay? The case law suggests the following list:

- physical incapacity
- absence abroad
- a postal strike
- a worker's failure to discover a fundamental fact until more than three months after the date of dismissal. For example, in *Churchill v. Yeates & Son Ltd* [1983] IRLR 187 the applicant, who did not discover evidence that his dismissal purportedly for redundancy may have been a sham until after the three-month deadline, had his claim admitted.[13]

In *Briggs v. Somerset County Council* [1996] IRLR 203 CA Neil L J said that while the phrase 'not reasonably practicable' might apply to a mistake of fact, it did not cover a mistake of law.

The Effective Date of Termination (EDT)

At various stages in this chapter, this phrase has been referred to. The identity of the date of termination will determine whether a claim is made in time, whether the

Figure 14.2: Excluded Employees

Workers who fail to satisfy the status of 'employee' (see Chapter 2).

Employees who have not worked for a continuous period of one year (ERA 1996, s. 108).

Share fishermen (ERA 1996, s. 199).

The police and prison officers (see ERA 1996, s. 200).

Members of the armed forces (ERA 1996, s. 192).

Crown employees where the relevant minister has issued an excepting certificate on grounds of national security (see ERA 1996, s. 193; *Council of Civil Service Unions* v. *Minister for the Civil Service* [1985] ICR 14).

Employees reaching retirement age: to claim employees must not have passed the 'normal retiring age' for employees in that position; or, where there is no normal retirement age, must not have passed their 65th birthday (ERA 1996, s. 109 [1]). It has been held that where a contract specifies retirement age then it can be presumed to be the 'normal retiring age' (see *Nothman* v. *Barnet London Borough Council* [1979] IRLR 35 HL). But this presumption can be rebutted by evidence that the contractual age has been abandoned in practice. The test of whether this has happened is to ascertain what would be the reasonable expectation or understanding of employees holding that position at the relevant time (*Waite* v. *Government Communications Headquarters* [1983] ICR 653 HL). *Hughes* v. *Department of Health & Social Security* [1985] AC 776, concerned the question whether employers can effectively alter a normal retirement age established by practice by a simple announcement to that effect. The House of Lords held that this was possible, since an announcement would vary the expectations of the employees affected. (See also *Brooks* v. *British Telecommunications plc* [1992] IRLR 66 CA.) In *Secretary of State for Trade and Industry* v. *Rutherford* (No. 2) [2003] IRLR 858, the EAT allowed the government's appeal and held that the exclusion of employees aged 65 and over from the statutory right not to be unfairly dismissed and the right to receive redundancy payment does not discriminate against men and is not contrary to EU law. The EAT ruled that the upper age limit does not have a disparity on men and that, in any event, the Secretary of State met the test of justifying the statutory exclusions.

Workers, who at the time of their dismissal, are taking official industrial action which has lasted more than eight weeks, locked out and there has been no selective dismissal or re-engagement of those taking the action. Unofficial strikers may be selectively dismissed or re-engaged (TULR[C]A 1992, ss. 237, 238, 238A; see Chapter 20).

Those employees covered by a disciplinary procedure, voluntarily agreed between employers and independent trade union, where the Secretary of State has designated it to apply instead of the statutory scheme. The designation will be granted only if the voluntary scheme is at least as beneficial to employees as statutory protection. Only one such scheme – between the Electrical Contractors Association and the EETPU – is in operation (ERA 1996, s. 110).

Illegal contracts: a contract of employment to do an act which is unlawful is unenforceable. The position is different, however, if the contract is capable of being performed lawfully, and was initially intended to be so performed, but which has in fact been performed by unlawful means. In this situation, the contract will be unenforceable only if the employee was a knowing and willing party to the illegality and stood to benefit – see *Hewcastle Catering Ltd* v. *Ahmed and Elkamah* [1991] IRLR 473 CA.

Where a settlement of the claim has been agreed with the involvement of an ACAS Conciliation Officer and the employee has agreed to withdraw his/her complaint (ERA 1996, s. 203 [e]).

Where the employee enters into a valid compromise agreement satisfying the conditions set out in s. 203 (3). These include the requirement that the employee should have taken independent legal advice (ERA 1996, s. 203).

applicant possessed the requisite continuity of employment at the date of dismissal, whether the retirement age exclusion is to operate in any particular case and, if the claim is successful, from when to calculate compensation.

ERA provides a definition of the date of termination for both unfair dismissal and redundancy payment claims and, although for unfair dismissal purposes it is called the 'effective date of termination' and for redundancy payments 'the relevant date', the definition is largely the same in both cases.[14]

(a)   Where the contract of employment is terminated by notice, whether by employer or employee, the date of termination is the date on which the notice expires. Where notice is given orally on a day when work is carried out, the notice period does not begin to run until the following day (*West* v. *Kneels Ltd* [1986] IRLR 430). If an employee is dismissed with notice but is given a payment in lieu of working out that notice, the EDT is the date when the notice expires (*Adams* v. *GKN Sankey* [1980] IRLR 416). As will be seen below, a fine distinction is drawn between the latter situation and one where the employee is dismissed with no notice with the payment being made in lieu of notice.

(b)   Where the contract of employment is terminated without notice, the date of termination is the date on which the termination takes effect. Two useful cases in this area are *Robert Cort & Sons* v. *Charman* [1981] IRLR 437 and *Stapp* v. *The Shaftesbury Society* [1982] IRLR 326, which both uphold the view that the effective date of termination is the actual date of termination regardless of whether the employment was lawfully or unlawfully terminated. So where, as in Cort's case, an employee is immediately dismissed with wages in lieu of notice, the effective date of termination is the actual date on which the employee is told of dismissal and not the date on which notice would expire.[15]

The only exception to this rule is provided by s. 97 (2), which artificially extends the EDT, either where summary dismissal has occurred despite a period of statutory minimum notice being due under s. 86, or where the statutory notice required to be given is longer than the actual notice given. In either case the date of the ending of the s. 86 notice period is treated as the EDT.

(c)   Where the employee is employed under a contract for a fixed term, the date of termination is the date on which the term expires.

Internal Appeals and the Effective Date of Termination

Where the dismissed employee exercises a right of appeal, the question may arise as to the EDT. Does the EDT become the date of the determination of the appeal, or does the original date of dismissal still stand as the EDT?

The leading case on this question is the Court of Appeal's decision in *J. Sainsbury Ltd* v. *Savage* [1981] ICR 1, where it was held that if the dismissed employee invokes an internal appeal which is subsequently rejected, the EDT is the date of the original dismissal, unless the contract provides to the contrary. This approach was expressly approved by the House of Lords in the important case of *West Midlands Cooperative Society* v. *Tipton* [1986] IRLR 112, which is discussed in more detail later in this chapter.

Stage Three: Is the Dismissal Fair or Unfair?

This involves the resolution of two issues:

(i)   has a potentially fair reason for the dismissal been established; and

(ii) whether, in the circumstances, the employer acted reasonably in treating that reason as a sufficient reason for dismissing the employee.

Potentially Fair Dismissals

It is for the employer to establish that there was a potentially facie reason for dismissal. These are as follows:

- capability or qualifications;
- conduct;
- redundancy;
- that the employee could not continue to work without contravention of a statute;
- some other substantial reason.

This stage in the process of justifying the dismissal will generally not be difficult for the employer to satisfy, since it does not involve any consideration of fairness and all that must be proved is the employer's subjective motivation for dismissal.

An employer will only be allowed to rely upon facts known at the time of dismissal to establish what was the reason for the dismissal. Facts which come to light after the dismissal cannot be relied on to justify the dismissal – though they may persuade a tribunal to reduce your compensation. This was the conclusion of the House of Lords in the important case of *W. Devis & Sons Ltd* v. *Atkins* [1977] AC 931.

In *Farrant* v. *Woodroffe School* [1998] IRLR 176 held that a dismissal is not necessarily unfair where the reason for it was the employer's genuine but mistaken belief that the employee was refusing to obey an instruction falling within the scope of his employment. Whether or not an instruction is lawful is relevant but not decisive.

In this case, the employers dismissed on the basis of a genuine, if mistaken, belief following advice they had received from the county council that they were entitled to require the employee to work to a new job description and, therefore, that he was guilty of gross misconduct in refusing to do so. The EAT upheld the finding that this was not unfair on the facts. However, as Rubenstein observes: 'That seems a harsh result, which treats the burden of showing the reason for the dismissal as entirely subjective. The decision illustrates that fairness will be judged from the perspective of the employer's actions and not from that of the employee' (Highlights, [1998] IRLR 166).

The Right to Receive Written Reasons for the Dismissal

ERA 1996, s. 92 provides that an employee who is under notice or who has been dismissed has the right, on request to the employer, to be provided within 14 days with a written statement of reasons for the dismissal. The period of continuous employment necessary for ex-employees to exercise this right was reduced from two years to one year with effect from 1 June 1999 (see the Unfair Dismissal and Statement of Reasons for Dismissal [Variation of Qualifying Period] Order 1999). The significance of s. 92 is that a written statement provided under the section is expressly made admissible in subsequent proceedings. Any basic inconsistency between the contents of the statement and the reason actually put forward before the tribunal could seriously undermine the employer's case.

If an employer unreasonably refuses to comply with the request or provides particulars which are 'inadequate or untrue', the employee may present a complaint to an employment tribunal, which may declare what it finds the reasons for dismissal are and also make an award of two weeks' wages to the employee.

The statement provided by the employer must at least contain a simple statement of the essential reasons for the dismissal, but no particular form is required. Indeed, it has been held that it is acceptable for a written statement to refer the employee to earlier correspondence which contain the reasons for dismissal: attaching a copy of that correspondence (*Kent County Council* v. *Gilham and Others* [1985] IRLR 16).

It does not matter whether the reason put forward by the employer is 'intrinsically a good, bad or indifferent one'; at this stage the ET is only concerned about identifying the genuine reason for the dismissal. So, in *Harvard Securities plc* v. *Younghusband* [1990] IRLR 17, where the employers stated that they had dismissed the employee for divulging confidential information to a third party, whether the employers were correct in describing that information as 'confidential' was irrelevant to the identification of their reason for dismissal.

Pressure on an Employer to Dismiss

ERA 1996, s. 107 states that, in determining the reason for the dismissal and its fairness, no account shall be taken of any industrial pressure (official or unofficial) exerted on the employer to dismiss the employee. It follows that if an employer cannot advance any reason other than the industrial pressure the dismissal will be held to be unfair.

Nevertheless, a trade union or union official who has exerted pressure to force the employer to dismiss a non-union member may be joined in subsequent unfair dismissal proceedings and be ordered to pay all or part of any compensation awarded (TULR[C]A 1992, s. 160).

Dismissals which are Deemed to be Unfair

Certain reasons for dismissal are regarded as automatically unfair and do not require two years' continuous employment before claims may be made. They are as follows:

(a) Dismissal for trade union membership and activity, or because of refusal to join a trade union or particular trade union; (TULR[C]A 1992, s. 152).
(b) Dismissal of a woman because she is pregnant or a reason connected with her pregnancy or childbirth (ERA 1996, s. 99).
(c) Dismissal because of a conviction which is spent under the terms of the Rehabilitation of Offenders Act 1974 (see s. 4 [3] [b]).
(d) Dismissal connected with the transfer of an undertaking unless there are economic, technical or organisational reasons entailing changes in the workforce (see the Transfer of Undertakings (Protection of Employment) Regulations 1981 (SI 1981 No. 17950), reg. 8, discussed in Chapter 8).
(e) Dismissal on the ground of redundancy if the circumstances constituting the redundancy also applied equally to one or more employees in the same undertaking who held posts similar to that held by the dismissed employee and they have not been dismissed and:
    (i) the reason (or, if more than one, the principal reason) for selecting the employee for dismissal was union-related (TULR[C]A, s. 153); or

    (ii)   the reason for selection was because of pregnancy or childbirth or because the employee had been involved in raising or taking action on health and safety issues (see (f) below); asserted certain statutory rights (see (g) below); performed (or proposed to perform) any functions as a trustee of an occupational pension scheme (see (h) below); performed (or proposed to perform) the functions or activities of an employee representative for the purpose of consultation over redundancies or the transfer of an undertaking; or as a 'protected' or 'opted out' shop or betting worker, refused to work on a Sunday (see (i) below) (ERA 1996, s. 105).

(f)   Dismissal on the grounds that the employee:
    (i)   carried out, or proposed to carry out, duties as a safety representative or as a member of a safety committee;
    (ii)   where there was no representative or committee, or it was not reasonable to raise the matter with them, brought to the employer's attention, by reasonable means, harmful or potentially harmful circumstances;
    (iii) left the place of work, or refused to return to it, in circumstances of danger which the employee reasonably believed to be serious or imminent and which s/he could not reasonably have been expected to avert; or
    (iv) in such circumstances, took or proposed to take appropriate steps to protect him/herself or others from danger (ERA 1996, s. 100).

(g) Dismissal where the employee had brought proceedings against the employer to enforce a 'relevant statutory right' or had alleged an infringement of such a right. 'Relevant statutory rights' are those conferred by ERA 1996 for which the remedy is by way of complaint to an employment tribunal; notice rights under ERA 1996, s. 86; and rights relating to deductions from pay, union activities and time off under TULR(C)A 1992. Similar protection is provided for those dismissed for those seeking to enforce the following more recently granted legal rights relating to: the national minimum wage; working time; public interest disclosure; working tax credit; parental leave; taking reasonable time off work to look after dependants; an application to work flexibly. There is no qualifying period of service or upper age limit for employees who wish to complain that they have been dismissed for any of the above reasons.

(h) An employee who is a trustee of an occupational pension scheme established under a trust will be regarded as unfairly dismissed if the reason (or, if more than one, the principal reason) for the dismissal is that the employee performed (or proposed to perform) any of the functions of a trustee (ERA 1996, s. 102).

(i)   A 'protected' or 'opted out' shop or betting worker who is dismissed for refusing to work on a Sunday shall be regarded as unfairly dismissed. Similarly, it will be unfair to dismiss a shop or betting worker because s/he gave (or proposed to give) an opting out notice to the employer (ERA 1996, s. 101). Broadly, shop or betting workers are 'protected' if, before the commencement dates of the legislation which liberalised Sunday trading and betting, they were not required under their contract of employment to work on Sunday. Shop or betting workers who are contractually required to work on a Sunday may give three months' written notice of their intention to 'opt out' of Sunday working at the end of the notice period but not before (ERA 1996, Part IV).

(j)   Dismissal for exercising the right to be accompanied or to accompany at a disciplinary or grievance hearing (ERA 1999, s. 12).

(k) Dismissal for exercising rights under the Part-time Workers (Prevention of Less Favourable Treatment) Regulations 2000 or the Fixed-term Employees (Prevention of Less Favourable Treatment) Regulations 2002.

Dismissal During an Industrial Dispute

It is automatically unfair to dismiss workers for taking official industrial action lasting eight weeks or less. It is also unfair to dismiss them where they have taken action for more than eight weeks if the employer has not first taken such procedural steps as are reasonable to resolve the dispute.

Otherwise, official strikers falling outside of the above provisos and all those taking *unofficial* industrial action will not be able to bring a complaint of unfair dismissal provided his or her employer

- has dismissed all who were taking part in the action at the same establishment as the complainant at the date of his or her dismissal; and
- has not offered re-engagement to any of them within three months of their date of dismissal without making him or her a similar offer.

Did the Employer Act Reasonably?

Prior to 1980, the burden of proof in unfair dismissal claims at this stage was on the employer. The Employment Act 1980 amended what was then s. 57 (3) of EPCA primarily by removing the requirement that employers shall satisfy the industrial tribunal as to the reasonableness of their actions and so rendered the burden of proof 'neutral'. A further amendment required tribunals to have regard to the size and administrative resources of an employer's undertaking in assessing the reasonableness of the dismissal. The specific reference to size and administrative resources is an encouragement to tribunals to be less exacting in their examination of the disciplinary standards and procedures of small employers.

In assessing the test of reasonableness, the question is what a reasonable employer would have done in the circumstances and not what a particular tribunal would have thought right. As such, the reasonableness test is viewed by a number of commentators as not unduly challenging managerial prerogatives in the matter of discipline and as a factor contributing to the low success rate of unfair dismissal applications. In its current formulation, the test is whether the dismissal fell within 'the band of reasonable responses to the employee's conduct within which one employer might take one view, another quite reasonably another' (*Iceland Frozen Foods v. Jones* [1982] IRLR 439 at 442; *Post Office v. Foley*; *HSBC Bank v. Madden* [2000] IRLR 827, CA; *Sainsbury's Supermarkets Ltd v. Hitt* [2003] IRLR 23, CA).

Provided the employment tribunal follows the 'band of reasonable responses' test and does not substitute its own view, it will have considerable discretion in reaching its decision and it will only be in rare cases that its decision will be overturned on appeal. This is because the fairness of the dismissal is essentially a question of fact, and so long as the tribunal has properly directed itself as to the law then its decision will only be overturned if it was perverse – that is, if no reasonable tribunal could possibly have come to that decision on the particular facts.

In reaching a conclusion on the reasonableness of the dismissal, the tribunal may have regard to two broad questions: the substantive merits and procedural fairness.

Substantive Merits

The substantive merits may involve the tribunal taking into account mitigating factors such as the employee's length of service, previous disciplinary record and any explanation or excuse. It is also important to maintain consistency in the application of disciplinary rules so that employees who behave in much the same way should have meted out to them much the same punishment. In *The Post Office* v. *Fennell* [1981] IRLR 221, the employee was instantly dismissed following an assault on a fellow worker in the works canteen. The Court of Appeal upheld a finding of unfair dismissal on the grounds that there was evidence that other workers had been guilty of similar offences but these had not been met by dismissal.

The principle of consistency, however, should not be interpreted so as to force the employer merely to adopt a 'tariff' approach to misconduct and apply rules in an inflexible manner: the mitigating factors in each individual case should be fully considered before deciding whether the circumstances are truly parallel (*Hadjioannou* v. *Coral Casinos Ltd* [1981] IRLR 352 EAT).

Inconsistency of treatment in relation to those fighting at work was again in issue in *Cain* v. *Leeds Western Health Authority* [1990] IRLR 168. The applicant, a hospital laundry worker, was dismissed on the grounds of misconduct for fighting with another employee while on duty. Mr Cain claimed that his dismissal was unfair because in the past other employees guilty of acts of gross misconduct, including fighting, had not been dismissed. The tribunal, in dismissing his complaint, disregarded the inconsistencies in treatment on the grounds that the relevant decision in the various cases were taken by different members of management. This view was overturned by the EAT who held that it is inconsistency of treatment by the employer rather than by individual line managers that is the crucial question:

> Because an employer is acting in one case through his servants A and B, and the other case through his servant C and D, it is no answer to a complaint of unfair dismissal to say that there were different employees considering the seriousness of the two alleged cases of misconduct. The consistency must be consistency as between all the employees of the employer.

Procedural Fairness

The second element of the test of fairness relates to the question of the fairness of the procedures adopted by the employer in the events leading up to the dismissal. The concept of procedural fairness is not expressly articulated in the legislation but its development was influenced by the codes of practice which were introduced to accompany the legislation. The provisions relevant to discipline and dismissal are presently contained in the ACAS Code of Practice on Disciplinary and Grievance Procedures. The Code was originally introduced in 1977. The most recent revision of the Code came into effect on 4 September 2000. The Code's guidelines do not carry the force of law, but any of its provisions which appear to a court or tribunal to be relevant to a question arising in the proceedings must be taken into account in reaching a decision (see TULR[C]A 1992, s. 207).

ACAS is updating the Code of Practice to take account of the new statutory procedures set out in the Employment Act 2002. A public consultation on the revised code ended on 14 April 2004. It is intended that the revised code will come into effect in October 2004 at the same time as the regulations giving effect to the new dispute resolution procedures. ACAS has also published an advisory handbook entitled *Discipline at Work*. In 2001, the handbook was revised and republished as *Discipline and Grievances at Work*. Though the handbook has no statutory force, given that it concisely summarises the views of the leading cases on what constitutes good disciplinary practice it is well worthy of careful study and may well be influential in employment tribunal adjudications.

Essential Features of Disciplinary Procedures – the ACAS Code

First, the ACAS Code emphasises that disciplinary procedures should not be viewed primarily as a means of imposing sanctions; they should also be designed to emphasise and encourage improvements in individual conduct.

Paragraph 9 of the Code recommends that disciplinary procedures should:

(i)   be in writing;
(ii)   specify to whom they apply;
(iii)   be non-discriminatory;
(iv)   provide for matters to be dealt with without undue delay;
(v)   provide for proceedings, witness statements and records to be kept confidential;
(vi)   indicate the disciplinary actions which may be taken;
(vii)   specify the levels of management which have the authority to take the various forms of disciplinary action;
(viii) provide for workers to be informed of the complaints against them and where possible all relevant evidence before any hearing;
(ix)   provide workers with an opportunity to state their case before decisions are reached;
(x)   provide workers with the right to be accompanied (see also section three for information on the statutory right to be accompanied);
(xi)   ensure that, except for gross misconduct, no worker is dismissed for a first breach of discipline;
(xii)   ensure that disciplinary action is not taken until the case has been carefully investigated;
(xiii) ensure that workers are given an explanation for any penalty imposed;
(xiv)   provide a right of appeal – normally to a more senior manager – and specify the procedure to be followed.

Second, on warnings, the Code recommends that in the case of minor offences there should be a formal oral warning (stage 1), followed by a written warning (stage 2), and then a final written warning (stage 3) which should make it clear that any recurrence will result in dismissal. However, as the ACAS advisory handbook makes clear, this does not mean that three warnings must always be given before dismissal action is taken. On occasion, the seriousness of the offence may make it appropriate to enter the procedure at stage 2 or stage 3. As we shall see below, there are also occasions when dismissal without notice is applicable.

The Code places emphasis on writing and retaining detailed personnel records by the employer who must be able if necessary to provide documentary proof of previous warnings. As a result a number of employers now adopt the practice of even giving written confirmation of an 'oral warning' and of requiring the employee's signature to acknowledge receipt.

The employer's system should include some time limit on warnings, so that after a set period they lapse; for example, warnings for minor offences may be valid for up to six months, while final warnings may remain active for 12 months or more. The life of a warning may also depend on the employee's previous disciplinary record. In rare cases, where there is serious misconduct, the employer may be held to be justified in refusing to set a time limit on the warning. Where this occurs, it should be made very clear to the employee that the final written warning can never be removed and that any recurrence will lead to dismissal.

A warning should be reasonably specific, identifying the precise ground of complaint by the employer. Commentators have suggested that one consequence of this is that a warning on ground A (such as bad language) should not be used as a step in the procedure to dismiss on ground B (such as bad timekeeping). This may mean that one employee may be subject to more than one series of warnings at the same time. Of course, there may come a point when the cumulative effect of a number of warnings on different matters provides reasonable grounds to dismiss on the grounds of generally unacceptable behaviour.

In *Auguste Noel Ltd* v. *Curtis* [1990] IRLR 326, however, we see the EAT taking a different approach in relation to previous warnings concerned with unrelated misconduct. Mr Curtis, a 'multi-drop' driver, was dismissed on 18 March 1988 for an act of misconduct involving mishandling company property. In deciding to dismiss him for that offence, the employer took into account two previous written warnings, one dated 16 October 1987 concerning his relationship with other employees and the other, dated 25 February 1988, referring to unsatisfactory documentation and absenteeism.

The EAT held that the tribunal had been wrong to find that the dismissal for mishandling company property was unfair because, in deciding to dismiss for that reason, the employers had taken into account two final written warnings for different offences.

Mr Justice Wood stated:

it can very rarely be said, if ever, that warnings are irrelevant to the consideration of an employer who is considering dismissal. The mere fact that the conduct was of a different kind on those occasions when warnings were given does not seem to us to render them irrelevant. It is essentially a matter of balance, of doing what is fair and reasonable in the circumstances and the employer is entitled to consider the existence of warnings. He is entitled to look at the substance of the complaint on each of those occasions, how many warnings there have been, the dates and the periods of time between those warnings and indeed all the circumstances of the case.

A third essential feature of disciplinary procedures concerns cases of gross misconduct. The ACAS Code of Practice advises that dismissal for a first breach of discipline should be restricted to cases of 'gross misconduct'. This phrase has no statutory definition, nor is it defined by the Code of Practice itself, but it is generally regarded as misconduct serious enough to destroy the relationship of trust and confidence between the employer and the employee. This would include:

- theft
- dishonesty
- violence at work

- serious incapability through drink or drugs
- deliberate damage to the employer's property
- serious acts of disobedience to lawful and reasonable orders
- gross negligence causing (or creating the risk of) significant economic loss, damage to property or personal injury.

In other cases, what constitutes gross misconduct may depend on the circumstances and the employer's own disciplinary rules. Employers may codify the orders and requirements for their employees in a series of disciplinary rules. Indeed, ERA 1996, s. 3 (1) (a) requires that the written statement of terms of employment must include 'any disciplinary rules applicable to the employee'. However, the Employment Act 1989 s. 13 removed the statutory requirement to provide a note of disciplinary rules and appeals procedure where the number of employees of the employer and any associated employer is less than 20. This amendment was yet a further example of the then Conservative government's policy of deregulation in the name of encouraging the growth of small businesses. However, given that a factor which will be influential in many dismissal cases is whether the employer adequately brought the existence of a particular disciplinary rule to the attention of an employee, small employers might have been well advised not to take advantage of this exemption. The 'fewer than 20' threshold was hard to justify and the Employment Act 2002 removed the exemption.

Disciplinary rules may be regarded as preliminary warnings to employees that the employer regards certain types of offence with particular gravity and that these will be likely to result in instant dismissal. However, while it is important that employees should be given a clear indication of the likely sanction consequent upon certain types of misconduct, imposition of that sanction should not be seen as following inexorably once the offence is committed. In other words, there is no such thing as an 'automatic' dismissal rule and employers must be prepared to exercise discretion, having allowed the employee to state his/her case and having considered such matters as the seriousness of the infringement of the rule, the employee's length of service and previous disciplinary record.

An illustration is provided by *Ladbroke Racing* v. *Arnott* [1983] IRLR 154. The applicants were employed in a betting shop. The employer's disciplinary rules specifically provided that employees were not permitted to place bets or to allow other staff to do so. Two of the applicants had placed such bets, one for her brother on one occasion and the other occasionally for old-age pensioners; the third, the office manager, had condoned these actions. All three employees were dismissed and a tribunal found the dismissals to be unfair. This decision was upheld by the EAT and the Court of Session on the basis that rules framed in mandatory terms did not leave the employer free from the obligation to act reasonably and to take into account the relatively minor nature of the offences in this particular case.

A final question concerns the situation where an employer summarily dismisses an employee for an offence which is not expressly set out in the disciplinary rules. The answer to this depends on fact and degree: the more serious the misconduct, the more likely the tribunal will find it reasonable for the employee to have anticipated the employer's reaction.

In *CA Parsons Ltd* v. *McLoughlin* [1978] IRLR 65, the dismissal of a shop steward for fighting was upheld although it was not included in the company's disciplinary rules as gross misconduct. Mr Justice Kilner Brown expressed the view that 'it ought not to be necessary for anybody, let alone a shop steward, to have in black and white in the form of a rule that a fight is going to be something that is to be regarded very gravely by management'.

Similarly, in *Ulsterbus* v. *Henderson* [1989] IRLR 253, the Northern Ireland Court of Appeal rejected a tribunal finding that it was unreasonable to dismiss a bus conductor for failure to give tickets in return for payment in circumstances where it was not made clear in the disciplinary procedure that offences of this nature would merit the ultimate sanction of dismissal. The court was of the view that it would be obvious to any employee that failure to give tickets in return for payment was a most serious offence which was likely to lead to dismissal.

Conversely, for offences whose gravity is not so immediately obvious there will be a requirement for the offence and likely sanction to be clearly expressed in the disciplinary rules – for example, consuming alcohol during working hours (*Dairy Produce Packers Ltd* v. *Beverstock* [1981] IRLR 265), or overstaying leave (*Hoover* v. *Forde* [1980] ICR 239).

While it is clear that the employer does not need to list every offence which could lead to dismissal, the offences which are listed will be taken as an indication of the character and class of offence which the employer views as gross misconduct. Therefore a dismissal for an offence of a less serious class or entirely different character than those set out in the disciplinary rules is likely to be regarded as unfair (see *Dietman* v. *London Borough of Brent* [1987] IRLR 299).

Hearings constitute a fourth key element of procedural fairness. Paragraph 14 of the ACAS Code states:

14. Before a decision is reached or any disciplinary action taken there should be a disciplinary hearing at which workers have the opportunity to state their case and to answer the allegations that have been made. Wherever possible the hearing should be arranged at a mutually convenient time and in advance of the hearing the worker should be advised of any rights under the disciplinary procedure including the statutory right to be accompanied (see section three). Prior to this stage, where matters remain informal, the statutory right of accompaniment does not arise.

Employees have the right to expect the following procedural guarantees when subject to disciplinary action:

(a) that they be informed of the nature of the allegations made against them;
(b) that they should be allowed to state their case;
(c) that those conducting the hearing should be free from bias.

However, the courts and tribunals have held that it is not necessary for the conduct of a fair hearing for the employee to be given the opportunity to cross-examine witnesses (*Ulsterbus* v. *Henderson* [1989] IRLR 251).

It is a general principle that a person who holds an inquiry must be seen to be impartial, that justice must not only be done but be seen to be done, and that if a reasonable observer with full knowledge of the facts would conclude that the hearing might not be impartial that is enough.

An illustration of an application of these principles is to be found in the decision of the EAT in *Moyes* v. *Hylton Castle Working Men's Social Club and Institute* [1986] IRLR 483, where two witnesses to an alleged act of sexual harassment by a club steward towards a barmaid were also members of the committee which dismissed the steward. The EAT held the dismissal to be unfair on the ground that it was a breach of natural justice for an apparently biased committee to decide the disciplinary matter. While the general rule is that if a person has been a witness s/he should not conduct the inquiry, the EAT did identify certain exceptions – for example, a firm which is owned and run by one person.

As for appeals, both the Code of Practice and advisory handbook lay great emphasis on the availability of an appeal against an initial decision to dismiss and tribunals have held dismissals to be unfair if such a procedure does not exist.

The handbook advises that an appeals procedure should:

- Specify any time limit within which the appeal should be lodged.
- Provide for appeals to be dealt with speedily, particularly those involving suspension without pay or dismissal.
- Wherever possible, provide for the appeal to be heard by an authority higher than that taking the disciplinary action.
- Spell out the action which may be taken by those hearing the appeal.
- Provide that the employee, or a representative if the employee so wishes, has an opportunity to comment on any new evidence arising during the appeal before any decision is taken.

The handbook recognises that in small organisations there may be no authority higher than the individual who took the original disciplinary action and that it is inevitable that they will hear the appeal. In such circumstances the handbook's advice is that the appeal hearing 'should be seen as an opportunity to review the original decision in an objective manner and at a quieter time. This can more readily be achieved if some time is allowed to lapse before the appeal hearing' (p. 33).

The importance of according the employee a right of appeal was underlined by the House of Lords in *W Midlands Cooperative Society* v. *Tipton* [1986] IRLR 112, where it was held that a dismissal will be unfair if:

(1) the employer unreasonably treated his/her real reason as a sufficient reason to dismiss the employee – either at the time the original decision to dismiss was made or at the conclusion of an internal appeal;
(2) the employer refused to entertain an appeal to which the employee was contractually entitled and thereby denied him or her the opportunity to show that, in all the circumstances, the real reason for dismissal could not reasonably be treated as sufficient.

Renewed Emphasis on Procedural Rectitude

In the early 1970s, the courts and tribunals laid much emphasis on the importance of employers adhering strictly to the basic procedural requirements of fairness, taking the Code as their guide. In one of the earliest cases, Sir John Donaldson thought that the only exception to the need for the employee to be allowed to state his/her case was 'where there can be no explanation which could cause the employer to refrain from dismissing the employee' (see *Earl* v. *Slater Wheeler (Airlyne) Ltd* [1972] IRLR 115). So it had to be almost inconceivable that the hearing could have made any difference. This test was, however, replaced by more lenient standards.

While the earlier approach could result in a dismissal being found to be unfair on procedural failings alone, the contemporary position is to view procedural matters as just one of a number of factors to be taken into account (see *Bailey* v. *BP Oil (Kent Refinery) Ltd*, cited in Note 9).

The high point of this dilution of procedural requirements is to be found in the test laid down by the Employment Appeal Tribunal in *British Labour Pump Co Ltd* v. *Byrne* [1979] IRLR. This test allowed the employer to argue that an element of procedural unfairness (such as a failure to give a proper hearing) may be 'forgiven' if the employer can show that, on the balance of probabilities, even if a proper procedure had been complied with the employee would still have been dismissed and the dismissal would then have been fair.

This decision received considerable academic and judicial criticism but was specifically approved of by the Court of Appeal in *Wass* v. *Binns* [1982] ICR 347. The major criticism of the *Labour Pump* principle was that it was irreconcilable with the ruling of the House of Lords in *W. Devis & Sons Ltd* v. *Atkin* [1977] AC 931, which held that the employer was not entitled to rely on evidence acquired after dismissal and that fairness must be judged in the light of facts known to the employer at the time of the dismissal.

This forceful criticism of the logic of *Labour Pump* was accepted by the House of Lords in *Polkey* v. *AE Dayton Services* (1987) IRLR 503 and the principle was overruled. This decision is perhaps the most important unfair dismissal decision of the last decade or so and in the judgments we find a re-emphasis on the importance of following a fair procedure. In the view of Lord Bridge:

> an employer having prima facie grounds to dismiss – will in the great majority of cases not act reasonably in treating the reason as a sufficient reason for the dismissal unless he has taken steps, conveniently classified in most authorities as 'procedural', which are necessary in the circumstances of the case to justify that course of action.

Lord Mackay was of the view that what must be considered is what a reasonable employer would have had in mind at the time he decided to dismiss:

> If the employer could reasonably have concluded in the light of circumstances known to him at the time of dismissal that consultation or warning would be utterly useless he might well act reasonably even if he did not observe the provisions of the Code.

It has been argued that there is a significant practical difference between asking whether at the time of the dismissal the employer had reasonable grounds for believing that a fair procedure would have been 'utterly useless' (the new test) and asking whether, in retrospect, it would have made any difference to the outcome (the old test). As a result it is likely that failure to follow a fair procedure may well lead to a finding of unfair dismissal in a much increased proportion of cases.[16]

Not all commentators are entirely convinced that the renewed emphasis on procedural rectitude will help applicants. McLean[17] suggests cynically that the renewed attachment to procedural justice is in inverse proportion to the likelihood of compensation being awarded to an 'undeserving' dismissed employee. In the early days of unfair dismissal, the tribunals could reduce compensation to nil where there had been a 'technical' unfair dismissal. When this power was removed with the introduction of the minimum basic award in EPCA 1978, the *British Labour Pump Co Ltd* v. *Byrne* principle developed. Following the repeal of the minimum basic award by the Employment Act 1980, there has been a return to the earlier approach. Of course, as McLean recognises, holding that the dismissed employee contributed to his/her own dismissal will not mean zero compensation in every case, whereas a finding of fair dismissal will mean just that.

Recent developments may confirm some of McLean's doubts. First, it is clear that the 'no difference' test still has a significant part to play in reducing compensation awards (see *Rao* v. *Civil Aviation Authority* [1994] IRLR 495 CA; *Red Bank Manufacturing Co. Ltd* v. *Meadows* [1992] ICR 204 EAT). Furthermore, in *Duffy* v. *Yeomans and Partners Ltd* [1994] IRLR 642 CA it was held that *Polkey* does not require that the employer must have consciously taken a decision not to consult with the employee. According to Balcome LJ it is sufficient that, judged objectively, the employer does what a reasonable employer might do. The danger inherent in this approach is that it resembles the 'did it make any difference' test that *Polkey* rejected.

Representation

The ACAS Code recommends that employees should have the right to be accompanied by a trade union representative or fellow employee of their choice. Employees should be informed of this right on being invited to attend the disciplinary interview, and a refusal to allow representation may well result in a finding of unfair dismissal (*Rank Xerox (UK) Ltd* v. *Goodchild* [1976] IRLR 185).

Given the potential damage to industrial relations where management propose to discipline a trade union official, the Code recommends that no action beyond an oral warning should be taken until the case has been discussed with a senior trade union representative or full-time official.

In *Fairness at Work*, Cmnd. 3968, May 1998, the government proposed to create a statutory right for employees to be accompanied by a fellow employee or trade union representative of their choice during grievance and disciplinary hearings.

The purpose of the Employment Relations Act 1999, s. 10 is to create a statutory right for a worker to be accompanied by a fellow employee or trade union official of his or her choice. The 1999 Act does not place a duty on trade union officials or fellow employees to perform the role as the accompanying individual.

Section 13 (4) and (5) define 'disciplinary' and 'grievance' hearings for the purposes of s. 10. A grievance hearing is defined as a hearing which 'concerns the performance of a duty by the employer in relation to a worker'. According to the explanatory notes produced by the Department of Trade and Industry to accompany the legislation, this means a legal duty, i.e. statutory, contractual or common law. The purpose of the subsection is to seek to ensure that workers do not have the right to be accompanied at hearings where trivial or minor complaints are dealt with.

Both the statutory provisions and the Code are silent regarding the situations in which the worker may ask to be legally represented. At present, the case law on this indicates that an employer is not obliged to afford legal representation, and s. 10's silence on the matter would appear to give this unsatisfactory position implicit statutory support. *Sharma* v. *British Gas Corporation*, EAT 495/82, 27 July 1983, is one example of where it was held that there is no requirement to afford legal representation. However, there are a number of possible situations where this might well be essential, particularly where the worker is due to be involved in criminal and civil proceedings, and where he or she may have wider concerns (commercial, intellectual property, etc.) to protect in addition to his or her job.

Section 10 (2) states that the companion is permitted to address the hearing and to confer with the worker during the hearing, but he or she is not permitted to answer questions on behalf of the worker.

Section 11 provides that a complaint may be made to a tribunal that an employer has failed, or has *threatened* to fail, to comply with the right to accompaniment. An award not exceeding two weeks' pay may be ordered. If the issue arises in the context of unfair dismissal proceedings, no award under this head may be made if the tribunal makes a supplementary award under ERA 1996, s. 127A (2) where the employer provided a procedure for appealing against the dismissal but has prevented the employee from using it.

Section 12 provides that the worker has the right not to be subject to any detriment by any act, or failure to act by his employer, on the grounds that he or she sought to exercise the right to be accompanied or sought to accompany a worker in accordance with s. 10. It expressly provides that accompanying workers have these rights whether or not they share the same employer as the worker seeking accompaniment. An employer will not, however, be required to pay his employee for time taken off to accompany another employer's worker.

By virtue of s. 12 (3), where the reason for a dismissal is the exercising of rights under s. 10, or the fact that a person has accompanied another in accordance with that section, the dismissal will be automatically unfair. Subsection (4) provides that rights under the section are not subject to any age limit or qualifying period. Subsection (5) extends the availability of interim relief, provided for by ss. 128–132 of ERA 1996, to dismissals for seeking the right to be accompanied.

For the purposes of these new rights, a 'worker' is defined in s. 13 in wider terms than just an 'employee'. It extends to 'worker' as already defined in ERA 1996, s. 230 (3) (contracts of employment and other contracts whereby the person undertakes personal services or work), and also to agency and homeworkers (as defined by s. 13 [2], [3]) and Crown servants, among others.

Some Common Disciplinary Issues

In this section, we discuss the scope of the five categories of potentially fair reasons for dismissal: capability/qualifications; conduct; redundancy; continued employment involving breach of the law; and some other substantial reason. In the course of this discussion we shall focus on the approaches adopted by the courts and tribunals in relation to a number of frequently recurring dismissal issues. These are as follows: sub-standard performance; absence (long-term illness, persistent absenteeism); dishonesty; and business reorganisation dismissals.

Capability/Qualifications

Under this head the employer has to show that the reason (or, if there was more than one, the principal reason) for the dismissal 'related to the capability or qualifications of the employee for performing work of the kind which he was employed to do' (ERA 1996, s. 98 [2] [a]). 'Capability' is defined in s. 98 (3) (a) (b) as 'capability assessed by reference to skill, aptitude, health or any other physical or mental quality' and 'qualifications' as 'any degree, diploma or other academic, technical or professional qualification relevant to the position which the employee held'. 'Qualifications' has to be construed in the light of the particular position which the employee held. Therefore, in certain circumstances, failure to pass a required aptitude test can be a reason for dismissal relating to qualification to do the job (*Blackman* v. *The Post Office* [1974] IRLR 46 NIRC). However, a mere licence, permit or authorisation is not a qualification unless it is substantially concerned with the employee's aptitude or ability to do the job (*Blue Star Ship Management Ltd* v. *Williams* [1979] IRLR 16 EAT).

Sub-standard Work

Sub-standard work may occur for a variety of reasons. It has been suggested that it is only when the employee is inherently incapable of reasonable standards of work that the dismissal is related to 'capability' within ERA 1996, s. 98 (2) (a). Where the employee has the capacity to do the job but produces poor performance because of carelessness or lack of motivation, then the matter is probably better dealt with as misconduct (*Sutton and Gates (Luton) Ltd* v. *Bloxall* [1978] IRLR 486).

Evidence of Incompetence

> Wherever a man is dismissed for incapacity or incompetence it is sufficient that the employer honestly believes on reasonable grounds that the man is incapable or incompetent. It is not necessary for the employer to prove that he is in fact incapable or incompetent.
>
> (Lord Denning in *Alidair Ltd* v. *Taylor* [1978] IRLR 82)

Therefore, the test is not purely subjective and the requirement of reasonable grounds dictates that the employer should have carried out a proper and full investigation into the question. However, as the above quote from Lord Denning suggests, the employer is not required to prove that the employee was in fact incompetent. In this sense, the test resembles the approach adopted in relation to suspected misconduct, discussed later in this chapter.

In the application of the test, the courts and tribunals have shown themselves prepared to give considerable weight to the employer's opinions and views concerning incapacity. In *Cook* v. *Thomas Linnell & Sons Ltd* [1977] IRLR 132, for example, the EAT expressed the view that although employers must act reasonably when removing from a particular post an employee whom they consider to be unsatisfactory, it was important that the unfair dismissal legislation did not impede employers unreasonably in the efficient management of their business. The tribunal went on to state: 'When responsible employers have genuinely come to the conclusion over a reasonable period of time that a manager is incompetent we think that it is some evidence that he is incompetent.'

The ACAS advisory handbook offers the following guidance on how alleged poor performance cases should be approached:

- The employee should be asked for an explanation and the explanation checked.
- Where the reason is the lack of the required skills, the employee should, wherever practicable, be assisted through training and given reasonable time to reach the required standard of performance.

- Where despite encouragement and assistance the employee is unable to reach the required standard of performance, consideration should be given to finding suitable alternative work.
- Where alternative work is not available, the position should be explained to the employee before dismissal action is taken.
- An employee should not normally be dismissed because of poor performance unless warnings and a chance to improve have been given.
- If the main cause of poor performance is the changing nature of the job, employers should consider whether the situation may properly be treated as redundancy rather than a capability issue.

While in most cases of poor performance a system of warnings should be operated, there are rare occasions where the employee commits a single mistake and the actual or potential consequences of that mistake are so serious that to warn would not be appropriate. This class of case was discussed by the Court of Appeal in *Taylor* v. *Alidair* [1978] IRLR 82, where it was stated that there are activities in which the degree of professional skill which must be required is so high, and the potential consequences of the smallest departure from that high standard are so serious, that one failure to perform in accordance with those standards is enough to justify dismissal. Examples might be the passenger-carrying airline pilot, the scientist operating the nuclear reactor, the chemist in charge of research into the possible effect of thalidomide, the driver of the Manchester to London express, the driver of an articulated lorry full of sulphuric acid.

Long-term Sickness Absence

One of the most common and difficult problems facing employers and trade union representatives in the realm of disciplinary practice and procedure is employee absence through sickness or injury. In these situations the employer will frequently have to resolve a conflict between economic considerations and the employee's claim for job security and fair treatment where s/he is absent through no fault of his/her own. Likewise, trade union representatives must protect those members who, in addition to shouldering the burden of ill-health, face the prospect of unemployment.

In cases of exceptionally severe and incapacitating illness where it is highly unlikely that the employee will ever be fit to return to work, the contract may be regarded as 'frustrated' and, therefore, terminated by operation of law rather than dismissal. The rules governing the doctrine of frustration and its relationship to long-term sickness absence and imprisonment were discussed in the previous chapter.

Given that the frustration doctrine offers employers a convenient way in which to avoid the unfair dismissal provisions, the courts are generally reluctant to apply it to contracts which are terminable by notice. Therefore, in less drastic cases of long-term sickness absence a body of case law has developed on the question of the fairness of a dismissal in such circumstances.

Two broad tests have been used by tribunals in determining fairness: the substantive and the procedural. The substantive aspect of the tribunal's inquiry revolves around the question of whether it was reasonable of the employer to dismiss in the particular circumstances of the case. In *Spencer* v. *Paragon Wallpapers Ltd* [1976] IRLR 373, Mr Justice Phillips set out the relevant consideration as follows:

the nature of the illness, the likely length of the continuing absence, the need for the employers to have done the work which the employee was employed to do ...

The basic question which has to be determined in every case is whether, in all the circumstances, the employer can be expected to wait any longer and, if so, how much longer? Every case will be different, depending on the circumstances.

Therefore a balance has to be struck between job security and the interests of the business (see para. 40 of the Industrial Relations Code of Practice, 1972). Where the absent employee holds a position which cannot be filled easily on a temporary basis and his/her continued absence is inconsistent with the operation efficiency of the undertaking, tribunals have held dismissals to be fair (see *Tan* v. *Berry Bros and Rudd Ltd* [1974] IRLR 244; *Coulson* v. *Felixstowe Docks and Railway Co* [1975] IRLR 11; *McPhee* v. *George H. Wright* [1975] IRLR 132).

The question of the time the employee must be away from work before it may be reasonable for an employer to dismiss him/her depends, as was stated in *Spencer*, on the circumstances of each case. A significant factor may be the size of the employer's undertaking. In a large firm, the disruption caused by sickness absence may be minimal, but in a small business such absences may be extremely serious.

Where an employee is covered by a contractual sick-pay scheme, can the employer dismiss before the sick-pay entitlement elapses? It may be assumed that if an employer has contracted to provide a certain period of sick pay it would not normally be reasonable to dismiss before this time span has elapsed. However, this does not mean that it will always be unfair to dismiss during the currency of a sick-pay period. In *Coulson* the company dismissed an employee whose lengthy absence over the previous two years had caused inconvenience from time to time when, because of a labour shortage, a replacement could not be found. He sought to argue before the tribunal, inter alia, that he should not have been dismissed before his sick pay entitlement was exhausted. This contention was rejected by the tribunal, which found that the sick-pay scheme was 'a financial provision and not a provision which in any event indicates the amount of absence to which an employee is entitled, if he is sick'. In line with this approach, merely because the absent employee has exhausted his/her sick-pay entitlement does not mean that an employer can automatically dismiss the employee even where the contract so provides (see *Hardwick* v. *Leeds Area Health Authority* [1975] IRLR 319).

The second aspect of the reasonableness test involves a consideration of the adequacy of the procedures the employer has adopted in coming to the conclusion that the dismissal was necessary. An employer will be expected to make a reasonable effort to inform him/herself of the true medical position and this will normally entail consulting the employee and seeking, with the employee's consent, a medical opinion. A model letter of enquiry to an employee's general practitioner, approved by the BMA, is included as Appendix 4 (vii) to the ACAS advisory handbook.

The Access to Medical Reports Act 1988, which came into force on 1 January 1989, now regulates the supply of medical reports on employees to employers. The Act obliges an employer to inform an employee of the intention to ask the employee's doctor for a medical report and to obtain the employee's consent. There is also a requirement that the employee be informed of the following rights under the Act: the right to refuse consent; the right of access to the report both before and after it is supplied to the employer; the right to refuse consent to the report being supplied to the employer; the right to amend the report where it is considered by the employee to be 'incorrect and misleading'. The right to amend is qualified by the fact that the Act allows the doctor to accept or reject the amendments. However, where the doctor does not accept the patient's amendments, s/he must attach a statement of the patient's views to the report (s. 5 [2] [b]).

If an employee does refuse to give consent to allow the employer to approach his/her GP, this may be taken by the tribunal to confirm the employer's doubts that the employee is fit to carry out his/her duties – see *Leeves* v. *Edward Hope Ltd* COIT 19464/77 July 1977.

Many employers now make it a term of employment that the employee agrees, if and when requested, to undergo a medical examination by the organisation's own occupational health practitioner or by an independent doctor to be nominated by the employer. The provisions of the Access to Medical Reports Act only apply to reports requested from the employee's own doctor.

The decision whether to dismiss is a managerial one rather than a medical question and, therefore, the medical opinion which the employer seeks must be sufficiently detailed to allow him/her to make a rational and informed decision (*East Lindsey District Council* v. *Daubney*). In the event of a conflict of opinion, some tribunal decisions have favoured the opinion of the employer's medical officer over that of the employee's own GP on the basis that the former is more aware of the demands of the job (see *Jeffries* v. *BP Tanker Co Ltd* [1974] IRLR 260; *Ford Motor Co Ltd* v. *Nawaz* [1987] IRLR 163; compare *Liverpool Area Health Authority* v. *Edwards* [1977] IRLR 471).

The need for consultation with the employee was stressed in *Spencer* v. *Paragon Wallpapers Ltd* and strongly affirmed by the EAT's decision in *E Lindsey District Council* v. *Daubney* [1977] IRLR 181. On the other hand, consultation has not always been required by tribunals. In *Taylorplan Catering (Scotland) Ltd* v. *McInally* [1980] IRLR 53 it was suggested that where a tribunal finds that the circumstances were such that a consultation would have made no difference to the result, lack of consultation could be justified. In this case, the EAT was of the view that the guidelines in *British Labour Pump* could be applied in cases involving ill-health. With the rejection of those guidelines by the House of Lords in *Polkey* it is likely that consultation will be required in the vast majority of cases.[18]

Assuming that the tribunal is satisfied that the employer could not be expected to wait any longer before replacing the sick employee and that he/she has made reasonable efforts to establish the true medical position, the employer may find that there is one further requirement to comply with before it is possible successfully to defend a claim of unfair dismissal: an obligation to look for alternative work for the sick employee within the organisation. Where there is a suitable job in existence which the employee is capable of performing, a failure to offer it to the employee may well cast doubt upon the fairness of the dismissal.

Therefore, if there is an existing job, even if it is lower paid, the employer should offer the alternative work to the employee. If the employee refuses any such offers, then it seems reasonable for the employer to dismiss the employee. This statement requires some qualification in the sense that the employer is only required to consider the employee's ability to perform existing jobs: there is no duty on the employer to create a new job (see *Merseyside and North Wales Electricity Board* v. *Taylor* [1975] IRLR 60). However, the employer may be expected to go to reasonable lengths to modify a particular job in order to meet the employee's needs (see *Carricks [Caterers] Ltd* v. *Nolan* [1980] IRLR 259).

For a checklist on handling long-term sickness absence see p. 42 of the ACAS advisory handbook, *Discipline and Grievances at Work* (1987: revised 2001).

Persistent Absenteeism

While long-term absence is treated as a matter of incapability it is clear that persistent absenteeism should be regarded as a matter of misconduct and can be dealt with under the ordinary disciplinary procedure (see *International Sports Ltd* v. *Thomson* [1980] IRLR 340; *Rolls Royce* v. *Walpole* [1980] IRLR 343).

The following extract from the ACAS handbook, *Discipline and Grievances at Work*, provides a checklist of what the courts and tribunals expect from employers in handling cases of frequent and persistent short-term absence:

- unexpected absences should be investigated promptly and the worker asked for an explanation at a return-to-work interview.
- if there are no acceptable reasons then the matter should be treated as a conduct issue and dealt with under the disciplinary procedure.
- where there is no medical certificate to support frequent short-term, self-certified, absences then the worker should be asked to see a doctor to establish whether treatment is necessary and whether the underlying reason for the absence is work-related. If no medical support is forthcoming the employer should consider whether to take action under the disciplinary procedure.
- if the absence could be disability related the employer should consider what reasonable adjustments could be made in the workplace to help the worker (this might be something as simple as an adequate, ergonomic chair, or a power-assisted piece of equipment (19)). Reasonable adjustment also means redeployment to a different type of work if necessary.
- if the absence is because of temporary problems relating to dependants, the worker may be entitled to have time off under the provisions of the Maternity and Parental Leave (time off for dependants in an emergency) Regulations 1999. This may be sufficient to improve the levels of absence and for the worker to resolve the difficulty. Other domestic problems may be solved through the worker taking holiday or by special leave arrangements, or by a rearrangement of hours worked. Collective or contractual agreements may also make provisions for such circumstances.
- in all cases the worker should be told what improvement in attendance is expected and warned of the likely consequences if this does not happen.
- if there is no improvement, the worker's length of service, performance, the likelihood of a change in attendance, the availability of suitable alternative work, and the effect of past and future absences on the organisation should all be taken into account in deciding appropriate action.

The Malingering Employee

Where the employer suspects that the absent employee is malingering, the issue should be treated as a matter of misconduct and normal disciplinary procedures followed. In *Hutchinson* v. *Enfield Rolling Mills Ltd* [1981] IRLR 318, it was held that a doctor's medical certificate was not conclusive proof of genuine sickness absence if the employer had other evidence that the employee was fit enough to attend work. This principle would, of course, apply with even more force where the employee has self-certificated absence.

Conduct

Dismissal for a reason related to the conduct of the employer covers a multitude of sins, encompassing those capable of amounting to gross misconduct (violence, theft, a serious act of disobedience, gross negligence) and also less serious infringements of discipline such as minor acts of insubordination, bad language and bad timekeeping. As we have seen, except in cases of dismissal for a single act of gross misconduct, the courts and tribunals expect employers to adopt the system of warnings discussed earlier.

Dishonesty and Other Criminal Offences

The courts and tribunals maintain a distinction between offences committed at work and those outside. Whether the commission of a criminal offence outside work merits an employee's dismissal depends above all on its relevance to the individual's duties as an employee. Tribunals take into account the following matters: the status of the employee; the nature of the offence; the employee's past record; the employee's access to cash (in cases of dishonesty); and proximity to members of the public (in cases of offences of violence).

In *P* v. *Nottinghamshire County Council* [1992] IRLR 362, the Court of Appeal stated that:

> in an appropriate case and where the size and administrative resources of the employer's undertaking permit, it may be unfair to dismiss an employee without the employer first considering whether the employee can be offered some other job, notwithstanding that it may be clear that he cannot be allowed to continue in his original job. (Lord Justice Balcombe)

Furthermore, where the alleged offence is committed outside employment, the Code of Practice advises that employees should not be dismissed 'solely because a charge against them is pending or because they are absent through having been remanded in custody' (para. 15 [c]). Nevertheless, there may be cases where the period of absence on remand is lengthy and the employer may be held to be justified, in the interests of the business, in seeking a permanent replacement (see *Kingston* v. *British Railways Board* [1984] IRLR 146 CA). Indeed, a lengthy period in custody on remand or a sentence of imprisonment on conviction may result in a finding that the employment contract has been 'frustrated', as discussed in the previous chapter.

An employee may be fairly dismissed where s/he conceals from his/her employer a criminal conviction imposed before the employment began and which is not a 'spent' conviction under the Rehabilitation of Offenders Act, 1974. Whether or not a conviction is spent and the individual is a 'rehabilitated person' under the Act depends upon the severity of the sentence and the time which has elapsed since it was imposed. (See Chapter 3 above for the rehabilitation periods.)

Section 4 (3) of the Act makes it automatically unfair to dismiss someone on the grounds of a conviction which is spent or because of failure to disclose it (see *Property Guards Ltd* v. *Taylor and Kershaw* [1982] IRLR 175). The scope of this provision is limited by subsequent regulations which exclude certain professions and employments from the Act. Exempted groups include: medical practitioners, lawyers, accountants, veterinary surgeons, dentists, nurses, opticians, pharmaceutical chemists, judicial appointments, justices' clerks, probation officers, those employed by local authorities in connection with the provision of social services, those offices and employments concerned with the provisions of services, schooling, training and so on to persons under the age of 18 where the holder will have access to young persons (or employment on premises used for providing such services) – see the Rehabilitation of Offenders Act 1974 (Exceptions) Order 1975 (SI 1975 No. 1023) as amended by the Rehabilitation of Offenders Act 1974 (Exceptions) (Amendment) Orders 1986 (SI 1986 No. 1249 and SI 1986 No. 2268).

An employer, when recruiting to an exempted occupation, should inform candidates in writing that spent convictions must be disclosed. If a person is then employed having failed to disclose a conviction, the employer may be held to have acted fairly if it dismisses on subsequent discovery of the conviction (see *Torr* v. *British Railways Board* [1977] ICR 785).

Suspected Dishonesty within Employment

As in all cases of misconduct, employers should not dismiss for dishonesty unless and until they have formed a genuine and reasonable belief in the guilt of the employee. The authoritative guidance on this issue is *BHS* v. *Burchell* [1978] IRLR 379 (approved by the Court of Appeal in *W. Weddel & Co Ltd* v. *Tepper* [1980] IRLR 96 CA). The test formulated by the EAT in Burchell is whether the employer:

(a) entertained a reasonable belief in the guilt of the employee;
(b) had reasonable grounds for that belief; and
(c) had carried out as much investigation into the matter as was reasonable.

What if the criminal court subsequently acquits a dismissed person? Remember that the employers are judged on the reasonableness of their actions at the time of the dismissal and not on the basis of what happens afterwards. Therefore, as long as the Burchell tests are satisfied then such a dismissal will be likely to be held to be fair. The standard of proof required in an unfair dismissal case (on the balance of probabilities) is not as onerous as in a criminal case (beyond all reasonable doubt).

A Reasonable Investigation

What constitutes reasonable investigation will very much depend on the circumstances of the particular case. At one extreme there is the employee who is caught red-handed, while at the other the guilt of the employee may be a matter of pure inference. The closer the case is to the latter end of the continuum, the more exacting the standard of inquiry and investigation required.

In cases where the position is less than clear-cut, it is clearly advisable for the employer to carry out an investigation before putting the accusation to the employee. This is because an accusation without reasonable foundation could entitle the recipient employee to resign and claim constructive dismissal (see *Robinson* v. *Crompton Parkinson Ltd* [1978] ICR 401).

Where an employee, having been charged with or convicted of a criminal offence, refuses to co-operate with the employer's investigation, it has been held that this should not prevent the employer from proceeding. In *Carr* v. *Alexander Russell Ltd* [1976] IRLR 220 it was suggested that it would be improper, after an employee has been arrested and charged with a criminal offence alleged to have been committed in the course of employment, for the employer to seek to question the employee. However, this approach was rejected in *Harris (Ipswich) Ltd* v. *Harrison* [1978] IRLR 382, where the view was expressed that there was nothing to prevent an employer in such circumstances from discussing the matter with the employee or his/her representative. What needs to be discussed is not so much the alleged offence as the action the employer is proposing to take and whether there are any mitigating circumstances, such as a lengthy and previously unblemished service record.

Therefore, where an employee – perhaps after having taken legal advice – chooses to remain silent, s/he should be given written warning that, unless s/he does provide further information, a disciplinary decision will be taken on the basis of the information that is available and could result in dismissal (see *Harris and Shepherd* v. *Courage (Eastern) Ltd* [1981] IRLR 153).

The ACAS handbook, *Discipline and Grievances at Work*, advises that where the police are involved they should not be asked to conduct the investigation on behalf of the employer nor should they be present at any disciplinary hearing or interview. Similarly, the employer cannot simply leave the disciplinary decision to the criminal justice system – deciding not to carry out an internal investigation but to dismiss the employee automatically if s/he is found guilty at trial (see *McLaren* v. *National Coal Board* [1988] IRLR 215).

'Blanket' Dismissals

The general rule is that employers may only dismiss for misconduct if they entertain a genuine and reasonable belief in the employee's guilt (see *BHS* v. *Burchell*, cited above). This rule was modified in cases where, despite all reasonable investigations, the employer is unable to identify the culprit but knows it must be one of two employees. In such a case the Court of Appeal has held that it is reasonable to dismiss both (see *Monie* v. *Coral Racing Ltd* [1981] ICR 109).

This principle concerning blanket dismissals has recently been extended by the EAT to cases of conduct or capability not involving dishonesty (see *Whitbread & Co* v. *Thomas* [1988] IRLR 43). According to this case, an employer who cannot identify which member of a group was responsible for an act can fairly dismiss the whole group, even where it is probable that not all were guilty of the act – provided three conditions are satisfied. First, the act in question must be such that, if committed by an identified individual, it would justify dismissal of that individual; second, the tribunal must be satisfied that the act was committed by one or more of the group, all of whom can be shown to be individually capable of having committed the act complained of; third, the tribunal must be satisfied that there has been a proper investigation by the employer to identify the person or persons responsible for the act.

This principle has been most recently applied by the EAT in *Parr* v. *Whitbread plc* [1990] IRLR 39. Mr Parr was employed as a branch manager of one of the respondent's off-licence shops. He was dismissed along with three other employees when the sum of £4,600 was stolen from the shop in circumstances which indicated that it was an inside job. Each of the four had equal opportunity of committing the theft and the employers found it impossible to ascertain which of them was actually guilty. The EAT upheld the IT's finding of a fair dismissal.

Unfair Redundancy Dismissals

As we have seen, redundancy is a prima facie fair ground for dismissal. It is important to note, however, that the statutory presumption that a dismissal is for redundancy under ERA 1996, s. 163 (2), which applies when the claim is for a redundancy payment, does not apply in relation to an unfair dismissal claim. Therefore it is up to the employer to prove that redundancy was the reason for dismissal.

Even where the employer has succeeded in this task, the dismissal for redundancy may still be attacked as unfair on one of two grounds:

(i)   If the circumstances constituting the redundancy also applied equally to one or more employees in the same undertaking who held posts similar to that held by the dismissed employee and they have not been dismissed and:

    (a) the reason (or, if more than one, the principal reason) for selecting the employee was union-related (TULR[C]A, s. 153); or

    (b) the reason for the selection was because of pregnancy or childbirth or because the employee had been involved in raising or taking action on health and safety issues; asserted certain statutory rights; performed (or proposed to perform) any functions as a trustee of an occupational scheme; performed (or proposed to perform) the functions or activities of an employee representative for the purposes of consultation over redundancies or the transfer of an undertaking; or, as a 'protected' or 'opted out' shop or betting worker, refused to work on a Sunday.

    The above reasons are regarded as automatically unfair and do not require two years' continuous employment before claims may be made.

(ii) Unreasonable redundancy under ERA 1996, s. 98 (4). Under s. 98 (4), the employment tribunal still has to decide whether an employer's selection of a particular employee for redundancy was reasonable (see *Watling* v. *Richardson* [1978] IRLR 255). Also certain types of selection agreements, such as 'part-timers first', may amount to indirect sex discrimination (see *Clarke and Powell* v. *Eley [IMI] Kynoch Ltd* [1982] IRLR 131 and compare with *Kidd* v. *DRG Ltd [UK]* [1985] IRLR 190).

Whether or not there is a redundancy agreement, the employee may challenge the fairness of the redundancy dismissal under s. 98 (4) (this was decided by the CA in *Bessenden Properties Ltd* v. *Corness* [1977] ICR 821).

The leading case in this area is *Williams* v. *Compair Maxam Ltd* [1982] IRLR 83, where the EAT laid down five principles of 'good industrial relations practice' which should generally be followed in redundancies where the employees are represented by an independent and recognised trade union. These guidelines were as follows:

(i)   to give as much warning as possible;

(ii) to consult with the union, particularly relating to the criteria to be applied in selection for redundancy; (Principles (i) and (ii) find an echo of what is now TULR(C)A 1992, ss. 188–192, as amended by the Collective Redundancies and Transfer of Undertakings (Protection of Employment) (Amendment) Regulations 1995 (SI 1995 No. 2587). Under the amended sections, there is an obligation to consult recognised trade unions or employee representatives 'in good time' as opposed to 'at the earliest opportunity' which was the phrase used prior to amendment. If the employer is proposing to dismiss 100 or more employees at one establishment over a 90-day period, consultations must commence not less than 90 days before the first dismissal. If it is proposed to dismiss 20 or more over a period of 90 days or less, consultations should take place at least 30 days before the first dismissal takes effect. There is no minimum period where the employer proposes to dismiss fewer than 20 employees. An employee who suffers loss through lack of consultation may receive compensation in the form of a 'protective award'. By virtue of the amendment, the threshold in TULR(C)A 1992, s. 188 for the obligatory 30 days' consultation was raised from 10 to 20 employees. Prior to amendment, the obligation was to consult with recognised trade unions. As stated above, the current situation is that the consultation is to be with either trade union representatives or with employee representatives elected by employees who may be made redundant. Where there are both elected representatives and a recognised trade union, consultation may be with either, as the employer chooses. This change has been criticised as allowing employers to block union involvement in the consultation process.)

(iii) to adopt objective rather than subjective criteria for selection; for example experience, length of service, attendance;

(iv) to select in accordance with the criteria, considering any representations made by the union regarding selection;

(v) to consider the possibility of redeployment rather than dismissal.

These guidelines have since been approved and applied by the Northern Ireland Court of Appeal in *Robinson v. Carrickfergus BC* [1983] IRLR 122, while in *Grundy (Teddington) Ltd v. Plummer* [1983] IRLR 98, the EAT emphasised that the guidelines should be applied flexibly, as one or more of the five points may not be appropriate in the particular circumstances of the case.

While the EAT in England has been in favour for a flexible but general application of the *Compair Maxam* guidelines, this approach has not found favour North of the Border. In *A. Simpson & Son (Motors) Ltd v. Reid and Findlater* [1983] IRLR 401, Lord MacDermott felt that the principles had been misapplied by the tribunals and that they only had application in situations where there was an independent recognised trade union. He was of the view that the principles had no relevance in a situation, such as that before the court, of a small business faced with a selection of two out of three people where no trade union was involved. In *Meikle v. McPhail (Charleston Arms)* [1983] IRLR 351, Lord MacDonald, referring somewhat disparagingly to the 'so-called principles' set out in *Compair Maxam* stated:

These principles must primarily refer to large organisations in which a significant number of redundancies are contemplated. In our view they should be applied with caution to circumstances such as the present where the size and administrative resources of the employer are minimal. (See also *Buchanan v. Tilcon Ltd* [1983] IRLR 417.)

We have been awaiting a decision from the Court of Appeal as to whether it approves of the *Compair Maxam* principles or adopts the restrictive Scottish approach. If the latter view is adopted, then the law will return to a pre-*Compair Maxam* state of affairs which rarely challenged management's approach to redundancy.

Strong implicit support for the need for the *Compair Maxam* principles, however, may now be derived from the House of Lords decision in *Polkey v. AE Dayton Services Ltd* which was discussed earlier in this chapter. As you will recall, this decision rejected the so-called no-difference rule – the rule that an unfair procedure leading to a dismissal does not render the dismissal unfair if it made no difference to the outcome. In the course of his judgment, Lord Bridge, while not referring to *Compair Maxam* by name, stated:

in the case of redundancy, the employer will not normally be acting reasonably unless he warns and consults any employees affected or their representative, adopts a fair basis on which to select for redundancy and takes such steps as may be reasonable to avoid or minimise redundancy by redeployment within his own organisation.

Lord Bridge felt that if a tribunal felt it likely the employee would have been dismissed even if consultation had taken place, the compensation could be reduced by 'a percentage representing the chance that the employee would still have lost his employment'. This was a better approach than the 'all or nothing' decision which resulted from the application of the no-difference rule. Moreover, Lord Bridge was of the view that:

> In a case where an Industrial Tribunal held that dismissal on the ground of redundancy would have been inevitable at the time it took place, even if the appropriate procedural steps had been taken, I do not, as presently advised, think this would necessarily preclude a discretionary order for re-engagement on suitable terms, if the altered circumstances considered by the Tribunal at the date of the hearing were thought to justify it.

For further discussion of redundancy dismissals see the following chapter.

Dismissal to Avoid Breach of a Statutory Duty or Restriction (ERA 1996, s. 98 [2] [d])

It is potentially fair for an employer to dismiss an employee because the employee 'could not continue to work in the position which he held without contravention (either on his part or on that of his employer) of a duty or restriction imposed by or under an enactment' (ERA 1996, s. 98 [2] [d]). Before proposing to act under this heading, the employee should seek legal advice as to whether the continued employment of the employee would involve a breach of the law. The courts and tribunals have taken a particularly strict view of the scope of the subsection and have held that it does not apply where the employer genuinely but mistakenly believes that continued employment would be unlawful (*Bouchaala* v. *Trusthouse Forte Hotels Ltd* [1980] IRLR 382).

The fact that the employer could not have lawfully continued to employ an employee without contravening the law does not inevitably lead to the conclusion that a dismissal falling within s. 98 (2) (d) is fair. In other words, the tribunal still has to be satisfied that the employer behaved reasonably within s. 98 (4) (*Sandhu* v. *1. Department of Education and Science 2. London Borough of Hillingdon* [1978] IRLR 208).

In practical terms, very few cases arise under this heading. The most common examples are cases where the individual employee is employed as a driver and then is disqualified from driving. In this sort of situation the employer should consider whether there is alternative work which can be offered to the disqualified driver before moving to dismissal (*Fearn* v. *Tayford Motor Company Ltd* [1975] IRLR 336).

Some Other Substantial Reason (ERA 1996, s. 98 [1] [b])

This is a catch-all category, intended to cover situations not encompassed by the four explicit admissible reasons (*RS Components Ltd* v. *Irwin* [1973] IRLR 239; and see *Alboni* v. *Ind Coope Retail Ltd* [1998] IRLR 131, CA). As with the other admissible reasons, the burden of proof is on the employer and if it cannot be shown that the reason which motivated the employer to dismiss was 'substantial', then the tribunal will find for the applicant.

Examples of dismissals which have been held to fall within this general residual category are given here.

Non-renewal of a Fixed-term Contract
This applies where it can be shown that there was a genuine need for fixed-term employment and the temporary nature of the employment was made known to the employee at the outset (see *Terry* v. *E Sussex County Council* [1976] IRLR 332; *N Yorkshire County Council* v. *Fay* [1985] IRLR 247).

Dismissal of Temporary Replacements
In two cases, statute provides that the dismissal of temporary replacement staff will constitute 'some other substantial reason'. The first is in respect of the dismissal of the replacement of an employee who has been on maternity leave (ERA 1996, s. 106 [2]) and the other concerns the dismissal of an individual employed to cover the absence of an employee who is suspended on medical grounds under ERA 1996, s. 64 (ERA 1996, s. 106 [2]). Such dismissals will be potentially justifiable, provided that the replacements have been informed in writing at the time of their engagement that their employment would be terminated on the return to work of the permanent employee. In addition, the tribunal must be satisfied that it was reasonable to dismiss and a relevant factor may be whether the employer has considered the availability of alternative work for the replacement employee.

Customer Pressure to Dismiss
Dismissal of an employee because an important customer of the employer was not willing to accept that employee doing the work has been held to constitute a substantial reason for dismissal (*Scott Packing & Warehousing Ltd* v. *Paterson* [1978] IRLR 166). However, if the employer wishes to rely on this ground for dismissal clear evidence must be produced that the valued customer had threatened to withdraw custom unless the employee was dismissed (*Grootcon [UK] Ltd* v. *Keld* [1984] IRLR 302).

In addition, before finally acceding to the demand, the employer should investigate the matter thoroughly in consultation with the customer and the employee, considering the possibility of deploying the employee on alternative work if it is available (*Dobie* v. *Burns International Security Services [UK] Ltd* [1984] IRLR 329).

Conflicts between Employees
Behaviour on the part of an employee which is causing disruption and discontent within the rest of the workforce has been held to constitute some other substantial reason for dismissal. For example, in *Treganowan* v. *Robert Knee & Co Ltd* [1975] IRLR 247, a female employee's frequent and open boasting about her sexual exploits had created tensions within the office which were affecting business. This behaviour was held to be some other substantial reason for dismissal and fair in the circumstances because she was completely insensitive to the effect she was having.

In such cases, however, dismissal must be viewed as a weapon of last resort and the employer must make sensible, practical and genuine efforts to see whether an improvement in relationships can be effected. The possibility of transferring the employee to another department should also be explored (*Turner* v. *Vestric Ltd* [1981] IRLR 23).

Finally, it should be borne in mind that pressure for the dismissal of an employee from the rest of the workforce which takes the form of industrial action will not help the employee justify the dismissal. As we saw earlier in this chapter, ERA 1996 s. 107 (2) specifically provides that, in determining the reason for the dismissal and its reasonableness, no account shall be taken of any industrial action threatened or taken against the employer.

Dismissal for Refusal to Accept Changes in Contractual Terms Resulting from a Business Reorganisation

One of the most controversial areas of unfair dismissal has concerned the correct approach to the situation where the employer wishes to reorganise the business in such a way that changes result in the employees' terms and condition of employment. These changes may not fall within the legal concept of redundancy because the work that the employee does is not diminished (see *Johnson* v. *Nottinghamshire Combined Police Authority* [1974] IRLR 20; *Lesney Products Ltd* v. *Nolan* [1977] IRLR 77).

The test of fairness is not inevitably controlled by the content of the contract of employment. As a result, the courts and tribunals have been prepared to hold as fair dismissals where the employee has refused to agree to a change in terms and conditions of employment in line with the employer's perception of business efficacy. Dismissals for refusal to agree to unilateral changes in job content, pay, location and hours of work have been held to be for some other substantial reason and fair (see, for example, *Ellis* v. *Brighton Cooperative Society* [1976] IRLR 419; *Hollister* v. *NFU* [1979] IRLR 23).

The tribunal will expect the employer to show evidence why it was felt to be necessary to impose the changes (*Banerjee* v. *City and E London AHA* [1979] IRLR 147) and it is also material for the tribunal to know whether the company was making profits or losses (*Ladbroke Courage Holidays Ltd* v. *Asten* [1981] IRLR 59).

On the other hand, the courts and tribunals have not imposed particularly strict criteria when judging the 'substantiality' of the decision to reorganise. In *Ellis* (above) it was suggested that the test was whether, if the changes were not implemented, the whole business would be brought to a standstill. A much less stringent test was formulated by Lord Denning in *Hollister* (above), where he felt that the principle should extend to situations 'where there was some sound, good business reason for the reorganisation'. In subsequent cases, the EAT has been prepared to dilute the test even further; in one case requiring only that the changes were considered as 'matters of importance' or to have 'discernible advantages to the organisation' (*Banerjee*, cited above) and in another demanding that the reorganisation be 'beneficial' (*Bowater Containers* v. *McCormack* [1980] IRLR 50).

Surveys of the case law on reorganisation or 'business efficacy' tend to show the adoption of a strong conception of managerial prerogative by the courts and tribunals.[19]

In *Evans* v. *Elementa Holdings* [1982] IRLR 143, a case involving the imposition of an obligation to work overtime, the EAT moved some way to redressing this imbalance in favour of managerial prerogative in holding that if it was unreasonable to expect an employee to accept the changes, it was unfair for the employer to dismiss. This view, however, was not accepted by a differently constituted EAT in *Chubb Fire Security Ltd* v. *Harper* [1983] IRLR 311. In its view the correct approach, in accordance with the decision of the Court of Appeal in *Hollister* v. *NFU* (above), is for the industrial tribunal to concentrate on whether it was reasonable for the employer to implement the reorganisation by terminating existing contracts and offering new ones.

It may be perfectly reasonable for an employee to decline to work extra overtime, having regard to his family commitments. Yet from the employer's point of view, having regard to his business commitments, it may be perfectly reasonable to require an employee to work overtime.

For a recent application of the approach adopted in *Chubb*, see *St. John of God (Care Services) Ltd* v. *Brooks* [1992] IRLR 546 EAT.

Some form of consultation over the reorganisation has been expected in the past in order to maintain the fairness of the dismissal. The dilution of the importance of consultation in *Hollister* – where the Court of Appeal held that consultation is only one of the factors to be taken into account when judging reasonableness and lack of it would not necessarily render a dismissal unfair – should be reassessed following the decision of the House of Lords in *Polkey* v. *AE Dayton Services Ltd* (above). Having said that, there is no clear guidance on the form the consultation should take. In *Ellis* v. *Brighton Cooperative Society Ltd* (above), the EAT was satisfied that the requirement of consultation had been fulfilled by union agreement to the scheme even though Ellis, as a non-union member, had little chance in participating in the scheme. In *Martin* v. *Automobile Proprietary Ltd* [1979] IRLR 64, on the other hand, there are suggestions that non-union members should expect to be individually consulted.

Dismissal on a Transfer of Undertaking

As we saw earlier, reg. 8 of the Transfer of Undertakings (Protection of Employment) Regulations 1981 provides that a dismissal of an employee of the transferor or transferee which is connected with the transfer of the business is automatically unfair unless it is for an 'economic, technical or organisational reason entailing changes in the workforce' – known as ETO. By virtue of reg. 8 (2) such dismissals are deemed to be for a substantial reason for the purpose of ERA 1996, s. 98 (1) (b), and are fair provided they pass the statutory test of reasonableness. It is now clear that, if the employer does successfully establish the ETO defence, an employee can claim a redundancy payment if redundancy was the reason for the transfer dismissal (*Gorictree Ltd* v. *Jenkinson* [1984] IRLR 391).

The scope of the ETO defence was considered by the Court of Appeal in *Berriman* v. *Delabole Slate Ltd* [1985] IRLR 305. The court held that in order to come within reg. 8 (2), the employer must show that a change in the workforce is part of the economic, technical or organisational reason for dismissal. It must be an objective of the employer's plan to achieve changes in the workforce, not just a possible consequence of the plan. So where an employee resigned following a transfer because the transferee employer proposed to remove his guaranteed weekly wage so as to bring his pay into line with the transferee's existing workforce, the reason behind the plan was to produce uniform terms and conditions and was not in any way to reduce the numbers in the workforce.

In order to counter the effects of the decision in *Berriman*, there was a developing practice of purchasers of a business insisting that the vendor dismisses the workforce before the transfer takes place. In this way, the transferee sought to avoid any liability for unfair dismissal and/or redundancy pay in relation to the transferor's workforce. In *Anderson* v. *Dalkeith Engineering Ltd* [1985] ICR 66, the Scottish EAT held that a dismissal by the transferor at the behest of the transferee was an 'economic' reason and therefore fell within reg. 8 (2). The EAT was of the view that to get the best deal for the sale of the business, the vendor had to accede to the purchaser's demand and that was clearly an 'economic reason'. This approach was not adopted by the English EAT in *Wheeler* v. *Patel* [1987] ICR 631, where it thought that the word 'economic' should be given a more restricted meaning. It was felt that an 'economic reason' must relate to the conduct of the business. A desire to obtain an enhanced price for the business or to achieve a sale was not a reason which related to the conduct of the business and was therefore not an economic reason. The *Wheeler* approach was subsequently supported by the EAT in *Gateway Hotels Ltd* v. *Stewart and Others* [1988] IRLR 287.

It is clear from the decision of the House of Lords in *Litster* v. *Forth Dry Dock & Engineering Co Ltd* [1989] IRLR 161 – discussed in detail in Chapter 15 below – that the mere insistence of the purchaser that the vendor dismiss as a condition of sale will not be regarded as an 'economic, technical or organisational reason entailing changes in the workforce'. As a result of the *Litster* decision, where an employee has been unfairly dismissed for a reason connected with the transfer, s/he is to be deemed to have been employed in the undertaking 'immediately before the transfer' and the employment is statutorily continued with the transferee.

Stage Four: Remedies for Unfair Dismissal

Once the tribunal is satisfied that an employee has been unfairly dismissed, it has to consider one of three forms of remedy:

- an order for reinstatement;
- an order of re-engagement;
- an award of compensation (see ERA 1996, ss. 112, 113).

Although reinstatement and re-engagement are regarded as primary remedies by the statute, in practice compensation is the normal remedy for unfair dismissal, the first two orders only being made by tribunals in roughly 0.2 per cent of cases proceeding to a hearing in 2002/03. As a result, the re-employment of dismissed workers has been described as 'the lost remedy'.[20] There may be many reasons for the low level of re-engagement/reinstatement orders. By the time the ET hearing is held – normally three to four months after the dismissal – the applicant may have found another job. Even if this is not the case, the passage of time and the adversarial nature of the proceedings may result in the relationship between the parties breaking down so severely that it would be unrealistic to expect them to resume a normal working relationship.[21]

The principles governing the normal remedies are set out below, together with the special rules and procedures concerning trade union related dismissals.

Reinstatement or Re-engagement

On finding the complaint well founded, the employment tribunal must explain to the applicant the availability of the orders of reinstatement or re-engagement and ask whether s/he wishes the tribunal to make such an order. Assuming that the applicant wishes to be reinstated or re-engaged, the tribunal must then take the following additional factors into account in exercising its discretion:

(a) whether it is practicable for an employer to comply with such an order; and
(b) whether the employee caused or contributed to his/her dismissal and, if so, whether it would be just and equitable to make the order.

An order for reinstatement is an order that the employer shall treat the applicant in all respects as if he/she had not been dismissed. An order for re-engagement is an order that the complainant be engaged by the employer, or by a successor of the employer or by an associated employer, in employment comparable to that from which he/she was dismissed, or to other suitable employment.

On making the order the tribunal shall specify:

(a) any amounts payable to the employee in respect of any benefit which the employee might have received but for the dismissal, including arrears of pay, for the period from the date of termination to the date of reinstatement, including any benefits which the employee might have enjoyed by way of improvements in terms and conditions but for the dismissal;
(b) any rights and privileges, including seniority and pension rights, which must be restored to the employee;
(c) the date by which the order must be complied with.

Is it Practicable to Reinstate or Re-engage?

Employers will not be able to argue that it is not practicable to reinstate/re-engage the employee because a replacement employee has been engaged unless they can show either:

*   that it was not practicable to arrange for the dismissed employee's work to be done without employing a permanent replacement; or
*   that the replacement was engaged after the lapse of a reasonable period of time, without having heard from the dismissed employee that s/he wished to be reinstated or re-engaged; it no longer being reasonable for the employer to have the dismissed employee's work carried out by anyone except a permanent replacement (ERA 1996, s. 116).

Partial or Total Failure to Comply with an Order for Reinstatement or Re-engagement

Where an order is made and the employee is taken back but the employer does not comply fully with its terms, the tribunal will make such an award of compensation as it thinks fit, having regard to the loss sustained by the complainant in consequence of the failure to comply fully with the order (ERA 1996, s. 117 [1]).

In the more frequent situation of a total failure to comply with the order, the tribunal will award compensation using the normal rules of computation plus an 'additional award' (see below). It is a defence to the granting of the additional award if the employer can show that it was not practicable to comply with the order.

Impracticability is therefore a possible defence at two stages in the process of ET decision-making. The following circumstances have been held to render a reinstatement/re-engagement impracticable:

- Where it would inevitably lead to industrial unrest (*Coleman v. Magnet Joinery Ltd* [1974] IRLR 343).
- Where there is no suitable vacancy. A re-engagement order does not place a duty on the employer to search for and find work for the dismissed employee irrespective of existing vacancies (*Freemans plc v. Flynn* [1984] IRLR 486).
- Where the employee believes him/herself to be a victim of conspiracy by his/her employers, s/he is not likely to be a satisfactory employee in any circumstances if reinstated or re-engaged (*Nothman v. LB Barnet (No. 2)* [1980] IRLR 65).
- Where there must exist a close personal relationship, reinstatement can only be appropriate in exceptional circumstances and to force it upon a reluctant employer is not a course which an employment tribunal should pursue unless persuaded by powerful evidence that it would succeed (*Enessy Co SA t/a The Tulchan Estate v. Minoprio and Minoprio* [1978] IRLR 489).

Compensation

The rules relating to the calculation of unfair dismissal compensation can be summarised as follows.

The Basic Award (ERA 1996, s. 119)

An award of half, one or one and a half weeks' pay for each year of continuous service (depending on age), subject to a maximum of 20 years. A week's pay is calculated in accordance with ERA 1996, ss. 220–229 and is based on gross pay. The maximum allowable for a week's pay is currently £270 (2004/05); this figure is reviewed each year and any changes made operate from 1 February.

Table 14.1: Basic Award and Age

If aged	But less than	No. of weeks pay for each year
	22	½
22	41	1
41	65	1½

If aged 64, entitlement goes down by one-twelfth for each month after your 64th birthday. Therefore, in general, the maximum payment under this head of calculation in the year 2004/05 will be:

$$£270 \times 20 \times 1\tfrac{1}{2} = £8,100$$

Compensatory Award

The tribunal may also make a compensatory award (ERA 1996, s. 123): This is an amount which the tribunal considers 'just and equitable'. Both the basic and compensatory award may be reduced if the applicant contributed to his/her own dismissal or as a result of any conduct before dismissal. The maximum award under this head is currently £55,000 (wef. 1 February 2004).

The aim of the award is to reimburse the employee for any financial loss experienced: interim loss of net earnings between the date of the dismissal and the tribunal hearing, and future losses that s/he is likely to sustain, including wages, pensions and other fringe benefits. For over thirty years, it was held that an award does not cover compensation for non-economic loss, such as injury to feeling arising from the dismissal itself or from the manner of dismissal (see *Norton Tool Co Ltd* v. *Tewson* [1972] IRLR 86, NIRC). This approach was questioned by Lord Hoffman in *Johnson* v. *Unisys Ltd* [2001] IRLR 279 when he expressed the opinion that he saw 'no reason why in an appropriate case compensation for unfair dismissal should not include compensation for distress, humiliation, damage to reputation in the community or to family life'. Subsequently, in *Dunnachie* v. *Kingston Upon Hull City Council* [2004] EWCA Civ 84, the Court of Appeal overruled the *Norton Tool* decision and held that the compensatory award for unfair dismissal can cover non-economic loss. The Court of Appeal decided that the award of £10,000 for emotional damage caused by the manner of Mr Dunnachie's dismissal was appropriate. The employee had been subject to a prolonged campaign of denigration and harassment by his employer. The Court noted that the employer's conduct: (i) seriously undermined the employee's health; (ii) caused him to go off work for three weeks because of stress; (iii) caused him to relocate his place of work which required some extra 64 miles per day of commuting and which impacted on his time with his family; and (iv) undermined his self-confidence and self-esteem so that he needed professional help. The House of Lords, however, allowed an appeal ([2004] UKHL 36). So 'loss' still does *not* extend to additional amounts for non-economic loss.

The Additional Award

This award is made where an order for reinstatement of re-engagement is not complied with. If the complaint is upheld, an award of compensation will be made and if there has been a total failure to comply with the order there will be an additional award over and above the basic and compensatory awards, unless the employer can show the tribunal that it was not practicable to comply with the order. The additional award will be between 26 and 52 weeks' pay. Where there is a *partial* failure by the employer to comply with a reinstatement/re-engagement order, the tribunal may make an additional award as it thinks fit having regard to the loss sustained by the complainant.

Remedies for Union-related Dismissals

By virtue of amendments introduced by the EA 1982, the amount of compensation to be awarded to employees who are unfairly dismissed (or selected for redundancy) on grounds of trade union membership and activities or non-membership was much higher than for other types of dismissal because a 'special award' was made in addition to the basic and compensatory elements. Also, unlike other cases, where the dismissal is union-related there is a minimum basic award (£3,600 in 2004/05).

With the raising of the compensation award limit to £55,000, and above there is less need for the 'special award' in trade union cases. Consequently, s. 33 of the Employment Relations Act 1999 simplifies arrangements by replacing special awards with additional awards.

Either the employer or the applicant may request that a trade union or other party be joined in the proceedings where they have exerted or threatened to exert industrial pressure on the employer to dismiss. If the tribunal finds the complaint of third party pressure well founded, the tribunal has the power to order the trade union or other party to pay any or all of the compensation awarded.

An employee who alleges that he or she has been dismissed for union/non-union membership or trade union activities can apply to the tribunal for an order for interim relief (TULR[C]A 1992, s. 161).

The order for interim relief is intended to preserve the *status quo* until full hearing of cases which by their very nature can be extremely damaging to the industrial relations in any organisation. Where relief is granted it will result in either the reinstatement/re-engagement of the employee pending full hearing or, in some cases, a suspension of the employee on continued terms and conditions (TULR[C]A 1992, ss. 161–166).

Recently, these provisions have been extended to dismissals of health and safety representatives, employee trustees of occupational pension schemes, and employee representatives for the purposes of consultation over redundancies and business transfers (see ERA 1996, s. 128).

The Law of Unfair Dismissal: A Critique

Critics of this legislation[22] argue that the law has been unsuccessful as an effective control upon managerial prerogative in relation to dismissals and that, far from acting as a constraint on power, the law actually legitimates managerial control. An explanation for the weakness of the law lies in the attitude of the appeal court judges to the legislation. The judges are not happy with the unfair dismissal provisions because they are perceived to be 'corporatist' in that they overstep the boundary between matters which are suitable for state intervention and those which are not. The judges feel unhappy about meddling in affairs they have always thought should be left to individuals to resolve. Consequently, the courts and tribunals are unwilling to substitute their own standards of fairness for management opinion and instead have the tendency to endorse the ordinary practices of employers. Once this occurs it is inevitable that the concept of fairness will tend to favour managerial control. Evidence of this approach can be seen in the following areas.

The Concept of the Reasonable Employer

Earlier in this chapter we saw that in assessing reasonableness, the question is what the reasonable employer would have done in the circumstances and not what the employment tribunal would have thought. In this sense, the courts do not set the norms of behaviour but merely reflect existing managerial standards. A notorious example of this approach can be seen in *Saunders* v. *Scottish National Camps Association Ltd* [1980] IRLR 174. The employee was a maintenance worker at a children's camp. He was dismissed on the grounds of being a homosexual. The dismissal was held to be fair because a considerable proportion of employers would take the view that the employment of a homosexual should be restricted, particularly when required to work in close proximity to children. Instead of setting its own standards, the court in this case accepted the commonly held and highly prejudicial views of some employers.

Overriding Contractual Rights

As we have seen, a dismissal may be held to be fair even when it is the employer who breaks the contract. So the courts and tribunals have been prepared to hold as fair dismissals where the employee has refused to agree to a change in terms and conditions of employment in line with the employer's perception of business efficiency.

The Dilution of Procedural Fairness

An additional criticism of the approach of the judges was their increasing willingness to put less emphasis on the need to follow a fair procedure. Since the *Polkey* decision, however, it may well be that flouting procedures will result in a finding of unfair dismissal in a much increased proportion of cases. But employees in such cases may find that they have achieved a Pyrrhic victory because the tribunal may reduce their compensation to nil if it is found that they were in any way at fault for their dismissal.[23]

These illustrations tend to confirm the view that the judges are most reluctant to trespass too far into the area of managerial prerogative. If they do intervene it has been to regulate the procedure by which the decision to dismiss is effected rather to question the substance of decision. This attitude is vividly illustrated by the following statement by Mr Justice Phillips in *Cook* v. *Thomas Linnell & Sons Ltd* [1977] ICR 770: 'It is important that the operation of the legislation in relation to unfair dismissal should not impede employers unreasonably in the efficient management of their business, which must be in the interests of all.'

Reform

These illustrations tend to confirm the view that the judges are most reluctant to trespass too far into the area of managerial prerogative. If they do intervene it has been to regulate the procedure by which the decision to dismiss is effected rather than to question the substance of the decision.

A number of reforms have been mooted by those who see the need to strengthen the present system, including amending the law so that a dismissal decision, if challenged, could not be implemented unless and until justified before an employment tribunal (a similar approach already exists under the 'interim relief' procedures presently used for dismissals for union reasons: see TULR[C]A 1992, ss. 161–167).

A more radical approach would be to remove unfair dismissal from the jurisdiction of employment tribunals and introduce a system of private arbitration which, it is claimed, would be cheaper, quicker and generally much less formal and legalistic. On this proposal and many other aspects of the working of the law of unfair dismissal see Dickens *et al.*, *Dismissed: A Study of Unfair Dismissal and the Industrial Tribunal System*, and Lewis and Clark, *The Case For Alternative Dispute Resolution*.[24]

The Employment Rights (Dispute Resolution) Act 1998 contained provisions designed to implement those aspects of the Green Paper, *Resolving Employment Rights Disputes: Options for Reform* (Cm 2707, 1994), which attracted wide support and which required primary legislation.

The most significant change under the Act was its requirement that ACAS should draw up an arbitration scheme for unfair dismissal claims and submit it to the Secretary of State for approval (see TULR[C]A 1992, s. 212A). The scheme was to be available as an alternative to an employment tribunal hearing and would be voluntary on both sides. The Secretary of State approved the ACAS Arbitration Scheme in April 2001 and it came into force in England and Wales from 21 May 2001 (and was extended to Scotland from April 2004). However, at the time of writing, the Scheme is contained in the Schedule to the ACAS Arbitration Scheme (England and Wales) Order 2001 (SI 2001/1185, updated by SI 2004/753). References below to the 'ACAS Guide' are to the ACAS publication, *The ACAS Arbitration Scheme for the Resolution of Unfair Dismissal Disputes: A Guide to the Scheme.*

Under the Scheme, where parties to an unfair dismissal claim agree in writing to submit their dispute to arbitration, ACAS will refer their dispute to an arbitrator. In order to ensure that claimants are not pressured into going down the arbitration route, the requirement of an 'Arbitration Agreement' must be satisfied. Part VI of the Scheme provides that the agreement must be in writing and may take the form of an ACAS-conciliated agreement or a compromise agreement and be accompanied by a completed 'waiver form' for each party. As a consequence of signing the waiver form, the parties are deemed to have agreed to waive certain rights that they would otherwise have had if the matter had been heard by an employment tribunal. The rights forfeited include: the right to a public hearing; the cross-examination of witnesses; obtaining orders for the production of documents; compelling the attendance of witnesses; the right to a published and fully reasoned decision; and the right to have the dispute resolved in strict law (except in cases involving points of EC law or issues under the Human Rights Act 1998, other than procedural matters within the Scheme).

ACAS will not provide a hearing under the Scheme if the Arbitration Agreement is notified to the ACAS Arbitration Section more than six weeks after the conclusion of the Agreement by the parties unless it was not reasonably practicable to notify ACAS within this time limit. In addition to the Agreement, ACAS should be sent a copy of the employee's application to the employment tribunal (Form IT1) and the employer's response (Form IT3). Where an Originating Application has not been submitted to the tribunal, the parties should advise the ACAS Arbitration Section in writing of the circumstances of the dispute.

Once the Arbitration Agreement has been concluded and forwarded to ACAS, the employee may withdraw from the process at any time provided that the withdrawal is in writing. In withdrawing the claim the employee will have no right to reopen the original claim to the employment tribunal. The employer, however, cannot unilaterally withdraw from the agreement to go to arbitration.

In anticipation of the Scheme's introduction, ACAS recruited a new dedicated panel of ACAS Scheme arbitrators, composed of around 30 members of its existing Arbitration Panel (which deals with 'trade dispute' arbitrations) plus about 60 new arbitrators who are not necessarily lawyers but have experience in employment relations. Once the parties have accessed the Scheme, an arbitrator is selected from the Arbitration Panel.

Arbitrators are under a general duty to:

(a) act fairly and impartially as between the parties, giving each party a reasonable opportunity of stating his or her case and dealing with that of his or her opponent; and

(b) adopt procedures suitable to the circumstances of the case; avoiding unnecessary delay or expense, so as to provide a fair means for the resolution of the matters falling to be determined (para. 48 of the Scheme).

The arbitrator will adopt an inquisitorial approach and encourage both parties and anyone they have called to be present at the hearing, to speak freely in order that as full a picture as possible of what happened can emerge. (The ACAS Guide, para. 77)

Parties and witnesses will not be examined on oath, and there will be no cross-examination by the other party and his/her representatives.

The terms of reference of the arbitrator under the Scheme will be to decide whether the dismissal is fair or unfair. In doing so, the arbitrator shall:

(i) have regard to general principles of fairness and good conduct in employment relations (including, for example, principles referred to in any relevant ACAS Disciplinary and grievance procedures Code of Practice ['the ACAS Code'] or Discipline at work Handbook ['the ACAS Handbook'], instead of applying legal tests or rules (e.g. court decisions or legislation);

(ii) apply EC law.

The arbitrator shall not decide the case by substituting what he or she would have done for the actions taken by the employer.

If the arbitrator finds the dismissal unfair, he or she shall determine the appropriate remedy under the terms of this scheme.

Nothing in the terms of reference affects the operation of the Human Rights Act 1998 insofar as this is applicable and relevant and (with respect to procedural matters) has not been waived by virtue of the provisions of this scheme. (para. 12 of the Scheme)

The Scheme does not extend to other kinds of claim, such as sex and/or race discrimination and claims for unpaid wages, which are frequently raised at the same time as a claim for unfair dismissal. These aspects of any dispute will have to be dealt with separately by an application to an employment tribunal made within the normal statutory time limits.

The Scheme is not intended for dismissal cases in which questions of EC law arise, e.g. dismissals relating to a transfer of undertaking or claims that the dismissal was related to exercising a right under the Working Time Regulations. The ACAS Guide strongly recommends that parties who have cases that raise such questions consider applying for their dispute to be heard by an employment tribunal.

If cases are referred to arbitration where EC law is relevant, the arbitrator may decide that a legal adviser be appointed by ACAS to report to the arbitrator on the EC law issue.

The Scheme is also not designed to deal with disputes raising jurisdictional disputes concerning the question as to whether or not an employment tribunal would have jurisdiction to hear the unfair dismissal claim. Such disputes include whether the applicant was an employee; whether the employee had the necessary period of service to bring a claim; whether a dismissal actually took place; or, whether the claim was within specified time limits. Accordingly, 'when agreeing to go to arbitration under the Scheme, both parties waive their ability to have such issues considered and are accepting as a condition of the Scheme that no such jurisdictional issue is in dispute between them' (ACAS Guide, para. 14).

The arbitrator's award is confidential, and will only be issued to the parties and their representatives. The remedies available under the Scheme largely mirror those available under Chapter II of Part X of ERA 1996; namely, reinstatement, re-engagement or compensation.

The Scheme makes it clear that there can be no appeal against an arbitrator's decision either on a point of law or fact, although if a party considers that there has been a 'serious irregularity' which has caused or will cause 'substantial injustice' to him/her, an appeal to the High Court under ss. 67–68 of the Arbitration Act 1996 is possible. The ACAS Guide envisages that this form of challenge is really only an option in extreme cases (ACAS Guide, para. 127).

The scheme has been slow to take off. During 2002, the first full year of operation, ACAS dealt with 23 cases compared with a mere 13 in the previous year. ACAS believe 'that the main barrier continues to be lack of understanding of the benefits of the process and its outcome compared to the more confrontational tribunal process' (ACAS Annual Report and Accounts 2002/03, p. 23).

However, there may be another reason why the parties and their advisers are suspicious of the Scheme. The absence of the obligation on the arbitrator to apply strict law in reaching a decision together with the lack of a right of appeal against that decision could lead to decision-making on the basis of 'unfettered pragmatism' and a two-tier system of unfair dismissal justice (see J. MacMillan, 'Employment Tribunals: Philosophies and Practicalities', *ILJ*, vol. 28 (1999), pp. 33–56; and J. Earnshaw, and S. Hardy, 'Assessing an Arbitral Route for Unfair Dismissal', *ILJ*, vol. 30 (2001), pp. 289–304.

New Statutory Procedures for Resolving Disputes

Most applications to employment tribunals come from employees who have not attempted to resolve their disputes privately. Indeed, some 60 per cent of small employers who defend claims in the tribunals have no internal disciplinary and grievance procedures. This, together with the three-fold increase in claims over the last decade, has persuaded the government to seek to reduce the number of claims reaching the employment tribunals. As we have seen, part of this strategy involved the introduction of the ACAS arbitration scheme described above. But this, to date, has had very limited success in diverting claims from the tribunals. More recently, the Employment Act 2002 has set out a scheme of minimum procedural standards for handling workplace disputes and grievances, and places obligations and incentives on both employer and employee to use them. The government predicts that its proposals will reduce the number of applications to employment tribunals by 30,000–40,000 a year.

The Act received Royal Assent on 8 July 2002. The statutory dispute resolution procedures are set out in detail in regulations which will come into force in October 2004.

The New Procedures

Two sets of procedure are introduced for each area: a standard procedure for dismissals and disciplinary action (DDPs) with a modified version for cases of gross misconduct. Similarly, grievance procedures (GPs) are also dealt with by a standard procedure and a modified one where the person raising the grievance is a former employee. The right to be accompanied will apply to both procedures.

The key procedures are:

A standard three-step dismissal and disciplinary procedure for all types of dismissal (e.g. on the grounds of capability, conduct, redundancy):

Step One: The employer sets down in writing the nature of the employee's conduct, capability or other circumstances which may result in dismissal or disciplinary action, and send a copy of the statement to the employee. The employer must inform the employee of the nature of his/her complaint.

Step Two: The employer should invite the employee to a meeting to discuss the issue. The employee should take all reasonable steps to attend. After the meeting, the employer must inform the employee about any decision, and offer the employee the right of appeal.

Step Three: If the employee wishes to appeal against any disciplinary action, s/he must inform the employer. The employer should invite the employee to a further meeting to discuss the appeal. The final decision must be communicated to the employee.

A modified two-step dismissal procedure can be followed only in exceptional circumstances where there has been actual gross misconduct leading to immediate dismissal or where employment cannot continue because of circumstances outside the employer's control (e.g. the employer becomes aware that the employer is working illegally or the employee becomes unable to carry out his/her duties):

Step One: The employer sets down in writing the nature of the alleged misconduct leading to the dismissal, the evidence for this decision, and the right to appeal against the decision and sends a copy of this to the employee.

Step Two: If the employee wishes to appeal against the dismissal, s/he must inform the employer. The employer should invite the employee to attend a further meeting to discuss the appeal. The final decision must be communicated to the employee.

There is also a standard three-step grievance procedure where an employee wishes to complain about action by the employer apart from actions within the dismissal procedure (e.g. warnings (oral and written), suspensions on full pay, constructive dismissal are all dealt with through the standard grievance procedure). A modified two-step grievance procedure only where employment has terminated and either both parties agree in writing to the modified procedure or it is not reasonably practicable for either party to use the standard procedure (e.g. the employee cannot get time off from his/her new job to attend a meeting).

The Standard (three-step) grievance procedure is as follows:

Step One: The employee sets down in writing the nature of the alleged grievance and sends the written complaint to the employer. S/he must inform the employer of the basis of his/her complaint.

Step Two: The employer should invite the employee to at least one hearing at a reasonable time and place at which the alleged grievance can be discussed. The employee should take all reasonable steps to attend. After the meeting, the employer must inform the employee about any decision, and offer the employee the right to appeal.

Step Three: If the employee considers that the grievance has not been satisfactorily dealt with, s/he should inform the employer that s/he wishes to appeal against the employer's decision or failure to make a decision. The employer should arrange a meeting to discuss the appeal. After the meeting, the employer's final decision should be communicated to the employee.

The modified (two-step) grievance procedure is as follows:

Step One: The employee sets down in writing the nature of the alleged grievance and sends the written complaint to the employer.

Step Two: The employer must set out his/her response in writing and send it to the employee.

General requirements are that each step and action under the procedures must be taken without unreasonable delay, and that the timing and location of the meeting must be reasonable, and allow both sides to state their case. A more senior manager than attended the first meeting should, as far as reasonably practicable, represent the employer at the appeal hearings.

However, when an employer dismisses an employee, going through the relevant procedure will not necessarily be sufficient to ensure that the dismissal is fair. The reasonableness of an employer's actions and adherence to the employer's own disciplinary procedures and to the ACAS Code of Practice on Disciplinary and Grievance Procedures will still be relevant. The Code is to be updated in October 2004 following a public consultation. The relationship between the new statutory minimum procedures and the guidance set out in the Code is one of the most confusing aspects of the new regime.

Sticks and Carrots

To seek to ensure that the employment tribunal is a place of last resort, the Act has included a number of 'sticks and carrots' into the process.

A new category of unfair dismissal is introduced for employees to seek redress against employers who fail to follow the relevant statutory dismissal procedure. Such a dismissal will result in the dismissal being held to be automatically unfair provided that employee has one year's continuous employment.

In addition, employment tribunals will be required to increase/reduce compensatory awards depending on whether it is the employer or employee who fails to use the procedures before a claim is brought before the tribunal. The reduction will range from 10 per cent to 50 per cent.

If an employee wishes to submit an employment tribunal application based on a grievance, s/he must write the Step One letter and wait 28 days or the tribunal will not accept the application. This will, however, prompt an automatic three-month extension of the time limit from the date when it would otherwise have expired. If the employee sends the Step One letter to the employer under the grievance procedure within the normal time limit for presenting an application (three months), this will trigger an automatic three-month extension of the time limit from the date when it would otherwise have expired. It will not be necessary for either party to have contacted the tribunal in any way for the automatic extension to be activated.

An applicant will not be *obliged* to delay submitting his/her claim until the expiry of the extended time limit. Of course, if statutory procedures have not been completed, then the award may be subject to adjustment (see above).

CHAPTER 15

Redundancy and Rights on Insolvency

Redundancy in Britain

One of the most significant but also controversial features of employment in Britain is the power of employers to dismiss workers for redundancy.[1] To some extent this is just an extension of a theme explored in Chapter 4, that the contract of employment does not provide a secure basis for key employment rights, and least of all job security. Nor has the position been improved greatly by statutory interventions. There is no 'right to remain in a job' in our employment system. Indeed quite the opposite as in formal terms the legal right of one side of the contract, the employer, to bring the employment relationship to an end is reinforced, and facilitated, by 'redundancy' as one of the potentially 'fair' reasons for dismissal listed in the ERA s. 98 (2). The fact is that it is relatively easy for an employer to dismiss staff for redundancy, subject to procedural requirements being adhered to. Even where the dismissal is procedurally defective, unfair, or wrongful, it will be virtually impossible to obtain an effective remedy to prevent a redundancy dismissal – or achieve reinstatement. Successive governments, including New Labour, have generally opted not to revisit or change the main features of the redundancy system in favour of arrangements more favourable to an employee's right to their job. This probably has much to do with the 'competitiveness' and 'flexible labour market' agendas. In terms of the two main competing pressures for regulating employment – fairness on the one hand, and regulation for 'competitiveness' and efficiency needs on the other as considered by Hugh Collins in 'Regulating the Employment Relationship for Competitiveness'[2] – it is always likely to be 'competitiveness', and business needs, that will win hands down.

Redundancy and Procedural Requirements

There are a number of important procedural safeguards designed, among other things, to facilitate retention of jobs when *alternatives* to dismissal can be proposed and negotiated. At the individual level, consultation is generally an essential element in the overall 'procedural fairness' requirement of any dismissal. Indeed, the leading case on procedural fairness *Polkey* v. *AE Dayton Services* (discussed in the last chapter) was a redundancy case. Discussion or negotiation may result in either withdrawal of the proposed redundancy or identification of alternatives to dismissal, such as retention through redeployment, or other options that are more favourable. For that reason collective redundancies are subject to procedures in the Trade Union and Labour Relations (Consolidation) Act 1992 (TULR[C]A) ss. 188–192, as amended, requiring consultation with union officials or employee representatives (see below).

Consultation and negotiation may also produce *better terms* than the basic statutory redundancy entitlements which, like the unfair dismissal regime, usually bear no relation to the dismissed employee's true financial loss, and the on-costs of dismissal – financial and otherwise.[3]

Not uncommonly, on closer scrutiny, a true 'redundancy' situation within the meaning of the legislation, may not exist. This may or may not assist the employees affected to achieve what they want. In some cases employees want redundancy, usually because of the uncertainty they have been facing – and being offered redundancy (or being made redundant) is, by then, seen as the best outcome available, giving at least a financial benefit. In other cases a proposed redundancy may be opposed, particularly if this is regarded as unjustifiable or unnecessary. Workplace reorganisations and restructuring are often contentious, particularly if part of the outcome is redundancy for just some of the workers affected. In technical terms, without a permanent cessation of work or a clear 'diminution' it may be difficult to demonstrate redundancy given its statutory definition in the ERA (see below). Worse, employees who do not co-operate in adapting to changes brought about by a reorganisation – whether they entail redundancy or not – may be at risk of dismissal: and such dismissals may be 'fair', as considered in the last chapter. In particular, a tribunal can conclude that an employee should have co-operated in the changes. The employer may well be able to use the 'some other substantial reason' head in the ERA s. 98 (1) (b), given the prevailing judicial perception which is that workers should be prepared to 'adapt'.

In some cases there is a fine line between 'redundancy', and a 'reorganisation' in which jobs (and job content) change significantly – but where it is unclear whether or not there has been a 'diminution' in work requirements needed to make it a 'redundancy' dismissal. In principle, a job may have changed *so* radically that it can be said that it is no longer the same job. Whether or not this has happened is now generally treated by the courts as an issue of 'fact' for a tribunal to decide on the evidence. However, whilst there may be no 'redundancy' the changes involved, and the way they have been managed by the employer, may nevertheless make the dismissal 'unfair' for a variety of reasons. For example, sizeable elements of a job as it was done before a reorganisation may have disappeared, but have then been replaced by other elements, some of them unwelcome; and this has not have been accompanied by adequate consultation or agreement. In practice, tribunals tend to find that jobs that have undergone significant changes are not redundant, but the change process itself has been unfair – a point illustrated by NHS reorganisation cases like *Shawkat* v. *Nottingham City Hospital (No. 2)* [2002] ICR 7, EAT, discussed below.

'Redundancy' means, basically, that an employee's services are no longer required. The likeliest reasons for this are business downturns and a consequent reduction in the need for staff. However, it may also have been precipitated by reorganisation, displacement as a result of the introduction of new technology, or the employer's business relocating, or running into financial difficulties.

In this chapter consideration is given to the exact extent of redundancy and the rights of workers affected by its use. Consideration will also be given to employees' rights when employers are hit by insolvency, that is, going into liquidation, receivership, or administration.

This will be dealt with in the following sections:

(1) Employers' use of redundancy
(2) Redundancy entitlements: ERA 1996 Parts XI, X

(3)   Redundancy payments
(4)   Redundancy: the present approach
(5)   Lay-off and short-time
(6)   Part-time workers and redundancy
(7)   Redundancy, unfair dismissal and breach of contract
(8)   Transfer of employer's business
(9)   Disqualification from entitlements: other claims issues
(10)   Insolvency-related rights.

(1) Employers' Use of Redundancy

People made redundant may often be given very little explanation of the reasons for it. Generally speaking, the redundancy decision-making process is, in legal and practical terms, completely within the employer's control – at least at the point dismissal procedures are initiated. If the employer has clearly gone insolvent and there is no realistic possibility of further employment (either from the employer or from a new owner of the business), there may be little alternative but to accept redundancy and try to get any compensation which is due. There may, however, be other situations where the position is *not* so clear-cut. In the *Shawcat* case, referred to above, the applicant was employed by a hospital trust as a staff grade doctor undertaking thoracic surgery. The trust then carried out a reorganisation, introduced a cardio-thoracic unit, and then required him to carry out a mix of cardiac and thoracic surgery. He refused to do this, and was dismissed. His complaint that he had been dismissed for redundancy failed. The ET concluded that there had been no 'diminution' in the requirements for work of a particular kind for the purposes of the key redundancy definition in the ERA s. 139 (1) (b) (i). The key point was that just because there has been a reorganisation, and jobs have changed in terms of content, demands, etc., it does not follow that the job is redundant. In the circumstances, however, and particularly given the way the changes were imposed on him, the dismissal was in any case unfair. The EAT upheld the finding that he had not been dismissed for redundancy. Among other things, whilst the tribunal had not made clear whether requiring the doctor to undertake a mix of cardiac and thoracic surgery was 'work of a different kind' within the definition of redundancy, this was implicit in its decision. The approach which is now generally adopted for determining if there is a redundancy or not, laid down by the House of Lords in *Murray* v. *Foyle Meats Ltd* (see below), was applied.

Opportunities for consultation provided prior to dismissal should generally be taken in both individual and collective redundancy situations.

Not surprisingly, perhaps, employers may not always want to co-operate in such a dialogue and may prefer to take the line that the problem is one over which they have no control. While there are undoubtedly situations in which job cuts are unavoidable, or have been forced on an employer, compulsory redundancy, as opposed to other alternatives such as redeployment, non-replacement of staff who take early retirement, etc., can often be shown to be unnecessary. The reasons given for a plant closure, 'reorganisation', or other organisational change leading to redundancies can be very controversial on purely business grounds. It is not unusual for large companies and multinationals to shut down even profitable operations if this is seen as advantageous to their corporate strategy. Another common scenario is for perfectly viable UK-based operations to be closed down, with consequent loss of jobs, when companies elect to transfer those operations abroad, and to locations where operating costs, including wages, social insurance costs, etc. are lower. This has been a common practice, with well-publicised examples in 2004 including transfers of telephone call centres abroad. In the context of globalisation, and in business terms, this may make sense, if it maximises profits for shareholders and (sometimes) assists the operation's longer-term viability – and the retention of remaining jobs. But the redundancy system does not require such companies to share any of the 'value' gained to staff who lose their jobs.[4] Whilst the Company Law regime does impose a statutory duty on directors *to have regard* to employees' interests (as well as shareholders' interests) – under the Companies Act 1985 s. 309 – the few cases that there have been which test the scope of this provision suggest that it does not alter their first priority, which is to run the company in the *shareholders'* interest. The Companies Act 1985 s. 719 gives directors the power to make financial provision for staff when there is a cessation of a business, or a transfer – something which on the face of it appears suited to map on to redundancy situations. In practice, though, it is used mainly to legitimise directors' severance arrangements, and senior managers' ill-health departures (particularly to maximise severance awards, or if they have no pension in place). Exceptionally a company could put the interests of shareholders ahead of those of stakeholders like employees, and continue running the company when it might otherwise be better (for shareholders and banks) for it to be sold off, the assets realised, and capital to be returned to them and other creditors. Recorded examples of this are few and far between, but reference may be made to cases like *Re Welfab Engineers* [1990] BCLC 833 and *Re Saul D Harrison & Sons plc* [1995] BCLC 14; and see on this the discussion in leading Company Law texts like *Farrar's Company Law*.[5] Arguably, given the high priority given by Company Law to directors' duties to shareholders and capital providers and other creditors, action which might put employees' interests ahead of those primary stakeholders could in some cases be beyond their management powers. It is certainly the case that employees probably lack sufficient legal standing to assert their rights under s. 309 against directors' decisions – for example in order to contest a closure, redundancies, etc.

Even if companies, or successful parts of them, could be sold off as going concerns it may be corporate policy *not* to do so – especially if they could be acquired by a competitor.[6] If redundancies *are* forced, managements often fail to take steps to avert job losses, or will be reluctant to give adequate consideration to alternatives to redundancy. This is not helped by the absence of effective legal obligations on them to do so. Redundancy therefore offers a relatively easy option to what may be just short-term problems.

Court Action to Stop Threatened Redundancy

In some circumstances, although this has been rare to date, there may be scope for going to court to try to get orders to prevent a management from carrying out redundancy dismissals. This could be a possibility, for example, where initiating a redundancy dismissal would be an anticipatory breach of contractual rights, or a breach of procedures laid down in a collective agreement requiring notice, consultation, or other preliminary steps. This is predicated on the assumption, however, that such procedures are apt and suitable for incorporation in individual members' and staff contracts. Collective agreements are not, in themselves, usually enforceable. There is then a further problem. The grant of court orders is a matter for judges' discretion, and in practice they may be reluctant to get involved in disputes at this stage.

Example
Members of the Transport and General Workers' Union working for Standard Telephones and Cables Ltd had rights under a collective redundancy agreement. This provided, among other things, that in the event of a compulsory redundancy selection for redundancy would be made on the basis of length of service with the company, that is to say a 'last in, first out' system (LIFO) was in operation. But when redundancies were made the company insisted that this should be the main consideration: and that the main criterion for selection should be its need for workers with the most suitable skills rather than a LIFO. The union members failed to get an injunction requiring the employers to treat them as continuously employed, and restraining the dismissals. The court's objection was that the provisions had to be seen as 'procedural', operating at the collective level as part of a consultative scheme, rather than incorporating rights into individuals' contracts. An injunction would effectively reinstate them and require the employment relationship to be reimposed on the employer. This it was not prepared to do, even if it would only have been a temporary measure until a proper trial of all the issues took place.[7]

A 1997 case, however, went the other way and confirmed that an interim order *was*, in the circumstances, appropriate to prevent the implementation of dismissals. In *Anderson* v. *Pringle of Scotland* [1998] IRLR 64 it was confirmed that the terms of a collective agreement dealing with redundancy selection (and providing for LIFO and length of service as the key criteria) *were* incorporated into each employee's individual contract; and that an interim order (or 'interdict') could be issued as an exception to the courts' usual reluctance to maintain the employment relationship. This was assisted by the finding that there was continuing trust and confidence in the worker. Later cases, however, have demonstrated the difficulties of demonstrating redundancy agreements are more than 'procedural'.[8]

As one of the authors has argued elsewhere, confidence in an employee is not destroyed purely because of an economic downturn: and the question for the court is whether the necessary trust and confidence that is needed to enable the employment relationship to continue still exists so as to grant the injunction. It should not be whether the employer has even more confidence in the workers it has *not* selected for redundancy.[9]

Public Sector Redundancies

Employees and unions in the public sector may be able to take advantage of the scope for bringing 'judicial review' proceedings to challenge the legality of what an employer which is a public body is doing, or proposing to do. Such proceedings, which must be started 'promptly' and in any case within three months in the Administrative Court, are regulated by the Supreme Court Act 1981 s. 31 and the Civil Procedure Rules 1998, SI 1998/3132 Part 54, may be brought if a public sector employer has not acted in accordance with its statutory duties, or incorrectly in procedural terms – for example by not consulting adequately with recognised unions before making redundancy decisions. The scope for such proceedings was demonstrated in the GCHQ case (*Council of Civil Service Unions* v. *Civil Service Minister* [1984] 3 All

ER 935; [1985] IRLR 28, HL), when ministerial action removing union membership rights was 'reviewed'; and again at the end of 1992 when miners' unions, including the pit deputies' union NACODS in Staffordshire, successfully obtained a court order, albeit temporary, that the government's British Coal's handling of the pits closure programme was unlawful.[10]

The Redundancy System

Before considering redundancy in more detail it is worth considering some of the background to the present legislation, if only to see how specific objectives map on to the statutory scheme. Redundancy law is largely contained in the Employment Rights Act 1996, ss. 135–165, replacing earlier redundancy legislation which started with the Redundancy Payments Act 1965. The 1965 Act introduced statutory compensation for redundancy for the first time, and its principal objective was to promote job 'mobility' – i.e. to make it easier to move workers between different areas of the economy in response to employers' changing demands for labour and skills. More specifically, said one leading commentator[11] the purpose was to 'mitigate the resistance of individual employees (and their unions) to the extensive changes which have accompanied and will continue to accompany the response of British industry ...' An early judicial perspective was that a worker, under the scheme, is recognised as having 'an accrued right in his job; and his rights gain in value with the years. It was, said the judge, 'compensation for long service'.[12] Unfortunately the levels of compensation required to be paid under the ERA are still so low (with no signs that they might be raised) that for most people they are hardly a realistic incentive to accept the loss of their job willingly.

Like other employment legislation of the 1960s and 1970s the redundancy regime, with its unnecessarily complex rules and procedures, has been seen as part of a policy of trying to remove industrial relations conflicts from the workplace by individualising and 'judicialising' them.[13] Despite its many elaborate provisions the legislation does not in fact do anything to give workers any greater job security; nor, arguably, has it in any way really restricted managerial power in redundancy situations. These and other limitations in the present scheme were, in fact, quickly realised within a few years of the 1965 Act coming into operation.[14] Arguably the rules simply institutionalise redundancy as a relatively easy and cost-effective way of sacking unwanted workers. They have also produced other consequences. First, that the TUC and unions routinely call for changes to be made to the scheme.[15] In practice, though, the main impetus for change has come from the EC – for example following an ECJ decision that Directive 75/129 on Collective Redundancies had not been properly implemented by the UK. Specifically, TULR(C)A 1992 s. 188A had to be enacted providing for employee representatives to be elected for the purposes of the duty to consult under s. 188 when the employer proposes to dismiss 20 or more employees within a 90-day period or less. Second, at the collective level, not surprisingly, unions continually seek to negotiate *improved* rights. Third, and perhaps most significantly, the way the scheme is structured, and the low level of statutory compensation, means there is every incentive for a worker and advisers to look for an unfair dismissal claim in redundancy situations. An 'unfair dismissal' generally takes one of two forms. First, that the selection for procedures used were unfair in terms of the ERA s. 98 (4). Second, that the *redundancy* is unfair because it was for reasons in the ERA s. 105. This stipulates that an employee is to be *treated* as 'unfair' if the reason for the dismissal is redundancy; that the circumstances constituting the redundancy applied equally to one or more other employees in the same undertaking who held positions similar to the employee (and who have not been dismissed); and any of the grounds listed in the rest of. s. 105 apply. These and other automatically unfair redundancy dismissals, including those under TULR(C)A s. 153, or the Maternity and Parental Leave Regulations 1999, SI 1999/3312, reg. 20, are considered later in this chapter.

In either case a successful unfair dismissal claim involves more compensation as it contains two elements. One is the *basic* award, which is assessed using a similar system to redundancy payments; and the second is the *compensatory* award. Where there is an unfair dismissal the compensation is regulated by the ERA Part IX, including ss. 118-127A. These, among other things, provide for the basic award to be reduced or 'further reduced', by the amount of any redundancy payment ordered by the tribunal or paid by the employer; s. 122 (4).

Redundancy and the Contract

As with other areas of Employment Law, the contract of employment can be the basis of redundancy rights. Among the other things this can use the contract to regulate the procedures that are to apply to the redundancy process including grounds, selection criteria and compensation levels. In one pre-1965 case it was held that by limiting the circumstances in which a worker could be dismissed the contract precluded dismissal for redundancy.[16] Arguably though, this will be rare: and the ERA s. 98 provides an employer with a pervasive power to dismiss for redundancy, subject to procedural safeguards that can be augmented by contractual procedures.[17]

(2) Redundancy Entitlements: ERA 1996 Parts XI, X

The statutory redundancy regime[18] provides two main rights:

- Redundancy payments for those who are eligible (Part XI).
- Unfair dismissal in some redundancy cases (Part X), and in union-related dismissal and redundancy selection cases.[19]

For both it will be necessary to demonstrate 'employee' status (as discussed in Chapter 2), and satisfy the other conditions in the ERA and redundancy scheme, and protective legislation. Among other things it is necessary, subject to exceptions (including some cases within s. 105), to have completed the appropriate period of service. This has been discussed in Chapter 2 and for unfair dismissal. The normal basic requirement for a redundancy payment is two years' continuous employment (ERA 1996, s. 155).

In most cases it will also need to be shown that there has been a 'dismissal' as a further pre-condition. This has already been discussed when looking at unfair dismissal. The principles are similar. For redundancy payment purposes and as set out in the ERA 1996, ss. 136–138, an employee is 'dismissed' if:

- the contract is terminated by the employer with or without notice; s. 136 (1) (a);

- a fixed-term contract under which the employee is employed, and that contract terminates by virtue of 'the limiting event' without being renewed under the same contract; s. 136 (1) (b) and SI 2002/2034;
- the employee terminates the contract (with or without notice) in circumstances in which he is entitled to terminate it without notice by reason of the employer's conduct; s. 136 (1) (c).

The s. 136 (1) (c) 'route' does not apply if the employee terminates without notice, even while being entitled to do so, by reason of a lockout; s. 136 (2). Apart from that statutory exception, the circumstances in which a constructive dismissal take place for redundancy purposes are similar to those in the ERA s. 95 (1) for unfair dismissal, discussed in the last chapter. Thus a change of core terms, such as a wages reduction and loss of seniority, is likely to be a 'dismissal'; *Marriott* v. *Oxford and District Co-operative Society* (No. 2) [1969] 3 All ER 1126. In most cases it should be clear whether there has been a dismissal. Nevertheless there are some specific circumstances in which, in law, there can be no 'dismissal' and therefore no entitlement to a payment. There are pitfalls which are similar to unfair dismissal, but which have other aspects. I.e.:

- there is no dismissal in cases of renewal of the contract, or re-engagement; ERA s. 138;
- agreements with the employer which are interpreted later as leaving 'voluntarily', or a consensual termination, are not treated as dismissals – either for unfair redundancy dismissal or, usually, redundancy payment purposes (see Chapter 14);
- volunteering for *redundancy* should be accompanied by the employer formally confirming that it *is* a redundancy situation, even if the employee is responding to an invitation by the employer for 'volunteers';
- employees should not leave before the redundancy is confirmed and are *dismissed*, as this can also be regarded as leaving voluntarily;
- although the scope for employees to 'waive' redundancy payments, since the repeal of the ERA s. 197 is restricted, it remains for some pre-1 October 2002 contracts (see, e.g., SI 2002/2034, Sched. 2).

(3) Redundancy Payments

The ERA provides compensation for loss of employment in the form of a redundancy payment. Specifically, the ERA s. 135 (1), in the lead provision states:

'An employer shall pay a redundancy payment to any employee of his if the employee –

(a) is dismissed by the employer by reason of redundancy, or
(b) is eligible for a redundancy payment by reason of being laid off or kept on short-time.

However, this is subject to other conditions and provisions in Part XI, in particular ss. 138–144, 149–152, and 155–161, 164.

In order to qualify the claimant must have been dismissed for 'redundancy'.

Dismissal for Redundancy

The Act in particular limits eligibility to situations in which the employee is 'dismissed by reason of redundancy'. This means, according to s. 139 (1), where the dismissal is 'wholly or mainly' attributable to:

(a) the fact that the employer has ceased, or intends to cease –
   (i) to carry on the business for the purposes of which the employee was employed by him, or
   (ii) to carry on that business in the place where the employee was so employed, or
(b) the fact that the requirements of that business –
   (i) for employees to carry out work of a particular kind, or
   (ii) for employees to carry out work of a particular kind in the place where the employee was employed by the employer,

have ceased or are expected to cease or diminish.

A payment may also be claimed:

- following a period of lay-off or short time (details are in ERA ss. 147, 148);
- on a transfer, in certain circumstances, of the employer's business; Transfer of Undertakings (Protection of Employment) Regulations 1981, SI 1981/1794, as considered below.

Disputed Redundancy Payment Claims

If the employer refuses to make a redundancy payment (or the employee believes the payment is too small) that refusal can be disputed by making a tribunal claim; ERA s. 163 (1). The employee making a claim for a redundancy payment is given a head start, if it is disputed, by a presumption that the dismissal *is* by reason of redundancy 'unless the contrary is proved'; s. 163 (2). In other words the employer could show, for example, that the dismissal was for other reasons, such as misconduct, 'some other substantial reason', etc. In some cases this will rebut the presumption, but still leave open a possibility of 'unfair dismissal', as in the *Shawcat* case, discussed above.

Dismissal for 'Redundancy'

At one time it was assumed, based on cases like *Lesney Products Ltd* v. *Nolan* [1977] ICR 235, CA, that if an employer contends the job losses arose out of a reorganisation then redundancy payment claims could not be made. In that case Lord Denning observed that an employer was entitled to reorganise his business, and propose to the staff affected that they should agree to changes in their terms and conditions – and to 'dispense with their services' if they did not want to agree: and that when this happened the changes did not give the staff a right to a redundancy payment. In fact what he said was that it does not give them an *automatic* right; and it is still open to them to show a 'redundancy situation' as part of the changes. This point was made in *Robinson* v. *British Island Airways Ltd* [1977] IRLR 477 at 478; [1978]

ICR 304; and it is more consistent with the present case-law including the *Murray* case and 'causation' test considered below.

Another scenario in which staff may be precluded from sustaining the presumption of dismissal 'by reason of redundancy' is where workers have been dismissed for taking strike action. In *Baxter* v. *Limb Group of Companies* [1994] IRLR 572, dock workers were sacked when they refused to undertake overtime, which was then followed by the employer contracting the work out. The Court of Appeal refused to accept the dismissals were for 'redundancy'. A similar result followed industrial action in the earlier case of *Sanders* v. *Ernest A. Neale Ltd* [1974] 3 All ER 327, in which workers took strike action after two colleagues were made redundant. The factory shut down, but redundancy payment claims were refused. The refusal was upheld by Mr Justice Donaldson, the President of the National Industrial Relations Court. Although he rejected the concept of a 'self-induced redundancy', it was for the employer to prove that the dismissal was not for redundancy. On the facts of the case there was a 'redundancy situation', but he then went on to hold that it was the dismissals, and the workers' 'misconduct' and strike which *caused* the redundancy. 'The appellants were dismissed because they persistently refused to work normally,' he said. It may be noted that strikes during the currency of an employer's notice of termination for redundancy may also prevent redundancy payments being paid; ERA s. 143.

It is important to note that there are exceptions to displacement of redundancy by 'misconduct'. Specifically, dismissal for misconduct, at least during the 'obligatory period' of notice for redundancy, can nevertheless result in some or all of the redundancy being paid, as the ET determines; s. 140 (1), (2) and *Lignacite Products Ltd* v. *Krollman* [1979] IRLR 22.

Unfair Dismissal Redundancies

An employee may claim a redundancy payment *and* that the dismissal was 'unfair'. The statutory presumption in s. 163 (2) assists the claim for a redundancy payment, but not the 'unfair dismissal' part of the claim. The two elements of the claim are separated off, procedurally, by the Employment Tribunals Act 1996, s. 7 (6).

In practical terms, the employer will need to raise a potentially fair reason for the dismissal, and 'redundancy' is one of the reasons which can be advanced as the reason, or the principal reason, for dismissal; ERA s. 98 (1). If this cannot be done, though, or having done so the employer is then held by the ET not to have acted reasonably in treating it as a sufficient reason for dismissal (and otherwise procedurally unfairly, in breach of statutorily implied terms, or as required by the ERA ss. 98 [4], 98A, etc.) – the employee's claim will succeed.

In practice the more important grounds for unfair dismissal, typically, include the following:

(1) selection for redundancy because of membership or proposed membership of an independent trade union; or because of participation in union activities at an 'appropriate time'; or because of reasons relating to non-membership of a union (under TULR[C]A Part III);

(2) the selection is related to maternity, the work of safety representation, or asserting a statutory right (see Chapter 14); or

(3) the process used for selecting staff for redundancy is not a reasonable one, and has not been administered properly (or fairly); (ERA s. 98 and related provisions)[20] or

(4) the employer has not in the particular circumstances of the case acted reasonably in managing redundancy and treating it as a sufficient reason for dismissal. There are different ways in which dismissal is 'unfair', including a failure to follow good industrial relations practices and ACAS guidance; or the statutory implied procedures in s. 98A (1) and the Employment Act 2002 Schedule 2, Part I.

The dismissal might also 'be unfair' if a 'points system' for staff for redundancy is a 'sham' because the employer refuses to divulge the points awarded, thus rendering the consultation process flawed; *John Brown Engineering Ltd* v. *Brown and Others* [1997] IRLR 90 EAT.

Unfair dismissal aspects of redundancy, including breach of contractual terms regulating redundancy selection and procedures, are considered again later in this chapter.

Redundancy Payments: The Key Issues

As already considered, s. 139 of the ERA sets out the key criteria for determining if a dismissal is 'by reason of redundancy'. These need to be examined more closely.

Employer's Business Ceasing: ERA 1996: s. 139 (1) (a)

Closure of an employer's business (or the part of it where the dismissals take place) is a redundancy situation – even if the 'cessation' is only temporary, as early cases like *Gemmell* v. *Darngavil Brickworks Ltd* (1967) 2 ITR 20 confirm. Rather more controversially, it does not matter what the employer's *motives* are: so that it is not permissible for an ET to inquire into whether the cessation or closure is out of spite or anti-union sentiments.[21] If the closure is due to the business becoming insolvent there may be problems in obtaining arrears of wages, redundancy pay and getting other debts paid. These are considered later in this chapter.

Change of Workplace (ERA 1996: s. 139 [1] [a] [ii])

This part of s. 139 highlights redundancy situations where the employer's business in a particular place comes to an end. There are, in fact, two aspects to this. The first part of s. 139 (1) reads:

(a)......
(ii) to carry on that business *in the place* where the employee was so employed ...

This may be contrasted with the second limb of the section, in s. 139 (1) (b), which refers to the fact that the requirements of that business '(ii) for employees to carry out work of a particular kind *in the place* where the employee was employed ... have *ceased or diminished* or are expected to cease or diminish.' In either scenario the employer may not just be ending the business operations, or reducing them in that particular location. It may be that the operation is being moved to a new location.

In both cases the problem is the same, though. Can the employee, under the contract, including any mobility clause, be *required* to work at the new location? If so, on one approach (focusing on the contract) a refusal to move might result in a fair dismissal, and no redundancy payment. This might be problematic, of course, for staff who are *not* able to readily adapt to such changes, particularly if increased travel time and costs would be involved, or changes to children's schools and other financial and social costs would make a move problematic.

If the employer's insistence is not based on any contractual authority such as a 'mobility' clause, there may be scope for a 'constructive dismissal' claim if an attempt is not authorised: and the employee would still be eligible for a redundancy payment. The other side of the coin, though, is that if there is such authority a refusal to move may justify dismissal. The reason for this is that the phrase 'the place where the employee was so employed' could be interpreted as meaning 'where under his/her contract s/he *could be required to work*'; *United Kingdom Atomic Energy Authority* v. *E.F. Claydon* [1974] IRLR 6.

Even if the employer does have the benefit of a mobility clause or other authority to move staff to another location, such contractual rights may not necessarily assist the employer – particularly if other factors come into play in deciding what is the employee's 'place of work'. In an important 1997 case the Court of Appeal held that the employee's 'place of work' should not just be determined in accordance with the contract, and a wider factual inquiry may be also necessary. For example, even where there is a mobility clause, if the employee has only ever worked in one place it may be wrong to use the clause to defeat a valid claim for a redundancy payment; *High Table Ltd* v. *Horst and Others* [1998] ICR 409; [1997] IRLR 513, CA.[22] The power to require staff to move may also be subject to an implied duty to give adequate notice and to pay expenses to do so (see the *Akhtar* case referred to in Chapter 5) – although the precise scope of such requirements is less certain. Nor is it clear whether the employer in any case can be expected to operate mobility clauses reasonably. In principle, trust and confidence requirements underline the need for such a 'reasonableness' factor.

Diminishing Requirements for Employees (ERA 1996, s. 139 (1) (b))

The key factor in this head of the section is that the dismissal must be '*wholly or mainly attributable* to

(a) ....
(b) the fact that the requirements of that business

    (i) for employees to *carry out work of a particular kind*, or
    (ii) for employees to carry out *work of a particular kind* in the *place* where the employee was employed by the employer

have ceased or diminished or are expected to cease or diminish'.

This is the most difficult aspect of the redundancy formula, and in practical terms the most important. It is concerned with situations where the business has not completely closed down but where the requirements for specific kinds of labour have, for whatever reason, come to an end or reduced. This might occur in a variety of ways. It could range from straightforward job cut-backs caused by a reduction in the amount of work coming into the business to rather more complex (and technically problematic and contentious) situations – for example, where new technology or changes in work patterns have been introduced.

In some cases a management will readily accept the existence of a 'redundancy' situation on the 'diminished requirements' basis, and pay the appropriate compensation as the price for effecting reorganisations and staffing reductions. In other cases it may seek to resist redundancy claims brought under this head, and defend unfair dismissal claims.

'Ceased or Diminished' – What Must be Shown?

Whatever the background to the claim, it will generally be necessary to demonstrate that there has been a clear reduction in the need for the person to undertake work of the particular kind which he or she is employed to do. Redundancy can also be maintained even if dismissal was anticipated when the employment began, for example where the employment is on a temporary contract.[23] A possibility also exists, under this head of redundancy, for it to be shown that the job has changed so significantly that it could be said to have 'gone' leaving the post 'redundant'.

The clearest scenario in which redundancy occurs is where there is a reduction in the amount of work required to be done, and therefore in the number of workers required to perform work which remains after a business downturn and loss of capacity and employment activity – and this has prompted an employer to dismiss workers who could otherwise do such work. But is there a 'redundancy', or is there some other explanation which could be put forward for the dismissal? As we have already seen when considering constructive dismissal claims (Chapter 14) the courts can be extremely sympathetic to employers undertaking reorganisations and wanting to reduce staff numbers – for example if they can establish a defence based on 'some other substantial reason', such as the need for a workplace reorganisation (see Chapter 5).

Changing the Work Requirements: What Does the Contract Say?

In some cases there may not necessarily be an overall change in employment activity. Nevertheless there can be a redundancy if there is sufficient diminution in specific *kinds* of work required. One important consideration in deciding whether there is such a diminished need – and therefore whether a 'redundancy' situation exists – has been to look at what the *contract* says the employee can be required to do. This may involve taking a very narrow approach, particularly when the formal contractual requirements of the employee being made redundant are compared with what they may *actually* be doing.[24]

Mr Pink was employed at a shoe factory as a making and finishing room operative. In practice, though, he spent most of his time specifically as a sole layer/pre-sole fitter. While he had been away a trainee had been brought in to carry out sole laying work. When redundancies were declared Mr Pink was selected rather than that person. His claim for unfair dismissal was rejected. It was held that he was 'redundant'. The tribunal reached this conclusion on the basis of his formal employment as a making and finishing room operative; and on that basis there had been a diminution in the employer's requirements for staff who could be asked to undertake work in his contract and job description. The EAT upheld the decision, saying it was irrelevant that there had been no diminution in the requirements for the sort of work Mr Pink was in *practice* doing most of the time.

Similarly, in *Johnson* v. *Peabody Trust* [1996] IRLR 387 a building worker complained of unfair dismissal when there was an apparent need to make a 'roofer' redundant. Rejecting the claim, and upholding the 'redundancy' finding, it was held that although his contract contained a flexibility clause enabling the employer to move him to non-roofing work if there was no roofing work to be done, his main *contractual* obligation was to perform roofing work. Accordingly it was that activity that had to be considered when considering whether there had been a 'diminution'.

(4) 'Redundancy': The Present Approach

In the EAT case of *Safeway Stores plc* v. *Burrell* [1997] IRLR 200, a move away from either a 'contract' approach or a 'function'-based approach was signalled. As discussed below, both approaches have been largely displaced by a more simple and pragmatic test focusing simply on whether there has been a diminution, and whether the dismissal is attributable to that diminution. In the *Safeway* case a petrol station manager was told that there would be a reorganisation of the management structure and that the post of 'petrol station manager' would disappear. It would be replaced by a new post of 'petrol filling station controller' (at a lower salary). Existing post-holders could apply for the posts. However, as there were fewer posts than managers there would be redundancies. Mr Burrell declined the invitation to apply and brought a complaint of unfair dismissal. He argued the new job was essentially the same as the old one so that there was no 'redundancy' situation. The employer contended that it was a genuine redundancy; or, alternatively, if there was no redundancy then (they said) there was justification for the dismissal on the basis of 'some other substantial reason' (see Chapter 14), namely because it was a necessary 'reorganisation'. The majority of the tribunal upheld his claim. Many of the jobs he had actually done (the 'function' test) were still required, albeit by someone with a different job title. The tribunal's Chairman (in the minority) looked at what Mr Burrell's contract required (the 'contract' test) and concluded that the job he was *employed* to do 'no longer existed'.

The EAT allowed the appeal and remitted the case for reconsideration by another tribunal. It said that the correct test involves *three* stages:

(1) Was the employee dismissed?
(2) If so, had the requirements of the business for employees to carry out work of a particular kind 'ceased or diminished' (or were they expected to do so)?
(3) If so, was the dismissal *caused* wholly or mainly by that state of affairs?

On stage 2, the key issue, said the EAT, was whether there was a diminution in the business requirements for *employees*, and in deciding this tribunals should not introduce a 'contract test' question whereby they just considered the specific tasks the applicant was employed to do. The tribunal majority had failed to consider the employer's alternative defence, however, namely that the dismissal was for 'some other substantial reason'.

Workplace Changes – 'Diminution' or 'Reorganisation'?
The points referred to in the last section beg the question whether all workplace changes and reorganisations *do* necessarily amount to 'redundancy'. It may be that a change in the type of work required can amount to a redundancy in appropriate

circumstances because it entails a diminution in 'work of a particular' kind. If, however, there is no overall reduction in demand, and staff are just being asked to do a job in different ways, then there is, in principle, generally no 'diminution' and therefore no 'redundancy'. The central question remains whether there has been either a clear diminution in the work required; or whether the job, as it has been reorganised, has become so 'different' to the point that it can be said that the existing job has gone.

The issue has arisen in earlier decisions, and it has frequently appeared that for policy reasons – and in particular a desire not to inhibit management's 'right to manage' – the courts often remain reluctant to recognise a redundancy situation. One early case in particular, has remained a benchmark for this important area of redundancy rights. This is the case of *Lesney Products Ltd* v. *Nolan*, referred to above.

Employees in that case were machine maintenance setters who worked in a toy factory where a three-shift system of day, evening, and night work was in operation. To cut operating costs the night shift was ended for both the direct workers and the setters. The latter, instead of working a day shift with long overtime periods and a night shift, were asked to work a double-day shift on alternate weeks. Among other things this reduced their opportunities to earn overtime pay, which was not fully recompensed as part of the changes, despite payment of a shift premium. Some of them were dismissed for refusing to accept the changes, and a number of them argued that the changes amounted to a 'redundancy'. The employers were able to show that the amount of work being done since the changes remained, broadly, the same. It was held by the Court of Appeal, which rejected their claim, that their dismissal was not 'wholly or mainly' due to a diminution in the requirements of the business. A reorganisation of hours did not, in itself, amount to 'redundancy'.[25]

Lord Denning referred to the earlier leading case of *Johnson* v. *Nottinghamshire Combined Police Authority* [1974] ICR 170 at 176 in which managements' right to reorganise for 'efficiency' reasons was seen as the main consideration in characterising changes as reorganisations: and making it clear that these do not automatically involve 'redundancy'. Police clerks had been working on a conventional day shift from 9.30 am to 5.30 pm. Not surprisingly, they were concerned when it was proposed to change to a system of work which required them to work from 8.00 am to 3.00 pm, and from 1.00 pm to 8.00 pm, in alternating weeks. They objected and were dismissed. Their case failed. It was not 'work of a particular kind' that was disappearing, or changing significantly, because of any significant change in the nature of the work. Under the changes the clerks would be doing the same job. It was just being done at different times, even though this was a lot less acceptable to them. The change was 'efficiency'-driven, but it was not 'redundancy' – and so redundancy payments did not have to be paid, held the Court of Appeal.

Not all the case law in this area can be easily reconciled, and in some cases the position has depended on the employees' contractual position in relation to the change process as much as the nature of the work they are asked to do after the changeover.

Example
Macfisheries Ltd decided to end night-shift working and asked Mrs Findlay and other workers to switch to days. However they wanted to work nights for domestic reasons, and it was an accepted point in the case that under their contracts they could not be required to make the change. The IT's decision that night-shift work

was 'work of a particular kind' and that it had ceased or diminished, thus making her redundant, was upheld by the EAT.[26]

S. 139 (1) (b): The Murray Test

In what is now the leading redundancy case on this part of the redundancy formula, *Murray* v. *Foyle Meats Ltd* [1999] IRLR 562; [1999] ICR 827; [2000] 1 AC 51, the Lord Chancellor giving the leading judgment described the statutory language in s. 139 (1) (b) as 'simplicity itself', saying that it asked 'two questions of fact'. The first is whether the requirements of the business for employees to carry out work of a particular kind have diminished. The second is whether the dismissal is attributable, wholly or mainly, to that state of affairs. He approved the analysis provided by the EAT in the *Safeway Stores* case (as discussed above). He called this a question of 'causation'.

In the *Murray* case itself the tribunal had found that the requirements of the business (for employees to work in the slaughter hall part of the operation) had diminished; and that this was what had led to their dismissal. That, he said, was 'the end to the matter'. He did, however, take the opportunity to put to rest the approach taken in earlier cases, including *Pink* v. *White* (and earlier 'contract' cases like *Nelson* v. *British Broadcasting Corporation* [1977] IRLR 148; and *Nelson No. 2* reported at [1979] IRLR 346, CA) 'which may have encouraged a belief that the statute had a different meaning'. Of *Pink* v. *White* he said the argument before the EAT turned on whether the 'contract' test ought to be applied (i.e. did the company need less employees of the kind specified in Mr Pink's contract?), in which case he was redundant. Or did the 'function' test apply (i.e. did the company need less staff to do the work he was actually doing?) in which case he was not. He had no doubt that on the facts the case was rightly decided, but added that both the contract and function tests 'miss the point'. He went on to say that 'the key word in the statute' was 'attributable' – and that there was no 'reason in law why the dismissal of an employee should not be attributable to a diminution in the employer's need for employees irrespective of the terms of his contract or the function which he performed'. He added the important point that 'the dismissal of an employee who could perfectly well have been redeployed or who was doing work unaffected by the fall in demand may require some explanation to establish the necessary causal connection'. But that, he said, was a 'question of fact, not law'.

The approach identified by the Lords has been applied in later leading cases like *Stankovic* v. *Westminster City Council* [2002] Emp. LR 68, EAT where a teacher was employed on a series of renewable fixed-term contracts. She was later offered a contract with reduced hours which she had to accept or not within a short period. Despite the council's contention that she was not redundant, as there was no reduction in the amount of work available in her area of expertise that she could have done, the EAT concluded that the facts showed there *was* an overall reduction in teaching required, and the reduction did not necessarily have to be in her area of expertise for a redundancy to arise. Redundancy could be the result of a 'knock on' effect from reductions in other related areas of work. Applying *Murray* and *Safeway Stores* the ET had correctly identified that there was a diminution in work, and that this was attributable wholly or mainly to that state of affairs. The dismissal was in any case flawed because of procedural unfairness, and lack of proper consultation – and so the case was remitted to another tribunal to consider.

Displacement and 'Bumping'

If workers are replaced by other workers, including 'contractors' they will normally be able to claim redundancy compensation on the ground that the employer's need for 'employees' has diminished.

The point is illustrated by a case in which two decorators were dismissed when their employer decided it was cheaper to employ 'self-employed' workers. The employer said this was not a redundancy situation – essentially because the business was actually expanding and the work *increasing*. Nevertheless, on appeal, it was held that there had been a reduction in the need for 'employees'. They were therefore entitled to redundancy payments.[27]

Displacement by another worker from *within* the organisation whose job has become redundant – a process sometimes called a 'transferred redundancy', or 'bumping' – has also generally entitled the worker dismissed to redundancy pay. Although this in many cases has been recognised by the courts, in order to qualify the employee must still be able to show that the dismissal *was* the result of a diminution in the employer's work requirements. In a leading case on the principle *North Yorkshire County Council* v. *Fay* [1985] IRLR 247 Mrs Fay was a teacher who had been employed on four successive short-term contracts. Each time she started a contract this was to fill a temporary shortfall in the staffing requirements of the department where she had worked. She was dismissed when the last contract was not renewed. She claimed both unfair dismissal *and* a redundancy payment. The redundancy claim was based partly on the fact that another teacher had been brought in from another school where there had been 'overstaffing'. The tribunal held that the dismissal had not been due to redundancy. Nevertheless it was 'fair' for 'some other substantial reason' (see Chapter 14), namely the expiry of her contract. The Court of Appeal, upheld the 'bumping' principle, but on the particular facts of the case decided that she had not lost her job for redundancy. On the evidence it had not been shown that there had been a diminution in either the school's or the authority's requirements for teachers.

Later cases illustrated how it is not always so clear that 'bumping' does entail dismissal for *redundancy*. The question the legislation seems to pose is whether the phrase 'work of a particular kind' means the work which the *dismissed employee* is required to do. On that basis, the employee dismissed must be redundant at the time of dismissal. If, for example, the employee has been asked to relinquish the job *before* a replacement has been put into the job there may already have been a 'dismissal' (*Church* v. *West Lancashire NHS Trust* (No. 1) [1998] IRLR 4).

In both the *Safeway Stores Ltd* and *Murray* v. *Foyle Meats Ltd* cases the principle that bumping redundancies are 'redundancies' has been re-affirmed, although as in *Church* there are still going to be cases where the 'causal link' between the circumstances affecting the post (and postholder) which has come to an end, and the dismissal of the 'bumped' employee, will require explanation. In a lot of such 'reorganisations' there may be an unfair dismissal of the employee dismissed rather than a redundancy.

(5) Lay-off and Short-time

The ERA allows an employee to claim a redundancy payment if he or she has been laid off or kept on short time for either four or more consecutive weeks, or for a series of six or more weeks (of which not more than three are consecutive) within a period of 13 weeks.[28] To do so, however, the procedural requirements in the ERA must be satisfied. Reference must be made to the detailed provisions in ss. 147–154, but in summary the process involves the following steps.

S. 147 (1) defines 'lay-off' and 'short-time'. An employee is taken to be laid off for a week if he works under a contract whereby remuneration depends on being provided with work, and where he is not entitled to be paid because no work is being provided. Not all contracts, of course, fit that description – and it may be that wages are payable even though no work is being provided. Short-time is defined by s. 147 (2). This requires that in any week where, by reason of a diminution in the work provided (which is work the employee is employed to do) remuneration must fall below half a week's pay.

If the lay-off or short-time lasts more than four consecutive weeks – or for a series of six or more weeks (of which not more than three were consecutive) within a period of 13 weeks – then the employee can give the employer a written notice of intention to claim a redundancy payment in respect of the lay-off or short-time; s. 148. An employer can either agree to accept the claim, or contest it. A redundancy payment entitlement is not made out if on the date of the employee's service it was reasonably to be expected that the employee, if he stayed, would not later than four weeks after that date enter a period of employment of not less than 13 weeks during which there are no further lay-offs, short-time periods and the employer serves a counter-notice within seven days after the service of the employee's notice. If the counter-notice is withdrawn, or there is a lay-off or short-time in the four-week period after the employee's notice, then the entitlement to a redundancy payment is made out; ss. 149–152. One of the disincentives to making such claims is that an employee, to be eligible, must resign by giving notice in accordance with s. 150 as a pre-condition.

A further problem is that an employer may offer alternative work during a short-time working period. In this case, even if the wages are low, as long as they exceed half a week's normal pay there is no 'short-time working'. This is illustrated by cases like *Spinpress* v. *Turner* [1986] ICR 433.

As discussed in Chapter 6 an employer's powers to lay off, introduce short-time working, etc., may be regulated by the individual contract and collective agreement procedures. There is generally no power to lay off without contractual authority, and it is difficult to demonstrate this by custom and practice even if this has traditionally been done in some industries. Such a lay-off, or introduction of short-time working – especially as it involves a reduction in pay and worsening of other conditions – may be repudiatory, and in appropriate cases it may enable a worker to resign and claim dismissal. This will not be the case, though, if the contract clearly authorises lengthy lay-offs.

(6) Part-time Workers and Redundancy

'Continuous employment' requirements have generally tended to discriminate against part-time workers, many of them women. Accordingly the requirements on hours and continuous service which blocked part-time employees' rights to unfair dismissal and other entitlements were withdrawn by the Employment Protection (Part-time Employees Regulations) 1995, SI 1995 No. 31. This has enabled part-time workers with the required continuous service to claim redundancy payment and make unfair dismissal claims. In addition, aspects of redundancy arrangements which impact less favourably on part-time staff when compared with full-timers doing comparable work may be the subject of complaints under the Part-time Workers (Prevention of Less Favourable Treatment) Regulations 2000, SI 2000/1551. However, the difficulties involved in using these regulations were illustrated in a 2003 case.[29]

(7) Redundancy: Unfair Dismissal and Breach of Contract

The ERA s. 98 (1), (2) (c) provides that redundancy is a potentially 'fair' reason for dismissal. Accordingly, if an employer manages the process correctly the only thing the employee gets is a redundancy payment, calculated in accordance with the ERA s. 162 and related provisions.

The process may, however, be handled in ways that breach contractual requirements. It is also clear that breach of implied terms, notably 'trust and confidence', can make dismissals unfair – for example if contractual enhancements in a redundancy scheme are offered to some staff rather than others; *Transco plc (formerly BG plc)* v. *O'Brien* [2001] IRLR 496. In that case the offer had not been extended as a result of a mistaken belief that the employee was not 'permanent' in status, but this did not make any difference to the EAT's finding.

The key factors for unfair dismissal purposes are:

- the employer has not satisfied the tribunal, particularly in terms of s. 98 (4) and procedural requirements, that the *selection process* was fair, or that other necessary *procedures*, including consultation, consideration of alternative employment, etc., were fair; or
- the *reason for dismissal* rendered the dismissal automatically 'unfair'; ERA s. 105, TULR(C)A, and related protective legislation; or
- the dismissal is unfair as a result of the TUPE Regulations if they apply to a 'transfer' (see below).

Unfair Selection for Redundancy

If other staff could have been dismissed for redundancy but were not, this then begs the question whether the staff selected have been selected fairly. The process used in this respect, as with other procedures, must be a reasonable one, and operated fairly. Otherwise the dismissal will be unfair. Examples include *British Areospace plc* v. *Green* [1995] IRLR 433, CA. A points system for determining who should go and who should be retained may be one way of ensuring redundancies are fair; but such systems are likely to be flawed if the points process, or points awarded, are not revealed, or the system is otherwise not fair and transparent – or if in effect it is used to obviate necessary consultations procedures, or render them ineffective; see, for example, *John Brown Engineering Ltd* v. *Brown and Others* [1997] IRLR 90, EAT. In *Constantine* v. *McGregor Cory Ltd* [2000] ICR 938 the employee was dismissed for redundancy unfairly because the selection criteria were misleading and unclear, and there had been no individual consultation. Although it is possible in such cases to conclude that this would not have made any difference to the outcome, or just award compensation to reflect the need for an extra period of consultation, on the facts the case was remitted by the EAT for reconsideration of remedy – especially as the options of reinstatement and re-engagement were not dealt with properly.

Procedural Requirements

The need for procedural fairness in redundancy was reiterated in *Polkey* v. *AE Dayton Services Ltd* [1987] IRLR 503, HL. Specifically, Lord Bridge said that in redundancy the employer will not normally have acted 'reasonably' for the purposes of what is now s. 98 (4) unless 'he warns and consults employees or their representatives, adopts a fair basis on which to select for redundancy, and takes such steps as may be reasonable to avoid or minimise redundancy by redeployment within his own organisation'. Guidance on consultation was also given in the leading case of *Williams* v. *Compair Maxam* [1982] ICR 156, EAT. Guidance is in the ACAS booklet *Redundancy Handling* (No. 12). The need for adequate procedural fairness, however, had already been well-established in early redundancy cases like *Vokes Ltd* v. *Bear* [1974] ICR 1, NIRC in which the employee was dismissed without warning and with no time off to find alternative employment in the company's other operations in its group. So that, despite there being a clear 'redundancy' situation, the dismissal was unfair.

Failing to consider, or consider properly, alternatives to redundancy will generally render a dismissal unfair; *Langston* v. *Cranfield University* [1998] IRLR 172.

TULR(C)A ss. 188–198, as amended, also requires consultation with any relevant trade union or employee representatives – not only with a view to provide information, consult and listen, but to try to reach agreement on ways of avoiding dismissals, and reducing the numbers involved (and their effects). If there is no union, arrangements to elect employee representatives must be made; TULR(C)A s. 188A.

In both individual and collective cases consultation must have the characteristics of a fair process, and this means 'fair' in terms of the timing it takes place, the information given, 'response time' afforded to staff, and evidence that points made by staff affected have been adequately considered. Similar shortcomings in the consultation process were identified in the 2002 case of *Stankovic*, discussed above, in which it was clear that the employee received information that she faced redundancy too late to enable her to do anything other than accept or reject the redundancy terms offered.

Exceptionally consultation may be unnecessary, for example in insolvency situations where there is a pressing need to find a purchaser quickly and consultation would have made no difference to the dismissal process; *Warner* v. *Adnet Ltd* [1998] IRLR 394. If, however, consultation cannot be waived in that way (as being 'futile') discussions with unions about selection criteria and systems does not prevent the need for consultation with the individuals affected. However, the precise scope of that stage in the process is dependent on the particular circumstances of each case and what 'fairness' standards require; *Mugford* v. *Midland Bank plc* [1997] ICR 399.

ERA s. 105; Automatically Unfair Dismissals

Under s. 105 (1) an employee who is dismissed is to be regarded for the purposes of Part X as unfairly dismissed if:

(a) the reason, or if more than one reason, the principal reason is that the employee is redundant;

(b) it is shown that the circumstances constituting the redundancy applied equally to one or more other employees in the same undertaking who held positions similar to that held by the employee and who have *not* been dismissed; and

(c)   it is shown that any of the reasons in s. 105 (2)–(7C), 7E, or 7F apply.

In summary, this includes dismissal in the following key types of case:

- health and safety (s. 100)
- shop workers and betting workers refusing to work on Sundays (s. 101)
- working time (s. 101A)
- trustees of occupational pension schemes (s. 102)
- employee representatives (s. 103)
- protected disclosure (s. 103A)
- assertion of a statutory right (s. 104)
- national minimum wage (s. 104A)
- tax credits (s. 104B)
- flexible working (s. 104C).

In addition certain union and employee representative-related cases may also be 'unfair' if the reasons for redundancy selection are within the protection afforded by the ERA Part X, TULR(C)A, and other employment protection legislation, including grounds relating to:

- trade union membership and activities, work as a representative, recognition, etc.; TULR(C)A, including s. 153
- participation in official industrial action, particularly during a protected period; TULR(C)A
- Transnational Information and Consultation of Employees Regulations 1999, SI 1999/3323.

Statutory protection is also afforded for redundancy dismissals connected with maternity and parental leave-taking, part-time rights, and TUPE transfers under the following schemes:

- Maternity and Parental Leave Regulations 1999, SI 1999, SI 1999/3312
- Part-time Workers (Prevention of Less Favourable Treatment) Regulations 2000, SI 2000/1551
- TUPE-related redundancies and dismissals (see below).

(8) Transfer of Employer's Business

Recent years have seen a massive increase in the number and scale of business transfers. Related developments, such as public sector compulsory competitive tendering, have involved use of the transfer legislation, and thereby impacted significantly on working conditions, as highlighted by research by one of the authors in *TUPE and CCT Business Transfers: UK Labour Market Views*.[30] For the workers involved this usually means not only a change of employer and management but also, possibly, significant changes in working conditions. Transfers may also involve enforced redundancies. The present rules, including the legislation which implements current EC measures, can often leave workers in an extremely vulnerable position – particularly in terms of job security and redundancies before and after a transfer.

There are three aspects to consider:

- 'continuity' of employment when there is a change of employer
- rules on transfers
- rights on a transfer.

Continuity

As already discussed (in Chapter 2) a period of continuous employment must be shown before redundancy, unfair dismissal and other rights can be claimed. In the case of a redundancy payment this is two years (ERA 1996, s. 155). Normally if the job finishes any rights will be exercisable against the employer at that time. Continuity of service will be broken on termination, however, and before the employee can assert rights against any new employer he or she would normally have to start accruing the appropriate service all over again. The ERA 'change of employer' rules[31] preserve continuity of employment in certain situations including:

(a) on trustees or personal representatives taking over from an employer who has died;
(b) on a change of partners if the employer is employed by a partnership;
(c) on a transfer of employment to an 'associated employer' (for example another company within a group);
(d) on a change of employer under an Act of Parliament (for example as a result of a privatisation Act);
(e) on a transfer of a trade, business or undertaking from one person to another.

Redundancy Payments on a Transfer

If there is a transfer of the ownership of the business and the new owner offers to renew the contract (or offers a new one), provisions in the ERA[32] have the effect that, despite the employment ending, the employee will only be entitled to a redundancy payment if that offer is refused *and* the refusal is 'reasonable'. If the offer is accepted point (e) above will apply and continuity of service will be maintained.

Another situation where a redundancy claim is preserved (because employment terminates without continuity being maintained) is where, instead of the entire ownership of the business being sold, the part of the business in which the employee is working is the subject of a so-called 'assets' sale. In general terms, if there is *no* transfer at that point, the contract is treated as terminating, even if the employee is re-employed at that time.

Example

Mrs Crompton worked at a children's clothing factory which, because business was slack, was sold off to another business. However, the company carried on making clothes at other factories. She was immediately re-employed on the same terms by the new owners of the factory. As there had not been a transfer of the business her continuity of service had been broken and she was eligible for redundancy pay.[33]

TUPE Regulations 1981

The Transfer of Undertakings (Protection of Employment) Regulations 1981, SI 1981, No. 1794 may or may not apply to a transfer, depending on the type of transaction involved. The basic principle is that the regulations apply if the transfer is effected 'by sale or by some other disposition or by operation of law'; reg. 3. If the change of ownership is effected by a transfer of shares there is no 'transfer' even, it would seem, if this is to avoid engaging the legal duties of TUPE; see *Brookes* v. *Borough Care Services* [1998] IRLR 636, discussed in Chapter 5. The rules in the ERA may still be relevant if the regulations do not apply; and regulations made under the Employment Relations Act 1999 s. 38 may also apply (few have been made to date). As originally enacted the regulations only applied to 'commercial' organisations or businesses. This had the potential effect of excluding workers in non-commercial parts of the economy – government, local government, and so on – from protection when their organisations were transferred or sold off. Non-commercial undertakings were subsequently covered following amendments by the Trade Union Reform and Employment Rights Act 1993, s. 33 (2). This change was needed in order to comply with the EC position and the consistently broad interpretation of the Acquired Rights Directive (EEC/77/187) given by the EC Commission and ECJ in deciding whether a 'transfer of an undertaking' has taken place.[34] The point was also illustrated by an important ECJ decision in a Dutch case,[35] when it was held that the withdrawal of a local government subsidy to a drugs rehabilitation organisation, and its reallocation to another organisation, the Sigma Foundation, in circumstances in which the operation was partly absorbed by Sigma, could amount to a 'transfer'. This gave continuity, and rights to maintain existing terms, to staff taken on by Sigma. It also assisted some of the staff who had been made redundant, who came within the directive's protection. A key factor was whether the organisation retains its 'identity' – even if it may not be the same as it was before the transfer transaction. Later case law has highlighted the difficulties in determining whether a particular situation amounts to a 'relevant transfer' or not. In particular, one key factor in determining whether an organisation has kept its identity and continued, is whether a majority of its staff have been retained. The 'identity' requirement has been developed and explained in important cases in the ECJ which have emphasised that for there to be a 'relevant transfer' there must be continuity in terms of the business's 'economic identity'. In *Merckx and Neuhuys* v. *Ford Motor Co. Belgium SA* [1996] IRLR 467, the ECJ held there was such a transfer when Ford transferred a dealership to new dealers who operated the same business but from a different location; nor did there have to be a direct contractual relationship between the 'transferor' employer and the 'transferee'.

Although there have been cases which confirm that there can be a 'relevant transfer' when services, including public sector services, are 'contracted out', the case of *Betts* v. *Brintel Helicopters Ltd and KLM* [1997] IRLR 361 CA, in which an oil company switched a helicopter services contract to new contractors did *not* involve a transfer, said the Court of Appeal. There was no identifiable economic identity transferred; the new contractor had not taken on any of the previous contractor's staff; and different assets and facilities were used in the new operation. The decision, which has been very significant in its implications for workers employed by private and public sector contractors, and in the context of the compulsory competitive tendering process, has to be considered in the context of another important ECJ decision, *Suzen* in which staff of a cleaning firm were affected when a school ended its contract with the firm and started using another firm. The ECJ did not consider the assets disposed of were significant enough and the main part of the business entity had not transferred (with the 'transferee' firm not taking most of the workers).[36] In essence the case established that there is *not* a 'transfer' where there is merely a change of contractors with no corresponding transfer of significant assets or a major part of the workforce. Post-*Suzen* cases have, on occasion, departed from such principles. One important case, for example, *ADI (UK) Ltd* v. *Willer* [2001] IRLR 542 CA, indicated that whilst *Suzen* principles must be adhered to, where business services are changed and staff are not retained or taken on, ETs should nevertheless enquire whether TUPE regulations are being circumvented *before* concluding there is no relevant transfer. In labour-intensive activities the key issue is likely to focus on the extent to which workers are re-engaged or not. If most of them are dismissed but then re-engaged by the transferor organisation it will still be necessary to ascertain whether assets have *also* been transferred in order to see if the organisation's 'identity' has remained; *Oy Liikenne Ab* v. *Liskojarvi and Another* (C-172/99) [2001] IRLR 171, ECJ.

If the regulations do not apply then workers will not have the protection which they give, although there may be scope for redundancy payments, and any available contractual entitlements.

A 'transfer' may, for the regulations to apply, include a transfer of an undertaking effected by a *series* of transactions, and it is not dependent on property being transferred.[37]

The Rules on Transfers and their Effects

If the regulations do apply to the transfer they do more than just preserve continuity. Their main effect, once the transfer is completed, should be to put the transferee employer in the same position as the original employer for most employment contract purposes including liability for the consequences of redundancy and dismissals.[38] It is not proposed to set out all the effects of the regulations, but the main consequences, as made clear by the key provision (reg. 5), are:

- unless the employee objects (which s/he can do under reg. 5 [4A] by informing the 'transferor' or the 'transferee') employment contracts with the old employer do not terminate at the time of the transfer, but will instead be treated as if they had been originally made with the new employer;
- all the old employer's 'rights, powers, duties and liabilities under or relating to any such contract' are transferred to the new employer: non-contractual benefits, for example in relation to pension benefits, do not have to be maintained by the new employer; *Adams* v. *Lancashire County Council and BET Catering Services Ltd* [1997] IRLR 436, CA;
- anything done in relation to the contract by the old employer before the transfer (including for example breaches of contract or statutory obligations) is generally to be treated as if done by the new employer.

Reg. 5 (5) preserves the right of an employee to leave without notice 'if a substantial change is made in his working conditions to his detriment'. The change of identity of the employer will not be such a change *per se*.

If an employee does object, the transfer will operate to terminate his/her employment with the transferor; reg. 5 (4B). But this will not constitute a 'dismissal' by the transferor giving rise to an unfair dismissal claim unless the employer's actions result in detrimental changes or, possibly, a 'redundancy' situation.[39] The effect of this is to *prevent* the employee initiating an unfair dismissal complaint, or getting a redundancy payment; see *Katsikas* v. *Konstantinidis* [1993] IRLR 179, ECJ.

Union consultation rights are given in transfer situations as discussed below.

Court Action to Prevent Transfers

As an employer's action in transferring a contract to another employer is, on the face of it, a repudiation of the employer's obligations under the contract, can an employee or union get a court order to stop it? This issue arose in 1992 when British Airways hived off part of the company to a subsidiary and simply notified staff of the changes. The TGWU and an employee tried unsuccessfully to get an injunction pending court action where the issue could be considered. In the *Newns* case the Court of Appeal ruled[40] that the effect of regulation 5 of the regulations overrode any rights an employee might otherwise have, and have at Common Law, and provided for a statutory change of employers. Nor, on the evidence, had any proposals relating to the transfer shown a breach of the implied duty of good faith by British Airways which could be restrained by injunction.

Which Employer is Liable; Employment 'Immediately before the Transfer'

In theory this question ought not to raise any problem, as the policy objective of the legislation is to try to maintain the acquired rights of workers employed by a transferor as a result of a transfer. In practice, however, there are pitfalls for workers caught up in some kinds of transfer situations.

One problem, put simply, is at what point in time before the transfer actually takes place must the employees be in the transferor's employment before they can come within the transfer rules and protection in regulation 5 referred to above?

The language in regulation 5 (3) suggests that this is, in fact, limited to anyone who is 'employed immediately before the transfer'. At first sight, then, this restriction seems to exclude any workers who are employed earlier than the point which is 'immediately before' the precise moment of transfer.

Of course this interpretation would be, potentially, a licence to evade the rules – for instance where a transferee employer arranges with the transferor to dismiss the workers before the transfer takes place, thus removing any responsibilities on the transferee (and thereby leaving the workers with what could be a worthless claim against an insolvent transferor employer).

In an earlier case *Secretary of State for Employment* v. *Spence* [1986] IRLR 248 this was exactly the interpretation that was adopted, with the Court of Appeal saying that for the purposes of reg. 5 (3) workers employed until several hours before a transfer were not employed 'immediately' before it.

Fortunately the full impact of this decision was averted by a judgment of the House of Lords in *Litster and Others* v. *Forth Dry Dock & Engineering Co Ltd* [1989] IRLR 161 – a case which illustrated the threat that some transfers and 'insolvency'-related corporate transactions can pose to workers' rights.

The case concerned 12 shipworkers employed by Forth Dry Dock (FDC), who were summarily dismissed when the company went into receivership and who were thereupon told that no funds could be 'made available' for wages, outstanding holiday pay or pay in lieu of notice. An hour later the company's assets were acquired by Forth Estuary (FE), a new company set up by people previously involved in the running of FDC, which immediately started recruiting workers (but not the dismissed workers).

As pointed out later by one of the judges in the Lords, FE very soon had a workforce the size of FDC, employed on similar trades but at lower rates of pay. The same judge also referred to 'one of the less creditable aspects of the matter'. When the shop steward had tried to get information about the transfer he was told by a director of FDC (who was also, by then, involved in FE) that he knew nothing about a new company taking over, and by a representative of the receivers that 'he knew nothing about a company called Forth Estuary Engineering'. This was described by the judge as a 'calculated disregard' of the workers' rights to information and to be consulted under regulation 10 of the regulations.

At the tribunal the shipworkers claimed they had been unfairly dismissed, but FE denied they were liable as the workers were not employed 'immediately' before the transfer. Any responsibility for them, they argued, remained with FDC as the transferor. The tribunal ruled against FE on this point and then went on to decide that:

- the dismissals had been automatically unfair (see the section on rights on a transfer below) as they had obviously been connected with the transfer: this was in line with guidance in an ECJ case which indicated that even if a dismissal had taken place before the transfer if it was due to the transfer, for example at the request of the transferee, the worker should be treated as still employed at that point (*P. Bork International A/S* v. *Foreningen af Arbejdsledere i Danmark* (101/87) [1989] IRLR 41, ECJ);
- even had the dismissals been for 'economic, technical or organisational' reasons (which could have given the employers a way out under reg. 8 [2]), the dismissals had still been unfair because they had been carried out unfairly.

The issue then went to three further stages of appeal, culminating in the House of Lords ruling.

The EAT said that the tribunal was wrong to say that the dismissal was not for an 'economic, technical or organisational' (ETO) reason. As it was caused by FDC's closure it was 'economic'. Nevertheless, the EAT agreed that the dismissal was unfair in terms of the 'reasonableness' requirement, as it had been unnecessary to sack the workers for redundancy.

The Scottish Court of Session reversed this, saying there had not been a 'transfer' as the employees had not been employed at the moment of transfer, and therefore FE should not have been held responsible.

The House of Lords overturned this and, in doing so, established several key ground rules which have generally applied to transfers of this kind. These are that:

- if workers are dismissed by the transferor employer prior to the transfer for a reason which is connected with the transfer, they must be treated as if they were still employed at the time of transfer;
- the regulations are to be applied to any worker who was either employed immediately before the transfer *or* who *would* have been employed at that time had s/he not been unfairly dismissed for a reason connected with the transfer: specifically, although the wording of reg. 5 (3) indicates that it only applies if the employee is 'employed immediately before the transfer' a purposive construction requires it to be read as if these were inserted 'or would have been so employed if he had not been unfairly dismissed in the circumstances described in regulation 8 (1)';
- transferees will be responsible for unfair dismissals *unless* they can be shown to be for an 'economic, technical or organisational' reason entailing a change in the workforce;
- the principle that a person must be employed at the exact moment of transfer will only apply if the reason for the dismissal is unconnected with the transfer; liability will then remain with the transferor up until the moment of transfer.

Redundancy and the ETO Defence

In the *Litster* case itself the Lords concluded that there had been no legitimate 'economic, technical or organisational' reasons for the dismissals, and the workers had not been 'redundant'. FE therefore was liable for the unfair dismissals.

Unfortunately the *Litster* decision did not address all the issues that can arise when businesses, or parts of them, are transferred. *Litster* was a case where there had clearly been collusion between the transferor employer and the transferee. Indeed the insolvency and business reconstruction was engineered by FDC. But it is by no means clear that a similar result would be achieved in other cases, and cases where ETO defence could be engaged. It is also clear that once workers are dismissed in such cases they *stay* dismissed. There is no provision to treat the dismissals as ineffective. Nor did the Lords deal with other issues in relation to pre-transfer changes, pre-'transfer' variations in contract terms, and redundancy dismissals which, although transfer-related, are assisted from employers' point of view by the ETO defence. There is also the problem of later implementation of planned changes.[41] Among other things, there is still uncertainty about the exact scope of the 'ETO' defence in cases where redundancy dismissals precede the transfer, but the link with the transfer is, arguably, broken; and where there are determinations by the tribunals or courts that organisational changes were essential to help the organisation survive. This has been highlighted by cases like *Wilson and Others* v. *St. Helens Borough Council* [1998] IRLR 706, HL (discussed in Chapter 5 in the context of workplace change).

Rights on a Transfer

(a) *Contractual and statutory rights.* If the regulations do apply then it follows from regs. 5 and 6 that an employee's rights under any contract with the transferor business (or collective agreement rights), including redundancy and contractual redundancy, and severance terms, will generally become enforceable against the new business. An important exception is occupational pension rights (reg. 7). Similarly, the new business could enforce any obligations owed under contract by the employee.

As well as the transferee employer being liable for its own actions after the transfer, that transferee can *also* be responsible for actions of the business prior to the transfer; reg. 5 (2) 9b); and *DJM International Ltd* v. *Nicholas* [1996] IRLR 76. In that case the transferor required the employee to retire at 60. She was then taken on as a part-timer, remaining with the transferee after a 'transfer'. Soon after, she was made redundant. The EAT confirmed she could maintain a sex discrimination claim against the transferee employer given the wide scope of reg. 5 (2) (b).

(b) *'Unfair' dismissals; redundancy dismissals.* If the regulations apply to the transfer, a dismissal (including a 'constructive' dismissal where, for example, significant changes are forced on the employee) will be automatically unfair if the transfer – or a reason connected with it – is the principal reason for it (reg. 8 [1]).

Redundancy compensation and redundancy-related dismissal rights are also available. In this respect, before employers can take advantage of the 'economic, technical or organisational reason entailing changes in the workforce of either the transferor or the transferee before or after a relevant transfer ...' (reg. 8 [2]) the change must be shown to be in the nature of workforce reorganisation.

Changes in terms and conditions *per se* are not, generally, sufficient. A change of job functions, particularly if this *is* part of a wider reorganisation may be within reg. 8 (2).[42] Dismissal for redundancy for business reasons is clearly within the scope of the ETO defence.[43]

As long as the employer can bring the reorganisation and changes within the terms of this exemption, and has otherwise acted 'reasonably', particularly in relation to the 'fairness' requirement (see Chapter 14), an unfair dismissal claim can be avoided.

(c) *Redundancy compensation.* Even if the employer can successfully avoid an unfair dismissal claim a redundancy payment may still be payable as long as the redundancy scheme conditions for obtaining this are met.

   Example
   Mr Jenkinson worked as a mechanic for Feastcroft Ltd (F Ltd), and the owners were a couple who also owned Gorictree Ltd (G Ltd). F Ltd was then sold to one of the couple. Six days later G Ltd started to trade and offered Mr Jenkinson a contract on a 'self-employed' basis. Although his dismissal was treated as being for an 'economic, technical or organisational' reason entailing a change in the workforce, and was not 'unfair', he was still held to be entitled to a redundancy payment. The normal test under ERA s. 139 applies, and there was a 'redundancy' on the basis that there had been a diminution in the requirements for employees.[44]

(d) *Consultation: union recognition.* Regs 10–11A of TUPE as amended[45] require the 'affected employees' of the transferor and transferee to inform and consult their union or employees' representatives about transfers *before* they happen. Among other things this must focus on the 'legal, economic and social implications' for the affected employees, and any 'measures' to be taken in connection with the transfer including the timetable for the transfer, the reasons for it, and the legal, economic, and social implications involved; reg. 10. There is a complaints procedure enabling complaints of a failure to inform or consult to be made to a tribunal (reg. 11). The process is assisted by the requirement that 'recognition' rights generally transfer under reg. 9. Consultation duties begin once 'measures' are to be taken; and consultation includes consideration of issues raised by the unions; *Transport and General Workers Union* v. *James McKinnon, JR (Haulage) Ltd* [2001] IRLR 597.

   A judicial review of amending regulations in 1995, brought on the grounds that they derogated from the Acquired Rights and Collective Redundancies Directives, e.g. because they did not provide the duty to consult where employers have less than 20 employees or in individual cases, failed in the case of *R* v. *Secretary of State for Trade and Industry, ex parte UNISON* [1996] ICR 1003. Consultation duties are also required by TULR(C)A 1992 ss. 188 (see below).

Disqualification and Offers of Alternative Employment

All the rules on disqualification from redundancy payments (and redundancy-related rights) (as discussed below) generally apply to 'transfer' redundancies. In particular the rules where offers of suitable employment are made will be relevant. This is because the new employer may well make such offers as part of a reorganisation within a short time of taking over the firm's management. If new working arrangements or different terms are required by the new employer there will be an opportunity for a statutory trial period (see below).

In the transfer context an important priority for the new employer will often be to 'standardise' working conditions and other arrangements between existing staff and the new workers who have been 'transferred in'. In this situation there is obviously considerable scope for disagreement if the new terms and conditions, or other arrangements, are worse or different than those that previously operated: and especially if they produce 'redundancy' situations, for example, where there is 'duplication' of staffing roles between staff transferring in and staff already employed by the transferor employer.

(9) Disqualification from Entitlements: Other Claims Issues

There are several ways in which entitlement to redundancy payments may be lost as a result of ERA provisions and each of these must be considered.

Offers of Renewal of Contract: Re-engagement

An employee who has been given notice of dismissal for redundancy will not be treated as 'dismissed', and will therefore be disqualified from receiving compensation, if the employer, before the employment is due to end, offers to renew the contract or engage the person on new terms – and that employment would begin either immediately on the ending of the existing contract, or within four weeks; ss. 138, 141. For this bar to operate, however, the new job offered must either be on the *same* terms or, if they are different, they must be 'suitable'. In this context 'suitable' means suitable in respect of the specific terms on which it is offered and in relation to any other personal considerations which are relevant. This is what is meant in the Act by 'suitable in relation to the employee'.

An unreasonable refusal by the employee of such an offer, whether it came from the employer or from an associated employer (such as another company in the same group of companies) or from a new owner of the business, will normally disqualify the employee.[46]

Such offers are not required to be in writing, but case law shows how it is prudent for the employee to require the employer to confirm all the relevant details in writing. This, of course, serves as a record in case of arguments over what was actually offered. It can, in fact, work to an employer's disadvantage not to co-operate over this as a tribunal could take into account any uncertainties the employee had about the offer in deciding if refusal was unreasonable, and the process was handled fairly.

If the offer is to keep the employee on the *same* terms it will usually be very difficult to justify a refusal without good reasons. Another important consideration is that it is not usually possible to argue that the new job would involve changes which he or she would find difficult to adapt to if what is proposed is something which could have been required under the existing contract. In this context the implied duty to co-operate with reasonable changes may become relevant (see further on this Chapter 5).

A proposal to re-engage on *different* terms in relation to capacity, place of employment, and other terms and conditions, puts the employee in a stronger position to reject the offer or to negotiate better terms. This is assisted by a four-week trial period provided under the scheme (see ss. 138–142 for the details). Tribunals are given a considerable amount of discretion in deciding whether a job offer amounted to suitable alternative employment, and whether the refusal was otherwise reasonable in the circumstances. It is not possible to lay down any hard and fast rules as to what sort of changes a person might reasonably rely on to justify refusal, although significant changes to things like job responsibility and status, earnings and the opportunity to enhance basic earnings, and more demanding travelling requirements, can constitute good reasons. In one leading case Gloucestershire County Council, as part of a cost-cutting exercise, reduced the number of its school cleaners and cut the hours of the remaining staff. This, it was accepted, meant reduced standards of cleanliness. Some of the remaining workers (who had been offered new terms) said they could not do a satisfactory job given the reduction in staff. The Court of Appeal held that this was something a tribunal *could* take into account in considering their refusal. It added that although there were usually two issues which tribunals had to consider, which could be categorised under the headings of suitability of the job offered in relation to the employee and the reasonableness of the employee in refusing the offer – a distinction developed in earlier cases – there was not always such a rigid distinction between the two questions in practice. Some objections which people raised could be relevant to both questions.[47]

Trial Period

As noted above, if employees are offered renewed employment, or a new contract, on different terms they have a statutory right to a trial period of four calendar weeks in that new job.[48] If a statutory trial period is 'refused', or not properly offered, there may be scope for an unfair dismissal claim.[49] A longer period may be agreed if this is done before the four-week period expires.

During the trial period the employee may decide to terminate the employment. Similarly, the employer could end the trial period, for example if the person is unsuitable. If this does happen – or notice is given which leads to eventual termination – the employee will generally be regarded as dismissed on the date the previous contract ended and for the reasons for which she or he was dismissed (or would have been dismissed) at that time.[50] If the employee completes the four-week trial period but then leaves voluntarily there will generally be no right to a redundancy payment or unfair dismissal award, even if it had been suggested the trial period should be for a longer period; *Meek v. J. Allen Rubber Co Ltd and Secretary of State for Employment* [1980] IRLR 21. This operates, in effect, as a form of waiver of the right to assert there has been a 'dismissal' – but not until the four-week period ends. There may be an *additional* 'reasonable period' added prior to the statutory period if the employee has been constructively dismissed.[51]

If the employer terminates the employment unjustifiably, or forces her to leave the organisation altogether, the reason for which she was originally dismissed (or would have been dismissed) – that is, redundancy, 'some other substantive reason', or similar – does not automatically operate. The way is therefore clear in this event to claim unfair dismissal. For example in one case the employer claimed the employee had to be dismissed because of 'unsuitability'. It was held, however, that an unfair dismissal claim was possible.[52]

Dismissal for Misconduct: Industrial Action

Employers can dismiss for misconduct rather than for redundancy and they may try to do so to avoid having to pay redundancy pay. The position is, however, affected by the ERA,[53] where redundancy is in the offing or has already been formally notified.

The exact position will depend on whether the employee is sacked *before* the obligatory statutory period of redundancy notice has begun or *during* that period.

If the dismissal takes place before the notice period has begun, the employer, in order to take advantage of the disentitlement provisions, must dismiss without notice or by reduced notice. If notice is to be 'worked out' a written statement explaining that the employee *could* have been dismissed without notice must be provided by the employer.

Dismissal during the obligatory period may result in disqualification for all, or just some, of the payment depending on what a tribunal decides is 'just and equitable'. It could decide that the dismissal was justified but that only a *partial* reduction should be made. For example it was held in one case[54] that 40 per cent of the compensation which would otherwise have been due should be withheld for stealing the employer's property after notice was given.

As already noted, strikes are treated in employment law as a form of 'misconduct' by the workers involved. This means that a strike prior to notice of dismissal being given will usually entitle the employer to dismiss, and redundancy payments may therefore be immediately forfeited.[55]

If an employee is dismissed for striking after notice of dismissal for redundancy has been given the right to a redundancy payment is preserved[56] – although the employer would be able to terminate the contract immediately. There are also provisions[57] whereby an employer can recoup any lost time due to the action taken. This involves serving a 'notice of extension' demanding an additional period to be worked to make up for time lost, and warning that the redundancy entitlement will be contested if it is not complied with. Non-compliance would result in either disqualification or a reduced award.

Leaving during Redundancy Notice Period

If the employee has been given notice of redundancy, and wants to leave before the notice expires, the employer can request him to withdraw his notice otherwise he will contest any liability to make a payment; ERA s. 142 (2). The ET then has power to decide whether the employer should make a payment, having regard to the reasons the employee wanted to leave and the employer wanted him to continue; s. 142 (3).

Fighting Redundancy by Industrial Action

There are obvious pitfalls in taking industrial action amounting to a strike, particularly if it is before any notice of redundancy/ies has been issued, for example when a management's decision is known and in an attempt to exert pressure to get that decision reversed. This was, no doubt, deliberately included in the legislation, and it creates a dilemma for many workers. Should proposed or expected redundancy be contested (in industrial action terms) before it is formally notified (and thereby risk forfeiture)? Or should industrial action which may be the only effective response to the threatened redundancy, be delayed, or not taken at all?

After Redundancy Notice is Given – the Steps to Take

Time Off

Once employees have been given notice of redundancy they may take advantage of the right to take reasonable time off to look for other work and for retraining.[58]

There is a right to be paid for this at the 'appropriate rate', and normal pay will satisfy the employer's obligations. The exact amount of time off to be permitted is a matter for agreement, although it may already be dealt with in the contract or in a collective agreement. The sanction if time off is refused, or not paid properly, is to go to a tribunal, which can award compensation.

Making Claims

Given the complexities of the redundancy scheme advice should always be sought, but several key points on claiming a payment can be considered. The key section of the ERA is s. 164 (1). This says that within six months of the 'relevant date'[59] the employee *must* have either:

(a) agreed and been paid a redundancy payment; or
(b) claimed a payment from the employer in writing; or
(c) made a claim to a tribunal which either relates to eligibility or the amount of entitlement; or
(d) made an unfair dismissal complaint to the tribunal under the ERA, s. 111. In this case the tribunal can deal with the complaint and the claim for a payment at the same time.

An extension of up to six months may be allowed under s. 164 (2), (3) within which to make a claim for payment in writing to the employer; to refer a case to the ET; or to present a complaint under the ERA s. 111 of unfair dismissal. But this is exceptional and depends on how 'good' the reason is for missing the deadline, and specifically whether an ET considers whether it is 'just and equitable' for the employee to get a payment.

Claims can be made against the receiver or liquidator if the business has become insolvent. If the business has been transferred to a new employer a claim should normally be made against that employer rather than the former employer. If in any doubt about who to make a claim against the claim can be made against both, and the tribunal can decide which is appropriate. If 'all reasonable steps' have been taken to recover payment from the employer, but still it has not been paid, or if the employer is insolvent and it remains unpaid, an application can be made for payment out of the government's National Insurance Fund.[60]

In redundancy cases advice should be sought from a local ACAS office, Citizens' Advice Bureaux, or other sources of specialist help such as a union.

Calculating the Payment; Enhanced Payment Offers

Information about the rules governing redundancy payments and their calculation, and unfair dismissal aspects, are provided by the Department of Work and Pensions (DWP) and are in guidance booklets (or on-line via the DWP website at www.dwp. gov.uk).[61]

Basically, the payment is calculated by reference to the 'week's pay' formula in the ERA, ss. 220–229, and redundancy calculation scheme in the Employment Rights Act 1996 s. 162. The exact payment will then depend on how much that week's pay amounts to (given the maximum limit and the employee's age). For each year of service that the employee is aged between 41 and 64 one and a half week's pay is paid for each year of service while aged between 22 and 40 it is one week's pay; and for each year between 18 and 21, half a week's pay. In calculating the payment any 'remuneration' paid under the contract (including contractual overtime) is included. Expenses, and 'perks' such as the value of a car are not included. There is a 'cap' on the maximum statutory redundancy payment.

The employer is required to provide a written statement of how the payment has been calculated. In practice, the statutory redundancy scheme's limits are so low that this prompts employers to negotiate improved arrangements in collective agreements (for good industrial relations reasons and to reduce the incentive to fight redundancies and reorganisations involving potential redundancy) and to offer enhanced benefits to individual workers.

Voluntary Redundancy: Additional Payments

As illustrated in a 1998 case *Sharpe* v. *SHS Handling Systems Ltd* (20 March 1998, Liverpool IT) additional payments offered to would-be volunteers for redundancy, as an incentive to agree to resign, if they are not paid, can be recovered as a breach of contract. Non-payment of such amounts may also constitute an 'unlawful deduction' from final wages in appropriate cases. The ET would also have jurisdiction to require them to be paid as a final payment of wages.

Collective Redundancies

As a result of EC legislation in the mid-1970s, including EC Directive 75/129 on collective redundancies, the Employment Protection Act 1975 gave unions rights to be consulted when employers propose to make redundancies. The procedures are now in TULR(C)A, ss. 188–198, as amended by SI 1995/2587, and SI 1999 Nos. 1925 and 2402 following EC Commission infringement proceedings as a result of not extending consultation rights (in earlier versions of the legislation) to employee as well as union representatives.

The key provision is s. 188 (1). This states that if an employer is proposing to dismiss as redundant 20 or more employees at one establishment within a period of 90 days or less, 'the employer shall consult about the dismissals all the persons who are appropriate representatives of any of the employees who may be affected by the proposed dismissals or may be affected by measures taken in connection with those dismissals'. Consultation must begin 'in good time', and in any event begin:

- at least 90 days before the first dismissal takes effect if 100 or more employees are to be made redundant;
- otherwise at least 30 days before the first dismissals take effect; s. 188 (1A).

S. 188 (1B) details the union or employee representatives who must be consulted. S. 188A provides for election of employee representatives.

An employer must disclose in writing details including the reasons for the proposals, the numbers of staff proposed for dismissal, and the method of calculating redundancy compensation; and

- the total number of any such employees of any such description employed at the establishment in question;
- the proposed method of selecting employees for dismissal;

- the proposed method of carrying out the dismissals, with due regard to any agreed procedure, including the period over which the dismissals are to take effect.

Consultation must, among other things, cover ways of avoiding dismissals, reducing the numbers of staff affected, and mitigating the consequences. It must be undertaken with a view to reaching agreement; s. 188 (2).

The employer is required to consider representations and must reply to them; *Rowell* v. *Hubbard Group Services Ltd* [1995] IRLR 195. If they are rejected reasons must be given. There is a possible defence, if the consultation requirements are not met, if the employer can show that compliance was not 'reasonably practicable'. An example of this would be a company suddenly going into receivership.

There are some important problems in the practical operation of these procedures, not least of which is the uncertainty about *when* an employer is required to tell the union that the redundancies are proposed. Arguably this is not until the employer has decided that redundancies will definitely be necessary and has determined a timetable for dismissals. Some cases indicate it is much earlier, for example when proposals (including redundancies as an option) are formulated; *Hough* v. *Leyland (DAF) Ltd* [1991] IRLR 194. In this case, though, consultation may be too late to have much effect on the process. Nor is it clear how much notice an employer needs to take of representations to satisfy the rules. As several EAT decisions have made clear, the policy considerations on which redundancy decisions are based, and the decisions themselves, remain a management responsibility despite the consultation requirements. On the other hand cases have also made it clear that the consultation process should not be a 'sham' as, for example, where redundancy notices were issued shortly after representatives were formally notified of the redundancies.[62]

Failure to Consult

A failure to comply with ss. 188, 188A, or to consult, or consult properly, entitles the union or employee representatives to make a complaint to a tribunal. The duty cannot be disregarded by an employer, and the process should be started in good time. To comply with EC Dir. 98/59 on collective redundancies that *should* mean at the point an employer contemplates making redundancies rather than proposes them; *MSF* v. *Refuge Assurance plc* [2002] IRLR 324. The tribunal can make a 'protective award' (ss. 189–192), that is, an award of remuneration for the employees affected for a 'protected' period. The claim must normally be made before the proposed dismissal takes effect, or within three months of the dismissal taking effect. The award is made in accordance with ss. 189 and 190, and can be for a maximum of 90 days. Individual employees can take enforcement action to recover the payment if it is not paid.

Although non-consultation with the union or employee representatives may be a relevant factor if a complainant is claiming unfair dismissal, in formal terms the main consequence is a claim for a protective award (s. 188 [8]). In practice, though, the issue of an employer's conduct may well be considered by the tribunal in the general context of procedural fairness.

Effect on Individuals

In cases where a union or employee representatives must be consulted, those consultation rights do not necessarily extend to individual employees; *Mugford* v.

Midland Bank plc [1997] IRLR 208. Early cases suggested that failures to implement the duty to consult collectively are not, in general, relevant to the 'fairness' of an individual employee's redundancy; see, for example, *Forman Construction* v. *Kelly* [1977] IRLR 468. However this depends on the circumstances in which the failure took place.

Rights on Insolvency

There are a number of ways in which an employer can be put out of business or affected by insolvency. Broadly speaking, insolvency means either that a company is going into liquidation (either voluntarily or compulsorily); or that a 'receiver' has been appointed; or that an 'administration' order has been made under which an administrator has taken over the running of the company for the time being. It can also mean an 'arrangement' has been made, for example to satisfy the company's creditors. In the case of individuals or partners in a partnership the equivalent of corporate insolvency is bankruptcy (or in Scotland, 'sequestration').

Most insolvency procedures are bad news for employees. In the first place they have little or no rights in the insolvency process, unlike shareholders and creditors. Apart from being wrong in principle, as employees have usually made an important contribution to a business, this treatment is inconsistent with the rights accorded to other stakeholders – especially as they are a form of 'creditor' with rights in respect of matters like outstanding pay, pension rights and possibly a variety of other claims on the company. To some extent this is recognised by giving employees 'preferential creditor' status (ranking with, for example, the tax and VAT authorities and ahead of unsecured creditors) with regard to certain unsatisfied debts. But, despite this employees are still in a vulnerable position and claims are often not settled until after long delays. As far as employment is concerned, there may be scope for continued or alternative employment depending on what course the insolvency takes and whether the business continues in some form or other, or is purchased by a new owner. In general terms it is a period of great uncertainty and insecurity for employees.

If during the course of the insolvency procedure employees are made redundant, a redundancy claim can be made against the liquidator, receiver or administrators. If there are problems in obtaining payment a claim can be made on the National Insurance Fund. If all reasonable steps have been taken to recover the redundancy payment from the employer, or the employer is clearly 'insolvent', a claim can be made on the Secretary of State (ERA 1996, ss. 166–170). There might, however, be other claims for debts which might not have been settled.

The ERA 1996, ss. 182–190, which implement EC Directive 80/987 on the protection of employees in the event of the insolvency of their employer, deals with insolvency of employers and establishes minimum rights and enables a limited range of claims to be made on the National Insurance Fund for certain debts. These include:

- arrears of pay up to a statutory weekly limit and in respect of a maximum period of eight weeks. This includes such things as overtime pay owed, any commission earned, and guarantee payments (relevant for those who were previously on short-time working);
- minimum periods of notice under the ERA, i.e. wages in lieu of notice;
- holiday pay up to a limit of six weeks and subject to a maximum limit;

- compensation for not getting the proper statutory notice;
- any unpaid 'basic award' made by a tribunal for unfair dismissal.

Rights to be paid out of the fund depend, however, on (a) the employer being 'insolvent' (as defined in s. 183); (b) the employment being *terminated*; and (c) the employee establishing *entitlement* to the debt. There can be difficulties in showing that an employer *is* 'insolvent', and delays in getting assistance can also arise unless the employer is insolvent *and* one of the heads in s. 183 is satisfied before the Fund can make a payment; *Secretary of State for Trade and Industry* v. *Walden* [2000] IRLR 168.

A complaint that payment has not been made following the required written application, or that the payment is less than that owed, may be made under s. 188 to a tribunal. If an insolvent employer has not paid contributions into an occupational pension scheme, the government may make up shortfalls to cover the unpaid amounts.[63] Scheme administrators will usually be responsible for ensuring scheme funds are maintained in this way. Unpaid debts to staff which are payable as preferential debts can be paid by the Secretary of State up to prescribed limits.

Claiming for Arrears and Debts

Claims for arrears of pay or other debts should be made to the 'proper officer' if one has been appointed, i.e. usually receiver, liquidator, administrator, trustee or equivalent, and this should be done on the appropriate forms without delay. It is then usually necessary, before payment is made, to sign a statement agreeing to transfer any rights to the Secretary of State for Work and Pensions.

Further information can be obtained from the Department of Work and Pensions and Jobcentre Plus offices (and see the DWP website referred to above).

(10) Insolvency-related Rights

Employees may also have a limited range of rights under insolvency legislation when their employer is insolvent. In the case of individuals this means she or he is adjudged bankrupt, or has made a 'composition' or arrangement with creditors (or has died, and the estate is being administered under the Insolvency Act 1986). With companies it means a winding up or administration order has been made, or the shareholders have passed a 'voluntary' winding up resolution. Another form of insolvency catered for by the 1986 Act is where a receiver has been appointed, or possession of company property has been taken by a receiver; or a 'voluntary arrangement' has been approved under the Insolvency Act 1986 (ERA 1996, s. 183).

Apart from rights under the ERA referred to above, employees may have certain rights under the Insolvency Act 1986, sched. 6 as 'preferential creditors' from the assets of the insolvent employer (although these rank *after* certain other creditors like lenders with 'fixed charges' over the business assets).[64] These include a right of employees and past employees to arrears of pay (wages and other specified items) for a period of up to four months prior to receivership or liquidation – up to a specified limit; and accrued holiday pay. Other amounts owed can generally only be pursued as ordinary non-preferential debts.

In the event of bankruptcy, employees' jobs usually end at that stage. Appointment of receivers, administrators and liquidators may in some circumstances mean automatic termination of employees' contracts of employment, but in some cases they may *continue*. This would be the case, for example, where a receiver is appointed as the company's agent (which most administrative receivers are). If the receiver then sells that part of the business, or shuts it down, employment contracts will normally end at that point. It is possible, however, that the business, or part of the business, is sold as a 'going concern' whereupon the transferee takes over all rights and liabilities in accordance with TUPE reg. 5 (discussed earlier in this chapter, and in the context of termination of employment in the preceding chapters). As part of a 'hiving down' process, an administrator, receiver, or liquidator may segregate the more profitable or saleable parts of an insolvent business, establish them as a 'subsidiary', and then sell them off. Reg. 4 of TUPE has special provisions which state that the 'transfer' does not take effect until the transferee company ceases to be a wholly owned subsidiary of the transferor, or the undertaking is transferred by the transferee to *another* entity. The transfer is taken to be effected immediately prior to that event and by *one* transaction.

There are situations in which an administrative receiver or administrator is treated as having 'adopted' employees' contracts of employment, so that they are then liable as employers for paying wages and honouring other commitments: to do this usually requires the employees' retention for 14 days following the receiver's appointment, and continuation of pay.[65]

Changes to EC Dir. 80/97

The EC Council of Ministers and Parliament decided in 2002 that Dir. 80/97 no longer provides an adequate basis for protection of employees affected by insolvency, and so Council Directive 2002/74 was passed which requires Member States to implement changes by 8 October 2005. Among other things this will mean improvements to the guarantees of payment of outstanding wages and other debts by State or other bodies when employers are unable to meet those obligations. The definitions of 'insolvency' currently in use will be broadened, and protection extended to part-time workers and other atypical groups at present outside the scope of protection under Dir. 80/97.

PART FIVE

Health and Safety

CHAPTER 16

Health, Safety and
the Work Environment

Introduction

The right to a working environment which is safe and free from risks to health is one of the most important aspects of modern employment rights. In this chapter we consider the specific ways in which the law deals with health, safety and working environment issues.

As with most other areas of employment, the establishment and maintenance of good standards of health and safety in the workplace are more readily achieved where there is union representation, and a joint approach by the employer and staff to maintaining acceptable standards. Ideally this means using the safety representative and safety committees system provided for in the legislation. The Robens Report in 1972 recognised this, and the Health and Safety at Work Act 1974 marked the start of formalised arrangements on employee involvement.[1]

Historically, health and safety issues have always been a key part of the remit of trade unions, both at a workplace level and as an issue on which they have campaigned for more legislation. Unfortunately, health and safety has been an area which has suffered as part of the general weakening of union organisation, and as a result of changes in employment patterns. Workers without union representation and groups like temporary, part-time and 'self-employed' workers are particularly vulnerable. It is also the case that atypical groups in the labour market, such as migrant workers employed as part of the Seasonal Agricultural Workers Scheme, are prone to poor safety standards and long hours, as highlighted in a TUC study *Gone West: The Harsh Reality of Ukrainians at Work in the UK* (9 March 2004).

While UK government policy in the 1980s and 1990s was characterised by deregulation in a number of areas of health and safety law and enforcement, and the UK's opt-out from the Social Chapter meant that important areas of legislation on the working environment did not operate pending the UK's return in 1997, the EC continued to introduce important legislation under art. 118A of the EC Treaty after it was added by the Single European Act 1986 (now in art. 137 of the Treaty). This required the EC Council to adopt, by the means of Directives, minimum requirements for improvements, especially in the working environment, and for improved health and safety standards. Council Directive 89/391 (the 'Framework Directive') then provided the framework for the more specific measures, so-called 'daughter' directives, which followed.

The scope of protection has broadened, too, by the move towards considering the working environment holistically, and addressing both physical and socio-psychological aspects of working, following Nordic traditions of occupational safety and health. This proved an important factor in the ECJ's rejection of UK arguments in the *United Kingdom* v. *Council of the European Union* case (discussed below and in Chapter 8) that working time was not an aspect of the employment relationship that should be the subject of health and safety restrictions (as discussed below, and in Chapter 8). Among other things, the court interpreted the EC's enabling legislation as wide enough to allow working hours to be regulated, assisted by World Health Organisation definitions of physical, mental and social well-being.[2] Dir. 89/391 is important in its application to 'all sectors of activity, both public and private' (art. 2), and it enjoins Member States to take the necessary steps to ensure that employers, workers and workers' representatives are subject to the legal provisions necessary to implement it (art. 4). More specific obligations are imposed on employers by art. 6 on the basis of 'general principles of prevention'. These are wide-ranging, and include, among other things: avoiding risks; evaluating risks which cannot be avoided; combating risks at source; adapting work to the individual in respect of the design of workplaces, choice of equipment, and working and production methods; adapting to technical progress; 'replacing the dangerous by the non-dangerous or less dangerous'; developing a coherent overall prevention policy which covers technology, organisation of work, working conditions, social relationships, and the influence of factors related to the working environment; giving collective protective measures priority over individual protective measures; and giving appropriate instructions to workers. The provision of information to workers is given a high priority (art. 10). So, too, is consultation in combination with participation rights (art. 11). The Directive marks an important step towards establishing minimum standards throughout the Member States, and particularly the UK,[3] where implementation began with measures like the Management of Health and Safety at Work (MHSW) Regulations 1999, SI 1999/3242.[4]

The Health and Safety at Work Act 1974 ('HSAWA')

The mid-1970s saw significant policy and legislative changes. In particular, the Health and Safety at Work Act 1974 laid down a series of minimum requirements for employers. It also provided an 'enabling' scheme whereby more detailed regulations on specific processes could be progressively introduced. Not all employers took kindly to the new legal regime, in particular those aspects which they saw as impinging on managerial prerogative – for example, being told to produce policy statements detailing their management structures, and the arrangements for implementing their legal responsibilities. Nor did they like other features of the Act, such as Health and Safety Executive (HSE) inspectors' powers to issue 'improvement' and 'prohibition' notices. Both these developments, and the other measures in the legislation, signalled important improvements in health and safety law. On the other hand the system introduced in the 1974 Act contains important weaknesses. Many of the duties on employers are limited by the proviso 'so far as is reasonably practicable'. In effect, this can provide a let-out for employers who can argue that the trouble, time and possibly costs, involved in dealing with a problem are not justified given the scale of the risk involved. Such an approach, involving, as it does, taking a 'cost-benefit' yardstick to safety measures, pre-dated the Act: and its negative effects could be seen in leading cases which set low thresholds of liability.[5] Also, in many areas of risk, detailed requirements have not been put into legislation or in regulations, but have been dealt with, if at all, in official 'guidance' or in codes of practice. This is made worse by the courts' reluctance at times to see the Act's 'general duties' as a springboard to extend employers' criminal and civil law responsibilities. Implementation of the EC Framework Directive in the UK, and in particular the Management of Health and Safety at Work Regulations 1999; SI 1999/3242 (the MHSW Regulations 1999) has helped to close some of these gaps.

Whilst the use of 'improvement notices' and 'prohibition notices' (under ss. 21–24 of the Act) have been an important part of the HSE's armoury, HSE and local authority inspectors do not have to use their powers in every case; and when they do it is possible for an employer to appeal against a notice to a tribunal. This has the effect of automatically suspending an improvement notice pending the tribunal's decision (which may take a long time). With prohibition notices the employer must apply to the tribunal for a suspension.

Other difficulties have been due, not to the legislation itself, but to failures of enforcement, and infrequent inspections resulting in poor awareness by HSE inspectors of what may be going on in some workplaces. This is not helped by a reluctance sometimes to consult closely with employees and their representatives, perhaps to avoid antagonising employers. There has also been a degree of suspicion in some unions that the HSE and employers' organisations co-operate *too* closely – particularly through industry groups and other consultative bodies – when fixing compliance standards. This has particularly been a concern when the system has looked to 'self-regulation' instead of direct policing of requirements. In practical terms it means important aspects of health, safety and occupational health standards being devolved to such bodies. It has also been clear from the outset of the post-1974 Act approach that to tackle health and safety issues effectively requires government commitment to provide adequate *resources* to enforcement agencies and in particular to increase the staffing levels of the HSE and its inspectorate. This has never happened on the scale that is needed. This has been due, in part, to a combination of cost-saving policies and a preference for 'self-regulation' rather than official enforcement activity (reflected in the tiny proportion of prosecutions actually brought by the HSE following accident investigations). In this way health and safety has become one of the casualties of the 'deregulation' process pursued in the 1980s and early 1990s.

This was clearly a stand-still period, both in terms of the failure to extend the scope and intensity of legislative requirements in areas where this was required, and in official unwillingness to take enforcement action against companies breaking the rules. This policy was facilitated by deregulatory measures signalled in a series of White Papers and Department of Employment documents.[6] One aspect of that policy was to single out 'small' companies, that is, workplaces of 20 or less people, for deregulation: for example by removing requirements such as the duty to produce company health and safety statements. Yet it is often in such small organisations that there are the worst health and safety standards. The effects of such government inaction, and its 'hands-off' were seen in the worsening statistics on fatal accidents and injuries, particularly in high-risk areas like construction work, North Sea oil operations, and agricultural work, as observed by Roger Moore in an influential study for the Institute of Employment Rights.[7] Official recognition of the problem was given when, on general accident statistics, the Director-General of the HSE admitted to the House of Commons Employment Select Committee that the number of workplace accidents had reached a 'disturbing and stubborn plateau'. Periods of recession had, he said, led to an erosion of the safety infrastructure with employers cutting corners and not investing in safety.[8]

Worse was to follow. In 1994 the government secured a 'fast-track' system of repealing 'burdensome' health and safety requirements when the Deregulation and Contracting Out Act 1994 was passed. In relation to EC initiatives the 'Framework' Directive set out general employers' responsibilities. However, the rights of UK workers suffered setbacks when, as a result of the UK's opt out from the Maastricht Treaty on political union, the benefits of social protection measures did not apply in some cases to the UK. The Social Chapter, signed by eleven Member States in December 1989 at Strasbourg (but not the UK) was accompanied by changes which extended the scope of qualified majority voting (QMV) to facilitate legislation in a much wider area of employment rights. These included health and safety, and the working environment. The UK government's refusal to co-operate in agreeing even watered-down proposals resulted in the position that in the period from 1 January 1993 until the Labour government took the UK back into the Social Chapter it was only the other Member States that made new legislation, and set new standards, on health and safety using the new procedures. Legislation made in this way was not, however, binding on the UK and UK employers in every case. Even when it was, the UK sought to contest the validity of health, safety and welfare at work measures in the ECJ, as in *United Kingdom* v. *Council of the European Union* [1997] IRLR 30. In that case the UK contended, unsuccessfully, that the Working Time Directive could not be adopted using art. 118A of the Treaty (now art. 138).

Employers' Contractual and Tort-based Duties

As a matter of contract an employer may have both express and implied duties in relation to the working environment. Express responsibilities can, and do, frequently derive from collective arrangements negotiated with unions – examples being the provision of rest periods for staff using visual display units (VDUs), safety training, or the supply of protective wear. Depending on the nature of the work and any special risks involved, it may also be possible to argue successfully that there are further implied obligations to be performed by the employer, or that there are limitations on what employees should be asked to do. This is, in part, due to the employer's 'duty of care', and tort-based duties. Excessive demands for overtime working, or requiring long hours doing stressful work, could fall into this category. The effect is to limit what could otherwise be required under the worker's contract.

Example
Junior hospital doctors' contracts required them to work 40 hours a week and to be 'available' for a further 48 hours a week on average. A doctor sued the employer, a health authority, on the basis that it was not taking reasonable care for his safety and well-being. In particular it was requiring him to work intolerably long hours and this was causing him stress and depression. He also argued the contract was void as being contrary to 'public policy' and not in the public interest.
The Court of Appeal, albeit only by a majority, held that, although the contract did allow the authority to require such overtime, the power to do so had to be exercised in a way that did not injure its employees. In other words, the express contractual powers of an employer must be read subject to implied limitations on *how* those powers can be used. If the facts of a case showed an employment contract was not being operated fairly then the employer would be in breach of that duty. The court refused, however, to entertain the other part of the claim. Issues

like inadequate funding of the Health Service (which has resulted in excessive hours of junior hospital doctors), they held, were matters for Parliament rather than the courts.

In the course of the judgment it was said that the duty in the case was no different from the duty owed to a factory worker not to expose him/her to noxious fumes. The exact scope of the employer's duty varied, however, depending on the particular employee's physical strength or weakness. The authority's lawyer argued that it could not be expected to treat its staff differently 'according to their physical stamina'. The court disagreed. The duty employers owe is a 'personal' one. Giving the example of back problems, it observed that: 'If employers know, or ought to know, that a workman has a vulnerable back they are in breach of duty in requiring him to lift and move weights which are likely to cause him injury even if a normal man can carry them without risk.'[9]

Use of implied terms in this way has become less important, in practical terms, since the Working Time Regulations 1998 imposed statutory limits on hours, and required rest periods, breaks, and annual leave (see Chapter 8). Nevertheless, in some cases implied duties remain important – for example in the context of breaches of the 'duty of care' and constructive dismissal cases (see below).

Hazardous Working Conditions
Earlier cases established that employers are not entitled, as a matter of contract, to require staff to do things which jeopardise health and safety, for example by instructing them to go to a country where personal safety is at risk.[10] This is reinforced by the ERA 1996, s. 44 (1) (d). This gives an employee the right not to be subject to any detriment if 'in circumstances of danger which the employee reasonably believed to be serious and imminent and which he could not reasonably have been expected to avert, he left (or proposed to leave) or (while the danger persisted) refused to return to his place of work or any dangerous part of his place of work ...'. That right is supplemented by a right not to be unfairly dismissed in such circumstances (ERA 1996, s. 100). Protection from fellow workers' hazardous activities is an employer's responsibility. So it is also arguable (although not yet clearly established) that employees have an implied contractual right not to be subjected to smoke from other employees' smoking. Employers now generally operate smoking bans and restrictions. As long as this is done fairly, disciplinary and dismissal action can be taken against people who ignore these. In one case a constructive dismissal claim failed when an employee unsuccessfully argued that he had an implied 'right to smoke'.[11]

Employers' Other Duties

The health and safety system makes employers legally responsible in other ways; and makes them potentially liable to criminal, administrative and civil sanctions.

The starting point is that employers are generally responsible for what happens on their premises, for deficiencies in the workplace environment, and for failures in their organisational and management systems – a principle estabished by both the HSAWA and the MHSW Regulations 1999. Although workers must co-operate in carrying out statutory requirements and must take reasonable care of themselves and others at the workplace,[12] the employer is given, and cannot transfer, responsibility for (or otherwise get out of) the key general duty by HSAWA, which is: 'to ensure, so far as is reasonably practicable, the health, safety and welfare at work of all his employees'.[13] The 1974 Act also makes clear, in s. 40, that the onus is on the employer to show that it is not reasonably practicable to do more than has been done to carry out the ss. 2–4 duties.

In some cases, responsibilities (and liabilities) lie with others besides employers – or, in appropriate cases, responsibility may be *shared*. For example, HSAWA s. 4 imposes duties on controllers of premises: e.g. landlords who have repair or maintenance duties. Manufacturers, designers, suppliers and importers also have duties; s. 6.

HSAWA duties are reinforced by legislation *deeming* the employer to be liable in certain situations, for example where workers are injured because of defective equipment, and the defect was the supplier's fault (Employers' Liability (Defective Equipment) Act 1969).

Employers are responsible at several levels for maintaining a safe working environment. If standards are below what is required, or an accident occurs, they will be subject to criminal or enforcement action by the HSE, local authority, or possibly other enforcement agencies (for example HM Pollution Inspectorate if an incident involves a wider threat to the environment). In addition, a worker can claim compensation in a civil action on the basis of the employer's civil duties (in particular for failure to provide a safe place of work or systems of work),[14] or for breach of a statutory duty where compensation is appropriate (see below).

Employers are required by law to take out insurance to cover their liability for personal injury to their staff. They are criminally liable if they fail to do so (under the Employers' Liability (Compulsory Insurance) Act 1969), but not, according to a 1995 Court of Appeal case,[15] liable in a *civil* claim for compensation. Detailed requirements are in the Employers' Liability (Compulsory Insurance) Regulations 1998, SI 1998/2573 (including restrictions on excluding liability, minimum sums to be insured, etc.). Insurance is an important requirement and provides workers with a safety net against workplace injuries when an employer may not be able to afford compensation. On the other hand courts have criticised the inadequacy and limitations of policies. Unions and staff are entitled to check the exact scope of workplace policies and insist on improvements if they are inadequate. If a duty to insure cannot be shown under the legislation it may arise as a result of implied duties, and the duty of care: but this may not extend to *every* risk, for example some which might be encountered while working overseas; *Reid v. Rush and Tomkins Group plc* [1989] IRLR 265, CA.

Although compulsory insurance has to some extent helped, despite the set-back from the Court of Appeal's judgment referred to, adequate compensation for accidents or occupational illness may depend on establishing fault on the employer's part. The difficulties and delays in doing this have been much criticised and the position was not helped when the Pearson Commission on civil liability and personal injuries compensation failed to recommend any significant changes.[16]

Overview

A summary of health and safety responsibilities is illustrated in Figure 16.1 below. This shows an employer's duties on the left, and the legal sanction/remedy on the right.

In the rest of this chapter a more detailed consideration is provided of the two most important areas of health and safety, namely HSAWA duties and rights; and employers' duty of care and compensation.

Employers' responsibilities in relation to fire hazards are generally set out in the Fire Precautions Act 1971, as amended, and related legislation and regulations (although HSAWA general duties to ensure employees' health and safety will still apply). Most workplaces are subject to local fire authority inspection certification, and enforcement procedures (mainly in ss. 5–9 of the 1971 Act).

HSAWA Duties and Rights

When Parliament passed the Health and Safety at Work Act in 1974 the intention was to get rid of much of the existing factories and other legislation, as proposed by the Robens Report (see above). In particular the intention was that the Factories Act 1961, containing important legislation affecting employers' duties as occupiers of workplaces, fencing and guarding of dangerous machinery and so on, which has been a basis of compensation claims for breach of statutory duty, would be progressively repealed.[17] Regulations made under the HSAWA set out more specific standards to supplement the general legal requirements that HSAWA lays down. Those regulations deal with particular processes and workplace health and safety problems.[18] Codes of Practice containing 'practical guidance' can be issued. Although a breach of them will not in itself render an employer liable, it could be important in establishing a contravention of the Act or Regulations (HSAWA, s. 17).

Figure 16.1: Health and Safety Responsibilities

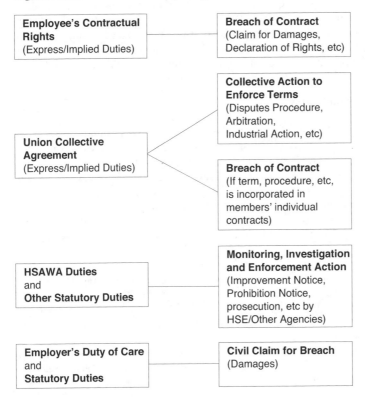

Enforcement and Civil Liability

A breach of the Act's general duties (as summarised below), and in most cases the regulations, will be a criminal offence, enforceable by the HSE or local authority. Allocation of responsibilities between the HSE and local authorities' officers is facilitated by the Health and Safety Regulations 1989, SI 1989/1903. A breach of the regulations, but *not* the general duties in the Act, may also be grounds for *civil* proceedings for compensation if injury and damage are caused (HSAWA, s. 47 [1], [2]). Civil claims for damages if an employer breaches the 'duty of care' are also still a possibility (see below). On unfair or 'constructive' dismissal, see Chapter 14.

Enforcement

Overall oversight and responsibility for health and safety rests with the Health and Safety Commission. Enforcement is mainly the responsibility of the Health and Safety Executive and, in some cases (see above) local authority inspectors. Powers include the ability to serve 'improvement notices' (HSAWA s. 21) if there have been contraventions of legislation, or these are likely to continue (or be repeated) and 'prohibition notices' (HSAWA s. 22). Both notices can be appealed to a tribunal, however; s. 24. The ability of inspectors to prevent operations resuming until corrective action *has* been taken was illustrated in the case of *Railtrack plc* v. *Smallwood* [2001] ICR 714.

Enforcement officers investigating potential health and safety problems have the power to require employers to answer questions about their operations; HSAWA s. 20. In the important case of *R (Wandsworth London Borough Council)* v. *South Western Magistrates Court* [2003] ICR 1287 it was held that such powers should be construed widely. In that case this enabled local authority officers to write, with detailed questions, about the training and competence of forklift truck drivers.

HSAWA: General Duties

Part I (ss. 1–9) of the Act is the most important part of the Act. Among other things it makes it clear that the scope of an employer's duties can go beyond employees and apply to other people. This will include workers on the site (such as visiting contractors) and people in the local community – for example by not exposing them to risks as a result of the way the undertaking is conducted (HSAWA s. 3).[19]

The key requirement in s. 2 is the duty of: 'every employer to ensure, so far as is reasonably practicable, the health, safety and welfare at work of all his employees'. The section then goes on to specify the particular matters to which that duty extends. These include in particular:

(a) the provision and maintenance of plant and systems of work that are, so far as is reasonably practicable, safe and without risks to health;

(b) arrangements for ensuring, so far as is reasonably practicable, safety and absence of risks to health in connection with the use, handling, storage and transport of articles and substances;

(c) the provision of such information, instruction, training and supervision as is necessary to ensure, so far as is reasonably practicable, the health and safety at work of the employees;

(d) so far as is reasonably practicable as regards any place of work under the employer's control, the maintenance of it in a condition that is safe and without risks to health, and the provision and maintenance of means of access to and egress from it that are safe and without such risks;

(e) the provision and maintenance of a working environment for employees that is, so far as is reasonably practicable, safe, without risks to health, and adequate as regards facilities and arrangements for their welfare at work.

By way of comment on the s. 2 General Duties, it must be said that their scope and enforcement largely depends on the extent to which enforcement agencies are prepared to use them in particular situations, and for particular purposes. The s. 2 general duties can be the basis for action against employers, and this can mean *corporate* liability in appropriate cases. Thus in fatal accident cases, when company managements fail to take reasonable precautions to avoid the risk of injury, the company can be convicted as well as specific managers; see the guidance in *R v. Gateway Foodmarkets Ltd* [1997] IRLR 189, CA on the scope of HSAWA s. 33 and the commission of offences when s. 2 duties are breached.

Without prejudice to the issuing of improvement and prohibition notices, and HSAWA prosecutions, fatal accidents may also result in prosecution of managers (and companies) for negligent manslaughter. Guidance on the test, which is an objective one (and does not necessarily require the accused to be 'subjectively reckless'), was given in *R v. Director of Public Prosecutions and Others, Ex Parte Jones* [2000] IRLR 373. The system of work used for unloading cargoes from ship holds at a dock was deficient in various respects, and resulted in a new worker, who had received no training, being fatally injured. The DPP's decision not to prosecute was quashed by the High Court.

Regulations on specific matters provide much of the detail needed to translate the general duties into specific requirements. Enforcement action, coupled with effective workplace monitoring of standards, are also needed as part of the promotion of proactive workplace health and safety policies.[20] The Act's effectiveness will also depend on how far the courts and tribunals *allow* them to be used, for example, in relation to workplace environment issues like smoking or employee behaviour and violence. Employees' rights to a safe working environment, such as protective measures against violent fellow workers, might, in some circumstances, be recognised through the operation of implied contractual duties, or the 'duty of care' employers owe staff (see below). There has, however, been judicial reluctance to recognise that HSAWA, s. 2 general principles can be used to impose duties on employers to protect staff from the risk of violence.[21] In the light of medical evidence about the effects of 'passive smoking' it is also arguable that s. 2 ought to be the basis for further action by employers to ban smoking in the workplace.[22]

Other key duties, in s. 2, are:

- To prepare and revise as appropriate a *written statement of general policy* with respect to employees' health and safety and the organisation and arrangements for carrying out that policy (and to bring the policy to employees' notice).
- To establish *safety representative arrangements* for the purposes of consultation (in accordance with regulations).[23] Employers have a duty to consult the representatives, who must have reasonable time off during working hours with pay, to carry out their prescribed duties 'with a view to the making and maintenance of arrangements which will enable him and his employees to co-

operate effectively in promoting and developing measures – and in checking the effectiveness of such measures'.

- If the safety representatives request this, to set up a *safety committee* to review the measure taken and to carry out any other functions prescribed by the regulations.

Safety Representation, Committees and Consultation

The safety representatives and safety committee system gives workers an important say in monitoring workplace hazards and in ensuring that employers implement health and safety requirements. The regulations make it clear, though, that the employer remains legally responsible – *not* the representatives or committee. Representatives are entitled to:

- training they might need;
- carry out inspections, and investigate accidents, dangerous occurrences and complaints;
- access to health and safety information held by the employer;
- make representations on health and safety issues;
- paid time off for union duties and activities.

The regulations, as reinforced by an HSC Code of Practice, require the employer to provide 'facilities and assistance' that are reasonably required.[24] The roles of safety representatives and committees have become increasingly important given there is now much greater worker involvement in risk assessment, workplace design and the like (see section on EC legislation below). In addition, workers have a right not to have action taken against them for stopping work in dangerous situations, particularly if there is a serious and imminent risk which cannot be averted. This is now provided for in the ERA 1996, ss. 44 and 100, which will, among other things, provide a right not to be dismissed or subjected to any detriment for exercising this right.

Where there is no recognised trade union the employer will still be required to consult employees (directly, or with elected representatives) by the Health and Safety (Consultation with Employees) Regulations 1996, SI 1996, No. 1513.

As far as employees are concerned the 1974 Act underpins the implied contractual duty of 'co-operation' by imposing duties to:

- take reasonable care of him/herself and 'other persons who may be affected' by acts or omissions;
- co-operate in enabling duties and requirements imposed on employers to be performed or complied with.

These requirements (in s. 7) permit enforcement action to be taken by the HSE (and other enforcement agencies) and they strengthen the employer's hand in taking disciplinary or dismissal action, for example if the employer unreasonably refuses permission to attend a safety training course.

Liability for Non-employees, Contractors' Staff and Others

It is not unusual for people working on site, or on activities not directly under the employer's control, to be injured while working. In this situation s. 3 (1) of the 1974

Act does make it clear that it is the duty of the employer to ensure that they are *not* exposed to risks to their health or safety (even if they are not in the employer's employment). The 1997 House of Lords case of *R v. Associated Octel Co. Ltd* [1997] IRLR 123, involving a serious accident resulting from unsafe working practices used by contractors (that led to injury to the contractor's employee) was, in fact, the responsibility of the employer occupying the site. The work being done was part of that employer's general undertaking. Employers' liabilities for accidents of their staff working abroad, on premises not owned or occupied by them, are generally less than in situations where the operations are in the UK – and which, as employers, they would be more aware; *Square D Ltd v. Cook* [1992] IRLR 35, CA.

Statutory duties are amplified by other liabilities of the employer, including the principle that in appropriate cases an employer can be vicariously liable for actions of staff, and injuries they inflict on others in the course of their employment. In the leading case on this *Mattis v. Pollock (t/a Flamingo Nightclub)* [2003] EWCA Civ. 887; [2003] IRLR 603, CA an unlicensed doorman was employed by a nightclub owner to provide security, and as part of his duties it was envisaged that he would engage in violent acts – and, indeed, he was encouraged to act aggressively. After a dispute with visitors the doorman knifed one of them. In holding the employer liable in damages, the court held that the question of vicarious liability depended on whether the action in question was so closely connected with what the employer had authorised or expected of the employee in the performance of his employment that it would be fair and just to conclude there was liability.

Detailed Requirements – Regulations

The detailed requirements that apply to particular kinds of operations, workplaces and operations are in regulations and codes of practice. The process is governed by HSAWA s. 15 and Schedule 3. S. 1 (2) deals with Codes of Practice relating to the 'general duties' in ss. 1–7 or regulations. The HSE also publishes guidance notes and booklets on most workplace activities involving hazards. If problems have been identified, or relevant regulations covering a particular process or activity have been identified, explanatory information and guidance can be obtained. A particularly useful source is the HSE's guidance series (HS[G]), or regulations booklets (HS[R]). As well as HSE advice help can also be obtained on detailed health and safety points from unions, and from health and safety organisations. The Labour Research Department provides advice for affiliated individuals and organisations, and there are local resource centres who may be able to assist.

Among the more important regulations, which will be relevant in most workplaces, and their key requirements, are:

Control of Substances Hazardous to Health Regulations 1999 (COSHH) (SI 1999, No. 437)

Employers must:

- carry out 'assessments' of risks from any substances hazardous to health in the workplace;

- detail the health and safety measures to be taken (which must be adequate and acceptable to enforcement inspectors) and implement those measures;
- monitor the measures taken;
- suspend operations/processes in prescribed cases.

The duty to carry out a risk assessment of workplace hazards was extended to *all* employers (as well as the 'self-employed') by the Management of Health and Safety at Work Regulations 1992; and requirements are now in the Management of Health and Safety Regulations 1999, SI 1999/3242 (see below).

Electricity at Work Regulations 1989 (SI 1989, No. 635)

- All systems must be constructed and maintained so as to prevent danger.
- Work activities on or near systems must be carried out so as not to give rise to danger.
- Work environment, lighting arrangements etc., near electrical systems must be suitable.
- Employees must be properly trained and supervised.
- Activities involving electricity must be assessed for suitability, design and siting.

The regulations are superseded for some purposes by later measures like the Provision and Use of Work Equipment Regulations 1998, SI 1998/2306 (for example on 'isolating' requirements, and warning devices).

Reporting of Injuries, Diseases and Dangerous Occurrences Regulations 1995 (RIDDOR) (SI 1995, No. 3163)

- Serious accidents, major injuries, and dangerous occurrences must be recorded and reported to the enforcement bodies as required, and to facilitate official action.
- Occupational diseases must, as prescribed, be reported.
- Reportable 'events' and other matters must be recorded.

Health and Safety (First Aid) Regulations 1981 (SI 1981, No. 917)

- Employers must provide appropriate first-aid materials and equipment.
- Sufficient trained first-aiders must be on site (the exact number depends on the workplace, size and hazards involved).

Noise at Work Regulations 1989 (SI 1989, No. 1790)

- Employers must assess noise hazards if 'action' levels are being exceeded (the first level over 85 dB(A)).
- Employers must reduce noise at *source* 'so far as reasonably practicable' in some cases (usually if 90 dB(A) is exceeded), rather than just relying on individual ear protection.

- Ear protection must be provided, and ear protection zones established as necessary.
- Information, training and instruction must be provided.

Health and Safety Information for Employees Regulations 1989 (SI 1989, No. 682)

- Details the posters to be displayed in workplaces.
- Requires leaflets and other information to be provided.

EC Legislation

As already discussed, EC policies have resulted in important policy changes affecting UK employment rights. The EC has now, arguably, become the most important source of new health and safety initiatives and legislation and workers' rights. Progress in implementing the 1988 Third Action Programme on health and safety has generally been good, and has been responsible for a variety of UK implementing regulations and proposals for action.[25] Prior to 1988, the Treaty of Rome allowed the Commission to make legislation on health and safety as part of the process of 'harmonising' Member States' standards, but it was not until the Single European Act 1986 that specific powers were given. Art. 118A in the treaty enabled legislation to be made by the Council of Ministers by qualified majority. What is now art. 137 provides for qualified majority voting, and this is currently the basis for much of the EC's legislative programme.

The Framework Directive on Health and Safety (EC Directive 89/391), as well as dealing with the matters referred to above:

- increased instruction and training, information and supervision for workers;
- required formal risk assessments and appropriate health and safety;
- implemented a right of worker to stop work in a dangerous situation, or to take 'appropriate steps' to protect themselves or others from danger (previously in the UK an employer could fairly dismiss staff doing this, unless procedural requirements were not followed);[26]
- provided for closer involvement of workers' representatives (unions and safety representatives) in health and safety issues and measures.

There are a variety of directives springing from these that have been progressively implemented by HSC regulations in the UK. Detailed information on the UK regulations which implement them are now available from the HSE, and are considered in more detail in specialist texts on the subject.[27] In some respects they impose 'absolute' duties on employers; but in others they impose more limited duties, and qualify them, for example by only requiring measures if they are 'practicable' or 'so far as is reasonably practicable'. In outline, key post-EC Dir. 89/391 regulations include:

- **The Workplace (Health, Safety and Welfare) Regulations 1992** (SI 1992, No. 3004) (identifying key requirements dealing with the state of premises and maintenance, cleanliness and repair: and setting new standards on buildings, equipment maintenance, fire-fighting arrangements, lighting, ventilation, sanitary and welfare facilities. Among other things facilities for pregnant women are required).

- **The Health and Safety (Display Screen Equipment) Regulations 1992** (SI 1992, No. 2792) (providing, among other things, for assessing risks at workstations and for minimum equipment standards, rest periods, proper training and education, regular eye-tests and suitable eye-wear, and the design of workstations. Arrangements should deal with physical and mental stress factors, including problems caused by software).[28]
- **The Manual Handling Operations Regulations 1992** (SI 1992, No. 2793) (requiring the avoidance of manual handling if possible, and where it is necessary laying down risk-avoidance requirements. If manual handling is necessay, and is then undertaken, operations must be properly assessed and work requirements must be adapted to the worker's abilities and limitations).
- **The Personal Protective Equipment at Work Regulations 1992** (SI 1992, No. 2966), and **The Provision and Use of Work Equipment Regulations 1998** (SI 1998, No. 2306) (setting minimum standards in relation to the selection, suitability, and use of equipment, and making the employer responsible for keeping equipment in good repair; and for training, instruction, provision to workers of information and use). The regulations also deal with measures to prevent access to dangerous machinery, and for isolating equipment from energy sources. There must also be compliance with EC standards and requirements in Directives. In general, the employer may not charge workers for the cost of health and safety arrangements, see HSAWA s. 9.
- **The Management of Health and Safety at Work Regulations 1999** (SI 1999, No. 3242) identifying key principles of 'prevention'; requiring risk assessments to be undertaken; and among other things, providing for health surveillance, and requiring information to be given by staff to the employer about the health and safety problems in the workplace's health and safety arrangements.

Other directives are directed at more specific problem areas, for example the Carcinogens, Asbestos and Biological Agents directives. Legislation is also being introduced in 'high-risk' industries such as construction and civil engineering, mining and offshore oil and gas production. On wider environmental issues, the EC Commission's legislation on company environmental audits is expected to include requirements on employee participation, particularly where these involve the integration of workplace health and safety problems and general environmental issues.

Civil Claims and Compensation

Broadly, employers have duties (and are liable) under two main 'heads':

- *Common Law* (including responsibilities arising under the contract, or in tort, including the 'duty of care'
- *Statute* (including HSAWA, regulations, and other legislation some of which may also give rise to civil claims based on breach of statutory duty

An injured employee, and the relatives of a worker killed at work,[29] may need to take legal action to get compensation.[30] This is because, as mentioned earlier in this chapter, the basis of the right to compensation is still 'fault' by the employer. Employers are usually covered by insurance, as required by law, but claims may have to be contested if liability is not accepted, or the scale of liability is not clear. For example, there may well be arguments over possible 'contributory negligence' by the worker, whether the worker was acting in the 'course of his/her employment' when the accident happened, whether there was 'third party' involvement, and other possible points that could be disputed. The outcome can be uncertain and compensation is often delayed.

In practice claims are often made under one or both of the two main heads: breach of the duty of care, or breach of statutory duty. In both cases the claim will be made in respect of the injuries suffered by the claimant.[31]

In one case employees had developed mesothelioma from working in conditions where they were exposed to asbestos; but such exposure had occurred while working with more than one employer. So it was difficult to establish, even on just a 'balance of probabilities' (the normal civil burden of proof) *which* employer was responsible. However, the claimants eventually succeeded in 2002 – but only after the House of Lords, reversing Court of Appeal decisions, adopted a modified approach to determining causation based on cumulative wrongful exposure; *Fairchild* v. *Glenhaven Funeral Services Ltd* [2002] ICR 798.

Employer's Duty of Care

There is no automatic liability on employers, even if injuries or illness occur at work or are work-related. It is generally necessary to base liability on specific duties the employer may have. The standard required is a 'reasonable' one and is measured by reference to factors which may be difficult to establish, such as foreseeability of an accident happening in the particular circumstances. Among other things, this aspect may well require a consideration of the state of knowledge and awareness of the particular risk among employers at the time of the accident. In some cases claimants may struggle to demonstrate 'causation'. In that that injury was caused by a breach of duty. This is illustrated by litigation against employers who subjected workers to exposure to asbestos dust. The duty is balanced by a requirement on workers to take care of themselves, and by the courts setting a standard which simply requires an employer to take steps which are 'reasonably practicable' and which would have been taken by a notional, reasonable and 'prudent' employer.[32] The duty is a 'personal' one, so that the scope of the duty may depend on the particular needs and characteristics of the worker concerned. This is illustrated in an important case *Tasci* v. *Pekalp of London Ltd* [2001] ICR 633 when a Kurdish worker, who spoke little English, was injured after receiving inadequate instruction and supervision. Among other things, an employer is liable for ensuring such workers receive adequate training, supervision, and support. The employer is also potentially liable for the acts and omissions of other workers, so that the duty of care cannot be delegated or passed on to others. As already noted, employers are normally 'vicariously liable' when an employee (or, possibly, contractor) causes injury to another employee and that injury is caused while the negligent employee is engaged on the employer's business, or is in the 'course of his employment'.[33]

There is extensive case law, and numerous precedents, in relation to particular types of accidents. There can be considerable overlap between different grounds for liability, but responsibilities can be grouped under headings which were initially identified in 1930 in *Wilson and Clyde Coal Co Ltd* v. *English* [1938] AC 57 and which have evolved since then in later leading cases.

Safe Systems and Place of Work

This covers the employer's site, the physical layout of the workplace and the area where the accident occurred, and the systems operated by the employer (including quality of training and supervision). 'Place of work' is a wide-ranging concept, and could, for example, include a van; *Bradford v. Robinson Rentals Ltd* [1967] All ER 267. The particular requirements of the worker concerned should have been met; for example, should specific types of personal protection have been provided to do the job? As a general rule it is not enough just to supply protective equipment, even if that equipment is suitable. There must be proper warnings given about any risks involved, and proper supervision given in safe *ways* of carrying out the job – for example if some working practices are better, and safer, than others.[34] The measures taken should be in line with any employer's assessment, and with the requirements of any relevant regulations, for example on personal equipment.

Employers are deemed to be responsible when employees suffer personal injuries in consequence of a defect in equipment provided by them (Employers' Liability (Defective Equipment) Act 1969).

Liability under the 'safe systems' heading may also include psychiatric and stress-related injury, although it would need to be shown that the illness was 'foreseeable' and that the illness *was* caused by the work system required (*Walker v. Northumberland County Council* [1995] IRLR 35). The requirements of demonstrating the employer is liable for stress and psychiatric injury were identified in the leading cases of *Hatton v. Sutherland* [2002] ICR 613; *Barber v. Somerset CC* [2004] IRLR 475, HL. These emphasise the need, first, for sufficient *knowledge* of the worker being at risk before a duty could arise. Second, there has to be a breach; and then, third, there must be proof that the alleged injury resulted *from* that breach, before liability arises. On compensation in Common Law actions for psychiatric injury, see also *Eastwood & Another v. Magnox Electric plc* [2004] UKHL 35 (and see Chapters 14 and 16).

Safe Plant, Appliances and Equipment

The test is, again, whether the employer has met the standards required of a 'reasonable' employer. There are numerous examples of employers failing to meet this requirement, including cases where they failed to keep abreast of knowledge and developments in the field of accident prevention and occupational health. An important area is noise, where employers' potential liability in the 1990s is enormous. The key considerations concern the adequacy of risk assessment, inadequate control measures, and unsuitable work arrangements and equipment. If the employer knows there is a potential problem, action should be taken.[35] This point is increasingly important in relation to claims relating to visual display unit use, and in particular to word-processor operation, where employers should by now be aware of the risk of repetitive strain injury and other hazards caused by badly designed workstations.

Competent Staff

Accidents are sometimes caused by other workers, either through their lack of training or supervision, or because the employer has not taken action to curtail potentially dangerous behaviour, despite knowing the risk they may represent. The basis of the employer's liability under this head is knowledge of a risk, and a failure to take preventative action. In one case the employer was held liable for a tripping injury caused by an employee who had previously engaged in such 'skylarking' and who had continued to do it without being restrained by the employer. *Hudson v. Ridge Manufacturing Co. Ltd* [1957] 2 QB 348.

Defences and Limitations

Even if, at first sight, it looks as if a claim is possible under one or more of these headings, there may be a defence to the claim (or a limitation on how much compensation is payable).

Defences and limitations include:

- Employee's own fault/absence of 'negligence'.
- Contributory negligence by the employee.
- Claim is 'out of time'.

Breach of Statutory Duty

In order to bring a claim there must be a statutory duty on the employer, that is a duty in an Act or regulations. There must have been a breach of that duty. This could be, but does not have to be, evidenced by a previous prosecution and conviction. The breach must have been the cause of injury for which compensation could be claimed.

The scope for starting proceedings will depend on the duty in question, and as the leading work on the subject[36] points out, this form of legal action is distinct from negligence (even if in practice claims are often made on *both* grounds). The basic principle is that the injury or damage sustained must be of a kind which the legislation was concerned to prevent.

The Health and Safety at Work Act 1974 s. 47 states that a civil action will not lie for breach of the *general* duties, i.e. ss. 2–8, but only for specific duties in health and safety regulations (and subject to any further restrictions them, or other provisions, limiting claims). This can be compared with other legislation which can, in appropriate cases, be the basis of a civil claim. As a general rule it must be shown that a duty on the defendant employer is in the legislation *and* that it is owed to the plaintiff worker; and that a breach of a duty of a kind envisaged by the legislation has occurred, resulting in injury, harm, etc. The precise requirements will depend on the legislation in question in each case, but there is no general requirement as to 'foreseeability' on the part of the employer – illustrated, for example, by cases on some of the key sections in the Factories Act 1961 s. 29; see *Mains* v. *Uniroyal Englebert Tyres Ltd* [1995] IRLR 544.

Other Legislation

Employers and occupiers may be subject to other legal duties (and liabilities) arising under legislation like the Occupiers Liability Acts 1957 and 1984. Among other things these may impose a common duty of care to visitors to premises. S. 2 (3) of the 1957 Act enables occupiers to rely on visitors, like contractors' staff, appreciating and guarding against risks for the purposes of civil liability. The position is, generally, that the employer of visiting staff (such as contractor's employees) is liable for health and safety – subject to HSAWA s. 3 responsibilities. The scope of occupiers' liability in such cases is governed, in part, by HSAWA s. 2 (4), and there may be no occupiers' liability if care is taken in selecting competent contractors, and the occupier observes other reasonable requirements.

PART SIX

Collective Rights

CHAPTER 17

Trade Unions and Their Members

The Legal Definitions

There are two parts to the legal definition of a trade union. First, it must be an organisation (permanent or temporary) that consists wholly or mainly of workers of one or more descriptions. Second, its 'principal purposes' must include 'the regulation of relations between workers of that description or those descriptions and employers or employers' associations'.

A federation, or similar organisation, may also be a 'trade union' if:

(1) it consists of constituent or affiliated organisations that are themselves trade unions (or their representatives); and
(2) its principal purposes include the regulation of relations between workers and employer or employers' associations, or the regulation of relations between its constituent or affiliated organisation. (This phrase would probably encompass the TUC.) Such bodies as the International Transport Workers' Federation are clearly within the definition. (TULR[C] Act 1992, s. 1).

In *British Association of Advisers and Lecturers in Physical Education* v. *National Union of Teachers and Others* [1986] IRLR 497, the Court of Appeal gave a broad interpretation to this definition so as to include an association 'concerned with the professional interests of its members'.

'Regulation of Relations'

This phrase was considered in *Midland Cold Storage Ltd* v. *Turner* [1972] ICR 773 NIRC.

The plaintiffs sought to prevent a joint shop stewards' committee from taking industrial action. The action was brought to restrain the commission of certain 'unfair industrial practices' created by the Industrial Relations Act. It was necessary to establish that the committee was an 'organisation of workers', a term defined by s. 61 of the Act in substantially the same words as s. 1 (TULR[C]A above).

The committee was held not to qualify within the definition because

its most apparent activity seems to consist of recommending the taking or abandonment of industrial action in the London Docks and organising any such action which may be decided upon. Thereafter, it does not seem to enter into negotiations with the employers, but leaves this task to the established union machinery.

Listing

Before 1971, the Registrar of Friendly Societies had the responsibility of maintaining a register of trade unions and most unions complied because there were tax advantages. The Industrial Relations Act 1971 introduced the office of Registrar of Trade Unions and made registration the precondition for any benefits to be gained under the Act. Since it also involved many interventions in the internal affairs of unions and control of the rule book, only a few registered. Any unions that did register were expelled from the TUC.

TULRA 1974 reverted to the substance of pre-1971 approach and the law is now set out in TULR(C)A 1992, ss. 2, 3, 4. By s. 2 the certification officer is charged with the duty of keeping a voluntary list of trade unions and employers' associations. The certification officer grants a listing if he or she is satisfied that the organisation comes within the appropriate definition.

Inclusion in the list is evidence that the organisation is a trade union. Unions on the list receive tax relief in respect of sums paid as 'provident benefits' (Income and Corporation Taxes Act 1988, s. 467) and listing is a precondition for a certificate from the certification officer that the union is 'independent'. Such status is an important attribute in relation to the following rights of unions' officials and members: to take part in trade union activities; to gain information for collective bargaining; to secure consultation over redundancies; to insist on time off for union duties and activities and to appoint health and safety representatives.

Certificate of Independence

Employers who wish to prevent trade unions recruiting their workforce may engage in two forms of 'peaceful competition'. They may ensure that the terms and conditions of their workforce are better than the negotiated rates, or they can encourage the formation of a staff association which does not pose an effective challenge to management's power. Such organisations are termed 'sweetheart unions'. The Certificate of Independence is the means by which the law seeks to ensure that such groupings do not receive the rights accorded to independent trade unions.

An independent trade union is defined by TULR(C)A, s. 5 as:

a trade union which:

(a)   is not under the domination and control of an employer or a group of employers or of one or more employers' associations; and

(b)   is not liable to interference by an employer or any such group or association (arising out of the provisions of financial or material support or by any means whatsoever) tending towards such control.

Item (b) of the test has caused the greatest difficulties in interpretation, requiring as it does a degree of speculation on the question as to whether the union is 'liable to interference'. In *Squibb UK Staff Association v. Certification Officer* [1980] IRLR 431, the Court of Appeal supported the certification officer's narrow interpretation of this phrase and held that 'liable to interference' means 'vulnerable to interference': being dependent on the employer for facilities and in a weak financial position. According to Lord Denning, the test was not satisfied merely because such interference was unlikely to occur in practice:

> One has to envisage the possibility that there may be a difference of opinion in the future between the employers and the staff association. It does not matter whether it is likely or not – it may be completely unlikely – but one has to envisage the possibility of a difference of opinion – But when it arises, the questions have to be asked. What is the strength of the employers? What pressures could they bring to bear against the staff association? What facilities could they withdraw?

Criteria Against Which Independence is to be Judged

These were set in *Blue Circle Staff Association* v. *Certification Officer* [1977] IRLR 20, EAT and are as follows:

1. Finance: If there is any evidence that a union is getting a direct subsidy from an employer, it is immediately ruled out.
2. Other Assistance: The certification officer's inspectors see what material support, such as free premises, time off work for officials, or office facilities a union is getting from an employer, and attempt to cost them out.
3. Employer Interference: If a union is very small, and weak, and gets a good deal of help, then on the face of it its independence must be in danger and liable to interference.
4. History: The recent history of a union, important in the case of the Blue Circle Staff Association which before February 1976 was dominated by the employers, is considered. It was not unusual for a staff association to start as a 'creature of management and grow into something independent'. The staff association had started on this road but still had a way to travel.
5. Rules: The applicant union's rule book is scrutinised to see if the employer can interfere with, or control it, and if there are any restrictions on membership. If a union is run by people near the top of a company it could be detrimental to the rank and file members.
6. Single Company Unions: Whilst they were not debarred from getting certificates, because such a rule could exclude unions like those of the miners and railwaymen, they were more liable to employer interference. Broadly based multi-company unions were more difficult to influence.
7. Organisation: The certification officer's inspectors then examine the applicant union in detail, its size and recruiting ability, whether it is run by competent and experienced officers, the state of its finance, and its branch and committee structure. Again, if the union was run by senior men in a company, employer interference was a greater risk.
8. Attitude: Once the other factors had been assessed, inspectors looked for a 'robust attitude in negotiation' as a sign of genuine independence, backed up by a good negotiating record ...

In coming to a decision, the certification officer is free to make such enquiries as he/she thinks fit and 'shall take into account any relevant information submitted to him [sic] by any person'. If an applicant union is refused a certificate, an appeal on fact or law may be made to the EAT. The right to appeal in TULR(C)A, s. 9 (2) is so worded that no other competing union can appeal against the certification officer's decision to grant a certificate: *General and Municipal Workers' Union* v. *Certification Officer* [1977] ICR 183.

A more recent application of the provisions relating to independence can be seen in *Government Communications Staff Federation* v. *Certification Officer* [1992] IRLR 260 EAT. Following the government's decision to ban trade unions at GCHQ, the GC Staff Association was formed. Its application for a Certificate of Independence was opposed by the TUC and the Council of Civil Service Unions, and was was rejected by the Certification Officer. Its appeal to the EAT was dismissed. Wood P held that it was 'liable to interference by an employer' because:

(a) it was a condition of service that staff were not allowed to be members of other unions, and any attempt to affiliate with another union would probably result in derecognition;
(b) approval or recognition could be withdrawn at any time by the employer on the ground of national security.

The Legal Status of a Trade Union

A trade union has a strange status in law. A trade union is not a body corporate, that is, a separate legal entity, existing independently of its members. It is an unincorporated association and its property must rest in the hands of trustees. When unions first received recognition under law, they were allowed, but not obliged, to register under the Trade Union Act 1871. Whether or not they were registered, unions remained unincorporated associations, and it was therefore assumed that it was impossible to sue them in their own name.

However, the notorious House of Lords decision in *Taff Vale Railway Co* v. *Amalgamated Society of Railway Servants* [1901] AC 426, held that a trade union registered under the 1871 Act could be sued in tort, as registered unions had a rather peculiar quasi-corporate status. The later House of Lords decision in *Bonsor* v. *Musicians Union* [1956] AC 104 confirmed this position.

The IRA 1971 then incorporated registered trade unions. TULRA 1974 essentially restored the pre-1971 position, except that no distinction was now drawn between listed and non-listed trade unions and their status was put on a more satisfactory legal footing.

The current position is that, with the exception of special registered bodies, no union, whether listed or not, is to be, or is to be treated as it were, a body corporate, except as specifically provided by the Act itself (TULR[C]A, s. 10 [2]).

Although the legal form is different from corporate entities, the underlying reality is not, since TULR(C)A, s. 10 (1) confers on unions many of the characteristics of legal corporate status, as indeed did the pre-1971 Acts. So:

(a) a trade union is capable of making contracts in its own name;
(b) all property belonging to a trade union shall be vested in trustees in trust for the union;
(c) it shall be capable of suing or being sued in its own name;
(d) proceedings may be brought against a trade union for a criminal offence;
(e) a trade union is liable for the enforcement of judgments as if it were a body corporate.

There are, however, some residual consequences of unincorporated status. Thus a trade union does not have the necessary legal personality to suffer injury to its reputation and so cannot sue for libel (*EETPU v. Times Newspapers* [1980] 1 All ER 1097).

Liability in Tort

Both employers' associations and trade unions used to have immunity from actions in tort for acts alleged or threatened, whether in their own name or by way of representative action. The immunity stemmed from the Trades Dispute Act 1906, passed in response to the *Taff Vale* decision (above).

Section 4 TDA 1906 stated that no action in tort was to be allowed against a trade union (whether in its registered name or through a representative action) 'in respect of any tortious act alleged to have been committed by or on behalf of a trade union'. The minor exception to this comprehensive immunity provided for tort actions against the trustees concerning a union's registered property outside trade disputes. Further, the union remained liable in contract; and individuals, officials and others remained liable in tort.

This blanket immunity was latched on to by critics of the unions – 'This is a Bill for legalising tyranny' (Lord Halsbury). Section 14 TULRA re-enacted this immunity but in a rather more restricted form. Actions in tort brought outside trade disputes for negligence, nuisance or other torts causing personal injury or connected with use of property were allowed.

This position was radically changed by the Employment Act 1982, which made unions liable in tort, made them vicariously liable for the unlawful actions of its officials and set out a scale of maximum damages depending on the size of the union. This scale applies unless the liability arises from personal injury caused by negligence, nuisance or other breach of duty, or a breach of duty which has arisen in connection with ownership, occupation, control or use of property, real or personal (TULR[C]A, s. 22).

Restraint of Trade

TULR(C)A, s. 11, provides immunity from the restraint of trade doctrine. This immunity is fundamental if unions are to operate lawfully. Where a union is empowered to take strike action or to impose various other forms of pressure on an employer, at common law these would be regarded as restraint of trade. Consequently, a union would be perceived to be an organisation pursuing purposes in a manner contrary to public policy, and as such would be unable to enforce its rules or protect its funds.

The vulnerability of the unions to the doctrine of restraint of trade was vividly illustrated in *Hornby v. Close* (1867) LR 2 QB 153. The United Order of Boilermakers, which had registered under the Friendly Societies Act 1855, wanted the help of the courts to prosecute an official who had embezzled its funds. It was refused: 'I do not say the objects of this society are criminal. I do not say they are not. But I am clearly of the opinion that the rules referred to are illegal in the sense that they cannot be enforced' (Mr Justice Blackburn).

Consequently, it was recognised by the framers of the Trade Union Act 1871 that if unions were to be made lawful they would need to be granted immunity from this doctrine. TULR(C)A, s. 11, retains this immunity but expands it slightly.

The provision declares that the purposes of a trade union are not, by reason only that they are in restraint of trade, to be regarded as unlawful so as:

(a) to make any union member liable to criminal proceedings for conspiracy or otherwise; or
(b) to make any agreement or trust void or voidable.

This protection is also provided for *rules* (in addition to purposes) which are not to be regarded as unlawful or enforceable by reason only that they are in restraint of trade. This extension to the immunity of rules was necessary because of the restrictive interpretation placed on 'purposes' by the Court of Appeal in *Edwards* v. *SOGAT* [1971] 3 All ER 689.

The plaintiff was expelled from the defendant trade union of which he had been classed a temporary member. His expulsion was carried out under rule 18 (4) (h), which provided for automatic termination of membership for arrears of subscription. The defendant conceded that the expulsion for this reason was unlawful because it was based on a misunderstanding about payment of his dues. However, the union argued that his damages should be nominal, since he could have been validly expelled under another rule, rule 18 (4) (j), which, it was argued, gave the union an unfettered right to terminate the membership of temporary members.

Lord Justice Sachs rejected this argument and found such an all empowering rule an unreasonable restraint of trade: 'It cannot be said that a rule that enabled such capricious and despotic action is proper to the purposes of this or indeed of any trade union.' This approach is now no longer possible given the extended s. 11. However, the reasoning adopted by another judge in the case, Lord Denning, was based on general public policy and a 'right to work' not tied to the doctrine of restraint of trade: if this approach is correct, then s. 11 would not offer immunity in such circumstances.

Political Funds and Objects

The Trade Union Act 1913 was enacted in order to restore the right of unions to spend money on political objects following the decision of the House of Lords in *Amalgamated Society of Railway Servants* v. *Osborne* [1910] AC 87 which held that it was unlawful for a union to impose on its members a compulsory levy for the purposes of creating a parliamentary fund to promote Labour MPs. However, whilst the Act allowed trade unions the right to maintain a political fund, it imposed a series of restrictive conditions on their ability to incur expenditure in respect of certain specified political objects. The union was required to ballot its members in order to approve the adoption of political objects – payments in furtherance of such objects had to be made out of a separate political fund, individual members were allowed to 'contract out' and were safeguarded against discrimination arising from their failure to contribute to the fund.

The two major changes introduced into this system by the Trade Union Act 1984 relate to the introduction of periodic ballots to test continued support for the political objects of the union and a new definition of 'political objects'. The law is now contained in the Trade Union and Labour Relations (Consolidation) Act 1992.

The Act provides that trade unions which maintain political funds must ballot their members at least every ten years to determine the continued operation of such funds. The Act stipulates rules regarding the conduct of political fund ballots which have to be approved by the certification officer. Most notably the ballot must be a fully postal ballot, with the papers sent out and returned by post. (The other ballot requirements are listed in our section on Union Elections and Ballots below.)

The second major change concerns the enlarged definition of those objects of expenditure which must be met out of the political fund. Political objects will now include expenditure:

(a) on any contributions to the funds of, or payment of any expenses incurred directly or indirectly by, a political party;

(b) on the provision of any service or property for use by or on behalf of any political party;[1]

(c) in connection with the registration of electors, the candidature of any person, the selection of any candidate or the holding of any ballot by the union in connection with any election to a political office;

(d) on the maintenance of any holder of political office;[2]

(e) on the holding of any conference or meeting by, or on behalf of, a political party or any other meeting the main purpose of which is the transaction of business in connection with a political party; and

(f) on the production, publication or distribution of any literature, document, film, sound recording or advertisement, the main purpose of which is to persuade people to vote for a political party or candidate or to persuade them not to vote for a political party or candidate (TULR[C]A, s. 72).

Perhaps the most far-reaching change concerns paragraph (f). First, it is much wider than the previous definition, covering not only literature and documents but other forms of publicity such as TV, radio and advertisements. Second, because the provision encompasses any publication whose main purpose is to persuade persons to vote or not to vote for a particular party or candidate, unions, particularly those operating in the public sector, will need to exercise care about the material they publish which is not paid for out of the political fund (see *Paul* v. *NALGO* [1987] IRLR 413). Publicity campaigns against privatisation or trade union legislation, for example, will need a thorough vetting if they are to be financed from the general fund. It is important to bear in mind that these changes affect all unions, whether or not they possess a political fund, since they limit the ways in which general funds can be spent.

Sections 89–91 of the 1992 Act deal with the case of a union which has a political fund but which fails to renew its resolution either by failing to get a majority in favour of renewal or by failing to call a ballot within a ten-year period.

In such situations, the trade union must ensure that the collection of contributions to the political fund is discontinued 'as soon as is reasonably practicable'. Any contributions which are received after a political resolution has lapsed may be paid into any of its other funds, subject to the individual member's right to claim a refund.

Where a union has held a ballot but fails to secure a majority for renewal, the union is allowed a period of six months during which it may continue to spend on political objects. Unions which fail to call a ballot within the ten-year period are penalised by not being allowed this 'breathing space'. Trade unions which do not run down their political funds in such situations may transfer the money into their non-political funds. Alternatively, the political fund is frozen until such time as the union can secure a majority in favour of renewal in a subsequent ballot.

Any member who claims that a union has failed to comply with the political fund ballot rules may apply to the High Court (Court of Session in Scotland) or the certification officer for a declaration to that effect. The High Court may, in addition, make an enforcement order specifying the steps the union must take and the time-scale within which they must be taken. The court order may be enforced by any individual who was a member both at the time the original order was made and when enforcement proceedings commenced. The right of enforcement is, therefore, not confined to the original litigant.

Contracting Out and the Check-off

Despite the fact that the Conservative government initially had proposed substituting contracting in for contracting out, ultimately it did not change the present system. Instead, discussions between the then Department of Employment and the TUC resulted in the latter's Statement of Guidance to its affiliates. The Secretary of State for employment, however, made it clear that the government would legislate if it believed that the TUC voluntary code was not working satisfactorily.

The Statement of Guidance advises unions to draw up an information sheet containing information, inter alia, on how to contract out, on the right not to be discriminated against for non-contribution and on the amount of the levy as a proportion of the normal subscription. The information sheet should be supplied to new members, existing members on request and all union members after any ballot concerning the establishment or continuation of the political fund.[3]

In relation to contracting out procedures, the statement advises that no obstacles should be placed in the way of members wishing to contract out and, in particular, that forms of exemption should be available through workplace representatives, union branches and the union's head office; that receipt of completed notices should be acknowledged; that exemption should be put into effect speedily,[4] and that unions should ensure that members who do not wish to pay the levy do not do so inadvertently (for instance, under check-off arrangements).[5]

Indeed, in order to safeguard against the latter eventuality, the 1992 Act itself makes it unlawful for employers operating the check-off system to deduct the political levy from the pay of an employee who has given notification that he/she has contracted out. Employees must certify to their employer in writing that they have contracted out and the employer must ensure as soon as is reasonably practicable that the political levy is not deducted from the employee's pay (s. 86).

Employers are often unwilling to deduct different amounts from employees' wages, according to whether or not they pay the political levy. As a result, unions have adopted the practice of periodically refunding to exempt members such amounts deducted by their employer as represents the political levy. This practice, held to be lawful by the EAT in *Reeves* v. *TGWU* [1980] ICR 728, is now outlawed by s. 86 (3) of the 1992 Act. Employers are now faced with the choice between the administrative burden of operating a check-off system which deducts variable amounts from pay, depending on whether the employee does or does not contribute to the political fund, or completely abandoning the check-off system.

Employees who wish to challenge their employer's actions in this area may apply to the county court for a declaration and an order requiring the employer to take remedial action.

Regulation of Trade Unions

The last three decades have witnessed an increasing tendency to subject internal union affairs to legal regulation. Although the Donovan Commission (1968), para. 622, found it 'unlikely that abuse of power by trade unions is widespread', it still recommended that the chief registrar of trade unions be given a supervisory role over the content of union rules and that an independent review body should be created to deal with arbitrary exclusion and expulsions. Section 65 IRA 1971 laid down a number of 'guiding principles' for trade union rules which forbid, inter alia, arbitrary or unreasonable exclusions from membership and unfair or unreasonable disciplinary action. In the 1980s, we witnessed considerable statutory intervention in this field. Moreover, judicial intervention via the common law has also played a major role in the trend towards intervention in internal union affairs.

The Residual Importance of the Common Law

Statutory protection for individuals has increased markedly since 1980, with the enactment of the right not to be unreasonably excluded or expelled from union membership where there is a closed shop in operation (Employment Act 1980, s. 4) and the right not to be disciplined for certain listed reasons (Employment Act 1988, s. 3). TURERA tightened the screw even further by exacting a general right not to be excluded and expanding the scope of unjustifiable discipline. However, as leading commentators have pointed out, an examination of the common law on admissions, disciplined expulsions is relevant, 'first, because common law actions may still have a considerable impact (as was seen particularly in the miners' strike of 1984/85) and secondly, because the statutory provisons for the most part build upon common law foundation rather than replacing it'.[6]

The Rule Book

The Rule Book and the Courts

The starting point for judicial involvement has traditionally been the contract of membership. The professed function of the law in this area is to strike a balance between the conflicting notions of union autonomy on the one hand and the rights of the individual member on the other.

In readily intervening to protect the individual, it may be that – as with strike law – the courts have shown little understanding of the need for collective solidarity within trade unions.

Means of Intervention

The foundation of the court's jurisdiction is contract, and the courts may regularly review affairs on that basis. But contract law has its limitations. In particular, members can sign away their rights and freedom of contract means that a union cannot be compelled to let an applicant join the group. The courts have therefore found new ways of intervening in the internal affairs of trade unions where contract fails to provide a satisfactory solution.

First, and most importantly, they have said that union committees and tribunals must observe the rules of natural justice in determining the rights of members. Second, they have developed the principle of the right to work. It is said that the common law recognises that every worker has a right to work, a right not to be arbitrarily and unreasonably prevented from earning his/her living as s/he wills. Third, on occasion, they have argued that the authority of the rule book derives from some other source other than the contract of membership and that certain actions were ultra vires (beyond the powers of) the union. An early and notorious example of this was the so-called *Osborne Judgment* in 1915 (*Amalgamated Society of Railway Servants* v. *Osborne* [1910] AC 87), where the House of Lords held that a trade union had no power to sponsor a member of Parliament. The Law Lords held that a union, whether registered or unregistered, had only the powers conferred on it by the Trade Union Acts 1871–6. That did not include the power to spend money on political objects. Rules allowing such expenditure were ultra vires the statute. The decision was reversed by the Trade Union Act 1913, which made it clear that a trade union could have other objects besides its 'statutory objects' of conducting industrial relations. That is the basis of the present law, as we saw from the definition in TULR(C)A, s. 1. The 1913 Act specifically enacted that a trade union had the power to apply its funds for any lawful object for any lawful purpose or object authorised by its constitution. Therefore, ever since 1913 it has been impossible to claim that any union rule was ultra vires the statute.

However, more recently it has been suggested that a union rule can be invalidated as 'ultra vires at common law'. The basis of the argument – the main proponent of which was Lord Denning – is that the rule book is not a contract at all, but akin to a legislative code of by-laws. It this is correct, then the court has the power to intervene, as in administrative law, if the rule is unreasonable. Having said that, Lord Denning's approach attracted little or no support from other judges and was unequivocally rejected by the House of Lords in *Faramus* v. *Film Artistes Association* [1964] AC 925.

Admission to a Union at Common Law

The lack of contractual relationship between the union and the applicant for membership has made it difficult for the courts to find a theoretical basis for review in exclusion cases. Indeed, in two decisions the House of Lords construed the fact that the plaintiffs had been admitted wrongly into membership as meaning that they had never been members of the relevant unions.

In *Faramus* v. *Film Artistes Association* [1964] 1 All ER 25 HL,[7] rule 4 (2) of the defendant association provided that: 'No person who has been convicted in a court of law of a criminal offence (other than a motoring offence not punishable by imprisonment) shall be eligible for, or retain membership of the association.' When he signed the application forms for membership, the appellant denied that he had been convicted of any offence, though he had twice been convicted of minor offences in Jersey several years earlier. After he had been in the union for eight years, his previous convictions were discovered and the union claimed that he was not, and had never been, a member. He sought a declaration that he was a member and an injunction restraining the union from excluding him from membership.

The House of Lords held:

(1) That Faramus had never in fact been validly elected a member.
(2) The membership contract, including the relevant rule, was validated as regards restraint of trade by s. 3 Trade Union Act 1871 (see now TULR[C]A, s. 11).
(3) The rules prescribing qualifications for entry into a union cannot be invalidated on the grounds of 'unreasonableness' or being contrary to natural justice.

The concept of the 'right to work', however, provided the most radical means of attack for the judges in their attempt to review decisions on admission. This was a development carried out almost single-handedly by Lord Denning. Although first discussed in 1952 (*Lee* v. *Showmen's Guild* [1952] 2 QB 329 CA), it was used for the first time in *Nagle* v. *Feilden* [1966] 2 QB 633 CA.

The stewards of the Jockey Club refused Mrs Nagle a licence to train racehorses in pursuance of their unwritten policy of refusing a licence to a woman. Mrs Nagle sued for an injunction and a declaration that the practice was against public policy, but her statement of claim was struck out as disclosing no cause of action. She appealed against this decision. The Court of Appeal granted an interlocutory injunction on the basis that she had an arguable case.

Lord Denning stated:

> The common law of England has for centuries recognised that a man has a right to work at his trade or profession without being unjustly excluded from it. He is not to be shut out from it at the whim of those having the governance of it. If they make a rule which enables them to reject his application arbitrarily or capriciously, not reasonably, that rule is bad. It is against public policy. The court will not give effect to it.

The interlocutory injunction enabled the parties to reach a settlement. Hence the case did not come to court for final judgment.

Edwards v. *SOGAT* (1971) Ch 354 CA, constituted the most radical application of the doctrine. The union's decision not to readmit Edwards into membership meant loss of employment. In such circumstances, Lord Denning offered the following opinion:

> I do not think the defendant union, or any other trade union, can give itself by its rules an unfettered discretion to expel a man or to withdraw his membership. The reason lies in the man's right to work. This is now fully recognised by law. It is a right which is of especial importance when a trade union operates a 'closed shop' or '100 per cent membership', for that means that no man can become employed or remain in employment with a firm unless he is a member of the union. If his union card is withdrawn, he has to leave the employment. He is deprived of his livelihood. The courts of this country will not allow so great a power to be exercised arbitrarily or capriciously or with unfair discrimination, neither in the making of rules, nor in the enforcement of them.

Prima facie the *Nagle* v. *Feilden* doctrine would seem equally applicable to those unions operating a closed shop. However, there is a fundamental difficulty. It is not clear that the concept of the right to work is anything more than the doctrine of restraint of trade reinterpreted from the standpoint of the individual. Whenever a union by its rules or policies arbitrarily or unreasonably restrains trade, it necessarily arbitrarily or unreasonably interferes with the right to work. This point is addressed in neither *Nagle* nor *Edwards*.

Discipline and Expulsion at Common Law

Two principal methods of judicial control of trade union disciplinary action are that:

(1) A union should comply strictly with its rules on a contract.
(2) Union rules and procedures must comply with the rules of natural justice.

Strict Compliance with Rules
Union rules can broadly be classified into two kinds:

(a) those which permit disciplinary sanctions to be imposed for some specific offence such as disobedience to instructions issued by the union executive; and
(b) those which leave the particular actions unspecified – for example, rules permitting sanctions to be imposed for such offences as conduct detrimental to the union, or prejudicial to its interests. Sometimes these rules are phrased subjectively, such as those that prohibit conduct which in the opinion of the executive committee might be detrimental to union interests.

The courts have construed both kinds of rules strictly, and they will resolve any ambiguity in favour of the member.

The following two cases illustrate the principles which the courts will adopt where the rules are general and inherently ambiguous.

In *Lee v. Showmen's Guild of GB* [1952] 1 All ER 1175 CA, the plaintiff was charged with 'unfair competition' under a union rule. An area committee of the union fined him for breaking the rule. Failure to pay the fine was, under the rules, to result in expulsion. The plaintiff did not pay the fine and was expelled. He sought an injunction to prevent the union from enforcing his expulsion. The Court of Appeal held that the courts will examine the decisions of domestic tribunals to see that the tribunal has observed the law, including the correct interpretation of the rules, which form the contract between the members. 'The true construction of the contract is to be decided by the courts and by no one else' (per Lord Justice Denning, at p. 344).

On the evidence in this case, the plaintiff could not properly have been found guilty of unfair competition and the committee was, therefore, acting without jurisdiction.

The basis for the intervention was described by Lord Justice Denning thus:

> the question whether the committee has acted within its jurisdiction depends, in my opinion, on whether the facts adduced before them were reasonably capable of being held to be a breach of the rules. If they were, then the proper inference is that the committee correctly construed the rules and have acted within their jurisdiction. If, however, the facts were not reasonably capable of being held to be

in breach and yet the committee held them in breach, then the only inference is that the committee have misconstrued the rules and exceeded their jurisdiction.

That is, it had come to a conclusion which no reasonable tribunal would have reached. Hence any purported expulsion was invalid. The effect of this decision, therefore, was to allow the courts to substitute their own view of the meaning of a blanket offence for that of the union.

The manner in which the courts have extended contractual principles to deal with blanket offence cases is most vividly illustrated by the case law on unions' powers to discipline members who have failed to participate in industrial action.

In *Esterman v. NALGO* [1974] ICR 625 ChD, there was a pay dispute and NALGO held a ballot on the question of selective strike action but only 49 per cent of the vote was cast in favour. Subsequently the union instructed its members not to assist in administering local elections. Esterman defied this instruction and, in consequence, was to be disciplined by the union on the basis that she was guilty of conduct rendering her unfit for membership. The relevant rule read: 'Any member who disregards any regulation issued by the branch, or is guilty of conduct which, in the opinion of the executive committee, renders him unfit for membership, shall be liable to expulsion.'

Esterman sought an injunction against the union to restrain it from taking disciplinary action against her. An injunction was granted on the basis that in the circumstances no reasonable tribunal could bona fide come to the conclusion that disobedience of the order to strike demonstrated any unfitness to be a member of NALGO.

The *Lee* and *Esterman* cases are important because they emphasise that the courts' jurisdiction between unions and members is based on contract, that questions of interpretation are reserved to the courts; and because it indicates the way in which the courts will control general blanket disciplinary provisions. *Esterman's* case shows that the mere fact that the provision is in subjective terms – 'in the opinion of' the disciplinary body – is unlikely to make a difference to the willingness of the courts to intervene.

Natural Justice

When exercising disciplinary functions, the trade union is taken to operate as a quasi-judicial body: 'although the jurisdiction of a domestic tribunal is founded on contract, express or implied, nevertheless the parties are not free to make any contract they like' (*Breen v. AEU* [1971] 2 QB 175). It is thus impossible to exclude, even by an express and unambiguous rule, the right of members to be heard in their own defence before disciplinary action is taken against them. This means that the rules of natural justice require two things:

(1) A disciplined member must have a proper notice of the complaint and an opportunity to be heard by the appropriate committee.
(2) The tribunal must act in an unbiased manner and reach an honest decision.

An example of a 'notice' is found in *Annamunthodo v. Oilfield Workers' Trade Union* [1961] 3 All ER 621. The appellant was charged in writing with four specific offences under a named union rule. None of the offences gave rise to the possibility of expulsion from the union. The initial hearing attended by the appellant was adjourned and he did not attend the remainder of the hearing. He was subsequently informed that he had been convicted on all four charges but had been expelled under a blanket rule with which he had not been charged. It was held by the Privy Council that he should have been given notice of the new charge and a fair opportunity of meeting it. The order for expulsion was set aside.

The other requirement of natural justice is for an unbiased tribunal to adjudicate on the merits of the case. Clearly, the disciplinary proceedings of trade unions are controlled by lay people and the law cannot demand the same level of impartiality that would be required of a judge or arbitrator. Instead their task is to have 'a will to reach an honest conclusion after hearing what was argued on either side and a resolve not to make their minds up beforehand' (per Viscount Simon in *White* v. *Kuzych* [1951] AC 585, Privy Council).

But this tolerance does not excuse the intervention of those with particular interests over and above those inevitable in such situations. *Roebuck* v. *NUM (Yorkshire Area) (No. 2)* [1978] ICR 676 arose after the union area president (Arthur Scargill), acting on behalf of the union, had successfully sued a newspaper for libel. In the action two union members had given evidence for the newspaper. At the instigation of Mr Scargill, the area executive resolved to charge those members with conduct detrimental to the interests of the union. The executive found the charges proved and this was confirmed by the area council which had originally referred the matter to the executive. Mr Scargill was president of both bodies and participated in their proceedings, questioning the plaintiffs and taking part in the deliberations. However, he did not vote on the resolution to suspend one of the plaintiffs from office as branch chairman and declare the other ineligible for office in the union for two years.

The judge found that it was irrelevant to consider whether Scargill's presence and conduct had an influence on the result. The real issue concerned the fact that his presence at all stages of the disciplinary procedure gave the impression that the dice were loaded against Roebuck. The decision to discipline Roebuck, therefore, could not stand since justice had to be seen to be done.

Excluding the Jurisdiction of the Court at Common Law

A union rule which seeks to bar the member from pursuing legal redress is void and unenforceable as against public policy.[8]

Less clear-cut is the validity of a rule that the union's internal disciplinary procedures must be exhausted before a member can apply to the court. Courts recognise that there are many advantages in internal resolution of the dispute. Thus in *Leigh* v. *NUR* [1970] Ch 326, Mr Justice Goff stated:

> [Wh]ere there is an express provision in the rules that the plaintiff must first exhaust his domestic remedies, the court is not absolutely bound by that because its jurisdiction cannot be ousted, but the plaintiff will have to show cause why it should interfere with the contractual position ...
>
> [In] the absence of such a provision the court can readily, or at all events more readily, grant relief without prior recourse to the domestic remedies, but may require the plaintiff to resort first to those remedies.

Exhaustion of internal procedures would not be required if the domestic proceedings were irretrievably biased; if they involve a serious point of law or fraud is at issue; or if the internal procedures would involve excessive delay.

In *Esterman* the court went further to hold that a plaintiff may bring an action to stop *impending* disciplinary action if s/he can show that there is no lawful basis for it.

Access to the Courts

The Employment Act 1988, s. 2, provided a new right for union members not to be denied access to the court to pursue a grievance against their union. The relevant provisions are now to be found in TULR(C)A 1992. Where court proceedings relate to a grievance which a member began to pursue against his/her union more than six months before applying to the court, the court must not: (a) dismiss; (b) stay or resist; or (c) adjourn the proceedings on the ground that further internal procedures for resolving the grievance are available under the union rules. (TULR[C]A, s. 63.)

However, TULR(C)A, s. 63 (6), states that this six-month rule is without prejudice to any rule of law by which a court could ignore any such union rule already – so the principles discussed in *Leigh* above are still relevant.

Refusals to Admit and Expulsions in the Interests of Inter-union Relations

The TUC has drawn up a set of 'Principles Governing Relations between Unions' – the so-called Bridlington Principles. They require every affiliated union to ask all applicants for membership if they are or have recently been a union member. The new union must then ask the old union whether the member has resigned, has any subscription arrears, is 'under discipline or penalty', or if there are any other reasons why s/he should not be accepted. If the old union objects, the dispute may be resolved by the TUC Disputes Committee. Most affiliated unions have a provision in their rule books providing for the automatic termination of membership, following a period of notice, in order to comply with the decision of the Disputes Committee. The courts have upheld the validity of such rules, provided that the power is exercised following a valid decision of the Disputes Committee itself.[9]

In *Cheall* v. *APEX* [1983] 2 AC 180, the House of Lords held that an individual trade unionist had no right to be heard by the TUC Disputes Committee before it made its determination. Furthermore, there was

> no existing rule of public policy that would prevent trade unions from entering into arrangements with one another which they consider to be in the interests of their members in promoting order in industrial relations and enhancing their members' bargaining power with their employers.

In its 1991 Green Paper, 'Industrial Relations in the 1990s' (Cm. 1602), the government expressed the view that the law should be amended so as to guarantee freedom of choice where more than one trade union can genuinely claim to be able to represent an employee's interests.

In the government's opinion, a union should not be obliged to accept someone into membership if it does not represent employees of a similar skill or occupation. Nor should it be obliged to accept an applicant who has been an unsatisfactory member of another union because, for example, of a record of refusing to pay subscriptions. However, a union should not be at liberty to refuse to accept an individual into membership simply because s/he was previously a member of another union, which gives that union sole recruitment rights in a particular company or sector. TURERA s. 14 contains provisions designed to implement these views (see now TULR[C]A 1992, s. 17).

The remedy for an infringement of this new right is by way of a complaint to an ET for a declaration and compensation. The remedies operate in a very similar way to those which already apply to unreasonable exclusion or expulsion from a trade union, and to unjustifiable discipline by a trade union (see below).

Statutory Controls over Admissions and Expulsions

Pre-1980 Law

As we have seen, in 1968 the Donovan Commission suggested that a review body should be created to hear complaints concerning arbitrary exclusions or expulsions. No such body was ever created by statute, although s. 65 IRA 1971 did contain provisions prohibiting arbitrary or unreasonable discrimination against applicants as members. A similar provision contained in s. 5 TULRA 1974 was repealed by TULR(A)A 1976. In response, the TUC established its own Independent Review Committee in April 1976 to provide a voluntary forum for hearing cases alleging unreasonable exclusion or expulsion from unions operating a closed shop.

The IRC's awards were not legally binding but the affiliates agreed to be bound by them. The remedy was a recommendation that a union admit or readmit the complainant into membership; it had no authority to award compensation. The major weakness was that an IRC recommendation could not be enforced against an employer – that is, even if the union reinstated a worker, there was nothing to force the employer to take that employee back if dismissed – though, of course, there is now the unfair dismissal remedy in such cases.

Once the government introduced legislation covering the area of admissions and expulsions in unions operating the closed shop, the voluntary machinery, in the words of the TUC, 'faded away'.

The Employment Act 1980

The Conservative government was not satisfied with the TUC's self-regulation and enacted s. 4 of EA 1980. This reverted the position to broadly that of the period of the IRA 1971, except s. 4 *only* applied where the employer operated a union membership agreement. This law is now set out in TULR(C)A, s. 174. This right remains alongside the more recent and general provisions on unjustifiable discipline by trade unions, which apply in all cases whether inside or outside closed shops (see below). Finally, pre-entry closed shops experienced yet a further legal onslaught as a result of the Employment Act 1990 which made it unlawful to refuse a person employment because s/he is not or does not wish to become a union member. (See now TULR[C]A, s. 137.)

Under the current statutory regime, an individual seeking a job where a closed shop – or 'union membership agreement' – operates has a right: (a) not to have his/her membership application unreasonably refused; and (b) not to be unreasonably expelled from the union (TULR[C]A ss. 174–177).

TURERA s. 14 replaces these provisions with new ss. 174–177 which provide a general right for workers not to be excluded or expelled from any union unless the exclusion or expulsion is for a statutory 'permitted' reason. The permitted exceptions are:

- The individual fails to satisfy an 'enforceable membership requirement' contained in the rules of the union. A requirement is 'enforceable' if it restricts membership solely by reference to one or more of the following criteria: employment in a specified trade, industry or profession; occupational description (including grade, level or category of employment); or possession of specified trade, industrial or professional qualifications or work experience.
- The individual does not qualify by reason of the union operating only in particular parts of Great Britain.
- The exclusion or expulsion is entirely attributable to the individual's conduct. But 'conduct' does not include ceasing to be, or having ceased to be, a member of another trade union or an employee of a particular employer or at a particular place. The definition also excludes any conduct to which TULR(C)A s. 65 – the right not to be unjustifiably disciplined by a trade union – applies (see below).

Remedies

These are complex. A person who has obtained a declaration from a tribunal that s/he was unreasonably excluded or expelled may claim compensation. The applicant must wait for at least four weeks after the date of the declaration (to give the union an opportunity to admit or readmit), but then has up to six months after the date of the declaration to present a claim for compensation. If s/he has been admitted/readmitted by the time of the application, complaint lies to an employment tribunal. If the union has refused to abide by the tribunal's initial declaration, complaint lies directly to the EAT. In both cases the amount of compensation will be such as is considered just and equitable in all the circumstances, subject to a maximum. The maximum compensation is 30 times the amount of a week's pay allowable in computing the basic award for unfair dismissal cases, plus the maximum compensatory award for the time being in force in respect of unfair dismissal (TULR[C]A 1992, s. 176 [4] [6]). The minimum award before the EAT is £5,900 (2004/05): there is no minimum award before an employment tribunal.

Where the industrial tribunal or EAT finds that the exclusion or expulsion complained of was to any extent caused or contributed to by the the action of the applicant, it shall reduce the amount of compensation by such proportion as it considers just and equitable in the circumstances (TULR[C]A, s. 176 [5]). In *Howard v. NGA* [1985] ICR 101, the EAT reduced the award by 15 per cent because the applicant had contributed to the refusal of membership by the union when he took a job with a company which he knew subscribed to the closed-shop agreement, while his application for union membership was still under consideration.

Other Relevant Provisions

Four other statutes are relevant to this area. RRA 1976, SDA 1975 and the DDA 1995 make it unlawful to discriminate on grounds of gender, race or on grounds of disability against an applicant for trade union membership. The Trade Union and Labour Relations (Consolidation) Act, s. 82 (c), states that where the union operates a political fund, it must not make contribution to the fund a condition of admission or discriminate against a non-contributor. Union rule books are required to contain a rule to this effect. Finally, as we see below, the EA 1988 provides a general prohibition on unjustifiable discipline of trade union members.

Unjustifiable Discipline

The Employment Act 1988, s. 3, provides that a union member may not be unjustifiably disciplined by his/her union. The law is now set out in TULR(C)A, s. 64.

This is a controversial provision, widely regarded by critics as a 'scab's charter'. The provision means that a union is prohibited from disciplining a member for not taking part in industrial action notwithstanding that a majority of that member's fellow workers voted in favour of the action in a properly held ballot. As such, s. 64 is understandably seen by the union movement as an attack on the fundamental concepts of union solidarity and collectivism.

Ewan McKendrick has argued:

> By prohibiting the exercise of disciplinary sanctions by unions, [s. 64] stacks all the disciplinary powers on the side of the employer. In sum [s. 64] is an objectionable intervention in union affairs, it is a possible violation of our international obligations and it elevates the individual interest of a union member to a point where it unacceptably undermines the collective strength of the union and represents an unwarranted intrusion into internal union affairs.[10]

It is deemed to be unjustifiable to discipline a trade union member for the following types of conduct:

(a) failure to participate in or support a strike or industrial action by members of his/her own trade union or any other or indicate opposition to the industrial action;

(b) failure to breach a contract of employment or any other agreement between the member and 'a person for whom he normally works' (this is a broader concept than 'employee and employer' and is likely to cover workers who are classified as self-employed);

(c) the making of an assertion (in legal proceedings or otherwise) that the union, or any official, representative or trustee, has contravened or is proposing to contravene a requirement imposed by the union's rules;

(d) encouraging or assisting a worker to perform his/her contractual duty or encouraging or assisting him/her to make or attempt to vindicate an allegation covered by (c) above;

(e) consulting the commissioner for the rights of trade union members or certification officer or asking them to provide advice or assistance;

(f) failing to comply with any requirement imposed as a result of unjustifiable disciplinary action, whether taken against the complainant or another, for example, refusing to comply with a ruling that a particular member should be fined or expelled;

(g) proposing to do any of the above, or doing acts which are preparatory or incidental to them.

TURERA extended the list of conduct for which it is unjustifiable for a trade union to discipline a member to include the following:

(h) failing to agree, or withdrawing agreement, to a check-off agreement;

(i) resigning, or proposing to resign, from the union, joining or proposing to join another union, or refusing to join another union;

(j) working with, or proposing to work with, individuals who are not members of another union; or

(k) working for, or proposing to work for, an employer who employs or who has employed non-members of the union, or non-members of another union;

(l) requiring the union to do an act which the union is, by virtue of TULR(C)A required to do on the requisition of a member (see now TULR[C]A 1992, s. 16).

Discipline is widely defined by TULR(C)A, s. 64 (2), and includes expulsion from a union or a branch of a union; fines; loss of any benefits, facilities or services; that another trade union, or a branch or section of another trade union, should be encouraged or advised not to accept that individual as a member; or that the individual should be subjected to any other detriment.

Procedure

A claim must be made to the ET within three months of the imposition of the disciplinary sanction. There is power to extend the period if the ET is satisfied:

(a) that it was not reasonably practicable for the complaint to have been presented within the three-month limit; and

(b) that any delay in making the complaint is wholly or partly attributable to any reasonable attempt to appeal internally against the determination to which the complaint relates.

Remedies

Where the ET find that the complainant has been unjustifiably disciplined, it will make a declaration to that effect. The complainant may then make a further application to the ET for compensation not earlier than four weeks but not later than six months after the date of the initial declaration.

What happens next depends on the trade union's response. If the union has revoked its disciplinary decision and taken all necessary steps to put that decision into effect, the further application is to the ET. If, on the other hand, the union fails to revoke its decision, the further application is to the EAT.

The amount of compensation to be awarded will be such as is considered to be just and equitable in all the circumstances of the case, subject to the usual rules relating to mitigation of loss and contributory fault.

Where the application is to the ET the maximum award is 30 times a week's pay together with the maximum compensatory award currently available. Where the application is to the EAT, the same maximum figure applies, but there is a fixed minimum award which in 2004/05 stands at £5,900 (s. 67 [8]).

Trade Union Democracy

Rule Book as Contract and Constitution

At common law, the government and administration of a union must be carried out in accordance with the terms of the contract of membership which are contained primarily in the rule book. A failure to do this will normally constitute a breach of contract, and the courts may well declare it ultra vires (beyond the powers of) the union.

The potential for challenging the action taken by a union in breach of its rules was repeatedly illustrated in the cases raised by working miners against various areas of the NUM during the miners' strike of 1984–85. In these cases, the judges relied on a strict construction of the NUM's rule book to establish the requirement for conducting ballots before authorising industrial action. In *Taylor v. NUM (Derbyshire Area) (No. 1)* [1984] IRLR 440, it was held that the local area was required by its rules to obtain 55 per cent support in a ballot for strike action before such action could be official; in *Taylor v. NUM (Yorkshire Area)* [1984] IRLR 445, it was held that an area ballot held some two and a half years previously was too remote to be capable of justifying a lawful call for strike action under the rules. In both cases the judges accepted that the strike in reality constituted national action, which was also unlawful in the absence of a national ballot.

Once the strike was called in breach of the rules, injunctions were granted preventing the issuing of instructions to the membership not to work or to cross picket lines (*Taylor v. NUM [Derbyshire Area] [No. 1]*). A second consequence of the holding that the action was beyond the rules was that the use of union funds to support the strike could be restrained. In *Taylor v. NUM (Derbyshire Area)(No. 3)* [1985] IRLR 99, the judge held that it was ultra vires for the union to authorise expenditure on strike action which had been called in breach of the area's rules. Further, the officials who had misapplied union monies in this way were in breach of the fiduciary duty which they owed to the members, and could be personally liable for such unauthorised expenditure. The miners' cases demonstrated the readiness of the judges to issue interlocutory injunctions to restrain the alleged unlawful behaviour and, as we shall see, the potential for using 'scab' workers to mount legal challenges against a striking union was not lost on the government when it framed the Employment Act 1988.[11]

Union Accounts

TULR(C)A lays down detailed rules for the carrying on of a union's financial affairs. The union must make annual returns to the certification officer (s. 32), including a profit and loss account, a balance sheet, an auditor's report and any other documents that may be required. All must be approved by auditors, who should be independent and professionally qualified. The overriding obligation is to present accounts which give a 'true and fair view' of the matters to which they relate (s. 32 [3]).

Failure either to submit an annual return or to maintain proper accounts and accounting controls is a criminal offence (s. 45 [1]). It is also an offence to falsify the accounts (s. 45 [4]).

Annual returns are open to public inspection at the offices of the certification officer (s. 32 [6]). The union itself must also provide a copy of its latest annual return to anyone who asks (s. 32 [5]). It may make a reasonable charge.

The 1991 Green Paper, 'Industrial Relations in the 1990s', contained a number of proposals for strengthening the law as it affects the responsibility of trade union leaders for union finances. In the government's view, the Lightman Inquiry into allegations of serious misconduct by senior officials of the NUM in the management of the union's finances indicated that the rights of union members in this area need further support.[12]

Consequently, TURERA contained provisions:

- providing the certification officer (CO) with wider powers to direct a trade union to produce documents relating to its financial affairs and to appoint inspectors to investigate the financial affairs of a trade union where it appears to the CO that there is impropriety in the conduct of those affairs. It requires reports of investigations to be published. Reports will be admissible in legal proceedings;
- creating new offences in connection with the CO's proposed powers of inspection and investigation. It will be an offence to: contravene any duty or requirement imposed by the CO or inspectors relating to the production of documents and so on; destroy, mutilate or falsify a document relating to the financial affairs of the union (unless there was no intention to conceal information or defeat the law); fraudulently part with, alter or delete anything in such a document; or provide or make an explanation or statement, either knowingly or recklessly, which is false;
- increasing the maximum penalty for an offence relating to the duty to keep accounting records or the duties as to annual returns, auditors or members' superannuation schemes from a fine not exceeding level 3 on the standard scale to a fine not exceeding level 5 (currently £2,000). The new offence of failing to comply with any requirements by the CO or inspectors relating to the production of financial documents and the like will attract a similar penalty;
- providing that certain offences relating to falsification, destruction, alteration or mutilation of financial documents may result in imprisonment for up to six months, a fine of up to £5,000, or both;
- that instead of a six-month limit, proceedings under the Act should be possible at any time within three years of the relevant offence, provided that the information is laid before the court within six months of the discovery of the offence;
- providing that persons convicted of offences in connection with the financial affairs of trade unions are disqualified from being a member of a union's executive or from being president or general secretary of a union. The disqualification periods are five years or ten years, depending on the gravity of the offence;
- a new statutory duty for a trade union to provide each of its members, on an annual basis, with a written summary of its financial affairs. The statement is to include an indication of what the member may do if s/he suspects an irregularity in the conduct of the union's affairs;
- annual returns to the CO to identify the salary or other remuneration (including loans and benefits in kind) provided out of union funds to each member of the union's principal executive committee, president and general secretary and to include a statement of the number of names on the union's register of members and how many are not accompanied by an address.

Members' Right of Access to a Trade Union's Accounts

Prior to 1988 an ordinary member did not possess a statutory right to inspect the union's accounts, though s/he may have been given that right under the rule book. If there was such a right under the rules, then the member also had the right to be accompanied by an accountant or other agent when inspecting the accounts – see *Norey* v. *Keep* [1909] 1 Ch 561 and *Taylor* v. *NUM (Derbyshire Area)* [1985] IRLR 65.

The first *statutory* provision giving right of access to union records, whether or not there is an express rule, was provided by the Employment Act 1988. The relevant provisions are now contained in TULR(C)A. Unions must:

(a) make their accounting records available for inspection by members for six years beginning with 1 January following the end of the period to which the records relate (s. 29);

(b) give members (but only members) the right to inspect such records on request (s. 30 [1]);

(c) allow members the right to inspect the records in the company of an accountant (s. 30 [2] [b]);

(d) supply members with copies or extracts from any such records as they may require (s. 30 [2] [c]).

The union may exact a charge to cover reasonable administrative expenses.

Where it is claimed that a union has failed to comply with a request within 28 days, a member may apply to the court for an order requiring inspection and so forth. It is also a criminal offence to fail to keep accounting records available for inspection (s. 31).

Indemnification by Unions of Officials

Prior to 1988 it was not clear as to what extent (if any) a trade union might use its funds to indemnify members for criminal sanctions imposed upon them for activities such as illegal picketing, or for being held in contempt of court.

The issue was first raised in *Drake* v. *Morgan* [1978] ICR 56. During the journalists' strike in 1977, a number of members of the NUJ were charged with offences in connection with picketing and fined. The union's national executive committee passed a resolution that it would indemnify members in respect of these offences, with the exception of cases involving physical violence. The judge refused the application for an injunction to restrain the union from implementing this resolution, on the basis that the resolution had been passed *after* the offences had been committed and therefore there was not a general indemnity for members who might commit offences. He thought that different considerations might apply if continued resolutions authorising expenditure from funds might lead to an expectation that a union would indemnify its members against the consequences of future offences (see also *Thomas* v. *NUM [S Wales Area]* [1985] IRLR 136).

The government was of the view that the common law position was unsatisfactory. It was anxious to ensure that union officials should take the full legal consequences of unlawful acts, and that they should not rely upon indemnification by their unions.

The EA 1988 banned all forms of indemnity, retrospective or prospective. Once again the law is now set out in TULR(C)A. Section 15 makes it unlawful for a union's property to be applied for the purposes of indemnifying individuals for any penalty imposed by a court for:

(a) contempt of court; or

(b) a relevant criminal offence as set out in an order.

As McKendrick wryly observes: 'Thus, even the payment of an individual's parking fine by the union will be caught, unless it is exempted by order.'[13]

Remedy

If the property of the union is applied in a manner caught by s. 15, the union may recover its value from the individual indemnified (s. 15 [2]).

Any member who claims that the union is unreasonably refusing to take steps towards recovery may apply to the court for authority to take such proceedings on behalf of the union – at the union's expense (s. 15 [3]). This special provision overcomes the procedural difficulties which might otherwise be created by the rule in *Foss* v. *Harbottle* (1843) 2 Hare 461,[14] often applied to unions, which provides that where a wrong has been done to a corporate body, a minority of the members will be bound by a decision of the majority to take no legal action to remedy the wrong, if none of the members in the minority has personally suffered any harm.

Section 15 is without prejudice to any other enactment, trade union rule or provision which would otherwise make it unlawful for trade union property to be used in a particular way (s. 15 [6]). Thus the expenditure of money may be restricted to lawful objects or objects other than industrial action in the union rule book.

McKendrick observes:

> As was pointed out in the Green Paper ['Trade Unions and Their Members'], the incorporation of contempt of court opens up considerable 'scope for willing martyrdom' where individual members of the union are named by the plaintiff in the proceedings. In the NUM dispute martyrdom for Mr Scargill was avoided by an anonymous donor paying Mr Scargill's fine but, presumably, were such a fine to be paid in such a way in the future, union members would be able to exercise their right to inspect the union accounts to ensure that the fine was not paid by their union. It is rather surprising that the Government has seen fit to include a provision which increases, rather than decreases, the prospect of martyrdom when they have consistently sought to ensure that remedies are enforceable against union property rather than individual union members.[15]

Control of Union Trustees

It will be remembered that the property of a trade union is vested in trustees in trust for the union (TULR[C]A, s. 12 [1]). This arises because a union is an unincorporated association and so, not being a legal person, it cannot hold property in its own name.

Union officials in general owe a fiduciary duty to their union. In *Taylor* v. *NUM (Derbyshire Area) (No. 3)* [1985] IRLR 99, Mr Justice Vinelott held that union officers who sanctioned payments to unofficial strikers, where such payments were in breach of union rules, were liable to reimburse the trade union.

The role of union trustees came into sharp focus during the miners' strike when there were allegations that the trustees – Scargill, McGahey and Heathfield – were in breach of their fiduciary position through repeatedly being in contempt of court. In November 1984 a receiver was appointed on the grounds that the trustees were 'not fit and proper people to be in charge of other people's money'.

The Employment Act 1988 gave members new powers against trustees of the union's property in respect of the unlawful application of its assets, or in cases where the trustees comply with any unlawful direction given to them under the rules of the union. A claim may be brought where the trustees are proposing or have already acted in this way, but to bring a claim in the latter case the claimant must have been a member at the time when the property was applied or the unlawful direction complied with (see now TULR[C]A, s. 16).

Commenting on the section, Bowers and Auerbach observe that it is:

> Another measure designed to give members powerful and effective controls over the use of the union's property and funds, thought to be particularly needed in the context of a later dispute which the union may be waging in the face of the law and the courts. Once again, the litigation of the miners' strike has helped to focus minds on the problem and to suggest a solution. That litigation demonstrated that the courts will not hesitate to respond to individual member actions brought where the union or its officials are thought to be ignoring the rule book or otherwise behaving unlawfully. However, as the Green Paper (*Trade Unions and Their Members*, Paragraph 3.9) pointed out, a right for members to restrain union officials from sponsoring unlawful industrial action, or behaving in an unlawful way, might in practice prove ineffectual, if the situation has been reached where those officials are committed to defying the courts in any event. S.9 therefore adopts a different strategy which might prove more effective: that of aiming at the union's trustees, who are the legal holders and controllers of its property. The powers to remove trustees and to appoint a receiver can thus be used to take the assets completely out of reach and control of officials.[16]

The Orders Which can Be Made

The court can make such orders as it considers appropriate including:

(a) a requirement that the trustees take all steps specified to protect or recover the union's property;
(b) a power to appoint a receiver;
(c) a power to remove the trustees (s. 16 [3]).

Where the property of the union has been applied, or the trustees are proposing to apply the union's property:

(a) in contravention of the order of any court; or
(b) in compliance with any direction given in contravention of a court order

then the court must remove all trustees except any trustee who satisfies the court that there are good reasons for being allowed to remain as a trustee.[17]

Union Elections and Ballots

Imposition of balloting requirements has been a central feature of Conservative governments' industrial relations policy, although views on the efficacy of ballots have varied over time. The Donovan Commission in 1968 rejected compulsory strike ballots on the ground that North American experience showed that they are seen as 'tests of solidarity' and nearly always favour industrial action.

The IRA 1971 contained compulsory balloting procedures but they were only employed on one occasion, the railwayworkers' dispute of 1972, when the subsequent vote was 5-to-1 in favour of strike action.

The 1979 Conservative government again tried to encourage trade union ballots, providing subsidies from public funds under EA 1980. The Trade Union Act went further and required ballots before industrial action, for the principal executive committee and on retaining the political fund. The EA 1988 refined and modified these requirements and also introduced the office of commissioner for the rights of trade union members.

State Funds for Union Postal Ballots

This measure was enacted to encourage unions to hold secret ballots in the hope that 'responsible' union leaders would be elected. It enabled the Secretary of State to create a scheme for the refund of certain expenses incurred in conducting secret ballots. The scheme was contained in the Funds for Trade Union Ballots Regulations, SI 1984, No. 1654.

Most TUC unions at first refused to accept government funds as part of their overall policy of non-co-operation with the government's employment legislation. The exceptions were the Electrical, Electronic, Telecommunications, Plumbing Union (EETPU) and the AUEW, who were threatened with TUC discipline for doing so. This policy was subsequently reviewed and the decision whether or not to claim was left to individual unions. By the late 1980s many unions were claiming under the 1980 Act. In 1991, 78 unions made applications in respect of 716 ballots; the certification officer made payments during that year of £4 million. This contrasts with applications in respect of 30 ballots and payments amounting to £72,498 in 1984.

At the end of 1992 the Employment Secretary, Gillian Shepherd, announced plans to phase the scheme out over the next three years. In her view: 'the scheme now operates largely as a public subsidy for ballots which unions are required to carry out to meet their obligations under the law'.[18]

The scheme ceased to operate from 1 April 1996 (TURERA, s. 7 [4]) (see The Funds for Trade Union Ballots [Revocation] Regulations [SI 1993, No. 233]).

Executive Elections

By the Trade Union Act 1984 every voting member of the principal executive committee of a trade union had to be elected every five years by all members of the union. The Act overrode anything provided in the rule book of the union, and the union could face an enforcement order in the High Court. The Act also overrode any provision to the contrary in a contract of employment of any executive committee member relating to the tenure.

The 1984 Act related only to a voting member of the executive. But in certain unions the president or general secretary does not have a vote. Even if they had a vote, there was nothing to stop unions changing their rules by constitutional means – to remove the right to vote and therefore avoid the application of the Act. Indeed, such a rule change was carried out by the NUM in 1985 to remove its president's vote.

This was seen by the government to be a weakness in its legislative framework and the law was considerably heightened by what Smith and Wood[19] describe as the 'We'll Get Scargill This Time' amendments in the Employment Act 1988 (see now TULR[C]A, s. 46).

The EA 1988 extended the provisions for the periodic re-election of the members of the principal executive committee of each trade union to:

(a) non-voting members of the principal executive committee who attend and speak at some or all of its meetings;
(b) a union's president and general secretary or any equivalent position.

The provisions do not apply to persons who attend the principal executive committee merely to provide:

(a) factual information (such as a research officer);
(b) technical or professional advice (such as union solicitors or accountants). (TULR[C]A, s. 46 [2] [3])

The Conduct of the Ballot

The Trade Union Act 1984 stipulated a postal ballot as the norm, but went on to allow a trade union to opt for a semi- or full workplace ballot if the union was satisfied that there were no reasonable grounds to believe that this would not result in a free election as required by the Act. The 1987 Green Paper, however, pointed to 'concern over ... the non-postal ballot held in 1984 for the election of the Transport and General Workers Union's General Secretary and more recent Civil and Public Services Association elections for General Secretary', as a 'justification for examining this issue more closely'. In the government's view, postal ballots offered less scope for manipulation in the context of executive elections and political fund ballots. This is despite the fact that the most infamous example of union election malpractice, the Electrical Trade Union (ETU) case, involved a postal ballot. EA 1988 ensured that such ballots are to be held by postal voting only. Ballot papers must now both be sent out and returned by post.

Election Addresses

The aim of this provision of the Employment Act 1988 is to allow all candidates an equal opportunity to set out their 'manifesto'. The relevant rule is now set out in TULR(C)A, s. 48. Under this section:

(a) the union must give every candidate in the election the right to have an election address in his/her own words distributed to members entitled to vote;
(b) the union must secure so far as is reasonably practicable that a copy of each election address is distributed by post to each voter at his/her proper address;
(c) none of the candidates should be required to bear the expense of producing those copies;
(d) no modification of any election address must be made by the union save:
    (i) at the request of or with the consent of the candidate;
    (ii) where the modification is necessarily incidental to the method adopted for producing that copy.

The same method of producing copies must be applied to each election address and no facility or information should be given to one candidate but not to others in respect of:

(a) the method by which copies of the election addresses are produced (by photocopying or printing); or
(b) the modifications which are necessarily incidental to that method.

So far as is reasonably practicable, the union should also secure the same facilities and restrictions for all candidates in relation to:

(a) preparation of election addresses;
(b) submission of election addresses;
(c) length of election addresses;
(d) modification of election addresses;
(e) the incorporation of a photograph or any other matter not in words.

A union may impose restrictions, provided they are applied equally to all candidates, in respect of:

(a) the length of the address, subject to a minimum of 100 words; and
(b) photographs and any other matter not in words.

Moreover,

(a) a deadline for the submission of election addresses must not be earlier than the latest time at which a person may become a candidate at that election;
(b) no person other than the candidate him/herself shall be subject to civil or criminal liability in respect of any publication of a candidate's election address.

Independent Scrutiny of Ballots

Under TULR(C)A, s. 49, both political fund and principal executive committee ballots must be independently scrutinised. TURERA extends this requirement to industrial action ballots and a failure to subject the ballot to independent scrutiny will render any subsequent industrial action unlawful (see s. 20).

The independent scrutineer must satisfy conditions set down in an order made by the Secretary of State (s. 49 [2]). Under this order, the following may be scrutineers:

(a) a solicitors or accountant qualified to be an auditor;
(b) the Electoral Reform Society, the Industrial Society or Unity Security Services Ltd (TU Ballots and Elections Independent Scrutineers Qualifications) Order 1988 (SI 1988, No. 2117).

Section 49 (4) sets out the following duties for the scrutineers:

(a) supervision of production and distribution of all voting papers;
(b) to be the person to whom the voting papers are returned;
(c) to retain custody of all voting papers:
   (i) for one year after the announcement of the ballot result; and
   (ii) if any application is made under s. 54 (complaint of failure to comply with election requirements) or s. 79 (complaint of failure to comply with political fund ballot rules), for a period extending beyond the year until the certification officer or the High Court orders disposal of the papers;

(d)   as soon as is reasonably practicable after the last date for return of voting papers, to make a report to the union.

The scrutineer's report must state:

(a)   the number of voting papers distributed;
(b)   the number of voting papers returned;
(c)   the number of votes cast for each proposition or candidate, as the case may be;
(d)   the number of spoiled or otherwise invalid voting papers returned.

The scrutineer must also state whether s/he is satisfied that:

(a)   there was no reasonable grounds for believing that there was any contravention of a requirement imposed by statute;
(b)   reasonable practicable steps were taken with regard to the security arrangements for the production, storage, distribution, return or other handling of the voting papers so as to minimise the risk of any unfairness or malpractice which might occur;
(c)   the scrutineer has been able to carry out his/her functions without interference (s. 52 [1] [2]).

The trade union must not publish the result of the election/ballot until this report is received. A copy of the report must also be sent by the trade union to every member of the union within three months of its receipt of the report. Alternatively, the union must take such other steps for notifying members of the contents of the report as is its practice when matters of general interest to all members need to be brought to their attention (s. 52 [4]). Where the union does not send a copy of the report to each member, it must include a statement that the union will on request supply any member with a copy of the report either free of charge or on payment of a reasonable fee.

Enforcement of Rules on Elections and Ballots

- Complaint to the certification officer or High Court for a declaration.
- In complaints concerning improperly held elections, the complainant must have been a member at the date of the election and when the application is made to the court.
- If the complaint is that the election has not been held, the complainant must be a member on the date of the application.
- Action must be taken within one year from the default.
- The court (but only the court) has the power to make an enforcement order. Such an order will require the union to hold an election, to take such other steps to remedy the declared failure within a specified time, or to abstain from certain acts in the future. Failure to comply with the order amounts to a contempt of court.

Ballots before Industrial Action
Part II of the Trade Union Act 1984 withdrew certain of the immunities contained in s. 13 TULRA in respect of industrial action not approved by a ballot. So, under the

original formulation it was the employers who were seen to be the potential plaintiffs: it did *not* provide a cause of action to trade union members themselves.

At common law the members' rights are very restricted. The member may apply to the High Court for an interlocutory mandatory injunction requiring the union to hold a ballot in accordance with its rules, but such an action requires that there is a positive obligation under union rules to hold a ballot and, even in such a case, an interlocutory injunction may be refused because it is a 'very exceptional form of relief' (see *Taylor* v. *NUM [Yorkshire Area]* [1984] IRLR 445). The Green Paper, 'Trade Unions and Their Members', pointed out (para. 2.5) that in the miners' strike (1984/85) there were 19 common-law actions brought against the NUM under the rule book for failing to hold a ballot.

The Employment Act 1988 changed the position in line with the proposals contained in the Green Paper and provided a cause of action to members themselves. The complex rules surrounding ballots before industrial action are discussed in detail in Chapter 19.

The EA 1988 created the office of the Commissioner of the Rights of Trade Union Members (CRTUM). The Commissioner's main functions were to provide assistance to individuals taking or contemplating certain legal proceedings against unions or union officials. From its inception, CRTUM assisted, on average, ten applications a year. The Employment Relations Act 1999, s. 28, implements the government's proposals in Chapter 4 of *Fairness at Work* to abolish the office. The Act gives new powers to the Certification Officer to hear complaints involving most aspects of the law where CRTUM was previously empowered to provide assistance. Section 29 gives effect to sched. 6, which amends the statutory powers of the Certification Officer as set out in the 1992 Act. The overall effect is to widen the scope for trade union members to make complaints to the CO of alleged breaches of trade union law or trade union rules, thereby enlarging the CO's role as an alternative to the courts as a means to resolve disputes. The Act achieves this by giving the CO order-making powers in areas of trade union law where he previously made only declarations, and by extending his powers to make declarations and orders into areas where previously he had no competence to hear complaints and issue orders.

Conclusions on the Recent Legislation on Trade Unions and their Members

The Trade Union Act 1984, the Employment Act 1988, and the Trade Union Reform and Employment Rights Act 1993 extended far-reaching controls over the internal affairs of trade unions. In the name of 'giving the unions back to their members', the legislation attempts to dissipate the strength of organised labour. Nowhere is this better highlighted than in the dual standard adopted by the law in relation to striking workers and those who, in the face of majority vote in favour, refuse to take strike action. Striking union members could be dismissed by the employer with virtual impunity, but if a union disciplines members who have undermined the solidarity of a strike by remaining at work, the prospect of 'pools win' compensation levels looms into sight. Whilst, the Labour government has introduced a degree of unfair dismissal protection for those on official strike, it has no plans to relax the extensive legal controls over the internal affairs of trade unions.

CHAPTER 18

Collective Bargaining

Introduction

Collective agreements are one of the main sources of employment rights and obligations. The central role which they play in the employment relationship and workplace relations, can be seen at every stage of employment, from recruitment through to termination.[1]

As well as dealing with a wide range of workplace issues affecting employees, collectively and individually, they are important to unions in organisational terms. This is because they are also often a source of terms and details about the collective bargaining process itself, such as precedural rights, consultation, and workplace organisational rights, including arrangements for meetings and the dissemination of information. For this reason they are a key factor in the success or failure of a union as a representative organisation which can promote and defend its members' interests.

Yet collective agreements are only one aspect of the bigger collective bargaining process. There are other important functions undertaken by unions and workers' representatives at the workplace, including individual representation in the course of disputes and grievances, and acting on behalf of members. These are often essential in order to assert the specific rights which operate under collective agreements and procedures during the period they run, and before they are re-negotiated and revised. On occasion this means entering into supplementary arrangements, even if such arrangements made with the employer are not necessarily legally binding. Some, however, are – or at least they produce significant legal *consequences* for the employment relationship collectively or individually. Workforce agreements for the purposes of the Working Time Regulations 1998, SI 1998/1833 (as formally provided for in Schedule 1 to the regulations) are an example. Another is annualised working and pay regulation, or modifications of pay and overtime systems, of the type that featured in *Ali* v. *Christian Salvesen Food Services Ltd* (discussed in Chapter 7). In some cases the system depends heavily on such mechanisms for regulating substantive terms on pay, hours, occupational benefits, etc. It also looks to so-called 'procedural' agreements which often amount to little more than verbal understandings. Indeed, as part of its analysis of collective agreements the Report of the Royal Commission on Trade Unions and Employers Associations (1968, Cm. 3623, at p. 36) observed how in practice the bargaining system not only produces formalised agreements at periodic intervals. It also relies on a continuous, more informal, system of 'understandings' and 'tacit agreements'. Unions and their paid or lay officials also undertake representational and campaigning activities which influence social and economic policies, and industry or national decision-making. It goes without saying that, without a legal framework to sustain trade unions' and members' organisational rights in these processes, especially at their principal power-base, the workplace and through legal rights, a viable system for producing and revising collective agreements is simply not possible.

In the wider context, collective labour relations and bargaining processes are inextricably linked with citizenship rights, including the three main facets of civil, political, and social rights identified by T.E. Marshall in *Citizenship and Social Class*.[2] Whilst State interventions like the National Minimum Wage (NMW), tax credits, and the regulation of working hours, have a general welfare-led function of setting minimum standards across the *whole* labour market, collective bargaining has an important role in *supplementing* such pervasive, redistributive measures – at least in those particular industries and workplaces where it operates. Essentially, it operates as a further redistributive mechanism for the two sides of a collective labour relationship, but with a specific industry or workplace focus – and one which is more effectively within the control of the two sides to the agreement. Advocates of unfettered collective bargaining, and what has been termed 'collective laissez-faire', have stressed the value of having institutions that can operate autonomously of the State.[3] However, it is precisely because of such autonomy that collective bargaining has been seen by governments, policy makers and economists as one of the key regulators in the labour market which affect income redistribution and impact on production costs and profitability. It is for that reason that for successive governments it merits close regulation. Conservative policy makers, in particular, have for most periods in which the party has been in government seen it as necessary to reduce the impact of collective bargaining as a labour market regulator which maintains wage levels and conditions 'artificially high'. In one Conservative White Paper, for example, it saw the system as synonymous with union power, and generating excessive costs and on-costs; sustaining unacceptable workplace practices; and otherwise producing 'rigidities' in the market.[4] With the reintroduction of legal rights to recognition, and a generally more supportive framework for collective bargaining (including 'protected industrial action' since the Employment Relations Act 1999) some of the conditions for a return to workplace bargaining as a means of setting and revising wage levels, and regulating working conditions, have been restored or put in place. In theory, if collective bargaining, as a primary means of setting and maintaining working conditions were to be established, then the conditions for interventions like the NMW, tax credits, and social security as earnings supplements, replacement, etc., would be obviated or at least reduced. The reality is, of course, very different. Apart from the continuing absence of collective bargaining in many sectors of the labour market, the system is often very fragile where it does operate (due in part to reduced union membership). What economists characterise as 'suboptimal income distribution', which translates, basically as workers and their families are poorer than they could (or should) be, and the resulting low consumption produced by such poor wages, still pervade sizeable sections of the economy. As the figures on the high take-up of tax credits and other in-work welfare support clearly indicate (see Chapter 22) low wages and the problems this produces for workers (and for the economy) remain the main drivers for continuing with such statutory interventions.[5]

In this chapter the following aspects are considered:

- Collective Bargaining in the UK
- EC Policies and UK Rights
- Collective Agreements: Status and Effects
- Legal Enforceability
- Incorporation into Employment Contracts

- Collective Bargaining and Union Organisation
- Recognition
- Other Elements of Collective Bargaining

Collective Bargaining in the UK

Collective bargaining as a means of agreeing workplace terms and conditions has a long history, and has been established in the UK since at least the eighteenth century, even if unions (or 'combinations') were not legalised until the Combination Laws Repeal Act 1824. However, unions' organisational rights, immunities from legal action, and freedom to function as independent workplace and national organisations have not always been so well established and recognised. The collective bargaining process received official encouragement after World War I, when joint industrial councils representing 'both sides' of industry were formed to negotiate, agree and periodically revise industry-wide agreements. This important development came at a time when there was intense debate between trade unionists about what the industrial role of unions should be, and how, and to what extent, they should be involved in fixing workers' terms and conditions.[6] As the Donovan Commission, in its 1968 report considered, the collective bargaining system developed in a piecemeal way and without much in the way of a coherent structure.

The attraction of collective agreements, however, is that they offer employers and unions consistency in setting and maintaining terms and conditions – and an effective means of revising them. In terms of international law, collective bargaining, and the processes that support it, is the main element in the general 'freedom of association' underpinned by key legal sources, namely the Universal Declaration of Human Rights, which in its adoption of the right to form and join trade unions for the protection of a person's interests implicitly extends to collective bargaining arrangements;[7] the European Convention for the Protection of Human Rights and Fundamental Freedoms 1950 (ECHR) art. 11;[8] and the International Labour Organisation Convention 1949 (Convention No. 98). Last, but by no means least, a new EC Social Charter was introduced in 1989, and includes as one of its 'fundamental social rights of workers' the 'right to conclude collective agreements'. More recently, there has been the Charter of Fundamental Rights of the European Union which will operate as part of the forthcoming EC Constitution. In regard to aspects like collective labour relations it will take effect in line with EC Law and national laws and practices and the Union's developing programme on employment and social policy discussed in Chapter 1. As discussed in Chapter 5 when considering the rights of workers on 'transfers', and the *Wilson* case, it is important to appreciate that there are many areas of EC law where the detailed interpretation of the legal effects of collective agreements, and transactions which affect workers, is left to national law and practice. In this respect the Charter itself does not, in itself, change things or have legal effect. Indeed, the UK was in the forefront of those seeking to ensure that it should *not* have legal effect in areas of employment and social policy like this, as noted by commentators at the time the basic principles of the Charter were agreed.[9] While that may be correct, and it was indeed a factor in resolving the *BECTU* case on the Working Time Regulations (discussed in Chapter 8), the collective bargaining system itself has not been accorded any additional specific protections in EC Law – largely, it would seem, because the process *already* enjoys protection as part of the general principle of 'freedom of contract'.[10] Nor is there in ECHR or EC law a legal right to recognition, or to protection of recognition arrangements, it would seem. This was considered in the *Wilson and Palmer* case in 2002 in the European Court of Human Rights as discussed below. The ECHR is incorporated in UK law by the Human Rights Act 1998, but to date this is an area of national competence in which there have been few inroads made by the ECHR.

The system in the UK that has developed, to date, includes bargaining arrangements at national, intermediate and workplace levels. In some cases national agreements are comprehensive, dealing with both procedural issues (such as the machinery for settling disputes, and redundancy selection) and more central issues like pay, hours and entitlements. An increasingly common approach, though, is that national agreements merely set *minimum* conditions, leaving it to local negotiations and agreements (or management discretion in some cases) to adopt those conditions, and apply them according to particular requirements and conditions at a workplace level.

Depending on the particular economic climate at the time, employers and unions have see-sawed between preferences for national, centralised bargaining or more 'localised' bargaining arrangements; and the picture can vary greatly between different industries and types of employment. This will also depend on the relative strengths and weaknesses of the unions involved.

Collective Bargaining 1968 to 1997

Soon after the Donovan Commission reported in 1968,[11] the collective bargaining system came under close political scrutiny. Worsening industrial relations problems were put down to a mixture of causes, but principally the uncertainty and unenforceability of collective agreements. 'Excessive union power' in workplaces was also identified by some sections of management, and politicians on the right, as a factor in undermining the stability of the collective agreement system. Such conclusions had not, in fact, been reached by Donovan. However the Commission did criticise the problems that can occur when workplace bargaining displaces, or overlaps with, agreements negotiated at a sectoral or national level. The report also identified a need for more orderly procedures resulting from decentralised power in some unions. But it specifically rejected calls to make unions' procedural obligations, and procedure agreements themselves legally enforceable; or to make arrangements for unions subject to more regulation (paras. 260–268). The courts by this time were also reluctant to treat collective agreements as legally enforceable – largely because of the difficulties of enforcement; *Ford Motor Co., Ltd* v. *Amalgamated Union of Engineering and Foundry Workers* [1969] 2 All ER 481. Nevertheless, the Industrial Relations Act 1971 was brought in to do exactly that, and it included a provision that collective agreements *were* to be presumed to be legally enforceable – something that had not been attempted since the nineteenth century. There were also elaborate arrangements made for making it an 'unfair industrial practice' to take industrial action which broke agreements (with punishing sanctions for unions and those concerned). This was facilitated by setting up a specialised court, the National Industrial Relations Court. The position was changed by the incoming Labour government in 1974, when agreements were, once again, 'conclusively presumed' not into be legally enforceable unless they are in writing, and there is a provision in it stating an intention that it should be enforceable; TULR(C)A s. 179. This has remained the position to date.

Since then, government policies towards collective bargaining have been contradictory under both Labour and the Conservatives. Labour has, at various times, tried to introduce greater elements of compulsion into the bargaining process, as seen when the Wilson government made reform proposals that were completely unacceptable to the labour movement.[12] But at the same time Labour legislation did try to *develop* collective bargaining, and put the system onto a more coherent footing, primarily by establishing statutory rights to recognition, giving unions legal rights to information for bargaining purposes, and giving the Advisory Conciliation and Arbitration Service (ACAS) a significant role in this. There was in the 1960s and 1970s a broad consensus on the desirability of such State support for collective bargaining.[13]

Conservative policy was, in theory, tolerant of the collective bargaining system, particularly in the initial phase of government after 1979. No doubt this was because it could still offer, particularly for larger enterprises, a disciplined framework within which corporate managements could operate. At the same time, however, the thrust of industrial relations policies, and then legislation, started to be directed against unions organisationally. Nor was there any attempt to develop or maintain procedures to give unions the ability to function effectively. The 1980s was a period in which Conservative legislation saw the progressive dismantling of the legislative framework supporting trades unions. These included the removal, or restrictions on, legal rights to recognition, union membership and organisational rights, and an individual's right to union representation (a right which was generally better established in other comparable jurisdictions and in international law).[14] There was also a reluctance to introduce effective rights to information and consultation. In the case of recognition procedures – an aspect of collective bargaining that was already fragile after two largely ineffectual schemes under the Industrial Relations Act 1971 ss. 44–60 and the Employment Protection Act 1975 ss. 11–21 – the mechanisms in place in 1979 for securing formal recognition were speedily removed by the Employment Act 1980. Even before that happened, the statutory recognition system had suffered a major body-blow at the hands of the judiciary in the House of Lords case of *Grunwick Processing Laboratories* v. *Advisory Conciliation and Arbitration Service* [1978] AC 655 – a decision which enabled a determined employer to obstruct the conduct of a ballot of workers in recognition disputes. Moreover, even where recognition arrangement remained in place (on a voluntary basis) – something which received no official encouragement from the government – there was no duty on UK employers to negotiate effectively (or at all) if they were unwilling to do so. Nor was there any requirement for employers to negotiate in good faith (unlike other countries, including the United States) in order to reinforce the responsibilities of employers in the bargaining process.

A further body blow to the collective bargaining process, and which significantly weakened the union side of it, was the government's (and sometimes the courts') attack on the closed shop in its various forms. In many cases the closed shop operated as an informal understanding, or custom and practice, wherby workers would join, and remain in, the union which bargained with their employer. The benefits, as well as any negative changes, in the bargains made from time to time would accrue to those members. In its more formalised state the system could be reinforced by a union membership agreement whereby the employer agreed with the union – either in a free-standing agreement, or as part of a wider-ranging collective agreement – to make it a condition of the worker's contract of employment that she should join and remain in the union. Some agreements permitted an employee to opt-out of this – for example on payment of an equivalent amount to union dues to a charity. Such arrangements suited both the employer and union. Not only did this make collective bargaining more cohesive, it also maintained consistency in terms and conditions. It also, of course, strengthened the union's ability to mount effective industrial action during disputes, and enabled it to exercise discipline over members at such times, and generally. In four successive Employment Acts between 1980 and 1990 legislation removed the legal basis for such arrangements, despite evidence going back to 1971 that the closed shop was widely in use and generally favoured by many employers and unions. Despite the introduction that year (in the Industrial Relations Act 1971) of a right *not* to join a union, the Act also rendered a dismissal 'fair' if the dismissal of an employee refusing to join (or remain) in the union occurred as a result of a legally effective union membership agreement. Such conditional legal support for the practice probably met with the approval of most companies involved in collective bargaining, and explains why they tended to discourage individuals from opting out of union membership, as suggested in a study by Brian Weekes and others *Industrial Relations and the Limits of Law: The Industrial Effects of the Industrial Relations Act 1971* (1975). An important factor that legitimised the post-1980 reforms was the judgment of the European Court of Human Rights in *Young James and Webster* v. *United Kingdom* [1981] IRLR 408; [1983] IRLR 35 that to the effect that the right to freedom of association in art. 11 of the ECHR encompasses a right *not* to belong to a union. The judgment also criticised a system that depends on compulsion and potential loss of employment. The present law in TULR(C)A does not specifically make the closed shop illegal. It simply renders it ineffective. For example, s. 69 implies a term in all contracts between a union member and the union preserving the right to terminate membership. Part III of the Act then regulates relations between the employer and employee, for example by making it unlawful to refuse a person employment who is not a union member, or who is unwilling to become (or remain) a member; s. 137. Dismissal is automatically unfair if the reason, or principal reason, was not being a union member; ss. 152, 153.

The impact of these changes on the collective bargaining process is clear. While many employers are still keen to maintain collective bargaining, and to keep the advantages it provides, the absence of a closed shop (or similar arrangement) means that the employer may often be bargaining with a union which may, in fact, only represent a small proportion of the employer's staff. From the employer's point of view it is necessary to ensure that there is a term in all individuals' contracts of employment to the effect that terms and conditions are in accordance with the collective agreement negotiated with the union, and as revised from time to time: and that this term is maintained throughout the relationship in order to maintain the 'bridge' between the collective agreement and the individual contract. This is essential given that the union will not be the agent for non-union members of staff; *Singh* v. *British Steel Corporation* [1974] IRLR 131. In the absence of such a so-called 'bridging term' the only other basis on which employees' terms and conditions could become subject to the collective bargain is an *implied* bridging term and custom and practice; *Henry* v. *London General Transport Services Ltd* [2002] IRLR 472, CA.

The migration of workers out of union membership, and out of collective bargaining systems, was also assisted by court decisions on 'personal contracts'. There was a spate of important cases which opened the door to a flurry of derecognition decisions throughout industry, and the start of a period of transition to alternative systems, including 'personal contracts'.

Personal Contracts

In *Wilson* v. *Associated Newspapers* [1995] 2 All ER 100, [1995] IRLR 258, HL, a particularly important leading case – which undoubtedly had a serious impact on collective bargaining arrangements – the House of Lords refused to accept that a financial inducement in the form of an offer of a 4.5 per cent wage increase, backdated by three months, in return for signing a personal contract with the company before the expiry of the collective agreement it had with the NUJ, the journalists' union, was barred out by the legislation as a form of 'action short of dismissal' taken against staff for the purpose of preventing or deterring them from being union members. Nor did it penalise them for their union membership.[15] In the *Wilson* case the employer had already announced in a letter to staff that it was not renewing a recognition agreement with the union, which until then had represented staff in negotiations on pay and conditions. On the face of it such action *was*, plainly, directed at preventing or deterring union membership – or at least it involved a form of penalty for remaining loyal to the union and preferring to have terms and conditions negotiated by the union. It also appeared to be well within the intended scope of the legislation, and the objective of barring out penalising workers for being in a union.[16] However, the tribunal's finding in favour of the employee (and the decision of the Court of Appeal upholding it) was overturned by the House of Lords. The government then moved speedily to legislate to impede further such litigation. It was indicative of the government's hostility to collective bargaining that soon after the Court of Appeal decision – even before the Lords' judgment – a late change in the Trade Union Reform and Employment Rights Act 1993 was hastily introduced at a late stage in the Lords debates on the Bill (the Ullswater amendment). This stipulated that even where an employer *was* found to have infringed employees' rights – this could be disregarded if the employer's motive was 'to further a change in the relationship' with employees. The full effects of this change are reversed in the proposed Employment Relations Act 2004, Part 3. Among other things a new TULR(C)A s. 145A has the right not to have an offer made by the employer for the purpose of inducing him to be or not to be a union member.

After the Lords' decision applications were made to the European Court of Human Rights asserting infringements of arts. 10, 11, and 14, based on the failure of the collective labour relations' system to maintain union rights, and infringment of Convention rights on the freedom of association, freedom of expression, and discrimination. These eventually led to favourable court decisions directed at protecting union members against such discrimination – but not until 2002.[17]

Despite these formidable setbacks, collective bargaining and the collective agreement system itself, has continued. It also functions notwithstanding significant changes in patterns of employment and a decline in union membership. 'Collective bargaining', observed ACAS in 1988, 'remains the dominant determinant, either directly or indirectly, of the terms and conditions of the majority of employees'.[18] That may have been correct, but the impact of Conservative policies and other factors were, by then, starting to reduce the proportion of UK workers with terms and conditions determined by collective agreements.[19] The process of moving workers out of collective arrangements accelerated, as well, after employers saw how easy it was to do, no doubt helped by the publicity given to high-profile cases of derecognition by large companies. This was a development charted by Robert Taylor in *The Future of Trade Unions*.[20] Intensification of ownership and control of companies, corporate takeovers and mergers and 'transfer' activity also put pressure on collective employment arrangements. Ironically, though, collective agreements have played a pivotal role in facilitating changes in corporate ownership and control, sometimes enabling transfers of large numbers of employees to take place between employers – or, more controversially, often facilitating job losses and diminution in terms and conditions. In many cases unions had little choice but to co-operate in much of the restructuring activity taking place. Needless to say such changes generally serve to undermine union membership and organisation, with acceptance of job losses or radical reductions in working conditions often being the price of preventing complete business closures and even more redundancies, as in *Ali v. Christian Salvesen Ltd* (Chaper 7) or *Wilson and others v. St Helens BC* (Chapter 5).

In the 1980s the pace of corporate takeovers and mergers quickened. So, too, did 'reconstructions': that is to say a process by which a company in voluntary liquidation can authorise the liquidator to sell off the business or parts of it in return for shares in the company to whom the assets are sold. The shares are then transferred to the shareholders of the company in liquidation. As with changes in ownership in the course of an involuntary liquidation, i.e. by liquidators and receivers, there is scope for such changes to be subject to the TUPE Regulations 1981, as discussed in Chapter 5. Indeed the transfer process is facilitated by TUPE. at the point of change collective arrangements, procedures, and collective agreements, should also, in theory (under TUPE regs. 4–6) 'transfer', and enjoy continuity. Under TUPE reg. 9, a union recognised by a transferor is also entitled to go on being recognised, after any transfer, by the transferee employer. In reality, transfers in the UK are often an opportunity for business owners and managers to make significant changes in bargaining arrangements – changes which may, indeed, see their disappearance altogether. This was made easier, at least until the reintroduction of a statutory process since 2000, by the absence of restrictions on derecognition, including the provision in TUPE reg. 9 (2) permitting agreements for recognition to be subsequently varied or rescinded. Nevertheless, it is still not unusual for a transferor employer to try to go further, and not just erode recognition and union bargaining rights, but to terminate collective agreements entered into by the previous employer. Whilst there is nothing to prevent a transferor employer withdrawing from collective agreements, even where there is still 'recognition' of the union, the consequences are not always clear. For example such withdrawal does not necessarily prevent the transferor's staff continuing to benefit from collective arrangements that may still operate having already 'crossed over' into individual contracts, or where the *process* of wage and conditions determination has already been established contractually. Thus in *Whent v. T Cartledge Ltd* [1997] IRLR 153 employees of Brent Council found themselves working for a private contractor who withdrew recognition from their union, and then purported to end the application of collective agreements made by their union with Brent Council prior to the transfer. In fact, during the Brent period, it was established that terms and conditions would be in line with the collective agreement made under a national joint council. That machinery was held to *continue* to apply as a result of TUPE reg. 5; and the staff could therefore insist on pay rates set by the NJC arrangements – despite the new employer no longer being a party to any such 'agreement'. Satisfactory though this position might seem it does not necessarily preserve continuity in every case. In any case it is only viable pending the expiry of the collective agreement or arrangements, or their displacement by another agreement – a position now facilitated by Dir. 2001/23, art. 3. Nor is it necessarily the case that all collective terms are always *apt* for incorporation into individual contracts in this way. In the context of 'contractualisation' and privatisation of governmental and local services it is very likely that employers of the kind in the *Whent* case may be very reluctant to continue to observe procedural or substantive rights for any longer than they are obliged to.

In the public sector, where compulsory competitive tendering, and then later versions like 'best value', were forced on local authorities and the NHS, collective bargaining was continued even in the face of privatisation and what, in some sectors, was an onslaught on workers' pay and conditions resulting from transfers to private contractors. In many instances unions had little choice but to negotiate reductions in pay and other entitlements, as seen in *Burke* v. *Royal Liverpool University Hospital NHS Trust* (referred to in Chapter 7) – a process which has continued. Unfortunately such involuntary changes were the price that often had to be paid to preserve bargaining systems.

EC Policies and UK Rights

Besides initiatives affecting collective bargaining through measures like Dir. Nos. 77/187 and 2001/23 on transfers of undertakings there have, in fact, been other early directives designed to assist collective rights. Examples include, Dir. 75/129 on collective redundancies, and Dir. 80/987 on insolvency. These provided unions with important workplace consultation and other procedural rights. Since then the EC has developed newer forms of participative rights based on 'partnership' and 'co-determination' (including representation on company boards).

The directive on European Works Councils (Dir. 94/95), which came into operation in September 1996, was implemented in the UK by the Transnational Information and Consultation of Employees Regulations 1999, SI 1999/3323 (from 15 January 2000). It requires a European Works Council, or information and consultation procedure (ICP) for the purpose of informing and consulting employees, to be set up in every 'Community-scale undertaking' if this is requested by at least 100 employees, or by employee representatives. The central management and a special negotiating body (established in accordance with art. 5 [2] and the regulations) must negotiate in a spirit of co-operation with a view to reaching agreement on prescribed arrangements and implementing information and consultation objectives. 'Community-scale undertaking is defined as an undertaking with at least 1,000 employees within the Member States, and applies to enterprises with at least 1,000 employees (or which have at least 150 employees in each of at least two Member States). The system has already led to significant changes, and new bargaining practices, in the larger UK and European companies; and it must be seen as a major development in collective labour law as suggested by Janice Bellace in *The European Works Council Directive: Transnational Information and Consultation in the European Union* in 'Comparative Labour Law Journal' (1997) 325. Such councils, and variants on the works council theme designed to give all staff participative rights, do not necessarily impact on established collective bargaining structures – although some UK unions are understandably wary when employers initiate their establishment. The directive's recognition and consultation requirements, for example with regard to the required Special Negotiation Bodies, and other mandatory procedures, has proven problematic in the UK. In some cases, proposals to introduce works councils have prompted unions with existing recognition arrangements to request more formalised recognition using the statutory procedure.[21]

'Europeanisation'

The realities of globalistion, and transnational aspects of business operations, have been taken on board by EC employment policies. Specifically, legislation caters for

'Europeanisation' of bargaining systems, and Europe-wide bargaining structures to reflect the increasing number of employers operating transnationally, and 'cross-border' mergers.[22] As well as formally establishing the right of employers' and workers' organisations to negotiate and conclude collective agreements (something UK legislation has never comprehensively done), art. 12 of the EC Charter of the Fundamental Social Rights of Workers (adopted by EC Heads of State and government on 10 December 1989) established the principle that 'the dialogue between the two sides of industry at European level which must be developed, may, if the parties deem it desirable, result in contractual relations, in particular at inter-occupational and sectoral level'. Guidelines on employment practices issued by the EC Commission since 1998 have also been directed at collective arrangements in key respects.

European norms in relation to collective bargaining, although they have positive features, can be criticised in important respects. A legal *duty* on employers to bargain with, or recognise, unions, for example, is not universally established throughout the European Community,[23] and neither the Action Programme for implementing the Social Charter, nor Guidelines have adequately addressed this problem.[24] Whilst the EC eventually adopted Regulation 2157/2001, and provided for the establishment of a European company (or 'SE'), arrangements made to date to accompany this important development do not go as far as they should, and fall a long way short of establishing clear union recognition, bargaining, and other participatory rights needed. Measures like Directive 2001/86, supplementing the Statute for a European Company, establish a basic negotiating machinery and employee 'involvement' rights, and a number of important principles such as the preservation of any acquired rights in employees' involvement in corporate decision-making established prior to the establishment of an SE. There is, however, still a substantial deficit in terms of legal requirements to establish and maintain basic bargaining systems.[25] In addition, some EC countries impose restraints on workplace bargaining that many UK trade unionists would find unacceptable.

In the UK the emphasis has generally been on voluntarism, but now reinforced by prescription when voluntary arrangements cannot be agreed. This can be seen in the preamble to the Trade Union Recognition (Method of Collective Bargaining) Order 2000, SI 2000/1300, where it refers to 'most' voluntary procedural agreements between employers and unions not being legally binding; and being concluded in a climate of trust and co-operation, so that bargaining processes do not need to be 'prescriptive'.

Labour Government Policies

In its election manifesto before coming to power, New Labour gave a clear commitment to reintroducing a balloting procedure by which workers could realise their wish to establish formal recognition by their employer of their union, and thereby establish basic collective bargaining procedures. Indeed, such empowerment was seen as an integral element in New Labour's social inclusion agenda, as explained by commentators like Martin Powell in *New Labour, New Welfare State: The Third Way in British Social Policy* (1999). Arrangements for implementing this, including detailed aspects such as the size of the majority required in a ballot for approval (and whether it should be a majority of those working for a business, or of those *voting*), proved problematic in the opening period of the Labour government. The impetus for delivering on this commitment was highlighted by high-profile recognition disputes like the 1998 one at Noon's Products. Despite 90 per cent of the workforce being members of the GMB union, the company *still* refused to accord recognition.[26]

Collective Agreements: Status and Effects

Before considering present arrangements on recognition, and bargaining methods, it is necessary to consider what collective agreements do, and their limitations. Although a collective agreement may have the characteristics of a contract – that is, there may be two parties (or 'sides') to it, and it contains rights and obligations – it is *not* in most cases a contract. Typically, collective agreements contain two types of provisions. The first are what are sometimes called 'substantive' or 'normative' terms dealing with issues like pay, overtime, hours and holidays. Second, they will often set out procedures for dealing with industrial relations issues and problems, for example representation on joint bodies, works councils, and procedures for dealing with individual and collective disputes.[27]

Agreements can be lengthy and very detailed documents, or they may amount to little more than locally agreed understandings, for instance based on a dialogue between a personnel manager and workplace shop stewards. There is no prescribed format for them, nor are there any legal requirements governing their content or how they are made. How they are expressed, and their intended scope, purposes and so on, will be relevant, though, if there is any argument about incorporation into the individual contract of employment and the legal enforceability of its terms, as discussed in the next section.

Legal Enforceability

A collective agreement generally operates on two levels. In the first place it is an agreement between the union(s) and employer(s) who made it. Second, as the agreement may have been made for *other* parties, that is, the workers and employers it covers, it may be the basis of more extensive rights and obligations (as considered in Chapter 4). In particular, all or some of its contents may be 'incorporated' into the individual contracts of employment between the workers and employers expressly within its scope. In some cases it may also be incorporated into *other* workers' contracts, for example those of any non-union members whose individual contracts state that agreements made between the union and the employer will apply to them; and workers in organisations where the employer has decided to adopt the agreement.

Employer(s) and Union(s)

Legislation, and the courts when they have had to deal with the issue, generally do not treat collective agreements as legally binding between the parties who make them. This has largely been due to the difficulties of interpreting and enforcing them, and because there is no tradition in industry of treating them as enforceable. It is also a recognition that employers and unions have preferred the use of industrial relations procedures to using the courts.[28] Following a brief period between 1971 and 1974 when there was a legal presumption in the Industrial Relations Act 1971 that agreements were enforceable, the position is now back to where it was. Specifically, the Trade Union and Labour Relations (Consolidation) Act 1992, s. 179, says that collective agreements are to be conclusively presumed *not* to have been intended to be legally enforceable unless they are in writing and clearly provide that they are to be legally enforceable.[29]

The practical effect of this position is that employers cannot sue unions (nor can they themselves be sued) to enforce the terms of a collective agreement.

'Incorporation' into Employment Contracts

The system by which collective agreements, or parts of them, become part of an individual's contract of employment has already been outlined in Chapter 4 above. That process is assisted by the legislative requirements in the ERA Part I that collective agreement terms which directly affect individuals' employment must be included in their written statement of initial particulars (see Chapter 4). From the union's point of view it will have a continuing interest, after a collective agreement has been made or revised, in ensuring that its terms *are* being properly observed. In practice most breaches and non-implementation are dealt with at an industrial relations level, either by the operation of 'disputes' procedures or through negotiations. Ultimately the union, or its members, may consider industrial action if the point in issue is sufficiently serious. The need for unions to have to do this is, of course, indicative of the problems associated with collective bargaining and the present legal regime that sustains it. Conciliation, mediation and arbitration may be possible to break a deadlock or to end a dispute, with arbitration providing a means of reaching a definitive and binding settlement of the point of difference. If the agreement itself does not contain disputes procedures, ACAS can provide conciliation, mediation and arbitration services.[30]

Taking Legal Action

For a variety of reasons, though, there may be no alternative to legal action, particularly if one side will not accept arbitration or other procedures, or because it is determined to pursue a particular course of action. It is not unusual for agreements (or important parts of them) to be terminated unilaterally, or simply to be ignored. In this case the scope for legal action will depend on whether individual members who have rights under the collective agreement *can* take action. As we have seen, the union itself cannot do so. In this sense members may be acting as the union's 'proxy'. Although the union may provide financial support and encouragement, a member does not need the union's formal support to take action.

There are many situations in which legal action will not be possible because the rights, which may be very important ones for both the union and its members, are not regarded as 'suitable' for incorporation. The courts may also decide that the rights in the collective agreement are rights of the union but not of its members. This artificial distinction can mean that the withdrawal of important collective rights like recognition of the union, organisational rights for its workplace representatives, consultation and participation procedures, and many other collective entitlements, can be undertaken without any legal means of prevention. The only way in which such action might be blocked is on the basis that the employer's action also infringes a personal entitlement which has become incorporated into an individual's contract. An example might be where a collective agreement gives a workplace representative rights to time off in lieu for approved industrial relations work that s/he does; or, possibly, personal facilities like accommodation expenses for union responsibilities.

In practical terms, though, such rights can be very hard to enforce in the courts, other than under ERA tribunal procedures when time off is unreasonably refused (see below).

Example
Following an industrial occupation at a hospital that was due to be closed, a shop steward was suspended from his job and barred from the building. He was successful, at first, in getting an injunction to lift the health authority's action. The Court of Appeal then reversed this decision. Even if the collective agreement gave a shop steward representational rights, and these operated on a personal level, the right depended on the normal continuation of the employment relationship between the employer and the person concerned. This was not the position following the suspension.[31]

'Implied' Rights

The absence of any formal statement in the member's individual contract, as evidenced by the statutory written statement, letter of appointment etc., expressly incorporating the relevant part of the collective agreement is not necessarily fatal to the member's (and union's) position. It may be possible, as discussed in Chapter 4 above, to demonstrate that particular parts of a collective agreement are implied. The difficulties of doing this, though, can be seen in cases where the courts have refused to accept that agreed redundancy procedures operate as a contractual 'right' when it actually comes to deciding how workers are to be selected for redundancy. See, the *Standard Telephones and Cables* case, discussed in Chapter 15 above. Other 'procedural' rights, such as disputes procedures, have also been held not to be incorporated.[32]

The Effects of Incorporation

Assuming the terms of a collective agreement *have* been effectively incorporated into members' contracts, there are a variety of practical consequences for both the union and members. Collectively, the position is strengthened because there will be scope to take court action to prevent breaches of members' rights taking place. In one case, for example, it was held that a guarantee payment scheme for dockworkers could not be terminated, as the scheme formed an integral part of their terms and conditions.[33] Individual members can obviously sue for entitlements given to them in the agreement, if necessary in a test case on behalf of other workers also covered by its terms. Conversely, where a collective agreement (even if it is only in the form of 'an exchange of letters') reduces entitlement, this can operate to *reduce* key rights to wages. This important point was confirmed in *Burke v. Royal Liverpool University Hospital NHS Trust* [1997] ICR 730 EAT (when an NHS union agreed to pay cuts in order to keep domestic services 'in house' rather than see the work transferred to another provider).

The terms of an agreement may also be the central issue in dismissal and constructive dismissal cases. Management's powers under an agreement to move workers between jobs and work locations are frequently tested in the context of such cases. Although there are examples of where collectively agreed 'mobility' arrangements are incorporated, and therefore do give a management the power it claims,[34] there is no hard and fast rule on the point. The outcome will depend – as in all incorporation issues – on the term in question, the intentions of the parties making the collective agreement (and the individual contract), and the particular circumstances in each case.

Procedural Requirements on 'Termination'

Even where an employer provides for schemes dealing with such matters as long-term sickness benefit, which have been incorporated into the individual contract of employment, and the arrangements also provide for such rights to be withdrawn (for example by a termination in the agreement), such termination must be properly effected. In an important case, *Bainbridge* v. *Circuit Foil UK Ltd* [1997] IRLR 305, the Court of Appeal treated an employee's rights under such a scheme as *continuing* when the employee had not been informed and notified of the changes.

Collective Bargaining and Union Organisation

For collective bargaining to work effectively, and for employees' interests to be properly represented in the process, unions must have the ability to function properly at national, regional, and workplace levels. Restrictions on trade unions are discussed elsewhere, in particular in relation to trade union government, and industrial action, in the previous chapter. In relation to collective bargaining, consideration must be given to certification, recognition, time off and facilities for union representatives and for union activities, disclosure of information, and the other essential elements that sustain the collective bargaining system. By the time the Employment Act 2004 is enacted there will be clarification of the precise rights of unions in the process of gaining recognition using the statutory procedure (see below), and in relation to the complex requirements relating to industrial action ballots and notices following a breakdown in the collective bargaining system.

Certification and Collective Bargaining

If a union is on the list kept by the certification officer it is entitled to a certificate that it is 'independent'.[35] Basically, this requires it to be free from domination or control of an employer or employers' organisation, and it should not run the risk of interference as a result of financial or other powers an employer might have. Not all organisations can meet these requirements, particularly smaller employer-financed staff associations.[36]

Certification is important for collective bargaining purposes because it is the key to significant bargaining rights. 'Independence' is generally a legal precondition for such rights. In most cases it must also be shown that the union is recognised by the employer (as discussed below). The most important rights are:

- time off for employees to take part in union activities (see Chapter 8 above);
- protection against dismissal, unfair selection for redundancy, 'detriment' etc., on union grounds, for employees who are members;
- information needed by union representatives for collective bargaining purposes (see below);

- information and consultation when there is a transfer of the employer's business (see below);
- details and supplementary information about pensions and employers' occupational pension scheme arrangements;
- time off for representatives to have industrial relations training (see Chapter 8);
- notification and consultation rights when collective redundancies are proposed by the employer (see Chapter 15);
- 'requests' under the statutory recognition procedure.

Recognition

Recognition by the employer of a union's right to negotiate terms and conditions on behalf of its members is an essential prerequisite to the collective bargaining process. Apart from establishing the employer's formal support, it opens the door to important statutory rights, including disclosure of information for bargaining purposes; consultation on transfers of undertakings; health and safety; training; contracting out of State pension arrangement; and redundancy dismissals. In formal terms 'recognition' simply means that an employer has agreed, or is required to discuss terms that will cover that employer's employees, either on all workplace issues or for more limited purposes. TULR(C)A s. 178 (3) defines 'recognition' in relation to a trade union as 'recognition by an employer, or two or more associated employers, to any extent, for the purpose of collective bargaining. It can be formally recorded, for example in correspondence or an agreement, or, more problematically, it can be implicit from previous dealings between the employer and union. If recognition is achieved using the statutory route it means that the union is entitled to conduct collective bargaining on behalf of a group, or groups, of workers in a specific bargaining unit. However, in this case the normal, wide definition of 'collective bargaining' in TULR(C)A s. 178 (1) is displaced by the more restrictive meaning of 'collective bargaining', referring to negotiations on pay, hours, and holidays or 'agreed matters' in Schedule A1, para. 3 (3), (4). This preserves the opportunity for the parties to reach agreement on bargaining on other areas of employment in addition to pay, hours, and holidays as well; para. 3 (4).

Recognition can take place at different levels. An employer can operate through an employers' association, and with other employers recognise a union (or unions) for the purposes of agreeing industry-wide arrangements. Recognition, however, may be more 'localised'. In the 1980s there was a tendency, particularly among some large employers, to break away from industry-wide arrangements. There have also been other important trends that have affected the position. In particular, there has been a movement away from multi-union representation in favour of the establishment of single-union and other bargaining structures. As considered below, the statutory procedure for recognition requires the CAC to look closely at applications, and in some cases they may not proceed at the 'admissibility' stage if more than one union is proposed at the same workplace.

Recognition: Voluntary Procedures

Recognition can be provided for in an agreement, reached voluntarily, which sets out the rights of the union and its representatives. Agreements deal with the scope of bargaining, and the matters which are negotiable. They also, commonly, deal with such matters as collection of union dues on behalf of the union, arrangements for holding union meetings, the timing and conduct of negotiating meetings and other organisational arrangements. Practice varies greatly, however, and some agreements are expressed in reciprocal terms, for example requiring unions to try to ensure that agreed procedures are maintained, and ensuring that arrangements for avoiding disputes are followed. Managements are sometimes prepared to agree to assist in encouraging staff to belong to the union. As noted already, however, TULR(C)A s. 137 makes it unlawful to go any further than this and make it a requirement to join a union.

In the absence of a formalised recognition arrangement, the issue of whether a union has been recognised will depend on previous evidence of its dealings with the employer. If consultation practices, routine representation at disciplinary and grievance proceedings, and involvement in other normal industrial relations can be shown, it will usually be possible to demonstrate recognition has been established (even if the employer denies it).[37] However, the courts have not, in general, readily accepted such implied recognition.

Example

Five polytechnic lecturers were members of the Association of Polytechnic Lecturers (APL). Their employers, Cleveland County Council, had repeatedly refused to recognise the association, and continued to recognise other established lecturers' organisations. The council did, however, answer queries on working conditions and there was some dialogue on matters like health and safety. The Secretary of State later indicated that he thought APL should attend Burnham Committee negotiations on pay.

Nevertheless, the council still refused to recognise the union. APL thereupon appointed safety representatives and then successfully persuaded an industrial tribunal to order that the representatives had formal rights (including time off and so on), on the basis that APL had been 'recognised'. The decision was overturned on appeal. The EAT held that the Secretary of State's actions and the other possible factors involved did not amount to 'recognition'. In particular, it said, recognition could not be foisted on unwilling employers as a result of actions over which they had no control (in this case the Secretary of State's views).[38]

Implied Recognition; Limited Recognition

A union may enjoy limited recognition, i.e. the employer recognises it for *some* of the purposes listed in TULR(C)A s. 178 (2). This is underlined by the phrase 'to any extent' in s. 178 (3). The problem is that such voluntary recognition is difficult to demonstrate, even for limited purposes – and it is dependent on clear evidence of past conduct, dealings, etc. Even if there has been negotiation on a particular matter in the past it does not necessarily mean it is *established*, or that the employer has not *withdrawn* the facility. Recognition can be implied: but as the courts have generally held this needs to be demonstrated over a period of time, and by simply stopping negotiation on a regular basis it may lapse.[39]

The uncertainties of establishing and maintaining recognition on a voluntary basis have highlighted the importance of a statutory system that enables workers to obtain legal protection for their bargaining rights. There is a further concern, which is that where there is a voluntary negotiating procedure, but it does not cover any of the so-called 'core' elements of the statutory procedure under the Employment Relations Act 1999, it is difficult to secure agreement to extend into such areas. Under changes proposed for later in 2004, and under new legislation, it will be possible to apply to the CAC to gain recognition on pay, hours, and holidays.

The need for a secure, statutory system has also been underlined by the reluctance of either EC Law or ECHR Law to introduce a Europe-wide right of workers to collectively bargain; or to laws requiring States to protect bargaining as an acquired right; or to bar out arbitrary derecognition. One of the shortcomings in the judgment of the European Court of Human Rights in the *Wilson and Palmer* case in 2002 (discussed above) is that the court stopped short of saying that the ECHR confers a *right* to collectively bargain, or that union recognition can be *imposed* on an employer as a necessary incident of trade union membership rights. It confirmed that the court had not, to date, been prepared to hold that 'the freedom of a trade union to make its voice heard extends to imposing on an employer an obligation to recognise a union'. It was merely concerned that a union and its members 'must be free in one way or another to seek to persuade the employer to listen to what it has to say on behalf of its members'. This falls a *long* way short of what UK unions would say is essential in the collective bargaining process (and which is now provided through the statutory recognition procedures introduced in 2000). The judgment necessitates amendments to be made to individual union members' rights in the TULR(C)A provisions (mainly ss. 146, 148, and 152), and to other provisions such as those dealing with the right to be accompanied, representation, etc., in the Employment Relations Act 1999 s. 10.[40] An opportunity to do this is provided by the Employment Relations Act 1994 – although it is apparent from the Explanatory Notes to the Bill that the changes will not provide a comprehensive re-working of that Act.

Statutory Recognition Procedure

After protracted consultations, and opposition from employers' organisations, the Employment Relations Act 1999 introduced a system of compulsory recognition.[41] This is in the TULR(C)A 1992 Schedule A1. Voluntary recognition is still available, but is underpinned by a statutory regime. Most aspects of the statutory recognition procedure (some of which has implications for voluntary arrangements) are in the nine Parts to Schedule A1:

- Part I: Statutory recognition
- Part II: Voluntary recognition
- Part III: Changes affecting the bargaining unit
- Part IV: Derecognition in general
- Part V: Derecognition where recognition is automatic
- Part VI: Derecognition where the union is not independent
- Part VII: Loss of independence
- Part VIII: Detriment
- Part IX: General issues.

Reference must be made to the legislation itself for the details, but what follows is a summary of the main features of the scheme, followed by a closer examination of its key elements.

Summary
Broadly, an independent trade union must initiate a formal request for recognition that it should be entitled to negotiate for a particular bargaining unit. If the request

is refused, or is not accepted after negotiations (which can be assisted by ACAS), the union (or unions) can request the Central Arbitration Committee (CAC) to issue a declaration requiring recognition if conditions are met. It can do this if a majority of workers in the proposed bargaining unit (once this has been agreed or determined by the CAC) already belong to the union at the time of a request. Otherwise, it will be necessary to conduct a ballot of the proposed bargaining unit's workers. The proposal that the union/s should undertake the collective bargaining for the unit must be supported by a majority of the workers voting, *and* at least 40 per cent of the workers in the unit. The bargaining system to be followed by the parties if recognition is agreed, or ordered, can be negotiated. Again, in the absence of agreement, the CAC may determine this, based on principles set out in the Trade Union Recognition (Method of Collective Bargaining) Order 2000, SI 2000/1300.

Statutory recognition gained in this way normally lasts for at least three years, and can only end in prescribed circumstances and accordance with the schedule's provisions, or in line with the statutory derecognition process in the TULR(C)A provisions.

The alternative 'route' to recognition is a recognition agreement. This can be reached independently of the statutory process: but the catalyst for negotiating a voluntary agreement may well be, initially, an application to the CAC for statutory recognition, and after the employer concedes recognition. Recognition arrangements can still be the subject of CAC intervention, and the system will, again, last for three years. The main difference, though, is that derecognition procedures are not the same. If recognition arrangements are no longer appropriate as a result of subsequent changes in the organisation then the employer or unions can make applications for new bargaining units and arrangements. Derecognition is automatic in some cases, and will occur in prescribed circumstances – for example, where the number of workers in the unit reduces to below 21; or when a secret ballot is conducted after the three-year period elapses, and there is no longer support. Employers may recognise non-independent unions outside the statutory procedure, but these can be derecognised. There are also procedures relating to trade unions which lose their independence.

In an attempt to avoid opportunities for judicial intervention in ways which rendered the last statutory scheme so unworkable, as shown by cases like *Grunwick Processing Laboratories v. Advisory Conciliation and Arbitration Service* [1978] AC 655, HL,[42] the system, deliberately, is detailed and prescriptive. In this respect the scheme has been successful, and given that there have been nearly sixty recognition awards, and over a thousand voluntary recognition agreements since 1999, it is remarkable that there have been only half a dozen judicial reviews of the CAC. That said, the Employment Relations Act 2004 will be concerned to address any scope there is for contesting CAC decisions. The scope for court actions is not altogether removed. There are still opportunities for an employer, as well as unions, to take action in certain cases, for example when it responds to union proposals on the proposed bargaining unit. In such cases it is essential that adequate consideration is given by the CAC to the employer's concerns and in ensuring statutory criteria are correctly taken in to account, as highlighted in *R (Kwik-Fit (GB) Ltd) v. CAC* [2002] IRLR 395, Court of Appeal.

Aspects of the statutory route are, undoubtedly, controversial, as considered below. Assuming the union (or unions) surmount the hurdles in the way of achieving a CAC declaration the end result is

(a) a formal declaration, and

(b) a prescribed method of bargaining.

Whilst (b) is enforceable as if it were a legal agreement this does not, in itself, address some qualitative shortcomings in what this gives unions. Specifically, even if the parties set up arrangements that mirror the main features identified in the 'model' in SI 2000/1300 that process says little to require an employer to bargain meaningfully, even on the core substantive areas of pay, hours, and holidays. The scheme does not, arguably, compare at all well with the arbitration methods that could apply to achieve changes and improvements to substantive conditions of work that was in the earlier legislation repealed by the Conservatives.

General Features

An independent trade union seeking recognition to be entitled to conduct collective bargaining can make a request for recognition under Schedule A1, Part I. The process looks to employers and unions to agree recognition wherever possible, but if this does not happen the CAC has powers to adjudicate and impose recognition. Recognition under the procedure brings with it the right to negotiate on pay, hours and holidays, but anything else requires agreement with the employer. For the purposes of this provision, though, 'pay' has been determined by the CAC to include pension contributions and benefits; *UNIFI v. Union Bank of Nigeria plc* [2001] IRLR 712. However, the Employment Relations Act 2004, Part I, reverses this decision by taking pensions out of the definition of 'pay' – but also gives the Secretary of State order-making powers to define what can or cannot be included in this 'core' area of pay.

As a general initial requirement a union must show that a minimum of 10 per cent of those in the proposed bargaining unit are members of the union, and other restrictions operate. For example, requests should not be made for recognition if recognition would disturb settled bargaining arrangements, i.e. if there is already recognition of another independent union.

The Main Process

Request for Recognition

To be a valid 'request' the conditions in paras. 4–9 must be met. Among other things this means a written request must be sent to the employer. The employer, taken with any associated employer or employers, must employ:

(a) at least 21 workers on the day the employer receives the request; or

(b) an average of at least 21 workers in the 13-week period ending with that day.

The request must identify the union or unions, and the proposed bargaining unit.

The CAC will normally determine bargaining units by reference to the separate entities in which workers are employed, taking into account that they are working for different companies. In exceptional cases, though, it may be permissible to lift the corporate veil and view two companies as one if the evidence supports this; *Graphical, Paper and Media Union v. Derry Print Ltd and another* [2002] IRLR 380, CAC.

Parties' Agreement

If before the end of the 'first period', which is ten working days from the day after the employer gets the request, agreement is reached on the bargaining unit, and that the union (or unions) are to be recognised as entitled to conduct bargaining for that unit, then no further steps need to be taken under Part I; para. 10 (1). Otherwise, if before the end of that period the employer does not accept this, but is willing to negotiate, then the parties conduct negotiations. Agreement before the end of the 'second period' (20 days starting with the day after the first period ends, or such longer period that is agreed) means, again, that no further steps are taken; para. 10 (4). ACAS can assist the negotiations reach a favourable outcome in these two phases.

If an agreement is reached in the first or second periods (or later at any point before the CAC orders recognition or a ballot for recognition purposes) it is treated as an 'agreement for recognition'; para. 52. The effect is that, subject to agreement, the agreement may not be terminated for three years. From that point, though, such agreements do not have the additional safeguards given to arrangements that have been ordered by the CAC.

If before the end of the first period the employer *fails* to respond to the request for recognition, or before the end of the first period the employer informs the union that the request is not accepted, without indicating a willingness to negotiate, the union can apply to the CAC to decide:

(i)   whether the proposed bargaining unit (or some other unit) is appropriate, and
(ii) whether the union has (or unions have) the support of the majority of the workers in the appropriate unit; (para. 11).

Failure of Negotiations

If the employer does not accept the request for recognition, is willing to negotiate, but no agreement is reached before the end of the second period, para. 12 applies. Basically, the union (or unions) can apply to the CAC to decide both the following questions:

(i)   whether the proposed unit is appropriate (or some other bargaining unit is appropriate);
(ii) whether the union has (or unions have) the support of the majority of the workers constituting the appropriate bargaining unit.

Provision is also made for situations when the employer agrees the bargaining unit, but does not agree that it should be the union (or unions) that should be recognised to conduct collective bargaining for it. This will usually prompt an application to the CAC to decide if the union has the support of a majority of the workers that make up that unit; para. 12 (4). Applications must be in accordance with the criteria laid down, and as the CAC requires.

The CAC must determine, within a ten-day period, if the application is validly made, has come after a valid 'request', and is otherwise admissible.

In some cases an application will be treated as *in*admissible by the CAC, notably if:

• *a collective agreement is already in force* recognising a union as the proposed bargaining unit: on the face of it this seems to extend to voluntary arrangements made with organisations such as staff associations or other representative bodies that are not certified as 'independent' under TULR(C)A, and which may indeed be under employers' control. There are other potential problems, and bars, which an employer might raise. Although these are not insuperable obstacles – for example there is provision for derecognition of non-independent bodies in later Parts of Schedule A1, they may in some circumstances act as disincentives to officials and members of a properly independent and certified union using the statutory recognition route.[43]

- the *level of union membership*, and *likely support for recognition*. A minimum of 10 per cent of the workers in the proposed bargaining unit must be in the union applying, and a majority of workers must be likely to support recognition. These are matters on which the CAC must decide based on evidence it is given and which it considers; para. 14.
- *more than one union has applied* under paras. 11, 12. However, in this case the unions may show that they will co-operate with each other in a manner likely to secure and maintain stable and effective arrangements: and that, if the employer wishes, they will enter into arrangements under which collective bargaining is conducted by the unions acting together on behalf of the workers constituting the relevant bargaining unit; para. 37.
- the CAC has *accepted an application in respect of a bargaining unit*, and the application is made in relation to substantially the same unit within a three-year period; para. 39.

What is the 'Bargaining Unit'?

This may already have been agreed by the employer and union/s. If so, the CAC is then only concerned with whether recognition should be given. Otherwise, if the application passes the tests for admissibility, the CAC must decide if what is proposed as the unit is appropriate or not. Initially it is for the parties, helped by the CAC, to try to agree what should be the unit within a 20-day period, assisted if they wish by ACAS; para. 18. Guidance on the process requires the employer to state its position on this to facilitate negotiation. Under an important change made by the Employment Relations Act 2004, Part 1, the CAC has the power to bring this initial bargaining phase to an end if there is no reasonable prospect of agreement on an appropriate unit; or it can extend the bargaining period. Otherwise the CAC must decide the issue (within ten days or any longer period it specifies, giving reasons for the extension), but taking into account the main criterion in para. 19 (3), which is 'the need for the unit to be compatible with effective management'; and 'the matters listed in para. 19(4) so far as they do not conflict with that need', namely:

(a) the views of the employer and the union/s;
(b) existing national and local bargaining arrangements;
(c) the desirability of avoiding small fragmented bargaining units within an undertaking;
(d) the characteristics of workers falling within the proposed bargaining unit and of any other employees of the employer of whom the CAC considers relevant;
(e) the location of workers.

If at that point the bargaining unit identified by the CAC (or by the parties through agreement) is different from the one originally proposed the CAC is supposed to determine the validity of the application within the terms of paras. 43–50, and the evidence of the employer and union/s; para. 20 (2). The union may, of course, decide whether to press on with its claim or not, especially if the bargaining unit is substantially different, or it risks losing a ballot of workers within the unit that has been identified.

Employers are able to contest CAC determinations as to what is or is not an appropriate bargaining unit, but Court of Appeal guidance in the *Kwik-Fit* case referred to above suggests that if there are good grounds on which the CAC adopts the unit proposed by the union, and takes employers' views and the other statutory criteria into account before reaching its conclusions, there is likely to be little scope for intervention in the way it exercises its powers.

Recognition Declarations

The CAC has power to decide whether recognition is appropriate or not. The key issue is the level of support within the proposed bargaining unit. If there is clear support for recognition among a majority of workers because they are members of the union then the CAC must make a declaration; para. 22 (2). However, even if there is such a majority of members the CAC must order a ballot in certain circumstances; paras. 22 (3), (4) if:

- this is in the interests of good industrial relations;
- a 'significant number of union members' in the unit inform the CAC that they do not want the union/s to conduct collective bargaining on their behalf;
- membership evidence is produced which leads the CAC to conclude that there are 'doubts' whether a significant number of the union members in the unit want the union/s to conduct collective bargaining on their behalf.

These further hurdles are controversial for a number of reasons, but mainly because they afford a determined employer a final late attempt to block recognition, and put pressure on workers in what could be a difficult and stressful phase (during which the employer may seek to influence the ballot). The counter-argument is that if there is any remaining doubt that the union has strong support for bargaining a ballot will resolve it.

Assuming the CAC orders a ballot this does not have to proceed, even at this late stage, if the union/s are opposed to it, and indicate within the prescribed notification period that they do *not* wish it to proceed. If it does proceed then the costs are shared between the parties, and it is carried out by an independent body appointed by the CAC. The employer is subject (under para. 26) to a number of duties during the ballot phase, including 'co-operation' with the person/body conducting the ballot and the union/s. The union/s must have reasonable access to the workers to enable information about the ballot to be given, and to seek their support – as indicated in a Code of Practice.[44] Up-to-date names and home addresses of workers making up the units must be given to the CAC. As an incentive to employers to co-operate on this essential requirement, the CAC has power to order the employer to 'take such steps to remedy the failure as the CAC considers reasonable'; and, if it decides there has been a failure to comply, and a ballot has not been held, the CAC may issue a recognition declaration even *without* a ballot; para. 27. Approval in the ballot must be by

(a) a majority of those voting, *and*

(b) over 40 per cent of the workers in the bargaining unit.

If this is secured in the ballot recognition at that point is assured, as the CAC *must* issue a declaration; para. 29 (3).

Recognition; Method of Bargaining

An important element in the statutory process is then to agree a *method* for the conduct of bargaining. This is meant to be achieved within a 30-day period of negotiation (or longer if this is agreed). The CAC's role after this period expires is that of facilitator, if requested by a party. If this still does not secure agreement the CAC can (and must) specify the method by which the parties are to conduct collective bargaining, assisted by the principles in the Trade Union Recognition (Method of Collectve Bargaining) Order 2000, SI 2000/1300; para. 30, 31. That 'method', once it is determined, takes effect 'as if it were contained in a legally enforceable contract made by the parties'. If there is non-compliance the arrangements are enforceable using the remedy of specific performance (backed up by contempt of court proceedings for a failure to comply).[45] However, this is subject to agreement by the parties in writing to disapply it, or parts of it – or to vary or replace the method specified by the CAC; para. 30 (3)–(6).

The CAC is given an on-going 'assistance' role by para. 32 in securing compliance with the method of collective bargaining.

Changes Affecting the Bargaining Unit

If there are changes in the composition of the bargaining unit, and one of the parties believes that the original unit is no longer appropriate, an application may be made to the CAC to decide if it is likely that it is no longer an appropriate bargaining unit. This is dealt with in Part III of Schedule A1, and could be triggered by the factors in para. 66 (2), namely a change in the organisation or structure of the business, changes in the activities pursued by the employer, or a substantial change in the number of workers employed in the original unit. If the application is admitted by the CAC the parties can negotiate a new unit, failing which the CAC decides whether to stay with the existing arrangements or replace it (if necessary after ordering a ballot to test support). An employer could also apply for the existing arrangements to end completely if the unit has ceased to exist – for example after a reorganisation or transfer of the undertaking; para. 74.

Derecognition

Unlike the position with voluntary recognition, where the employer generally has unregulated control over derecognition, and changing arrangements, if recognition has been agreed after a request is made under the statutory procedure the position is heavily regulated – at least during the three-year period after an 'agreement for recognition' or CAC declaration. Normally recognition must be maintained except where a union loses its 'independence', or the other specific statutory criteria are satisfied; Parts IV–VI. These are similar to the criteria needed before a union or unions achieve recognition, i.e. having fewer than 21 workers in the unit, more than 10 per cent want an end to recognition (and it is likely a majority would favour this), and so forth.

Employment Protection

In anticipation of the possibility that workers may be subjected to pressure, including threats of dismissal, 'detriment', etc., during phases when recognition or derecognition are being mooted, Part VIII contains a range of employment protection measures (including 'automatically unfair' dismissal rights, and compensation if employers subject workers to detriments) – with Employment Tribunal proceedings including powers to grant interim relief.

Other Elements of Collective Bargaining

Business Transfers and Collective Agreements

The Transfer of Undertakings (Employment Protection) Regulations 1981, reg. 6, provides for collective agreements in respect of employees whose employment contracts are 'preserved' (reg. 5) to be deemed to be made with the transferee employer. There is nothing, however, to prevent collective agreements being terminated (or not being renegotiatied by the new employer) *after* the transfer. As far as recognition is concerned a union recognised by the transferor employer should continue to enjoy recognition rights, especially when these have been secured under the statutory procedure (subject to the derecognition possibilities permitted in Schedule AI to TULR[C]A).

TUPE reg. 9 applies where, after a relevant transfer, the undertaking or part of the undertaking transferred 'maintains an identity distinct from the remainder of the transferee's undertaking'. Assuming this *is* the case, the union is deemed to be recognised 'to the same extent in respect of employees of that description so employed': but it adds '... and any agreement for recognition may be *varied* or *rescinded* accordingly'. There may, of course, be changes in the bargaining unit following reorganisations and changes, and (as discussed above) transfers – and this may trigger an application to the CAC for recognition to cease, or for arrangements to be varied; Part III of Schedule A1. Reference must also be made to the codified provisions of EC Directive 2001/23 which now supplement the TUPE position.

Time Off and Facilities for Union Representatives and Union Activities

The rights of shop stewards and other union officials working for an employer, and of employees, to reasonable, paid time off have been described in Chapter 8 above. In the case of representatives' time off for collective bargaining, including 'negotiations with the employer related to or connected with matters within s. 178 (2)' (collective bargaining), this is clearly covered by the Trade Union and Labour Relations (Consolidation) Act 1992, s. 168. Problems usually arise, though, over activities which may be *related* to negotiating but for which an employer is less willing to provide time off. These include training courses and time spent on communicating information to members, meetings with full-time officials and so forth. The ACAS Code of Practice 'Time Off for Trade Union Duties and Activities' lists the specific activities which require paid time off. They only extend to collective bargaining on matters for which the union is recognised. Examples of 'trade union duties' for which the right applies are provided in Section 1, and include reasonable time off for negotiation or, where the employer has agreed, 'for duties concerned with other functions related to or connected with the matters listed in para. 12 of the Code. This is an extensive list, but as might be expected includes terms and conditions of employment; physical working conditions; engagement or non-engagement, or termination or suspension of employment of workers; disciplinary matters; trade union membership or non-membership; machinery for negotiation or consultation. Section 2 deals with training of officials, and Section 3 relates to 'trade union activities'. In practical terms one of the most important parts of the Code is Section 4 which provides important guidance on the amount and frequency of time off, and 'request' procedures.

Ideally, the needs of representatives should be dealt with in detail in written arrangements agreed with the employer. Among other matters, these should provide people with sufficient time to carry out the specific responsibilities for which they have been elected, and this will obviously depend on the extent to which they have to be involved in collective bargaining issues. Arrangements should be designed to avoid problems in relations with immediate supervisors, particularly if absence means work commitments could be affected. Workplace representatives who take on union responsibilities should not have to accept worse working conditions or career disadvantages.[46]

In some aspects of lay officials' work, for example the role of 'companion' in disciplinary or grievance hearings, the role is underpinned and defined by statute s. 10 of the Employment Relations Act 1999, as extended by Part 3 of the Employment Relations Act 2004, implicitly giving such officials time off to attend meetings – and this function is an important one which can often have wider implications for bargaining.

If disputes do arise tribunals have the basic task of deciding whether or not a refusal of time off is 'reasonable' in the particular circumstances.[47]

Disclosure of Information: Legal Duties

The Trade Union and Labour Relations (Consolidation) Act 1992, s. 181, imposes a duty on employers to disclose information at all stages of collective bargaining relating to their undertakings, without which union representatives involved in collective bargaining would be 'to a material extent' impeded. The CAC, as a general principle, looks to a test of whether the information sought is 'relevant' to the matter being negotiated, as can be seen from its decisions; and in its Annual Reports. If the employer does not recognise the union (or decides not to recognise it for the specific purpose for which the information is claimed) the duty does not apply. Guidance is contained in the ACAS Code of Practice *Disclosure of Information to Trade Unions for Collective Bargaining Purposes* (and in other ACAS published information). The Code gives examples of information which could be relevant in different contexts, including pay, conditions of service, performance data, and financial matters relating to profits and liabilities.

There are limitations on what the employer is required to produce in ss. 181, 182. The information must be relevant and it must be sufficiently important to the negotiations and the claim in respect of which it is claimed. Disclosure is required if it would be in accordance with 'good industrial relations practice', and in some cases disclosure has been refused on the basis that it would not be in line with normal practice. In addition, disclosure can be specifically refused (s. 182) in certain cases. The main ones concern:

- national security interests;
- data held subject to legal and 'confidentiality' requirements, for example in tenders to a government department in a private cleaning contractor's tender (*Civil Service Union v. CAC* [1980] IRLR 274);
- information held on individuals (like personnel data) unless consent to disclose it has been given;
- information which, if disclosed, would cause 'substantial injury' to the employer's undertaking (but only for reasons other than the effect on collective bargaining);
- information obtained by the employer for legal proceedings.

Employers are also able to take advantage of a restriction whereby the amount of work, or expenditure, involved in compiling the information would be 'out of reasonable proportion to the value of it in the conduct of collective bargaining'; s. 182 (2) (b).

Failure to Disclose

Complaints of non-disclosure can be taken under s. 183 to the Central Arbitration Committee (CAC) and if ACAS cannot settle the claim, after the matter has been referred to it by the CAC for conciliation (if this could produce a settlement), the CAC can make a ruling. The procedure is a difficult one, though, and there can be significant delays before disclosure is obtained.[48] The CAC's powers extend to requiring an employer to observe the terms and conditions specified in the claim that the union has made or 'other terms which the Committee consider appropriate'. The effect of this is to give the employees covered contractual entitlements pending a later collective agreement or improved terms.[49] By way of comment on the CAC's powers and the disclosure regime, it can be said that ss. 181 and 182 strike an uneasy balance between the union's general right of access and the wide-ranging restrictions afforded to employers. In practice, employers can be reluctant to reveal details of their operations which are not specifically within the specific heads of collective bargaining in s. 178 (2), or within a narrow range of examples in the ACAS Code. Nor is disclosure likely if the matter does not concern a collective bargaining issue that is under discussion, such as future redundancy intentions and staffing projections something borne out by research by Gospel and Willman in 1980 (reported in the *Industrial Law Journal* at vol. 10 (1981), p. 10). In some cases an employer subject to a duty to disclose financial information (under para. 11 of the ACAS Code examples for guidance in the 'financial' head) will seek to impose conditions on *further* disclosure by the recipient (using the Supreme Court Act 1981 s. 31/CPR Part 54).

There is no appeal process, and this means that a party who is dissatisfied with the CAC's decision would have to seek a judicial review of the decision, or the way it was reached, in the Administrative Court (using the Supreme Court Act 1981 s. 31/CPR Part 54).

In order to facilitate the introduction of requirements on employers to provide information, and to consult, the Employment Relations Act 2004 gives the Secretary of State regulation-making powers. The regulations can prescribe the specific 'matters' on which employees and representatives are entitled to be informed or consulted. This can be done by requiring employers and employees to initiate and conduct negotiations on 'information and consultation' agreements, and dispute resolution elements in such agreements (backed up by an ET jurisdiction to hear complaints). In consultations on EC Dir. 2002/14 (establishing a general framework for informing and consulting employees) the TUC supported, broadly, the approach which the government has taken to getting such agreements in its detailed responses in *High Performance Workplaces* (Nov. 2002). Some aspects of the scheme remain unresolved, however, and will need to be addressed in regulations: as will the interaction between agreements and employers' duties under other legislation, including TUPE, collective redundancies' requirements and the Transnational Information and Consultation of Employees Regulations 1999, SI 1999/3323; and the Information and Consultation Directive (2002/14/EC); and Information and Consultation of Employees Regulations 2004 (Draft, June 2004).

On information requirements relating to redundancy and transfers of the employer's business, see Chapter 15.

CHAPTER 19

Industrial Conflict I: Industrial Action

In the UK, there is no positive right to strike. Instead there is merely a system of immunities from liability which offer a limited shield of protection to trade unions and strike organisers. This shield, always vulnerable to attack by an unsympathetic judiciary, has been weakened still further by the changes introduced by the government since 1980. Moreover, those workers who take strike or other industrial action may have some or all of their pay 'docked' and may incur the risk of dismissal with no right to challenge its fairness before an industrial tribunal.[1]

In this chapter, we will start by examining the scope of the employer's power lawfully to sack its striking workforce or make deductions from wages. In the second part of the chapter, we will look at the liability of trade unions and strike organisers for unlawful industrial action. Finally, we will identify those groups of workers who are denied the right to withdraw their labour and examine recent proposals to control industrial action in public services.

The changes to collective labour law introduced during the 1980s were consolidated in one Act of Parliament: the Trade Union and Labour Relations (Consolidation) Act 1992, or TULR(C)A. The relevant provisions of this Act are referred to in the text.

Sanctions against Individual Strikers

Dismissal

Where dismissal is for taking part in a strike or other industrial action, where all those still on strike have been dismissed and there has been no selective re-engagement of those dismissed within a three-month period, the law prevents an industrial tribunal from hearing an unfair dismissal claim (TULR[C]A 1992 s. 238).

'Other industrial action' is not defined by the Act but it is now clear that it can cover forms of action which do not constitute a breach of the contract of employment. In *Faust* v. *Power Packing Casemakers Ltd* [1983] IRLR 117, three employees refused to work overtime because of a dispute over wages. The IT found the dismissals unfair on the grounds that there was no contractual obligation to work overtime. Both the EAT and the Court of Appeal rejected this view, stating that any action taken against employers during the course of a dispute which was designed to extract some benefit from them constituted 'other industrial action' – whether or not it was in breach of contract.

In determining whether there has been a selective dismissal or re-engagement of strikers, the tribunal must have regard to the 'relevant employee'. These are defined as those employees at the establishment who were taking part in the industrial action at the date of the complainant's dismissal. In other words, those who have been on strike but who have returned to work before that date are not included and the fact that they are not dismissed does not entitle the dismissed employees to present a claim.

The time at which it must be shown that one or more relevant employees who took part in a strike were not dismissed, for the purposes of deciding whether an ET has jurisdiction to hear the unfair dismissal claim, is the conclusion of the relevant hearing at which the tribunal determines whether it has jurisdiction (*P&O European Ferries (Dover) Ltd* v. *Byrne* [1989] IRLR 254). This is an extremely favourable interpretation for employers because if the identities of those strikers which the employer has, by mistake, failed to dismiss are revealed during the proceedings, then the employer can escape liability by dismissing them before the conclusion of those proceedings.

Whether a particular employee is taking part in a strike within the meaning of s. 238 is a question of fact for the employment tribunal to decide. In *Coates* v. *Modern Methods and Materials Ltd* [1982] IRLR 318, however, the majority of the Court of Appeal expressed the view that the matter should be judged by what the employee does and not by what s/he thinks or why s/he does it. Reasons or motives are irrelevant. Therefore, an employee who does not support a strike but who does not cross a picket line because of fear of abuse could reasonably be regarded as taking part in the strike.

The Employment Act 1990 tightened the law even further. The effect of this amendment is that, henceforth, no employee can complain of unfair dismissal if at the time of the dismissal s/he was taking part in unofficial industrial action. In such a situation the employer may selectively dismiss or re-engage any participating employee without risking unfair dismissal liability (see now TULR[C]A 1992, s. 237).

An employee's action will be unofficial unless:

- s/he is a member of a trade union and the action is authorised and endorsed by that union; or
- s/he is not a trade union member, but members of a union which has authorised or endorsed the action also take part; or
- no trade union members are taking part in the industrial action.

It is interesting to note that this provision, although substantially strengthened by the Tories in 1982 and 1990, owes its origins to the last Labour government. The policy underlying it is that the courts and tribunals are not appropriate places in which to decide the rights and wrongs of industrial disputes. As such, the provision is very much in line with the earlier abstentionist tradition in British industrial relations.

The fact that the employer has the legal freedom to sack those taking industrial action, even if the action has been sanctioned by a properly conducted ballot, may come as a surprise to many trade unionists. Indeed, research conducted by Roger Welch in 1987 established that almost 45 per cent of his sample of active trade unionists believed that employers could not dismiss strikers. This proportion increased to 70 per cent if the industrial action involved was short of a strike, such as an overtime ban.[2] This misconception is entirely understandable. After all, how can we talk of a right or freedom to strike unless it is possible for workers to withdraw their labour, in whole or in part, without fearing lawful dismissal? Those workers to whom the existence of this legal prop to managerial prerogative will come as no surprise are the News International printers and the P&O seafarers who during the 1980s fell victim to its use in defeating strikes.

In Chapter 4 of *Fairness at Work*, the government proposed to extend the protection against dismissal to workers taking *official* industrial action in certain circumstances. In proposing the new rights the government said it believed that 'in general employees dismissed for taking part in lawfully organised official industrial action should have the right to complain of unfair dismissal to a tribunal' (para. 4.22). It then invited views on the tests which should be applied to determine whether dismissals in such circumstances are fair. Subsequently, s. 16 and sched. 5 of the Employment Relations Act 1999 introduced a new s. 238A into TULR(C)A 1992.

From a trade unionist perspective, the end result is rather disappointing, with only a limited protection against dismissal being extended to those engaged in industrial action. The protection covers only lawfully organised official industrial action and *generally* lasts only for the first eight weeks of the employee's involvement. Given the massive complexity of the law relating to industrial action, it will rarely be the case that workers can be certain that the action they are taking is lawful. If it is found to be unlawful, or their involvement in the dispute extends beyond eight weeks, they risk dismissal without redress unless they can establish selective dismissal/re-engagement within the terms of s. 238. Where the dispute is unofficial, the employee has no protection against dismissal unless it is shown that the reason or principal reason for dismissal or selection for dismissal was one of those specified in ss. 99 (1)–(3), 100, 101A (d) or 103 of ERA 1996 (dismissal in maternity, health and safety and employee representative cases) or s. 103A (making a protected disclosure).

The changes introduced by the 1999 Act still fail to guarantee an effective right to strike and are unlikely to satisfy International Labour Organisation Standards.

The new rights under s. 238A are not dependent on length of service, so that all employees are covered immediately from the start of their employment.

Possible Loss of Redundancy Payments

Strikes and other types of industrial action have often been called as a defensive response to an employer's announcement of impending redundancies. It is also the case that employers will often threaten redundancies during a strike: on occasions these threats may be genuine; at other times they may merely form part of the employer's bargaining strategy. We have examined the legal position in some detail in our chapter above on redundancy but, given the importance of issue for strikers, it is worthwhile summarising the possible outcomes here:

Scenario One
Employees at Capital plc take strike or other industrial action in breach of their contracts either before they are given their redundancy notices, or after receipt but before the obligatory period of notice (the minimum contractual and/or statutory notice to which each employee is entitled). In this situation, Capital plc dismisses the strikers without incurring liability for redundancy payments.

Scenario Two
Employees at Capital plc take strike action after having received the obligatory period of notice. If they are then dismissed for taking part in the strike, they are entitled to a full redundancy payment. This entitlement is subject to the employer's statutory right to serve a written notice of extension on the striking employees requiring

them to work extra days after the expiry of the redundancy notice, equivalent to the number of days lost during the strike. If the employees fail without reasonable cause to comply with the notice, they will lose their right to claim all or any part of the redundancy payment.

Scenario Three
Employees at Capital plc take industrial action short of a strike involving a breach of their contracts after having received the obligatory period of notice. If Capital's response is dismissal, the employees may apply to an employment tribunal, which has discretion to award some or all of the redundancy payment.

Suing for Breach of Contract

As we shall see below, most forms of industrial action will involve a breach of the worker's contract of employment. Consequently, the employer has the option to sue the worker for damages. Employers rarely do this because the amount of damages recoverable is likely to be extremely small. The employer is limited to claiming the loss caused by the individual contract-breaker – normally the cost of employing a substitute. In order to recover something approaching actual loss, the employer would have to sue each and every striker individually: hardly a realistic proposition. A far more effective sanction is to deduct the whole or part of the worker's pay.

Deductions from Wages of Those Taking Industrial Action

As we saw in Chapter 7 above, Part II of ERA 1996 allows employers to make deductions from a worker's pay provided written 'consent' has been given by the worker. But deductions from the wages of those taking industrial action are exempt from the requirements of the Act (see ERA 1996 s. 14 [5]). Whether the employer can make deductions from the wages of any employee who is engaged in industrial action remains a question governed by the common law: hence the importance of *Miles* v. *Wakefield Metropolitan District Council* [1987] IRLR 193.

The central question in this case was: if an employee, entitled to a weekly wage for a defined number of hours, refuses to work the whole or part of a week, is the employer entitled, without terminating the contract and without relying on damages for breach of contract, to withhold the whole or a proportion of a week's pay?

The House of Lords upheld the principle of 'no work, no pay' as the basis for the mutual obligations between employer and employee. This principle was described by Lord Templeman as follows: 'In a contract of employment wages and work go together ... In an action by a worker to recover his pay he must allege and be ready to prove that he is ready and willing to work.' Therefore in Miles' case the employer was entitled to withhold wages for the Saturday mornings on which the superintendent registrar of births, marriages and deaths, in furtherance of industrial action, had refused to carry out marriage ceremonies as part of his normal contractual duties.

In disputes where the action being taken does not involve clearly defined periods where work is not being done the legal position has never been clear. An example would be where normal hours were being worked but selective aspects of the job, such as providing cover for absent colleagues, or answering correspondence, are withdrawn. In this case the employer's main options have generally been either to sack staff or to carry on paying wages. Another local authority case has, however, widened the employer's options.

Example
Housing Department officials took industrial action by refusing to deal with certain telephone enquiries. Although this was a minor part of the job the council told staff they would not be needed at work unless they worked properly, and if they did come to work and carry on the action they would not be paid. One of the staff got a Court Order that normal wages should continue to be paid, as there had been substantial performance. This was reversed by the Court of Appeal. As the employer had confirmed that it would not pay for incomplete performance, it was entitled to withhold pay for the period of the dispute.[3]

The Effect of a Strike or a Lock-out on an Employee's Continuity of Employment[4]

In Chapter 2 we saw that, in order to qualify for most employment protection rights, it was necessary for employees to show that they had been continuously employed for the appropriate length of time, such as two years in the case of unfair dismissal or redundancy payment claims. It was also noted that certain events could break continuous service.

Strikes
If an employee is on strike during the whole or part of any week, that week does not count in aggregating the period of time the employee has been employed (ERA 1996, s. 216 [1]). However, continuity of employment is not broken by a strike (ERA 1996, s. 216 [2]).

It is often the case that an employer will dismiss its striking workers and then re-engage them on settlement of the dispute. Does the dismissal break continuity? No, according to the decision in *Bloomfield* v. *Springfield Hosiery Finishing Co Ltd* [1972] 1 All ER 609, the rules made no distinction between strikes where there are dismissals and those where there are not. Moreover, an employer cannot re-engage a striker on the basis that service prior to the dismissal will not count for continuity purposes (*Hamson* v. *Fashion Industries [Hartlepool] Ltd* [1980] IRLR 393).

Lock-outs
It is also the case that continuity is not broken when an employee is absent from work because of a lock-out. However, whether the period during which the employee is locked-out counts for aggregation purposes is not specifically dealt with in the legislation. It would appear that, so long as the employer does not dismiss those who have been locked-out, the employee will be able to include the period in the total period of continuous service.

Guarantee Payments

In Chapter 6 we saw that ERA provides a very limited right to a guaranteed payment to workers who are laid off through no fault of their own. However, the employee loses the right where the lay-off is in consequence of a strike, lock-out or other industrial action involving any employee of his/her employer or of an associated employer (ERA 1996, s. 29 [3]). Although the disqualification only involves disputes 'internal' to the company or group for which the employee works, it can produce some rather surprising and unjust results. This is illustrated in *Garvey* v. *J. and J. Maybank (Oldham) Ltd* [1979] IRLR 408:

> Maybanks were paper merchants. Paper supplies to their works were made using their own fleet of lorries and those of haulage contractors. As a result of a road haulage strike, Maybanks could only rely on their own drivers to make deliveries but they refused to cross the picket lines set up by the road haulage drivers. Consequently, no supplies were delivered and approximately 50 workers were laid off by Maybanks. It was held that these workers had no entitlement to guarantee payments because they were laid off in consequence of a dispute between Maybanks and its own lorry drivers.

Strikers and Social Security

Workers who are involved in industrial action are normally denied entitlement to jobseeker's allowances or income support to meet their own personal income requirements during the currency of the dispute. The rationale for this disqualification (the details of which are laid down in the Social Security Contributions and Benefits Act 1992, s. 27; the Income Support [General] Regulations 1987 [SI 1987/1967]; and the Jobseeker's Allowance Regulations 1996 [SI 1996/207]) is the same one which underlies the exclusion of unfair dismissal claims from strikers – the perceived need to maintain state neutrality in industrial disputes. Both exclusions, however, totally ignore the inequality of economic power between employers and workers and further weaken the ability of workers to defend their interests.

Benefits Disqualification

This will apply where the loss of employment arises out of a 'trade dispute' at the claimant's place of work.

The statutory definition of a 'trade dispute' in the benefits legislation is based on that contained in the Trade Disputes Act 1906 and it is wider than the current definition of trade dispute used for determining immunity from tort liability for trade unions and strike organisers. It is a bitter irony that a wide definition that is beneficial to strikers in the context of immunity from tort liability, has major disadvantages when applied to benefit claims, because it increases the scope for disqualification.

Disqualification is generally maintained throughout the duration of the dispute for the striker (although not for his/her dependants) but it can cease before the end of the stoppage in the following situations:

- If the employee can show that s/he has become bona fide employed in new employment, s/he will again be eligible for benefit if the new employment then terminates (although this may be subject to normal sanctioning).
- If the employee's contract has been terminated by redundancy in certain cases. This provision was originally inserted by the Social Security Act 1986 in order to counteract the harshness of the Court of Appeal's decision in *Cartlidge* v. *Chief Adjudication Officer* [1986] IRLR 182. Cartlidge was a miner who was already under notice of redundancy when the miners' strike of 1984/85

commenced. As a result, he was unable to work during his notice period. The court had determined that he was not only prevented from claiming benefit during his notice period but was, in addition, precluded from benefit for the duration of the strike.

- If the employee can establish that s/he bona fide resumed employment with his/her employer but then left for genuine reasons other than the dispute, eligibility may return.
- If the employee can establish that s/he was not 'directly interested' in the dispute eligibility is restored. This phrase was given a wide definition by the House of Lords in *Presho* v. *DHSS (Insurance Officer)* [1984] IRLR 74. Employees, who were members of the AUEW, took strike action in support of a pay rise. The claimant, a member of USDAW, was laid off as a result and claimed benefit. The insurance officer refused her claim on the basis that she and the other USDAW members were directly interested in the dispute, since there was evidence of a custom and practice that USDAW members would automatically get the same pay rise if they asked for it. This decision was upheld by the Law Lords.

Disqualification from Benefits: Dependants' Entitlements
The specific rights of a striker's dependants to receive benefits will depend on their 'income' and notional needs. I.e. for IS and JSA purposes the 'applicable' amount (consisting of allowances, premiums, and housing costs if they have a mortgage). S. 126 (3) of the 1992 Act specifies that for a childless couple, where only one of them is involved in the dispute, *half* the couple's personal allowance and couple rate of premium can be claimed, and children's personal allowances and any eligible disability premium can be claimed.

For a family with children (either one-parent or a couple), children's allowances, the family premium and any housing costs that are normally included with IS or JSA as part of the 'applicable amount', i.e. to cover mortgage interest costs, will be payable but only to the extent that these can be attributed to the non-striking partner (as provided in the regulations). Eligibility for rent assistance through the Housing Benefit system (Housing Benefit [General] Regulations 1987 [SI 1987/1971]) will also be restricted.

The benefits system deliberately imposes tougher rules on strikers, for example by modifying the normal rules by which 'income' is assessed. Consequently s. 126 of the 1992 Act and the regulations treat employers' loans or advances, and tax refunds, as 'income' so that they are assessed, for eligibility purposes, as income available to the claimant. Payments from a trade union which the striker receives, or is entitled to receive, is normally disregarded as 'income' – but at the same time the rules stipulate that a deduction is to be made from benefit which is equivalent to the maximum available (s. 126 [5]).

People who are engaged in industrial action (or who are about to do so) should obtain specialist benefits advice, either from the CAB or other appropriate advisers.

Legal Action against the Trade Union and Strike Organisers

Attempting to Demystify the Law

The incremental approach to strike law 'reform' adopted by the Conservative governments of 1979–97 obviously proved a successful political strategy, but it meant that an already complex area of law has become even more difficult to unravel. Of course, the sheer complexity of the legislative framework is in itself a powerful weapon against trade unions and their members. It will often be the case that the legality of the proposed action cannot be determined with any certainty and this may encourage trade unions to adopt a 'safety-first' attitude so as not to put union funds at risk.[5]

In trying to make sense of the law relating to industrial action it is important that you adopt a structured approach. We suggest that you adopt the following three-stage framework of analysis:[6]

- Stage one. Does the industrial action give rise to civil liability at common law?
- Stage two. If so, is there an immunity from liability provided by what was s. 13 of TULRA, 1974 (now TULR[C]A 1992, s. 219)?
- Stage three. If so, has that immunity now been removed by virtue of the changes introduced by the Employment Acts 1980, 1982, 1988, 1990, the Trade Union Act 1984 and TURERA 1993?

Let us try and add a little detail to our analytical framework.

Stage One: Civil Liabilities for Industrial Action

Industrial Action and How it Affects Your Contract of Employment

Your contract of employment is not suspended during a strike. The traditionally accepted view is that a strike is a breach of contract: it is a breach of the obligation on the part of the employee to be ready and willing to work. This is so even if strike notice has been given: this is merely construed as notice of impending breach.

Most other forms of industrial action short of a strike also amount to contractual breaches. If workers boycott (refuse to carry out) certain work then they are in breach for refusing to comply with a reasonable order. A go-slow or work-to-rule probably breaks an implied term not to frustrate the commercial objectives of the business. This last point is illustrated by a case which arose under the now-repealed Industrial Relations Act 1971, *Secretary of State for Employment v. ASLEF* (No. 2) [1972] 2 QB 455.[7]

> The railwayworkers embarked on a work-to-rule and the question arose whether there was a breach of contract (under the law as it then was, if the action amounted to a breach of contract, a 'cooling-off' period could be ordered, followed by a ballot). The Court of Appeal found that there was a breach because, although the workers claimed to be strictly working to the terms of their contracts, what in fact they were doing was giving their contracts a wholly unreasonable interpretation and working on the basis of that interpretation. (A cooling-off period and ballot were ordered and the ballot secured a massive majority in favour of industrial action. The procedure was never used again.)

An overtime ban will also certainly amount to breach of contract if the employer is entitled under the contract to demand overtime, but not if overtime is voluntary on the part of the employee. However, as you saw earlier in this chapter, a ban on voluntary overtime was classed as 'industrial action' for the purposes of s. 238 of

TULR(C)A 1992 in *Faust v. Power Packing Casemakers Ltd* [1983] ICR 292, with the somewhat surprising result that the IT had no jurisdiction to hear the workers' unfair dismissal claims.

As we have seen, where the industrial action does constitute breach, the employer may summarily dismiss or also sue for damages. But, in relation to strike organisers, the true significance of a finding of breach is that it constitutes the 'unlawful means' element necessary for certain of the economic torts to which we will now turn our attention.

The Economic Torts

It is possible to place the torts relevant to industrial action under four broad headings:

(a) Inducement of breach of contract
(b) Interference with contract, trade or business
(c) Intimidation
(d) Conspiracy

Inducement of Breach of Contract

This is the main economic tort and derives from *Lumley v. Gye* [1853] 2 E&B 216. In this case, it was established that it was a tort to induce a person to break a contract to which s/he was a party. Since, as we have seen, virtually all industrial action involves a breach of contract you can readily appreciate that anyone who calls on workers to take industrial action commits the tort. The inducement may take one of two forms: direct and indirect.

Direct inducement occurs where the defendant induces a third party to break an existing contract which that third party has with the plaintiff who thereby suffers loss. It may help you conceptualise this and other torts if you express the position in diagram form:

	Inducement		Breach of contract of employment	
Ann	—————————	>Brenda	—————————	>Capital plc
(union official)		(employee)		(employer)

In this example Brenda is employed by Capital plc. Ann, a trade union officer, instructs her to strike. Ann is directly inducing Brenda to break her contract with Capital and is therefore committing a tort.

The necessary elements of this form of the tort are:

(a) Knowledge of the contract
(b) Intention to cause its breach
(c) Evidence of an inducement
(d) Actual breach

Note also that this form of the tort can also be committed where a union directly puts pressure on one of the employer's suppliers to cease delivery of vital supplies, thereby inducing a breach of a commercial contract. However, boycotting the employer in dispute usually arises in the second form of the tort, that is, indirect inducement.

Indirect inducement occurs where the unlawful means are used to render performance of the contract by one of the parties impossible.

```
                          Breach of              Breach of
        Ann————>Brenda————————>Capital————————>Delta
                          employment             commercial
                          contract               contract
```

In this example, Delta plc's workers are in dispute with their employer. Capital plc is a supplier of Delta. Brenda is employed by Capital as a lorry driver. Ann, a union official, persuades Brenda not to make deliveries to Delta. Not only has Ann directly induced Brenda to break her contract of employment with Capital, she has also used unlawful means through which she has indirectly induced a breach of commercial contract between Capital and Delta.

Interference with Contract, Trade or Business

In contrast to the well-established inducement to breach of contract, this tort is of more recent vintage. In several cases, Master of the Rolls Lord Denning expressed his view that 'if one party interferes with the trade or business of another, and does so by unlawful means, then he is acting unlawfully, even though he does not procure or induce any actual breach of contract'.[8] Therefore it will be unlawful to interfere with a contract short of breach, for example, by preventing performance in cases where the contract contains a force majeure clause, exempting a party in breach from liability to pay damages. (For an interesting application of this tort, see the county court judgment in *Falconer* v. *ASLEF and NUR* [1986] IRLR, where a commuter succeeded in claiming damages for the expenditure and inconvenience caused to him by a rail strike.)

More recently, it would appear that this head of liability is even broader in scope, encompassing any intentional use of unlawful means aimed at interfering with the plaintiff's trade or business. The existence of this 'super tort', as Smith and Wood aptly describe it,[9] was recognised by Lord Diplock in *Merkur Island Shipping Corporation* v. *Laughton* [1983] 2 All ER 189.

Intimidation

The tort of intimidation may take the form of compelling a person, by threats of unlawful action, to do some act which causes him/her loss; or of intimidating other persons, by threats of unlawful action, with the intention and effect of causing loss to a third party. Prior to 1964 it was assumed that the tort was confined to threats of physical violence, but in that year the House of Lords held that threats to break a contract were encompassed by the tort (*Rookes* v. *Barnard* [1964] AC 1129).

Conspiracy

This tort may take two forms:

(i)   Conspiracy to commit an unlawful act. A conspiracy to commit a crime or tort is clearly included in this category.

(ii) Conspiracy to injure by lawful means. It is, however, the second form of conspiracy which is most dangerous, because it makes it unlawful when two or more people do something which would have been quite lawful if performed by an individual. A conspiracy to injure is simply an agreement to cause deliberate loss to another without justification. The motive or purpose of the defendants is important. If the predominate purpose is to injure the plaintiff, the conspiracy is actionable. If, on the other hand, the principal aim is to achieve a legitimate goal, the action is not unlawful, even if in so doing the plaintiff suffers injury. While it took the courts some time to accept trade union objectives as legitimate (see *Quinn* v. *Leathem* [1901] AC 495), later decisions adopted a more liberal stance (see *Crofter Handwoven Harris Tweed Co* v. *Veitch* [1942] AC 435). As a result, this form of the tort does not pose the threat it once did to trade union activities.

Stage Two: the Immunities

The next stage of our analysis is to examine the scope of the statutory immunities from liability for the four categories of economic torts which we have just described. These are now contained in TULR(C)A 1992, s. 219.

Inducement to Breach of Contract

Under the Trade Disputes Act 1906, the immunity for inducements to breach in contemplation or furtherance of a trade dispute only extended to contracts of employment. This had allowed the courts in the 1960s to find ways of holding trade unionists liable for inducing breaches of commercial contracts (see *Stratford* v. *Lindley*, [1965] AC 269).

In the mid-1970s immunity was extended to cover the breach of 'any' contract. The relevant provision states that an act performed by a person in contemplation or furtherance of a trade dispute shall not be actionable in tort on the ground only 'that it induces another person to break a contract or interferes or induces any other person to interfere with its performance' – now in TULR(C)A 1992, s. 219 (1) (a).

As we shall see, however, it is important to view this immunity in the context of subsequent legislative developments. Section 219 (1) (a) provides a prima facie immunity, but this immunity may be lost in certain instances: by taking unlawful secondary action; engaging in secondary picketing; enforcing trade union membership; or taking 'official' industrial action without first having called a secret ballot.

Interference with Contract, Trade or Business

Section 219 (1) (a) provides an immunity against the tort of interference with contract. It does not, however, offer any explicit protection against the wider 'genus' tort of interference with trade or business by unlawful means. As a result it is of crucial importance to discover whether an act which is immune by virtue of s. 219 (inducement to breach of contract, for example) may nonetheless constitute the 'unlawful means' for the tort of interference with trade or business. Before the passage of the Employment Act 1980, s. 13 (3) of TULRA 1974 (as amended) had stated that 'for the avoidance of doubt' acts already given immunity could not found the unlawful means element of other torts. When the 1980 statute repealed s. 13 (3), the legal position became confused. However, it would appear that the correct view is that the repeal of s. 13 (3) has not changed the position. According to the House of Lords in *Hadmor Productions Ltd* v. *Hamilton* [1982] IRLR 102, s 13 (3) merely confirmed what was obvious anyway from s. 13 (1) – that is, inducement is 'not actionable'. So if the unlawful means are immune, then no liability in tort can arise.

Intimidation

This immunity is contained in TULR(C)A, s. 219 (1) (b) which states that an act committed by a person in contemplation or furtherance of a trade dispute shall not be actionable in tort on the ground only

> that it consists of his threatening that a contract (whether one to which he is a party or not) will be broken or its performance interfered with, or that he will induce another person to break a contract or to interfere with its performance.

Conspiracy

Section 219 (2) now provides the immunity against simple conspiracy originally contained in the Trade Disputes Act 1906.

The Trade Dispute Immunity

In order to gain the protection of the immunities the individual must be acting in contemplation or furtherance of a trade dispute. For analytical purposes you should ask yourself four questions in order to determine whether the industrial action qualifies:

(a) Is it between the correct parties? (See below.)
(b) Is there a dispute? (Note that there may still be a dispute even if the employer is willing to concede to the demands of the union [s. 244 (4)]. Thus if an employer ceases to supply another company on receiving a threat of strike action by its workforce if it continues supplies, there is still a dispute.)
(c) Is the subject matter of the dispute wholly or mainly related to one or more of the matters listed in s. 244 (1)? (See below.)
(d) Is the action in contemplation or furtherance of a trade dispute (ICFTD)?

The scope of the 'golden formula' was amended by the Employment Act 1982 and significantly narrowed in the following ways:

(i) A trade dispute must now be 'between workers and *their* employers' (our emphasis), not between 'employers and workers' which was the previous position. Furthermore in repealing what was s. 29 (4) of TULRA, the Act no longer allowed trade unions and employers' associations to be regarded as parties to a trade dispute in their own right. Under the law as it stood before the 1982 Act, it was possible for there to be a 'trade dispute' between a trade union and an employer, even if none of the employer's workforce were involved in the dispute. In *NWL* v. *Woods* [1979] IRLR 478, for example, the House of Lords held that there was a trade dispute between the owners of a 'flag of convenience' ship and the International Transport Workers' Federation, although there was evidence that the crew did not support the union's action. As a result of the 1982 amendment, the ITF's action would not now be protected within the ICFTD formula. (See now TULR[C]A, 1992, s. 244 [1], [5]; see *UNISON* v. *UK* [2002] IRLR 497, ECHR).

(ii)   Disputes between 'workers and workers' are now omitted from the trade dispute definition. While this means that disputes not involving an employer are unlawful, in practice it is rare for an employer not to be party to interunion disputes. A demarcation dispute between unions will usually involve a dispute with an employer regarding terms and conditions of employment.

(iii) A trade dispute must now relate 'wholly or mainly' to terms and conditions of employment and the other matters listed as legitimate in TULR(C)A 1992, s. 244. Under the law existing prior to the 1982 Act, the dispute merely had to be 'connected' with such matters. The amended phrase marks a return to the form of words used under the Industrial Relations Act and was inserted to overrule another aspect of the decision of the House of Lords in *NWL* v. *Woods* (cited above). In this case it was argued that the predominant purpose behind the 'blacking' of the Nawala was the ITF's campaign against 'flags of convenience' shipping, and little to do with a trade dispute. The House of Lords did not agree, stating that as long as there was a genuine connection between the dispute and the subjects listed in the 1974 Act, it did not matter that other issues were predominant. The amendment wrought by the 1982 Act means that a mere connection with the matters specified in s. 244 will no longer suffice. So a dispute which is held to be predominantly a trade dispute will fall outside the trade dispute formula. In many instances it will be extremely difficult to decide which is the predominant element in the dispute and this can be illustrated by the first case which dealt with the issue: *Mercury Communications Ltd* v. *Scott-Garner* [1983] IRLR 494. Mercury had been granted a government licence to run a private telecommunications system. The Post Office Engineers Union (POEU) objected to the government's policy of 'liberalisation' and ultimate privatisation of the industry. The union instructed its members employed by British Telecom (BT) to refuse to connect Mercury's telecommunication system to the BT network. The Court of Appeal, in granting an injunction to prevent the union continuing its instruction, held that this action related wholly or mainly to opposition to the government's policy, rather than fear of future redundancies in the industry should those policies be implemented (see *P* v. *National Association of Schoolmasters/Union of Women Teachers* [2003] IRLR 307).

(iv)   Since 1982, disputes relating to matters occurring outside the UK are excluded from the immunity, unless the UK workers taking action in furtherance of the dispute are likely to be affected by its outcome in terms of the matters listed in s. 244 (see s. 244 [3]). This means that sympathy action taken by British workers in order to advertise the plight of workers in other countries will be unlawful. In any event, this sort of solidarity action would probably be regarded as a political rather than a trade dispute (*BBC* v. *Hearn* [1977] IRLR 269).

In Contemplation or Furtherance

In several cases in the mid-1970s the Court of Appeal held that individuals could not properly claim to be within the trade dispute immunity if, objectively, the action they had taken was not furthering the trade dispute because it was too remote from it. This meant that certain types of 'secondary action' – action taken against a customer or supplier of the employer in the dispute – lost their immunity.

A classic example of this approach is the case of *Express Newspapers Ltd* v. *McShane* [1980] AC 672. In the course of a dispute with provincial newspapers, the National Union of Journalists (NUJ) called on journalists employed by the Press Association (who were still supplying vital copy to the newspapers) to strike. When this call was not fully supported, the NUJ called on its members on the national newspapers to refuse to handle any copy from the Press Association. This action was restrained by the CA on the ground that it was not reasonably capable of achieving the objective of the trade dispute.

The Court of Appeal's attempt to restrict secondary action, however, was subsequently rejected by the House of Lords. The main thrust of the decision of the Lords in the *McShane* case was that if a person taking the action honestly believes it will further the trade dispute, then this is all that matters: there was no room for an objective test (see also *Duport Steels Ltd* v. *Sirs* [1980] 1 All ER 529).

It was, however, the approach of the Court of Appeal, and Lord Denning in particular, which most closely accorded with the newly elected Conservative government's perspective on industrial relations. As a result, the Employment Act 1980 included provisions which aimed, inter alia, to control secondary action and, to use the words of one government spokesman, to 'return the law to Denning'. This legislation commenced the new legislative policy of stripping away the immunities.

Stage Three: Removal of the Immunities

The scope of the immunities has been restricted by the legislation of the 1980s: The Employment Acts of 1980, 1982, 1988 and 1990, and the Trade Union Act of 1984, and the Trade Union Reform and Employment Rights Act 1993. In this section we examine the restriction of secondary action; the loss of immunity for unlawful picketing; the provisions removing immunity in respect of actions aimed at enforcing the closed shop or trade union recognition on an employer; the requirements for secret ballots before industrial action; and industrial action taken in support of dismissed 'unofficial strikers'.

Statutory Control of Secondary Action

Section 17 of the Employment Act 1980 removed the protection provided by s. 13 (1) TULRA 1974 (as amended) against liability for interfering with commercial contracts by secondary action unless it satisfies conditions which enable it to pass through one of three 'gateways to legality', the most important of which is the so-called first customer/first supplier gateway. This permitted secondary action to be organised if it involved employees of persons who were in direct contractual relations with the employer involved in the primary dispute. The second gateway extended the first customer/first supplier rule to cover cases where the supply which was disrupted was between the secondary employer and an employer 'associated' with the primary employer. This gateway only applied where the supplies which were disrupted were in substitution for the goods which, but for the dispute, would have been supplied by or to the primary employer. The third gateway maintained immunity where the secondary action was a consequence of lawful picketing.

While the policy behind s. 17 is straightforward, its drafting was massively complex. Indeed, Lord Denning described it as 'the most tortuous section I have ever come across' (*Hadmor Productions* v. *Hamilton* [1981] IRLR 210). The complexity of the section was one of the reasons put forward for its repeal by s. 4 of the Employment Act 1990. The aim of s. 4 of the 1990 Act is that only direct disputes between an employer and its workers should attract immunity under s. 13 of TULRA. The only exception was to be secondary action arising out of lawful picketing – the only gateway to legality to be retained from the repealed s. 17 of the 1980 Act. The relevant law is now consolidated in TULR(C)A 1992, s. 244.

Determining whether secondary action attracts immunity is much simpler than it used to be. Ask yourself the following questions:

(i) Is there a trade dispute within TULR(C)A, s. 244?
     If so,
(ii) Does the basic immunity contained in s. 219 apply?
     If so,
(iii) Is there secondary action as defined by s. 224?

This occurs if a person:

(a) induces another to break a contract of employment or interferes or induces another to interfere with its performance, or
(b) threatens that a contract of employment under which he or another is employed will be broken or its performance interfered with, or that he will induce another to break a contract of employment or interfere with its performance, and the employer under the contract of employment is not a party to the trade dispute.

At this point, we have to establish which employer is in dispute with its workers (the primary dispute). If a person acting in support of this primary dispute induces a breach of the employment contracts of the employees of a different employer, then there is secondary action.

Example
Company A's employees are on strike for higher wages. Company B supplies Company A. Company B's employees are instructed to strike in furtherance of the trade dispute with A.

The instruction to Company B's employees constitutes secondary action.

Section 224 (4) seeks to limit any attempt to extend the notion of the primary employer. The section states that an employer is not to be regarded as party to a dispute between another employer and its workers. This section would appear to confirm the thinking of the House of Lords in *Dimbleby & Sons Ltd* v. *National Union of Journalists* [1984] ICR 386, that an employer, even though associated with the employer involved in the primary dispute, was not to be regarded as party to that dispute.

If there is secondary action, then we move to the final question:

(iv) Does the case pass through the lawful picketing 'gateway' in s. 224 (1), (3)? If not, immunity is lost and the action is unlawful. The basic immunity of s. 219 only applies if the picket is acting lawfully within s. 220, of which the main requirement is that workers may only picket their own place of work.

Even if the workers do picket their own place of work, their actions may still amount to secondary action because they may induce a breach of the contracts of employment of employees of other employers.

Unlawful Picketing

Unlawful picketing, such as picketing a place other than your own place of work, will not attract immunity under s. 219 (see TULR[C]A, s. 219 [3] and the next chapter here).

Enforcing Union Membership

We have already referred to the fact that the EA 1988 put further curbs on the closed shop. Section 10 removed the immunities contained in s. 13 of TULRA 1974 (as amended) from primary industrial action where the reason, or one of the reasons, for the action is that the employer is employing, has employed or might employ a person who is not a member of a trade union or that the employer is failing, has failed or might fail to discriminate against such a person. As we saw in our chapter on unfair dismissal, s. 11 made it unfair for an employer to dismiss or to take action short of dismissal against an employee on the ground of the employee's non-membership of a union or a particular union. In both the situations covered by ss. 10 and 11, the fact that the closed shop may have been approved in a ballot is an irrelevancy. (See now TULR[C]A, s. 222.)

Section 14 of the EA 1982 withdrew the immunity where the reason for the industrial action is to compel another employer to 'recognise, negotiate or consult' one or more trade unions or to force the employer to discriminate in contract or tendering on the ground of union membership or non-membership in the contracting or tendering concern. (See now TULR[C]A, s. 225.)

Secret Ballots before Industrial Action (TULR[C]A, ss. 226–235)

Official industrial action will only attract the immunity offered by TULR(C)A 1992, s. 219, if the majority of union members likely to be called upon to take industrial action have supported that action in a properly conducted ballot. As we have already seen, the requirements for a lawful ballot and the ways in which a union can be held to be vicariously responsible for industrial action saw considerable additions and modifications as a result of the Employment Acts 1988 and 1990. Yet further requirements were added by TURERA 1993. To supplement these requirements, the Department of Employment issued a Code of Practice on Trade Union Ballots on Industrial Action. Originally issued in 1990, it was revised in 1991 and 1995. The current Code of Practice on Industrial Action Ballots and Notice to Employers came into effect on 18 September 2000. Breach of the Code does not of itself give rise to civil or criminal liability, but any court or tribunal must, where it is relevant, take it into account as evidence of good industrial relations practice (TULR[C]A 1992, s. 207).

The ballot and notice requirements are set out in TULR(C)A 1992, ss. 226–235B. The provisions are complex. The government invited suggestions in *Fairness at Work* to clarify and simplify the law in this area. A large number of responses were received, especially from trade unions and legal bodies. The Employment Relations Act 1999, s. 4 gives effect to sched. 3, which, drawing on some of the suggestions, amends the law in certain respects.

When is a Ballot Required?

A ballot is only required in respect of an 'act done by a trade union'. An act is taken to have been authorised (beforehand) or endorsed (afterwards) by a trade union if it was done, or was authorised or endorsed, by:

- any person who is empowered by the rules so to do;
- the principal executive committee, the president, or
- any other committee of the union or any official of the union (whether employed by it or not) (TULR[C]A, s. 20 [2]).

The third provision, originally introduced by the EA 1990, will mean that a shop steward could render a union liable where s/he authorises or endorses action without a ballot. Moreover, by virtue of a further amendment, it is sufficient that such an official is a member of a group, the purpose of which includes organising or co-ordinating industrial action, and that any member of that group has authorised or endorsed the action (see now TULR[C]A, s. 20 [3] [b]). The insidious nature of this provision was highlighted by Lord Wedderburn during the House of Lords debates on the new legislation:

under this Bill the union is at risk from an act of an unknown person, some mysterious stranger acting unilaterally after the gathering of an unknown, shadowy group to which the official, at a material time, at some point entered and became, for a few moments, a member.[10]

A union may repudiate the purported authorisation or endorsement by the third group (other committees and officials), but can never repudiate the actions of the principal executive committee, president, general secretary or those acting under the rules. The requirements for an effective repudiation are far more stringent and complicated as a result of changes introduced by the 1990 Act. To escape liability, the action must be repudiated by the principal executive committee or the president or the general secretary as soon as reasonably practicable. Furthermore:

- written notice of the repudiation must be given to the committee or official in question without delay, and
- the union 'must do its best' to give individual written notice of the fact and date of repudiation, without delay, (i) to every member of the union who the union has reason to believe is taking part, or might otherwise take part, in industrial action as a result of the act; and (ii) to the employer of every such member (see now TULR[C]A, s. 21 [2]).

The notice given to members must also contain the following 'health warning':

> Your union has repudiated the call (or calls) for industrial action to which this notice relates and will give no support to unofficial action taken in response to it (or them). If you are dismissed while taking industrial action, you will have no right to complain of unfair dismissal.

Should these requirements not be complied with, the repudiation will be treated as ineffective. In addition, there is no repudiation if the principal executive committee, president or general secretary subsequently 'behaves in a manner which is inconsistent with the purported repudiation'.

At this stage, we think it important to emphasise the fundamental point that while a properly conducted ballot is vital to maintain the protection of the immunities for any action authorised or endorsed by the union, a lawful ballot per se will not accord immunity to the action if it is unlawful for other reasons – such as secondary action or action to enforce the closed shop.

Moreover, official industrial action will only attract immunity if the following conditions are met.

Separate Ballots for Each Workplace

As originally enacted, the Trade Union Act 1984 required a single ballot of all those who were expected to take part in the industrial action. This position was, however, changed by the EA 1988; a union intending to organise industrial action, generally speaking, must organise separate ballots for each place of work. Industrial action may not be lawfully taken at a particular workplace unless a majority of members have voted in favour of the action at that workplace (see now TULR[C]A, s. 228).

The requirement of separate ballots is subject to the following major exceptions:

(i)   Where the union reasonably believed that all the members had the same workplace.
(ii)   Where there is some factor:

    (a)   which relates to the terms, conditions or occupational description of each member entitled to vote;
    (b)   which that member has in common with some or all members of the union entitled to vote.

This allows a trade union to hold a single aggregated ballot covering members from different places of work if all belong to a complete bargaining unit – for instance, all electricians or all members employed by that employer. If you can make sense of this highly convoluted provision, you will also note that there does not have to be a factor which is common to all voters. There can be several factors, each of which is common to some – such as all skilled and semi-skilled grades, all part-time workers and electricians. The union must ballot all its members who possess the same relevant factor. So, for example, if it wishes to conduct a ballot of part-time employees employed by a particular employer, it cannot ballot those at workplace A but not those at workplace B.

Ballot Papers (TULR[C]A, s. 229)

The ballot paper must ask either whether the voter is prepared to take part or continue to take part in a strike; or whether the voter is prepared to take part or continue to take part in action short of a strike; or it may ask both questions separately. The voter must be required to answer 'Yes' or 'No' to each question and the questions must not be rolled up into one (see *Post Office* v. *Union of Communication Workers* [1990] IRLR 143). Every voting paper must contain the following statement: 'If you take part in a strike or other industrial action, you may be in breach of your contract of employment'.

The ballot paper must also specify the identity of the person(s) authorised to call upon members to take industrial action in the event of a vote in favour. This person need not be authorised under the rules of the union, but he or she must be someone who comes within TULR(C)A, s. 20 (2)–(4) (see above).

Section 20 (2) of TURERA provides that ballot papers must also state the independent scrutineer's name, the address for return and the date by which votes must be returned. The papers will also have to be marked with consecutive numbers.

Conduct of the Ballot

The Trade Union Act 1974 offered a union a choice of voting methods: fully postal; semi-postal (voting papers are returned but not distributed by post) or workplace balloting. However, the Code of Practice on Trade Union Ballots in Industrial Action strongly advocated the fully postal method as the most desirable (see para. 20) and TURERA 1993, s. 17 has now made it a legal requirement (see now TULR[C]A, s. 230 [2]).

Section 227 (1) provides that all those who the union might reasonably believe will be induced to take part, or to continue to take part, in the strike or industrial action should be entitled to vote. Section 227 (2) provides that requirement is not satisfied where a trade union member who is called out on strike 'was denied entitlement to vote in a ballot'. Section 230 (3) relates to the opportunity to vote and provides that: 'So far as is reasonably practicable, every person who is entitled to vote in the ballot must' be given an opportunity to vote.

In *British Railways Board* v. *NUR* [1989] 349, the Court of Appeal rejected the employer's argument that what is now s. 227 (2) invalidates a ballot if anyone who is entitled to vote but did not have an opportunity of voting is invited to strike. The court held that there was a profound difference between denying someone's entitlement to vote and inadvertently failing to give an individual an opportunity to vote. Wrongly denying a member's entitlement to vote is an absolute obligation with draconian consequences. However, s. 230 (3) expressly makes the opportunity to vote subject to a test of practicability. Therefore, a 'trifling error' – 200 members out of 60,000 not having an opportunity to vote – did not invalidate the ballot (cf. *RJB Mining (UK) Ltd* v. *NUM* [1997] IRLR 621, QBD).

Timing of the Industrial Action

The normal rule is that the action must be called within four weeks, beginning with the date of the ballot (see s. 234 [1] and *RJB Mining (UK) Ltd* v. *NUM* [1995] IRLR 556 CA). However, the 1989 docks dispute and the litigation surrounding it showed the harsh effect of this time limit where the union was prevented from calling industrial action during the four-week period because of an injunction. The TGWU succeeded in getting the injunction lifted but then had to reballot because it was outside the four-week limit.

Under s. 234 (2), a union may now apply for an extension of time to allow for the period during which it was prohibited from calling the action. An application has to be made 'forthwith upon the prohibition ceasing to have effect' and no application may be made after the end of a period of eight weeks, beginning with the date of the ballot. The Employment Relations Act 1999 amends s. 234 (1) of the 1992 Act so that the four-week period may be extended by up to a maximum of four more weeks if both the union and the employer agree to the extension. The purpose of the amendment is to avoid circumstances where a union feels obliged to organise industrial action within the four-week period before a ballot becomes ineffective, even though the parties might be able to reach a settlement through further negotiation.

We saw earlier the ballot paper must identify the person(s) authorised to call for industrial action and, indeed, industrial action will only be regarded as having the support of the ballot if called by this 'specified person' (s. 233 [1]). Finally, there must be no authorisation or endorsement of the action before the date of the ballot.

The courts have taken a realistic view of the requirement that the 'call for industrial action' must be by a specified person and have held it to include the case where the specified person authorises a subordinate (such as regional or local officials) to call for industrial action if a final 'make or break' negotiation fails: *Tank and Drums Ltd* v. *Transport and General Workers' Union* [1991] IRLR 372 CA.

In the Green Paper, 'Industrial Relations in the 1990s',[11] the government proposed that, once a ballot has produced a majority in favour of (or continuing with) industrial action, a union should be required to give the employer seven days' written notice of any industrial action to which the ballot relates. The notice would have to identify which workers were to be called upon to take industrial action, and on which specific date the industrial action would begin. Where a union proposes to call for intermittent action, such as a series of one-day strikes, it would be required to give at least seven days' notice of each day or other separate period of industrial action. Moreover, if the union suspends or withdraws its support for the action, further notice would be required before there is any subsequent call to resume the action. These proposals were given statutory force by TURERA 1993 and are now contained in an amended TULR(C)A 1992, s. 234A.

The Green Paper also proposed that employers should have the right to receive the following information:

- notice of intent to hold the ballot, with details of which of the workers will be entitled to vote;
- a sample copy of the ballot paper, to enable the employer to know which questions are to be asked and what other information is to appear on the ballot paper; and
- the same details of the result as the law requires to be given to the union's members, and a copy of the report of the independent scrutineer for the ballot.

These proposals are now enshrined in TULR(C)A 1992, ss. 226A, 231A and 231B.

A particular difficulty is the legal requirement of trade unions in certain circumstances to give to employers the names of those they will ballot. Trade unions are reluctant to do so because some members may not wish their trade union to disclose their names to the employer. The law had been interpreted by the courts (most notably, in the case *Blackpool and the Fylde College* v. *National Association of Teachers in Further and Higher Education* [1994] ICR 648, CA, and [1994] ICR 982, HL) as requiring the union in certain circumstances to give to the employer the names of those employees which it is balloting or calling upon to take industrial action. The Employment Relations Act 1999 amends the 1992 Act so as to ensure that a union is required to provide only information in its possession relating to number, category or workplace of the employees concerned and that it is not required to name the employees concerned (see *RMT* v. *London Underground Ltd* [2001] IRLR 228, CA; c.f. *Westminster City Council* v. *UNISON* [2001] IRLR 524, CA; see Clause 21 of the Employment Relations Bill 2004).

The Member's Statutory Right to Prevent Unballoted Action

While the failure to hold a ballot will result in the loss of immunities, the Employment Act 1988 created an additional legal consequence. Where a trade union authorises or endorses 'industrial action' without first holding a ballot, one of its members who has been, or is likely to be, induced to take part in this may apply to the High Court for an order requiring the union to withdraw the authorisation or reverse the effect of its authorisation or endorsement (see now TULR[C]A 1992, s. 62). In bringing this action, the member may be assisted by the Commissioner for the Rights of Trade Union Members.

The precise scope of the phrase 'industrial action' is unclear. But interpretation of that phrase under what is now TULR(C)A, s. 238 (dealing with the dismissal of those taking part in a strike or other industrial action) would suggest it encompasses action which does not necessarily involve a breach of contract (see *Power Packing Casemakers* v. *Faust* [1983] QB 471). The practical significance of this is not lost on the editors of *Harvey on Industrial Relations and Employment Law*.[12]

> One purpose of balloting members over industrial action is to preserve the union's statutory immunity from a suit in tort brought by a plaintiff employer. The tort concerned will be or involve the tort of inducing a person to break a contract; and there is no need for any tort immunity. Therefore, for the purposes of the 1984 Act, the union does not need to ballot the members unless there is going to be a *breach* of contract. However under the 1988 Act, a member of the union can ask the court to restrain unballoted industrial action whether that industrial action involves breaches of contract or not. Ergo, the union, to be safe, needs to ballot *all* industrial action, whether or not there is going to be any breach of the member's contracts of employment.

Industrial Action in Support of Dismissed 'Unofficial Strikers'

In our earlier chapter dealing with unfair dismissal, we have described how the 1990 Act removed the limited unfair dismissal protection to 'unofficial' strikers (see now TULR[C]A, s. 237). In order to strengthen the employer's position in such a situation the 1990 Act removed the statutory immunity from any industrial action if 'the reason, or one of the reasons, for doing it is the fact or belief' that an employer has selectively dismissed one or more employees who were taking unofficial action (see now TULR[C]A, s. 223).

Civil Remedies and Enforcement

Currently, if a trade union organises industrial action which is unlawful, it can be restrained by an injunction from the courts on an application from the employer involved in the dispute, or from any other party whose contractual rights have been infringed. Union members also have the right to restrain industrial action if they are, or are likely to be, induced to participate in industrial action which does not have the support of a ballot. TURERA 1993 extended the right of action to members of the public who suffer, or are likely to suffer, disruption from unlawful industrial action (see now TULR[C]A 1992, s. 235A).

Injunctions

An injunction is either an order requiring the defendant to cease a particular course of action (a negative injunction) or, in its mandatory form, an order requiring the defendant to do something. The most frequent form of order in industrial disputes is the interlocutory injunction requiring the organisers to call off the industrial action pending full trial of the action. Employers who succeed at this stage rarely proceed to full trial: they have achieved their aim of halting the action. They know the suspension of the industrial action, although theoretically on a temporary basis, will defeat the strike in practical terms because the impetus will be lost. Given the crucial effect the obtaining of injunctive relief will have on the outcome of a dispute, the principles on which the court's discretion is based are of great importance. It used to be the case that in order to be granted interim relief the plaintiff had to establish a prima facie case. However, in *American Cyanamid Co v. Ethicon Ltd* [1975] AC 396 (a case involving patents law), the House of Lords substituted a less arduous test: namely, whether there is 'a serious issue to be tried'.

Moreover, the plaintiff must show that the defendant's conduct is causing him/her irreparable harm: harm that cannot be remedied by a subsequent award of damages (the status quo concept).

Finally, the plaintiff must convince the court that the harm being suffered by him or her is greater than will be incurred by the defendants if they are ordered to cease their activities pending full trial (the 'balance of convenience' test).

The application of these tests generally produced a favourable result for the plaintiff employer. In determining the status quo and balance of convenience tests, it is easy to quantify the economic loss to an employer as a result of a strike but far more difficult to assess the enormous damage that can be done to a union's bargaining position if an injunction is granted. This, together with the fact that interlocutory relief can be obtained on affidavit evidence, at very short notice and without the defendants even having an opportunity to answer the complaint, meant that the process was very much tilted in favour of management.

TULR(C)A s. 221 contains two provisions which seek to do something to redress the imbalance:

(a) Section 221 (1) requires reasonable steps to be taken to give notice of the application and an opportunity to be heard to a party likely to put forward a trade dispute defence.

(b) Section 221 (2) provides that where a party against whom an interlocutory injunction is sought claims that he or she acted in contemplation or furtherance of a trade dispute, the court shall have regard to the likelihood of that party succeeding in establishing a trade dispute defence. This was an attempt to mitigate the effects of *Cyanamid* in labour injunction cases.

In *NWL* v. *Woods* [1979] 3 All ER 614, Lord Diplock was of the view that the provision was intended as a reminder to judges that, in weighing the balance of convenience, they should consider a number of 'practical realities', particularly the fact that the interlocutory injunction stage generally disposes of the whole action. However, in *Dimbleby & Sons Ltd* v. *NUJ* [1984] ICR 386, his Lordship revised his view of the practical realities, given that in the interim period the Employment Act 1982 had made it possible to pursue actions for damages against trade unions themselves and therefore it was wrong to assume that the matter would be disposed at the interlocutory stage. Lord Diplock appeared to suggest that this should make a judge more willing to grant an interim injunction. But surely this factor should weight the balance of convenience against the granting of an injunction, given that the employer is now able to recover damages and costs at full trial from a solvent defendant.

You will find suggestions in several cases (*NWL Ltd* v. *Woods*; *Express Newspapers* v. *MacShane* [1980] AC 672; and *Duport Steels Ltd* v. *Sirs* [1980] ICR 161) that the courts have a residual discretion to grant an injunction. Consequently, in cases where a strike poses serious consequences to the employer, a third party or the general public, what is now s. 221 (2) might be overridden. This possibility is now of much less practical importance given the considerable narrowing of the scope of the immunities which has taken place (for a detailed discussion of this highly complex area see Wedderburn, *The Worker and the Law*, pp. 681–717).

Damages

Probably the most significant change in the structure of labour law during the 1980s was made by the Employment Act 1982, enabling a trade union itself to be sued for unlawful industrial action. In doing so, the Act 'broke the mould' of British labour law which had held sway, but for the brief interlude of the Industrial Relations Act, since 1906.

We have already seen that a union will be held vicariously liable for the unlawful industrial action of its membership where such action was authorised or endorsed by those identified in the TULR(C)A, s. 20 (2) (see pp. 448–9 for a full discussion and the circumstances in which a trade union may repudiate a purported authorisation or endorsement).

Limits on Damages Awarded against Trade Unions in Actions in Tort
The TULR(C)A, s. 22 places limits on the amounts which can be awarded against trade unions in actions brought against them where they have authorised or endorsed unlawful industrial action. The limits, which depend on the size of the trade union, have been as follows since 1982 (although the Secretary of State does have power to vary them – s. 22 [3]):

(a)   £10,000 for unions with less than 5,000 members.
(b)   £50,000 for unions between 5,000 and less than 25,000 in membership.
(c)   £125,000 for unions with more than 25,000 but less than 100,000 members.
(d)   £250,000 if the union has 100,000 or more members.

These limits apply in 'any proceedings in tort brought against a trade union'. The effect of this phrase is that where a union is sued by various plaintiffs (for example, the employer in dispute, customers, or suppliers) for the damages caused to them by the unlawful action, then the maximum will be applied to them separately. In this way a large union, such as the TGWU, could find it will be liable to pay well over the £250,000 in damages arising from any one dispute. You should also note these maxima do not apply in respect of the size of any fine imposed for contempt of court where there is a failure to comply with the terms of the injunction. Nor do the limits on damages include the legal costs the defendant union may have to pay. Hepple and Fredman cite the example of the *Stockport Messenger* action in 1983 against the National Graphical Association as a result of which the union lost one-tenth of its assets.

The damages against the union were assessed at £131,000 plus interest (which included aggravated and exemplary damages in relation to proved losses). When this was added to the £675,000 fines for contempt of court for non-compliance with an injunction, and legal costs of sequestration, it was estimated in December 1985 that the union had lost over £1 million.[13] (see also *Messenger Newspapers Group Ltd v. National Graphical Association* (1982) (1984) ICR 345)

Workers whose Right Lawfully to Withdraw Their Labour is Wholly or Partly Restricted

The Armed Forces

Industrial action would constitute desertion or mutiny and those who organised a strike would commit the crime of incitement to disaffection or sedition.

The Police

Following the abortive strike in 1919, it was made a criminal offence to take any actions likely to cause disaffection or breach of discipline among members of the police force. This law is now contained in the Police Act 1996, s. 91. This statute also forbids police officers the right to join a trade union, though, if they are already union members when they enlist, permission may be granted to retain that membership. The police may join the Police Federation but that is not a trade union as such and it is not affiliated to the TUC.

Prison Officers

As a result of the Criminal Justice and Public Order Act 1994, s. 127, it is unlawful to induce a prison officer to take industrial action. As in other, similar torts, it is the inducement that is unlawful: actually withholding services or committing breaches of discipline will not be within the section. The tort created by this section is only actionable by the Home Secretary. S/he is entitled to apply for an injunction to present an apprehended breach of duty without the need to show that he would suffer any actual loss or damage.

Merchant Seafarers

The Merchant Shipping Acts create a variety of criminal offences which could be used against those who organise or take part in industrial action *while the ship is at sea* – for example, in breach of duty endangering a ship, life or limb (Merchant Shipping Act 1995, s. 58. There is also a crime of concerted disobedience 'at sea' which carries the maximum statutory fine or summary conviction, or two years' imprisonment and/or a fine on indictment (s. 59).

Communications Workers

The Post Office Act 1953 makes it a criminal offence for postal workers wilfully to delay or detain any postal packet (ss. 58, 68; see also Telecommunications Act 1984, ss. 44, 45). The 1984 Act also created a new civil liability of inducing a breach of the licensed operator's duty to operate the telecommunications system or to interfere with the performance of that duty. Liability is established when the action is taken wholly or partly to achieve such a result (s. 18 [5]–[7]). Industrial action by telecommunications workers could clearly fall foul of this form of liability and, in this context, it will be irrelevant if they are acting in contemplation or furtherance of a trade dispute.

Aliens

The Aliens Restriction (Amendment) Act 1919, s. 3 (2) makes it a crime punishable by three months' imprisonment for an alien to promote industrial unrest unless engaged bona fide in the industry for at least two years. This piece of xenophobic legislation owes its place on the statute book to the panic which followed the Russian Revolution of 1917 and the fear that foreign agitators were plotting a similar insurrection in Britain.

Endangering Life

Any worker who breaks a contract of service or hiring knowing or having reasonable cause to believe that the probable consequence of so doing, either alone or in combination with others, will be to endanger human life, cause serious bodily harm or expose any property to destruction or serious injury, commits a crime (originally enacted as Conspiracy and Protection of Property Act, s. 5; now TULR[C]A, s. 240).

This offence might be relevant to a wide range of occupations engaged in industrial action, such as hospital workers, firefighters and refuse collectors, but there is no record of this mid-Victorian provision ever being used.

Emergency Powers

In the event of a national emergency, the government possesses extremely wide powers to intervene in an industrial dispute. The Emergency Powers Acts of 1920 and 1964 empower the government to proclaim a state of emergency and make regulations where there have occurred 'events of such a nature as to be calculated by interfering with the supply and distribution of food, water or light, or with the means of locomotion, to deprive the community or a substantial proportion of the community of the essentials of life'. The proclamation must be renewed after one month and Parliament must approve the regulations made by the government.

While the Act gives almost unlimited power to the government to make regulations, it cannot make it an offence to take part in a strike or to persuade others to do so and it cannot introduce military or industrial conscription. An emergency has been proclaimed 12 times since 1920 (including the seamen's strike in 1966, the docks strike in 1972, the miners' strike in 1972 and coal and electricity workers in 1973).

In addition, the government has the power to call in the armed forces to be used on 'urgent work of national importance' and this power may be exercised without any proclamation or consultation with Parliament (see the Defence [Armed Forces] Regulations 1939, now made permanent by the Emergency Powers Act 1964, s. 2).

More recently, the legislation which privatised the electricity and water industries provides ministers with wide powers to issue confidential directions to the relevant operators for purposes which include 'mitigating the effects of any civil emergency which may occur'. The Secretary of State must lay a copy of every direction s/he gives before Parliament unless s/he 'is of the opinion that disclosure of the direction is against the interests of national security' or, in the case of electricity supply, s/he 'considers that it would be against the commercial interests of any person'.[14]

On the assumption that industrial action could come within the definition of a 'civil emergency', Gillian Morris has observed:

> In the event of industrial action taking place, the powers to regulate supplies which previously would have required approval under the Emergency Powers Act 1920 may now be exercised without the need for parliamentary involvement. At the same time as privatizing these services, therefore, the Government has increased considerably its scope for taking measures on a wholly unaccountable basis to counter the impact of industrial action.[15]

Proposals to Ban Strikes in Essential Services

The increasing militancy of workers in essential services during the 1970s, particularly during the so-called winter of discontent of 1978/79, brought calls from certain sources for a general constraint to be placed on industrial action by such workers. However, the promise of legislation, though contained in both the 1979 and 1983 Conservative election manifestos, has not come to fruition. The matter was last mooted by the government in 1989, following the 'summer of discontent' and the disruption on the railways and London Underground. Once again, no legislation was forthcoming. One difficulty is in coming up with a definition of what constitutes an 'essential service'. No doubt it would cover those working in health and burial services, the fire brigade and those in gas, water, sewage and electricity. But what about the railways, docks, air and road transport? As the Green Paper, 'Trade Union Immunities', observed in 1981: 'so interdependent and interconnected are firms and industries that there is almost no major strike which will not ultimately affect the interests of the economy or community as a whole'.[16]

An alternative reason for the lack of legislation is offered by Gillian Morris, who speculates that financial considerations may have played some part:

> Prominent advocates of restrictions all recognized the need for some form of pay guarantee or alternative method of dispute resolution, such as compulsory binding arbitration, in return. To the Government such suggestions were anathema; from an early stage it made clear its antipathy to unilateral arbitration, and it refused to countenance any index-linking arrangement beyond those already in existence for the police and fire service. In the light of this attitude, it was unlikely to pay a price for limiting recourse to industrial action in essential services.[17]

But Morris' central argument is that even though the government has not acted directly to outlaw industrial action in essential services, it has severely constrained the freedom to strike in these areas by more subtle means. First, as we have already seen, the privatisation legislation contains new and enhanced powers to defeat industrial action. Second, there are elements of the general legislation on industrial action which will have a particular impact on unions proposing to organise industrial action in essential services. The structural and organisational changes which have taken place in a number of essential services, such as water, electricity and the Health Service, with the decentralisation of the employer function could make action taken by workers taken in support of those employed in the same service unlawful 'secondary action'. In addition, the complexities surrounding the appropriate constituency for a lawful ballot on industrial action would pose particular difficulties for essential service unions who wished to preserve emergency cover during disputes.

In April 1993, according to a leaked letter from Mrs Gillian Shepherd, then employment secretary, to John Patten, another education minister, the government had been considering outlawing any industrial action aimed at frustrating the carrying out of a specific statutory duty. Such a change would affect all five million public sector staff and thousands of others working on services contracted out to public companies.

Mrs Shepherd's letter, written against the background of the teachers' boycott of tests under the national curriculum, alleged that the boycott was 'clearly designed to frustrate the carrying out of a specific statutory duty', namely that of schools to deliver the national curriculum.

On this occasion at least, the government received no help from the courts, with both the High Court and a unanimous Court of Appeal declaring that the tests boycott was against the workload caused by the curriculum and testing arrangements, and that it therefore was a lawful trade dispute.[18]

The Citizen and the Control of Industrial Action

The Green Paper, 'Industrial Relations in the 1990s', while not proposing an outright ban on strikes in the public services, did advocate further legal constraints. It proposed that customers of public services within the scope of the so-called Citizen's Charter should have the right to bring proceedings to prevent or restrain the unlawful organisation of industrial action in, or affecting, any such service.

The proposed right would be exercised where:

(a) a relevant public service was, or would be affected by, unlawful industrial action; and

(b) the unlawful industrial action had not been restrained by proceedings brought
     by an employer or union member.

The new right would be available to anyone who was, or was likely to be, a customer
of the relevant public service when it was affected by industrial action. Proceedings
could be brought if unlawfully organised industrial action either brought the service
to a total standstill or resulted in its operating at a reduced level. Failure to comply
with the resultant Court Order would put the union or strike organisers in contempt
of court and fines and sequestration of assets might then follow.

While the Green Paper concerned itself solely with industrial action in the public
services, TURERA extended this to cover *all* industrial action, whether it takes place
in either the public or private sector. Moreover, unlike the Green Paper, the Act did
not make the exercise of the right conditional on no employer or union member
having sought to challenge the legality of the industrial action in the courts (see
now TULR[C]A 1992, s. 235A).

These proposals were presented by the Conservative government as complementing
the proposals for extending consumer protection through the Citizen's Charter (Cm.
1599), but they could have potentially disastrous effects on industrial relations.
Even with the legal power which has been handed to employers in the 1980s and
beginning of the 1990s, there will still be occasions when an employer will judge
it more appropriate to pursue further negotiations rather than to go rushing to the
courts. These provisions rob the employer of that choice and allow individuals backed
by such right-wing groups as the Freedom Association to get involved, risking an
increase in the bitterness of the dispute.

The 1993 Act also created a new Commissioner for Protection Against Unlawful
Industrial Action, who would have the power on application, to grant assistance for
proceedings against a trade union under the right in TULR(C)A 1992, s. 235A. In
1996–97 only two formal applications for assistance were received. Of these, one was
granted assistance. In addition, the Commissioner's Office issued 1,027 information
sheets, 233 guides and 369 reports at a cost the taxpayer of £91, 388. The office was
abolished by the Employment Relations Act 1999, s. 28.

CHAPTER 20

Industrial Conflict II: Picketing

Introduction

The practice of picketing a place of work in order to persuade other workers not to enter the workplace has been traditionally perceived by trade unions as an essential weapon when they are involved in disputes. The vast majority of pickets lines are conducted in an entirely peaceful and orderly manner, often without the need for a police presence.[1] During the 1970s and 1980s, however, we witnessed the practice of 'mass-picketing' and instances of violent confrontation between strikers and the police – for example, the miners' strikes of 1972, 1974 and 1984/85, Grunwick in 1977 and Wapping in 1986. Such atypical *causes célèbres* provided the rationale for statutory intervention aimed at controlling more closely the conduct of picketing through the use of both the civil and criminal law.

While it is true that picketing is one area of industrial conflict where the criminal law plays a significant part in regulation in addition to the civil law, it should be stressed that secondary picketing – picketing a workplace other than your own – is not in itself a criminal offence. Since the early 1980s there has been a blurring of the distinction between the civil and the criminal law in the case of picketing and this causes confusion in the minds of trade unionists themselves. Welch's survey of active trade unionists found that nearly 80 per cent of the sample believed that they would automatically commit a criminal offence if they peacefully picketed the premises of a supplier of their employer. Commenting on this legal mystification, Welch argues:

> This has important ideological connotations, particularly when the participants in such an activity are not aware that at a factual level they may be able to counter claims by employers, the media and the police that they are acting illegally or committing the 'offence' of secondary picketing. Moreover, such misconceptions of the criminal law may result in pickets obeying police instructions to leave or disperse even when they are within their strict legal rights.[2]

The law's approach to picketing raises the question of whether there is an adequate recognition of an individual right of assembly.

The Freedom to Picket

As with strike action, the law provides no right to picket. Instead it offers an extremely limited immunity from civil and criminal liability. This is now contained in TULR(C)A 1992, s. 220. Section 220 (1) (a) states that:

> It shall be lawful for a person in contemplation or furtherance of a trade dispute to attend –

(a) at or near his own place of work; or

(b) if he is an official of a trade union, at or near the place of work of a member
     of that union whom he is accompanying and whom he represents, for the
     purposes only of communicating information or peacefully persuading any
     person to work or abstain from working.

Notice that picketing will only receive the protection of the immunities if the pickets
are attending at or near their own workplace. So-called secondary picketing was
rendered unlawful by the amendments made by the Employment Act 1980. There is
no statutory definition of 'place of work'. However, the Code of Practice on Picketing,
published in 1980 to accompany the amendments to the statute and revised in 1992,
offers the following guidance:

> The law does not enable a picket to attend lawfully at an entrance to, or exit from any
> place of work other than his own. This applies even, for example, if those working
> at the other place of work are employed by the same employer, or are covered by
> the same collective bargaining arrangements as the picket. (para. 18)

In *Rayware Ltd* v. *TGWU* [1989] IRLR 134, pickets assembled on the public highway
at an entrance to an industrial estate which included the factory unit where they
worked. They were actually three-quarters of a mile from their factory unit. The
majority view of the Court of Appeal was that the pickets were 'near' their workplace
and therefore acting lawfully.

The statute provides three exceptions to the 'own place of work' requirement:

(i)   If workers normally work at more than one place (mobile workers) or if it is
      impractical to picket their place of work (for instance, an oil rig), then the section
      allows them to picket the place where their work is administered by the employer
      (s. 220 [2]).

(ii) Workers who are dismissed during the dispute in question are permitted to picket
      their former place of work (s. 220 [3]).

(iii) As you will see from s. 220 (1) (b), a trade union official may attend at any place
      of work provided that:

      (a) s/he is accompanying a member or members of his/her trade union who
           are picketing at their own place of work; and

      (b) s/he personally represents those members within the trade union. An official
           – whether lay or full-time – is regarded for this purpose as representing only
           those members s/he has been specifically appointed or elected to represent.
           So it is lawful for a regional official to attend a picket at any place within
           that region, whereas a shop steward can only picket the workplace of the
           work group s/he represents (see s. 220 [4]).

Civil Liabilities

The Economic Torts

Without the protection of the immunities, picketing will generally result in an
economic tort being committed. If workers assemble at the entrance to a workplace

and attempt to persuade other employees not to work, the pickets could be liable for inducing a breach of contracts of employment. However, provided the picketing is lawful within s. 220, the general immunity provided by s. 219 in respect of tortious liability applies (see s. 219 [3]).

Private Nuisance

Private nuisance is an unlawful interference with an individual's use or enjoyment of his/her land. Unreasonable interference with that right by, for example, blocking an access route to the employer's property may give rise to a cause of action. So, even if the pickets stand outside the employer's premises they may be liable for the tort of private nuisance.

Picketing which exceeds the bounds of peacefully obtaining or communicating information may involve liability for private nuisance. However, there is still doubt whether peaceful picketing itself amounts to a nuisance when not protected by the 'golden formula'. In the case of *Lyons* v. *Wilkins*, the Court of Appeal held that peaceful picketing which involved persuasion went beyond mere attendance for the purpose of informing, and was a common law nuisance. In *Ward Lock & Co* v. *Operative Printers' Assistants' Society* [1906] 22 TLR 327, a differently constituted Court of Appeal thought otherwise. In this case it was said that picketing a person's premises is not unlawful unless it is associated with conduct which constitutes nuisance at common law: some independent wrongful act such as obstruction, violence, intimidation, molestation or threats.

In *Hubbard* v. *Pitt* [1975] ICR 308 (a rare non-industrial picketing case), Lord Denning sided with the view of the Court of Appeal in *Ward Lock*, stating:

> Picketing is not a nuisance in itself. Nor is it a nuisance for a group of people to attend at or near the plaintiff's premises in order to obtain or communicate information or in order to peacefully persuade. It does not become a nuisance unless it is associated with obstruction, violence, intimidation, molestation or threats.

The majority of the Court of Appeal, on the other hand, merely affirmed the exercise of the High Court judge's discretion to grant an interlocutory injunction to the plaintiffs whose premises were being picketed and had little to say on the substantive issue. However, Lord Justice Orr did feel that the defendants' intentions and states of mind formed what he called 'a crucial question' in this matter and he was satisfied that in this case the pickets intended to interfere with the plaintiff's business.

This sort of reasoning was applied subsequently in *Mersey Dock & Harbour Co Ltd* v. *Verrinder* [1982] IRLR 152, where the High Court held that the picketing of the entrances to container terminals at Mersey Docks amounted to private nuisance despite the fact that the picketing was carried out in an entirely peaceful manner by a small group of pickets.

On the basis of this approach, it would appear that if the intention of the pickets is to achieve more than the mere communication of information and actually to interfere with the picketed employer's business, then the picket will be tortious.

As you can see, the conflict between the *Lyons* and *Ward Lock* approaches is unresolved, though you will find the weight of academic opinion favouring the *Ward Lock* approach.[3]

You will also find that the tort of nuisance was interpreted to be considerably broader in scope in *Thomas v. NUM (South Wales Area)* [1985] IRLR 136, a case arising out of the protracted miners' strike of 1984/85. In this case, a group of working miners obtained injunctions restraining the area union from organising mass picketing at the collieries where they worked. While Mr Justice Scott expressed his agreement with the *Ward Lock* approach that picketing per se does not amount to a common law nuisance, he held that it could be tortious if it amounted to an unreasonable interference with the victims' rights to use the highway. This was the situation in the case before the court:

> the picketing at the colliery gates is of such a nature and is carried out in a manner that represents an unreasonable harassment of the working miners. A daily congregation on average of 50 to 70 men hurling abuse in circumstances that require a police presence and require the working miners to be conveyed in vehicles does not in my view leave any room for argument.

Two important points arise from this decision:

- Private nuisance is concerned with interference with the use or enjoyment of land in which the plaintiff has an interest. In this case, a species of the tort was held to extend to interference with the right to use the highway.
- The terms of the injunction granted by the court restricted picketing at the collieries to communicating and obtaining information peacefully and in numbers not exceeding six. This number is not a purely arbitrary figure; it comes from the Code of Practice on Picketing which at para. 51 advises that: 'pickets and their organisers should ensure that in general the number of pickets does not exceed six at any entrance to a workplace; frequently a smaller number will be appropriate'.

This would suggest that the judge was using the guidance in the Code to fix the parameters of lawful picketing. If this view is correct, then any picketing numbering more than six will lose the immunity offered by s. 220 and will be tortious.

Trespass
Section 220 tells us that picketing is lawful where pickets attend 'at or near' their own place of work. To mount a picket on the employer's land without consent will mean that the immunity will be forfeited and that the tort of trespass has been committed (see *British Airports Authority v. Ashton* [1983] IRLR 287).

Criminal Liability

While it is important to grasp the range of possible civil liabilities which may attach to certain types of picketing, it is the criminal law which is of the greatest practical significance in terms of the control of the activity. This can be clearly seen from the employment of the criminal law during the miners' strike, where over 11,000 charges were brought in connection with incidents arising out of the dispute. These ranged in gravity from the serious offences of riot and unlawful assembly to the less serious charges of obstruction of the highway. Additional criminal offences which may be relevant to the conduct of picketing have been created by the Public Order Act 1986. We shall offer you a brief survey of the potential criminal liability of pickets.[4]

Obstructing a Police Officer

If a police officer reasonably apprehends that a breach of the peace is likely to occur, the officer has the right and duty at common law to take reasonable steps to prevent it. If the officer is obstructed in the exercise of this duty then an offence is committed (s. 51 [3] of the Police Act 1964). In practice, this gives the police a wide discretion to control picketing. While there must be an objective apprehension that a breach of the peace is a real as opposed to a remote possibility, the courts tend to accept the officer's assessment of the situation. The leading case on this question is *Piddington* v. *Bates* [1960] 1 WLR 162, where the officer's decision to restrict the number of pickets at an entrance to a workplace to two was held to be legally justified. (You should note that the Code of Practice on Picketing makes it clear that its recommended number of six pickets does not affect in any way the discretion of the police to limit the number of people on any one picket line – para. 47.)

The common law duty to preserve the peace also allows the police to set up roadblocks to prevent pickets joining picket lines some distance away, provided that there is a reasonable apprehension that the risk to the peace is 'in close proximity both in time and place' (see *Moss* v. *McLachlan* [1985] IRLR 76 and the commentary on the case by Morris).[5] Under s. 4 of the Police and Criminal Evidence Act 1984, police officers may also operate 'road checks' for purposes which include ascertaining whether a vehicle is carrying a person intending to commit an offence which a senior officer has reasonable grounds to believe is likely to lead to serious public disorder.

Obstruction of the Highway (s. 137 of the Highways Act 1980)

Under this provision, it is an offence wilfully to obstruct free passage along a highway without lawful authority or excuse. Before the offence is established, there must be proof of an unreasonable use of the highway. This is a question of fact and depends upon all the circumstances, including the length of time the obstruction continues, the place where it occurs, its purpose and whether it causes an actual as opposed to potential obstruction (*Nagy* v. *Weston* [1965] 1 All ER 78). It would appear that peaceful picketing carried out in the manner envisaged by s. 15 TULRA and within the numbers advised by the Code will be held to be a reasonable user. If, however, these boundaries are crossed an offence will be committed, as, for example, where pickets stood in front of a vehicle in order to stop it entering the employer's premises (*Broome* v. *DPP* [1974] AC 587) or walked in a continuous circle in a factory entrance (*Tynan* v. *Balmer* [1967] 1 QB 91).

Public Nuisance

This offence derives from common law and is committed where members of the public are obstructed in the exercise of rights which are common to all Her Majesty's subjects, including the right of free passage along the public highway. As with the more frequently charged offence under the Highways Act, it is necessary for the prosecution to prove unreasonable use.

Where an individual suffers special damage, over and above that suffered by the rest of the public, an action in tort for public nuisance may also be brought.

The Conspiracy and Protection of Property Act 1875
This Victorian statute made the following five acts criminal if they are done 'wrongfully and without legal authority' with a view to compelling any person to do or abstain from doing any act which that person has a legal right to do (the gender-biased language follows the wording in the Act):

(i)   using violence or intimidating that person or his wife or children or injuring his property;
(ii)   persistently following that person about from place to place;
(iii)   hiding any tools, clothes or other property owned or used by such other person, or depriving him or hindering him in the use thereof;
(iv)   watching or besetting his house, residence or place of work, or the approach to such house, residence or place, or wherever the person happens to be;
(v)   following such a person with two or more other persons in a disorderly manner in or through any street or road. (Now TULR[C]A s. 241)

Until relatively recently, it was assumed that this quaintly worded provision was only of historical interest and virtually obsolete in practical terms. During the miners' strike of 1984/85, however, at least 643 charges were brought under what is now TULR(C)A, s. 241, mainly to deal with 'watching and besetting' working miners' homes. In the view of the government, the section had demonstrated its continued efficacy in the circumstances of the strike and should not only be retained but strengthened (see White Paper, 'Review of Public Order Law').[6]

Consequently, the Public Order Act 1986 increased the maximum penalty of three months' imprisonment and a £100 fine to six months' imprisonment and/or a fine (currently £5,000). The Act also made breach of what is now s. 241 an arrestable offence.

Of the five offences listed in s. 241, watching and besetting is the one which is most likely to arise out of the course of picketing. As we have seen earlier in this chapter, the weight of authority would suggest that the watching and besetting must be of such a nature as to amount in itself to tortious activity before it can give rise to liability under s. 241. If peaceful picketing is not tortious, then it cannot amount to a criminal watching and besetting either.

One final point in this section concerns the question of whether mass picketing amounts to intimidation. In *Thomas* v. *NUM (South Wales Area)* (cited above), Mr Justice Scott was of the view that not only was mass picketing a common law nuisance but it also amounted to intimidation under what is now s. 241, even where there was no physical obstruction of those going to work.

The Public Order Act 1986

In putting forward the proposals which were later largely translated into the provisions of the Public Order Act, the White Paper of 1985 stated:

The rights of peaceful protest and assembly are amongst our fundamental freedoms: they are numbered among the touchstones which distinguish a free society from a totalitarian one. Throughout the review the Government has been concerned to regulate those freedoms to the minimum extent necessary to preserve order and protect the rights of others.[7]

A number of commentators, however, have expressed a general concern that the provisions contained in the Act impose a dangerous restriction on the civil liberties of assembly and protest and, particularly in the light of events during the 1984/85 miners' strike, make it increasingly more difficult for the police to be seen to maintain a position of neutrality in the policing of industrial disputes.[8]

Part I of the Public Order Act, as amended contains five new statutory offences which may have a relevance in the context of picketing. Sections 1–3 of the Act contain the offences of riot, violent disorder and affray, and replace the common law offences of riot, rout, unlawful assembly and affray whose ambit was confused and uncertain. Sections 4 and 5 contain the more minor offences of causing fear or provocation of violence and causing harassment, alarm or distress.

Riot (s. 1)

Where 12 or more people are present together and use or threaten violence for a common purpose and their conduct (taken together) is such that a person of reasonable firmness – if present – would fear for his/her safety, each person using the violence is guilty of riot an liable on conviction to a maximum possible penalty of ten years' imprisonment (or a fine or both).

Violent Disorder (s. 2)

Where three or more people who are present together use or threaten violence and their conduct, taken together, would cause a person of reasonable firmness – if present – to fear for his/her safety, each person using or threatening violence is guilty of the offence and liable on conviction to a maximum of five years' imprisonment (or a combination of fines and imprisonment, or just a fine).

Note the contrast with the more serious offence of riot: less people are required; the accused need only threaten violence as opposed to using it; and there is no requirement for a common purpose.

Affray (s. 3)

The offence is committed if a person uses or threatens unlawful violence towards another and his/her conduct is such as would cause a person of reasonable firmness – if present – to fear for his or her personal safety. The maximum sentence on conviction is three years (or a combination of fines and imprisonment, or just a fine).

You should note that 'violence' is given a wide definition by s. 8 of the Act and, except in the context of affray, includes violent conduct to property as well as towards persons. In addition, the term is not restricted to conduct intended to cause injury or damage: it covers any 'violent conduct'. Rather unusually, the section provides us with an example of what it means – throwing at or towards a person a missile of a kind capable of causing injury which does not hit or falls short.

Note also that it is not necessary for the prosecution to prove that anyone actually did fear for their safety: the fear of a hypothetical bystander is sufficient.

Causing Fear of or Provoking Violence (s. 4)

The most frequently charged public order offence prior to the passage of the 1986 Act was that contained in s. 5 of the Public Order Act 1936. This section made it an offence to use threatening, abusive or insulting words or behaviour with intent to cause a breach of the peace or whereby a breach of the peace was likely to be occasioned. During the miners' strike in 1984/85, some 4,107 prosecutions were brought under this section.

Section 4 of the 1986 Act replaces s. 5 of the 1936 Act with a modified and extended version of the offence. A person is guilty of the offence if s/he:

(a) uses towards another person threatening, abusive or insulting words or behaviour; or

(b) distributes or displays any writing, sign or other visible representation which is threatening, abusive or insulting, with intent to cause that person to believe that immediate unlawful violence will be used against him/her or another by any person, or to provoke the immediate use of unlawful violence by that person or another, or whereby that person is likely to believe that such violence will be used or it is likely that such violence will be provoked.

The new provision is broader in scope than its predecessor in two respects. First, the new offence can be committed in either a public or a private place. The limitation of s. 5 of the 1936 Act to conduct in public places meant that during the miners' strike a number of summonses were dismissed where people charged with threatening words or behaviour were able to show they were on National Coal Board or other private property at the time of the alleged offence. (Indeed, the extension of coverage to both public and private places applies in respect of all five of the statutory public order offences contained in the Act.) Second, case law suggested that s. 5 did not cover a situation where the victim (for example, an elderly person) was someone who was not likely to be provoked to breach the peace. Under the new provision, a belief that immediate violence will be used against oneself or another is sufficient.

The maximum penalty on conviction is six months' imprisonment and a fine.

Causing Harassment, Alarm and Distress (s. 5)

This 'catch-all' and controversial offence is committed where a person:

(a) uses threatening, abusive or insulting words or behaviour, or disorderly behaviour, or

(b) displays any writing, sign or other visible representation which is threatening, abusive or insulting, within the hearing or sight of a person likely to be caused harassment, alarm or distress thereby.

The maximum penalty is a £1,000 fine.

It is easy to foresee that this offence will be readily employed to control the conduct of picketing. Shouts of abuse to workers as they cross the picket line, offensive gestures and insulting placards or banners may all fall foul of this section.

One of three defences provided by s. 5 (3) is if the accused can prove that his/ her conduct was reasonable. The scope of this defence for the picket is untried and uncertain, though Bowers and Duggan are not optimistic:

> A picket might claim that his conduct was reasonable when he called the strike-breaker names such as 'scab', because it is in the collective interest that the strike is successful and his conduct ought to achieve that result. One cannot, however, imagine the courts being very sympathetic to such a plea.[9]

(S. 154 of the Criminal Justice and Public Order Act 1994 inserted s. 4A of the Public Order Act 1986 and creates the more serious offence of causing intentional harassment, alarm or distress.)

Marches and Assemblies

Part II of the Public Order Act 1986 imposes new controls over the conduct of marches or processions and static assemblies.

Section 11 imposes a new national requirement for organisers of 'public processions' to give at least six clear days' notice of their intention to the police. The notice must specify the date of the procession, its proposed starting time and route, and the name and address of one of the organisers.

Picketing, by definition, is a static assembly outside the entrance of a workplace. However, protest marches are now a relatively frequent feature of larger industrial disputes, for instance the protest marches held in support of the striking miners in 1984/85 and the marches, culminating in a mass picket outside the Wapping plant of News International, during 1986 in protest at the dismissal of some 5,500 printworkers (see *News Group Newspapers Ltd* v. *SOGAT 82* [1986] IRLR 337). In future such marches will have to comply with the terms of s. 11, though you should note that the notice requirement does not apply to processions 'commonly and customarily held' – for example a march by trade unionists on May Day.

A notice may be delivered by post but only if it is by recorded delivery; otherwise it must be delivered by hand to a police station in the police area in which it is proposed the procession will start. The Act allows an exception to the six-day notice requirement in the case of a delivery by hand where it is not reasonably practicable to give that amount of advance notice. An example where this exception may be relevant in an industrial dispute would be the need for a rapid protest response to the summary dismissal of a shop steward or management's announcement of immediate plant closure and redundancies.

Failure to give the appropriate notice renders the organisers liable to a fine. It is also made an offence to organise a march which differs in terms of start and route from the information given in the notice. Defences are available if it is proved that the accused did not know of, and neither suspected nor had reason to suspect, the failure to satisfy the requirements or the different date, time or route. In relation to a march being held on a different date or time, or along a different route, it is also a defence to prove that the difference arose from circumstances beyond the control of the accused or from something done with the agreement of a police officer.

The Power to Impose Conditions on Processions (s. 12)
This section enables the most senior police officer present to impose conditions, including route and timing, on processions when the officer reasonably believes that it

may result in serious public disorder, serious damage to property or serious disruption to the life of the community, or that the purpose of the organisers is to intimidate others. Where a march or procession is *intended* to be held, 'the senior police officer' with the power to impose conditions is the chief officer of police.

The organiser of a march who knowingly fails to comply with a condition imposed under this section commits an offence, whose maximum punishment is three months' imprisonment and/or a fine. In addition, those who participate in a march who knowingly fail to comply with any imposed condition commit a summary offence punishable with a fine. Finally, those who incite marchers to break a condition are also guilty of a summary offence and are liable on conviction to a maximum of three months' imprisonment or a fine.

Bans on Marches

The power to ban marches for up to three months under the Public Order Act on the grounds of reasonable belief that it will result in 'serious public disorder' is retained. The major change is that the 1986 Act makes it an offence to participate in a banned march, punishable with a maximum fine, in addition to organising or inciting others to participate in one.

Static Assemblies

The Act provided the police, for the first time, with a clear statutory power to impose conditions which prescribe the location, size and maximum duration of 'public assemblies' (defined as assemblies of 20 or more people in a 'public place' which is wholly or partly open to the air). As with processions, the most senior officer present will be able to impose such conditions where s/he reasonably believes that it may result in serious disorder, serious damage to property, serious disruption to the life of the community or the 'intimidation of others with a view to compelling them not to do an act they have a right to do, or to do an act they have a right not to do'.

This provision has the clearest relevance for pickets and provides a potent additional weapon of control for the police. As the White Paper 'Review of Public Order Law' observed: 'at Grunwick's or Warrington, for example, the police could have imposed conditions limiting the numbers of demonstrators, or moving the demonstration in support of the pickets further away from the factory'.[10] Where conditions are imposed in advance of the assembly, then they may only be imposed by the chief officer of police or that officer's deputy or assistant. The organisers of a static assembly which fails to abide by the conditions or those who incite disobedience face a maximum penalty of three months' imprisonment and/or a fine. The participants in such an assembly risk a fine. See also the Criminal Justice and Public Order Act 1994, s. 68 which creates the offence of aggravated trespass and s. 70 which empowers chief police officers to seek an order from the district council prohibiting the holding of trespassory assemblies in the district for a specified period.

PART SEVEN

Legal Action and Welfare Benefits

CHAPTER 21

Tribunal and Court Claims

Introduction

Depending on the kind of issue involved, and the size of the claim (if the proceedings in the courts are for damages), there are four different tribunals or courts in which an employment case can begin. If an appeal is made against a decison, each one of them then has a possible appeal 'route', as shown in Figure 21.1 below. In the case of work-related welfare benefits rights adjudication and appeals are dealt with by different procedures, including a separate system of tribunals.[1]

The Employment Tribunal deals with most of the ERA and other statutory issues discussed in the previous chapters. The matters dealt with include unfair dismissal, redundancy, discrimination, most (but not all) wages problems, and contract-related issues on termination of employment. The ET also hears appeals against health and safety improvement and prohibition notices (see Chapter 16). It may still be necessary for some contract cases to be heard in the courts rather than in the tribunal, and this means either by the County Court or by the High Court, despite the Employment Tribunal's increasingly important judridiction.[2]

As well as the important area of personal injuries, the courts deal with other civil claims based on torts (civil wrongs) – an important example being damages claims in 'duty of care' cases (see Chapter 16). They also deal with disputes over post-termination contract restrictions or intellectual property rights involving court action for injunctions and damages (see Chapter 9 above). The High Court will usually be the relevant court in such cases. Collective issues, including actions by employers, unions and, sometimes, individuals who want to get court orders, are also usually dealt with by the High Court. The Central Arbitration Committee has an important jurisdiction in relation to recognition and disputes over access to information for collective bargaining purposes.

As a comment on the present system, there is obviously a strong argument for moving to a less fragmented and more integrated labour court structure. Ideas on this, and on a generally more 'autonomous' employment law system, have been discussed extensively. The proposal for a 'labour court' begs the question, though, what *sort* of system that should be. The Conservative government's National Industrial Relations Court in the 1970s was regarded by the labour movement as highly pro-employer, and there is still a significant distrust of judicial involvement in industrial relations issues since that era.[3] There are, in any case, quite a few different possible models, including those operating in Europe, which could be adopted (with varying degrees of integration into their general court systems and appeal structures).

Workers employed in countries outside the UK sometimes have problems in bringing cases, even when their employer is UK-based. Generally the position is dealt with under the Civil Jurisdiction and Judgments Act 1982 (giving effect to the Brussels Convention, as amended), and the Contracts Law (Applicable Law) Act 1990.

Figure 21.1: Different Courts Applicable to Different Types of Claim

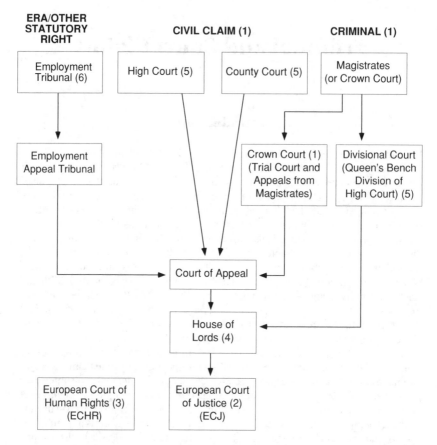

Notes:
(1) Criminal cases can begin in the Magistrates or Crown Court, depending on how serious they are. In Scotland the Sheriff's Court deals with criminal cases, and the Court of Session with civil claims.

(2) The ECJ is the highest court on EC employment points, and cases can also be 'referred', to decide preliminary EC points, by lower courts or tribunals.

(3) Employment issues involving infringements of the European Convention on Human Rights can be taken to the ECHR (normally only after UK courts have failed to implement the Convention's requirements). Under the Human Rights Act 1998, ECHR points can be dealt with, initially, by UK courts.

(4) In some cases it is possible to appeal directly from the High Court to the House of Lords (leap-frogging the Court of Appeal).

(5) Whether a claim begins in the High Court or the County Court depends principally on its size. Claims for breach of contract, or tort, will generally be dealt with in a County Court and larger (or more technical and complex) claims in the High Court. Cases are, however, allocated in accordance with rules which allow for transfer of cases between courts and which, among other things, allow the parties to agree on where a case should be dealt with. On Administrative Court remedies against public sector employees, see CPR Part 54.

(6) As well as its jurisdiction in relation to ERA and other employment rights, the tribunal may deal with some contract-related matters (see text above).

Broadly, the effect is that a worker with an individual contract of employment may sue in the State of the employer's domicile, or where the work is habitually carried out: or, if the employee does not habitually work in any one country in the courts of the country, where the business which employed him or her was (or is) situated.[4]

Starting a Tribunal Claim

There are generally no difficult formalities in starting a tribunal claim. To begin a claim it is always advisable to use a Form ET1 (copies are obtainable from regional offices of employment tribunals), or other forms provided by the Employment Tribunal Service (ETS), even when alternative methods or documents are permitted. In doing so, the applicant provides details about the complaint, the compensation, relief and so on being claimed which are legally required before the claim will be heard. Applications may be made on-line after advice, and accessing the Employment Tribunals website at www.employmenttribunals.gov.uk. A specimen copy showing the sort of information required is shown in Appendix II below, although it is always essential to access up-to-date guidance from the ETS. On receipt of the ET1, the tribunal office sends a copy of the completed form and a 'Notice of Originating Summons' to the employer. To defend the claim the employer must return a 'Notice of Appearance' form.

The important sections are those where the complainant/applicant is asked to state the type of complaint to be dealt with, and the details of the complaint. Assistance with this is provided in the information from the ETS (including *How to Apply to an Employment Tribunal* (Booklet 2)). It is always advisable to get assistance from a union, solicitor, or Citizens' Advice Bureau: and help is also available from the Advisory Conciliation and Arbitration Service (ACAS), and organisations like the Equal Opportunities Commission (for sex discrimination and equal pay claims); the Commission for Racial Equality (for race discrimination claims); and the Disability Rights Commission (on disability-related issues).

Advice can be obtained from solicitors. This does not usually include representation, however; and without guidance and representation the chances of success are generally much reduced.[5] Guidance on legal advice can be sought from the Legal Services Commission (website www.legalservicescommission.gov.uk).

Eligibility, Procedure, and Time Limits

Most employment rights are subject to eligibility requirements; and in particular, one year's continuous service is normally (but not in all cases) required for unfair dismissal claims (see Chapter 14). Service and other eligibility requirements are referred to earlier in the relevant subject chapters. In addition, there are procedural conditions which must be carefully followed. The most important of these is that claims should be presented as quickly as possible, and *within the statutory time limits*. ET proceedings are otherwise closely regulated, and reference must be made to the guidance provided by the Employment Tribunals Service and by the legislation. The Employment Tribunals have a website (www.employmenttribunals.gov.uk), as does the Employment Tribunal Service (www.ets.gov.uk). Procedural requirements governing ET proceedings are in the ERA and other legislation referred to in the preceeding chapters, and in the Employment Tribunals (Constitution and Rules of Procedure) Regulations 2001, SI

2001/1171. Schedule 1 to the regulations contains the ET Rules of Procedure to which reference must be made for the detailed provisions. In particular they provide for:

- The responsibilities of applicants, originating applications, and action on them.
- Respondents' 'appearances', and failures to enter an appearance.
- Case management and tribunals' power to issue directions.
- Pre-hearing reviews by ETs to consider applications and notices of appearance, and requiring deposits from parties (up to £500) if their contentions have 'no reasonable prospect of success'.
- Hearings and procedure at hearings.
- ET decisions and 'reasons' for decisions. These are normally in summary form unless the ET decides to give them in 'extended' form – or this is requested by a party after the hearing (and before summary reasons are sent to the parties). They should be requested within 21 days of the date on which summary reasons are sent to the parties. Extended reasons must be obtained if there is to be an appeal to the EAT. Although cases may, exceptionally, be allowed to proceed without them the prospects of success in the EAT will be much reduced – and some points may, in practice, not be appealable. This is sometimes a problem when unrepresented parties at the ET do not request extended reasons at the end of a hearing or within the time limit; or before they then go to see an advisor.

The regulations also enable a tribunal to review its own decision, and exceptionally, to correct errors in a review (see 'Appeals' below).

Costs are also dealt with in the regulations. This includes cases where in the opinion of the ET a party in *bringing* the proceedings, or a party or a party's representative has in *conducting* the proceedings, acted vexatiously, abusively, disruptively or otherwise unreasonably – or the bringing or conducting of the proceedings by a party has been 'misconceived'.

Schedules 2–6 provide rules of procedure for other specific aspects of the ET's jurisdiction.

The Overriding Objective
An important feature of the procedure rules in Schedules 1–6 since 2001 is that proceedings are subject to the 'overriding objective' of dealing with cases 'justly'. This means under reg. 10, so far as practicable, ensuring that the parties are on an equal footing; saving expense; dealing with the case in ways which are proportionate to the complexity of the issues; and ensuring that it is dealt with expeditiously and fairly. ETs are expected to give effect to the principle in the way they exercise their powers and interpret the rules in the Schedules – and the parties are also expected to assist tribunals in furthering the objective.

Changes to ET Regulations and Rules of Procedure
Changes come into operation from 1 October 2004. Among other things these include standard claim and response forms; tougher rules on extensions to time limits; procedures for 'sifting out' claims and responses that should not go forward to the tribunal, and striking out cases at pre-hearing reviews; and new costs rules so that

representatives (other than not-for-profit representatives) can incur costs awards against them for their conduct. Details can be accessed on the Department of Trade and Industry website (www.dti.gov.uk), and the ACAS and ETS websites contain up-to-date guidance on the procedures, codes, and ET's powers.

Time Limits

A time limit of three months from the date of the matter complained of applies in several cases, but limits can be shorter than that – for instance, within seven days from dismissal for union victimisation cases where reinstatement is claimed as interim relief. Exceptionally, time limits can be longer, as in the case of redundancy payments where the limit is six months. A tribunal has only *very* limited scope for allowing an extended period in which to claim, so it is vital to check what the relevant limit is, and comply with it. The ET could allow an extension, but only in very exceptional circumstances. The tribunal will consider *why* the application was late and what action, if any, it can then take. Reference must be made to the specific legislation and time limits relating to specific types of complaint or proceedings, but among the kinds of complaint which have different or special rules are: redundancy payment claims (there is a redundancy 'helpline' available at the Department of Work and Pensions, and in ETS guidance); national minimum wage proceedings (again there is a 'helpline'); union activities and membership, and health and safety-related activities; complaints relating to activities undertaken by employee representatives, pension scheme trustees; shop workers and betting shop workers refusing to undertake Sunday working; and working-time complaints. In particular, such complainants may request a 're-employment order' within seven days of dismissal – and this and other forms of interim relief may be sought, but without delay. Guidance is given by the ETS (including its Guidance Notes in *Application to an Employment Tribunal*).

Processing the Claim

Copies of claims are sent to the employer and to the ACAS conciliation officer who may conciliate and try to settle the claim after the completed application has been received. Assistance at this stage from a conciliation officer (who also sees the employer's response) may avoid the need to pursue tribunal proceedings. If a claim is formally settled[6] tribunal proceedings will normally not be possible. As noted above, if the claim is to be defended, the employer must send a completed form 'Notice of Appearance' within 21 days, although extensions may possibly be obtained.

The role of conciliation[7] is an important one in practice, and it is set to change before the end of 2004 as a result of changes to the regulations. These provide a more time-regulated framework in which parties are encouraged to conciliate with a short period for claims considered suitable for fast-tracking (normally seven weeks), and a standard period for other claims (13 weeks) – but with equal pay and discrimination claims excluded from such fixed period rules.

If, on receipt of the form ET1, the tribunal secretary can decide that the tribunal does not have power to make an award, applicants are notified of this. If, despite this, the claim is maintained, there is a risk of a 'costs' award being made. Costs awards can be made against parties (and their representatives) in some circumstances if cases are brought or conducted frivolously, vexatiously, or unreasonably, and if it is decided that a party is abusing the system – for example, by bringing the case for malicious motives, or by forcing unnecessary adjournments.

The tribunal rules govern parties' rights at tribunals, but otherwise ETs have discretion in how cases are dealt with. Among other things:

- A party (or the ET) can require the other party to provide 'further and better' particulars to clarify their case.
- The ET can be asked, prior to a hearing, to order disclosure of documents which a party has if these are necessary to decide the case fairly.
- Witness orders can be made, requiring witnesses to attend (if their evidence could be useful).

Before the main hearing there may be scope for obtaining interim remedies and relief.

After hearing both parties' cases (including documentary evidence, witnesses, cross-examination, and closing statements by the parties), the ET will make a decision. This will normally be a brief verbal decision, and fuller reasons are posted to the parties later.

The ET can order:

- compensation; or
- reinstatement or re-engagement (in unfair dismissal cases); or
- a declaration of rights (which is not legally enforceable).
- other remedies provided in the relevant legislation: the wide range of remedies available now to ETs have been considered in Chapter 14 and preceding chapters.

As considered below, awards may be affected in some circumstances where an applicant has not made use of available internal appeals procedures provided by the employer; or has not complied with statutory procedures set out in Schedule 2 to the Employment Act 2002 (s. 31 of the 2002 Act). In some ET jurisdictions, notably those listed in Schedule 4 to the 2002 Act, complaints relating to grievances may not be presented to an ET if the requirements in Schedule 2 have not been complied with.

Appeals

The losing party can ask the tribunal to review its own decision in some cases under the 2001 regulations. This must be requested at the hearing, or within 14 days of the decision being recorded. The grounds are limited. They might include, for example, the decision being made when a party is not present, or where important new evidence becomes available after the hearing. The ET can order a review if this is required in 'the interests of justice', but such reviews are rarely allowed except where there has been an obvious mistake or procedural error.

Appeal to the EAT is possible (as shown in Figure 21.1 above) and the appeal must be lodged within the prescribed time limit. This normally means within 42 days from the date on which extended reasons for the decision or order of the ET were sent to the appellant (or otherwise as provided in the Employment Appeal Tribunal Rules 1993, SI 1993/2854, rule 3, and the Employment Appeal Tribunal Practice Direction 2002, Direction 3). The jurisdiction of the EAT is provided by the Employment Tribunals Act 1996, and appeals are regulated by those 1993 Rules and the 2002 Direction. As with ET time limits for appealing, time limits are strictly adhered to, and extensions to the limits are not given unless 'good excuse' for the delay has been shown; Direction 3 (5), (6). The dangers of not ensuring appeals are brought in time were highlighted in *Peters v. Sat Katar Co. Ltd* [2003] IRLR 574. However, in that case – a litigant in person won her appeal in the Court of Appeal on the basis that even if her appeal notice to the EAT was not received until after the 42-day time limit (which runs from the date the ET decision is sent to the parties) she had posted it within that period. As an unrepresented litigant she had not acted unreasonably in assuming the notice would arrive in time; and even if she had not checked to see if it had arrived safely she could not be said to be 'at fault' in not doing so.

For further guidance on contesting ET decisions, and appeals to the EAT, reference may be made to the guidance on the EAT's website; and to specialist publications on appeals.[8] Appeals are normally only allowed on a point of law (as the ET generally decides factual points). However, this could include errors or misunderstanding the facts amounting to errors of law or making a decision that is 'perverse' or not supported by evidence. A copy of the ET chair's notes may be requested, although this is subject to ET and EAT guidance on the criteria for providng them. The ET's full written reasons ('extended reasons') will need to be obtained for the appeal (and lodged with other documentation).

Other documents which must normally be provided include:

- A notice of appeal in the form prescribed.
- A copy of the decision or order or the ET, certification officer, etc.
- A copy of the ET's 'extended reasons'.
- In the case of appeals against orders of the CAC a copy of its declaration or order.

Assistance under Legal Commission schemes may be available, and the EAT can assist on advice and representation needs prior to an appeal.

The EAT has a website with guidance on appeals procedures (www. employmentappeals.gov.uk).

Court Claims

It is possible to initiate or defend legal claims in the courts without professional assistance, but there are many good reasons for not doing so. The first step should be to get assistance, if possible, through support organisations like unions, law centres or CABx. Advice from a solicitors' firm that does employment work and civil appeals is recommended, and the Legal Services Commission provides a list of such firms in different areas of the UK – and can provide guidance on financial assistances.

Claims in the County Court (which might be suitable for a variety of employment disputes where the ET may not have jurisdiction) are often pursued without legal help, and these may provide the opportunity of getting a claim dealt with by informal arbitration at minimal costs.[9] Even for these claims advice should be obtained if possible.

Disputes: Alternative Procedures

Under the Employment Rights (Dispute Resolution) Act 1998 a number of additional features of tribunal procedure need to be considered. Among other things, the Act provides alternatives to formal proceedings, and provides a system of penalising employers (and employees in some circumstances) where internal appeals procedures have not been used. It also widened the scope for non-lawyers ('independent advisers') to be involved in assisting with compromise agreements. Employees need to be aware of the potential for compensatory awards to be reduced if internal procedures are not used before a tribunal claim is started.

Other features of the legislation included:

- a wider role for ACAS conciliation officers e.g. in relation to statutory redundancy payment rights;
- a power enabling ACAS to provide and promote arbitration schemes relating to unfair dismissal. The 2004 scheme gives ETs power to enforce re-employment orders (SI 2004/753, r. 6);
- a power to enable ACAS to provide (and promote) arbitration schemes relating to unfair dismissal – with possible extension of such schemes to other types of workplace dispute;
- the removal of tribunals' jurisdiction for some kinds of dispute which have been referred to arbitration;
- the possible settlement of some types of proceedings without the necessity of a full hearing, e.g. if respondents have not defended the case, or the parties agree;
- changes to enable EAT to have jurisdiction to hear appeals from tribunals about 'breach of contract' matters.

For details, see the ACAS Arbitration Scheme (Great Britain) Order 2004, SI 2004/753 and TULR(C)A s. 212A; and see pp. 315–17.

The Employment Act 2002, which has made important changes affecting the unfair dismissal jurisdiction (see Chapter 14) contains important statutory dispute resolution procedures in Part 3. Among other things all contracts of employment are subject to requirements of employees and employers to comply with the procedures in Schedule 2: and sanctions in the form of reduced awards for non-compliance (or increased awards for employers in the face of non-compliance by an employee) are provided by s. 31 of the 2002 Act.

CHAPTER 22

Employment-related
Welfare Benefits

Introduction and Overview

State welfare benefit rights which support the employment relationship are not considered in detail in this book. There are other texts on the subject to which reference may be made.[1] It is necessary, however, in any meaningful consideration of employment rights to consider several important aspects of the employment–welfare interface. Despite significant retreats in key areas of State welfare provision, and continuing shifts in policy reshaping modern welfare since the post-Beveridge Welfare State[2] under New Labour (and in the preceding Conservative period),[3] the employment relationship is often heavily reliant on State welfare provision. Indeed, a large section of the UK's labour force, especially part-timers and those on low incomes may well receive more income from the State than they do from their wages.

State support can be seen at all three main stages in the employment cycle:

- **Pre-employment**: assistance and financial incentives in the transition from the State benefits system, support from the family, and other welfare sources, to employment and wages as the primary source of income and welfare (*welfare-to-work*).
- **In-work**: although a lot of workers may be able to look to occupational income/welfare in the form of contractual sickness, injury, income replacement during periods away from the workplace (maternity and paternity leave, for example), and occupational income is therefore a primary source of financial support and 'welfare'[4] in these periods, State benefits also play an important role in sustaining employment at these times. This is done mainly through replacement earnings and income delivered through a mix of contributory, non-contributory, and means-tested benefits. Despite interventions in the employment relationship to raise wages (such as the National Minimum Wage, discussed in Chapter 7) a large section of the labour market is now supported by tax credits under the Tax Credits Act 2002, and these are now an integral part of their income. For many workers the State's input into their 'wage' can be significantly greater than their occupational earnings, as shown by the 'Rona and Children' worked example below (in the section *In-work Welfare*).
- **Pre-termination/Post-termination**: in the lead-up to termination of the employment relationship workers may often be dependent on State benefits as replacement income, for example during periods of short-time working, lay-offs, long-term illness, and periods of incapacity following accidents. Post-termination workers and their dependants in such cases must look to State benefits rather than other forms of social insurance to meet income needs.

This is the point at which the community takes responsibility for such workers and their dependants. It has long been the policy of the unfair dismissal system that employers do not bear the full financial costs and on-costs of dismissals, redundancy, and other actions that bring employment to an end.[5] The burden of dismissal, and costs, fall on the worker, and on the rest of the community through the welfare and tax systems. In addition, State Retirement Pension, income guarantees, and tax credits (and benefits) deliver a large proportion of income in retirement – if only as supplements to pensions representing workers' as deferred remuneration.[6]

Active Labour Market Policies

The government's *Welfare to Work* programme, its general approach to the role of State welfare systems, and its support of active labour market policies, made the subject of in-work support important as soon as it took office in May 1997. In its *Case for Welfare Reform* in January 1998 the government declared 'work is the best route out of poverty', thereby building on approaches developed by the Conservatives and under Ministers like Peter Lilley. In particular, New Labour inherited, and adapted, measures like the Jobseeker's Act 1995, and the Jobseeker's Allowance (JSA) whereby unemployed workers became 'jobseekers'. In 1995 this not only legislated away many workers' accrued contributory benefits rights, including the right to a year's worth of contribution-based JSA (replaced by a heavily conditioned six months JSA), it also represented the point at which an increasing range of State welfare provision began to be made conditional on engaging with the jobseeking process. By 1997 New Labour had fully embraced Third Way approaches to turning State welfare into a vehicle for promoting active labour market policies, and 'positive welfare'.[7] This also resulted in a mix of welfare-led interventions in the employment relationship, including easements and regulation of part-time working while claiming JSA,[8] as well as the NMW for low-paid workers. EC-led interventions came later with the regulation of working time, and newer forms of State in-work support. The most significant change in welfare and employment policy, however, was the approach dictated by the assumption that it is better (as well as cheaper) to have someone in employment, supported by the State, than on out-of-work State benefits – a shift in direction with enormous (and on-going) implications for current employment rights. It can be traced back to Kenneth Clarke's Social Market Foundation speech on 12 July 1993 at the LSE which heralded, by the end of the Conservative period in government, a dozen or more welfare-to-work measures for 'building bridges out of dependence'. These mirrored US 'active labour' schemes designed to use welfare support and sanctioning as incentives to take up jobs, implementing Clinton 'hand up, rather than hand out' principles.[9]

In the UK, as in the US, tax credits – the UK equivalent to the US Earned Income Tax Credit (but with some important differences) – have become, since the Tax Credits Act 2002, the centrepiece of in-work State support. Earlier versions of the present regime, such as Family Credit and Earnings Top-Up, introduced by the Conservatives, were driven, in part, by the need to address the problems of under-consumption, low demand, high levels of unemployment, and low wages. They were also the inevitable consequences of Conservative successes in driving down wages, dismembering the collective labour relations system, and creating large sections of the labour market that became (and which are still) dependent on State in-work welfare. This was a development exacerbated by other developments such as the deregulation of the housing market, and rise in rents (and consequent explosion in take-up and reliance on Housing Benefit as an in-work benefit for many workers).[10] The most important legacy inherited by New Labour, however, was the expansion of the in-work welfare system, driven largely by deteriorating working conditions and the growing cost of social security (representing by 1998 one pound in every three of State expenditure).[11] As one commentator put it, 'The benefit system was being slowly moved from one which paid people in the main on condition that they did not work, to one that was having to subsidise them to be in work or at least actively looking for it.'[12] The twin problems of the 'unemployment trap', whereby a person is better off financially by staying *out* of a job, and the 'poverty trap' (where workers are not much better off after getting a pay rise or moving to another job) were exacerbated by policies which succeeded in keeping wages down, while at the same time offering few incentives through tax and benefits regimes of entering or remaining in work. The problem was made worse by deregulation of the rented housing market, and cuts in Housing Benefit which impacted severely on low-paid workers both in the private and public sectors. In *Benefits and Work: A CAB Perspective on the Welfare to Work Debate* (NACAB, 1997) it was noted (at p. 33) how government policies in simultaneously encouraging the growth of low-paid employment and higher rents, while at the same time cutting Housing Benefit, had 'led to a situation where the net income of low-paid workers after housing costs can be little more than they would get if unemployed'.

In the earlier phases of active labour market policies not much consideration was given to the qualitative aspects of work, or the kind of employment people were being expected to take up. Added to that, the flexible labour market, and competitiveness and flexible labour market agendas, have consistently dictated minimal intervention in the dismissal and workplace reorganisation regimes.[13] The result is that the employment of many entry-level and part-time jobs is insecure, poorly paid, and heavily reliant on State support through the tax credits regime – a support system which has also produced a number of negative effects, including distortion of wage systems, and disincentives to employers to deliver acceptable levels of occupational income and benefits.[14]

The later variant of 'work is the best route out of poverty' theme, namely that 'work is the best form of welfare', remains a cornerstone of New Labour thinking about the welfare function of a job. Directed initially at the unemployment trap and the poverty trap, the theme now takes on other aspects of the inter-action of occupational earnings, tax, and in-work benefits. It seeks to implement other tenets of Third Way employment and social policy – notably the need to reduce 'dependency' and welfare fraud (particularly people working while claiming out-of-work benefits), the promotion of 'personal responsibility'; and the importance of introducing incentives for sections of the community on the fringes of paid work, and who are affected by labour market segmentation and long-term unemployment.[15]

Accordingly, groups like lone parents, disabled people, those over the age of 50, and, more recently, pensioners faced with the prospect of having to work beyond State retirement age (largely as a result of failing occupational pensions and other private social insurance sources), have been targeted for *New Deal* or other support programmes like Pension Credits under the State Pension Credit Act 2002. In some cases schemes like the Working Tax Credit (WTC), Child Tax Credit (CTC), and State Pension Credit, which are essentially means-tested benefits (or what ECHR jurisprudence calls 'schemes of social solidarity') – and non-contributory benefits like Statutory Maternity Pay (SMP), Statutory Paternity Pay (SPP), and Statutory Adoption

Pay (SAP) (provided for under the Employment Act 2002) – may just complement employment sources like wages, pension income, and intra-family redistributions from working adults, especially couples who are both working. But as Treasury and Department of Work and Pensions policy dictates, they are also intended, to supplement *other* household income streams and sources – some of which are the product of welfare-led interventions developed as part of the wider welfare reform programme. One such source is Child Support, and the income which a working single parent receives from a former partner. This is based on compulsorily redistributing a proportion of his net weekly earnings and income[16] as the 'non-resident parent' to the 'parent with care'. Both parents may be working. But based on the principle that the parent with care is more likely to be a woman, and more likely to be in a lower-paid job, the system now contains a number of important features designed to maximise the earnings of a working mother, and to raise the value of overall household income. Welfare objectives are assisted by other interventions targeted on employers (such as stakeholder pensions), but accompanied by regulatory measures designed to make such 'private' sources of welfare income more secure, within a more intensely regulated social market of pensions, insurance, and financial products.[17]

Working Single Parents: The Wages-Tax Credits-Benefits 'Triangle'

In the case of the Child Support system, lone parents make up a sizeable proportion of those officially designated 'unemployed' (or engaged in employment below the 16-hour weekly threshold, claiming Income Support or income-based JSA as in-work benefits) – as confirmed by the CSA's official 'caseload' in 2003/04, although of the 1.4 million people on its books, an increasing proportion have made the transition from IS to in-work benefits like WTC. The strategy of assisting lone parents into paid employment has been developed in a number of ways; and in a labour market which looks to groups like single parents to take up part-time work in ways that can maintain incentives, and maximise income, the emphasis is still on 'making work pay'; *The Child and Working Tax Credits: the Modernisation of Britain's Tax and Benefit System* (No. 10) (HM Treasury, April 2002, at p. 1). Primarily, as with other groups on the fringes of the labour market, the principal means is to create financial incentives, using a mix of tax and benefits measures to 'make work pay', and to create discernible differentials in the income position of working parents and those deemed by the system to be 'unemployed' – including those working below the 16-hour threshold. Consequently, whereas a lone parent electing *not* to work, and claiming Income Support, has her Child Benefit and child maintenance taken fully into account as 'income' in the assessment of benefits – subject to a small disregard for child maintenance received, and weekly earnings – a lone parent who increases her hours (or takes on new employment) so that she is working *more* than 16 hours a week, has both these key elements fully disregarded. She and her dependants will also enjoy a range of more advantageous arrangements including a generally more 'responsive' system. When earnings go down in-work support will promptly go up. Similar approaches to 'incentivising' other atypical employment groups, including the disabled, over-50s, and older workers are being developed, with mixed success. In terms of in-work 'welfare' these and other elements that go to make up the remuneration package of groups like the young and long-term unemployed, lone parents, the over-50s, and pensioners, and *New Deal* benefits, must now be seen as an integral part of modern employment rights.

The key elements of these approaches are in the *New Welfare Contract* as it is set out in the analysis of the four ages of welfare in *New Ambitions for Our Country: A New Contract for Welfare*.[18] The reform programme which, in its implementation by measures like the Social Security Act 1998, the Tax Credits Act 2002, the State Pension Credit Act 2002, and Disability Act 2004, is set, if it runs to plan, to culminate in the so-called Fourth Age (by 2020), by when the institutions of welfare will have been 'restructured' to promote people's opportunity and independence, with protection for the vulnerable 'so that everyone can enjoy a secure and dignified life'. The *New Welfare Contract* is a product of Third Way thinking about welfare and work which dictates that having assisted people into employment it is the State's on-going task to 'make work pay' and promote welfare at work – utilising a mix of interventions in the employment relationship, such as the National Minimum Wage, working time restrictions, etc.; and distributive mechanisms and State welfare like tax credits, pension credits, and means-tested in-work welfare.

However, it has a *lot* less to say about aspects like job security, qualitative aspects of work, or compensating people when they are unfairly dismissed from jobs which in the face of globalisation and competition have become increasingly less secure. Some of the more vulnerable groups in the labour market like the disabled enjoy a measure of protection through legislation like the Disability Discrimination Act 1995. This was an Act passed by the Conservatives under duress, and as a means of blocking a much more demanding legal regime put forward with all-party support, and backed by the disability organisations. It was amended by the Disability Discrimination Act 1995 (Amendment) Regulations 2003, SI 2003/1673 (from 1 October 2004), extending protection into newer areas like harassment, and supplemented by a Disability Act 2004.[19] As Catherine Casserly has said in *Law, Rights and Disability* (2000, at p. 139) the Act is not the 'fully comprehensive civil rights legislation' that had been campaigned for. Nevertheless it does contain a number of important welfare-led aspects to it. Under it, employers are obliged to at least consider making 'reasonable adjustments' to facilitate employment and retention (s. 6); and in many cases this is assisted by in-work welfare schemes like the disability element of WTC (considered below). Such interventions plainly assist workers, such as those who have had accidents or long-term illness to be retained in alternative employment, rather than going out of the labour market and onto out-of-work benefits. Yet even with the assistance of judicial interpretations of the DDA which facilitate claims of constructive dismissal, or other forms of discrimination, such measures still do not adequately address the need for better employment protection – particularly given the disproportionate impact job loss has on such groups.[20]

Welfare-to-Work

There are several ways in which people are assisted by the welfare benefits system. At the outset, for example, benefits like Housing Benefit (HB) and Council Tax Benefit may be claimed as 'run ons' during the first month of employment at the same rate at which they were paid while 'out of work' benefits were received. This eases the transition into work (and recognises that many workers may find it difficult to meet living costs until wages are paid). Income Support and HB have also undergone transformations in order to facilitate take-up and retention of employment in a variety of ways. In the case of HB, the changes introduced from the end of 2003, and the standard local housing allowance system operating from 2004 in the unregulated private housing sector, are expected to produce faster adjudications for job starters, and more responsiveness to in-work changes and fluctuations in income.[21] State assistance towards the incidental costs of employment, including mortgage and rental housing costs, child care, Council Tax, school meals etc., is also available. Such assistance is being progressively replaced by more focused forms of assistance for particular groups experiencing problems moving into employment – such as payments for lone parents (from 2004), giving them weekly income supplements for up to a year while they are actively looking for employment, and £40 when they get a job. Job Grant and other changes being introduced to replace run-ons (initially set at £100 for single people, and those with no children: and £250 for single parents and couples with children) are among the 'new generation' benefits developed. Most claimants are subject to mandatory 'work-focused' interviews, designed to make them aware of welfare-to-work options;[22] and such welfare-to-work strategies now operate with modifications, and in conjunction with New Deal schemes, for target groups like lone parents.[23]

Another group with difficulties in accessing employment, and returning to the labour market, are people on Incapacity Benefit (IB) who may have (or have had) long-term incapacity and disability. In this case claimants have been subjected (since June 2003) to more demanding 'work-focused interviews', the first one coming just eight weeks after claiming, with follow-up interviews thereafter at monthly intervals. Changes to the IB regime, designed to 'restore the link between IB and employment', were discussed by the Ministers responsible in an article 'Reforming Disability Benefits'.[24] Later, after the Welfare Reform and Pensions Act 1999 had introduced major changes to eligibility criteria for IB, designed to make the benefit harder to access, important easements were introduced which now enable IB claimants to undertake a limited amount of paid work while still claiming. Strict restrictions have traditionally been maintained on *any* kind of working by incapacitated and disabled claimants claiming benefits like IB and Disability Living Allowance unless it came within highly restrictive exceptions, an example being 'therapeutic' work. This has generally been the case whether claimants are claiming the benefit as an in-work earnings replacement benefit – usually when SSP is not payable, or has ceased to be paid after 28 weeks (see Chapter 8) – or as an out-of-work benefit on a long-term basis. The bar has been maintained by a tough system of civil overpayments and criminal law sanctions directed at underpinning the Social Security (Incapacity for Work) (General) Regulations 1995, SI 1995/311. Under that system a person who is 'incapable of work' (under regs. 10–15, 27, 28) is to be *treated* as 'capable of work' if she works. Most kinds of employment are barred out, even work which had been undertaken without expectation of payment (reg. 16). However, as a result of government *welfare-to-work* initiatives, designed to promote take-up of work options among long-term incapacitated claimants, easements have taken a variety of forms. These have included the introduction of 'linking periods', so that any two periods of incapacity for work separated by a period of less than 52 weeks is treated as one period of incapacity,[25] thereby facilitating periods of employment, and work experience, without being penalised by the welfare scheme. In addition, restrictions may be disapplied in any week in which employment (which has been notified and approved) can come within the scope of the Permitted Work scheme, and certain categories of 'exempt work' (reg. 17). Such work must, in general terms, be done within strict earnings limits, and limits on hours (usually up to 16 hours a week) in the scheme which is set out in the Social Security (Incapacity from Work) Regulations

1995, SI 1995/311, as amended after 2002: and its 'exempt work' provisions are backed up by DWP guidance on notifications and eligibility.

Employment Gateways

At the interface of employment law and social welfare law there are, in theory, effective rights (and duties on both the employer and the State) designed to assist vulnerable claimants into jobs; to assist them in retaining an acceptable quality of life at work; and to provide them with a measure of security once they are in employment. However, in areas of employment rights like disability discrimination, as discussed in Chapters 12 and 14, that interface does not always deliver effective results. Even when employers comply with the requirements of measures like the Disability Discrimination Act 1995, including implementation of reasonable adjustments to facilitate take-up of employment opportunities, the special needs which entrants to employment may require are not always met, as they should be, by State welfare agencies. To promote welfare-to-work among disabled people who are able to work, the *New Deal for Disabled People* (NDDP) provides a range of support measures. There are also other services provided by Pathfinder offices of Jobcentre Plus, Personal Adviser assistance, a Job Broker Service, Access to Work, and other support to assist disability benefits claimants to connect (or re-connect) with the labour market. Among other things such policies match disabled applicants' skills and abilities with job opportunities and the needs of employers; and target financial assistance which can provide the necessary incentives for employers to employ applicants.

In practice, though, there can be shortcomings in the delivery of support. An unfortunate example was the case of *Kenny* v. *Hampshire Constabulary* [1999] IRLR 76, EAT. This was a case in which a person with cerebral palsy, Mr Kenny, was offered employment – having demonstrated his aptitude and suitability as a good candidate for the post. Delays in arranging a personal assistant through the Access to Work scheme unfortunately prompted the employer to withdraw the job offer. Although Mr Kenny was a 'disabled person', and the Disability Discrimination Act applied because of his 'disability', it was held that the personal support that he needed was not 'job-related', in the sense that it was the employer's legal responsibility to provide it. The responsibility lay with the State, and withdrawal of the offer was therefore 'justified', held the tribunal.[26] The further changes due to be implemented in the Disability Discrimination Act 1995 (Amendment Regulations 2003, SI 2003/1673 (from 1 October 2004) have increased employers' responsibilities as required by EC Dir. 2000/78 (establishing a general framework for equal treatment in employment). But neither those new laws, nor the expected Disability Act 2004, impose any additional responsibilities or liabilities on welfare agencies. *Towards Equality and Diversity* (Cabinet Office, 13 December 2001), the paper setting out government proposals for implementing EC Law requirements, made it clear that the disability discrimination legislation would not extend to State welfare systems. There may, however, be liability for such failures as those which prevented Mr Kenny from taking up work opportunities as a result of remedies under the Human Rights Act 1998, as being developed in Community Care Law.[27]

Other sizeable, but also vulnerable, groups of atypical entrants to the labour market include young people who have been in the care system. This is a group which can have considerable problems in accessing jobs, especially as they tend to have poor qualifications and skills. Reforms include the Children (Leaving Care) Act 2000 which has imposed on local authorities and other agencies a range of work (as well as general welfare) responsibilities for carrying out assessments of their needs, and then supporting such entrants (through funding, training, housing, etc.).[28]

Although interventions in the employment relationship like the national minimum wage is designed, in part, to reduce the reliance of workers on State in-work benefits, it is unlikely that it could ever remove, entirely, the level of financial support provided by present welfare-to-work measures.

In-Work Welfare

In-work State welfare support takes two main forms:

- assistance for those in *'remunerative employment'*: the lead in-work benefit is WTC/CTC;
- assistance for those who are *not in 'remunerative employment'* (a status which includes those undertaking part-time work up to 16 hours a week) as well as being assisted by welfare-to-work programmes: the lead in-work benefits are IS and JSA.

For those working 16 hours or more each week, assistance usually takes the form of Working Tax Credit (WTC) and Child Tax Credit (CTC) for workers with child dependants (supplemented by Housing Benefit (HB) Council Tax Benefit, and other available benefits, subject to means tests and other eligibility criteria).

Remunerative Employment: WTC and CTC

Eligibility criteria for WTC and CTC are in the Tax Credits Act 2002 and regulations.[29]

Basically, the system assists:

- claimants (single or couples) who are in qualifying 'remunerative employment' for **16 hours or more a week** and responsible for a child; or
- those working at that level, but who have a **disability** (mental or physical); or
- **single claimants aged 25 or more**, working for at least 30 hours a week.

'Remunerative employment' has an extended meaning to bring into eligibility those on maternity leave claiming Statutory Maternity Pay or Maternity Allowance. This is an incentive for workers to remain in paid employment (and within the in-work welfare/tax credits system) during such periods.

WTC requires a *basic element* or a *disability element*, although there are other work-related elements as well – for example to reward those who increase their hours to 30 or more a week, and childcare assistance of up to 70 per cent of the weekly costs (up to prescribed limits).

Other Key Features/Requirements

Tax credits are assessed and paid separately from other in-work benefits like Child Benefit, and they contain a 'family element' and a 'child element'. There is no capital limit (unlike earlier versions of the scheme). Their precise value depends on the earners' (and families') income and circumstances, including the number of their children living with them.

As with other income-related benefits the credits are means-tested, and take into account spouses'/partners' income. This makes partners' wages and income resources during periods of 'cohabitation' relevant to the assessment – with resources being aggregated and treated as if they are available to both parties, subject to any available 'disregards'.

Payments of tax credits are usually made at the same time as other payments of net wages; i.e. through the employer's payroll, or directly if the claimant is self-employed (or other 'direct payment' cases). Amounts of tax credits paid should be shown on the itemised pay slip. CTC is paid separately, and usually directly to the main carer, who may well be a different partner to the one receiving the WTC. The rationale for paying WTC with wages, and for requiring the value of tax credits to be shown on itemised pay statements (and otherwise treating them in the same way as wages) is to create the sense that they are a form of wages. More specifically, the intention was to remove the perceived 'stigma' of welfare: a feature introduced after the Taylor Report.[30]

Changes in Earnings: 'Responsiveness'

Claimants are normally assessed on their previous tax year's gross income (or current year's projected income in some cases, for example after it is expected to reduce or increase significantly, as determined by the Inland Revenue). Despite this use of historic financial information, WTC and CTC, once assessed, are much more responsive to income changes, and other changes, than their predecessors. In particular, as of right, when a recipients' earnings go down – for example during periods of short-time working, loss of overtime opportunities, or on a change in job – they can immediately require the Inland Revenue to reassess their income. This will result in a new, higher award to reflect the reduction (without the need to wait for the end of the award, and a re-assessment, as in the case of WTC's predecessor, the Working Families Tax Credit). Awards are also adjusted, following mandatory reporting, if other changes impact on eligibility and the household's income – such as a couple separating, a child's childcare ending, or children leaving the premises to live in another household.

The benefits are assessed by reference to gross income before tax and National Insurance contributions, partly to enable claimants and advisers to assess eligibility and entitlement using Form P60 and other tax records. Despite the tax credit system's reliance on the tax and NI systems in this way they can still be claimed and paid as a State 'benefit', using other data sources, including information provided by the claimant, and independently of tax data systems. The importance of this is that a person can be paid them even if they are not paying tax or NI contributions, as well might be the case if they are on very low earnings.

Assessment

A detailed examination of tax credits assessment is not proposed.[31] In outline, assessment involves the following 'stages'. In the 'Rona and Children' worked example that follows it can be seen just how important tax credits have become, given the respective value of her wages (£6,500 a year) and her tax credits (£11,392.86 a year).

Stage 1 – Relevant Period

A 'relevant period' is identified, and this is usually, for most claimants, one year (although more than one period is possible to cater for some groups like those on short-term, or fixed-term contracts with varying pay and income periods).

Stage 2 – Maximum WTC/CTC including Childcare Costs

The claimant's maximum WTC and/or CTC is identified by aggregating all the elements for which the claimant is eligible, including basic, child, 30 hours, lone parent, etc.

Childcare costs, having been assessed separately, are added in. The system, among other things, depends on what the claimant pays, number of children, average charges in relevant period, and whether the charges are a fixed amount or variable.

Stage 3 – 'Income'

In most cases previous year's income will be used. The Inland Revenue, at the end of each tax year, determines whether tax credits should be assessed using the previous year's income or *current* income in the year in question having regard to s. 7 (3) of the Act and other provisions.

If income in the current year is less than, or is *likely* to be less than, income in the previous tax year, the current tax year's income will be used. On the other hand, if income in the current year has *increased* when compared with the previous year, it will depend on how much the increase is, or is expected to be. If the increase is less than £2,500, the previous tax year's income is used: if the increase is more than £2,500 the current year is used – but there is a deduction of £2,500 from the total amount of the increase.

Stage 4 – Income and 'Threshold' Comparison

A comparison is made between income and threshold amounts. The figures that follow are those used for assessments in 2004, and these will change in later years: so reference must be made to up-to-date Inland Revenue figures. For those claiming WTC the threshold in 2003/04 is £5,060; and this is also the amount that applies to those claiming *both* WTC and CTC.

The CTC threshold, for those only eligible for CTC/not on IS/JSA income-based is £13,320.

Stage 5 – Assessment of Tax Credits

If income is *below* the threshold then the maximum amount of tax credits is payable. If it is *above* the threshold it is necessary to identify the excess, i.e. take the threshold amount from the income, and apply the 37 per cent taper to the excess.

The excess is deducted from the maximum amount of tax credits to produce the amount payable. 'Tapering' is applied to any excess income according to a prescribed priority, starting with WTC other than the childcare element, and then:

- childcare element of WTC;
- child elements of CTC, and any disability/severe disability elements for children;
- family element of CTC, but only if there is income in the tax year that exceeds the £50,000 second threshold. The family element then reduces at the rate of £1 for each £15 above £50,000.

The Value of Tax Credits

For a large number of workers, tax credits awards are worth substantially more than their occupational earnings. As important, in terms of employment rights, they facilitate access to (and retention of) employment in a number of important ways, for example by:

- targeting assistance on groups who might otherwise find take-up of employment difficult – for example, single parents through childcare costs, and by maximising the value of child maintenance payments and Child Benefit (both of which are wholly disregarded as 'income' in the assessment of WTC, thereby keeping them as separate income streams);
- assisting employers redeploy/retain staff with disabilities and long-term incapacity in part-time or less well-paid jobs – for example when dismissal might otherwise be a likely option after accidents or long-term illness absence. This is clearly something that complements employers' duty to consider 'reasonable adjustments' to working conditions and the contract of employment under the Disability Discrimination Act 1995;
- making part-time work pay, and therefore a more viable option for atypical groups. It therefore complements employment measures such as flexible working, and reduced hours to reconcile work and home commitments, as permitted by the ERA ss. 80F–80I, and the Flexible Working (Eligibility, Complaints and Remedies) Regulations 2002, SI 2002/3236; and Part-Time Workers (Prevention of Less Favourable Treatment) Regulations 2000, SI 2000/1551. The fact that part-time workers in some sectors of the labour market like emergency services may have a large proportion of tax credits claimants in them does not preclude them asserting employment rights if they are treated less favourably than full-time staff, or, if using such employment procedures, they can enhance their working conditions and earnings; see, for example, observations in the leading case of *Matthews & Others* v. *Kent & Medway Towns Fire Authority* [2003] IRLR 732, EAT.

The 'Rona and Children' worked example that follows, using tax credits rates as at March 2004, illustrates the system's operation. NB Inland Revenue rates are revised in April each year, with details announced in the preceding November by the Inland Revenue and Treasury.

Worked Example: 'Rona and Children'

Rona separated from Mike in 2000. The children now live with her throughout the week, and she receives Child Benefit for them. She works for 20 hours a week, and rents the home she and the children live in. She has made a claim for tax credits for 2003/04. In 2001/02 she earned £6,500 a year. She spends £150 a week on childcare for the two children. She receives child maintenance payments from Mike.

Although her income increased recently, following a pay rise, the Inland Revenue confirms the rise was not a significant one, and so they use her income in 2001/02 as the basis for assessing her claim for WTC and CTC.

Her household's income derives from the following five sources:

- net occupational earnings;
- Child Benefit;
- Child Support payments;
- WTC and CTC;
- Housing Benefit and CTB.

As shown below her income from tax credits, paid on top of Child Benefit and child maintenance is worth £11,392.86 a year. Wages from her employer are worth £6,500 a year.

Stage 1 – Relevant Period

Rona's 'relevant period' is 366 days.

Stage 2 – Maximum WTC/CTC including Childcare Costs

Maximum WTC for the relevant period is:

Basic Element	£1526.20
Lone Parent Element	£1500.60
Childcare Element	£5462.10

Maximum CTC for the relevant period is:

Family Element	£545.34
Child Element (Child 1)	£1445.70
Child Element (Child 2)	£1445.70

Total: £11,925.64

NB The amounts shown in this example are higher than the annual amounts provided in the table of tax credits 'elements' because of the effect of 'rounding up' rules, and multiplication of the number of actual days in the tax year (366 in 2003/04).

Stage 3 – Income

Rona's income in 2001/02, the year being used by the Inland Revenue, is £6,500. Her relevant period is 366.
So her income for the period is £6,500 divided by 366. It is multiplied by 366 = £6,500

Stage 4 – Compare Income and 'Threshold'

Rona's annual 'threshold' is £5,060 as she claims WTC and CTC.
For the relevant period it is £5,060 divided by 366, and multiplied by 366 = £5,060

Stage 5 – Assess Tax Credits for the Relevant Period

Rona's income is compared with her threshold to identify any 'excess'.
The excess is £6,500 – £5,060 = £1,440
Taper @ 37% is applied
£1,440 × 0.37 = £532.80

This amount is applied to reduce her WTC (other than the childcare element).
i.e. Basic Element (£1526.22) + Lone Parent Element (£1500.60) = £3026.82.
So £3026.82 – £532.80 = £2494.02

Rona's Tax Credits:

WTC (excluding Childcare Element) = £2494.02
Childcare Element = £5462.10
CTC = £3436.74

Total = **£11,392.86**

Rises in Earnings

If earnings rise the State's support goes down. In many cases, however, increases do not have an immediate impact on a worker's take-home pay. On the other hand, if the earnings *increase* (such as through a promotion or re-grading, or a different job altogether) is set to continue, so that annual income is set to rise by more than £2,500 a year, WTC changes *are* made during the award year.

In effect, this means there is a temporary 'disregard' of earnings rises of up to £2,500. Reassessment at the end of the year will take into account such rises that have taken place during the year, and that reconciliation may mean an adjustment is made which is reflected in the next year's award.

In practice, the process is managed in the following way:

Worked Example: 'Moira and Child'

Moira works in a full-time job. She has one child, Ami. In the last tax year she earned £8,000, an average of £153.85 a week. As the excess income above the threshold being tapered she gets less than the full WTC/CTC.

Having changed jobs two months after her award was notified (taking on a new job that pays £11,500 a year) she decides to advise the Inland Revenue of the change, and ask for a reassessment.

The first £2,500 of the £3,500 earnings increase is 'disregarded' until the end of the year. So the reassessment is based on £1,000 difference. Her income is treated as £9,000 rather than £8,000.

The award is re-calculated, and is reduced to £79.95.

Other In-Work Benefits

Other benefits for which tax credits claimants may be eligible include Housing Benefit and CTB. However, unlike Income Support and income-based Jobseeker's Allowance working claimants who automatically receive these benefits in full (and so get all their rental and Council Tax costs paid) WTC/CTC claimants do not necessarily receive these benefits in full. Tax credit income counts in full as 'income' in the HB and CTB assessments, so that as income rises so the support reduces.[32]

Disability Living Allowance (DLA)

Other important benefits which can be paid to workers include Disability Living Allowance (DLA) Care and Mobility Components. In the case of DLA the injury or disability must give rise to a 'frequent attention' or 'continual supervision' need, or other criteria (including the 'cooking test' must be satisfied).[33] People working full-time can and do receive DLA. In practice, though, many DLA claimants work (usually part-time employment) assisted in some cases by benefits like Income Support. In this case their benefit income is increased by the disregard of DLA as 'income' in the means-test. In many cases DLA at the lower rate is paid on the basis of the so-called 'cooking test', a test based on ability to cook a main meal which assesses need based on the severity of disability, but which the House of Lords in 2003 confirmed is essentially just an 'indicative' assessment.[34] A lot of workers as well as out-of-work claimants experience problems in the DLA claims and adjudication process, as highlighted in an influential survey by the RNID *Can't Hear, Can't Benefit: A Survey of Deaf People's Experiences of Claiming DLA.*[35]

Disablement Benefit (DB)

Like DLA, Disablement Benefit is another important in-work benefit. However, like DLA, this is a benefit which is also claimed by a large number of part-time workers, many of whom also experience problems of disability discrimination. In theory the benefit is relatively easy to claim by an employee who has had a workplace injury, or is suffering from a work-related industrial illness.[36] She or he must be suffering long-term disablement, and have an assessment that s/he is at least 14 per cent 'disabled' (1 per cent for some industrial diseases will suffice), resulting from an 'accident' sustained in the course of the claimant's employment. Yet the case law shows how problematical it can be to demonstrate eligibility. For example, in the case of work-related stress, or psychiatric illnesses, the scheme still requires evidence of an 'accident', or series of 'accidents', as highlighted by the House of Lords judgment in *Chief Adjudication Officer* v. *Faulds* [2000] ICR 1297, HL in which a fireman suffered post-traumatic stress disorder as a result of attending fatal accidents and other distressing incidents that adversely affected his health. In principle, said the Lords, the benefit is available to workers in such situations – but it is still necessary to show, evidentially, that the illness resulted from an incident or series of incidents, and there is a procedure whereby decisions can be contested in the tribunal if a 'Certificate of Accident' is refused.

In a later case, involving an ambulance person suffering from stress and depression, the *Faulds* principle was applied to refuse a claim made for work-related stress.[37] In practice, groups like teachers suffering the effects of stress can and do regularly claim the benefit, at the same time as asserting other employment rights based on the same facts – such as compensation claims based on breach of the employer's 'duty of care', or constructive dismissals (see Chapter 16).

Awards can be aggregated with *other* awards, and it is not uncommon for workers to have the benefit of two or more DB awards.[38] This improves claimants' financial position considerably.[39]

The need to demonstrate causation, i.e. that an injury or illness derived from a work-related incident or cause, involves several elements, as shown by cases where a 'certificate of accident' has been refused, and appeals are made against the refusal.[40] In the leading Court of Appeal case of *Chief Adjudication Officer* v. *Rhodes* [1999] IRLR 103, CA[41] it was confirmed that personal injury must have been suffered, and that the injury arose 'out of and in the course of' the employed earner's employment; s. 94 (1) of the SSCBA. S. 94 (3) assists by stating that for the purposes of the benefit an accident arising in the course of the employment is to be taken 'in the absence of evidence to the contrary' to have arisen out of the employment. But that presumption is not always decisive. In the *Rhodes* case the claimant was an employee of the Benefits Agency. She was assaulted (while she was at home) by a neighbour she had reported earlier for suspected benefits fraud. She claimed benefit on the basis that it was work-related. Her appeal to the tribunal was successful (by a 2 to 1 majority). A Commissioner concluded that she was in 'earner's employment' at the time of her injury, given that the assault was related to and referable to her employment.

However, the Court of Appeal (by 2 to 1) allowed the appeal, holding that there are two key requirements for DB:

(1) the injury must arise *out of* the employment; and
(2) it must have occurred *in the course of* the employment.

On the facts she failed to satisfy point (2). They accepted that she might have qualified had she been doing something 'reasonably incidental' to her job at home when the incident occurred, but that this had not been the case.

Workers not in 'Remunerative Employment': IS and JSA

Workers/Claimants not in 'Remunerative Employement'

In the case of somebody who is working less than 16 hours a week (or who has a partner working up to 24 hours a week), the key benefits are Income Support (IS) or Jobseeker's Allowance (JSA).

These are important in-work benefits payable to people who are, in formal terms, treated as not in 'remunerative employment'. The rules allow claimants to claim IS and JSA while they can be claimed as an important supplement to'such income, assisted by 'earnings disregards' and capital disregards, which may assist claimants with capital or realisable assets which could take them over the £8,000 capital limit.

As a group, workers in part-time employment (with weekly hours below 16), and thus eligible for IS or income-based JSA (or contribution-based JSA during the first six months of their 'unemployment'), have become an important group for a number of reasons. First, lone parents opting to stay below the 16-hour threshold are still a sizeable group. Second, it may be financially advantageous for some workers to keep their hours below 16 a week – particularly as tax credits claimants do not benefit from the IS Mortgage Interest scheme (ISMI) which assists those with mortgage liabilities, for example after separation. Third, as indicated from research into claims made for 'flexible working' (see Chapter 8), there may be good reasons for reducing hours (usually because of parental commitments), and electing to access both IS *and* other key family benefits. A good example of this is Carer's Allowance. Carer's Allowance is paid to those who undertake regular and substantial care for a 'severely disabled person' (including children, partners, or older relatives with special needs, and who are in receipt of DLA at the middle rate of Care Component, or Attendance Allowance), and there are an estimated 4–5 million carers in the UK according to the main carer's organisation Carers UK.[42] However, it is a requirement of Care Allowance that working does not interfere with their care work and the need to undertake at least 35 hours 'regular and substantial care' each week. Weekly earnings must not exceed the Lower Earnings Limit for National Insurance contributions.[43]

IS/Income-Based JSA Eligibility

Workers who keep their weekly hours below 16 and who claim IS or JSA are subject to other eligibility requirements. A detailed consideration is not provided, but reference may be made to the legislation and guidance.[44] Key requirements and eligibility points are:

- *capital limit* of £8,000 capital;
- claimant's *'income' must be below their weekly 'applicable amount'*. Most forms of income, such as net earnings, child maintenance, etc., are 'income' for the IS/JSA assessment;
- *employment below 16 hours* (if s/he has a partner that partner must not work for 24 hours or more);
- not be in *'full-time education'* (subject to exceptions);
- be within a Schedule 1B of the Income Support (General) Regulations *'prescribed category'* e.g. carer, lone parent, over 60, disabled, incapacitated worker, etc.;
- be *'habitually resident'* in GB.

Income-based JSA is subject to similar rules, and is calculated in a similar way. The claimant is subject, however, to 'jobseeking' requirements, including being 'available for work', and 'actively seeking work'; and compliance with jobseeking responsibilities in the jobseeker's agreement, and jobseeking directions.

Amount Payable

IS (or JSA income-based): the amount payable is the amount needed in order to raise the claimant's income up to his/her 'applicable amount', i.e. the aggregate of the claimant's and dependants'

- personal allowances;
- premiums;
- mortgage costs (if any, assessed under the Income Support Mortgage Interest scheme).

Useful guidance on mortgage assistance is in *Help with Housing Costs* (DWP, IS8) Child-related additions are paid as part of the IS 'Applicable Amount' (see below). Under the Tax Credits Act 2002, they are delivered through Child Tax Credit (in most cases from April 2004 for IS and JSA income-based claimants).

A worked example of how a worker on IS is assisted is provided below.

Worked Example: 'Rachel and Children'

Rachel is a teacher, and aged 40. Following a period of stress and work-related depression, she was off work – and eventually lost her job. She separated from her husband Tony a year ago. She receives child maintenance of £60 a week from Tony for the children (who live with her throughout the week).

She rents the accommodation they live in, and pays £90 a week rent. There are three children in the family, Daniel (aged 9), Sandra (aged 13), and Julian (aged 14). She has a part-time job which pays £40 net of tax and National Insurance.

Assessed on State benefits rates as at March 2004, she gets £37.55 Child Benefit. She has no other weekly income, or capital.

Rachel's Housing Costs

As Rachel is on Income Support, she automatically gets 'maximum HB' (after a claim to her local authority); i.e. all her housing costs are paid.

Had she been paying a *mortgage* her housing costs would be assessed as part of her Income Support 'Applicable Amount'. To assess how much she would get her up-to-date amount outstanding mortgage amount is identified. This is multiplied by the 'standard interest rate' (an amount set from time-to-time, in line with the interest rates of the top mortgage lenders). It is then divided by 52 weeks to produce an average weekly amount which is added to the applicable amount (and paid after a 39-week 'wait' for most post-2 October 1995 mortgages, unless the claimant is within an exempt category, e.g. carer, partner of person in prison on remand, 'abandoned' spouse with a child, etc., in which case it is paid sooner, i.e. at 50 per cent of the amount after eight weeks, and then in full after a further 18 weeks' 'wait'.

Rachel and Children

**Income Support/Income Based JSA
Worked Example**

'Step 1'

APPLICABLE AMOUNT

Personal Allowances	Premiums	Housing Costs (for Mortgage)	Applicable Amount
54.65	15.75	–	
+ 38.50		–	
+ 38.50			
+ 38.50			
170.15 +	15.75 +	– =	185.90

'Step 2'

WEEKLY INCOME

Net Earnings apply appropriate disregard	From Benefits Income	'Tariff' Income	Income from other sources	Total Weekly Income
40.00	37.55	–	60.00	
		–	–	
–20.00				
20.00 +	37.55 +	– +	60.00 =	117.55

NB Rates are based on figures as at March 2004 (these are revised in April each year). Standard rate CB is shown. In some cases a higher rate for older child (£17.55) may be payable. As a lone parent Rachel's earnings disregard is £20.

Child Support payments count in full as 'income', as shown above in the 'Income from Other Sources' column: Child Support Premium (up to £10 each week of any maintenance paid) may be available for Rachel to reduce this (plus transitional rights for any accrued child maintenance bonus before it is abolished). This is not shown (for details see SI 2003/231).

'Step 3'

Deduct Weekly Income from Applicable Amount

185.90 – 117.55 = 68.35

Rachel's Income Support is £**68.35**. In later weeks it may go up or down in response to changing circumstances, including increases or reductions in net earnings. After April 2004, child-related support is delivered through Child Tax Credit.

IS/JSA as Earnings Replacement

For many workers who do not qualify for benefits like Statutory Sick Pay or Statutory Maternity Pay (usually because their earnings are below the Lower Earnings Limit, or because of employment status problems), these benefits, and in particular, Income Support, are an essential source of earnings replacement. They are also important if a claimant is ineligible for contributory benefits like Incapacity Benefit, as is often the case for many low-paid workers, and workers in 'atypical' employment. Of the estimated 6.8 million or more part-time workers in the UK – now representing over a quarter of the labour force according to the Labour Force Survey – many are women working on low wages and insecure employment terms. As an Equal Opportunities Commission in a submission to the Low Pay Commission[45] pointed out, 4.2 million of the 6.5 million workers earning less that £4.50 an hour are women. Not surprisingly therefore, the EOC has always had an important interest in the operation of the in-work benefits system and in its effects on women in low-paid jobs, as well as in employment measures like the national minimum wage and its impact on the gender pay gap.

Atypical and Migrant Workers

Public International Law[46] requires States to support workers, migrants, asylum seekers,[47] and their dependants in a number of ways. The problem is that such rights may only have limited effect at the national law level. In Europe, the ECHR (now part of UK law since the Human Rights Act 1998) has at different times assisted claimants of State support – for example in demonstrating that without support there would be a 'threat to life', thereby enabling art. 2 to be invoked.[48] ECHR case law is sometimes useful in securing welfare entitlements when they can be characterised as forms of 'property' – for example if they are based on NI contributions, or are accrued rights deriving from the employment relationship, thereby attracting the protection given by art. 1 of Protocol 1.[49] Discrimination in the payment of benefits, or the processes of adjudicating rights, is another potent basis on which to engage ECHR rights.[50]

     EC Law sets out a number of important basic work-related welfare principles in the Social Charter 1989, and in the Charter of Fundamental Rights of the European Union 2000. Whilst not delivering substantive rights, the latter can be an authoritative legal source when determining the scope of 'social rights', for example payments during periods of annual leave.[51] More specifically, EC legislation extends rights to work-related social security, and other forms of welfare support, to EC workers residing in other Member States. The main objective is to facilitate EC workers' freedom of movement, access to work, and residence during periods of work and work-seeking.[52] Such access cannot be restricted by the application of national rules, for example if these try to require a claimant to have 'habitual residence'; *Swaddling* v. *Adjudication Officer* (C90/97) [1999] 2 CMLR 679, ECJ. However, the requirement can still apply to some workers – including some categories of British citizens, who can be treated as a 'person from abroad',[53] and be required to have lived in the UK for 'an appreciable period'.[54]

EC Law in some cases extends rights to workers from outside the EC, for example those with refugee and stateless person status;[55] and more recently EC measures have secured minimum levels of State welfare support for non-EU workers and others. This is now an area of EC competence under the Title IV of Part 3 (arts. 61–69) of the EC Treaty. Art. 63 has produced measures like EC Directive 2003/9 which lays down minimum standards in all Member States on the reception of asylum seekers in Member States, thereby securing rights of access to the labour market after an initial period when work is not permitted (art. 11); 'material reception conditions', i.e. support for subsistence, and health needs (art. 13); and housing (art. 15). In practice, though, those subject to immigration control, and asylum seekers, are still subject to tough restrictions on State welfare assistance,[56] and can not only be prevented from working but at the same time be excluded from all forms of State welfare support (including the minimal subsistence and housing afforded by the National Asylum Support Service).[57] A residual level of Community Care support is available when destitution goes beyond mere financial destitution, assisted by ECHR requirements.[58] Even when asylum status is secured, and work obtained, such workers face considerable problems – for example in accessing support in the form of housing, and assistance with housing costs.[59]

Since 1 May 2004, and the accession of East European and other States, workers from those States and their dependants have new rights including freedom of movement in other EU countries. Those rights have been restricted, though, and do not extend a general right to seek and obtain work (and State welfare) in *all* EU States. In fact the UK is one of only several countries to agree to take such workers, and to pay work-related as well as general benefits.[60] However, the government, largely under pressure from the media and after a barrage of scare stories in the tabloids, in the weeks before 1 May, sought to mollify its critics of unrestricted entry by imposing strict conditions on take-up by such workers, notably by withholding benefits for those without a job (to bar out 'benefit tourists'). It also limited access to State support until completion of an initial period of 12 months' employment in the UK.[61] In doing so, it failed to address the problem of how workers and their dependants are supposed to get by in intervals between short-term jobs – or if employment ends without the 12 months qualifying period being completed. Given that many of the jobs being taken up are in sectors like agriculture, hotels, and catering, the availability of WTC and CTC has been a major factor in supplementing what would otherwise be very low wages. Such support has made employment in the UK a more attractive option for migrant workers than it would otherwise be. Some of the workers now resident in the UK have come from some of the poorest parts of post-Communist Eastern Europe.[62]

In the case of workers from *outside* the EU, often working illegally after they arrive in the UK, unable in practice to secure employment protection, and excluded from State welfare support, housing, or health care, the reality is that they can be easy prey for exploitation – particularly by gangmasters acting as intermediaries for employers in sectors with some of the very worst pay and working conditions in the country. The reality is that significant sections of the UK's labour market have started to become dependent on such workers. This seemed to be readily acknowledged by the Environment, Food and Rural Affairs Minister, Lord Whitty, in the aftermath of the tragic drowning of young Chinese cockle pickers in Morecambe Bay when confirming that the government would support the setting up of a licensing scheme for their work under the Gangmasters (Licensing) Bill 2004. The legislation itself is plainly deficient, and goes nowhere near addressing the problems involved;[63] and even newspapers not usually noted for their support for migrants' rights were shocked by the affair, and by the lack of an effective response. This was evident in one front-page report headed 'Slavery 2004 – How Migrants are Lured to Britain to Work for 10p a Day and Fed on Dog Food'.[64] Nor has Parliament been impressed. The Environment, Food and Rural Affairs Select Committee criticised what it called 'the government's lack of a concerted approach', which 'still leaves many thousands of people vulnerable to both exploitation and danger'.[65]

Notes and References

Chapter 1: Employment Rights: Past, Present and Future

1. Anthony Giddens, *The Third Way: The Renewal of Social Democracy* (Cambridge: Polity Press, 1998). Giddens' influence, even before New Labour came to power, is evident for example in *Social Justice: Strategies for National Renewal*, The Report of the Commission on Social Justice (London: Vintage, 1994).
2. Otto Kahn-Freund, *Labour and the Law* (Hamlyn Lectures) (London: Stevens, 1972).
3. Hugh Collins, 'Is there a Third Way in Labour Law?' in J. Conaghan, R. Fischl, K. Klare (eds.), *Labour Law in an Era of Globalisation – Transformative Practices and Possibilities* (Oxford: OUP, 2002), p. 449; discussed by Claire Kilpatrick in 'Has New Labour Reconfigured Employment Legislation?', *ILJ*, vol. 32 (2003), pp. 136–40.
4. *New Ambitions for Our Country: A New Contract for Welfare* (1998, Cm. 3805) at pp. (iii), (iv) of the Prime Minister's Foreword; and pp. 28, 29.
5. *ILJ*, vol. 26 (1997), p. 295.
6. Under the *New Welfare Contract*, in return for government providing assistance to find work, make work pay, etc., the 'duty of the individual' includes taking up the opportunity to 'be independent'; see *New Ambitions for Our Country: A New Contract for Welfare* (1998, Cm. 3805), at p. 80.
7. The centrepiece of the government's White Paper *Fairness at Work* (May 1998) was the government's intention 'to replace the notion of conflict between employers and employees with the promotion of partnership' – an ideal which permeated all three sections of the paper: new rights for individuals; collective rights; and family-friendly policies.
8. As discussed in later chapters, the Employment Act 2002 backs this responsibility up with legal sanctions. The Explanatory Notes to the Act provided insights into government thinking on individuals' and their employers' responsibilities as part of this approach to employment rights.
9. Official Journal C340, 10 November 1997, p. 1, in force from 1 May 1999. The Treaty of Nice changes came into force from 1 December 2002 with effect from 1 December 2002.
10. M. Pollack, 'A Blairite Treaty – Neo-Liberalism and Regulated Capitalism in the Treaty of Amsterdam' in K. Neunreither and A. Wiener (eds.) *European Integration after Amsterdam: Institutional Dynamics and Prospects for Democracy* (Oxford: OUP, 2000).
11. Originally viewed sceptically by many European unions as little more than a 'wish-list'. That was the opinion of IG Metall, the German metalworkers union, quoted in Silvia, 'The Social Charter of the European Community. A Defeat for European Labour', 44, *Industrial and Labour Relations Review*, 626. See also Vogel-Polsky, 'What Future is there for a Social Europe Following the Strasbourg Summit?', *ILJ*, vol. 19 (1990), p. 65.
12. See Paul Davies and Mark Freedland, 'The Impact of Public Law on Labour Law, 1972–1977', *ILJ*, vol. 26 (1997), p. 311.
13. Awareness of dismal working conditions in Eastern European countries like Romania has not prevented EC-based companies transferring their operations because of lower

rates of pay and lack of union organisation – an issue highlighted by articles like 'Slum in Hell of IKEA's Low-Paid Suppliers' (*Sunday Times*, 22 February 1998). The migration of service industry jobs like rail enquiries and insurance to India, where workers may have better academic qualifications, but worse employment conditions, caused consternation in 2003.

14. See Fran Bennett and Donald Hirsch, *The Employment Tax Credit: Issues for the Future of In-Work Support* (York: J. Rowntree Foundation/YPS, 2001). The reality, however, is that a large number of lower-paid UK workers receive substantial in-work financial support, and may get a much larger 'wage' from the State than they do from their occupational wage. This is something employers, through their wages systems, have started to adapt to; see Keith Puttick, 'Welfare as "Wages": Benefits, Low Pay and the Flexible Labour Market', *ILJ*, vol. 27, no. 2, June 1998; and Keith Puttick, 'New Generation Tax Credits', *Family Law Journal*, May 2003, no. 5. See also Chapter 22.

15. The government sees, as a positive feature of adaptability and flexibility, opportunities for employers to adopt 'innovative approaches' to managing change – for example in introducing schemes for flexible working arrangement; see *Balancing Work and Family Life: Enhancing Choice and Support for Parents* (HM Treasury and DTI, 2003).

16. Sandra Fredman, 'Labour Law in Flux: The Changing Composition of the Workforce', *ILJ*, vol. 26 (1997), p. 311.

17. For a comprehensive discussion of the evolution of legal policy in this area, and the impact of deregulation, see Roy Lewis, 'The Role of Law in Employment Relations', in Lewis (ed.) *Labour Law in Britain* (Oxford: Blackwell, 1986) and Roy Lewis, 'Reforming Labour Law: Choices and Constraints', *Employee Relations* (1987) vol. 9, no. 4, pp. 28–31.

18. H. Phelps Brown, *The Growth of British Industrial Relations*, quoted in Lord Wedderburn of Charlton, *The Worker and the Law*, 3rd edn (Harmondsworth: Penguin, 1986), p. 1.

19. On the legal regulation of unions, see Gillian Morris and Timothy Archer, *Collective Labour Law* (Oxford: Hart Publishing, 2000).

20. See F. Von Hayek, *1980s Unemployment and the Unions* (London: Institute of Economic Affairs, 1980). For a more detailed analysis of the views of Hayek, see Wedderburn, 'Freedom of Association and Philosophies of Labour Law', *ILJ*, vol. 18 (1989), pp. 1–38.

21. A survey by the National Association of Citizens' Advice Bureaux found that some employers routinely dismiss staff weeks or even days before they complete two years in the job and thereby qualify for unfair dismissal protection. The report recommended cutting the qualifying period for employment protection from two years to six months, regardless of the number of hours worked each week ('Job Insecurity: CAB Evidence on Employment Problems in the Recession', London: National Association of Citizens' Advice Bureaux, March 1993, pp. 1–55). A later NACAB study, 'Flexibility Abused' (November 1997), recommended employment protection law has to be reviewed for such reasons.

22. Morris and Archer, *Collective Labour Law*, p. 45.

23. A campaign and 'Charter for Pension Fund Democracy' was launched by the TUC in September 1992. On the issues involved in protecting pension rights, see Richard Nobles, *Controlling Occupational Pension Schemes* (London: Independent Institute of Employment Rights, 1992).

24. *New Ambitions for Our Country: A New Contract for Welfare* (1998, Cm. 3805), at p. 80.

25. On employers' responsibilities, and employees' rights, under the SSP, SMP and other more recent schemes like Statutory Paternity Pay, see Keith Puttick *Welfare Benefits: Law and Practice* 9th edn (Welwyn Garden City: EMIS Professional Publishing, 2004).

26. See S. Evans, 'The Use of Injunctions in Labour Disputes', *BJIR*, vol. 25 (1987), p. 419.

27. Evans found that injunctions resulted in an immediate lifting of the industrial action or withdrawal of official support in three-quarters of the cases surveyed; unions ignored injunctions in approximately 25 per cent of cases – see endnote 5 in that study.

28. See M. Cully and S. Woodland, 'Trade Union Membership and Recognition', *Labour Market Trends*, June 1997, pp. 231–9.

29. See K. Sweeney and J. Davies, 'International Comparisons of Labour Disputes in 1995', *Labour Market Trends*, April 1997, pp. 129–33.

30. See W.W. Daniel and E. Stilgoe, *The Impact of the Employment Protection Laws* (London: Policy Studies Institute, 1978); A. Clifton and C. Tatton-Brown, 'The Impact of Employment Protection on Small Firms', Department of Employment Research Paper 7 (London: HMSO, 1979).

31. S. Evans, J. Goodman and L. Hargreaves, 'Unfair Dismissal Law and Employment Practice in the 1980s', DES Research Paper 53 (London: HMSO, 1985).

32. I. Wood and P. Smith, 'Employers' Labour Use Strategies: First Report on the 1987 Survey', Department of Employment Research Paper 63 (London: HMSO, 1989).

33. *Labour Market Trends*, April 1997, pp. 151–6.

34. B. Hepple, 'Individual Employment Law' in G.S. Bain (ed.), *Industrial Relations in Britain* (Oxford: Blackwell, 1983), pp. 393–417 at p. 393.

35. The UK government's policy of deregulation also forced it to denounce four International Labour Organisation (ILO) conventions. These included Convention no. 94 (Labour Clauses [Public Contracts] Convention 1949) and Convention no. 95 (Protection of Wages Convention 1949). The denunciation of Convention no. 94 enabled the government to rescind the Fair Wages Resolution, while the denunciation of Convention no. 95 enabled it to introduce the Wages Act 1986 and to repeal the Truck Acts. The UK was later held to have breached other ILO conventions dealing with Freedom of Association and the Right to Organise (see Chapter 16).

36. *United Kingdom* v. *Council* [1997] IRLR 30; [1997] ICR 443, ECJ. For commentary on the directive, see B. Bercusson, *European Labour Law* (London: Butterworths), ch. 21. See also Barry Fitzpatrick, 'Straining the Definition of Health and Safety?', *ILJ*, vol. 26 (1997), p. 115.

37. London: Sweet and Maxwell, ch. 12; and on appeals, see John Bowers QC, 'Employment Appeals' in Sir Michael Burton (ed.), *Civil Appeals* (Welwyn Garden City: EMIS Publishing).

38. *Grunwick Processing Laboratories* v. *Advisory Conciliation and Arbitration Service* [1978] AC 655. A decisive issue in that case was the difficulty ACAS had in obtaining the employer's co-operation, and so to enable a ballot of workers to be properly conducted. The legislation was complex, however, and it was not difficult for the Lords to hold that ACAS had got it wrong. See, now, the requirements of Schedule A1 to TULR(C)A discussed in Chapter 18.

39. Puttick, 'Welfare as "Wages"', Note 14 above, at p. 162. On in-work welfare, and 'making work pay' measures like the Tax Credits Act 1999, see Keith Puttick, '2020: A Welfare Odyssey – A Commentary on *Principles into Practice* and the Reform Programme', *ILJ*, vol. 28 (1999), p. 19.

40. Developments in ECHR rights may assist in securing various accrued benefits arising from the employment relationship, including wages, some State benefits paid for out of wages (and through National Insurance contributions), and other elements with 'property' characteristics (such as pensions and accrued rights under the contract); John Bowers QC and Jeremy Lewis, *Employment Law and Human Rights* (London: Sweet and Maxwell, 2001). But there is still no legal recognition, statutory or otherwise, that a job *per se* is capable of legal protection as a form of 'property'. See, generally, on this Hugh Collins, *Justice in Dismissal: The Law of Termination of Employment* (Oxford: Clarendon Press), in which he comments that in a market economy in which demand for labour directs workers to jobs 'the market would cease to function efficiently if employers were not permitted to enter and to terminate contracts of employment at

their discretion in the light of market conditions'; and see Hugh Collins, 'The Meaning of Job Security', *ILJ*, vol. 20 (1991), p. 227; and see Chapter 22.

41. For a union to be legally liable for industrial action there must be civil liability in the first place. However, not *all* action involves a breach of contract, e.g. some types of ban on voluntary overtime. See *Burgess and Others* v. *Stevedoring Services Ltd* [2002] IRLR 210.

42. Bob Hepple QC and Gillian Morris, 'The Employment Act 2002 and the Crisis of Individual Employment Rights', *ILJ*, vol. 31 (2002), p. 245. Criticisms of the changes were also made by Lord Wedderburn in 'Common Law, Labour Law, Global Law' in Bob Hepple (ed.), *Social and Labour Rights in a Global Context* (2002).

43. For a commentary on changes in the family leave regime, and benefits, by Joanna Wade of the Maternity Alliance, see 'Maternity and Parental Rights for the New Millennium', *Welfare Benefits*, vol. 8, issue 5. On parental leave, adoption leave, and maternity leave benefits generally, including procedures for contesting refusals, see Keith Puttick, *Welfare Benefits: Law and Practice* 9th edn (Welwyn Garden City: EMIS Professional Publishing).

44. Employment Lawyers' Association *Briefing*, vol. 10 (no. 10) Dec. 2003.

45. Flexible Working Survey, by Lovells and the Chartered Institute of Personnel and Development (Sept. 2003).

46. Research commissioned by the Joseph Rowntree Foundation, and published by The Policy Press (July 2003).

Chapter 2: The Gateways to Employment Rights

1. In 1951, only 4 per cent of employees worked fewer than 30 hours a week.

2. Labour Force surveys show that 60 per cent of all part-timers are found in retail distribution, hotels and catering, education and other services.

3. Women working part-time earn 75 per cent of average full-time female hourly earnings and under 60 per cent of average male full-time hourly earnings (see K. Osborne, 'Earnings of Part-time Workers: Data from the 1995 New Earnings Survey', *Labour Market Trends*, May 1996, pp. 227–35). In 1992, about half of workers in part-time, temporary and casual jobs were receiving hourly earnings in the lowest quartile. This compared with 10 per cent of men and 23 per cent of women in permanent full-time jobs; see B. Anderton and K. Mayhew, 'A Comparative Analysis of the UK Labour Market', in R. Barrell (ed.) *The UK Labour Market: Comparative Aspects and Institutional Developments* (Cambridge: Cambridge University Press, 1994), p. 24.

4. House of Lords, Select Committee on the European Communities, 'Voluntary Part-time Work', session 1981–1982, 19th report (London: HMSO, 1982).

5. The spring 1988 Labour Force survey indicated that 55 per cent of all part-time workers were not covered by the main employment protection rights through a combination of the hours and service requirements, compared with the 29 per cent of full-timers who were disqualified because they lack two years' service then required to claim.

6. P. Heather, J. Rick, J. Atkinson and S. Morris, 'Employers' Use of Temporary Workers', *Labour Market Trends*, September 1996, pp. 403–11.

7. See ERA 1996, s. 197.

8. ERA 1996, s. 230 defines an employee as 'an individual who has entered into or works under ... a contract of employment'; a contract of employment is defined as 'a contract of service or apprenticeship, whether express or implied, and (if it is express) whether it is oral or in writing'.

9. See *Ready Mixed Concrete (South East) Ltd* v. *Minister of Pensions and National Insurance* [1968] 1 All ER 433, *Market Investigations* v. *Minister of Social Security* [1969] 2 QB 173, *Lee* v. *Chung and Shun Sing Construction and Engineering Co Ltd* [1990] IRLR 236, and *Hall* v. *Lorimer* [1994] 1 WLR 9.

10. See the EC Directive on Acquired Rights (77/187); *Dr Sophie Redmond Stichting* v. *Bartol and Others* [1992] IRLR 366, ECJ and *Rask and Christensen* v. *ISS Kantineservice A/S* [1993] IRLIB 464, ECJ.
11. For a detailed analysis of the issues see L. Dickens, *Whose Flexibility? Discrimination & Equality Issues in Atypical Work* (London: Institute of Employment Rights, 1992).
12. B. Hepple, 'Restructuring Employment Rights', *ILJ*, vol. 15, p. 69.
13. Patricia Leighton, 'Marginal Workers', in R. Lewis (ed.), *Labour Law in Britain* (Oxford: Blackwell, 1986), ch. 18.

Chapter 3: Job Applications and Recruitment

1. *Allen* v. *Flood* [1898] AC 1. This position still applies if legislation or case law has not modified it. One reason for the Common Law on this has been the law's refusal to force a party to enter into a contract against their will; D. Newell, *Understanding Recruitment Law* (London: Waterlow, 1984), p. 1.
2. For guidance, see *Sexual Orientation and the Workplace – A Guide for Employers and Employees* (ACAS).
3. ACAS website is www.acas.gov.uk.
4. *An Inquiry into Employment Practice and Procedures in the London Borough of Hackney* (Lincoln Crawford, 1998: commissioned by Hackney London Borough Council).
5. To access tax credits it is necessary to be working, on average, at least 16 hours a week; for details, see the Tax Credits Act 2002. On low pay, benefits, and tax credits see Keith Puttick, 'Welfare as "Wages": Benefits, Low Pay and the Flexible Labour Market', *ILJ*, vol. 27, no. 2 (June 1998), p. 162. As the government made clear in 1998, the need to reduce the cost of in-work welfare benefits was part of the reason for the Act; see observations at 303 HC Official Report (6th Series) at cols. 163 and 164.
6. The Conduct of Employment Agencies and Employment Businesses Regulations 2003, SI 2003/3319.
7. *E. Pascoe* v. *Hallen & Medway* [1975] IRLR 116 (asthma attack at work).
8. The Disability Rights Commission can advise those experiencing discriminatory recruitment practices; and see its comprehensive guidance to applicants and employers.
9. Exclusions from the rights in the Act apply to designated professions; see the Rehabilitation of Offenders Act 1974 (Exceptions) Order 1975, SI 1975/1023.
10. Section 4 (3) of the Act says non-disclosure of a spent conviction is not a ground of dismissal or exclusion from employment, or for prejudicing a person 'in any way'; *Property Guards Ltd* v. *Taylor and Kershaw* [1982] IRLR 175.
11. *Pedersen* v. *Camden London Borough Council* [1981] ICR 674.
12. If the offer, or important parts of it, are too vague (or there is no agreed means for settling details of important terms later) there is the possibility that, in law, there is no contract; *Loftus* v. *Roberts*, 18 TLR 532.
13. *Laws* v. *London Chronicle (Indicator Newspapers)* [1959] 2 All 285 and 287. For a general guide, see Cheshire Fifoot and Furmston's *Law of Contract* (London: Butterworths, 2000).
14. *Newland* v. *Simons & Willer (Hairdressers) Ltd* [1981] ICR 521.
15. *Wishart* v. *National Association of Citizens' Advice Bureaux* [1990] IRLR 393, CA.
16. *Spring* v. *Guardian Assurance plc and others* [1994] IRLR 460, HL, [1994] ICR 596.
17. *Dalgleish* v. *Lothian & Borders Police* (1991); see LRD, *The Law at Work* (March 1992).
18. *Gill and Others* v. *Cape Contracts Ltd* [1985] IRLR 499.
19. *Powell* v. *London Borough of Brent* [1987] IRLR 466.

Chapter 4: The Contract of Employment

1. Discussed comprehensively by Robert Palmer in *English Law in the Age of Black Death 1348–1381* (1993).
2. Simon Deakin and Gillian Morris, *Labour Law* 3rd Edn (London: Butterworths, 2001), p. 6.
3. Bob Hepple, 'Restructuring Employment Rights', *ILJ*, vol. 15 (1986), p. 69.
4. On contracts of employment generally, see Mark Freedland, *The Personal Employment Contract* (Oxford: OUP, 2003); Deakin and Morris, *Labour Law* 3rd Edn; Paul Davies and Mark Freedland, *Labour Law: Text and Materials* (London: Weidenfeld and Nicolson, 1984).
5. On this role for contracts, see Anthony T. Kronman, 'Contract Law and Distributive Justice', *Yale Law Journal*, vol. 89: 472 (1980); and Hugh Collins *Regulating Contracts* (Oxford: OUP, 1999). Distributive justice and corrective justice, as concepts, have their origins in Aristotle *The Nichomachean Ethics*.
6. On relevant criteria, see the leading case of *Secretary of State for Trade and Industry* v. *Bottrill* [1999] IRLR 326; [2000] 1 All ER 915.
7. *Diocese of Southwark* v. *Coker* [1998] ICR 140.
8. *Buchan* v. *Secretary of State for Employment* [1997] IRLR 80.
9. *Dryden* v. *Greater Glasgow Health Board* [1992] IRLR 469. Introducing such a ban was held not to infringe employees' contractual rights and was an action an employer could take. An employee could not therefore claim 'constructive dismissal'.
10. See A. Flanders, 'What are Trade Unions For?', ch. 1 in W.E.J. McCarthy (ed.), *Trade Unions* (Harmondsworth: Penguin, 1985), p. 26.
11. See A. Fox, *Beyond Contract: Work, Power and Trust Relations* (London: Faber, 1974). Appraisal systems, and job evaluation and analysis, are important examples of this, especially when they are linked to pay and rewards and to disciplinary systems.
12. *Associated Newspapers Ltd* v. *Wilson*; *Associated British Ports* v. *Palmer* [1995] IRLR 258, HL. See, however, the follow-up proceedings in the European Court of Human Rights, reported as *Wilson and the National Union of Journalists; Palmer, Wyeth and National Union of Rail, Maritime and Transport Workers; Doolan and others* v. *United Kingdom* [2002] IRLR 128, EctHR, and changes made to the relevant provisions of TULR(C)A, including ss. 146–167; and for a commentary, see Keith Ewing, 'The Implications of Wilson and Palmer', *ILJ*, vol. 32 (2003), p. 1.
13. On employees' rights (and employers' powers) in the transfer process, see J. McMullen, *Business Transfers and Employees' Rights* (London: Butterworths, 1992); and S. Anderman, *Labour Law: Management Decisions and Workers' Rights* (London: Butterworths, 2001).
14. It has been argued, for example, that employment contracts can be used to strengthen job security, by including 'no compulsory redundancy' clauses and restrictions on dismissal powers; K.D. Ewing, 'Job Security and the Contract of Employment', *ILJ*, vol. 18 (1989), p. 217.
15. On the changes affecting employment contracts, see Keith Ewing (ed.), *Working Life: A New Perspective on Labour Law* (London: Lawrence and Wishart/Institute of Employment Rights, 1996), ch. 2.
16. Unfair Contract Terms Act 1977.
17. White Paper, 'People, Jobs and Opportunity' (February 1992).
18. Reporting to Parliament on the Amsterdam summit meeting of the EC Council; see *Hansard*, 18 June 1997, col. 315.
19. These were adopted by the EC Social Affairs Council on 15 December 1997, and confirmed in June 1998.
20. Even if details of wages have not been agreed the court (or the tribunal if it has jurisdiction) can make an order for remuneration based on what the parties would have agreed; or on the basis of what would be reasonable.
21. *Eagland* v. *British Telecommunications plc* [1990] ICR 248.

22. ERA, sections 1–3. For guidance on statements, see *Written Statement of Initial Particulars* (DTI, PL700). Subject to the requirement that certain particulars (in s. 1 [3], [4] [a]–[c], d [i], [f] and [h]) must all be contained in one single statement, it is permissible for an employer to provide the statements in 'instalments'; s. 1 (2), 2 (4). Other key provisions, which may need to be referred to, include s. 2 (which stipulates that in some cases, even if there are no particulars to be entered, that fact must be stated: and that even if the employment has ended before the statement was due to be provided it must still be given); s. 3 (disciplinary procedures and pensions); s. 4 (statement of changes); s. 5 (exclusion of rights to statements); s. 6 (the need for documents or collective agreements to be reasonably accessible).

23. *Gascol Conversions Ltd* v. *J.W. Mercer* [1974] IRLR 155 at 156–7 laid down the principle that documents signed as contracts generally trigger the parole evidence rule (excluding the admission of other evidence contradicting the contract). In the later leading case of *Systems Floors (UK) Ltd* v. *Daniel* [1982] ICR 54 it was made clear, developing guidance in *Turriff Construction Ltd* v. *Bryant* [1967] 2 KIR 659, that statements are not, in themselves, the contract of employment (or conclusive evidence of the terms of the contract), subject to the exceptional situation in the *Gascol Conversions* case where both parties had signed the statement *as* the contract. Said the EAT: 'In the absence of an acknowledgment by the parties that the statement is itself a contract and that the terms are correct, such as that contained in the *Mercer* case, the statutory statement does not itself constitute a contract in writing.'

24. If, for example, a letter of appointment provides for a bonus, but the statement says something different (and this prompts the employer to cancel that bonus) it might be open to argue that the employer is *not* entitled to do so – particularly if the bonus has been incorporated into the individual contract, and that entitlement has not been the subject of an effective contract variation; see, for example, the principles considered in *Robertson* v. *British Gas Corporation* [1983] ICR 351.

25. 27th edition, para. 2–042.

26. ERA 1996, ss. 11 and 12.

27. *Cadoux* v. *Central Regional Council* [1986] IRLR 131. The case may be compared with the different approach taken in *Marley* v. *Forward Trust Ltd* [1986] IRLR 369; and for a critical commentary see Brian Napier, 'Incorporation of Collective Agreements', *ILJ*, vol. 15, no. 52 (1986). Public sector workers may in certain circumstances be able to take advantage of a public law requirement to consult before action is taken which removes established employment rights; *Council of Civil Service Unions* v. *Civil Service Minister* [1985] IRLR 29.

28. *Robertson* v. *British Gas Corporation* [1983] ICR 351. In *Marley* v. *Forward Trust Group Ltd* (see Note 27 above), it was held that the terms of a collective agreement on redundancy had become incorporated into a person's individual contract. Those terms could therefore be relied upon when the employer tried to invoke the requirements of the original 'mobility' clause. Cases can go the other way, though, as in *Alexander* v. *Standard Telephones and Cables plc* [1990] IRLR 55; No. 2 [1991] IRLR 286.

29. TULR(C)A, s. 179. It is possible, but uncommon, for agreements to state that they will be enforceable; *NCB* v. *NUM* [1986] IRLR 439 at 449.

30. *Maclea* v. *Essex Line Ltd* [1933] Lloyd's Report vol. 45, p. 254.

31. Kahn-Freund, critically discussed in Paul Davies and Mark Freedland, *Kahn-Freund's Labour and the Law* (London: Stevens, 1983), pp. 168 et seq.

32. *C. Singh* v. *British Steel Corporation* [1974] IRLR 131.

33. *Petrie* v. *MacFisheries Ltd* [1940] 1 KB 258.

34. *International Packaging (UK) Ltd* v. *Balfour and others* [2003] IRLR 11.

35. In *Meek* v. *Port of London Authority* [1918] 1 Ch 415, it was suggested that such knowledge was necessary; but cf. *Sagar* v. *H. Ridehalgh & Son Ltd* [1931] 1 Ch 310.

36. *F.G. Samways* v. *Swan Hunter Shipbuilders Ltd* [1975] IRLR 190.

37. *Scally* v. *Southern Health and Social Services Board* [1992] IRLR 523.

38. *Ibekwe* v. *London General Transport Services Ltd* [2003] EWCA Civ. 1075, CA.

39. *Murco Petroleum Ltd* v. *Forge* [1987] IRLR 50.
40. *Miles* v. *Wakefield District Council* [1987] IRLR 193, [1987] 1 All ER 1089, House of Lords.
41. *Secretary of State for Employment* v. *ASLEF* (No. 2) [1972] 2 All ER 949.
42. *Johnstone* v. *Bloomsbury Health Authority* [1991] 2 All ER 293, CA; discussed in Chapter 16 below.
43. By Douglas Brodie, *ILJ*, vol. 27, no. 2 (June 1998), p. 79.
44. *ILJ*, vol. 30, no. 1 (March 2001).
45. An appeal to the Lords is expected. See also *Pratley* v. *Surrey County Council* [2003] EWCA Civ 1067, [2003] IRLR 794, CA which shows how difficult it can be to demonstrate that there has been a breach of duty, even where it was foreseeable, on the facts, that the system of work involved might lead to the claimant's nervous breakdown and illness, and after undertakings which had been given to modify that system had not been carried out.
46. 'Incorporation of the ECHR and its Impact on Employment Law', *EHRLR*, 560 (1998). See also S. Palmer 'Human Rights – Implications for Labour Law', *CLJ*, 168 (2000); John Bowers and Jeremy Lewis, *Employment Law and Human Rights* (London: Sweet & Maxwell, 2001); and, on 'proportionality', and its impact on rights like 'whistleblowing' (discussed in Chapter 9), 'Whistleblowing: The New Law', *EHRLR*, 13 (1999).
47. In effect from 1 December 2003.

Chapter 5: Workplace Change

1. Wedderburn, *The Worker and the Law* 3rd Edn (London: Penguin Books, 1986).
2. EC Council Directive 94/95, OJ 254 (on European Works Councils for the purposes of informing and consulting employees); and the European Social Charter (Revised 1996), article 21. On workers' rights to participation on the board of the European Company, see Paul Davies, 'Workers on the Board of the European Company', *ILJ*, vol. 32 (2003), p. 75.
3. See, further, Richard Painter and Ann Holmes, *Cases and Materials on Employment Law* (Oxford: OUP, 2004), ch. 7.
4. See, for example, cases on TULR(C)A ss. 152, 153 like *Dundon* v. *GPT Ltd* [1995] IRLR 403; and *O'Dea* v. *ISC Chemicals Ltd* [1995] IRLR 799, CA.
5. Case 324/86 *Foreningen af Arbejdsledere i Danmark* v. *Daddy's Dance Hall* A/SC 324/86 [1988] IRLR 315, ECJ.
6. [2002] IRLR 629, CA; IRLB 699, p. 10. The referral to the ECJ by the HL was made on 10 November 2003. See IRLB 726 (Dec. 2003), p. 3.
7. Mark Freedland, *The Personal Employment Contract* (Oxford: OUP, 2003), p. 51.
8. The Companies Act 1985 (Table A) Regulations, SI 1985/805.
9. Companies Act 1985 s. 309.
10. Wedderburn, 'Consultation and Collective Bargaining in Europe: Success or Ideology?', *ILJ*, vol. 26, no. 1 (1997). For commentary on the change process, and useful guidance, see *Contracts of Employment: Defending Legal Rights* (LRD 1996).
11. 'The Onward March of Workers', *Business Law Review*, Nov. 2003, p. 263.
12. EC Reg. 2002/14, OJ L 2002 80/29 directed at UK employers with more than 50 employees, but coming into operation in stages: employers with more than 150 employees, by 23 March 2005; 100 employees, by 23 March 2007; and 50, by 23 March 2008.
13. EC Council Directive 93/104, OJ L307/18 on working time. This is implemented in the UK by the Working Time Regulations 1998, SI 1998 No. 1833.
14. In an influential report in September 1997 the CABx highlighted the widespread changes (including increased use of 'zero hours' contracts) affecting the employment conditions of millions of low-paid workers (*Flexibility Abused: A CAB Evidence Report on*

Employment Conditions in the Labour Market (NACABx, September 1997). In another report, *Zero Hours Contracts* (Katherine Care/University of Huddersfield, January 1997) the incidence of 'zero hours' working arrangements and their legal implications was considered (also see Linda Dickens 'Exploring the Atypical: Zero Hours Contracts', *ILJ*, vol. 26 (1997), p. 262). On the difficulties of part-time and atypical workers accessing State benefits, see Keith Puttick, 'Welfare as "Wages": Benefits, Low Pay and the Flexible Labour Market', *ILJ*, vol. 27, no. 2 (June 1998), p. 162.

15. Whilst earlier initiatives like company law reform, e.g. in the Draft EC Fifth Company Directive on Company Law 1972 (and amended proposals in 1983 and 1991, OJ, C176, 8 July 1991), progressed slowly, other employee stakeholder initiatives have been developing fast since ratification of the Treaty of Amsterdam.

16. *Hollister* v. *National Farmers Union* [1979] ICR 542; and *Woods* v. *W.M. Car Services (Peterborough) Ltd* [1982] IRLR 413, CA.

17. *Smith* v. *Stockport Metropolitan Borough Council*, 8 August 1979, Stockport County Court; [1979] CLY 905.

18. For example, where an employer's arrangements for transferring staff are in breach of the implied duty to act fairly (the 'fair dealing' requirement); *Newns* v. *British Airways plc* [1992] 575, CA; and Chapter 4, Note 36. But cf. the *White* case cited in Note 22 below.

19. *Haden Carrier Ltd* v. *Cowen* [1982] IRLR 314. However, see the later cases discussed in Chapter 15 showing a move away from a 'contract' approach in the context of reorganisation and redundancy.

20. *Cresswell and Others* v. *Board of Inland Revenue* [1984] IRLR 190.

21. *United Bank Ltd* v. *Akhtar* [1989] IRLR 507, where a bank's insistence on an employee moving job locations without adequate notice or financial assistance was held to be a constructive dismissal.

22. *White* v. *Reflecting Roadstuds Ltd* [1991] IRLR 331.

23. *Waine* v. *R. Oliver (Plant Hire) Ltd* [1977] IRLR 434.

24. See the ERA 1996, s. 4 and Chapter 4 on statutory written statements; note that the tribunal has power to decide the terms being worked on (including any new terms) if they have not been provided, or they are incorrect (ERA 1996, ss. 11, 12).

25. *Burdett Coutts and Others* v. *Hertfordshire County Council* [1984] IRLR 91.

26. *Rigby* v. *Ferodo Ltd* [1987] IRLR 516.

27. Alterations in the *way* pay is calculated, e.g. commission earnings, may also be a breach of contract; see *R.F. Hill Ltd* v. *Mooney* [1981] IRLR 258.

28. *Jowitt* v. *Pioneer Technology (UK) Ltd* [2002] IRLR 790 and [2003] 356, CA; and *Manchester City Council* v. *Thurston* [2002] IRLR 319.

29. *New Century Cleaning Co. Ltd* v. *Church* [2000] IRLR 27, CA.

30. *Chubb Fire Security Ltd* v. *Harper* [1983] IRLR 311.

31. *Safeway Stores plc* v. *Burrell* [1997] IRLR 200.

32. *Mennell* v. *Newell & Wright (Transport Contractors) Ltd* [1996] IRLR 384, [1997] 519, CA. To come within the protection in the ERA s. 104 it is not necessarily a requirement for the employee to have taken action to enforce the right. But he must show that his assertion was the reason for his dismissal (Court of Appeal, 10 July 1997). The scope of s. 104 is also illustrated by *Jenvey* v. *Australian Broadcasting Corporation* [2002] IRLR 520, discussed in Chapter 4.

Chapter 6: Reductions in Work

1. *Bond* v. *CAV Ltd*; *Neads* v. *CAV Ltd* [1983] IRLR 360.

2. See, for example, *Millbrook Furnishing Industries Ltd* v. *McIntosh* [1981] IRLR 309.

3. *Kenneth MacRae & Co Ltd* v. *Dawson* [1984] IRLR 5.

4. *International Packaging Corporation (UK) Ltd* v. *Balfour and others* [2003] IRLR 11.

5. ERA, ss. 28–35.

6. On welfare benefits and tax credits entitlements during periods of reduced earnings, see specialist texts like CPAG's *Welfare Benefits and Tax Credits Handbook* (London: CPAG Publications 2004, published annually); and Keith Puttick, *Welfare Benefits: Law and Practice* (Welwyn Garden City: EMIS Professional Publishing, 2004/5 published annually). See further, on in-work benefits, Chapter 22.

Chapter 7: Pay

1. On wages and wage systems, see K. Puttick (with R. Painter, I. Henn, S. Evans), *Wages and the Law* (London: Shaw & Sons, 1989); A.M. Bowey, *Handbook of Salary and Wages Systems* (London: Gower, 1982); ACAS advisory booklet, *Introduction to Payments Systems*.
2. As to which, see Paul Davies and Mark Freedland, *Labour Law – Text and Materials* 2nd Edn (London: Weidenfeld and Nicolson, 1984).
3. *Miles* v. *Wakefield Metropolitan District Council* [1987] IRLR 193. See also *Cresswell* v. *Board of Inland Revenue* [1984] IRLR 190.
4. Robert Palmer in *English Law in the Age of Black Death 1348–1381* (1993).
5. Poor Law Act 1388; Poor Law Acts 1598, 1601; and the Poor Law Amendment Act 1834.
6. Speenhamland Poor Relief Scheme 1795.
7. See J. Prebble, *The Highland Clearances* (London: Martin Secker & Warburg, 1963).
8. *The Modernisation of Britain's Tax and Benefit System* (no. 2, 1998); *New Tax Credits: Supporting Families, Making Work Pay and Tackling Poverty* (Inland Revenue, 2001); and Keith Puttick, 'New Generation Tax Credits', *Family Law Journal* (June 2003).
9. Inland Revenue Statement 89/03, '5.9 Million Families Now Benefiting from Tax Credits', 31 October 2003.
10. See M. White, *Payment Systems in Britain* (London: Gower, 1981); and A.M. Bowey, *Handbook of Salary and Wages Systems* (London: Gower, 1982).
11. In *Mallone* v. *BPB Industries Ltd* [2002] ICR 1045 discretion in relation to share options had to be exercised reasonably. On discretionary pay systems, see I. Smith, *The Management of Remuneration: Paying for Effectiveness* (London: IPM/Gower, 1983).
12. Not surprisingly, the changeover to such contracts has often been accompanied by the removal, by employers, of union rights, and union derecognition. See *Associated Newspapers Ltd* v. *Wilson*; *Associated British Ports* v. *Palmer and Others* [1995] IRLR 258, HL; and the discussion of the change process in Chapters 5, 16, 18.
13. *Pedersen* v. *Camden LBC* [1981] IRLR 173. On job advertisements, and their effects on wages, see D. Newell, *Understanding Recruitment Law* (London: Waterlow, 1984); and see Chapter 3 above.
14. *Robertson* v. *British Gas Corporation* [1983] ICR 351 where the letter promising incentive bonus created a contractual right in the individual's contract.
15. In *Re Famatina Development Corporation Ltd* [1914] 2 Ch 271.
16. *Way* v. *Latilla* [1937] 3 All ER 759.
17. *Gaumont British Picture Corporation Ltd* v. *Alexander* [1936] 2 All ER 1686.
18. Keith Puttick, 'Welfare as "Wages": Benefits, Low Pay and the Flexible Labour Markets', *ILJ*, vol. 27 (1998), p. 162. On tax credits and how they supplement wages, see Keith Puttick, *Welfare Benefits: Law and Practice* 9th Edn (Welwyn Garden City: EMIS Publishing, 2004).
19. *Gill and Others* v. *Cape Contracts Limited* [1985] IRLR 499.
20. *R.F. Hill Ltd* v. *Mooney* [1981] IRLR 258.
21. *Bauman* v. *Hulton Press Ltd* [1952] All ER 1121. In the case of performance-related pay, such as piecework, there is an implied duty on employers to give workers the opportunity to earn; *Devonald* v. *Rosser & Sons* [1906] 2 KB 728.
22. B. Bercusson, *Fair Wages Resolutions* (London: Mansell Publishing, 1978).
23. F. Bayliss, *British Wages Councils* (Oxford: Blackwell, 1962). See also Keith Puttick et al, *Wages and the Law* (London: Shaw & Sons, 1990).

24. B. Simpson, 'A Milestone in the Legal Regulation of Pay: The National Minimum Wage Act 1998', *ILJ*, vol. 28 (1999), p. 1.
25. Simpson, 'A Milestone in the Legal Regulation of Pay', (Note 24 above) pp. 1–3.
26. K. Puttick, '2020: A Welfare Odyssey – A Commentary on "Principles into Practice" and the Reform Programme', *ILJ*, vol. 29, no. 2 (1999); Puttick, 'Welfare as "Wages"' (Note 18 above); and Puttick, 'New Generation Tax Credits' (Note 8 above).
27. H. Collins, 'Regulating the Employment Relation for Competitiveness', *ILJ*, vol. 30 (2001).
28. Simpson, 'A Milestone in the Legal Regulation of Pay', p. 3.
29. *British Nursing Association v. Inland Revenue* [2003] ICR 19, Court of Appeal.
30. *A. Hanlon v. Allied Breweries* (UK) Ltd [1975] IRLR 321.
31. *Adams v. C. Zub Associates Ltd* [1978] IRLR 551.
32. *Bond v. CAV Ltd* [1983] IRLR 360. Cf, however, the *Miles* case (Chapter 19).
33. *Bridgen v. Lancashire County Council* [1987] IRLR 58.
34. A feature of personalised contracts and performance-related pay is the use of management discretion in determining remuneration and the timing of any increases, as illustrated by *Clark v. Nomura International plc* [2000] IRLR 766.
35. *Murco Petroleum v. Forge* [1987] IRLR 50.
36. *F.C. Gardner Ltd v. Beresford* [1978] IRLR 63; and *Murco Petroleum Ltd v. Forge* above.
37. See *Wilson and the National Union of Journalists; Palmer, Wyeth and National Union of Rail, Maritime and Transport Workers; Doolan and others v. United Kingdom* [2002] IRLR 128, ECtHR. The concept of 'action short of dismissal', or 'detriment', in relation to wages and other conditions, when this relates to union membership or activities, was reviewed, and modified by the Employment Relations Act 1999. Employees' rights on this are now in the Trade Union and Labour Relations (Consolidation) Act 1992, ss. 146–167. For a useful commentary on the case, see K.D. Ewing, 'The Implications of Wilson and Palmer', *ILJ*, vol. 32 (2003), p. 1.
38. *Lavarack v. Woods of Colchester* [1967] 1 QB 278.
39. *Smith v. Stockport Metropolitan Council* [1979] Current Law Yearbook 905.
40. ERA 1996, s. 8.
41. ERA 1996, s. 13–15.
42. ERA 1996, s. 27.
43. ERA 1996, s. 13 (3), (4).
44. This defines the type of cases the tribunal has jurisdiction over; and the limits on payments (£25,000 in 2003).
45. ERA 1996, s. 14.
46. ERA 1996, s. 18.
47. This can amount to a 'double indemnity'; see R.W. Painter and P. Leighton, 'The Wages Act: A Critical Guide' in *Employee Relations*, vol. 8 (1986), no. 6, p. 27.
48. ERA 1996, s. 20.
49. ERA 1996, ss. 23–26.
50. *Group 4 Nightspeed Ltd v. Gilbert* [1997] IRLR 398, EAT.
51. *Menell v. Newell & Wright (Transport Contractors) Ltd* [1996] IRLR 384 (but varied on appeal by the Court of Appeal [1997] IRLR 519).
52. As in *Legal & General Assurance Co Ltd v. Kirk* [2002] IRLR 124, CA.
53. *Clayton Newbury Ltd v. Findlay* [1953] 2 All ER 826.

Chapter 8: Holidays, Working Hours and Absence from Work

1. EC Council Directive 93/104, OJ L307, 13 Dec. 1993, p. 18.
2. In addition, Clause 8 of the EC Social Charter states: 'Every worker of the European Community shall have a right to a weekly rest period and to annual paid leave.'

3. Details of collective agreements' provisions on holidays are published in the *Department of Employment Gazette* and in Labour Research Department (LRD) *Collective Bargaining* series.
4. *Tucker and Others* v. *British Leyland Motor Corporation Ltd* [1978] IRLR 493.
5. Nick Adnett, *European Labour Markets: Analysis and Policy* (New York: Addison Wesley Longman, 2000).
6. See Barry Fitzpatrick, 'Straining the Definition of Health and Safety', *ILJ*, vol. 26 (1997), p. 115.
7. *Gibson* v. *East Riding of Yorkshire Council* [2000] IRLR 598.
8. *R* v. *Attorney-General for Northern Ireland, ex parte Burns* [1999] IRLR 315.
9. ACAS *Code of Practice on Disciplinary and Grievance Procedures* (2002), paras. 19, 20 which is often relied on by tribunals, makes the distinction between cases of absence (including sickness-related absences) which, after investigation, may be a 'conduct' issue, and those which are 'capability'-related.
10. *Notcutt* v. *Universal Engineering Ltd* [1982] IRLR 218. As later cases have shown, though, it is often difficult for an employer to show that a contract of employment *is*, in any particular circumstances, and by reference to the contract, 'frustrated'. More often than not it is not frustrated; and there will therefore, in the absence of agreement to terminate, be a 'dismissal' if the worker's employment is ended by the employer.
11. *Clark* v. *Oxfordshire Health Authority* [1998] IRLR 125.
12. See also *Marrison* v. *Bell* [1939] 2 KB 187.
13. *Eagland* v. *British Telecommunications plc* [1992] IRLR 323, CA.
14. In *Howman & Son* v. *Blyth* [1983] ICR 417, the EAT adopted the approach of asking what is the 'common position' in industry – something that also assists in determining how much should be paid, and over what period. Generally, tribunals now imply a term that is for net pay, i.e. after tax, National Insurance etc., and which is finite rather than 'open-ended' (as is the case with most sick pay schemes), which provide for full net pay for a specified period; followed by a period of reduced pay; and then no sick pay.
15. Workers will be able to access State benefits like Incapacity Benefit, Industrial Injuries Benefit, and Income Support (as it is paid to incapacitated workers) if eligible. Subject to means-tests Housing Benefit (for rented accommodation) or IS mortgage interest costs for assistance with the interest element of a mortgage liability. If they are working reduced hours, but more than 16 hours a week on average (for example after an accident or illness) they may also claim Working Tax Credit with a 'disability' element to supplement their earnings. See, further, Chapter 22. For a more detailed guide to in-work and sickness/disability-related benefits, see Keith Puttick, *Welfare Benefits: Law and Practice* 9th Edn (EMIS Publishing, 2004/5).
16. EAT 0159/03; Case Report ELA *Briefing*, vol. 10 (no. 10) Dec. 2003 and article by Joanne Keddie and Kirsten Sparrow.
17. Appeal rights are in ss. 10–13 of the 1999 Act and the Social Security Contributions (Decisions and Appeals) Regulations 1999, SI 1999/1027. For guidance, see also *Taylor Gordon & Co. Ltd* v. *Stuart Timmons* (EAT Case 0159/03).
18. SSCBA s. 163 (1) and reg. 16.
19. SSCBA s. 151 (1), but only if the conditions in ss. 152–154 are met.
20. SSCBA s. 151 (2).
21. This depends on her particular circumstances, though, and on the expected period of employment; see, for example, *Brown* v. *Chief Adjudication Officer* [1997]IRLR 110, CA.
22. SSCBA s. 155.
23. For authoritative and up-to-date information reference must be made to the legislation, as amended, and Inland Revenue guidance.
24. SSCBA s. 156.
25. For details see the SSP (General) Regulations 1992 reg. 7.

26. The Inland Revenue can take over responsibility for SSP; and in some cases must do, e.g. if the employee is insolvent. See, generally, regs. 9A–9C.

27. For a fuller account, reference should be made to specialist health and safety texts like Redgrave, Fife and Machin (eds. J. Hendy, M. Ford, and D. Brodie), *Health and Safety* (London: Butterworths, 1997); the *Encyclopaedia of Health and Safety at Work – Law and Practice* (London: Sweet & Maxwell); Jeremy Stranks, *Health and Safety Law* (London: Prentice Hall, 2002). For an interesting commentary on restrictions on women's working hours, and the impact of equal opportunities policy and legislation, see Diana Kloss, *Occupational Health Law* (Oxford: Blackwell, 1994), ch. 9.

28. On the judgment and its implications, see Anna Edwards, '*Barber v RJB Mining* in the Wider Context of Health and Safety', *ILJ*, vol. 29 (2000), p. 280.

29. Working Time (Amendment) Regulations 2002, SI 2002/3128.

30. WTR reg. 5A.

31. WTR reg. 6A.

32. WTR reg. 7.

33. The key provisions are in WTR regs. 10 (2), (3); 11 (3); 12 (4), (5).

34. WTR reg. 8.

35. WTR reg.9.

36. WTR reg. 10 (2), (3).

37. WTR reg. 11.

38. WTR reg. 11 (4)–(8)

39. WTR regs. 11 and 12, as substituted in part by the WT (Amendment) Regulations 2002, SI 2002/3128.

40. WTR reg. 12.

41. WTR reg. 16 (2), (3). *Bamsey* is reported at [2003] ICR 1224, EAT.

42. WTR reg. 13 (4), Schedule 2.

43. WTR reg. 13 (5).

44. WTR reg. 13 (6).

45. WTR reg. 13 (9) (a).

46. Under WTR reg. 14 (3).

47. Under WTR reg. 16.

48. 'Pay-back' arrangements must set out in a relevant agreement; WTR reg. 14 (4).

49. Other EAT cases confirm this; see *Canada Life Ltd* v. *Gray* EAT 13 January 2004; and *IRC* v. *Ainsworth* EAT 4 February 2004. To exercise a right to annual leave under the WTR notice must be given by the worker (as required by reg. 15); and the days must be specified beforehand. There is no 'right' to holiday pay under reg. 13 (9), said the EAT in the *Kigass* case, where the entitlement is not actually exercised.

50. Complying with WTR reg. 15 (2)–(5).

51. WTR reg. 15 (5).

52. WTR reg. 15A.

53. Part of the rationale for the decision in *MPB Structures Ltd* v. *Monro* [2003] IRLR 350 CS, [2002] IRLR 601, EAT was that compliance with the WTR requires holiday pay to be paid when holidays are taken, although the reasoning of the Court of Session was different – so that although the employer's appeal failed, it was not unlawful *per se* for an employer and worker to agree that annual leave can be paid for as part of wages as long as certain WTR conditions are met.

This is in line with a Court of Appeal decision *Blackburn* v. *Gridquest Ltd* [2002] IRLR 604 CA.

54. WTR reg. 17.

55. WTR regs. 28–35A.

56. As defined in WTR reg. 28.

57. WTR reg. 29.

58. Notably under WTR regs. 10–13, 24, 25, 27, 27A.

59. WTR reg. 30 (2).

60. For commentary, see Anna Edwards, '*Barber v RJB Mining* in the Wider Context of Health and Safety', *ILJ*, vol. 29 (2000), p. 280.

61. ERA s. 45A.
62. ERA ss. 101A and 105 (4A) respectively.
63. It is important to note, however, that tribunals decide such cases on their particular facts; and in other cases such absence might well be treated, in the circumstances, as more serious – meriting a final warning or even dismissal.
64. *Nethermere (St. Neots) Ltd v. Taverna and Gardiner* [1984] IRLR 240.
65. Government policy at the time had been to 'encourage' employers to operate supportive time-off arrangements rather than to require employers to make provision; White Paper, 'People, Jobs and Opportunity' (February 1992).
66. See the White Paper *Fairness at Work* (May 1998), which was prompted, in the main, by EC legislation, including measures like EC Directive 92/85 aimed at requiring Member States to improve maternity-related rights. On the work–family life balance, see S. Lewis and J. Lewis, *The Work/Family Challenge: Rethinking Employment* (London: Sage, 1996).
67. *Warner v. Barbers Stores* [1978] IRLR 109.
68. Concluded by international/European regional bodies, UNICE, CEEP and the ETUC; see the EC's 'Official Journal' OJ L145 p. 4.
69. ERA s. 57A.
70. ERA s. 57A (2).
71. ERA s. 57B.
72. For details, see the ERA ss. 36–43. For the background and guidance, see 'Sunday Trading Act 1994: New Employment Rights for Shopworkers', DTI Guidance PL960.
73. TULR(C)A, s. 168. Learning representatives also have time off for prescribed purposes, see s. 168A.
74. TULR(C)A, s. 169.
75. TULR(C)A, s. 170. The Code of Practice is *Time Off for Trade Union Duties and Activities* (ACAS) No. 3 (1998). S. 170 also contains rights of learning representatives.
76. SI 1996, No. 1513.
77. Safety Representatives and Safety Committees Regulations 1977, SI 1977 no. 500, reg. 4 (2) (6), and Code of Practice 'Time Off for the Training of Safety Representatives' paras. 3–5 (available from HSE).
78. ERA 1996, ss. 50, 51. For guidance, see *Borders R.C. v. Maule* [1993] IRLR 199.
79. ERA 1996, ss. 52–54.
80. ERA 1996, ss. 55–57.
81. *Day v. T. Pickles Farm Ltd* [1999] IRLR 217.
82. ACAS, *Maternity Leave and Pay*; and *Maternity Rights: A Guide for Employers and Employees* (PL958).
83. Advice on tax credits, to see what the precise support is, should be sought ahead of leave-taking. One of the objectives, explained in *New Tax Credits: Supporting Families, Making Work Pay and Tackling Poverty* (Inland Revenue, July 2001), is to maintain income during periods of reduced earnings, and to create a 'portable and secure income bridge spanning welfare and work'.
84. For the form and guidance, see ACAS website www.acas.gov.uk.
85. ELA 'Briefing' vol. 10 (no. 10) Dec. 2003.
86. Conducted by Lovells and the Chartered Institute of Personnel and Development, September 2003. Feinstein and Turner comment that the survey shows employees have not been reticent in exercising their right.

Chapter 9: Conflicts of Interest, Competition and Confidentiality

1. Mr Justice Lindsay, 'The Implied Term of Trust and Confidence', *ILJ*, vol. 30 (2001), no. 1.
2. Theft Acts 1968 and 1978.

3. *Boston Deep Sea Fishing and Ice Co.* v. *Ansell* (1888) LR 39 Ch. D 339; and *Reading* v. *Attorney General* [1951] 1 All ER 617, HL.
4. *Janata Bank* v. *Ahmed* [1981] IRLR 457, CA. It is an implied term of a contract, subject to express provision modifying this, that the worker must use his or her skills and perform the duties with 'reasonable care' and is liable to damages for loss resulting from a breach; *Lister* v. *Romford Ice and Cold Storage Co. Ltd* [1957] 1 All ER 125 (at 130).
5. *Sinclair* v. *Neighbour* [1967] 2 QB 279.
6. A duty to disclose earnings from another employer, or other source, generally only arises if there *is* either a fiduciary obligation, or an express term requiring this.
7. See also *Robb* v. *Green* [1895] 2 QB 315, CA in which the court implied a duty of good faith which made an employee liable for copying customer lists before leaving the employer's business.
8. *Hivac Ltd* v. *Park Royal Scientific Instruments Ltd* [1946] Ch 169.
9. *Nova Plastics Ltd* v. *Froggatt* [1982] IRLR 146.
10. *Printers and Finishers Ltd* v. *Holloway* No. 2 [1965] 1 WLR 1.
11. *Attwood* v. *Lamont* [1920] 3 KB 571; *Wallace Bogan & Co.* v. *Cove* [1997] IRLR 453, CA.
12. *Provident Financial Group plc* v. *Hayward* [1989] IRLR 84.
13. *Faccenda Chicken Ltd* v. *Fowler and others* [1986] IRLR 69, CA. To come within a 'category 3', under which an ex-employee owes a continuing duty of confidence after leaving, it is not incumbent on the employer to point out the precise limits of the information he seeks to protect as 'confidential', especially if a defendant must have known that the processes involved are secret.
14. *Symbian Ltd* v. *Christensen* [2001] IRLR 77, CA.
15. *Spafax Limited* v. *Harrison* [1980] IRLR 442.
16. *Bents Brewery Co. Ltd* v. *Hogan* [1945] 2 All ER 570. Although in this case liability was founded on the economic torts.
17. *Faccenda Chicken Ltd* v. *Fowler and others* [1986] IRLR 69.
18. [1988] 3 All ER 545, HL.
19. *ILJ*, vol. 30 (2001) no. 2169 at 171. See also cases like *Lion Laboratories* v. *Evans* [1984] 2 All ER 417 where an application for an order to restrain publication of information about breathalyser equipment, and its effectiveness in testing alcohol levels, failed. The court considered the staff involved had a just cause or excuse for the revelation.
20. *Re a Company's Application* [1989] ICR 449.
21. *British Syphon Co. Ltd* v. *Homewood* No. 2 [1956] 2 A11 ER 897.
22. *Reiss Engineering Co Ltd* v. *Harris* [1985] IRLR 232.
23. Copyright, Designs and Patents Act 1988, s. 11.

Chapter 10: Equal Pay

1. This decision is perhaps less important than it would be given the subsequent ruling of the ECJ in *Francovich* v. *Italian Republic* [1992] IRLR 84. In *Francovich* the ECJ ruled that when an individual suffers damage as a result of a Member State's failure to correctly implement a directive which confers rights for the benefit of the individual, the individual can sue the State directly under European law for the damage suffered by the State's failure. This ruling considerably strengthens the position of private sector workers.
2. *Steincke* v. *Bundesanstalt Fur Arbeit* [2003] IRLR 892.
3. *Mirror Group Newspapers Ltd* v. *Gunning* [1986] ICR 145.
4. *Meeks* v. *National Union of Agricultural and Allied Workers* [1976] IRLR 198.
5. *Ainsworth* v. *Glass Tubes and Components Ltd* [1976] IRLR 74.

6. A.E.M. Holmes and R.W. Painter, *Cases and Materials on Employment Law*, 5th edn (London: Blackstone, 2004).
7. Michael Rubenstein, 'Highlights' [1988] IRLR 324.
8. EOC, 'Equal Pay for Men and Women: Strengthening the Acts' (London: EOC, 1990), p. 6.
9. The EOC has suggested that the amendments to equal pay law could make it harder for women to pursue successfully equal value claims. (Annual Report 2002/03.)
10. EOC, 'Equal Pay for Men and Women: Strengthening the Acts' (London: EOC, 1990), p. 6.
11. Twice as many women as men are paid below the national minimum wage levels – 'Low Pay Estimates' (Spring 2002) – National Statistics Website (www.statistics.gov.uk).
12. EOC response to the Consultation paper on *Equality and Diversity: The Way Ahead* – www.eoc.org.uk.

Chapter 11: Race and Sex Discrimination

1. C. Brown and P. Gay, *Racial Discrimination 17 Years after the Act* (London: Policy Studies Institute, 1985). For a survey of the literature see P. Iles and R. Aulick, 'The Experience of Black Workers', in M.J. Davidson and J. Earnshaw (eds), *Vulnerable Workers: Psychosocial and Legal Issues* (Chichester: Wiley, 1991).
2. For a detailed discussion see A.E. Morris and S.M. Nott, *Working Women and the Law: Equality and Discrimination in Theory and Practice* (London: Routledge/Sweet & Maxwell, 1991), ch. 4.
3. S.D. Anderman, *Labour Law: Management Decisions & Workers' Rights* 4th edn (London: Butterworths, 2000).
4. It should be noted that sex discrimination cases dropped by 20 per cent in 2002–03. There is generally a low success rate for discrimination cases at between 3 to 4 per cent.
5. Under the Fair Employment (Northern Ireland) Acts 1976, 1979 it is unlawful for employers to discriminate against employees or applicants for employment on the grounds of their religious belief or political opinion.
6. Morris and Nott, *Working Women and the Law*.
7. Michael Rubenstein, *The Dignity of Women at Work: A Report on the Problem of Sexual Harassment in the Member States of the European Communities* (Luxembourg: Office for Official Publications of the European Communities, 1988), p. 16. Moreover, a survey by Alfred Marks in 1990/01 found that around two-thirds of employees surveyed had experienced some form of sexual harassment on several occasions, usually by a colleague or a senior person. Eighty-eight per cent of employers were aware of incidents of sexual harassment. However, only a quarter of those who experienced harassment reported it and many had little confidence in the employer's ability to deal with the harassment effectively (see 'Sexual Harassment in the Office: A Quantitative Report on Client Attitudes and Experiences 1990/92', available from Alfred Marks).
8. For some examples of policy statements on sexual and racial harassment which have been issued by employers see 'Combating Harassment at Work', IDS study 513 (London: Incomes Data Services Ltd, September 1992).
9. See *Marleasing SA v. La Comercial Internacional de Alimentacion SA* 13/11/90 European Court of Justice case no. 106/89.
10. For an overview of the current position on maternity and parental rights – see 'Maternity and Parental Rights 2003', J. Wade and C. and Palmer (2003) EOR 115.
11. EOC has launched an investigation into occupational segregation – 'No more "jobs for the boys" or "jobs for the girls"'. See EOC www.eoc.org.uk.

12. *Perera* v. *Civil Service Commission* [1982] IRLR 147.
13. The EOC advocated a return to the stricter test of justification in *Equal Treatment For Men And Women: Strengthening The Acts*.
14. Morris and Nott, *Working Women and the Law*, p. 88.
15. See Alice Leonard, *Pyrrhic Victories* (London: EOC, 1986).
16. *Trial by Ordeal: A Study of People who Lost Equal Pay and Sex Discrimination Cases in the Industrial Tribunals during 1985 and 1986* (London: EOC, 1989).
17. See also *Wylie* v. *Dee & Co Ltd* [1978] IRLR 103.
18. This provision was inserted by the SDA 1986.
19. See *Alexander* v. *Home Office* [1988] IRLR 190. Currently, it would appear that exemplary damages covering oppresive, arbitrary or unconstitutional action by the servants of the government, are not available in discrimination cases (see *Ministry of Defence* v. *Meredith* [1995] IRLR 539.
20. Alice Leonard's survey of successful sex discrimination applicants in 1980–84 found the median average award in recruitment cases was £291; Leonard, *Pyrrhic Victories*, p. 14, cited above. Clearly the removal of the upper limit will impact on the average award.
21. '... Aggravated, exemplary and restitutionary damage', Law Com, No. 247.
22. See also *British Gas plc* v. *Sharma* [1991] IRLR 101, EAT.
23. A single Commission for Equality and Human Rights was proposed in 2004.
24. See above, Note 3. The government has put forward plans for a single equality commission. The new body would bring together the work of the existing commissions and also take responsibility for discrimination relating to age, religion and sexual orientation, as well as supporting the promotion of human rights.
25. Bob Hepple *et al.*, *Improving Equality Law: The Options* (Justice and The Runnymede Trust, 1997).

Chapter 12: Other Forms of Discrimination

1 However, on the status of post-operative transexuals see *A* v. *Chief Constable of West Yorkshire Police* [2003] IRLR 103, the Gender Recognition Bill, and *KB* v. *National Health Service Pensions Agency* [2004] IRLR 240.
2. For an examination of five case studies of HIV in the workplace see P. Wilson, *HIV and AIDS in the Workplace: An Examination of Cases of Discrimination* (London: National AIDS Trust, 1992). For an overview of the legal implications for HIV-Positive employees see S. Podro, 'A Positive Future', (2003) EOR 116.
3. See K. Widdows, 'AIDs and the Workplace: Some Approaches at the National Level', *International Journal of Comparative Labour Law and Industrial Relations*, vol. 4 (1988), p. 140.
4. See *AIDs and the Workplace – A Guide for Employers* (London: Department of Employment/Health and Safety Executive, 1990).
5. B.W. Napier, 'AIDS Sufferers at Work and the Law' in M.J. Davidson and J. Earnshaw (eds), *Vulnerable Workers: Psychosocial and Legal Issues* (Chichester: Wiley, 1991).
6. For a review of the DDA see C. Casserley, 'The Disability Discrimination Act 1995: One Year On', *Legal Action*, December 1997.
7 The Disability Discrimination Bill 2004 (published 3 December 2003) proposes new positive duties to promote equality, and extensions of existing duties.
8. In 2002–03 disability discrimination cases rose to 2,716 from 2,100.
9. The DRC has undertaken a review of the legislative provisions on disability and has made recommendations for change. *Disability Equality: Making It Happen*, www.drc-gb.org.
10. 'Legislation Comes of Age', *Employment Trends* (2003) ER 782 p. 8.
11. 'Employment Policies and Practices Towards Older Workers: France, Germany, Spain and Sweden', *Labour Market Trends*, April 1997, pp. 143–8.

12. Equality and Diversity: Age Matters, DTI Consultation July 2003. There has also been an evaluation of the Code of Practice on Age Diversity in Employment Interim Review, DFEE, July 2000.

Chapter 13: Terminating the Contract

1. The court expressed the opinion that where an offer of employment is conditional upon 'satisfactory' references, that is likely to have a subjective meaning of 'satisfactory to the defendants'. It is highly probable that no objective test is applicable and there is no obligation in law upon the employers in considering the references other than to consider in good faith whether they were satisfactory to them. Nevertheless, it is still prudent to use wording such as 'references satisfactory to us' so as to avoid any doubt.
2. See also *Waddock* v. *LB Brent* [1990] IRLR 223.

Chapter 14: Unfair Dismissal

1. See *Addis* v. *Gramophone Co Ltd* [1909] AC 488 HL and *Bliss* v. *South East Thames Regional Health Authority* [1985] IRLR 308 CA.
2. See *Ridge* v. *Baldwin* [1964] AC 40 HL.
3. In 2002/03 26 per cent of cases dealt with by tribunals concerned unfair dismissal. However, this proportion has been falling since 1986/87, when unfair dismissal cases represented 74.5 per cent of all complaints (*Employment Tribunal Service, Annual Report and Accounts 2002/03*, London: The Stationery Office, 2003).
4. See Kevin Williams, 'Unfair Dismissal: Myths and Statistics', *ILJ*, vol. 12, no. 3, pp. 157–65.
5. Statistical source: *Employment Tribunal Service, Annual Report and Accounts 2002/03*, London: The Stationery Office, 2003.
6. See *Irani* v. *South West Hampshire Health Authority* [1985] ICR 590; *Powell* v. *London Borough of Brent* [1987] IRLR 466 CA; *Hughes* v. *London Borough of Southwark* [1988] IRLR 55.
7. See W.R. Hawes and G. Smith, 'Patterns of Representation of the Parties in Unfair Dismissal Cases: a Review of the Evidence', DE Research Paper no. 22 (1981); H. Genn and Y. Genn, *The Effectiveness of Representation at Tribunals* (London: Lord Chancellor's Department, 1989).
8. The following are examples of this policy of classifying issues as question of fact and thus limiting the possibility of appeals: whether a worker is an 'employee' (*O'Kelly* v. *Trusthouse Forte plc* [1983] IRLR 369 CA); whether a 'constructive dismissal' has taken place (*Pedersen* v. *Camden London Borough Council* [1981] IRLR 173 CA); whether an employee resigned or was forced to do so (*Martin* v. *Glynwed Distribution Ltd* [1983] IRLR 198 CA); whether it was reasonably practicable to present an unfair dismissal claim on time (*Palmer* v. *Southend-on-Sea Borough Council* [1984] IRLR 119 CA).
9. See *Bailey* v. *BP Oil (Kent Refinery) Ltd* [1980] IRLR 287.
10. *Dedman* v. *British Building & Engineering Appliances* [1974] ICR 53; *Walls Meat Co Ltd* v. *Khan* [1978] IRLR 499).
11. *Riley* v. *Tesco Stores Ltd* [1980] IRLR 103. Compare with *Jean Sorelle Ltd* v. *Rybak* [1991] IRLR 153 EAT where erroneous advice concerning the final date for presentation of claim by an industrial tribunal clerk provided grounds to excuse a late claim. See also *London International College* v. *Sen* [1993] IRLR 333, CA, for signs of a less rigid approach to cases where the applicant receives misleading advice as to the time limit from his/her solicitor.
12. See *Palmer* v. *Southend-on-Sea Borough Council* [1984] IRLR 119.

13. The decision in *Churchill* has received the approval of the House of Lords in *Machine Tool Industry Research Association* v. *Simpson* [1988] IRLR 212.
14. See ERA 1996, ss. 97, 145.
15. See also *Batchelor* v. *British Railways Board* [1987] IRLR 136.
16. Even post-*Polkey*, the courts and tribunals have still shown a propensity to forgive minor procedural lapses, provided that in the overall context of the case they did not result in unfairness: see *Fuller* v. *Lloyds Bank plc* [1991] IRLR 336, EAT and *Eclipse Blinds Ltd* v. *Wright* [1992] IRLR 133, EAT.
17. See H. McLean, 'Fair Procedure and Contribution' (1986) 15 *ILJ*, 205–207.
18. Minor or understandable breaches of procedure in ill-health dismissals may be excused: see *A Links & Co Ltd* v. *Rose* [1991] IRLR 353 and *Eclipse Blinds Ltd* v. *Wright* [1992] IRLR 133.
19. See R.W. Painter, 'Any Other Substantial Reason: A Managerial Prerogative?', *New Law Journal* (1981) p. 131; Bowers and Clark, 'Unfair Dismissal and Managerial Prerogative: A Study of "Other Substantial Reason"', *ILJ*, vol. 10 (1981), p. 34.
20. See L. Dickens, M. Jones, B. Weekes and M. Hart, *Dismissal: A Study of Unfair Dismissal and the Industrial Tribunal System* (Oxford: Basil Blackwell, 1985).
21. P. Lewis, 'An Analysis of Why Legislation has Failed to Provide Employment Protection for Unfairly Dismissed Employees', *BJIR*, vol. XIX, no. 3, November 1981, pp. 316–26.
22. See Hugh Collins, 'Capitalist Discipline and Corporatist Law', *ILJ*, vol. 11 (1982), pp. 78, 170; also D.J. Denham, 'Unfair Dismissal Law and the Legitimation of Managerial Control', *Capital & Class*, 41, summer 1990, p. 83 and Hugh Collins, *Justice in Dismissal* (Oxford: Oxford University Press, 1992).
23. In *Rao* v. *Civil Aviation Authority* [1992] IRLR 203, the EAT held that where a dismissal is unfair because of a procedural defect, compensation should be assessed first by deciding whether the award based on loss should be reduced on grounds of contributory fault; the resultant sum could then be further reduced to reflect the likelihood that the employee would have been fairly dismissed if the proper procedure had been followed. The EAT did not perceive this approach as imposing a double penalty. See also *Red Bank Manufacturing Co Ltd* v. *Meadows* [1992] IRLR 209.
24. Dickens et al., *Dismissed*; R. Lewis and J. Clark, *The Case For Alternative Dispute Resolution* (London: Institute of Employment Rights, 1993).

Chapter 15: Redundancy and Rights on Insolvency

1. The main legal authority which legitimises redundancy dismissals is the ERA s. 98 (2) (c).
2. *ILJ*, vol. 30 (2001), no. 1.
3. See Hugh Collins, *Justice in Dismissal* (Oxford, Clarendon, 1993).
4. The government and DTI reviews since 1998 have opted not to intervene in this area.
5. *Farrar's Company Law* 4th Edn (London: Butterworths, 1998), pp. 385, 386.
6. S.D. Anderman, *Management Decisions and Workers' Rights* (London: Butterworths, 1992), pp. 138–9.
7. *Alexander and Others* v. *Standard Telephones & Cables Ltd* [1990] IRLR 55; (No. 2) [1991] IRLR 286.
8. *Griffiths* v. *Buckinghamshire CC* [1994] ICR 265.
9. Richard Painter in Richard Painter and Ann Holmes *Cases and Materials on Employment Law* (Oxford, OUP, 2004), p. 461.
10. For a discussion of pit closures in relation to the 1984 miners' strike, see W.M. Rees, 'The Law, Practice and Procedures Concerning Redundancy in the Coal Mining Industry', *ILJ*, vol. 15 (1985), p. 203. The successful 1992 court action was based,

in part, on the fact that pit closure and redundancy consultation procedures had been well established, making it harder for British Coal to ignore them.

11. Cyril Grunfeld, *Law of Redundancy* (London: Sweet and Maxwell, 1989).

12. Lord Denning in *Lloyd* v. *Brassey* [1969] 2 QB 98.

13. H. Collins, 'Capitalist Discipline and Corporatist Law', *ILJ*, vol. 11 (1982), p. 78.

14. R.H. Fryer, 'The Myths of the Redundancy Payments Act', *ILJ*, vol. 2, (1973), p. 1.

15. See K. Ewing (ed.), *Working Life: A New Perspective on Labour Law* (London: Institute of Employment Rights, 1996) particularly in relation to 'economic dismissals', pp. 300–3; and the TUC General Council's statement 'Employment Law: A New Approach', June 1990.

16. In *McClelland* v. *Northern Ireland General Health Services Board* [1957] 2 All ER 129 the contract said that dismissal could only be for 'gross misconduct, inefficiency, and unfitness': and this was held to prevent dismissal on any other grounds. So the dismissal for redundancy was a breach of contract.

17. On the use of contract terms, see K.D. Ewing, 'Job Security and the Contract of Employment', *ILJ*, vol. 18 (1989), p. 217, which discusses *McClelland*.

18. Redundancy rights are mainly in the ERA 1996, ss. 135–70, Part VIII (maternity rights) and Part X (unfair dismissal aspects); and in the Trade Union and Labour Relations (Consolidation) Act 1992 (TULR[C]A).

19. TULR(C)A ss. 152, 153. Unfair selection for redundancy on union grounds is not subject to a service qualification.

20. *British Aerospace plc* v. *Green* [1995] IRLR 433 CA.

21. *Moon* v. *Homeworthy Furniture* [1977] ICR 117 at 121.

22. See also the earlier case, to the same effect, *Bass Leisure Ltd* v. *Thomas* [1994] IRLR 104.

23. As in *Lee* v. *Nottinghamshire County Council* [1980] IRLR 284 where a teacher taken on for only temporary periods was still held to be eligible for redundancy pay.

24. *Pink* v. *White and White and Co. (Earls Barton) Ltd* [1985] IRLR 489.

25. *Lesney Products & Co Ltd* v. *Nolan* [1977] IRLR 77.

26. *Macfisheries* v. *Findlay* [1985] ICR 160.

27. *Bromley & Hoare Limited* v. *Evans* (1972) 7 ITR 76, NIRC.

28. ERA 1996, ss. 147–154. Constructive dismissal and/or redundancy pay may also be possible if you have been kept on such working for longer than your contract allows.

29. *Matthews and others* v. *Kent and Medway Towns Fire Authority* [2003] IRLR 732.

30. S.T. Hardy, N.J. Adnett and R.W. Painter, *TUPE and CCT Business Transfers: UK Labour Market Views* Report No. 1, Staffordshire University Law School, 1997 (discussed in T. Colling, 'Views of TUPE and CCTT', *ILJ*, vol. 27 (1998), p. 152).

31. ERA 1996, s. 218. On 'continuity' generally, see ss. 210–219 of the Act. As far as part-timers are concerned, continuity provisions restricting redundancy and other rights were removed as noted above. This opened the door to claims for redundancy payments in appropriate cases.

32. ERA s. 141.

33. *E. Crompton* v. *Truly Fair (International) Ltd* [1975] IRLR 250.

34. *Berg and Busschers* v. *Besselsen* [1989] IRLR 447, ECJ; and *Rask and Christensen* v. *ISS Kantineservice A/S* (1993) IRLIB no. 464; IRLR 133, ECJ. For a discussion of the case law and principles involved, see Stephen Hardy, 'Acquiring Revised Rights: TUPE Regulations and Recent Developments', in Gary Slapper (ed.), *Companies in the 1990s* (London: Cavendish Publishing).

35. *Dr Sophie Redmond Stitching* v. *Bartol and Others* [1992] IRLR 366, ECJ. The decision has been important for UK workers affected in a similar way, for example when governmental grants are withdrawn or local authority services are 'contracted out' to organisations that are competing for work.

36. *Süzen* v. *Zehnacker Gebaudereinigung GmbH Krankenhaussevice and Lefarth GmbH* [1997] ICR 662; [1997] IRLR 255 ECJ; and see, for a discussion of the implications of the

case in the context of compulsory competitve tendering, V. Shrubsall, 'Competitive Tendering Outsourcing and the Acquired Rights Directive', *Modern Law Review*, vol. 61 (1998), p. 85.

37. Reg. 3 (4), as substituted in part by the Trade Union Reform and Employment Rights Act 1993 s. 33.

38. See guidance on TUPE, changes to the legislation, and the effects of the scheme, on the DTI, DWP, and TUC websites and in Department of Work and Pensions booklets like PL 699, 'Employment Rights on the Transfer of an Undertaking'. For detailed commentary, see specialist texts like *Harvey on Industrial Relations* sections F1, R, U5; and J. Bowers et al *Transfer of Undertakings* (London: Sweet and Maxwell, updated service).

39. For example, when there is a partial transfer of assets; see *Melon* v. *Hector Powe Ltd* [1980] IRLR 477, HL.

40. *Newns* v. *British Airways plc* [1992] IRLR 575, CA. Regulation 5 now enables an employee to object to a transfer of his/her contract, although this may bring it to an end without there being a 'dismissal' by the transferor.

41. For discussion of this, see Hugh Collins, 'Transfer of Undertakings and Insolvency', *ILJ*, vol. 18 (1989), p. 144.

42. *Crawford* v. *Swinton Insurance Brokers Ltd* [1990] IRLR 42; and *Berriman* v. *Delabole Slate Ltd* [1985] IRLR 305. In *Cornwall Country Care Ltd* v. *Brightman and Others* [1998] IRLR 228, EAT it was held that dismissal and re-engagement on worse terms following a transfer of council carers to a private company was deemed 'unfair' by reg. 8 (1); but that they should just receive a 'one off' compensation payment.

43. *Whitehouse* v. *Charles A Blatchford & Sons Ltd* [1999] IRLR 492, CA.

44. *Gorictree* v. *Jenkinson* [1985] IRLR 391.

45. By the Collective Redundancies and Transfer of Undertakings (Protection of Employment) (Amendment) Regulations 1995, SI 1995/2587; the Collective Redundancies and Transfer of Undertakings (Protection of Employment) (Amendment) Regulations 1999, SI 1999/1925; and the Transfer of Undertakings (Protection of Employment) (Amendment) Regulations 1999, SI 1999/2402. Further changes will be made to implement the EC Directive on Information and Consultation from 2004. Changes may be monitored on the DTI and TUC websites.

46. ERA 1996, s. 141 (1), 146.

47. *Spencer and Griffin* v. *Gloucestershire CC* [1985] IRLR 393, CA.

48. ERA 1996, s. 141 (1).

49. *Elliot* v. *Richard Stump Ltd* [1987] IRLR 215.

50. ERA 1996, s. 138.

51. *G.W. Stephens* v. *Fish* [1989] ICR 324, EAT.

52. *Hempell* v. *W.H. Smith & Sons Ltd* [1986] IRLR 95.

53. ERA 1996, s. 140.

54. *Lignacite Products Ltd* v. *Krollman* [1979] IRLR 22.

55. ERA 1996, s. 140.

56. ERA 1996, s. 140.

57. ERA 1996, s. 143.

58. ERA 1996, s. 52.

59. Section 145 defines this but it is usually the date when the job finishes, i.e. when notice expires; or, if no notice is given, when the termination takes effect.

60. ERA 1996, ss. 166–170. For guidance, see DTI and DWP websites at www.dti.gov. uk and www.dwp.gov.uk, and guidance booklets, e.g. *Employees' Rights on Insolvency of an Employer*, PL 718.

61. See also DTI Booklet PL 808, *Redundancy Payments* and other official guidance.

62. *TGWU* v. *Ledbury Preserves (1928) Ltd* [1986] IRLR 492. See also *John Brown Engineering Ltd* v. *Brown and Others* [1997] IRLR 90.

63. Rights were introduced by the Pension Schemes Act 1993, s. 134.

64. See generally on insolvency, Pennington's *Corporate Insolvency Law* (London: Butterworths, 1991).
65. *Powdrill v. Watson* (the 'Paramount Airways' case) [1994] IRLR 295, CA; [1995] IRLR 269 HL. Following the case the Insolvency Act 1994 was speedily passed, so that in the event of 'adoption' only a specified range of employee benefits need be paid.

Chapter 16: Health, Safety and the Work Environment

1. The Robens Committee Report (Report of the Committee on Health and Safety at Work 1972, Cmnd. 5034). See P. James and D. Lewis, 'Health and Work' in Roy Lewis (ed.), *Labour Law in Britain* (Oxford: Basil Blackwell, 1986).
2. Diana Kloss, *Occupational Health Law* (Oxford: Blackwell, 1994), pp. 11–13.
3. See Alan Neal, 'The European Framework Directive on the Health and Safety of Workers: Challenges for the United Kingdom?', *International Journal of Comparative Labour Law and Industrial Relations*, vol. 16 (1990), p. 80; and R. Eberlie, 'The New Health and Safety Legislation of the European Community', *ILJ*, vol. 19 (1990), p. 81.
4. On these and other regulations, see Redgrave, Fife and Machin, *Health and Safety* (eds. J. Hendy, M. Ford and D. Brodie) (London: Butterworths, 1997).
5. For example *Latimer v. AEC Ltd* [1953] 2 All ER 449.
6. Dept. of Employment papers: *Lifting the Burden* (London: HMSO, 1985); *Building Business – Not Barriers* (HMSO, 1986); *Releasing Enterprise* (HMSO, 1988).
7. On the effects of deregulation and inadequate monitoring and enforcement, see Roger Moore, *The Price of Safety: The Market, Workers' Rights and the Law* (London: Institute of Employment Rights, 1991).
8. Reported in *Health and Safety at Work – The Journal of the Working Environment* (March 1992), p. 8.
9. *Johnstone v. Bloomsbury Health Authority* [1991] 2 All ER 293, CA.
10. *Ottoman Bank v. Chakarian* [1930] AC 277.
11. *Rogers v. Wicks & Wilson Ltd* (1988), IDS Brief 366 HSIB 148; see also *Dryden v. Greater Glasgow Health Board* [1992] IRLR 469; and see R.W. Painter, 'Smoking Policies – The Legal Implications', *Employment Relations*, vol. 12, no. 4, p. 17.
12. HSAWA, s. 7. See also the MHSW Regulations 1999, SI 1999/3242, reg. 14.
13. HSAWA, s. 2. See also the MHSW Regulations 1999.
14. The leading case is *Wilson and Clyde Coal Co Ltd v. English* [1938] AC 57.
15. *Richardson v. Pitt-Stanley and Others* [1995] 1 All ER 460.
16. The Royal Commission on Civil Liability and Compensation for Civil Injuries (1978).
17. Although much of that repeal process has been completed, there are several 'residual' areas; and case law is still relevant.
18. For detailed coverage, see Redgrave, Fife and Machin, *Health and Safety*; *Encyclopaedia of Health and Safety at Work – Law and Practice* (London: Sweet & Maxwell, 1992). See also J. Stranks, *Handbook of Health and Safety Practice* (London: ROSPA/Pitman, 1992).
19. On companies' wider environmental obligations see S. Ball and S. Bell, *Environmental Law* (London: Blackstone Press, 1995).
20. See *Health and Employment*. ACAS, 1992.
21. See Kate Painter, 'It's Part of the Job: Violence at Work', in *Vulnerable Workers in the UK Labour Market*, (eds. Patricia Leighton and Richard Painter), *Employee Relations*, vol. 9, no. 5, 1987, pp. 30–40, discussing *Dutton & Clark Ltd v. Daly* [1985] IRLR 363.
22. On 27 January 1993 it was announced that an employee of Stockport Council had secured an out-of-court settlement (reportedly £15,000) for the effects of smoking by other staff which, it had been claimed, caused bronchitis. This had an immediate

impact on companies nationwide. The introduction of 'no-smoking' policies by employers will not normally be a ground for an employee who wants to smoke at work to leave and claim constructive dismissal (*Dryden* v. *Greater Glasgow Health Board* [1992] IRLR 469).

23. The Safety Representatives and Safety Committees Regulations 1977, SI 1977, No. 500. As a result of EC legislation, the Management of Health and Safety at Work Regulations 1992 (SI 1992, No. 2051) include requirements, including provision for the appointment of 'competent persons', to evaluate risks and assist with health and safety procedures. Protection from victimisation is provided in the ERA 1996, s. 44 for employees with safety responsibilities. Specifically, it gives representatives and other employees a right not to suffer a 'detriment' or to be dismissed for undertaking health and safety work, bringing health and safety matters to the employer's attention, leaving a dangerous workplace, and so forth.

24. For a useful guide, see *The Safety Reps' Action Guide*, LRD booklets.

25. See Eberlie, 'The New Health and Safety Legislation of the European Community', *ILJ*, vol. 81 (1990); and standard health and safety texts like Redgrave, Fife and Machin, *Health and Safety.*

26. Provisions to give employees a right not to have action taken against them (or to be dismissed) for exercising the rights are now in the ERA 1996, ss. 44 and 100.

27. Redgrave, Fife and Machin, *Health and Safety*, Note 4 above.

28. For guidance, see *VDUs and Health and Safety: A User's Guide on Safe VDU Use and 1992 UK Implementing Legislation* (LRD booklets, October 1991).

29. The most important claim possible is by dependants for their loss of financial support; Fatal Accidents Act 1976.

30. Until compensation is paid, Income Support and other assistance must be obtained from the employer, or from State benefits. These include Industrial Injuries Disablement Benefit, Disablement Allowance, Incapacity Benefit and means-tested benefits; see, further, Chapter 22.

31. A child suffering a pre-natal injury can also sue; Congenital Disabilities (Civil Liability) Act 1976.

32. *Paris* v. *Stepney Borough Council* [1951] AC 367. On the scope of the duty, see J. Munkman, *Employer's Liability at Common Law* (London: Butterworths, 1980).

33. *Smith* v. *Stages* [1989] 1 A11 ER 833 HLs; and see the later case of *Mattis* v. *Pollock (t/a Flamingos Nightclub)* [2003] IRLR 603, CA.

34. *Pape* v. *Cumbria County Council* [1991] IRLR 463 (dermatitis caused by cleaning agents).

35. *Baxter* v. *Harland & Wolff plc* [1990] IRLR 516, CA. Adequate risk-assessment procedures are now, in any case, a pivotal requirement.

36. Redgrave, Fife and Machin, *Health and Safety*, Note 4 above.

Chapter 17: Trade Unions and Their Members

1. This embodies the EAT's approach to the trade union provision of property for use by a political party in *ASTMS* v. *Parkin* [1983] IRLR 448. In this case, the EAT upheld the decision of the certification officer that a contribution towards the Labour Party headquarters should have come out of the political fund even though it was by way of commercial investment.

2. The term 'political office' referred to in paras (c) and (d) covers MPs, MEPs, local authority councillors and any position within a political party, for example ward secretaries.

3. Section 5 (1) of the 1913 Act already provided that when a union adopted a political fund, existing members must be informed of their right not to contribute and the CO's model rules currently contain a provision requiring that new members shall be

supplied with a copy of the political fund rules. This right to be informed of exemption from the political level now appears as TULR(C)A, s. 84 (2) (b).

4. The CO's model rules state that, with the exception of new members, a member who gives notice of exemption shall be exempt from contributing to the political fund from the following 1 January. New members who give notice of exemption within one month of receiving a copy of the rules must be exempt from the date of the notice (see also TULR[C]A, s. 84 [2] [b]).

5. The statement also exhorts unions, where they do not already do so, to provide a right of access for members to the accounts of the political fund. Also unions should, in completing their returns to the CO, attach a list showing each payment over £250 made from their general funds to external bodies not falling within the 'political objects' definition, specify the source and amount of any investment income to the political fund, and show the administrative costs connected with the political fund.

6. I.T. Smith and G.H. Thomas, *Smith and Wood's Industrial Law*, 8th edn (London: Butterworths, 2003), p. 700.

7. See also *Martin v. Scottish TGWU* [1952] 1 All ER 691.

8. See *Lee v. Showmen's Guild* [1952] 2 QB 329.

9. See *Rothwell v. APEX* [1975] IRLR 375.

10. Ewan McKendrick, 'The Rights of Trade Union Members – Part I of the Employment Act 1988', *ILJ*, vol. 17, no. 3, September 1988, pp. 141–50 at p. 149.

11. For a penetrating analysis of the litigation during the miners' strike see K D. Ewing, 'The Strike, the Courts and the Rule-Books', *ILJ*, vol. 14, no. 3, pp. 160–75.

12. See *The Lightman Report on the NUM* (Harmondsworth: Penguin, 1990).

13. McKendrick, 'The Rights of Trade Union Members', p. 152.

14. The rule has several exceptions, including the following:

    - it does not apply to actions which infringe the individual rights of the member;
    - the rule does not apply so as to prevent a member suing to restrain an ultra vires act, for that cannot be cured by a simple majority.

    The occasions upon which a member is most likely to want to sue his/her union are: first, to remedy a wrong done to him/her personally (and especially to complain of wrongful discipline or expulsion) and, second, to restrain the union from committing an ultra vires act. As we have seen, both of these are the principal exceptions where the rule does not apply anyway.

15. McKendrick, 'The Rights of Trade Union Members' above, p. 152.

16. John Bowers and Simon Auerbach, *Blackstone's Guide to the Employment Act 1988* (London: Blackstone Press, 1988), p. 45.

17. The appointment of a receiver of the funds of the NUM during the miners' strike was the first recorded receivership of a trade union. The NUM's trustees were also removed by the court (*Clarke v. Heathfield* [1985] ICR 203, 606).

18. *Hansard* (House of Commons), 10 December 1992, cols. 797–8.

19. Ian Smith and John Wood, *Industrial Law*, 4th edn (London: Butterworths, 1989), p. 478.

Chapter 18: Collective Bargaining

1. On collective bargaining, and unions' role in it, see Gillian Morris and Timothy Archer, *Collective Labour Law* (Oxford: Hart Publishing, 2000); Lord Wedderburn, *The Worker and the Law* (Harmondsworth: Penguin, 1986); W.E.J. McCarthy (ed.), *Trade Unions* (Harmondsworth: Penguin, 1985); S. Deakin and G. Morris, *Labour Law* (London: Butterworths, 2001); B. Perrins, *Trade Union Law* (London, Butterworths, 1985); S. Anderman, *Labour Law: Management Decisions and Workers' Rights* (London: Butterworths, 1993); Paul Davies and Mark Freedland, *Kahn-Freund's Labour and the*

Law (London: Stevens, 1983); Simon Honeyball and John Bowers, *Labour Law* (Oxford: Oxford University Press, 2002) and K. Ewing (ed.), *Working Life: A New Perspective on Labour Law* (London: Lawrence and Wishart/Institute of Employment Rights, 1996); *Harvey on Industrial Relations and Employment Law* (London: Butterworths).

2. T.E. Marshall, *Citizenship and Social Class* (Cambridge: Cambridge University Press, 1950).

3. Kahn-Freund, 'Legal Framework' in Allan Flanders and Hugh Clegg (eds.) *The System of Industrial Relations in Britain* (Oxford: Blackwell, 1954); and 'Labour Law' in M. Ginsberg (ed.), *Law and Public Opinion in Britain in the Twentieth Century* (London: Stevens, 1959). The problem is that such systems operated in conjunction with supplemental arrangements like trade boards and then wages councils which provided minimum wages and conditions coverage for those areas *not* benefiting from effective collective arrangements. Commentators have pointed out that collective laissez-faire also produced a degree of structural inequality between the voluntary and regulated sectors, and an absence of legal guarantees of universal social and economic rights for all employees; Deakin and Morris, *Labour Law*, Note 1 above at p. 22.

4. See *Employment – the Challenge for the Nation*, White Paper, Cm 9474. Labour governments were also, at times, not slow to intervene to curb the impact of collective bargaining as it affected the economy; see Paul Davies and Mark Freedland, *Labour Legislation and Public Policy* (Oxford: Clarendon Press, 1993). On the 'welfare' function of wages and occupational income, as determined by labour agreements, see Nicholas Barr, *The Economics of the Welfare State* (Oxford: OUP, 1998).

5. It may also be a by-product of regulatory measures like the NMW that employers tend to set wage levels in line with the NMW norm, unless other competitive pressures dictate higher levels – a syndrome not assisted when they know the State will also then top up NMW-level wages by tax credits. On the interaction of systems for determining occupational income, like bargaining, and other sources of 'welfare', including State provision, see, generally, Gospa Esping-Anderson, *The Three Worlds of Welfare Capitalism* (Cambridge: Polity Press, 1990) and *Welfare States in Transition: National Adaptations in Global Economies* (London: Sage, 1996).

6. G.D.H. Cole (1913), 'Trade Unions as Co-managers of Industry' in McCarthy (ed.), *Trade Unions*, pp. 76–82.

7. On implementation, including the International Covenant on Economic, Social and Cultural Rights, see Matthew Craven, *The International Covenant on Economic, Social and Cultural Rights* (Oxford: Clarendon, 1998).

8. As to which, see John Bowers and Jeremy Lewis, *Employment Law and Human Rights* (London: Sweet & Maxwell, 2001).

9. Bob Hepple, 'The EU Charter of Fundamental Rights', *ILJ*, vol. 30, no. 2 (2000), pp. 225–31. The Prime Minister told the House of Commons that 'our case is that it [the Charter] should have no legal status', and he reiterated the government's intention to maintain that stance; see HC Deb 11 December 2000, col. 354. As Hepple argues, though, there is no reason *why* UK courts and tribunals should not have regard to the Charter when interpreting domestic legislation which implements Community obligations (at p. 231).

10. See, for example, the opinion on this point of the Advocate-General in EC Case C-67/96 *Albany International BV v. Stichting Bedrijfspensioenfonds Textielindustrie* [1999] ECR I-5751.

11. Royal Commission on Trade Unions and Employers' Associations (1965–8, Cmnd. 3623) the 'Donovan Report' (London: HMSO).

12. *In Place of Strife*, Department of Employment and Productivity (1969).

13. Bob Simpson, *Trade Union Recognition and the Law* (London: Institute of Employment Rights, 1991); and 'The Summer of Discontent and the Law', *ILJ*, vol. 18 (1989), p. 234.

14. See John Hendy QC and Michael Walton, 'An Individual Right to Union Representation in International Law', *ILJ*, vol. 26 (1997), p. 205.

15. For the Court of Appeal decision, which was part of a joined appeal with another case, see *Associated British Ports v. Palmer; Associated Newspapers v. Wilson* [1994] ICR 97.
16. Employment Protection (Consolidation) Act 1978 s. 23. The thrust of the Lords' decision was that the legislation did not encompass omissions or failures to act, as opposed to 'action'.
17. *Wilson and the National Union of Journalists; Palmer, Wyeth and the National Union of Rail, Maritime and Transport Workers; Doolan and others v. United Kingdom* [2002] 35 EHRR 20, ECtHR. For a fuller analysis of the judgment, and its implications, see Keith Ewing, 'The Implications of Wilson and Palmer', *ILJ*, vol. 32, no. 1 (2003), p. 1.
18. ACAS, *Annual Report* (1988), p. 8.
19. Surveys indicated that in the mid-1980s the coverage was above 70 per cent. By 1998, though, according to one source it had fallen to little more than 40 per cent; M. Cully, S. Woodland, A. O'Reilly and G. Dix, *Britain at Work* (based on a 1998 workplace employment relations survey) (London: Routledge, 1999).
20. R. Taylor, *The Future of Trade Unions* (London: Andre Deutsch, 1994).
21. See Keith Ewing (ed.), *Working Life: A New Perspective on Labour Law* (London: Institute of Employment Rights, 1996), ch. 7; and Wedderburn, 'Consultation and Collective Bargaining in Europe: Success or Ideology?', *ILJ*, vol. 26, no. 1 (1997). For useful guidance see *European Works Councils: Negotiating the Way Forward* (LRD, 1997).
22. Precedents exist in the case of single-employer agreements, but European unions have already started to negotiate multilateral bargaining arrangements that are transnational, covering different employees within particular industries and economic sectors. Details are reported in the DWP's *Employment Gazette*.
23. Lord Wedderburn, *The Social Charter, European Company and Employment Rights: An Outline Agenda* (London: Institute of Employment Rights, 1990), providing a useful commentary and insights into the problem, and UK aspects, ahead of EC Reg. 2157/2001 on European Company Statute.
24. Simpson, *Trade Union Recognition and the Law*, p. 7.
25. In 2002 the European Parliament and Council adopted Directive 2002/14 establishing a general framework for informing and consulting employees in the European Community.
26. 'Union Rights Battle Hots Up', *Guardian* (14 February 1998).
27. ACAS, *Industrial Relations Handbook*. See also *Employment Policies*, ACAS, and other ACAS guidance.
28. *Ford Motor Co Ltd v. Amalgamated Union of Engineering and Foundry Workers* [1969] 2 All ER 481.
29. In *National Coal Board v. National Union of Mineworkers* [1986] IRLR 439 the potential for legally enforceable agreements was discussed.
30. See the ACAS website www.acas.gov.uk.
31. *City and Hackney Health Authority v. National Union of Public Employees* [1985] IRLR 252.
32. *Tadd v. Eastwood and Daily Telegraph Ltd.* [1983] IRLR 320. High Court affirmed [1985] IRLR 119, CA.
33. *Gibbons v. Associated British Ports* [1985] IRLR 376.
34. *Joel v. Cammel Laird Ltd* (1969) 4 ITR 207.
35. TULR(C)A, ss. 1–10. Guidance is available from the Certification Officer on the factors considered.
36. A leading case is *Squibb United Kingdom Staff Association v. Certification Officer* [1977] IRLR 355; [1979] IRLR 75, CA.
37. *J. Wilson & Bros Ltd v. USDAW* [1977] ICR 530.
38. *Cleveland County Council v. Springett and Others* [1985] IRLR 131.
39. On the difficulties of voluntary recognition, see cases like *National Union of Gold, Silver and Allied Trades v. Albury Bros Ltd* [1978] IRLR 504; *Union of Shop Distributive and Allied Workers v. Sketchley Ltd* [1981] IRLR 291.

40. See further on the specific changes that may be needed to give effect to the judgment, Ewing, 'The Implications of *Wilson and Palmer*'. Such a weak perception of unions' role (and rights) as a bargaining agent does little to prevent future domestic legislation making incursions into the mandatory aspects of the statutory recognition procedure introduced in the UK from 6 June 2000.

41. For commentary, and criticisms, see Bob Simpson, 'Trade Union Recognition and the Law, a New Approach – Parts I and II of Schedule A1 to the Trade Union and Labour Relations (Consolidation) Act 1992', *ILJ*, vol. 29, p. 193; and Lord Wedderburn, 'Collective Bargaining or Legal Enactment? The 1999 Act and Union Recognition', *ILJ*, vol. 29 (2000), p. 1; Gillain Morris and Timothy Archer *Collective Labour Law* (Oxford: Hart Publishing, 2000); and Tonia Novitz and Paul Skidmore, *Fairness at Work: A Critical Analysis of the Employment Relations Act 1999 and Its Treatment of Collective Rights* (Oxford: Hart Publishing, 2001).

42. For a commentary on the courts' role at the time, see Bob Simpson 'Judicial Review of ACAS', *ILJ*, vol. 8 (1979), pp. 420–25.

43. On this, see Keith Ewing, 'Trade Union Recognition and Staff: A Breach of ILO Standards?', *ILJ*, vol. 29 (2000), p. 267.

44. Code of Practice 'Access to Workers during Recognition and Derecognition Ballots' (2000).

45. Code of Practice on Access to Workers during Recognition and Derecognition Ballots (2000).

46. For general guidance, see paras. 1–7 of the ACAS Code.

47. *Thomas Scott & Sons (Bakers) Ltd* v. *Allen and Others* [1983] IRLR 329 CA.

48. H. Gospel and G. Lockwood, 'Disclosure of Information for Collective Bargaining: The CAC Approach Revisited', *ILJ*, vol. 28 (1999), p. 233.

49. See TULR(C)A, s. 185.

Chapter 19: Industrial Conflict I: Industrial Action

1. For a detailed analysis of the effect of strikes and other industrial action on the contract of employment, the question of the payment of wages to those taking industrial action and the social security implications of unemployment caused by trade disputes see K.D. Ewing, *The Right to Strike* (Oxford: Oxford University Press, 1991).

2. Roger Welch, *The Right to Strike: A Trade Union View* (London: Institute of Employment Rights, 1991), p. 25.

3. *Wiluszynski* v. *London Borough of Tower Hamlets* [1989] IRLR 259; see also *British Telecommunications plc* v. *Ticehurst and Thompson* [1992] IRLR 219, CA.

4. For the purposes of the continuity provisions, the terms 'strike' and 'lock-out' are defined by EPCA 1978, sched. 13, para. 24 (1). A strike involves the cessation of work by a body of employees acting in combination or a concerted refusal to work. A lock-out involves the closing of a place of employment, the suspension of work or the refusal by the employer to continue to employ any number of employees. In the case of both strike and lock-out, the action taken must be in consequence of a dispute and its purpose must be to coerce the other party to accept or not accept terms and conditions of or affecting employment.

5. See ILO Committee of Experts, Observation 1989 on Convention 87, discussed in Chapter 17 above.

6. This approach was developed by Lord Justice Brightman in *Marina Shipping Ltd* v. *Laughton* [1982] 481 at 489 and was subsequently employed by Lord Diplock in *Merkur Island Shipping* v. *Laughton* [1983] 2 All ER 189.

7. See also *Drew* v. *St Edmondsbury BC* [1980] ICR 513.

8. *Daily Mirror Newspapers* v. *Gardner* [1968] 2 All ER 163; see also *Torquay Hotels Co Ltd* v. *Cousins* [1969] 2 Ch 106.

9. I.T. Smith and G.H. Thomas, *Industrial Law*, 8th edn (London: Butterworths, 2003), p. 768.
10. *Hansard* (House of Lords) 23 July 1990, col. 1272.
11. Cm. 1602 (London: HMSO, 1991).
12. London: Butterworths, 1993, II M, para. 3610.
13. B.A. Hepple and S. Fredman, *Labour Law and Industrial Relations in Great Britain* (Deventer: Kluwer, 1986), p. 212.
14. Electricity Act 1989, s. 96; Water Act 1989, s. 170. The Telecommunications Act 1984, s. 94, provides grants powers of direction.
15. Gillian Morris, 'Industrial Action in Essential Services', *ILJ*, vol. 20 (1991), p. 92.
16. Cmnd. 8218, 1981, paras 330–4.
17. Morris, 'Industrial Action in Essential Services', p. 90.
18. *Guardian*, 23 April 1993; *London Borough of Wandsworth* v. *National Association of Schoolmasters/Union of Women Teachers* [1993] IRLR 344, CA.

Chapter 20: Industrial Conflict II: Picketing

1. S. Evans, 'Picketing under the Employment Acts', in P. Fosh and C. Littler (eds), *Industrial Relations and the Law in the 1980s: Issues and Trends* (Aldershot: Gower, 1985).
2. Roger Welch, *The Case for Positive Trade Union Rights* (Employment Relations Research Centre, Anglia Higher Education College, 1989).
3. See, for example, R. Lewis, 'Picketing', in R. Lewis (ed.), *Labour Law in Britain* (Oxford: Blackwell, 1986), p. 199; P.L. Davies and M. Freedland, *Labour Law: Text & Materials*, 2nd edn (London: Weidenfeld & Nicolson, 1984), p. 852.
4. More detailed accounts of developments in this area are provided by Gillian Morris, 'Industrial Action & the Criminal Law', *Industrial Relations Legal Information Bulletin*, 5 May 1987, pp. 2–9, and J. Bowers and M. Duggan, *The Modern Law of Strikes* (London: Financial Training Publications, 1987), ch. 4.
5. Gillian Morris commentary, *ILJ*, vol. 14, p. 109.
6. Cmnd. 9510, May 1985.
7. Ibid.
8. See Lewis, 'Picketing', pp. 216–19, and Lord Wedderburn, *The Worker and the Law* (Harmondsworth: Penguin, 1986), pp. 550–3.
9. Bowers and Duggan, *The Modern Law of Strikes*, p. 44.
10. Cmnd. 9510, para. 5.7.

Chapter 21: Tribunal and Court Claims

1. Reference may be made to specialist texts, including those referred to in Chapter 22.
2. See the Employment Tribunals Act 1996 and regulations and orders made under it for details of the jurisdiction, including the Employment Tribunals Extension of Jurisdiction (England and Wales) Order 1994, SI 1994/1623 (in Scotland SI 1994/1624). On procedural aspects, see the Employment Tribunals (Constitution and Rules of Procedure) Regulations 2001, SI 2001/1171.
3. Lord Wedderburn, 'Labour Law – From Here to Autonomy', *ILJ*, vol. 16 (1987), p. 1; the Labour Party Manifesto 1992 also proposed a labour court, although this proposal has not resurfaced. On the labour court issue it has been said that 'if you want to adopt a dog and would like to have a corgi, you do not want to end up with a rottweiler'; Lord Wedderburn, 'The Social Charter in Britain: Labour Law – and

Labour Courts', in Wedderburn, *Employment Rights in Britain and Europe – Selected Papers* (London: Cent, 1991), p. 375.

4. Art. 5 (1) of the Brussels Convention, and SI 1990/1591; see further Richard Kidner, 'Jurisdiction in European Contracts of Employment', *ILJ*, vol. 27 (1998), p. 103.

5. *The Effectiveness of Representation at Tribunals* (Lord Chancellor's Department, 1989); and Philip Parry, *Industrial Tribunals: How to Present Your Case* (London: Industrial Society, 1991). To *some* extent the imbalance seen when one side is represented and the other is not is redressed by the 'overriding objective' (in SI 2001/1171, reg. 10 [2] [a]) which requires cases to be dealt with 'justly' by ensuring, so far as practicable, parties are 'on an equal footing'.

6. For guidance and commentary, see *Harvey on Industrial Relations and Employment Law* (London: Butterworths). On settlement, and COT3 forms, see p. 269.

7. For guidance on conciliation, see ACAS *Conciliation in Tribunal Cases*; and other guidance (see the ACAS website www.acas.gov.uk).

8. On employment appeals, see *Civil Appeals* (General Editor Sir Michael Burton, President of the EAT; Employment Section Editor John Bowers QC) (Welwyn Garden City: EMIS Professional Publishing).

9. See *Small Claims in the County Court* and the other guidance available from county court offices, CABx, and the Court Service; see also G. Appleby, *A Practical Guide to the Small Claims Court* (Welwyn Garden City: EMIS, 1998).

Chapter 22: Employment-related Welfare Benefits

1. More specialised texts include CPAG's *Welfare Benefits and Tax Credits Handbook* (London: Child Poverty Action Group); Keith Puttick, *Welfare Benefits: Law and Practice*, 9th edn (Welwyn Garden City: EMIS Publishing, 2004); Wikeley, Ogus and Barendt, *The Law of Social Security* (London: Butterworths, 2002).

2. The blueprint was in *Social Insurance and Allied Services*: Report by Sir William Beveridge (Cm. 6404, 1942); and see also the White Paper *Employment Policy* (Cm. 6527, 1944); and Beveridge's, *Full Employment in a Free Society* (London: George Allen & Unwin, 1944); and Jose Harris, *William Beveridge, A Biography* (Oxford: OUP, 1977).

3. For a general history of the Welfare State since the Second World War, see Nicholas Timmins, *The Five Giants: A Biography of the Welfare State* (London: Harper Collins, 2001). On New Labour's reforms to welfare aspects of employment rights, see Keith Puttick, '2020: A Welfare Odyssey – A Commentary on *Principles into Practice* and the Reform Programme', *ILJ*, vol. 28 (1999), p. 190.

4. Income deriving from the employment relationship and wages is arguably the most important source in the welfare 'mosaic'; see Nicholas Barr, *The Economics of the Welfare State* (Oxford: OUP, 1998), p. 6.

5. Several parts of the Lords' judgment in *Johnson* v. *Unisys Ltd* [2001] IRLR 279, HL, explain how Parliament, when it created the unfair dismissal jurisdiction, and provided for compensation for those found to have been unfairly dismissed (in the Industrial Relations Act 1971), deliberately set low financial compensation limits. Basically, the scheme facilitates dismissal, and preserves it as a viable option by not making it too expensive for employers to dismiss. See also Hugh Collins, *Justice in Dismissal* (Oxford: OUP, 1992).

6. The failure of private pensions, and State-regulated stakeholder pensions (introduced under the Welfare Reform and Pensions Act 1999), has put even greater burdens on State pensions, and necessitated much more extensive measures to supplement income in retirement – such as the State Second Pension from 2001, and the State Pension Credit Act 2002; see Puttick, *Welfare Benefits*, Note 1 above, in ch. 6. This was not what was intended in the original blue-print, and was not envisaged by *A New Contract for Welfare: Partnership in Pensions* (1998, Cm. 4179).

7. See, for example, Anthony Giddens, *The Third Way: The Renewal of Social Democracy* (Cambridge: Polity Press, 1998), especially ch. 4 (which focuses on what Giddens calls the Social Investment State); and Anthony Giddens, *The Third Way and Its Critics* (Cambridge: Polity Press, 2000).

8. Formally, JSA is conditional on entry into, and observance of, the Jobseeker's Agreement, but it may *also* be claimed by part-time workers doing less than 16 hours' work each week, and those with partners who work up to 24 hours a week. Although a Conservative measure, introduced in the Jobseeker's Act 1996, and which Labour was pledged to repeal (Ian McCartney, Commons *Hansard* 17 January 1996 col. 765), it has been retained and progressively used as the centrepiece, and springboard for other *welfare-to-work* initiatives – and as a gateway to tax credits and State-supported full-time employment.

9. Bringing with it, in its wake, a lot of unwelcome, negative implications. On US in-work welfare systems, and aspects of active labour market policies operating at the work–welfare interface, see Helen Hershkoff and Stephen Loffredo, *The Rights of the Poor* (American Civil Liberties Union/SUP, 1997); and Joel F. Handler, 'Welfare Reform in the United States', 35 *Osgoode Hall Law Journal* (no. 2), p. 290. One of the important elements in US welfare-to-work strategy, which like WTC and CTC assists a lot of low-paid US workers, is the Earned Income Tax Credit, as to which see Anne L. Alstott, 'The Earned Income Tax Credit and the Limitations of Tax-Based Welfare Reform', *Harvard Law Review*, vol. 108, p. 533.

10. The rise in take-up of HB, and increased costs to the State, in the 1980s and 1990s has been linked directly to deregulation of the private sector housing market, as observed in CABx reports from its offices – something which impacted particularly on low-paid workers. *Benefits and Work: A CAB Perspective on the Welfare to Work Debate* (London: National Association of CABx/Janet Allbeson, 1997); and *Flexibility Abused: A CAB Evidence Report on Employment Conditions in the Labour Market* (London: National Association of CABx, 1997). It also produced serious difficulties in motivating unemployed workers, and workers in low-paid jobs enjoying support from the State with housing and other work costs, to move into better-paid jobs. See, generally, Peter Robinson, 'Employment and Social Inclusion' and Paul Gregg, 'Employment, Taxes and Benefits' in Carey Oppenheim (ed.) *An Inclusive Society: Strategies for Tackling Poverty* (London: Institute of Public Policy Research, 1998), chs 9, 10, respectively.

11. See the Preface to *New Ambitions for Our Country: A New Contract for Welfare* (1998, Cm. 3805); and in relation to the costs of disability and incapacity benefits for workers affected by long-term incapacity, see Hugh Bayley and Stephen Timms, 'The Government's Proposals for Reforming Disability Benefits', *Welfare Benefits*, vol. 6, issue 3, pp. 28 et seq.

12. Timmins, *The Five Giants*, Note 3 above at p. 531.

13. As to which, see Hugh Collins, 'Regulating the Employment Relation for Competitiveness', *ILJ*, vol. 30 (2001), p. 17.

14. See Fran Bennett and Donald Hirsch, *The Employment Tax Credit: Issues for the Future of In-Work Support* (with contributions by Frank Wilkinson, Mark Pearson, and Stefano Scarpetta) (York: J. Rowntree Foundation/YPS, 2001). See also Keith Puttick, 'Welfare as "Wages": Benefits, Low Pay and the Flexible Labour Market', *ILJ*, vol. 27 (1998), p. 162; and Keith Puttick, 'New Generation Tax Credits', *Family Law Journal*, May 2003, no. 5.

15. See, generally, A.B. Atkinson, 'Social Exclusion, Poverty and Unemployment' in A.B. Atkinson and J. Hills (eds.) *Exclusion, Employment and Opportunity: Paper 4*, Centre for Analysis of Social Exclusion, London School of Economics.

16. On the simplified Child Support system, as it has operated since March 2003, and the policy background to welfare-to-work aspects, and in-work support for lone parents and non-resident parents, see Keith Puttick, *Child Support Law: Parents, the CSA and the Courts* (Welwyn Garden City: EMIS Publishing, 2003).

17. The government's undertaking in the *New Welfare Contract* produced a number of regulatory measures, the main one being the Financial Services and Markets Act 2000.
18. 1997, Cm. 3805.
19. As it is due to be when it is enacted in 2004.
20. Disabled workers fare particularly badly, and the employment and welfare systems present innumerable obstacles to returning to paid employment; see, for example, Alan Hedges and Wendy Sykes, *Moving Between Sickness and Work* (DWP Research Report Series No. 151, 31 October 2001); and Julia Louinidis, Rachel Youngs, Carli Lessof and Bruce Staffod, *The New Deal for Disabled People: National Survey of Incapacity Benefits Claimants* (DWP Research Report Series No. 160, 19 December 2001).
21. See the Housing Benefit (General) (Local Housing Allowance) Amendment Regulations 2003, SI 2003/2399.
22. Social Security (Jobcentre Plus Interviews) Regulations 2001, SI 2001/3210.
23. Social Security (Work-focused Interviews for Lone Parents) Amendment Regulations 2003, SI 2003/400. Lone parents claiming IS since 7 April 2003, once their youngest child reaches the age of 5 years and 3 months are officially seen at that point as suitable entrants to the labour market: and so must participate in a work-focused interview from the date that their child reaches that age.
24. Bayley and Timms, 'The Government's Proposals for Reforming Disability Benefits', *Welfare Benefits*, vol. 6, issue 3 (1999), p. 28 responding to a critique in *Welfare Benefits* by Lorna Reith, Director of the Disability Alliance.
25. Social Security (Welfare to Work) Regulations 1998/2231. See Grainne McKeever, 'Welfare to Work for the (In)Capacitated – The Reform of Incapacity Benefit', *ILJ*, vol. 29 (2000), p. 145.
26. Changes made to the DDA by the Disability Discrimination Act 1995 (Amendment) Regulations 2003, SI 2003/1673 (from 1 October 2004), implementing EC Directive 2000/78/EC establishing a general framework for equal treatment in employment and occupations.
27. On Community Care provision and liabilities, see Luke Clements, *Community Care and the Law* (London: Legal Action Group, 2004).
28. On the legislation, and the difficulties in this area of employment and welfare rights, see Jim Goddard, 'Children (Leaving Care) Act: A Commentary', *Welfare Benefits*, vol. 8, issue 3 (2001). For implementation of the scheme, see the Children (Leaving Care) (England) Regulations 2001, SI 2001/2874.
29. For a more detailed guide to tax credits, and eligibility criteria, see Puttick, *Welfare Benefits: Law and Practice*, Note 1 above; and the *CPAG Welfare Benefits and Tax Credits Handbook* (London: CPAG, 2004 (both published annually)). Key regulations include Working Tax Credit (Entitlement and Maximum Rate) Regulations 2002, SI 2002/2005; Tax Credits (Definition and Calculation of Income) Regulations 2002, SI 2002/2006; Child Tax Credit Regulations 2002, SI 2002/2007; Tax Credits (Income Thresholds and Determination of Rates) Regulations 2002, SI 2002/2008. On tax credits appeals, see *Civil Appeals* (General Editor Sir Michael Burton, President of the EAT) (Welwyn Garden City: EMIS Professional Publishing, 2004 (revised biannually)); Social Security and Community Care Section, Keith Puttick.
30. *The Modernisation of Britain's Tax and Benefits System* (No. 2 Work Incentives) – A Report by Martin Taylor (April 1988, HM Treasury).
31. For details, and worked examples, see Puttick, *Welfare Benefits*, Note 1 above ch. 9.
32. For further guidance on HB and CTB, see the *CPAG Handbook*, and Puttick, *Welfare Benefits*. Note 1 above.
33. For eligibility criteria, see the Social Security Contributions and Benefits Act 1992 (the SSCBA) ss. 72, 73 and the Social Security (Disability Living Allowance) Regulations 1991, SI 1991/2890.
34. *Moyna v. Secretary of State for Work and Pensions (formerly against the Social Security Commissioner)* [2003] UKHL 44.

35. Duleep Allirajah, 'How the DLA System is Failing Deaf People', *Welfare Benefits*, vol. 9, issue 1 (2002), p. 16.

36. For eligibility, see the SSCBA ss. 94–110.

37. Commissioner's Decision CI/3511/2002 (*Welfare Benefits*, vol. 10, issue 2, March 2003). The appeal for a certificate failed due to lack of supporting evidence showing the link between his work and the illness.

38. Guidance is in Commissioners' Cases *51/2000 and CI/1698/1997; *Welfare Benefits*, vol. 8, issue 1 (2001), and in DWP Guidance (with Claim Form DBA 1).

39. See *Welfare Benefits*, vol. 7, issue 5 (2000).

40. Appeals can be made under the Social Security Act 1998; and Social Security and Child Support (Decisions and Appeals Regulations 1999, SI 1999/99).

41. *Welfare Benefits*, December 1999, pp. 32, 33.

42. *We're in this Together* (Carers National Association/Loughborough University, June 1999); and see the government's National Carers Strategy. *Caring about Carers: A National Strategy for Carers* (1999).

43. For eligibility criteria for Carer's Allowance see the SSCBA s. 70; Social Security (Care Allowance) Regulations 1976, SI 1976 No. 409. Carers also have rights to be assessed and supported by the Community Care regime, with assessments and provision under the Carers and Disabled Children Act 2000, extending rights under the Carers (Recognition and Services) Act 1995. See, further, Luke Clements, *Community Care and the Law* (London: Legal Action Group, 2004).

44. See the SSCBA s. 124, and IS (General) Regulations 1987, SI 1987/1967; and for JSA, the Jobseeker's Act 1995, and Jobseekers Allowance Regulations 1996, SI 1996/207, and related regulations. For detailed commentary, see *CPAG Handbook*; and Puttick, *Welfare Benefits* (Note 1 above).

45. *EOC Backs National Minimum Wage as Good for Women*, EOC Press Release, 26 January 1998.

46. The UN Declaration of Universal Human Rights 1948, General Assembly Resolution 217A, 10 December 1948 includes arts. 7 (equal protection of the law without discrimination); 13 (freedom of movement and residence); 14 (the right to seek and enjoy, in other countries, asylum from persecution); 22 (the right to social security); 23 (the right to work, free choice of employment, just and favourable conditions of work, and protection against unemployment); and 25 (a standard of living adequate for health and well-being, housing, social security in the event of unemployment, sickness, disability, widowhood, etc.). Conventions of the International Labour Organisation may also be relevant: of the Conventions ratified by the UK at least ten are concerned with welfare-related matters such as income replacement, incapacity and unemployment benefits, and so forth. An example is No. 95 on wages protection; and see EC Dir. 2003/9.

47. Convention Relating to the Status of Refugees, Geneva, 28 July 1951. The main welfare-related provisions include arts. 17 (wage-earning employment rights); 18 (self-employment); 21 (housing); 22 (education); 23 (public relief); 24 (labour legislation and access to social security).

48. *R (On the Application of S) v. Secretary of State for the Home Department* [2003] EWCA Civ. 1285, applying *Pretty v. United Kingdom* [2002] EHRR 1 at 33, para. 5.

49. Thereby engaging protection under art. 1 of Protocol 1; *Gaygusuz v. Austria* [1996] 23 EHRR 364; and *Stigson v. Sweden* App. 12264/86 (13 July 1988). See Jeremy Lewis and John Bowers QC, 'Article 1 of Protocol 1, ECHR – the Peaceful Enjoyment of Property?' in *Welfare Benefits*, vol. 7, issue 6, p. 17. On ECHR aspects of in-work welfare, see John Bowers QC and Jeremy Lewis, *Employment Law and Human Rights* (London: Sweet and Maxwell, 2001). See also Peter Billings and Richard Edwards, 'Safeguarding Asylum Seekers' Dignity: Clarifying the Interface between Convention Rights and Asylum Law', (2004) 11 *Journal of Social Security Law* 83.

50. *Willis v. UK* [2002] FLR 582. EC Law also bars out discrimination in the payment of benefits like Jobseeker's Allowance; *Hockenjos v. Secretary of State for Social Security*

[2001] EWCA Civ. 624; [2001] 2 CMLR 51, Court of Appeal. See also Sue Smith, 'Joint Residence, Benefits, and Discrimination' in Welfare Benefits, vol. 8, issue 3, p. 13.

51. As in R v. Secretary of State for Trade and Industry, ex parte Broadcasting, Entertainment, Cinematographic and Theatre Union [2001] IRLR 559, European Court of Justice.

52. Art. 42 of the Treaty authorises the EC to enact social security measures to facilitate freedom of movement; and for specific examples, see EC Regs. 1612/68 (freedom of movement); 1408/71 (ensuring the same access to benefits that is available to nationals of the State they are in); and 98/49 (safeguarding pension rights of the employed and self-employed moving within the Community). For an excellent account of support arrangements, see Pieter van der Mei, Free Movement of Persons within the European Community: Cross-Border Access to Public Benefits (Oxford: Hart Publishing, 2003).

53. For the purposes of claiming benefits like Income Support; Income Support (General) Regulations 1987, SI 1987/1967, reg. 21 (3).

54. As in Gingi v. Secretary of State for Work and Pensions [2001] 1 CMLR 20; [2002] Eu. LR 37, Court of Appeal; and Nessa v. Chief Adjudication Officer [1999] 1 WLR 1937, HL.

55. See EC Reg. 1408/71, art. 1 (d) and (e): consolidated by Reg. 118/97.

56. Mainly under the Immigration and Asylum Act 1999; and the Nationality, Immigration and Asylum Act 2002. For detailed consideration, see Mark Symes and Peter Jorro, Asylum Law and Practice (London: Lexis Nexis Butterworths, 2003).

57. Immigration and Asylum Act 1999 ss. 94–101 and the Asylum Support Regulations 2000, SI 2000/704; the Nationality, Immigration and Asylum Act 2002; and the Asylum and Immigration (Treatment of Claimants) Act 2004. The courts' position is supportive of restrictions which ban working while at the same time limiting State welfare take-up; R v. Secretary of State for the Home Department, ex parte Jammeh [1998] INLR 701, CA. On asylum support, see Sue Willman, Stephen Knafler, and Stephen Pierce, Support for Asylum Seekers (London: Legal Action Group, 2001).

58. R v. Wandsworth LBC, Ex Parte O [2000] 1 WLR 2539, applied in R (On the Application of Mani) v. Lambeth London Borough Council [2003] EWCA Civ 836; and see R (On the Application of Westminster City Council) v. NASS [2002] 1 WLR 2956; [2002] 4 All ER 654 (which clarifies that while a local authority has a duty to support an asylum-seeker it is that authority, and not the National Asylum Support Service, that must provide the necessary Social Security assistance). Housing and other assistance under Part VI of the 1999 Act is largely discretionary, with little or no scope for appeal. However, once support is given, if it is withdrawn unlawfully the decision can be quashed in judicial review proceedings; see Keith Puttick, 'Social Security and Community Care' in Civil Appeals (ed. Sir Michael Burton) (Welwyn Garden City: EMIS, 2004); and see R (Hamid Ali Husain) v. Asylum Support Adjudicator and Secretary of State for the Home Department 5 October 2001, reported at [2001] EWHC Admin 852; Times 15 November 2001.

59. R v. City of Westminster HB Review Board, Ex parte Mehanne [2001] 2 All ER 690; [2001] 1 WLR 539, HL.

60. Prakash Shah and Werner Menski, 'UK and Ireland Only States to Accept Full Free Movement for EU Accession Countries?', Immigration and Nationality Law, vol. 18, no. 1 (2004), p. 7.

61. The right to work is dependent on registration and satisfying other conditions in the Accession (Immigration and Worker Registration) Regulations 2004, SI 2004/1219. For the purposes of accessing benefits claimants must be 'habitually resident' in the UK (subject to exceptions), and this is linked to citizenship of the accession States, and the ability to meet employment requirements, etc. On residence conditions, see the Social Security (Habitual Residence) Amendment Regulations 2004, SI 2004/1232. On EU Law aspects of employment and welfare post-1 May, see Keith Puttick, Towards a Just European State? The Welfare System for Immigrants and Asylum Seekers Conference Paper, W.G. Hart Workshop, 'The Challenge of

Migration to Legal Systems' (London: Institute of Advanced Legal Studies, London University, June 2003).

62. On poverty and working conditions in the Eastern European accession States, see David Gordon and Peter Townsend, *Breadline Europe: The Measurement of Poverty* (Bristol: The Policy Press, 2000).

63. Although ECHR art. 4 prohibits forced labour, and there are many other aspects of working conditions in the gangmaster system that may breach international and UK national labour standards (NMW requirements, working time, restrictions on pay deductions, etc.), this legislation does not address these directly. It does little more than require gangmasters to register and be licensed. Two types of activities are regulated. First, when they supply 'gang' workers to employers; and, second, when the gangmasters themselves contract to complete tasks using gang labour. The scheme does not add to the employment rights of gang labourers, or assist them, directly, in meeting their welfare needs. Nor does it deal with problems that may link to the workers' entry status – e.g. when there are restrictions on working after temporary admission has been granted. There are usually clear restrictions on working in the case of asylum seekers, i.e. before their refugee status is determined, or before six months has elapsed since their application was made: as a matter of policy work is usually permitted when there has been no decision on their application within six months; Symes and Jorro (Note 56 above), at pp. 444–5. When State welfare support is not available (for example after covert entry to the UK, or when claimants fall foul of the requirement in the Nationality, Immigration, and Asylum Act 2002 s. 55 preventing support if a claim for asylum is not made as soon as reasonably practicable after arrival in the United Kingdom), or it has been refused or withdrawn – for example following an adverse decision on an application, under powers in the Asylum and Immigration (Treatment of Claimants) Act 2004, then engaging in employment provided by gangmasters may become a person's *only* source of income. In some cases decisions refusing support may be contested, especially given that s. 55 (5) of the 2002 Act implicitly requires support to be given to prevent a breach of an applicant's Convention rights (and the ECHR art. 3 provides that no one shall be subjected to 'inhuman or degrading treatment'); and s. 6 of the Human Rights Act 1998 forbids the Secretary of State to act incompatibly with the Convention rights); *R (Q and Others)* v. *Secretary of State for the Home Department* [2003] EWCA Civ 364, Court of Appeal. Contesting such decisions takes time, though; and the kind of unregulated employment available assists claimants to meet short- and long-term income needs.

64. *London Evening Standard*, 13 February 2003.

65. Report of the Select Committee, Food and Rural Affairs (Follow-up Report on Gangmasters), published on 20 May 2004; and see Felicity Kendal, 'MPs Condemn Inaction over Gangmasters', *Guardian*, 20 May 2004.

Appendices

Appendix I
Useful Organisations & Websites

Advisory, Conciliation and Arbitration Service (ACAS)
Publicly-funded organisation providing expertise and services relating to dispute resolution – but also general information and publications.
www.acas.org.uk

Central Arbitration Committee (CAC)
Statutory body with responsibilities in relation to union recognition claims, de-recognition by employers, access to information for collective bargaining purposes, voluntary arbitration, etc – and decision-making powers under TULR(C)A 1992.
www.cac.gov.uk

Certification Officer
Information on the work of the Certification Officer, with guidance for trade unions and employers' associations. Also provides a lists of trade unions and employers' associations, with hyperlinks to individual websites, decisions made by the Certification Officer; and guidance on procedures for complaints against trades unions.
www.certoffice.org

Child Poverty Action Group
Campaigns on child poverty and welfare benefits issues in general, including in-work welfare support.
www.cpag.org.uk

Commission for Racial Equality (CRE)
Main body with statutory responsibilities for race relations (also gives guidance and information).
www.cre.gov.uk

Community Legal Service (CLS)
Valuable source of information about sources of advice and legal information (including organisations, law firms, etc offering employment advice services).
www.legalservicescommission.gov.uk

Confederation of British Industry (CBI)
The main employers' organisation in the UK.
www.cbi.org.uk

Department of Trade and Industry (DTI)

Government department with responsibilities for employment and social policy (shared with the Department of Work and Pensions). The website has information for employees, business, and new legislation and policy developments: and details of regulatory requirements.

www.dti.gov.uk

www.dti.gov.uk/er/regs.htm

See also, for other government advice services and information points/e-services

www.gateway.gov.uk

Department of Work and Pensions (DWP)

Government department responsible for in-work benefits, pensions, and other work-related support such as Access to Work.

www.dwp.gov.uk

Department of Work and Pensions Disability Unit

Provides information about DWP disability policies.

www.disability.gov.uk

Disability Rights Commission (DRC)

Responsible for assisting those with disabilities, and giving advice and support for employers and staff. Site has useful information about legislation, guidance, test cases to help eliminate discrimination against disabled people and to promote equality of opportunity. The site contains a significant amount of campaign and resource information.

www.drc.org.uk

EC Employment Law and Social Policy: Europa

Useful website with information about EC Law and developments.

www.europa.eu.int/futurum/index_en.htm

Equal Opportunities Commission

Body with responsibilities for combating discrimination, and promoting equality and equal opportunities at work.

www.eoc.org.uk

Employment Tribunal Service

Has essential information about Employment Tribunals, and guidance on claims procedures.

www.ets.gov.uk

Employment Appeal Tribunal

Site with information about employment appeals, and EAT cases data-base.

www.employmentappeals.gov.uk

Health and Safety Executive

Main health and safety organisation with statutory responsibilities for health, safety, and the working environment.

www.hse.gov.uk

Institute of Employment Rights
Undertakes research and publishes papers on topical issues.
www.ier.org.uk

Labour Research Department
Researches workplace issues, and publishes guidance.
www.lrd.org.uk

LAGER (Lesbian and Gay Employment Rights)
Offers support and information on lesbian and gay rights at work, with support service.
www.lager.dircon.co.uk

Involvement and Participation Association
IPA is a centre of excellence for companies developing world class strategies for employee involvement and partnership. A focal point for best practice, the IPA has a wide experience of what works best in any situation.

Liberty
Concerned with civil liberties issues, including work-related rights.
www.liberty-human-rights.org.uk

Low Pay Commission
Keeps low pay and NMW issues under review.
lpc@gtnet.gov.uk

Maternity Alliance
Campaigns and advises on maternity and work issues.
www.maternityalliance.org.uk

National Association of Citizens Advice Bureaux
Citizens' Advice Bureaux provide advice and support for those with work-related problems, as well as meeting other mainstream advice needs.
For information about the organisation, publications, reports, etc:
www.nacab.org.uk
For information about services, local CABx, etc:
www.adviceguide.org.uk

National Pensioners Convention
Represents pensioners, and active on pensioners and pensions issues.
www.natpencon.org.uk

TIGER
Valuable official website providing information on workplace rights, including National Minimum Wage, maternity and paternity leave and benefits, working time, etc.
www.tiger.gov.uk

Trades Union Congress
Body representing UK trades unions. Valuable source of information and advice, and links to other sites.
www.tuc.org.uk

The Work Foundation (formerly Industrial Society)
Researches and publishes material on workplace issues.
www.theworkfoundation.com

WorkSmart
Provides information about workplace rights including working-time rules, and workplace organisation.
www.worksmart.org.uk

Appendix II
Application to an
Employment Tribunal

Application to an
Employment Tribunal

For office use

- If you fax this form you do not need to send one in the post.
- This form has to be photocopied. Please use CAPITALS and black ink (if possible).
- Where there are tick boxes, please tick to one that applies.

Received at ET

Case number

Code

Initials

1 Please give the type of complaint you want the tribunal to decide (for example, unfair dismissal, equal pay). A full list is available from the tribunal office. If you have more than one complaint list them all.

2 Please give your details

Mr ☐ Mrs ☐ Miss ☐ Ms ☐ Other _____

First names

Surname

Date of birth

Address

Postcode

Phone number

Daytime phone number

Please give an address to which we should send documents if different from above

Postcode

3 If a representative is acting for you please give details (all correspondence will be sent to your representative)

Name

Address

Postcode

Phone

Fax

Reference

4 Please give the dates of your employment

From _____ to _____

5 Please give the name and address of the employer, other organisation or person against whom this complaint is being brought

Name

Address

Postcode

Phone number

Please give the place where you worked or applied to work if different from above

Address

Postcode

6 Please say what job you did for the employer (or what job you applied for). If this does not apply, please say what your connection was with the employer

IT1(E/W)

7 Please give the number of normal basic hours worked each week

Hours per week

8 Please give your earning details

Basic wage or salary

£   :   per

Average take home pay

£   :   per

Other bonuses or benefits

£   :   per

9 If your complaint is not about dismissal, please give the date when the matter you are complaining about took place

10 Unfair dismissal applicants only

Please indicate what you are seeking at this stage, if you win your case

☐ Reinstatement: to carry on working in your old job as before (an order for reinstatement normally includes an award of compensation for loss of earnings).

☐ Re-engagement: to start another job or new contract with your old employer (an order for re-engagement normally includes an award of compensation for loss of earnings).

☐ Compensation only: to get an award of money.

11 Please give details of your complaint

If there is not enough space for your answer, please continue on a separate sheet and attach it to this form.

12 Please sign and date this form, then send it to the appropriate address on the back cover of this booklet (see postcode list on pages 13-16).

Signed

Date

IT1/F/V/V

Index

Compiled by Auriol Griffith-Jones